Poverty in America: A Book of Readings

Poverty

Edited by

Louis A. Ferman
Joyce L. Kornbluh
and # Alan Haber

Introduction by Michael Harrington

in America
A Book of Readings

Ann Arbor
The University of Michigan Press

*To Norman Thomas in his eighty-first year
in tribute to a lifetime of crusading
against the causes of poverty.*

*Such poverty as we have today in all our great cities degrades
the poor, and infects with its degradation the whole neighborhood
in which they live. And whatever can degrade a neighborhood can
degrade a country and a continent and finally the whole civilized world,
which is only a large neighborhood. . . . The old notion that
people can "keep themselves to themselves" and not be touched
by what is happening to their neighbors, or even to the people who live
a hundred miles off, is a most dangerous mistake. The saying that
we are members one of another is not a mere pious formula
to be repeated in church without any meaning: it is a literal truth;
for though the rich end of the town can avoid living with the poor end,
it cannot avoid dying with it when the plague comes.
People will be able to keep themselves to themselves as much as
they please when they have made an end of poverty; but until
then they will not be able to shut out the sights and sounds
and smells of poverty from their daily walks, nor feel sure
from day to day that its most violent and fatal evils will not reach
them. through their strongest police guards.*

—From *The Intelligent Woman's Guide to Socialism and
Capitalism* (New York, 1928), by George Bernard Shaw

Introduction

Michael Harrington

THE ISSUES RAISED by this book of readings, *Poverty in America,* are not simply those of the problems of poverty, but the problem of poverty in its larger context and how, in a sense, that problem meets the issue of the Great Society. For, when we declare a war against poverty, we are reaching out to touch a problem which has first come to the poor but which, if not solved in terms of the poor, will threaten to engulf the entire society.

Individual articles in this comprehensive anthology focus on definitions and prevalence of poverty, the structure of poverty, the relationship of poverty to the economy, the values and life styles of poor people, and various programs and proposals that have been suggested to meet the problems of social, economic, and cultural deprivation.

The point is made in this book that in contrast to the old poverty of immigrants who came with high hopes to a new land and an expanding economy and found unskilled or semi-skilled factory jobs, the new poor are internal aliens in this affluent country. They are the rejects of the past. They are the people who have been driven off farmlands, workers displaced by technological advancement, old folks who face poverty in their declining years, women left alone to raise their children, unemployed teenagers and youths who have dropped out of school but can't find jobs. This is a new kind of poverty in a new kind of society. This is the first poverty of automation, the first poverty of the minority poor, and a poverty that under present conditions could become hereditary, transmitted from generation to generation unless the typical cycles of poverty are broken. Let me share some observations about the growing edge of poverty in this society.

We now have a five percent unemployment figure in this country, but that figure is an understatement. It is possible, according to the Senate Committee on Manpower and Employment Report of last spring, that a million and a half people have been driven out of the labor market who don't show up as statistics, because a person must be looking for work to be an unemployment statistic. Secretary of Labor Willard Wirtz has told us that last year there were three hundred and fifty thousand young Americans between ages 16 and 21 not in school, not at work, and not looking for work. In addition, there is tremendous underemployment in dead-end jobs.

Between 1962 and 1963, this economy increased the number of manufacturing jobs by 152,000 and the number of service industry jobs by 283,000. The production worker earned an average of $99.63 a week and the typical service worker received a weekly pay of $47.58. Between 1962 and 1963, this economy created almost three times as many jobs for people in the field of education as it did for factory hands. All this means is that this economy is going through a fundamental change in the way it produces goods and services. At some point we must face up to the social consequences of technology and what it is doing to the skill levels of our society.

America's automating technology has already created a tremendous number of social problems in addition to persistent and chronic rates of high unemployment during this decade: the devastation of regions such as Appalachia; a setback to the economic progress of the Negro; and a tremendously bleak future for the one-third of the young generation lacking a high school education in a time of increasing demands for skilled workers within the economy.

These are only a few instances of deepgoing problems which cannot be wished away, and an indication of possibly greater difficulties in the future. One need not predict a Thirties-type crash to say that America has not solved all of its contradictions. And, more importantly, the solutions to problems such as automation-induced unemployment, the plight of uneducated youth, the tenacious fact of the slums, all point toward the need for some fairly basic—and controversial—changes in the social and economic institutions of the United States.

By 1980, the government tells us, America will have to have over one hundred and one million jobs, and even that incredible figure is projected on the assumption that unemployment will remain well above three percent. This figure, and many others that have come out of Washington in recent months, defines one of the most fundamental problems in the United States. It raises two basic questions: Will the economy generate this many new employments? And if so, what will the work be—poverty jobs, or Great Society jobs?

Both President Johnson's manpower message and the 1965 Manpower Report predict that the decline in the number of blue-collar workers will continue into the indefinite future. It was in 1956 that the white-collar work force became more numerous than the blue, and there is nothing in the present technology that would make one expect a reversal of this trend. This of course means that the United States confronts a critical challenge: With millions of young people coming into the labor force in the next fifteen years, a third of them with less than a high-school diploma, where will they go? The jobs which are on the ascendant are either highly skilled, requiring an education well beyond that possessed by the typical poor, working-class youth, or else they are miserably paid, unorganized jobs in the service sector of the economy, menial tasks in hospitals, schools, hotels, and restaurants.

These considerations make it fairly clear that the nation is going to have to go well beyond its present commitments to deal with the problems of poverty and unemployment. And this raises a basic question. It was assumed by the New Dealers in the Thirties that the government's function was to prime the pump—and the private economy would do the rest. This policy was fixed at the time of the "second" New Deal when Roosevelt abandoned the corporate-dominated, planned economy perspective of the NRA. And it was reasserted by John F. Kennedy when social change was once more put on the agenda in 1961.

Full employment will require much more massive outlays for expanding the public, social sector of our economy. And although business has learned the profitable common sense of a tax cut, and even of pump priming in its patriotic noncompetitive form of defense spending, it has been something else again to speak of the government's helping to redesign the cities and rural areas of this country and plan some changes in our institutions that would lead to a qualitatively better life for its citizens—the Great Society that President Lyndon Johnson has so eloquently suggested.

American liberalism is now in favor of government social investments, i.e., in direct federal participation in the building of housing, schools, transportation systems and the like. This point of view is represented by the A.F.L.–C.I.O., the Americans for Democratic Action and thinkers like John Kenneth Galbraith and Leon Keyserling. On the other hand, the more conservative Keynesians—and that camp now includes the sophisticated, tax-cutting corporation presidents—do not want direct government investments but indirect stimulation of the economy.

The new debate of the coming period will not be over whether the government should intervene in the economy, but how the intervention will take place, for Keynes has finally conquered the entire political spectrum. However, the manner of federal intervention is, to put it mildly, a most crucial question. A conservative intervention which limits itself to stimulating the economy through fiscal and monetary means will have the most reactionary consequences. It may well achieve business "prosperity" but there is no evidence that it will generate sufficient new employments, or the right kinds of new jobs to give youths their economic opportunity.

The labor-liberal view avoids these pitfalls. As the Clark Senate Subcommittee demonstrated in the spring of 1964, had the Administration then pledged itself to annual increments of five billion dollars in social spending, unemployment would have been reduced to three percent by 1968. Secondly, the direct federal outlay approach—the technique of making investments—consciously allocates the funds to make up the enormous deficiencies in our social consumption.

In addition, this debate raises the question of fundamental economic power in the society. In the face of these tremendous transformations of the work force and technology, what is being timidly posed is that most basic of all issues: the necessity of subjecting economic power to the democratic will of the people. Or, in classic terms, this is a first and tiny installment in the ideological struggle to make human need, rather than private profit, the criterion for economic decisions.

By now, America has had its first glimpse of the war on poverty and it is now possible to take its resulting proposals with the seriousness that they deserve. The ideas of massive social investment in low-cost housing, schools, hospitals, and transportation systems have now become politically relevant. The various pre-school education proposals and demonstration projects indicate the beginning of an awareness that the slum child is frequently educationally retarded before he even sees the inside of a school. Finally, all these programs are profoundly related to the most dynamic component of the social change movement in the United States: the Negro freedom struggle. As even the FBI understood, the causes of the riots in the summer of 1964 were not to be found in the Communists, the Nationalists, or any other organized group, but rather in the unspeakable conditions under which Negroes live, North and South.

Beyond the immediate proposals of the war on poverty, there lies the extraordinary fact that the President of the United States is talking in the historic vocabulary of utopianism: "Ahead now is a summit where freedom from the wants of the body can help fulfill the needs of the spirit."

But there are some problems with the war on poverty which I raise within the context of an enthusiasm that we have a government program at all. In this society we need to create jobs for the people. It is good under the program of the Economic Opportunity Act of 1964 to train people for jobs, but in addition, jobs must be created for which people can be trained. I would suggest as a strategy in the war against poverty the following simplified slogan: Let us abolish poverty by hiring the poor to abolish poverty. Let us make a massive social investment in the destruction of the slums. Just think of that for a moment.

In 1949, Senator Robert Taft said that we needed to build 810,000 new units of low cost housing in four years. In 1968, if the present housing program goes through, we will have just about reached Senator Taft's 1953 goal. How can we have a really profound and serious war against poverty that does not have a pledge to tear down every slum in the United States; could we not, by tearing down these slums, create employment for the people who need work? By building schools, hospitals, and transportation systems, could we not hire the poor to help us build the Great Society?

I think it is clear that we are going to have national economic planning in the United States. The United States is a curious exception in the world, because the typical American reaction to the word "planning" is that it equals red revolution, and bringing Brezhnev to the White House, and having some bureaucrats determine the brand of toothpaste which the citizens use. We are the only people who think this way. In France, a conservative general and a banker Premier plan. In Britain's last election, the Tory Party ran against the Labor Party on the antisocialist program that businessmen can plan better than trade unionists. In Italy, the Vatican knows about planning. And in the United States we are going to have to understand that a modern, integrated economy needs national economic planning.

In this context, the Majority Report of the Senate Subcommittee on Manpower and Employment published under the direction of Senator Joseph S. Clark of Pennsylvania is one of the most significant public documents of recent times. This report poses concretely the need for national planning in this country based on the premise stated in Senator Clark's foreword that there is a "manpower revolution" taking place in American society. The Clark Subcommittee proposes that a goal be set: the reduction of unemployment to three percent by 1968. The President should, in his economic report, estimate the size of the gross national product required to attain this objective, and the Council of Economic Advisors should engage in even longer range projections. If the rate of unemployment is greater than three percent, the President is legally obliged to submit governmental programs which would increase the gross national product to such a level that will reduce unemployment below three percent. Americans must understand, as Europeans have for some time, that if a country's gross national product is unsuitable, that country goes out and makes one that is. And it makes one based on social standards. In other words, the poor are hired not only to abolish poverty but to help to begin to build a Great Society.

What are some other relationships between the war on poverty and the Great Society? It is excellent that we are at least talking about a Great Society and that Americans have their eyes lifted up beyond this year or next, or even this decade and the next, to the idea of a new society with qualitative social changes.

Far from being rhetoric, Lyndon Johnson's concept of a Great Society is a very serious intellectual proposition, behind which is an implied political science and sociology. The Great Society will be, presumably, the creation of business, labor, the consumer, the religious believers, the atheists. It will be, it is implied, brought about through the consensus of all these groups. In a sense, the President is participating in the mood which first appeared among intellectuals around the phrase, "the end of ideology," popularized in this country by Daniel Bell. The President is saying that we are going to have a revolution without the painful inconvenience of changing basic institutions and the reason we can do so is that now we live in a society which is so abundant that it need no longer have class conflict in order to make economic decisions, because all reasonable claims can now be satisfied and politics will now proceed by way of consensus rather than by way of conflict.

It seems to me that this view of reality fails because if we are going to eliminate poverty and create a qualitatively new society, we are in for some radical changes. There are going to be more than a few conflicts when we throw so much of the conventional and outlived wisdom overboard and start acting a new way.

For example, we now have to begin to redefine work in this country. First of all, we have to redefine what we mean by public work. The concept of public work grew up in the United States in the 1930's and was based on the theory that the private economy had temporarily broken down in providing employment for willing workers and that the government would temporarily provide public work until the private economy could be put back together again. As a result, the concept of public work had a temporary and pejorative aspect to it; many people regarded it as a form of relief. But, faced with the new economic and social conditions in our society, confronted with the problems raised by automation in the private sector of our economy and the greater social consumption needs of the public sector, our concept of public work has to change.

There has already been a tremendous growth of one type of public work: in the field of education more new jobs have been opened in the last several years than in any other sector of the economy. If we can do that for school teachers with college degrees, why can't we do it for other people, too?

Secondly, the concept of education must be brought more and more under the heading of productive work. I would argue that we should have a GI bill in the war against poverty and pay people to go to school, pay for their tuition, their books, and give them an additional living allowance if they have a family. The GI bill was one of the most successful social experiments this society has ever had. Why does it require a shooting war for us to be so smart? Why can't we in the war on poverty say that the most productive thing a young person between ages 16 and 21 can do is go to school, and that this is an investment in the Great Society?

In addition, I think we need to go out and invent new kinds of work, a new concept of work, creative work, the kind of work that a computer can't do. This year, the star of the antipoverty program is the concept of the indigenous worker. People have discovered, for example, that you can have a social worker with less than an eighth grade education, and that a bright, talented, and sympathetic slum dweller has some abilities that a person with a master's degree in social work may not have. If we look, we can find all kinds of new jobs to create for people if we are willing to make these investments.

We are now making a change in our whole social philosophy. We are breaking with the theory of custodial care for the poor, the supportive care for the poor. We are now taking on a much greater obligation as a nation—to lift people out of poverty and change the quality of their lives. And I think in order to do so, we must change some of the ways we think, establish new definitions of work, pay people for things we once called leisure-time activities, and invent new kinds of jobs. The government has made a start in this direction in the war on poverty through such programs as the Economic Opportunity Act, Medicare, the Appalachian Development Act, but only a start, which thus far has fallen short of what needs to be done to liberate people from poverty by involving them in planning and working to abolish poverty and to start creating a Great Society.

In his *Politics*, Aristotle indirectly referred to the subject of automation with a simile which is relevant today. In the course of defending slavery, Aristotle said that slavery was inherent and necessary to a society. There was, however, one circumstance under which masters would not need slaves, and managers would not need subordinates. He said that a slaveless society could come about if the statues of Daedelus were to come to life--if inanimate objects could, by intelligent anticipation, do things.

I suggest that we are living through that period of mankind when the statues of Daedelus, that cunning craftsman of Greek legend, have come from myth and are becoming reality, that automation and cybernation are the statues of Daedelus and that we are coming into a period when inanimate objects will, by intelligent anticipation, do the things which the slaves and underlings of former societies were set to do. If we want to look into the future, maybe we are talking about the creation of a new Athens. In the old Athens there were human slaves at the bottom of the society. But the Greek citizen knew that the proper work of man was the work of the intellect, the work of the body in sports, the work of the arts. I am suggesting that perhaps we are entering a period when it will be possible for advanced technology to abolish progressively the menial, routine, and bitter work and to liberate this society for the things that are truly human: the sports, the thought, or the arts.

Thus, when one looks at the question of poverty and the issues that are raised in the war on poverty and discussed in the articles included in this collection, we are not just looking at the poor people whom we are going to help. We are looking from a particular vantage point at the problem of the Twentieth Century, and more so, of the Twenty-first. For I suggest that in abolishing poverty in the United States, we will have begun to construct a Great Society for us all.

In *Poverty in America,* the causes of, and cures for, the types of poverty in our country are described by government and labor leaders, economists, social workers, psychologists, and other specialists. The result is a balanced, comprehensive book which presents an up-to-date and accurate picture of this nation-wide problem. It is a collection which should prove useful in raising issues for continued discussion and research.

Editors' Preface

SERIOUS PUBLIC CONCERN with the problem of poverty is not a new phenomenon on the American scene, although the present excitement about poverty and its consequences may have created such an impression. Henry George in his *Progress and Poverty* referred to the United States of 1869 as a land where "amid the greatest accumulation of wealth, men die of starvation and puny infants suckle dry breasts." In 1890, Jacob Riis wrote *How the Other Half Lives*, a reporter's observations and anecdotes on life in the New York slums, which created a sensation at the time. In his State of the Union Message in 1933, Franklin D. Roosevelt referred to "one third of the nation that is ill-clothed, ill-housed, and ill-nourished." There has always been a "lowest third" or a "lowest fifth" in the sense that some groups of people in the nation have always been *relatively* disadvantaged in their access to opportunities and adequate financial resources. However, the composition of these groups, the nature and prevalence of poverty, attitudes toward the poor, and government involvement in the solution to the problem have varied over time.

The Changing Structure of Poverty

The great majority of the Negroes in America have always been among the poor—first as slaves in the plantation system, then as indentured sharecroppers in the rural areas of the country, and finally as the residents of the black ghettoes of the large cities. Until recent years, the remainder of the poor were largely immigrants from other lands—the bondservants of colonial times, followed by the immigrant masses from western and eastern Europe. With the recession of immigration, the poverty-stricken have included farm workers displaced by the advent of the large mechanized farm; white and Negro migrants from the rural areas to eroded urban city centers; unskilled workers in unprotected and underpaid industries; displaced workers, victimized by technological change, who cannot find new roles in the labor market; and finally those individuals who because of age, physical or emotional disability, undereducation or lack of skill do not participate in the labor market, or if they do, only in marginal roles.

Changes in the Nature of Poverty

The nature of poverty changed with these shifting groups. The immigrant saw poverty as a *temporary state* and looked forward to the day when he or his children could gain a greater access to opportunity and financial resources. The poor of today are more inclined to regard poverty as a *permanent way of life* with little hope for themselves or their children. This change in the outlook of the poor can be explained by changes in the opportunity structure. Unlike earlier times, the labor market of today does not have a place for the undereducated, the underskilled or the old. Increasing technological sophistication makes the future prospects of these groups even bleaker than they are at the present time. Disadvantage breeds disadvantage, and the offspring of today's poor, even though more educated than their parents, will find serious limitations in opportunities for employment and social participation. The general affluence of the society means very little to this underclass of individuals and families.

Changes in Attitudes Toward the Poor

Early attitudes toward the poor in America were compounded by feelings of contempt, repugnance and fatalism. For the most part, the affluent ignored the plight of the poor. Poor people were "the damned" or they were "the losers" who could never be righted to a decent life but were committed to a lifetime of inequality. In a society committed to success and achievement, the poor could only be viewed as an abnormality. Although this view was softened with time, it was still popular to assume that the roots of poverty were in *individual* laziness, thriftlessness, and immorality.

The post-Civil War period posed the problem of new poverty in the wake of industrialization, immigration, and urban growth. The new poor lived in the filth and squalor of the urban ghettoes, which were only too visible. These ghettoes posed a twofold problem for the affluent in the cities. First, it became recognized that the substandard living conditions of the poor were breeding grounds for the dread epidemics of the period—typhoid, cholera, and smallpox. Second, the slum environment was viewed as the incubator of the undesirable and lawless groups that posed a direct threat to the institutions of the society. Thus, the city dweller found himself forced to recognize the existence of poor people and their problems. The proximity and interdependence of city life brought a new attention to poverty, its causes, and its cures.

The post-Civil War period also marked the beginnings of the new philanthropy. The conscience of liberal reformers was awakened to the problems of poverty and a subtle shift of attitudes toward the poor occurred. Attention was focused on systemic and structural causes of poverty rather than on properties of the individual. *The individual was viewed as a victim and not as a causal agent of poverty*. It became popular to discuss faulty resource allocation and structural impediments to opportunity. The classic analysis by Henry George was typical of this shift of emphasis which reached its culmination in the 1930's in the policies of the New Deal.

Public attitudes toward the poor today are a mosaic. The poor are viewed with some compassion but are also frequently seen as immoral, unmotivated, and childlike in their behavior. There is still a public lack of appreciation of the debilitating effects of poverty and the stresses that result from a lack of adequate resources. Hostility and racial prejudice may be directed toward some of the poor. In some cases, these attitudes permeate the leadership elites of communities, making the task of poverty reduction more difficult. In truth, history has widened the social distance between the poor and the affluent since life in suburbia makes it possible for the affluent to carry on day-to-day activities with little intimate awareness of the poor or their problems in the crowded urban ghettoes.

Federal Involvement in Antipoverty Programs

Although humanitarian reformists of the nineteenth century pressed for aid and relief to the poor, the main response came from private charity groups. These efforts were uncoordinated and "brushfire" in emphasis. It was not until the Depression of the 1930's that the full resources of the federal government were mobilized to deal with the problem. In his first campaign for the presidency, Franklin Roosevelt pledged participation by the federal government in an antipoverty drive and a good share of New Deal legislation was aimed at improving the minimum purchasing power of every family regardless of their personal circumstances. The Social Security retirement system was set up to maintain income for persons too old to work; unemployment compensation aimed to sustain younger families while the breadwinner looked for work; public assistance was to provide for those unable to work or ineligible for other benefits. These measures undoubtedly made a substantial contribution to the relief of the impoverished during the Depression, but they did not eliminate poverty. Although some of these measures were subsequently broadened, at least one-half of the people now classed as poor were not eligible for these transfer payments. These were the people with low paying jobs, unstable work histories and disabilities that prevented their qualifying for these benefits. The people who needed transfer payments most, received them least.

The 1960's have seen a turning point in federal involvement with antipoverty programs and the greatest outpouring of poverty reducing legislation since the New Deal. Under President Kennedy, the contract compliance machinery of the federal government was strengthened to provide equal employment opportunities for disadvantaged minority groups, a measure extended under President Johnson. The Area Redevelopment Act of 1961 and the Manpower Development Act of 1962 were developed to revitalize economically distressed communities and to provide more vocational training for the underskilled. The Vocational Education Act of 1963 emphasized training for the disadvantaged, especially youth. In 1964, the Economic Opportunity Act provided funds for a direct attack on the problems of poverty, and the Appalachia Regional Development Act of 1965 developed a program of poverty reduction for a single area in the United States. Of equal importance is the recognition in the 1960's that the problems of the poor will not be solved by magic market forces or the resources of the poor themselves, but only by a comprehensive program touching all segments of their lives.

The New Awakening to Poverty

Why has poverty gained a new prominence in the current arena of public issues? Certainly, the issue of poverty has always existed, although it was undoubtedly dulled by the economic prosperity of World War II and the post-war years. We can identify six social currents that have given a sudden urgency to the reduction of poverty. These are: (1) the technological revolution of the fifties and sixties with consequent erosion and dislocation of manpower resources; (2) the internal challenge to our economy posed by the Cold War; (3) the Civil Rights movement of the 1960's; (4) the increased financial costs of social welfare programs; (5) the increase in crime and juvenile delinquency; and (6) the youth and school crisis.

Automation and Mechanization

Although technological change has become deeply imbedded in the American industrial process, the *rate of change* has shown a remarkable increase in the post-war period and will continue to increase in the predictable future. The immediate effect of these changes is to eliminate low-skilled jobs or to create a demand for skills that require extensive preparation. The shrinking of this job base has posed a threat to the employment opportunities of the undertrained and underskilled, and has resulted in a concern for improving vocational opportunities for these groups.

Cold War Pressures

The advent of the Cold War has also created pressures to examine our current patterns of resource allocation. The best answer to external criticisms of our political economy would be a viable economic system with an adequate allocation and distribution of resources to individuals. It could be argued that a country that cannot solve this problem is ill-prepared to exert international leadership and provide a useful model for developing nations to follow.

The Civil Rights Movement

The rise of the Civil Rights movement has also contributed a new sense of urgency to the question of poverty reduction. The core issue in the Civil Rights movement is a maldistribution of economic resources and opportunities to Negroes. Even though the majority of the poverty-stricken are not Negro, the majority of Negroes are poverty-stricken. If one could point to a single current impetus for poverty reduction, it would be the pressures generated by the Civil Rights movement: the demands for better housing, better jobs and better education.

Increased Costs of Welfare Programs

As the number and quality of welfare programs have changed, there has been increasing attention given to the *costs* of these programs. This pressure has been felt at the local and state levels where welfare program financing must compete with other social priorities (e.g. industrial development, service improvement, education, and road construction). Welfare costs have expanded considerably and account for a large proportion of local expenditures. As pressures mount for tax reduction and better services, more and more attention has been given to the financial costs of poverty.

The Increase in Crime and Juvenile Delinquency

The increased rates of social deviancy have focused attention on "the breeding grounds" of such social ills—the slum and the ghetto. The attention has been twofold: (1) what specific conditions of poverty generate these forms of social deviancy and (2) what specific programs can be used as preventive. Basic to this new concern is a desire to treat the cause rather than the symptom.

The Youth and School Crisis

Finally, the recognition of the growing armies of youth who are inadequately prepared for military and occupational service has strengthened the concern with poverty reduction. In an age where better educational preparation is demanded, there has been considerable searching and questioning about possible revisions of the educational system to meet the needs of disadvantaged youngsters.

These are some of the pressures, then, that have generated current interest in poverty, its causes, and its cures. This interest has been articulated in a number of articles and books that, in turn, helped to influence public opinion. Undoubtedly two of the most important were Michael Harrington's *The Other America* (New York: The Macmillan Co., 1962) and Dwight Macdonald's article "Our Invisible Poor" in *The New Yorker* magazine. Both works came to the attention of Presidents Kennedy and Johnson and other public officials and admittedly helped shape action proposals for the current "war on poverty." We are witnessing an intellectual reawakening to the issue of poverty in the United States and an outpouring of popular and technical articles and books on many phases of the subject.

The Purpose and Scope of the Book

In preparing this book, it was our intention to present a selection of articles that reflected both variety and diversity in describing and analyzing the many-faceted problems of poverty in order to contribute to a better understanding of the issue. The book presents an overview of the poverty problem and it is an analytic tool, synthesizing some of the best thinking on the subject. This collection of articles may be as noteworthy for what is *not* included as for what is included. Very little current analyses exist, for example, on the health of the poor, their employment experiences, and their politics. We reached the conclusion in preparing the book that poverty as a subject of inquiry has many unresearched areas and it is hoped, therefore, that this book may prove to be a stimulant for needed research and analyses in these fields.

Acknowledgments

Many individuals contributed to this report. We especially thank the following people. First, we would like to express our gratitude to the Institute of Labor and Industrial Relations, the University of Michigan–Wayne State University, and especially to its co-directors, Ronald W. Haughton and Charles M. Rehmus, who saw the value of the project and made available technical and financial assistance. We were also encouraged and supported in this work by Dean William Haber of the College of Literature, Science and the Arts of The University of Michigan.

A number of people proved to be valuable resources in the development of this book. Space limitations permit us to name only a few: Eugene Feingold, Sydney Bernard, and Benjamin Darsky of The University of Michigan; S. M. Miller of Syracuse University; Hylan Lewis of Howard University; Hyman Rodman of the Merrill Palmer Institute; Robert Lampman of the University of Wisconsin; Sar Levitan of the Upjohn Institute for Employment Research; Irving Jacobs of the Social Security Administration; and Nat Goldfinger of the A.F.L.–C.I.O. Research Department. We are grateful also to the national office and to the Detroit chapter of the American Jewish Committee for their financial assistance to this project.

Our work was also facilitated by the yeomanlike services of William Murphy, Mrs. Alfreda Wilson, and Mrs. Vicki Wittlich who helped in assembling and typing the materials for this book. We are also indeed grateful for the support and encouragement given to us by Patricia Ferman, Hy Kornbluh, and Barbara Haber.

Contents

Chapter 1

Definitions and Prevalence of Poverty

To all too many people, poverty means merely the absence of money. This is a definition influenced, perhaps, by the belief in American society that if money is lacking, work and determination will provide it, and that in our affluent society no one need starve. Admittedly, nobody starves today and apples will probably never again be sold on the street corners. But it must also be remembered that poverty is not merely a question of food, or of money, or of determination. For poverty deprives the individual not only of material comfort but also of human dignity and fulfillment. Its causes are much more complex, and its cure requires more than merely a relief check or the creation of one or two programs of training and retraining. It must be realized that, because of the growing complexity of modern society, the disadvantaged, in particular, more and more lose the very ability to make choices, to be responsible, to know what must be done, and to take action. In short, poverty has today become a complex interlocking set of circumstances, caused by and in turn reinforcing each other, that combine to keep the individual without money, without help, without work. It can truly be said that today those people are poor who can least afford it.

—From Hearings before the Select Committee on Poverty of the Committee on Labor and Public Welfare, United States Senate, 88th Congress, Second Session on S.2642.

How IS POVERTY DEFINED in the United States and how many people are impoverished? The definition of poverty has implications both for statements about its magnitude and about programs for its reduction. There are four different criteria that could be used to analyze the nature and extent of poverty in this country: (1) the limitation of income resources of a single person or a family; (2) the deficiency of community resources and income substitutes; (3) the combination of negative characteristics for labor force participation; and (4) the presence of a "culture of poverty."

1. *The income criteria:* The most common definition of poverty stresses the lack or inadequacy of income as the distinguishing characteristic of poor individuals or families. Below a defined "poverty-line" individuals are said to have insufficient income to meet the minimum daily needs of life, and above which, it is held, people are able to meet these needs. The "poverty-line" varies depending on assumptions as to what constitutes "the daily needs of life" and the cost of these items.

Current poverty-line definitions vary. In a 1964 report on poverty the President's Council of Economic Advisors used a cash income of less than $3,000 in 1962 as a poverty-line for families of two or more persons, and an income of less than $1,500 for unattached individuals living alone or with nonrelatives. In all, the Council estimated that between thirty-three million and thirty-five million Americans were "living at or below the boundaries of poverty in 1962—nearly one fifth of our nation."

A variation of the poverty-line definition is urged by liberal economist Leon H. Keyserling who has classified families with an income of less than $4,000 (in 1960 dollars), and unattached individuals with an income of less than $2,000 as poverty-stricken. By this standard, there were ten and a half million families and four million unattached individuals in poverty in 1960. But, in addition to his poverty classification, Keyserling adds a category of *deprivation*. This includes unattached individuals whose income ranges from $2,000–$3,999, and multi-person families with incomes of $4,000 to $5,999, a sum which leaves them in a constant climate of economic insecurity, unable to meet adequate living standards and vulnerable to a marginal social existence. Keyserling estimates that the number of persons in both the poverty and deprivation categories equals about seventy-seven million Americans (forty-three percent of the population) who have less than an acceptable standard of living. This estimate is almost double that made by the President's Council of Economic Advisors.

Until recently, a "poverty-line" definition has failed to distinguish the different minimum needs of families of different sizes, different stages in the life cycle, and different geographic location. Thus, the $3,000 standard would give lead to the impression that a very large, female-headed Harlem family which receives $4,300 in welfare payments was more affluent and less poverty-stricken than a small farm family which earns $2,500. The Social Security Administration has developed a standard which accounts for these differences, but the invariant $3,000 is still widely used.

A second difficulty in using a "poverty-line" is that the line is relative to time. No attempt has been made to use the same methodology to calculate equivalent poverty lines for a number of time periods. For example, the $2,000 guide used in 1949 by the Joint Economic Committee of Congress to define poverty for a four-person urban family has little meaning in current definitions. It was probably too low even in 1949. This fact casts serious doubts on any statements comparing the magnitude of poverty today with that of the 1949 standard.

In calculating the reduction of poverty over time, there is controversy over the relative advantages of a "fixed poverty-line" definition (based on the amount of money in current dollars needed for an unchanging list of goods and services), or a "shifting poverty-line" (where the goods and services considered as the necessary minimum are not fixed but increase with the general increase in the American living standards). As Herman Miller has said in a recent paper, "Changes in the Number and Composition of the Poor,"

> The essential fallacy of a fixed poverty line is that it fails to recognize the relative nature of 'needs.' The poor will not be satisfied with a given level of living year after year when the levels of those around them are going up at the rate of about 2½ per cent per year. Oldtimers may harken back to the 'good old days' when people were happy without electricity, flush toilets, automobiles, and television sets; but, they must also realize that once it becomes possible for all to have these 'luxuries,' they will be demanded and will quickly assume the status of 'needs.' For these reasons, it is unrealistic in an expanding economy to think in terms of a fixed poverty line.

Regardless of where the "poverty-line" is set, it is considerably below what is needed to lead a full and fruitful life in American society, a point that will be explored later in this chapter.

2. *Community resource criteria:* Frequently, we hear about pockets of poverty or "communities of poverty." These are communities in which the occupational base has eroded, or employment opportunities are limited to low paid and unskilled jobs. This limited opportunity fosters the outmigration of the young, the skilled, and the energetic, leaving the community with an underskilled, nondiversified labor force, a situation that makes future economic redevelopment of the community even more difficult.

The key to this type of definition is the use of community attributes (e.g., skill composition, unemployment rate, wage levels) as a guideline to the welfare of its inhabitants. In recent years, the Area Redevelopment Administration has used this approach in designating areas in need of federal redevelopment aid. This agency uses as its guide the unemployment rate of the community in relation to the national rate to define a deficiency of community resources. If the unemployment rate is fifty percent or more above the national rate for three consecutive years then the community is designated a redevelopment area in need of program aid.

The area designation approach to poverty has advantages and disadvantages. It is an advantage that special emphasis is placed on areas of substantial and enduring economic problems. Programs can be designed for the particular needs of the distressed community. However, this area designation also has certain disadvantages. It overlooks the large number of economically impoverished individuals and families that live in affluent communities and would not be served by such a community designation system. Also, such an approach rests largely on the willingness and cooperation of community power leaders in accepting a "distressed area" definition of their community and developing a grass roots program coordinated with federal aid. The experience of the ARA program indicates that such federal programs may frequently meet with resistance from local power groups.

There are other ways of looking at community resources as criteria for a definition of poverty. A community may provide public services which serve as *income supplements:* medical care, job training, relocation assistance, surplus foods, retirement pensions, income maintenance during unemployment or disability, and child care centers. The elimination of poverty in Scandinavian countries, for example, relies heavily on such community income supplements. A community may also provide other resources which serve as *adjustment or coping aids.* These provide an individual or family with needed services or emergency assistance, such as psychiatric and other counseling, consumer education, or legal aid. And, a community may provide a *wide opportunity field* for individual development and involvement: cultural activities, good schools, adult and remedial education, voluntary organizations, recreation areas, quality housing, adequate public transportation, and an open political structure where people can play meaningful roles in making community decisions.

Some communities, when viewed in terms of available resources, are poverty-sustaining; others are poverty-reducing. There is a need to develop a "Community Resource Scale" as a component of any adequate measure of poverty. Community resource deficiency handicaps the poverty-reducing potential of personal income; resource richness decreases the income needed for adequate quality of life.

3. *Negative risk criteria:* Frequently we speak of individuals who are undereducated, underskilled, and old as having a *combination of*

risk characteristics which make it difficult to take part in the labor force in anything more than a marginal role. This definition emphasizes finding and holding a satisfactory role in the labor market, since access to economic resources and the rewards of society is largely dependent on adequate income from a steady job.

Education, skill level, and age are not the only characteristics that may combine to affect a person's chances in the labor market. Work experience, previous training, race, seniority record, occupation and industrial attachment are other factors which can combine to limit effectively the labor market opportunities of the individual. This type of definition has a certain utility in isolating the people who are most likely to be economically deprived and providing guidelines for the content of rehabilitation programs. The definition has weaknesses, however, in implying that the cause of poverty lies within the individual and that the treatment of poverty must be oriented toward the individual. This view may bring about a neglect of factors outside of the individual (e.g., the opportunity structure) in the development of an anti-poverty program.

4. *Behavior or attitudinal criteria:* A group of individuals or families may be said to be in poverty when they *share* a distinctive set of values, behavior traits, and belief complexes that markedly set them off from the affluent groups in the society. This set is a *derivative* of prolonged economic deprivation, lack of adequate financial resources, and socialization in an environment of economic uncertainty. This "culture of poverty" is characterized by an intergenerational persistence and transmission to the children of the poor.

There is both agreement and disagreement among scholars and critics as to what themes run through a "culture of poverty." Anthropologist Thomas Gladwin noted in a recent speech before the National Conference of Social Workers that the life of the poor is dominated by two themes: a sense of powerlessness about the events in everyday life (i.e., a sense of failure in the control of the social environment) and a sense of pessimism about the future. Michael Harrington in *The Other America* points to "a personality of poverty, a type of human being produced by the grinding, wearing life of the slums."

The definition of poverty by reference to a culture complex offers certain objections of which the anthropologist is only too aware. The investigators are looking at *different* groups of the poverty-stricken in *different* geographical locations and in *different* opportunity structures. It may well be that we should refer to "*cultures of poverty*" rather than a single "*culture of poverty*."

One general point should be noted about all of these definitions:

they are criteria for classifying individuals and families as poverty-stricken. But this classification system is developed and applied from the viewpoint of the outside observer. To what extent do these individuals and groups *see themselves* as impoverished? Do they accept this judgment of their life situation by outside observers? There is evidence to indicate that some of them do not. When the Area Redevelopment Administration first began labeling areas as "distressed," some of the very individuals who were the object of this program denied that they were "impoverished" or that their areas were "distressed." The officials of anti-poverty programs are beginning to realize that some individuals and families resent receiving anti-poverty aid because to accept such help is to admit personal failure by the standards of American society. A low-paid worker who earns $3,000 may feel the pinch of inadequate economic resources, but he is not likely to think of himself as a failure, which indeed he is not.

Definitions of poverty are classification systems, designed to suit particular policy or program purposes. They do not reflect the psychological reality of the poor, nor any value judgments as to the quality of life or the actual and potential social contributions of people in America who lack an adequate income.

In this chapter, Dwight Macdonald critically discusses various definitions of poverty and the measure of its prevalence. Oscar Ornati analyzes some of the risk characteristics associated with poverty. In the third article, the authors raise some pointed questions regarding the current use of "poverty budgets." Finally, Mollie Orshansky details a new approach to "counting the poor."

Our Invisible Poor
Dwight Macdonald
The New Yorker

[This reprint was adapted by the Sidney Hillman Foundation from an article which originally appeared in The New Yorker, *January 19, 1963, and is included by permission of the author and the Sidney Hillman Foundation.]*

IN HIS SIGNIFICANTLY TITLED "The Affluent Society" (1958) Professor J. K. Galbraith states that poverty in this country is no longer "a massive affliction [but] more nearly an afterthought." Dr. Galbraith is a humane critic of the American capitalist system, and he is generously indignant about the continued existence of even this nonmassive and afterthoughtish poverty. But the interesting thing about his pronouncement, aside from the fact that it is inaccurate, is that it was generally accepted as obvious. For a long time now, almost everybody has assumed that, because of the New Deal's social legislation and—more important—the prosperity we have enjoyed since 1940, mass poverty no longer exists in this country.

✗ Dr. Galbraith states that our poor have dwindled to two hard-core categories. One is the "insular poverty" of those who live in the rural South or in depressed areas like West Virginia. The other category is "case poverty," which he says is "commonly and properly related to [such] characteristics of the individuals so afflicted [as] mental deficiency, bad health, inability to adapt to the discipline of modern economic life, excessive procreation, alcohol, insufficient education." He reasons that such poverty must be due to individual defects, since "nearly everyone else has mastered his environment; this proves that it is not intractable." Without pressing the similarity of this concept to the "Social Darwinism" whose fallacies Dr. Galbraith easily disposes of elsewhere in his book, one may observe that most of these characteristics are as much the result of poverty as its cause.

Dr. Galbraith's error is understandable, and common. Last April the newspapers reported some exhilarating statistics in a Department of Commerce study: the average family income increased from $2,340 in 1929 to $7,020 in 1961. (These figures are calculated in current dollars, as are all the others I shall cite.) But the papers did not report the fine type, so to speak, which showed that almost all the recent gain was made by families with incomes of over $7,500, and that the rate at which poverty is being eliminated has slowed down alarmingly since 1953. Only the specialists and the statisticians read the fine type, which is why illusions continue to exist about American poverty.

Now Michael Harrington, an alumnus of the *Catholic Worker* and the Fund for the Republic who is at present a contributing editor of *Dissent* and the chief editor of the Socialist Party biweekly, *New America,* has written "The Other America: Poverty in the United States" (Macmillan). In the admirably short space of under two hundred pages, he outlines the problem, describes in imaginative detail what it means to be poor in this country today, summarizes the findings of recent studies by economists and sociologists, and analyzes the reasons for the persistence of mass poverty in the midst of general prosperity.

In the last year we seem to have suddenly awakened, rubbing our eyes like Rip van Winkle, to the fact that mass poverty persists, and that it is one of our two gravest social problems. (The other is related: While only eleven per cent of our population is non-white, twenty-five per cent of our poor are.) What is "poverty"? It is a historically relative concept, first of all. "There are new definitions [in America] of what man can achieve, of what a human standard of life should be," Mr. Harrington writes. "Those who suffer levels of life well below those that are possible, even though they live better than medieval knights or Asian peasants, are poor. . . . Poverty should be defined in terms of those who are denied the minimal levels of health, housing, food, and education that our present stage of scientific knowledge specifies for life as it is now lived in the United States." His dividing line follows that proposed in recent studies by the United States Bureau of Labor Statistics: $4,000 a year for a family of four and $2,000 for an individual living alone. (All kinds of income are included, such as food grown and consumed on farms.) This is the cutoff line generally drawn today.

Mr. Harrington estimates that between forty and fifty million Americans, or about a fourth of the population, are now living in poverty. Not just below the level of comfortable living, but real poverty, in the old-fashioned sense of the word—that they are hard put to it to get the mere necessities, beginning with enough to eat. This is difficult to believe in the United States of 1963, but one has to make the effort, and it is now being made. The extent of our poverty has suddenly become visible. The same thing has happened in England, where working-class gains as a result of the Labour Party's post-1945 welfare state blinded almost everybody to the continued existence of mass poverty. It was not until Professor Richard M. Titmuss, of the London School of Economics, published a series of articles in the *New Statesman* last fall, based on his new book, "Income Distribution and Social Change" (Allen & Unwin), that even the liberal public in England became aware that the problem still persists on a scale that is "statistically significant," as the economists put it.

The Limits of Statistics

Statistics on poverty are even trickier than most. For example, age and geography make a difference. There is a distinction, which cannot be rendered arithmetically, between poverty and low income. A childless young couple with $3,000 a year is not poor in the way an elderly couple might be with the same income. The young couple's statistical poverty may be temporary inconvenience; if the husband is a graduate student or a skilled worker, there are prospects of later affluence or at least comfort. But the old couple can look forward only to diminishing earnings and increasing medical expenses. So also geographically: A family of four in a small town with $4,000 a year may be better off than a like family in a city—lower rent, no bus fares to get to work, fewer occasions (or temptations) to spend money. Even more so with a rural family. Although allowance is made for the value of the vegetables they may raise to feed themselves, it is impossible to calculate how much money they *don't* spend on clothes, say, or furniture, because they don't have to keep up with the Joneses. Lurking in the crevices of a city, like piranha fish in a Brazilian stream, are numerous tempting opportunities for expenditure, small but voracious, which can strip a budget to its bones in a surprisingly short time.

How Many Poor?

It is not, therefore, surprising to find that there is some disagreement about just how many millions of Americans are poor. The point is that all recent studies* agree that American poverty is still a mass phenomenon.

Thus the Commerce Department's April report estimates there are 17,500,000 families *and* "unattached individuals" with incomes of less than $4,000. How many of the latter are there? "Poverty and Deprivation" (see note below) puts the number of single persons with under $2,000 at 4,000,000. Let us say that in the 17,500,000 under $4,000 there are 6,500,000 single persons—the proportion of unattached individuals tends to go down as income rises. This homemade estimate gives us 11,000,000 families with incomes of under $4,000. Figuring the average American family at three and a half persons—which it is—this makes 38,500,000 individuals in families, or a grand total, if we add in the 4,000,000 "unattached individuals" with under $2,000 a year, of 42,500,000 Americans now living in poverty, which is close to a fourth of the total population.

The reason Dr. Galbraith was able to see poverty as no longer "a massive affliction" is that he used a cutoff of $1,000, which even in 1949, when it was adopted in a Congressional study, was probably too low (the c.i.o. argued for $2,000) and in 1958, when "The Affluent Society" appeared, was simply fantastic.

The model postwar budgets drawn up in 1951 by the Bureau of Labor Statistics to "maintain a level of adequate living" give a concrete idea of what poverty means in this country—or would mean if poor families lived within their income and spent it wisely, which they don't. Dr. Kolko summarizes the kind of living these budgets provide:

---

*The studies, all of which are referred to by the author, include, Dr. Gabriel Kolko, *Wealth & Poverty in America* (Praeger); Dr. James N. Morgan, et al, *Income and Welfare in the United States* (McGraw-Hill); "Poverty and Deprivation" (pamphlet), Conference on Economic Progress, Leon H. Keyserling and others.

Three members of the family see a movie once every three weeks, and one member sees a movie once every two weeks. There is no telephone in the house, but the family makes three pay calls a week. They buy one book a year and write one letter a week.

The father buys one heavy wool suit every two years and a light wool suit every three years; the wife, one suit every ten years or one skirt every five years. Every three or four years, depending on the distance and time involved, the family takes a vacation outside their own city. In 1950, the family spent a total of $80 to $90 on all types of home furnishings, electrical appliances, and laundry equipment. . . . The family eats cheaper cuts of meat several times a week, but has more expensive cuts on holidays. The entire family consumes a total of two five-cent ice cream cones, one five-cent candy bar, two bottles of soda, and one bottle of beer a week. The family owes no money, but has no savings except for a small insurance policy.

One other item is included in the B.L.S. "maintenance" budget: a new car every twelve to eighteen years.

This is an ideal picture, drawn up by social workers, of how a poor family *should* spend its money. But the poor are much less provident—installment debts take up a lot of their cash, and only a statistician could expect an actual live woman, however poor, to buy new clothes at intervals of five or ten years. Also, one suspects that a lot more movies are seen and ice-cream cones and bottles of beer are consumed than in the Spartan ideal. But these necessary luxuries are had only at the cost of displacing other items—necessary, so to speak—in the B.L.S. budget.

The Conference on Economic Progress's "Poverty and Deprivation" deals not only with the poor but also with another large section of the "underprivileged," which is an American euphemism almost as good as "senior citizen"; namely, the 37,000,000 persons whose family income is between $4,000 and $5,999 and the 2,000,000 singles who have from $2,000 to $2,999. The authors define "deprivation" as "above poverty but short of minimum requirements for a modestly comfortable level of living." They claim that 77,000,000 Americans, or *almost half the population,* live in poverty or deprivation. One recalls the furor Roosevelt aroused with his "one-third of a nation—ill-housed, ill-clad, ill-nourished." But the political climate was different then.

The distinction between a family income of $3,500 ("poverty") and $4,500 ("deprivation") is not vivid to those who run things—the 31 percent whose incomes are between $7,500 and $14,999 and the 7 percent of the top-most top dogs, who get $15,000 or more. These two minorities, sizable enough to feel they *are* the nation, have been as unaware of the continued existence of mass poverty as this reviewer was until he read Mr. Harrington's book. They are businessmen, congressmen, judges, government officials, politicians, lawyers, doctors, engineers, scientists, editors, journalists, and administrators in colleges, churches, and foundations. Since their education, income, and social status are superior, they, if anybody, might be expected to accept responsibility for what the Constitution calls "the general welfare." They have not done so in the case of the poor. And they have a good excuse. It is becoming harder and harder simply to *see* the one-fourth of our fellow-citizens who live below the poverty line.

> The poor are increasingly slipping out of the very experience and consciousness of the nation [Mr. Harrington writes]. If the middle class never did like ugliness and poverty, it was at least aware of them. "Across the tracks" was not a very long way to go. . . . Now the American city has been transformed. The poor still inhabit the miserable housing in the central area, but they are increasingly isolated from contact with, or sight of, anybody else. . . . Living out in the suburbs, it is easy to assume that ours is, indeed, an affluent society. . . .
>
> Clothes make the poor invisible too: America has the best-dressed poverty the world has ever known. . . . It is much easier in the United States to be decently dressed than it is to be decently housed, fed, or doctored. . . .
>
> Many of the poor are the wrong age to be seen. A good number of them are sixty-five years of age or better; an even larger number are under eighteen. . . .
>
> And finally, the poor are politically invisible. . . . They are without lobbies of their own; they put forward no legislative program. As a group, they are atomized. They have no face; they have no voice. . . . Only the social agencies have a really direct involvement with the other America, and they are without any great political power. . . .
>
> Forty to fifty million people are becoming increasingly invisible.

These invisible people fall mostly into the following categories, some of them overlapping: poor farmers, who operate 40 percent of the farms and get 7 percent of the farm cash income; migratory farm workers; unskilled, unorganized workers in offices, hotels, restaurants, hospitals, laundries, and other service jobs; inhabitants of areas where poverty is either endemic ("peculiar to a people or district"), as in the rural South, or epidemic ("prevalent among a community at a special time and produced by some special causes"), as in West Virginia, where the special cause was the closing of coal mines and steel plants; Negroes and Puerto Ricans, who are a fourth of the total poor; the alcoholic derelicts in the big-city skid rows; the hillbillies from Kentucky, Tennessee, and Oklahoma who have migrated to Midwestern cities in search of better jobs. And, finally, almost half our "senior citizens."

The Wrong Color

The most obvious citizens of the Other America are those whose skins are the wrong color. The folk slogans are realistic: "Last to be hired, first to be fired" and "If you're black, stay back." There has been some progress. In 1939, the non-white worker's wage averaged 41.4 percent of the white worker's; by 1958 it had climbed to 58 percent. A famous victory, but the non-whites still average only slightly more than half as much as the whites. Even this modest gain was due not to any Rooseveltian or Trumanian social reform but merely to the fact that for some years there was a war on and workers were in demand, whether black, white, or violet. By 1947, the non-whites had achieved most of their advance—to 54 percent of white earnings, which means they have gained, in the last fifteen years, just 4 percent.

The least obvious poverty affects our "senior citizens"—those over sixty-five. Mr. Harrington estimates that half of them—8,000,000—live in poverty, and he thinks they are even more atomized and politically helpless than the rest of the Other America. He estimates that one-fourth of the "unrelated individuals" among them, or a million persons, have less than $580 a year, which is about what is allotted *for food alone* in the Department of Agriculture's minimum-subsistence budget. (The average American family now spends only 20 percent of its income for food—an indication of the remarkable prosperity we are all enjoying, except for one-quarter of us.) One can imagine, or perhaps one can't, what it would be like to live on $580 a year, or $11 a week. It is only fair to note that most of our senior citizens do better: The average per capita income of those over sixty-five is now estimated to be slightly over $20 a week. That is, $1,000 a year.

The aged poor have two sources of income besides their earnings or savings. One is contributions by relatives. A 1961 White House Conference Report put this at 10 percent of income, which works out to $8 a week for an income of $4,000—and the 8,000,000 aged poor all have less than that. The other is Social Security, whose benefits in 1959 averaged $18 a week. Even this modest sum is more than any of the under-$4,000 got, since payments are proportionate to earnings and the poor, of course, earned less than the rest. A quarter of them, and those in general the neediest, are not covered by Social Security. The last resort is relief, and Mr. Harrington describes most vividly the humiliations the poor often have to put up with to get that.

The whole problem of poverty and the aged is especially serious today because Americans are living longer. In the first half of this century, life expectancy increased 17.6 years for men and 20.3 years for women. And between 1950 and 1960 the over-sixty-five group increased twice as fast as the population as a whole.

The worst part of being old and poor in this country is the loneliness. Mr. Harrington notes that we have not only racial ghettos but geriatric ones, in the cheap rooming-house districts of large cities. He gives one peculiarly disturbing statistic: "One-third of the aged in the United States, some 5,000,000 or more human beings, have no phone in their place of residence. They are literally cut off from the rest of America."

Ernest Hemingway's celebrated deflation of Scott Fitzgerald's romantic notion that the rich are "different" somehow—"Yes, they have money"—doesn't apply to the poor. They are different in more important ways than their lack of money, as Mr. Harrington demonstrates:

> Emotional upset is one of the main forms of the vicious circle of impoverishment. The structure of the society is hostile to these people. The poor tend to become pessimistic and depressed; they seek immediate gratification instead of saving; they act out.
>
> Once this mood, this unarticulated philosophy becomes a fact, society can change, the recession can end, and yet there is no motive for movement. The depression has become internalized. The middle class looks upon this process and sees "lazy" people who "just don't want to get ahead." People who are much too sensitive to demand of cripples that they run races ask of the poor that they get up and act just like everyone else in the society.
>
> The poor are not like everyone else. . . . They think and feel differently; they look upon a different America than the middle class looks upon.

The poor are also different in a physical sense: they are much less healthy. According to "Poverty and Deprivation," the proportion of those "disabled or limited in their major activity by chronic ill health" rises sharply as income sinks. In reasonably well-off families ($7,000 and up), 4.3 percent are so disabled; in reasonably poor families ($2,000 to $3,999), the proportion doubles, to 8 percent; and in unreasonably poor families (under $2,000), it doubles again, to 16.5 percent. An obvious cause, among others, for the very poor being four times as much disabled by "chronic ill health" as the well-to-do is that they have much less money to spend for medical care—in fact, almost nothing. This weighs with special heaviness on the aged poor. During the fifties, Mr. Harrington notes, "all costs on the Consumer Price Index went up by 12 percent. But medical costs, that terrible staple of the aged, went up by 36 percent, hospitalization rose by 65 percent, and group hospitalization costs (Blue Cross premiums) were up by 83 percent."

The Defeat of Medicare

This last figure is particularly interesting, since Blue Cross and such plans are the A.M.A.'s alternative to socialized medicine, or, rather, to the timid fumblings toward it that even our most liberal politicians have dared to propose. Such figures throw an unpleasant light on the Senate's rejection of Medicare. The defeat was all the more bitter because, in the usual effort to appease the conservatives (with the usual lack of success—only five Republicans and only four Southern Democrats voted pro), the bill was watered down in advance. Not until he had spent $90 of his own money—which is 10 percent of the annual income of some 3,000,000 aged poor—would a patient have been eligible. And the original program included only people already covered by Social Security or Railroad Retirement pensions and excluded the neediest of all—the 2,500,000 aged poor who are left out of both these systems.

Mental as well as physical illness is much greater among the poor, even though our complacent cliché is that nervous breakdowns are a prerogative of the rich because the poor "can't afford them." (They can't, but they have them anyway.) This bit of middle-class folklore should be laid to rest by a study made in New Haven: "Social Class and Mental Illness," by August B. Hollingshead and Frederick C. Redlich (Wiley). They found that the rate of "treated psychiatric illness" is about the same from the rich down through decently paid workers—an average of 573 per 100,000. But in the bottom fifth it shoots up to 1,659 per 100,000. There is an even more striking difference in the *kind* of mental illness. Of those in the four top income groups who had undergone psychiatric treatment, 65 percent had been treated for neurotic problems and 35 percent for psychotic disturbances. In the bottom fifth, the treated illnesses were almost all psychotic (90 percent). This shows there is something to the notion that the poor "can't afford" nervous breakdowns—the milder kind, that is—since the reason the proportion of *treated* neuroses among the poor is only 10 percent is that a neurotic can keep going, after a fashion. But the argument cuts deeper the other way. The poor go to a psychiatrist (or, more commonly, are committed to a mental institution) only when they are completely unable to function because of psychotic symptoms. Therefore, even that nearly threefold increase in mental disorders among the poor is probably an underestimate.

The main reason the American poor have become invisible is that since 1936 their numbers have been reduced by two-thirds. Astounding as it may seem, the fact is that President Roosevelt's "one-third of a nation" was a considerable understatement; over two-thirds of us then lived below the poverty line, as is shown by the tables that follow. But today the poor are a minority, and minorities can be ignored if they are so heterogeneous that they cannot be organized. When the poor were a majority, they simply could not be overlooked. Poverty is also hard to see today because the middle class ($6,000 to $14,999) has vastly increased—from 13 percent of all families in 1936 to a near-majority (47 percent) today. That mass poverty can persist despite this rise to affluence is hard to believe, or see, especially if one is among those who have risen.

Two tables in "Poverty and Deprivation" summarize what has been happening in the last thirty years. They cover only multiple-person families; all figures are converted to 1960 dollars; and the income is before taxes. I have omitted, for clarity, all fractions.

The first table is the percentage of families with a given income:

	1935–6	1947	1953	1960
Under $ 4,000	68%	37%	28%	23%
$4,000 to $ 5,999	17	29	28	23
$6,000 to $ 7,499	6	12	17	16
$7,500 to $14,999	7	17	23	31
Over $15,000	2	4	5	7

The second table is the share each group had in the family income of the nation:

	1935–6	1947	1953	1960
Under $ 4,000	35%	16%	11%	7%
$4,000 to $ 5,999	21	24	21	15
$6,000 to $ 7,499	10	14	17	14
$7,500 to $14,999	16	28	33	40
Over $15,000	18	18	19	24

Several interesting conclusions can be drawn from these tables:

(1)   The New Deal didn't do anything about poverty: The under-$4,000 families in 1936 were 68 percent of the total population, which was slightly *more* than the 1929 figure of 65 percent.

(2)   The war economy (hot and cold) did do something about poverty: Between 1936 and 1960 the proportion of all families who were poor was reduced from 68 percent to 23 percent.

(3) If the percentage of under-$4,000 families decreased by two-thirds between 1936 and 1960, their share of the national income dropped a great deal more—from 35 percent to 7 percent.

(4) The well-to-do ($7,500 to $14,999) have enormously increased, from 7 percent of all families in 1936 to 31 percent today. The rich ($15,000 and over) have also multiplied—from 2 to 7 percent. But it should be noted that the very rich, according to another new study, "The Share of Top Wealth-Holders in National Wealth, 1822–1956," by Robert J. Lampman (Princeton), have experienced a decline. He finds that the top 1 percent of wealth-holders owned 38 percent of the national wealth in 1929 and own only 28 percent today.

(5) The reduction of poverty has slowed down. In the six years 1947–53, the number of poor families declined 9 percent, but in the following seven years only 5 percent. The economic stasis that set in with Eisenhower and that still persists under Kennedy was responsible. (This stagnation, however, did not affect the over-$7,500 families, who increased from 28 percent to 38 percent between 1953 and 1960.) In the New York *Times Magazine* for last November 11th, Herman P. Miller, of the Bureau of the Census, wrote, "During the forties, the lower-paid occupations made the greatest relative gains in average income. Laborers and service workers . . . had increases of about 180% . . . and professional and managerial workers, the highest paid workers of all, had the lowest relative gains—96%." But in the last decade the trend has been reversed; laborers and service workers have gained 39% while professional-managerial workers have gained 68%. This is because in the wartime forties the unskilled were in great demand, while now they are being replaced by machines. Automation is today the same kind of menace to the unskilled—that is, the poor—that the enclosure movement was to the British agricultural population centuries ago. "The facts show that our 'social revolution' ended nearly twenty years ago," Mr. Miller concludes, "yet important segments of the American public, many of them highly placed Government officials and prominent educators, think and act as though it were a continuing process."

The post-1940 decrease in poverty was not due to the policies or actions of those who are not poor, those in positions of power and responsibility. The war economy needed workers, wages went up, and the poor became less poor. When economic stasis set in, the rate of decrease in poverty slowed down proportionately, and it is still slow. Kennedy's efforts to "get the country moving again" have been unsuccessful, possibly because he has, despite the suggestions of many of his economic advisers, not yet advocated the one big step that might push the economy off dead center: a massive increase in government spending. This would be politically courageous, perhaps even dangerous, because of the superstitious fear of "deficit spending" and an "unbalanced" federal budget. American folklore insists that a government's budget must be arranged like a private family's. Walter Lippmann wrote, after the collapse of the stock market last spring:

> There is mounting evidence that those economists were right who told the Administration last winter that it was making the mistake of trying to balance the budget too soon. It will be said that the budget is not balanced: it shows a deficit in fiscal 1962 of $7 billion. . . . But . . . the budget that matters is the Department of Commerce's income and product accounts budget. Nobody looks at it except the economists [but] while the Administrative budget is necessary for administration and is like a man's checkbook, the income budget tells the real story. . . .
>
> [It] shows that at the end of 1962 the outgo and ingo accounts will be virtually in balance, with a deficit of only about half a billion dollars. Thus, in reality, the Kennedy administration is no longer stimulating the economy, and the economy is stagnating for lack of stimulation. We have one of the lowest rates of growth among the advanced industrial nations of the world.

One shouldn't be hard on the President. Franklin Roosevelt, a more daring and experimental politician, at least in his domestic policy, listened to the American disciples of J. M. Keynes in the early New Deal years and unbalanced his budgets, with splendid results. But by 1936 he had lost his nerve. He cut back government spending and there ensued the 1937 recession, from which the economy recovered only when war orders began to make up for the deficiency in domestic buying power. "Poverty and Deprivation" estimates that between 1953 and 1961 the annual growth rate of our economy was "only 2.5 percent per annum contrasted with an estimated 4.2 percent required to maintain utilization of manpower and other productive resources." The poor, who always experience the worst the first, understand quite personally the meaning of that dry statistic, as they understand Kipling's "The toad beneath the harrow knows / Exactly where each tooth-point goes." They are also most intimately acquainted with another set of statistics: the steady postwar rise in the unemployment rate, from 3.1 percent in 1949 to 4.3 percent in 1954 to 5.1 percent in 1958 to over 7 percent in 1961. (The Tory Government is worried because British unemployment is now at its highest point for the last three years. This point is 2.1 percent, which is less than our lowest rate in the last fifteen years.)

It's not that Public Opinion doesn't become Aroused every now and then. But the arousement never leads to much. It was aroused twenty-four years ago when John Steinbeck published "The Grapes of Wrath," but Mr. Harrington reports that things in the Imperial Valley are still much the same: low wages, bad housing, no effective union. Public Opinion is too public—that is, too general; of its very nature, it can have no sustained interest in California agriculture. The only groups with such a continuing interest are the workers and the farmers who hire them. Once Public Opinion ceased to be Aroused, the battle was again between the two antagonists with a real, personal stake in the outcome, and there was no question about which was stronger. So with the rural poor in general. In the late fifties, the average annual wage for white male American farm workers was slightly over $1,000; women, children, Negroes, and Mexicans got less. One recalls Edward R. Murrow's celebrated television program about these people, "Harvest of Shame." Once more everybody was shocked, but the harvest is still shameful. One also recalls that Mr. Murrow, after President Kennedy had appointed him head of the United States Information Agency, tried to persuade the b.b.c. not to show "Harvest of Shame." His argument was that it would give an undesirable "image" of America to foreign audiences.

There is a monotony about the injustices suffered by the poor that perhaps accounts for the lack of interest the rest of society shows in them. Everything seems to go wrong with them. They never win. It's just boring.

"Address Unknown"

Public housing turns out not to be for them. The 1949 Housing Act authorized 810,000 new units of low-cost housing in the following four years. Twelve years later, in 1961, the a.f.l.-c.i.o. proposed 400,000 units to complete the lagging 1949 program. The Kennedy administration ventured to recommend 100,000 to Congress. Thus, instead of 810,000 low-cost units by 1953, the poor will get, if they are lucky, 500,000 by 1963. And they are more likely to be injured than helped by slum clearance, since the new projects usually have higher rents than the displaced slum-dwellers can afford. (There has been no dearth of government-financed *middle*-income housing since 1949.) These refugees from the bulldozers for the most part simply emigrate to other slums. They also become invisible; Mr. Harrington notes that half of them are recorded as "address unknown." Several years ago, Charles Abrams, who was New York State Rent Administrator under Harriman and who is now president of the National Committee Against Discrimination in

Housing, summed up what he had learned in two decades in public housing: "Once social reforms have won tonal appeal in the public mind, their slogans and goal-symbols may degenerate into tools of the dominant class for beleaguering the minority and often for defeating the very aims which the original sponsors had intended for their reforms."

And this is not the end of tribulation. The poor, who can least afford to lose pay because of ill health, lose the most. A National Health Survey, made a few years ago, found that workers earning under $2,000 a year had twice as many "restricted-activity days" as those earning over $4,000.

Although they are the most in need of hospital insurance, the poor have the least, since they can't afford the premiums; only 40 percent of poor families have it, as against 63 percent of all families. (It should be noted, however, that the poor who are war veterans can get free treatment, at government expense, in Veterans Administration Hospitals.)

The poor actually pay more taxes, in proportion to their income, than the rich. A recent study by the Tax Foundation estimates that 28 percent of incomes under $2,000 goes for taxes, as against 24 percent of the incomes of families earning five to seven times as much. Sales and other excise taxes are largely responsible for this curious statistic. It is true that such taxes fall impartially on all, like the blessed rain from heaven, but it is a form of egalitarianism that perhaps only Senator Goldwater can fully appreciate.

The final irony is that the Welfare State, which Roosevelt erected and which Eisenhower, no matter how strongly he felt about it, didn't attempt to pull down, is not for the poor, either. Agricultural workers are not covered by Social Security, nor are many of the desperately poor among the aged, such as "unrelated individuals" with incomes of less than $1,000, of whom only 37 percent are covered, which is just half the percentage of coverage among the aged in general. Of the Welfare State, Mr. Harrington says, "Its creation had been stimulated by mass impoverishment and misery, yet it helped the poor least of all. Laws like unemployment compensation, the Wagner Act, the various farm programs, all these were designed for the middle third in the cities, for the organized workers, and for the . . . big market farmers. . . . [It] benefits those least who need help most." The industrial workers, led by John L. Lewis, mobilized enough political force to put through Section 7(a) of the National Industrial Recovery Act, which, with the Wagner Act, made the c.i.o. possible. The big farmers put enough pressure on Henry Wallace, Roosevelt's first Secretary of Agriculture—who talked a good fight for liberal principles but was a Hamlet when it came to action—to establish the two basic propositions of Welfare State agriculture: subsidies that now cost $3 billion a year and that chiefly benefit the big farmers; and the exclusion of sharecroppers, tenant farmers, and migratory workers from the protection of minimum-wage and Social Security laws.

No doubt the Kennedy administration would like to do more for the poor than it has, but it is hampered by the cabal of Republicans and Southern Democrats in Congress. The 1961 revision of the Fair Labor Standards Act, which raised the national minimum wage to the not exorbitant figure of $1.15 an hour, was a slight improvement over the previous act. For instance, it increased coverage of retail-trade workers from 3 percent to 33 percent. (But one-fourth of the retail workers still excluded earn less than $1 an hour.) There was also a considerable amount of shadow-boxing involved: Of the 3,600,000 workers newly covered, only 663,000 were making less than $1 an hour. And there was the exclusion of a particularly ill-paid group of workers. Nobody had anything against the laundry workers *personally*. It was just that they were weak, unorganized, and politically expendable. To appease the conservatives in Congress, whose votes were needed to get the revision through, they were therefore expended. The result is that of the 500,000 workers in the laundry, dry-cleaning, and dyeing industries, just 17,000 are now protected by the Fair Labor Standards Act.

Perpetuating Poverty

It seems likely that mass poverty will continue in this country for a long time. The more it is reduced, the harder it is to keep on reducing it. The poor, having dwindled from two-thirds of the population in 1936 to one-quarter today, no longer are a significant political force, as is shown by the Senate's rejection of Medicare and by the Democrats' dropping it as an issue in the elections last year. Also, as poverty decreases, those left behind tend more and more to be the ones who have for so long accepted poverty as their destiny that they need outside help to climb out of it. This new minority mass poverty, so much more isolated and hopeless than the old majority poverty, shows signs of becoming chronic. "The permanence of low incomes is inferred from a variety of findings," write the authors of the Morgan survey. "In many poor families the head has never earned enough to cover the family's present needs."

> For most families, however, the problem of chronic poverty is serious. One such family is headed by a thirty-two-year-old man who is employed as a dishwasher. Though he works steadily and more than full time, he earned over $2,000 in 1959. His wife earned $300 more,

but their combined incomes are not enough to support themselves and their three children. Although the head of the family is only thirty-two, he feels that he has no chance of advancement partly because he finished only seven grades of school. . . . The possibility of such families leaving the ranks of the poor is not high.

Children born into poor families today have less chance of "improving themselves" than the children of the pre-1940 poor. Rags to riches is now more likely to be rags to rags. "Indeed," the Morgan book concludes, "it appears that a number of the heads of poor families have moved into less skilled jobs than their fathers had." Over a third of the children of the poor, according to the survey, don't go beyond the eighth grade and "will probably perpetuate the poverty of their parents." There are a great many of these children. In an important study of poverty, made for a Congressional committee in 1959, Dr. Robert J. Lampman estimated that eleven million of the poor were under eighteen. "A considerable number of younger persons are starting life in a condition of 'inherited poverty,'" he observed. To which Mr. Harrington adds, "The character of poverty has changed, and it has become more deadly for the young. It is no longer associated with immigrant groups with high aspirations; it is now identified with those whose social existence makes it more and more difficult to break out into the larger society." Even when children from poor families show intellectual promise, there is nothing in the values of their friends or families to encourage them to make use of it. Of the top 16 percent of high-school students—those scoring 120 and over in I.Q. tests—only half go on to college. The explanation for this amazing—and alarming—situation is as much cultural as economic. The children of the poor now tend to lack what the sociologists call "motivation." At least one foundation is working on the problem of why so many bright children from poor families don't ever try to go beyond high school.

Mr. Raymond M. Hilliard, at present director of the Cook County (i.e., Chicago) Department of Public Aid and formerly Commissioner of Welfare for New York City, recently directed a "representative-sample" investigation, which showed that more than half of the 225,000 able-bodied Cook County residents who were on relief were "functionally illiterate." One reason Cook County has to spend $16,500,000 a month on relief is "the lack of basic educational skills of relief recipients which are essential to compete in our modern society." An interesting footnote, appropos of recent happenings at "Ole Miss," is that the illiteracy rate of the relief recipients who were educated in Chicago is 33 percent, while among those who were educated in Mississippi and later moved to Chicago it is 77 percent.

Slums and Schools

The problem of educating the poor has changed since 1900. Then it was the language and cultural difficulties of immigrants from foreign countries; now it is the subtler but more intractable problems of internal migration from backward regions, mostly in the South. The old immigrants wanted to Better Themselves and to Get Ahead. The new migrants are less ambitious, and they come into a less ambitious atmosphere. "When they arrive in the city," wrote Christopher Jencks in an excellent two-part survey, "Slums and Schools," in the *New Republic* last fall, "they join others equally unprepared for urban life in the slums—a milieu which is in many ways utterly dissociated from the rest of America. Often this milieu is self-perpetuating. I have been unable to find any statistics on how many of these migrants' children and grandchildren have become middle-class, but it is probably not too inaccurate to estimate that about 30,000,000 people live in urban slums, and that about half are second-generation residents." The immigrants of 1890–1910 also arrived in a milieu that was "in many ways utterly dissociated from the rest of America," yet they had a vision—a rather materialistic one, but still a vision—of what life in America could be if they worked hard enough; and they did work, and they did aspire to something more than they had; and they did get out of the slums. The disturbing thing about the poor today is that so many of them seem to lack any such vision. Mr. Jencks remarks:

> While the economy is changing in a way which makes the eventual liquidation of the slums at least conceivable, young people are not seizing the opportunities this change presents. Too many are dropping out of school before graduation (more than half in many slums); too few are going to college. . . . As a result there are serious shortages of teachers, nurses, doctors, technicians, and scientifically trained executives, but 4,500,000 unemployables.

The federal government is the only purposeful force—I assume wars are not purposeful—that can reduce the numbers of the poor and make their lives more bearable. The effect of government policy on poverty has two quite distinct aspects. One is the indirect effect of the stimulation of the economy by federal spending. Such stimulation—though by war-time demands rather than government policy—has in the past produced a prosperity that did cut down American poverty by almost two-thirds. But I am inclined to agree with Dr. Galbraith that it would not have a comparable effect on present-day poverty:

> It is assumed that with increasing output poverty must disappear [he writes]. Increased output eliminated the general poverty of all who

worked. Accordingly it must, sooner or later, eliminate the special poverty that still remains. . . . Yet just as the arithmetic of modern politics makes it tempting to overlook the very poor, so the supposition that increasing output will remedy their case has made it easy to do so too.

He underestimates the massiveness of American poverty, but he is right when he says there is now a hard core of the specially disadvantaged—because of age, race, environment, physical or mental defects, etc.—that would not be significantly reduced by general prosperity. (Although I think the majority of our present poor *would* benefit, if only by a reduction in the present high rate of unemployment.)

To do something about this hard core, a second line of government policy would be required; namely, direct intervention to help the poor. We have had this since the New Deal, but it has always been grudging and miserly, and we have never accepted the principle that every citizen should be provided, at state expense, with a reasonable minimum standard of living regardless of any other considerations. It should not depend on earnings, as does Social Security, which continues the inequalities and inequities and so tends to keep the poor forever poor. Nor should it exclude millions of our poorest citizens because they lack the political pressure to force their way into the Welfare State. The governmental obligation to provide, out of taxes, such a minimum living standard for all who need it should be taken as much for granted as free public schools have always been in our history.

"Nobody Starves"

It may be objected that the economy cannot bear the cost, and certainly costs must be calculated. But the point is not the calculation but the principle. Statistics—and especially statistical forecasts—can be pushed one way or the other. Who can determine in advance to what extent the extra expense of giving our 40,000,000 poor enough income to rise above the poverty line would be offset by the lift to the economy from their increased purchasing power? We really don't know. Nor did we know what the budgetary effects would be when we established the principle of free public education. The rationale then was that all citizens should have an equal chance of competing for a better status. The rationale now is different: that every citizen has a right to become or remain part of our society because if this right is denied, as it is in the case of at least one-fourth of our citizens, it impoverishes us all. Since 1932, "the government"—local, state, and federal—has recognized a responsibility to provide its citizens with a subsistence living. Apples will never again be sold on the street by jobless accountants, it seems safe to predict, nor will any serious political leader ever again suggest that share-the-work and local charity can solve the problem of unemployment. "Nobody starves" in this country any more, but, like every social statistic, this is a tricky business. Nobody starves, but who can measure the starvation, not to be calculated by daily intake of proteins and calories, that reduces life for many of our poor to a long vestibule to death? Nobody starves, but every fourth citizen rubs along on a standard of living that is below what Mr. Harrington defines as "the minimal levels of health, housing, food, and education that our present stage of scientific knowledge specifies as necessary for life as it is now lived in the United States." Nobody starves, but a fourth of us are excluded from the common social existence. Not to be able to afford a movie or a glass of beer is a kind of starvation—if everybody else can.

The problem is obvious: the persistence of mass poverty in a prosperous country. The solution is also obvious: to provide, out of taxes, the kind of subsidies that have always been given to the public schools (not to mention the police and fire departments and the post office)—subsidies that would raise incomes above the poverty level, so that every citizen could feel he is indeed such. *"Civis Romanus sum!"* cried St. Paul when he was threatened with flogging—and he was not flogged. Until our poor can be proud to say *"Civis Americanus sum,"* until the act of justice that would make this possible has been performed by the three-quarters of Americans who are not poor—until then the shame of the Other America will continue.

Poverty in America

Oscar Ornati

The New School for Social Research

[Reprinted by permission of the National Policy Committee on Pockets of Poverty, Washington, D. C.]

How Many Americans Are Poor?

TRADITIONALLY, A "LINE OF POVERTY" is drawn to separate the poor from the non-poor. The line is drawn at a specific dollar-income level reflecting a judgment as to the minimum needs below which an individual cannot "subsist" or does not live "adequately," or lives in "deprivation." The line is drawn at different levels by different people and reflects differing concepts of justice, of needs, of values and of the influence of geography and occupation.

A survey of the contemporary practice of private and public agencies concerned with the problems of the poor reveals a great variety of definitions. In spite of these differences clusters appear at three levels. The three levels of poverty most generally used are:

1. Minimum subsistence ($2500 per year for a family of four)
2. Minimum adequacy   ($3500 per year for a family of four)
3. Minimum comfort   ($5500 per year for a family of four).

By these standards there are 20, 46, or 70 million "poor" in the United States today.

By whatever standard poverty is measured there are today a very large number of poor Americans. To act against poverty no precise calculation is required. While differences in the use of available statistics explain how various recent studies have arrived at different counts of the poor, once agreement on the standards of poverty is reached no significant difference in the estimate of the number of the poor flows from the use of different statistics, or different imputations of "non-money income" and the like.

Is the Situation Improving?

Various statisticians and government agencies are in disagreement as to whether there are now more or less poor today than in the past. Here different judgments as to how the comparisons are to be made explain the differences. Should the standards of the past be taken as a guide and, having corrected for changes in the value of the dollar, applied to the present? Or, should the opposite be done and current standards be deflated and the extent of poverty of the past so measured?

By taking past standards that go back far enough we are bound to find that there are *no* poor today, which is a patent absurdity.

The President's Economic Report in its statement that "since 1947, prosperity and progress have reduced the incidence of substandard incomes from one-third to one-fifth" suffers from this bias. It is based on the substandard income level used in 1947—17 years ago.

Conversely, by taking present standards and projecting them backwards we would find that Franklin D. Roosevelt's "one-third of a nation" would have been one-half of the nation.

Either exercise tells us more about changing standards than about the number of the poor. If comparisons are to be made, they should be made in terms of contemporary standards. What should be compared is the number who lived "below adequacy" in 1947 by 1947 standards of adequacy with those who lived "below adequacy" in 1960 by 1960 standards. When this is done, we find that the numbers of abject poor, the numbers of those living "below adequacy" and below minimum comfort levels have not changed very much. In 1947, by 1947 standards, 27 percent of all people lived below levels of minimum adequacy and in 1960, by 1960 standards, they amounted to 26 percent. The 1947 proportion living below minimum comfort was 39 percent while in 1960 it was 40 percent.

The story is different when abject poverty is considered. Here, when the number of poor, living at or below subsistence levels in 1947 and 1960 are compared, the proportion decreased from 15 percent to 11 percent although their actual number only decreased from 21 to 20 million.

To do away with poverty the line of poverty approach is *not* useful because:

1. Consensus on the meaning of poverty is hard to obtain and searching for it will delay policy action to do away with poverty; and
2. Viewing poverty as the condition of large but ill-defined populations does not give policy guidance on which action should be taken or on which individuals would be the beneficiaries of which programs.

Far more important than a count of the poor is the identification of the groups that are poor and of the relative risk of poverty that individuals incur because of conditions which are beyond their control.

The Risk of Poverty

For most of the economic history of the United States low income and poverty characterized a considerable part of the population. The old and the young, man and woman, farmer and city dweller, black and white, North and South, almost all shared in the national insufficiency; if one were black or a female family head or Southern, the risk of poverty was greater but not much greater. Many without these attributes shared their fate. The few that escaped from poverty did so by chance, by stubbornness or by personal qualities much more than because they belonged to a particular group.

Since World War II, it has been quite another story. Poverty has become increasingly a burden carried by "special" groups and individuals.

In the United States of the 1960's poverty is more properly and more effectively approached in terms of the programs necessary to improve conditions in which certain groups live, and of the characteristics which they possess.

The contemporary poor are the non-whites, families with no earners, families whose heads are females and men aged 14 to 25 or over 65. The contemporary poor are also those with less than eight years of education, inhabitants of rural farm areas, members of families in which there are more than six children under 18, and residents of the South. These characteristics are, for brevity, called poverty-linked.

Table A shows the proportion of people with poverty-linked characteristics according to the 1960 census that are found at three low income groups.

TABLE A
Poverty-Linked Populations vs. Total Population
1960
Per Cent Distribution

Poverty-Linked Characteristics	Income Class				
	$0–500		$0–2,000		$0–4,500
	Families	Individuals	Families	Individuals	Families
Percent of Total Population	2.5	14.6	13.0	54.1	36.7
Non-white	5.7	19.7	31.7	66.7	65.8
Female	8.0	17.1	34.0	60.9	68.0
Age:					
65 and over	3.2	13.7	31.4	79.4	68.0
14 to 24	3.2	25.9	18.3	54.9	58.0
Residence:					
Rural Farm	9.3	32.0	35.8	79.9	70.3
Southern[a]					
All	N.A.	N.A.	21.3	66.3	50.3
Non-white	N.A.	N.A.	44.0	78.7	80.8
Non-earner	12.1	27.7	57.9	88.7	93.4
Work Experience:					
None	7.2	21.0	40.3	86.3	76.8
All Part Time	6.2	20.6	39.6	80.4	71.0
0-26 weeks	8.0	26.3	49.3	86.5	81.9
27-49 weeks	4.2	12.0	32.3	82.4	64.0
Six plus children Under eighteen	6.2	—	22.0	—	54.2
Education:					
Less than 8 years[b]	6.2	22.6	33.2	80.3	69.7

Sources: Data for all characteristics except education and southern residence from *Current Population Reports,* Bureau of the Census, 1960, Series P60-37. Education data from *Current Population Reports,* Bureau of the Census, 1956, Series P60-27. Southern residence material from special tabulation Census Bureau (unpublished data).

[a] Total population for southern residence: $0-500, not available for both families and unrelated individuals. For families, $0-2,000, 13.1; $0-4,500, 30.9. For unrelated individuals, $0-2,000, 58.5. Data from *Census Supplementary Report,* PC(S1)—18.

[b] Total population for 1956: (Used because educational income data not available for 1960, see source). For families, $0-500, 3.2; $0-2,000, 15.4; $0-4,500, 46.1. For unrelated individuals, $0-500, 17.7; $0-2,000, 61.1.

Data in Table A involve characteristics and not people. They therefore cannot be added. Indeed the characteristics are overlapping as the individuals involved may have—and, in most cases, do have— more than one such characteristic.

For example, the category "family headed by a female" contains also families with more than six children and such families are often non-white, rural farm, etc. Later, this problem of overlap is dealt with; here we simply examine the extent to which the low income population consists of people with such characteristics.

The major finding highlighted in Table A is that the characteristics studied show a clear, significant and strong association with poverty. Indeed, compared to all families, a much greater proportion of those with poverty-linked characteristics had less than $500 income. Of course, not all the traits are equally tied to low income. But for nine of the fourteen poverty-linked characteristics, possession doubled the risk of abject poverty. For a few traits the risk was even higher. Only very youthful and aged families did not deviate much from the percentage of all families with less than $500 income. Old Age Assistance, Social Security, pensions and savings have insured that only three aged families out of 100 need try to live on an income of less than $500 per year.

At the $2000 income level the situation changes. Here possession of any one of eleven poverty-linked characteristics means a family has twice the normal possibility of living in poverty. At this level, Social Security and Old Age Assistance no longer provide a floor under which income cannot fall. The gap between aged families and families in general has widened; only 13 percent of all American families have incomes under $2,000 as compared with 31 percent for aged families. The same widening of the risk holds for many other categories (non-white, rural farm, etc.).

At the $4,500 income level *all* of the characteristics studied are firmly related to poverty. Indeed, more than half of the families with any one of fourteen traits have less than $4,500 in income, while less than 37 percent of all families are in this situation. The most extreme group is families with no earners, where over 93 percent had incomes of less than $4,500 in 1960.

Unattached individuals with the same characteristics run similarly high risks of being poor. One special feature is added. As the table makes clear, being an unrelated individual is in itself a poverty-linked attribute.

It should be noted that the relative portion of those with poverty-linked characteristics is here understated since comparisons are made with the *total* population, which includes the poverty-linked groups. Had the poverty-linked population been compared with the non-poverty-linked population the contrast would be even more striking.

The importance of poverty-linked characteristics as the most effective approach to poverty analysis depends upon our knowledge as to the changing makeup of the total population.

The numerical changes in poverty-linked groups between 1947 and 1960, as well as a tentative forecast for the year 1980, are shown in Table B.

Families and individuals with poverty-linked characteristics are now a larger part of the total population than they were in 1947. If our population forecasts are valid, this trend will continue. By 1980 non-whites will account for more than 11 percent of all families whereas in 1947 they were only 8.4 percent. The growth of the aged in the United States is the best publicized of any poverty-linked group. Again,

TABLE B

Poverty-Linked Characteristics, 1947, 1960 and 1980 (Projected)
Per Cent and Per Cent Change

Families

Characteristics	Per Cent			Per Cent Change		
	1947	1960	1980ª	1947-60	1960-80ª	1947-80ª
Non-white	8.4%	9.5%	11.2%	13.1%	17.9%	33.3%
Female	10.1	10.1	9.7	No Change	—4.0	—4.0
Rural-farmᵇ	14.7	11.3	5.6	—23.1	—50.6	—73.7
Age 65 and Over	11.7	13.7	14.0	17.1	2.2	19.7
Age 14-24	4.9	5.1	8.2	4.1	60.8	67.3
No Earners	6.0	7.3	9.8	22.0	32.1	63.3
Six or More Children Under 18	1.8	2.5	4.2	39.0	68.0	133.0

Unrelated Individuals

Characteristics	Per Cent			Per Cent Change		
	1947	1960	1980ª	1947-60	1960-80ª	1947-80ª
Non-white	11.9%	13.7%	15.9%	15.1%	16.1%	33.6%
Female	53.8	61.5	61.5	14.0	No Change	14.0
Rural-farmᵇ	6.4	5.7	—	—10.9	—	—
Age 65 and Over	28.6	33.5	44.0	17.1	31.3	53.8
Age 14-24	10.3	10.0	10.5	—3.0	5.0	1.9
Non-Earners	33.5	37.0	42.9	10.4	15.9	28.1

Source: Data for 1947 from *Current Population Reports,* Bureau of the Census, Series P60-5; data for 1960 from *Current Population Reports,* Bureau of the Census, Series P60-37.

ª For method of projection see forthcoming *Poverty in an Affluent Society.*

ᵇ For consistency of definition data for 1949, 1958 and 1960 were used instead of 1947 and 1960. Other periods in this line conform to these dates, i.e., 1960-1980 is 1958-60 and 1947-1960 is 1949-1958.

if population forecasts to 1980 are correct, there will be only a small proportional increase in the characteristic "aged family heads," but there will be a proportionately very large increase in the characteristic "unattached individuals over 65." The number of unattached females grew in the fourteen-year span analyzed, but the proportion of families headed by females remained unchanged. In the future this group might diminish in their relative importance. The proportion of families headed by persons 14 to 24 years old increased while the proportion of unattached individuals of the same age group declined. In the future young families can be expected to increase sharply, while young individuals will, by 1980, record only a modest increase. One poverty-linked family group, those with six or more children under 18, increased sharply between 1947 and 1960. This group is expected to increase even more sharply but, in evaluating this change, the smallness in absolute numbers of this group should be kept in mind.

Rural farm residence, a very important poverty-linked characteristic, has declined sharply. Between 1949 and 1958, the number of those residing in rural farm areas declined sharply. It is difficult to forecast rural farm residence for the year 1980. The variables are many and difficult to assess with precision. Our forecast, however, points to a continuing decline in the number of people engaged in agriculture.

The unique behavior of rurality as a poverty-linked characteristic undoubtedly reflects the fact that aside from the non-earner characteristic this is one characteristic from which the individual can theoretically escape by moving. This does not mean that a former rural farm resident is automatically not poor when he reaches the city. All it says is that the moment he reaches the city, he joins a population group whose risk of being poor is lower. One might argue also that education provides another escape. This holds true for the younger person, but less so for the adult currently living on a farm. Historically, Americans escape poverty by pulling up stakes. This is still the case. It has been noted how unattached individuals for the most part fare worse than families. But this is not the case with the locational traits: rural farm and southern residence. For southern residence no reliable forecast could be developed and therefore this characteristic was not included in Table B. Again mobility is the key and unattached individuals behaved as expected: they moved.

An exception which throws light on the interplay of the impact of poverty-linked traits and economic conditions is the curse of the non-white southern individual. The poverty percent of southern individuals is lower than that for southern families. For southern non-whites, as the same table shows, this is not the case. This is not an unreasonable or illogical development. Although as individuals they have greater potential mobility than families, as non-whites poverty already has a hold on them. It prevents them from taking full advantage of their potential mobility. As non-whites they may have discounted the possible benefits of moving which, by itself, does not help them shed the more pervasive poverty-linked trait: color.

In summary, it is clear that population characteristics associated with low income have all increased in importance over the past fourteen years. An exception, and possibly an important offset, to this pattern has been in the declining numerical importance of rural farm dwellers. It is impossible, however, to gauge the total impact of the changes described above by using an additive technique since many of the characteristics are not mutually exclusive. For example, an increase in families with no earners in part reflects the higher proportion of older families. This qualification tempers, rather than contradicts, the initial generalization.

Changes in the Risk of Being Poor

Using data about the risk of poverty of various groups to formulate anti-poverty policies is useful also as it permits comparison over time. What is important is to be able to measure how the risk of being poor for persons with a given characteristic has changed over time correcting the data for the change in the number of people with these characteristics. Such comparisons have been done, where the data were available for 1948 through 1960 on the basis of contemporary standards.

A check on the validity of this whole approach and on the particular findings reported for 1960 is provided by repeating the analysis of the characteristics for a population with *non-poverty-linked characteristics*. This was done for families with the characteristics: white, male head aged 25–34, with two children under 18. The data showed that in 1960 this constellation of attributes was much less frequent in the low income brackets and much heavier in the higher income brackets. Thus individuals with these characteristics appear *not to have a high risk of poverty* which can for 1960 be interpreted as meaning that such individuals are not poor. In 1948 the risk of this type of individual being poor was almost twice as great even by 1948 standards.

The comparison with 1948 strikingly shows that people with low income in 1960 had more frequently those demographic characteristics that have been found to be linked with poverty than did persons with comparable income in 1948.

The fact that in 1960, at income equivalents to those of 1948, poverty-linked demographic characteristics were more frequent is not due to increases in the number of persons at the low end of the income scale. In fact a modest decline in the total number of people in these groups has occurred. *The greater concentration of the population with poverty-linked characteristics at the low income levels of 1960 appears due rather to the fact that persons that moved out of low levels of income since 1948 were predominantly those without those social and demographic characteristics* which have been found to be associated with a high risk of poverty. Obviously the data do not suggest that in 1948 and 1960 the same persons were necessarily involved—some died, new ones were born, some managed to earn more, others less and so on. The data indicate only that populations with poverty-linked characteristics, irrespective of who the particular persons with such characteristics may be, have a greater risk of finding themselves in the low income groups.

The changes in the risk of being poor that have taken place for each of the major groups involved tell a complicated story that is only briefly summarized here:

Non-earners

Despite unemployment benefits, welfare payments, insurance and aid from relatives, living with a non-earner exposes the family to a high risk of being poor. The risk of being poor is *unaffected by changes in business conditions* and *has increased* over the last decade.

Non-earners who do not live in families have a high risk of poverty. The risk of poverty for the unattached individual is not as high as for other poverty-linked characteristics nor has it increased with time.

Non-white

Being non-white makes for a very high risk of poverty. Since 1954 the risk of poverty has increased for all non-whites. The general improvement in business conditions which took place after 1954 and after 1957 was not felt by the non-white families living below subsistence and below adequacy. Following the 1958 recession, improvement was not apparent until 1960. Non-white families living below minimum comfort on the other hand, had a smaller risk of being poor with business expansion and a greater risk of poverty with business contractions. The pattern for non-white individuals was like that of families.

Age 65 and Over

In the last decade the aged seem to have "detached" themselves from abject poverty more than any other group. There is much evidence that, from 1947 to 1960—probably mostly because of Social Security—families with heads 65 and over have moved up, if not out of, abject poverty.

At the level of adequacy and comfort an aged head still exposes the family to a considerable risk of being poor and this risk has increased. The reason the upward movement was limited may reflect the problem older workers have in finding employment to supplement Social Security payments.

The unattached individuals over 65 are worse off than families and, if anything, less sensitive to the cycle. At the lower levels their status has improved somewhat in recent years.

The effect of Social Security is less manifest among the unattached. One possible explanation is that there is a disproportionate number of women among older single individuals and many of them may not have qualified for OASI benefits, since their labor force participation rate in covered employment is, and has been, considerably below the male rate.

Rural Farm

This poverty-linked family group is numerically less important today than in 1948. *The association of the now smaller population with low income, however, has become stronger. Their risk of being poor is much greater.* An additional finding—not unexpected—is that the association appears closely related to the economy's cyclical path. In the 1948 and 1949 recession period, for example, the association became much stronger at all levels of low income and particularly at the $4,500 level. The association weakened somewhat following the recession. A significant tightening of the relationship paralleled the second postwar recession. *Since 1954 the risk of poverty at the abject poverty ($2,500) and minimum adequacy ($3,500) income levels have been less sensitive to the movements of the general economy.*

Although there is some indication that the risk of poverty has increased for rural farm individuals, the trend lacks the strength found for families.

Females

The risk of poverty for a family headed by a female is high, and growing.

Changes in attachment to poverty for such families conflict sharply with changing business conditions. The increase in the risk of poverty for female heads of families was often apparent when the rest of the population was relatively prosperous. The worsening condition of these families appeared to be arrested in years when the rest of the population suffered serious economic setbacks.

The wedding between poverty and single females is not as serious as that in which a family is involved. Their condition is not comparable with that of the female head of household, nor has their risk of being poor increased.

This is not unexpected. Single females suffer from only one economic disadvantage, their sex, while female heads of families face a complex of problems which impinge on their ability to be viable in our economy. There is also no clear relationship between changes in the value of the coefficients measuring attachment to poverty and the postwar business fluctuations. A factor which blurs whatever relationship there might be is the age composition of this group. It contains a large group of elderly women who were never or are no longer in the labor force, women who are living on their own or their husband's pension, or on welfare or gifts, all of which are sources of income less sensitive to changes in business conditions.

The Large and Young Families

Since 1947 the number of large families has increased. The average increase in the size of the American family does not seem to have affected the poor population very significantly (indeed, different sized families are scattered fairly evenly among consumer units of all incomes). Among low income families, the number with four, five and six persons, has fallen drastically.

Very young families—with the family head between 14 and 24—*comprised a slightly smaller segment of the total population in 1960 than in 1947 but their incidence in the low income population has increased.* Thus, in spite of the lack of any relationship to business conditions, the honor of being called "family head" bestowed too soon brings with it a greater likelihood of poverty, particularly since 1957. For part of this group, poverty may be only a temporary condition. For most, low income is no momentary detour, but the foreshadowing of a life of poverty.

The Convergence of Poverty-Linked Characteristics

The demographic characteristics discussed so far obviously overlap; being non-white may also mean being a farmer, or being aged, or being a female head of family. The poor do not usually have only one problem and many poor families are classified as "multi-problem" families. Available data point clearly to low education and shrinking occupational mobility as one of the major causes of poverty. Here the increased requirements in education for employment are one of the major causes of poverty. In addition, bad physical and mental health contribute to poverty to an undetermined but clearly significant degree.

Our rough estimate is that of the 20 million abject poor more than two-thirds, or somewhere between 12 and 14 million, are deficient in either health, mental or physical, or education, and a very large number of individuals are affected by more than one disadvantage. The proportions do not change significantly at the $3,500 or $4,500 level.

If we are to move against poverty, we must understand the dynamics of the process. Then we can move from the broad discussions of complex causality which determines an individual's risk of being poor to the isolation of characteristics which, in the aggregate, appear to contribute more, and of those that contribute less, to poverty.

Analysis of the 1960 census data allows, at least for that year, a precise count, at different levels of income, of population units which had one or more of four key poverty-linked characteristics. It also provides a set of major preliminary clues as to how to move against poverty along the lines suggested above. Fifteen different poverty-linked family populations were constructed, ranging from units possessing one characteristic to those with all four. Here the problem of overlapping characteristics is eliminated. A non-white family is only non-white. There is no aged family head, no female family head, and no rural-farm resident. The same for the other characteristics. The cumulative total of all families with one characteristic holds no duplication—each family is counted only once. Nor is there duplication when families with two or more characteristics are examined.

As expected, by correcting for overlap, we note that: (1) there are more families with only one poverty characteristic than with two, with three or four; (2) the risk of poverty increases with the number of characteristics. The data in Table C indicate that while the relationship is not perfect, the possession of two characteristics means a greater chance of very low income than the possession of one, three a greater chance than two, etc. The degree of poverty, measured by the proportion of families below the three budget levels varies considerably.

Families that have only one characteristic find between 30 and 40 percent of their membership at or below subsistence, between 55 and 60 percent below the minimum adequacy level and roughly 70 percent below minimum comfort.

Possessing two characteristics condemns a considerably larger portion of the population to subsistence living. For all but one of the six sub-populations with two attributes the proportion below $2,600 is

TABLE C

The Percentage of Each Poverty-Linked Population Below
Three Low Income Levels
(1960)

Characteristic(s) of Family Head	# of Units	%	Per Cent Below		
			2,500	4,500	5,500
One Characteristic					
Aged	4,276,016	100%	39.6%	60.2%	70.5%
Female	2,387,443	100	38.0	60.4	73.3
Rural-farm	2,434,041	100	34.5	57.5	71.0
Non-white	2,786,211	100	28.6	54.7	70.9
Two Characteristics					
Non-white, Female	743,115	100	64.6	82.2	88.4
Aged, Female	787,975	100	37.2	56.1	68.4
Aged, Rural-farm	489,732	100	54.9	74.7	83.2
Aged, Non-white	331,316	100	62.6	80.1	87.5
Non-white, Rural-farm	208,047	100	78.3	90.8	94.8
Rural-farm, Female	73,842	100	54.8	73.9	83.1
Three Characteristics					
Non-white, Aged, Female	115,444	100	67.5	83.5	89.8
Non-white, Rural-farm, Aged	40,901	100	81.1	91.9	95.4
Rural-farm, Aged, Female	55,444	100	52.5	70.8	80.3
Rural-farm, Non-white, Female	22,784	100	86.6	94.9	97.8
Four Characteristics					
Non-white, Rural-farm, Aged, Female	7,698	100	84.0	93.9	97.0

better than half. For non-white families with the added characteristic of rural farm residence, the probability of abject poverty is three out of four. The chance of living at or below the minimum adequacy level is 75 percent or better for all but one of these twice-cursed families. Ninety percent of all non-white farm families, 80 percent of all the non-white aged and 82 percent of all the non-white families with female heads lived under this level. For all but one of these combinations the chance of escaping from the poverty band is less than 2 in 10. Conversely, families with two poverty-linked attributes rarely have incomes placing them above the poverty level. Extreme poverty is the fate of families with 3 or 4 poverty attributes. For three groups the figure is 8 in 10, for one, 7 in 10, and for one 5 in 10.

The Policy Implications of Convergence

The policy implications of the data and the analysis presented so far should be clear. On the one hand, families with one poverty characteristic make up the largest part of the low income population; on the other hand, families with more than one attribute, although less numerous, suffer the heavier burdens. Noting that they are less numerous in no way means they are insignificant. Families with two characteristics involve roughly ten million men, women and children.

Half of these live below the contemporary subsistence level. Another quarter of a million families are marked by the even more extreme poverty associated with three or four characteristics. They contribute another million human exceptions to American affluence.

Examination of the differential impact of particular characteristics sharpens the focus of policy. Not only does this provide guidelines for the future, it also gives insight into the effect of past policies.

Table D *measures the income effect of removing one poverty-linked characteristic from the population of families with three such characteristics.* The table shows how, in every case, the removal of the *characteristic non-white reduces the percentage of families below subsistence to a greater degree than removing the characteristic rural-farm.* The effect is least marked in terms of removing any third characteristic from families with rural-farm as one of their three poverty-linked characteristics.

TABLE D

The Effect of Removing a Poverty-Linked Characteristic
From a Family Possessing Three Characteristics
(Changes in Percentages of Families Below the Subsistence Level)

Characteristic		%	Characteristic		%
Non-white, Rural-farm, Female		86.6%	Non-white, Rural-farm, Aged		81.1%
Minus:			Minus:		
Non-white	=	54.8	Non-white	=	54.9
Rural-farm	=	64.6	Rural-farm	=	62.6
Female	=	78.3	Aged	=	78.3
Non-white, Aged, Female		67.5	Aged, Rural-farm, Female		52.5
Minus:			Minus:		
Non-white	=	37.2	Rural-farm	=	37.2
Aged	=	64.6	Aged	=	54.8
Female	=	62.6	Female	=	54.9

Table E shows—in a manner similar to Table D—the effect of *removing one poverty-linked characteristic from families with two.* The pattern that emerges throws some light on the success of a past policy, Social Security. In the first set of percentages and the fifth set we find that subtracting the aged has a modifying rather than a depressing effect on the percentage of extremely low income units. Rural-farm families headed by aged females were slightly better off than rural-farm families headed by non-aged females. Age is the one area where, adequate or not, there does exist a national policy and program of insurance. Removing the non-white characteristic helps here, too, but less so.

Defining poverty through poverty-linked characteristics leads to the following major conclusions: First, the poverty population in

TABLE E

The Effect of Removing a Poverty-Linked Characteristic
From a Family Possessing Two Characteristics
(Changes in Percentages of Families Below the Subsistence Level)

Characteristic	%	Characteristic	%
Non-white, Rural-farm	78.3%	Non-white, Female	64.6%
Minus:		Minus:	
Rural-farm =	28.6	Female =	28.6
Non-white =	34.5	Non-white =	38.0
Non-white, Aged	62.6	Rural-farm, Aged	54.9
Minus:		Minus:	
Aged =	28.6	Aged =	34.5
Non-white =	39.6	Rural-farm =	39.6
Rural-farm, Female	54.8	Aged, Female	37.2
Minus:		Minus:	
Female =	34.5	Aged =	38.0
Rural-farm =	38.0	Female =	39.6

1960 is characterized by identifying specific socio-demographic attributes. Families that are aged, rural-farm, non-white, headed by females,
or combinations of these, account for 70 percent of the abject poor.
Second, in absolute terms, the largest groups are those families possessing only one characteristic. Third, the most severe poverty exists
among families with more than one attribute and, fourth, among the
multi-characteristic families, non-whiteness is most damaging.

In the strictest sense of the word, the poor of today are less endowed. "Underprivileged" has long been a fashionable word. It seemed
less offensive than "poor." On the whole, until recent years, it was an
inappropriate euphemism. Now it fits. It means those who are less
endowed and less able to participate in the Affluent Society. It means
those who are out of the mainstream of American life.

The underprivileged are not of, even though they are in, the
market society. Their poverty is a poverty of structure. They sit outside as marginal sellers and weak buyers. They are economic as well
as physical invalids and are discriminated against socially and economically. *Their poverty is the result of special circumstances,* rather than
of the rate of economic activity. They do not directly reflect an inadequate growth rate as they are not part of the economic structure. Our
economy takes care of those who are within its embrace, but it does
not take care of the underprivileged.

The policy implications are clear. The redefinition presented
here casts poverty in a context in which action is possible. Poverty is
a structural problem and thus policies to deal with it must be struc-

turally-oriented. This presents many problems. Many policy-makers and economists contend that poverty will be done away with by policies aimed at bringing about full employment. Such policies are necessary prerequisites and have a social and economic value and priority of their own. But, the elimination or drastic reduction of poverty in America demands additional measures pinpointed to those structural characteristics of the affluent society that have permitted a large pool of underprivileged in the midst of a relatively efficient economy.

How Much Is Enough? A Note on Poverty Budgets
The Editors

THE MOST COMMON CONCEPTION of poverty refers to the adequacy or inadequacy of financial resources to meet family needs. We can speak then of a "poverty-line" above which people are supposed to have adequate resources and below which people are said to lack adequate resources. Such a definition inevitably poses a problem: where is the "poverty-line" to be drawn. In Galbraith's *Affluent Society*, the line was set at $1,000; a figure that Galbraith has since admitted was too low and for which he has been criticized. The most prevalent tendency has been to draw the line at $3,000 although Keyserling makes a distinction between families in poverty (under $4,000) and families in deprivation (between $4,000 and $6,000). The problem of where the line is to be drawn is an important one not only for gauging the prevalence of poverty but also for the development of programs to reduce poverty. The major problem in setting the poverty-line is a determination of a "true level" of needs of the family and this, of course, involves a question of value judgments. All too often, the value judgments are not examined in a particular definition of poverty and this definition becomes an article of faith rather than a critically developed set of guidelines.

The current "poverty-line" is defined at $3,130 annual income for a nonfarm family of four and $1,850 for an elderly couple. Those below that line are defined as "poor." Those above it are seen as able to carry on without being the special object of social policy.

This concept of poverty is based on the "'economy plan" budget of $3,165 developed by the Social Security Administration for a city family of four people. The economy diet plan was developed, in turn, by the Department of Agriculture as a guide for "temporary or emergency use when funds are low." It was a downward modification of the "low-cost diet plan," the minimum diet consistent with food preferences of the lowest third of the population and adequate to avoid basic nutritional deficiencies.

The economy plan budget on which government transfer payments are made, allows about $800 a year for housing and $1,040 a year for food ($5 a week per person). It leaves a family of four with a little over $22 a week for all other living expenses—housing supplies, clothes, transportation, medical care, insurance, recreation, etc.

The food allowance of both the economy plan and low-cost budgets is based on certain assumptions. First of all, the $1,040 food allowance of the economy plan assumes that the low-income housewife will be "a careful shopper, a skillful cook, and a good manager who will prepare all the family meals at home." The emergency diet budget of the economy plan assumes maximum shopping effectiveness, although the poverty budget allows little transportation money to leave the neighborhood and thus restricts shopping choice for food, clothing and durables. The economy plan budget fails to take into account that low financial resources mean more frequent use of credit (with no money in the budget for costs of credit), more frequent use of "the friendly neighborhood grocery store" where credit is available but where prices are higher than at the supermarket. Lack of money means that poor people are less able than the more affluent to buy groceries in quantity, or to take advantage of special sales. Limited literacy, inability or inexperience in reading the fine print of contracts or labels, and lack of knowledge of various packaging deceptions also tend to make the low-income consumer an inefficient shopper.

In addition, the value of the poor man's dollar is further undermined by a variety of illegal or quasi-legal practices in consumer purchases by the poor. As Caplovitz points out in the selection from his book, *The Poor Pay More* (Glencoe, Ill.: Free Press of Glencoe, 1963), in Chapter 4, shoddy or misrepresented merchandise, high pressure selling, loan sharking, illegal or exorbitant credit charges, repossession procedures may also make the price that the low-income consumer pays for goods and services well above the standard on which government budgets and transfer payments are calculated.

The economy plan budget also fails to take into account the realistic needs of the poor. For example, it does not allow for the cost of any meals eaten away from home. It makes no provision for lunches at work or at school or the need to escape inadequate or tiring kitchen facilities, overcrowded housing, monotonous daily existence, irregular work patterns by an occasional meal eaten in a restaurant.

The final and ultimately most serious problem with the economy plan budget on which the government's poverty cut-off point is gauged, is that the food-to-income ratio is too high at low-income levels. Any family having to spend one-third or more of its income on food will be deprived of other necessities. Families at the lower end of the economic scale need proportionately more money to repair and replace lower quality clothing, furniture, and household appliances than do higher income purchasers of higher quality goods. The lower-income family needs more funds available for contingencies. With one-third of the budget irreducibly allocated for food, the absolute amount of funds available may be insufficient to meet the minimum costs of other irreducible necessities such as housing, clothing, and medical care let alone emergency situations.

The privation of families whose income is below the government's poverty-line may be seen by comparing the economy plan budget with the City Workers' Family Budget (cwfb) calculated by the Bureau of Labor Statistics of the U.S. Department of Labor. The "modest but adequate" bls cwfb represents "an estimate of the total cost of a representative list of goods and services considered necessary by four-person city families . . . to maintain a level of adequate living according to standards prevailing in large cities of the United States." Based on costs of living in 20 large cities in 1959, the most recent estimates of the bls found that expenditures for a city worker's family of four would range from $6,567 in Chicago to $5,370 in Houston. Since that time, consumer prices have risen over 7.3 percent.

The failure to determine and calculate the actual costs of necessary goods and services for a minimum nonpoverty living standard ties the poverty definition to a food standard. The poverty budget is really a food maintenance budget, and a deficient one at that. It is unrealistic in terms of the life conditions of the poor and it is inadequate for a decent level of living. It makes no allowance for travel, education, recreation, contacts with kin, participation in voluntary organizations.

A new approach is needed to the definition of poverty—an approach based on social goals and the realities of the social environment. Such a definition would see the poverty-stricken as having inadequate financial resources to maintain minimum standards of food, shelter, clothing, and physical health, *and* to achieve a full development of individual talents and social participation. Income is necessary to avoid poverty of life, as well as poverty of diet. A definition of poverty must be based on two social goals beyond biological maintenance: individual fulfillment and satisfying involvement in the larger society. These goals relate poverty to a desired *quality* of life. The productive capacity of the American economy and the potential of our developing technology make these goals possible. No longer can it be argued that the necessity of scarcity restricts them to a privileged few.

Counting the Poor: Another Look at the Poverty Profile

Mollie Orshansky

U.S. Department of Health, Education, and Welfare

[Reprinted from the Social Security Bulletin, *January, 1965.]*

A REVOLUTION OF EXPECTATIONS has taken place in this country as well as abroad. There is now a conviction that everyone has the right to share in the good things of life. Yet there are still many who must watch America's parade of progress from the sidelines, as they wait for their turn—a turn that does not come. The legacy of poverty awaiting many of our children is the same that has been handed down to their parents, but in a time when the boon of prosperity is more general the taste of poverty is more bitter.

Now, however, the Nation is committed to a battle against poverty. And as part of planning the how, there is the task of identifying the whom. The initiation of corrective measures need not wait upon final determination of the most suitable criterion of poverty, but the interim standard adopted and the characteristics of the population thus described will be important in evaluating the effectiveness of the steps taken.

There is not, and indeed in a rapidly changing pluralistic society there cannot be, one standard universally accepted and uniformly applicable by which it can be decided who is poor. Almost inevitably a single criterion applied across the board must either leave out of the count some who should be there or include some who, all things considered, ought not be classed as indigent. There can be, however, agreement on some of the considerations to be taken into account in arriving at a standard. And if it is not possible to state unequivocally "how much is enough," it should be possible to assert with confidence how much, on an average, is too little. Whatever the level at which we peg the concept of "too little," the measure of income used should reflect at least roughly an equivalent level of living for individuals and families of different size and composition.

In such terms, it is the purpose of this paper to sketch a profile of poverty based on a particular income standard that makes allowance for the different needs of families with varying numbers of adults and children to support. It recognizes, too, that a family on a farm normally is able to manage on somewhat less cash income than a family living in a city. As an example, a family of father, mother, two young children, and no other relatives is assumed on the average to need a minimum of $1,860 today if living on a farm and $3,100 elsewhere. It should go without saying that, although such cutoff points have their place when the economic well-being of the population at large is being assessed, they do not necessarily apply with equal validity to each individual family in its own special setting.

The standard itself is admittedly arbitrary, but not unreasonable. It is based essentially on the amount of income remaining after allowance for an adequate diet at minimum cost. Under the criteria adopted, it is estimated that in 1963 a total of 7.2 million families and 5 million individuals living alone or with nonrelatives (excluding persons in institutions) lacked the wherewithal to live at anywhere near a tolerable level. Literally, for the 34½ million persons involved—15 million of them children under age 18 and 5 million persons aged 65 or older—everyday living implied choosing between an adequate diet of the most economical sort and some other necessity because there was not money enough to have both.

There are others in need not included in this count. Were one to add in the hidden poor, the 1.7 million elderly and the 1.1 million members of subfamilies—including 600,000 children—whose own income does not permit independent living at a minimum standard but who escape poverty by living in a household with relatives whose combined income is adequate for all, the number of poor rises to nearly 37.5 million persons.

The aggregate income available to the 7.2 million families and 5 million individuals in 1963 was only 60 percent as much as they needed, or about $11½ billion less than their estimated minimum requirements.

The Poverty Profile

From data reported to the Bureau of the Census in March 1964, it can be inferred that 1 in 7 of all families of two or more and almost half of all persons living alone or with nonrelatives had incomes too low in 1963 to enable them to eat even the minimal diet that could be expected to provide adequate nutrition and still have enough left over to pay for all other living essentials. Such a judgment is predicated on the assumption that, at current prices and current standards, an average family of four can achieve an adequate diet on about 70 cents a day per person for all food and an additional $1.40 for all other items—from housing and medical care to clothing and carfare.[1] For those dependent on a regular paycheck, such a budget would mean, for the family of four, total family earnings of $60 a week.

By almost any realistic definition, individuals and families with such income—who include more than a fifth of all our children—must be counted among our undoubted poor. A somewhat less conservative but by no means generous standard, calling for about 90 cents a day for food per person and a total weekly income of $77, would add 8.8 million adults and 6.8 million children to the roster. There is thus a total of 50 million persons—of whom 22 million are young children—who live within the bleak circle of poverty or at least hover around its edge. In these terms, though progress has been made, there are still from a fifth to a fourth of our citizens whose situation reminds us that all is not yet well in America.

Who are these people who tug at the national conscience? Are they all social casualties, visited by personal misfortune, like the woman left alone to raise a family? Are they persons who find little opportunity to earn their living, like the aged and the unemployed? Or are they perhaps mainly Negroes and members of other minority groups, living out the destiny of their years of discrimination? These groups, to be sure, are among the poorest of the poor, but they are not alone.

The population groups most vulnerable to the risk of inadequate income have long been identified and of late much publicized, but they make up only a small part of all the Nation's poor.

Families headed by a woman are subject to a risk of poverty three times that of units headed by a man, but they represent only a fourth of all persons in families classed as poor. Indeed, almost three-fourths of the poor families have a man as the head.

Children growing up without a father must get along on less than they need far more often than children living with both parents. In fact, two-thirds of them are in families with inadequate income. But two-thirds of all the children in the families called poor do live in a home with a man at the head.

---

[1] Estimates are based on a per capita average for all 4-person nonfarm families. Costs will average slightly more in small households and less in larger ones. A member of a 2-person family, for example, would need 74 cents a day for food and $2 a day for other items.

Many of our aged have inadequate incomes, but almost four-fifths of the poor families have someone under age 65 at the head. Even among persons who live alone, as do so many aged women, nearly half of all individuals classified as poor have not yet reached old age.

Nonwhite families suffer a poverty risk three times as great as white families do, but 7 out of 10 poor families are white.

And finally, in our work-oriented society, those who cannot or do not work must expect to be poorer than those who do. Yet more than half of all poor families report that the head currently has a job. Moreover, half of these employed family heads, representing almost 30 percent of all the families called poor, have been holding down a full-time job for a whole year. In fact, of the 7.2 million poor families in 1963, 1 in every 6 (1.3 million) is the family of a white male worker who worked full time throughout the year. Yet this is the kind of family that in our present society has the best chance of escaping poverty.

All told, of the 15 million children under age 18 counted as poor, about 5¾ million were in the family of a man or woman who had a full-time job all during 1963.

Defining the Poverty Line

Poverty has many facets, not all reducible to money. Even in such terms alone, it will not be possible to obtain unanimous consent to a list of goods and services that make up the *sine qua non* and the dollars it takes to buy them. The difficulty is compounded in a country such as ours, which has long since passed the stage of struggle for sheer survival.

In many parts of the world, the overriding concern for a majority of the populace every day is still "Can I live?" For the United States as a society, it is no longer whether but how. Although by the levels of living prevailing elsewhere, some of the poor in this country might be well-to-do, no one here today would settle for mere subsistence as the just due for himself or his neighbor, and even the poorest may claim more than bread. Yet as yesterday's luxuries become tomorrow's necessities, who can define for today how much is enough? And in a society that equates economic well-being with earnings, what is the floor for those whose earning capacity is limited or absent altogether, as it is for aged persons and children?

Available Standards for Food Adequacy

Despite the Nation's technological and social advance, or perhaps because of it, there is no generally accepted standard of adequacy for essentials of living except food. Even for food, social conscience and custom dictate that there be not only sufficient quantity but sufficient variety to meet recommended nutritional goals and conform to customary eating patterns. Calories alone will not be enough.

Food plans prepared by the Department of Agriculture have for more than 30 years served as a guide for estimating costs of food needed by families of different composition. The plans represent a translation of the criteria of nutritional adequacy set forth by the National Research Council into quantities and types of food compatible with the preference of United States families, as revealed in food consumption studies. Plans are developed at varying levels of cost to suit the needs of families with different amounts to spend. All the plans, if strictly followed, can provide an acceptable and adequate diet, but—generally speaking—the lower the level of cost, the more restricted the kinds and qualities of food must be and the more the skill in marketing and food preparation that is required.[2]

Each plan specifies the required weekly quantities of foods in particular food groups for individuals of varying age and sex. The Department regularly publishes cost estimates at United States average prices based on the assumption that all meals are prepared at home from foods purchased at retail. Because no allowance is made for using any food from the home farm or garden, the cost estimates are not applicable to farm families without some adjustment, although the quantities presumably could be.

The low-cost plan, adapted to the food patterns of families in the lowest third of the income range, has for many years been used by welfare agencies as a basis for food allotments for needy families and others who wished to keep food costs down. Often, however, the actual food allowance for families receiving public assistance was less than that in the low-cost plan. Although spending as much as this food plan recommends by no means guarantees that diets will be adequate, families spending less are more likely to have diets falling below the recommended allowances for some important nutrients.

Recently the Department of Agriculture began to issue an "economy" food plan, costing only 75–80 percent as much as the basic low-cost plan, for "temporary or emergency use when funds are low." In January 1964, this plan suggested foods costing $4.60 a week per person, an average of only 22 cents a meal per person in a 4-person family.[3]

---

[2] See U.S. Department of Agriculture, *Family Food Plans and Food Costs*, Home Economics Research Report No. 20, November 1962.

[3] With recommended adjustments for family size, small families are allowed somewhat more and larger families somewhat less, and for all families the actual

For some family members, such as men and teen-age boys, the cost was higher; for others—young children and women, for example—it was less.

The food plan as such includes no additional allowance for meals eaten out or other food eaten away from home. Meals eaten by family members at school or on the job, whether purchased or carried from home, must still come out of the same household food allowance.

The food costs for individuals according to this economy plan, at January 1964 prices, were used as the point of departure for determining the minimum total income requirement for families of different types. An additional set of poverty income points was computed, using the low-cost plan with its average per capita weekly cost of $5.90.

Income-Food Expenditure Relationship

It has long been accepted for individuals as for nations that the proportion of income allocated to the "necessaries," and in particular to food, is an indicator of economic well-being. A declining percentage has been associated with prosperity and higher income, and the rising percentage associated with lower income has been taken as an indicator of stringency.

The fact that larger households tend to spend a larger share of their income for food has not been so readily recognized as an indicator of economic pressure because of the assumed economy of scale. Yet, on the whole, larger families are less likely to have diets that satisfy the recommended allowances in essential nutrients. The dearth of data on expenditures of families classified by both size and income has made it difficult to assay the situation, and the fact that as families increase in size the age and sex distribution of the members changes too further obscures the picture.

In its 1955 study of household food consumption, the Department of Agriculture found that the diets of almost a fourth of the 2-person households but about half of the households with six or more members had less than the recommended amounts of calcium—a nutrient found mainly in milk products. Similarly, large households were

---

amounts of food suggested will vary with the sex and age of the members. Even in a 4-person family, the per capita cost will vary slightly from the figure cited, depending upon whether it includes teen-agers with high food requirements or a younger child or an aged member with food needs less than average.

Recent revisions in suggested food quantities to allow for changes in the Recommended Dietary Allowances result in almost no change in the costs of the plans on the average. Foods for men of all ages and girls aged 9–12 cost slightly less than before, and foods for women under age 55 cost slightly more. (*See Family Economics Review* (U.S. Department of Agriculture), October 1964.)

twice as likely as small households to have diets lacking in ascorbic acid and two and a half times as likely to have diets short in protein. The latter situation is particularly striking because, though lack of protein is far less common in this country than deficiency in other nutrients, it is more telling. Diets too low in protein are more likely than other diets to have deficiencies in other essential nutrients also.[4]

It thus appears that what passes for "economy of scale" in the large family may in part reflect a lowering of dietary standards enforced by insufficient funds. Support for this thesis may be gained from the fact, illustrated later in this report, that families with large numbers of children do indeed have lower incomes than smaller families. Moreover, analysis of recent consumption data suggests that large families, given the opportunity, prefer to devote no larger a share of their income to food than do smaller families with the same per capita income.

The Agriculture Department evaluated family food consumption and dietary adequacy in a 1955 survey week and reported for all families of two or more—farm and nonfarm—an expenditure for food approximating one-third of money income after taxes.[5] Two-person nonfarm families used about 27 percent of their income for food, and families with three or more persons about 35 percent. A later study made in 1960–61 by the Bureau of Labor Statistics found for urban families that nearly a fourth of the family's income (after taxes) went for food. There is less variation by size of family than might have been anticipated, ranging between 22 percent and 28 percent, as Table 1 shows.

The data suggest that the declining income per person in the larger families may have been responsible for the different rate of spending as well as possibly more efficient utilization of food. Indeed, on more critical examination of the complete income-size distributions, it would appear that, given the same per capita income, the spending patterns appear to converge considerably.* Urban families in 1960–61, for example, spending on the average approximately every third of their available dollars for food, are estimated to have had incomes of approximately $1,000 per person when there were two in the family, $900 when there were three, $910 when there were four, $915 for five, and $800 for six or more.

---

[4] U.S. Department of Agriculture, Household Food Consumption Survey, 1955, *Dietary Evaluation of Food Used in Households in the United States*, Report No. 16, November 1961, and *Food Consumption and Dietary Levels of Households of Different Size, United States, by Region*, Report No. 17, January 1963.

[5] See U.S. Department of Agriculture, *Food Consumption and Dietary Levels of Households in the United States* (ARS626), August 1957.

* Illustrative tables omitted.

TABLE 1

Family size	USDA 1955, nonfarm[1]		BLS 1960-61, urban[2]	
	Average per capita income	Percent spent for food	Average per capita income	Percent spent for food
1	(3)	(3)	$2,967	23
2 or more, total	$1,328	33	1,886	22
2..........................	2,036	27	2,750	22
3..........................	1,603	31	2,302	22
4..........................	1,299	35	1,854	24
5..........................	1,067	36	1,512	26
6..........................	837	40 ⎫	1,944	28
7 or more	616	46 ⎭		

[1] Derived from U.S. Department of Agriculture, Food Consumption Survey, 1955, Report No. 1, December 1956.

[2] Derived from Bureau of Labor Statistics, *Consumer Expenditures and Income,* Supplement 3, Part A, to BLS Report No. 237-38, July 1964.

[3] Because of the housekeeping eligibility requirement for this study, the single individuals included are not representative of all persons living alone.

Some of the difference in the results of the two studies cited may be attributed to differences in methodology. The questions employed by the Bureau of Labor Statistics to obtain the data on annual food outlays usually have yielded lower average expenditures than the more detailed item-by-item checklist of foods used in a week that serves as a questionnaire for the Agriculture Department. Moreover, since the Department studies are limited to families who have 10 or more meals at home during the survey week, they leave out some high food spenders represented in the bls figures. On the other hand, the decreases undoubtedly reflect in part the general improvement in real income achieved by the Nation as a whole in the 6 years elapsed between the two studies.

For the present analysis, the earlier relationship was adopted as the basis for defining poverty—that is, an income less than three times the cost of the economy food plan (or alternatively the low-cost plan)— for families of three or more persons. For families with two members the ratio of 27 percent observed in that study was applied partly because it is generally acknowledged that a straight per capita income measure does not allow for the relatively larger fixed costs that small households face. Moreover, the more recent consumption curves themselves indicate that the 1- or 2-person families, who as a group are less homogeneous in composition, seem to be "out of line" with larger families with respect to the spending pattern.

For 1-person units, for whom the consumption data are hard to interpret because of the heavy representation of aged individuals not shown separately, the income cutoff at the low-cost level was taken at 72 percent of the estimated $2,480 for a couple, following BLS recent practice.[6] For the economy level, the income cutoff was assumed at 80 percent of the couple's requirement, on the premise that the lower the income the more difficult it would be for one person to cut expenses such as housing and utilities below the minimum for a couple.[7]

As stated earlier, for each family size several income points were developed in relation to the sex of the head and different combinations of adults and children. When weighted together in accordance with the distribution of families of these types in the current population,* they yield a set of assumed food expenditures and income that can be compared with the income of families of the same size who spend that amount per person for food, as estimated roughly from the 1960–61 consumption study.

It may be mentioned that the low-cost food plan criterion, derived correspondingly, can be taken as a rough measure of the results that would obtain if the income-food ratios in the BLS study were accepted as the guideline and applied to the lower food standard. Inasmuch as the economy plan for many families requires roughly three-fourths as much to buy as does the low-cost plan, multiplying by three the purchase requirement in the low-cost food plan yields approximately the same income point as multiplying the economy-plan cost by four.

---

[6] Willard Wirtz, statement in *Hearings Before the Ways and Means Committee, House of Representatives, Eighty-eighth Congress, on Medical Care for the Aged, November 18–22, 1963 and January 20–24, 1963.*

[7] See Mollie Orshansky, "Budget for an Elderly Couple," *Social Security Bulletin,* December 1960.

* Descriptive table omitted from original.

TABLE 2

Family size	SSA poverty index— economy level (nonfarm)		BLS 1960-61 average (urban)[1]— estimated income corresponding to economy food expenditure
	Per capita food expense	Income	
1	[2]	$1,540	[2]
2	$240	1,990	$1,560
3	270	2,440	2,475
4	260	3,130	3,120
5	245	3,685	3,600
6	230	4,135	4,020
7 or more	210	5,090	[2]

[1] Derived from BLS Report 237-38, July 1964.
[2] Not estimated.

The Farm-Nonfarm Adjustment

One additional adjustment was made to allow in some degree for the lesser needs of farm families for cash income. Farm families today buy much of their food, in contrast to the situation 40 or 50 years ago when they depended almost entirely on their own production. Yet it was still true in 1955 that about 40 percent of the food items consumed by all farm families—valued at prices paid by any families who did buy them—came from their home farm or garden. On the other hand, the food purchased represented—as it did for nonfarm families—a third of total cash income for the year after deductions for operating expenses.[8]

Farm families generally can count not only some of their food but most of their housing as part of the farm operation. Thus, it was assumed that a farm family would need 40 percent less net cash than a nonfarm family of the same size and composition.

The Resultant Standard

The poverty lines thus developed served to classify a representative Bureau of the Census population sample as of March 1964 for comparison of characteristics of poor and nonpoor units in terms of 1963 money income.[9] That is, for the farm and nonfarm population separately, unrelated individuals were classified by age and sex, and families by sex of head, total number of members, and number of related children under age 18. The income of each unit was then compared with the appropriate minimum. The households thus classified as poor and nonpoor were then analyzed for characteristics other than income.[10]

With the information on how the population is divided into units by size and number of children, it is possible to condense the 248 separate criteria into an abbreviated set for families of different size. As Table 3 indicates, the income cutoff points in the economy food plan

---

[8] See U.S. Department of Agriculture, Household Food Consumption Survey, 1955, *Food Production for Home Use by Households in the United States, by Region,* Report No. 12, January 1958, and *Farm Family Spending in the United States,* Agriculture Information Bulletin No. 192, June 1958.

[9] An earlier analysis related to 1961 income, along the same lines but restricted to families with children, was reported in the *Bulletin* for July 1963. For that earlier estimate, since family income data were available only by number of own children, not crossed with total number of persons, it was necessary to make arbitrary assumptions about the additional relatives. The present figures, based on a more refined income grid and incorporating 1960 Census data not previously available on characteristics of families and persons, represent not only an updating but, it is hoped, a refinement.

[10] Acknowledgement is made of the helpful assistance of Bureau of the Census staff in the preparation of the special tabulations for this purpose.

TABLE 3

Weighted average of poverty income criteria[1] for families of different composition, by household size, sex of head, and farm or nonfarm residence

Number of family members	Nonfarm			Farm			Nonfarm			Farm		
	Total	Male head	Female head	Total	Male head	Female head	Total	Male head	Female head	Total	Male head	Female head
	Weighted average of incomes at economy level						Weighted average of incomes at low-cost level					
1 (under age 65)	$1,580	$1,650	$1,525	$960	$990	$920	$1,885	$1,970	$1,820	$1,150	$1,185	$1,090
1 (aged 65 or over)	1,470	1,480	1,465	885	890	880	1,745	1,775	1,735	1,055	1,065	1,040
2 (under age 65)	2,050	2,065	1,975	1,240	1,240	1,180	2,715	2,740	2,570	1,640	1,645	1,540
2 (aged 65 or over)	1,850	1,855	1,845	1,110	1,110	1,120	2,460	2,470	2,420	1,480	1,480	1,465
3	2,440	2,455	2,350	1,410	1,410	1,395	3,160	3,170	3,070	1,890	1,895	1,835
4	3,130	3,130	3,115	1,925	1,925	1,865	4,005	4,010	3,920	2,410	2,410	2,375
5	3,685	3,685	3,660	2,210	2,210	2,220	4,675	4,680	4,595	2,815	2,815	2,795
6	4,135	4,135	4,110	2,500	2,495	2,530	5,250	5,255	5,141	3,165	3,165	3,165
7 or more	5,090	5,100	5,000	3,055	3,065	2,985	6,395	6,405	6,270	3,840	3,850	3,750

1 For definition of poverty criteria, see text.

for nonfarm units would range from $1,580 for a single person under age 65 to $5,090 for a family averaging eight members—that is, seven or more persons. At the low-cost level, the corresponding income range runs from $1,885 to $6,395. A nonfarm family of husband, wife, and two young children would need $3,100 or $3,980.

When applied to the Census income distributions the cutoff points are being related to income before income taxes, although they were derived on an after-tax basis. At the economy level the incomes are so low that for most families of more than two persons and for aged unrelated individuals no tax would be required. By contrast, the BLS "modest but adequate" budget for a similar family of four in autumn 1959 in 20 large cities ranged from $4,880 to $5,870, not including taxes, and from $5,370 to $6,570 with taxes included.[11]

How Adequate Is the Standard?
The measure of poverty thus developed is arbitrary. Few could call it too high. Many might find it too low. Assuming the homemaker is a good manager and has the time and skill to shop wisely, she must prepare nutritious, palatable meals on a budget that for herself, a husband, and two young children—an average family—would come to about 70 cents a day per person.

For a meal all four of them ate together, she could spend on the average only 95 cents, and to stay within her budget she must allow no more a day than a pound of meat, poultry, or fish altogether, barely enough for one small serving for each family member at one of the three meals. Eggs could fill out her family fare only to a limited degree because the plan allows less than 2 dozen a week for all uses in cooking and at the table, not even one to a person a day. And any food extras, such as milk at school for the children, or the coffee her husband might buy to supplement the lunch he carries to work, have to come out of the same food money or compete with the limited funds available for rent, clothing, medical care, and all other expenses. Studies indicate that, on the average, family members eating a meal away from home spend twice as much as the homemaker would spend for preparing one for them at home. The 20–25 cents allowed for a meal at home in the economy plan would not buy much even in the way of supplementation.

There is some evidence that families with very low income, particularly large families, cut their food bills below the economy plan

---

[11] Helen H. Lamale and Margaret S. Strotz, "The Interim City Worker's Family Budget," *Monthly Labor Review*, August 1960.

level—a level at which a nutritionally good diet, though possible, is hard to achieve. Indeed, a study of beneficiaries of old-age, survivors, and disability insurance—limited to 1- or 2-person families—found that only about 10 percent of those spending less than the low-cost plan (priced about a third higher than the economy plan) had meals furnishing the full recommended amounts of essential nutrients. Not more than 40 percent had even as much as two-thirds the amounts recommended. Only when food expenditures were as high as those in the low-cost plan, or better, did 90 percent of the diets include two-thirds of the recommended allowance of the nutrients, and 60 percent meet them in full.[12] Few housewives with greater resources—income and other—than most poor families have at their disposal could do better. Many might not do as well.

Varying the Reference Point

Much of the recent discussion of the poor has centered about an ad hoc definition adopted in 1963. Under this definition a family of two persons or more with income of less than $3,000 and one person alone with less than $1,500 were considered poor. At the time, a more refined poverty income test was believed to be desirable. The hope was expressed that, although the statistical magnitude of the problem would undoubtedly be altered by a different measure, "the analysis of the sources of poverty, and of the programs needed to cope with it, would remain substantially unchanged."[13] Since programs are selected on other than purely statistical considerations, this part of the statement is unchallenged. But at least the relative importance of various phases of the poverty question does depend on the criterion used.

The present analysis pivots about a standard of roughly $3,130 for a family of four persons (all types combined) and $1,540 for an unrelated individual—a level in itself not materially different from the earlier one. The standard assumes in addition that families with fewer than four persons will, on the average, require less and that larger families will need more, despite the fact that in actuality they do not always have incomes to correspond. The resulting count of the poor therefore includes fewer small families and more large ones, many of them with children. Moreover, the preceding standard treats farm and nonfarm families alike, but the one discussed here assumes a lower cash requirement for families receiving some food and housing without direct out-

---

[12] U.S. Department of Agriculture, *Food Consumption and Dietary Levels of Older Households in Rochester, New York,* by C. LeBovit and D. A. Baker (Home Economics Research Report No. 25), 1964.

[13] Council of Economic Advisors, *Annual Report 1964,* chapter 2.

lay, as part of a farming operation. Accordingly, farm families, despite their low cash income, have a somewhat smaller representation in the current count of the poor for 1963 than in the earlier statistic.

The gross number of the population counted as poor will reflect, in the main, the level of living used as the basis. In this respect the old definition and the present one are much alike: Twenty-eight and one-half million persons in families would be called poor today because their families have income less than $3,000; 29¾ million persons in families would be poor because their family income is considered too low in relation to the number it must support. What is more telling, however, is the composition of the groups selected, for in considerable measure they are not the same.

To the extent that families differing in composition tend also to differ in income, the power of the poverty line to approximate an equivalent measure of need determines how accurately the selected group reflects the economic well-being of families of different composition. It may be that the consistency of the measure of economic well-being applied to different types of families is even more important than the level itself.

Though one may question the merits of a food-income relationship alone as a poverty index, it probably does serve as an interim guide to equivalent levels of living among families in different situations. Additional variables could improve it, as, for example, allowance for geographic variables of community size and region, and indeed further study of the income-consumption patterns themselves. Even as it stands, however, this index is undoubtedly a better leveler than a single income applied across the board.

As a comparison of four different measures of poverty illustrates (table 4), the flat sum of $3,000 for a family and $1,500 for an individual would indicate that 33.4 million persons were living in poverty in 1963. One in 7 of them would be a farm resident, and 1 in 3 a child under age 18. The modification of this scale to allow $1,500 for the first person and $500 for every additional family member raises the number of the poor to 34.5 million, and the percent who are children to more than 40, but the ratio of 1 in 7 on a farm remains unchanged. Under the economy plan definition, the most complex and differentiated of the standards compared, there are 34.6 million poor—almost the same number as under the $500 per person modification of the single $3,000 standard—but the number of poor children, who now represent 43 percent of the population living in poverty, is 1 million greater. As would be expected, the proportion of the poor who live on farms is considerably lower, or only 1 in 11.

TABLE 4

Persons in poverty status in 1963, by alternative definitions
(In millions)

Type of unit	A[1]	B[2]	C[3]	D[4]	Total U.S. population
Total number of persons.........	33.4	34.0	34.5	34.6	187.2
Farm	4.9	6.4	5.1	3.2	12.6
Nonfarm	28.5	27.6	29.3	31.4	174.6
Unrelated individuals	4.9	[5]4.0	4.9	4.9	11.2
Farm	.2	1.4	.2	.1	.4
Nonfarm	4.7	2.6	4.7	4.8	10.8
Members of family units	28.5	30.0	29.6	29.7	176.0
Farm	4.7	5.0	4.9	3.1	12.2
Nonfarm	23.8	25.0	24.6	26.6	163.8
Children under age 18	10.8	15.7	14.1	15.0	68.8
Farm	1.8	2.4	2.1	1.5	4.8
Nonfarm	9.0	13.3	12.0	13.5	64.0

[1] Under $3,000 for family; under $1,500 for unrelated individuals (interim measure used by Council of Economic Advisers).

[2] Level below which no income tax is required, beginning in 1965.

[3] $1,500 for first person plus $500 for each additional person, up to $4,500. See testimony by Walter Heller on the Economic Opportunity Act, *Hearings Before the Subcommittee on the War on Poverty Program of the Committee on Education and Labor, House of Representatives, Eighty-eighth Congress, Second Session,* Part 1, page 30.

[4] Economy level of the poverty index developed by the Social Security Administration, by family size and farm-nonfarm residence, centering around $3,100 for 4 persons.

[5] Estimated; income-tax cutoff is $900; Census 1963 income data available only for total less than $1,000; this figure has been broken into less than $500 and $500-999 on basis of 1962 proportions.

Of particular significance is the incidence of poverty among different kinds of families. The uniform $3,000 test, which designated 9.3 million families as poor in 1962, by 1963 counted 8.8 million, or about 1 out of 5. By contrast, in 1963 the economy plan standard would tag only 1 in 7 families as poor, or 7.2 million all told. Although half the families poor by the $3,000 income test include no more than two members, 2-person units represent only a third of the families poor according to the economy level definition. In corresponding fashion, only 1 in 8 of the families with less than $3,000 had four or more children, but among those poor according to the economy level every fourth family had at least four children. Families with an aged head represented more than a third of all the families with less than $3,000 but only a fifth of those with incomes below the economy plan standard (table 5).

Clearly a profile of the poor that includes large numbers of farm families and aged couples may raise different questions and evoke different answers than when the group is characterized by relatively more

TABLE 5

Incidence of poverty by two measures: Families with 1963 incomes below $3,000 and below the economy level of the SSA poverty index, by specified characteristics

(Numbers in millions)

Characteristic	Total number of families	Poor— with incomes under $3,000[1]		Poor—with incomes below economy level[2]		
		Number	Percent of total	Number	Percent of total	Percentage distribution of all poor families
All families	47.4	8.8	19	7.2	15	100
Residence:						
Farm	3.1	1.3	43	.7	23	10
Nonfarm	44.3	7.5	17	6.5	15	90
Race of head:						
White	42.7	6.8	16	5.2	12	72
Nonwhite	4.7	2.0	43	2.0	42	28
Age of head:						
14-24	2.7	.8	30	.7	26	10
25-54	30.6	3.6	12	4.0	13	54
55-64	7.4	1.3	18	1.0	13	14
65 and over	6.7	3.1	45	1.5	24	22
Type of family:						
Husband-wife	41.3	6.2	15	5.0	12	70
Wife in paid labor force	13.4	1.0	8	.9	7	13
Wife not in paid labor force	27.9	5.2	19	4.1	15	57
Other male head	1.2	.3	23	.2	17	3
Female head	4.9	2.3	47	2.0	40	27
Number of persons in family:						
2	15.3	4.6	30	2.5	16	34
3	9.8	1.5	16	1.0	11	14
4	9.4	1.0	10	1.0	10	14
5	6.3	.7	11	.9	14	13
6	3.3	.4	12	.6	19	9
7 or more	3.3	.6	18	1.2	35	16
Number of related children under age 18:						
None	19.1	4.7	25	2.4	13	34
1	8.7	1.4	16	1.1	12	15
2	8.6	1.0	11	1.0	11	13
3	5.5	.7	14	1.0	17	14
4	2.9	.4	15	.6	23	9
5	1.4	.3	18	.5	36	7
6	1.2	.3	30	.6	49	8
Number of earners:						
None	3.7	2.8	76	2.0	53	27
1	20.8	3.9	19	3.3	16	46
2	17.3	1.8	10	1.5	9	21
3 or more	5.6	.3	6	.4	7	6

TABLE 5 (cont'd)

Incidence of poverty by two measures: Families with 1963 incomes below $3,000 and below the economy level of the SSA poverty index, by specified characteristics

(Numbers in millions)

Characteristic	Total number of families	Poor— with incomes under $3,000[1]		Poor—with incomes below economy level[2]		
		Number	Percent of total	Number	Percent of total	Percentage distribution of all poor families
Employment status and occupation of head:						
Not in labor force[3]	8.8	4.3	49	3.0	34	42
Unemployed	1.4	.4	28	.4	28	6
Employed	37.2	4.1	11	3.7	10	52
Professional, technical, and kindred workers	4.7	.1	3	.1	3	2
Farmers and farm managers.	1.8	.9	48	.5	29	8
Managers, officials, and proprietors (except farm).	6.0	.4	6	.3	5	4
Clerical, sales, and kindred workers	4.9	.2	6	.2	4	3
Craftsmen, operatives, and kindred workers	14.5	1.1	8	1.2	8	17
Service workers, including private household	3.0	.7	23	.6	20	8
Laborers (except mine)	2.3	.7	33	.7	30	10
Work experience of head in 1963:[4]						
Worked in 1963	40.7	5.1	13	4.6	11	64
Worked at full-time jobs	37.9	3.8	10	3.6	10	50
50-52 weeks	30.7	2.1	7	2.0	7	28
Worked at part-time jobs ...	2.8	1.4	49	1.0	36	14
Did not work in 1963	6.7	3.7	54	2.6	38	36

[1] Prepared by the Bureau of the Census from P-60, No. 43, *Income of Families and Persons in the U.S., 1963.*

[2] Derived from special tabulations by the Bureau of the Census for the Social Security Administration. For definitions of poverty criteria, see text.

[3] Includes approximately 900,000 family heads in the Armed Forces, of whom about 100,000 have incomes under $3,000.

[4] All work-experience data, including data for year-round, full-time workers, limited to civilian workers.

young nonfarm families—many of them with several children. Non-white families, generally larger than white families, account for about 2 million of the poor units by either definition. Because the total number of families counted among the poor by the economy standard is smaller, however, the nonwhite families make up a larger part of them.

Because the measure of poverty for nonfarm unrelated individuals is almost the same under the economy level definition as under the earlier one—and 1-person households seldom live on a farm—characteristics of the 4.9 million unrelated persons now labeled poor are almost the same as those thus identified earlier (table 6).

TABLE 6

Incidence of poverty by two measures: Unrelated individuals with 1963 incomes below $1,500 and below the economy level of the SSA poverty index, by specified characteristics
(Numbers in millions)

Characteristic	Total number	Poor—with incomes under $1,500[1]		Poor—with incomes below economy level[2]		
		Number	Percent of total	Number	Percent of total	Percentage distribution of all poor unrelated individuals
All unrelated individuals ...	11.2	4.9	44	4.9	44	100
Residence:						
Nonfarm	10.8	4.7	43	4.7	44	97
Farm	.4	.2	67	.2	40	3
Race:						
White	9.7	4.1	42	4.1	42	83
Nonwhite	1.5	.8	56	.8	58	17
Age:						
14-24	1.0	.5	47	.5	48	10
25-64	5.9	1.8	31	1.9	56	38
65 and over	4.3	2.6	62	2.5	59	52
Sex:						
Male	4.3	1.4	33	1.4	34	30
Female	6.9	3.5	51	3.5	50	70
Earner status:						
Earner	7.0	1.8	26	1.8	26	37
Nonearner	4.2	3.1	75	3.1	74	63
Work experience in 1963[3]						
Worked in 1963	6.7	1.8	26	1.8	26	36
Worked at full-time jobs ...	5.5	1.1	20	1.2	21	23
50-52 weeks	3.7	.5	12	.5	13	10
Worked at part-time jobs ...	1.2	.7	55	.6	54	13
Did not work in 1963	4.5	3.1	72	3.9	80	64

[1] Prepared by Bureau of the Census from P-60, No. 43, *Income of Families and Persons in the U.S., 1963.*

[2] Derived from special tabulations by the Bureau of the Census for the Social Security Administration. For definition of poverty criteria, see text.

[3] All work-experience data, including data for year-round, full-time workers, limited to civilian workers.

The Income Deficit

Before elaborating further on who is poor and who is not, it may be well to assess the magnitude of the poverty complex in dollar terms. Just how much less than the aggregate estimated need is the actual income of the poor? Does it fall short by much or by little?

In the very rough terms that the selected income standard permits, it can be estimated that the 34.6 million persons identified as poor needed an aggregate money income of $28.8 billion in 1963 to cover their basic requirements. Their current income actually totaled about $17.3 billion, or only 60 percent of their estimated needs. Some of the deficit could have been—and no doubt was—offset by use of savings. By and large, however, it has been well documented that the low-income persons who could benefit most from such additions to their meager resources are least likely to have the advantage of them. And it is not usually the poor who have the rich relatives.

Unquestionably the income of the poor included the $4.7 billion paid under public assistance programs from Federal, State, and local funds during 1963. In December of that year such payments were going to a total of 7¾ million recipients. Not all persons who are poor receive assistance, but all persons receiving assistance are unquestionably poor. It cannot be said for sure how many of the poor were benefiting from other public income-support programs such as

TABLE 7

Income deficit of families and unrelated individuals below the economy level of the SSA poverty index, 1963[1]

Type of unit	Dollar deficit (in billions)			Percentage distribution		
	Total	Male head	Female head	Total	Male head	Female head
Total	$11.5	$6.4	$5.1	100.0	56.1	43.9
Unrelated individuals	3.1	1.0	2.1	27.2	8.5	18.7
Families with 2 or more members	8.4	5.4	3.0	72.8	47.6	25.2
With no children under age 18	1.8	1.4	.4	15.1	12.4	2.7
With children under age 18	6.6	4.0	2.6	57.7	35.2	22.5
1	1.0	.6	.4	8.5	4.9	3.6
2	1.0	.6	.4	8.9	5.2	3.7
3	1.3	.7	.6	11.7	6.2	5.5
4	1.0	.6	.4	9.1	5.8	3.3
5	1.0	.6	.3	8.5	5.6	2.9
6 or more	1.3	.9	.4	11.0	7.5	3.5

[1] For definition of poverty criteria, see text.

old-age, survivors, and disability insurance, unemployment insurance, veterans' payments, and the like.

Of the total deficit, about $5 billion represented the unmet needs of families headed by a woman. About three-fifths of the total ($6.6 billion) represented the shortage in income of families with children under age 18 and about 60 percent of this shortage was in the income of families with a man at the head (table 7). It is estimated that $600 million represented the deficit of poor persons on farms.

Even among the needy, there are some who are worse off than others, and in dollar terms the families consisting of a mother and young children must rank among the poorest. Such families as a group had less than half the money they needed, and the greater the number of children the greater the unmet need: Poor families with a female head and five or more children, including altogether about 1,650,000 children, as a group were living on income less by 59 percent than their minimum requirement. Of the total family units of this type in the population—that is, of all families with female head and five or more children—9 out of 10 were poor. As the following tabulation shows, for both male and female units, those families with the highest poverty rate—the families with several children—tended also to include the poorest poor.

TABLE 8

Income and family size: Median money income of nonfarm families, 1963, by number of members, number of children, and sex of head

Number of family members	Total	Number of related children under age 18						
		None	1	2	3	4	5	6 or more
		Male head						
Total	$6,745	$6,045	$6,960	$7,290	$7,095	$7,080	$6,590	$5,765
2	5,400	5,415	[1]	.....	.....	.....	.....	.....
3	6,901	8,260	6,450	[1]	.....	.....	.....	.....
4	7,490	11,410	8,810	7,000	[1]	.....	.....	.....
5	7,390	[2]12,570	9,640	8,680	6,900	[1]	.....	.....
6	7,290	[1]	[1]	9,860	8,365	6,865	[1]	.....
7 or more	6,870	[1]	[1]	[1]	[2]10,770	8,430	6,590	5,765
		Female head						
Total	$3,245	$4,585	$3,080	$2,940	$2,160	$2,260	[2]$1,660	[2]$2,230
2	3,340	3,955	2,115	.....	.....	.....	.....	.....
3	3,885	6,480	4,225	2,335	.....	.....	.....	.....
4	3,151	[1]	[2]6,000	[2]3,230	1,940	.....	.....	.....
5	2,625	[1]	[1]	[1]	[1]	[2]2,050	.....	.....
6	[2]2,120	.....	.....	[1]	[1]	[1]	[2]1,575	.....
7 or more	2,575	.....	.....	[1]	[1]	[1]	[1]	[2]2,230

[1] Not shown for fewer than 100,000 families.
[2] Base between 100,000 and 200,000.

For unrelated individuals, among whom are many aged persons poverty rates are high too, and their income deficits substantial (table 11).

Children and Poverty

Of all the persons in family units with income below the economy level (that is, disregarding for the moment persons living alone), half were

TABLE 9

Persons in poverty in 1963: Total number of persons in units with income below the economy level of the SSA poverty index, by sex of head and farm-nonfarm residence[1]

(In millions)

Type of unit	Total	Sex of head		Residence	
		Male	Female	Farm	Non-farm
	Number of persons				
Total	34.6	23.5	11.1	3.2	31.4
Unrelated individuals	4.9	1.4	3.5	.1	4.8
Under age 65	2.4	.9	1.4	.1	2.3
Aged 65 or over	2.5	.5	2.1	(2)	2.5
Persons in families	29.7	22.1	7.6	3.1	26.6
With no children	5.3	4.4	.9	.6	4.7
With children	24.4	17.7	6.7	2.5	21.9
Adults	9.4	7.3	2.1	1.0	8.4
Children under age 18	15.0	10.4	4.6	1.5	13.5
Head year-round, full-time worker[3]	5.7	5.2	.5	(4)	(4)
Other	9.3	5.2	4.1	(4)	(4)
	Number of family units				
Total	12.1	6.7	5.4	0.9	11.2
Unrelated individuals	4.9	1.4	3.5	.2	4.7
Year-round, full-time workers	.5	.2	.3	(2)	(2)
Under age 65	.4	.2	.2	(2)	(2)
Aged 65 or over	.1	.2	.1	(2)	(2)
Other	4.4	1.2	3.2	(2)	(2)
Under age 65	1.9	.7	1.2	(2)	(2)
Aged 65 or over	2.5	.5	2.0	(2)	(2)
Families	7.2	5.2	2.0	.7	6.5
With no children	2.5	2.1	.4	.3	2.2
Head year-round, full-time worker[3]	.4	.4	(2)	(2)	(2)
Other	2.1	1.7	.4	(2)	(2)
With children	4.7	3.2	1.5	.4	4.3
Head year-round, full-time worker[3]	1.6	1.5	.1	(2)	(2)
Other	3.1	1.7	1.4	(2)	(2)

[1] For definition of poverty criteria, see text.
[2] Less than 50,000.
[3] One who worked primarily at full-time civilian jobs (35 hours or more a week) for 50 weeks or more during 1963. Year-round, full-time workers exclude all members of the Armed Forces. "Other" workers include members of the Armed Forces living off post or with their families on post.
[4] Not available.

TABLE 10

(Percent)

Type of unit	Male head		Female head	
	Incidence of poverty at economy level	*Income of poor as proportion of required income*	*Incidence of poverty at economy level*	*Income of poor as proportion of required income*
Total	14	64	46	53
Unrelated individual	34	57	50	58
Family	12	65	40	49
With no children	12	64	19	62
With children	12	65	55	47
1 or 2	8	68	42	53
3 or 4	14	66	72	45
5 or more	36	62	92	41

children under age 18. These 15 million youngsters represented more than 1 in 5 of all children living in families. Because poor families sometimes find it necessary to "double up" in order to cut down their living expenses, about 9 percent of the children in the poor families were designated as "related" rather than "own" children. In other words, they were not the children of the head of the family but the children of other relatives making their home with the family. Among the poor families with a woman at the head, one-seventh of the children were "related" rather than "own," and nearly a third of these related children were part of a subfamily consisting of a mother and children. Among poor families with a male head, 6 percent of the children in the households were children of a relative of the head.

A considerable number of subfamilies that include children are poor—a third of those with a father present and nearly three-fourths of those with only a mother. But from 50 percent to 60 percent of all subfamilies with inadequate income manage to escape poverty by living with relatives. Counting as poor the children in subfamilies whose own income is inadequate but who live as part of a larger family with a combined income above the poverty level would add 580,000 to the number of children whose parents are too poor to support them even at the economy level. Together with their parents, these children are part of a group of 1.1 million persons under age 65 not included in the current count of the poor, although they would be if they had to rely solely on their own income.

In contrast to this total of 15.6 million needy children, in December 1963 only 3.1 million children were receiving assistance in the form of aid to families with dependent children, the public program

TABLE 11

The poverty matrix: Number of families and unrelated individuals (and total number of persons) below the economy level of the SSA poverty index,[1] by sex of head, number of children, and work experience of head in 1963
(Numbers in thousands)

Type of unit	U.S. population		The poor						
			Units					Number of persons	
	Number of units	Percent	Number	Percent	Poverty rate (percent)	Head year-round full-time worker[a]	Other head	Total	Children
All units	58,620	100.0	12,100	100.0	21	2,510	9,590	34,580	14,970
Unrelated individuals, total	11,180	19.1	4,890	40.4	44	480	4,410	4,890	....
Under age 65	6,910	11.8	2,360	19.5	34	400	1,960	2,360	....
Aged 65 or over	4,270	7.3	2,540	21.0	59	80	2,460	2,540	....
Families, total	47,440	80.9	7,210	59.6	15	2,030	5,180	29,690	14,970
With no children	19,120	32.6	2,460	20.3	13	370	2,080	5,340	....
With children	28,320	48.3	4,750	39.3	17	1,660	3,090	24,340	14,970
1	8,680	14.8	1,050	8.6	12	270	780	3,060	1,050
2	8,580	14.6	980	8.1	11	320	660	3,830	1,950
3	5,550	9.5	960	7.9	17	340	620	4,770	2,880
4	2,860	4.9	650	5.4	23	290	360	3,960	2,600
5	1,430	2.4	520	4.3	36	200	310	3,910	2,580
6 or more	1,210	2.1	600	5.0	49	240	370	4,810	3,910

Units with male head	46,830	79.9	6,670	55.1	14	2,090	4,580	23,500	10,420
Unrelated individuals	4,280	7.3	1,440	11.9	34	240	1,200	1,440	.....
Under age 65	3,110	5.3	940	7.8	30	220	720	940	.....
Aged 65 or over	1,170	2.0	500	4.2	43	20	480	500	.....
Families	42,550	72.6	5,220	43.2	12	1,850	3,370	22,060	10,420
With no children	17,070	29.1	2,040	16.9	12	350	1,690	4,400	4,400
With children	25,480	43.5	3,180	26.3	12	1,500	1,680	17,660	10,420
1	7,650	13.0	650	5.4	9	240	420	2,160	650
2	7,830	13.4	620	5.1	8	280	340	2,630	1,230
3	5,070	8.6	620	5.2	12	300	320	3,280	1,870
4	2,600	4.4	460	3.8	18	270	180	2,920	1,820
5	1,280	2.2	380	3.2	30	180	200	3,070	1,920
6 or more	1,050	1.8	450	3.7	43	220	220	3,590	2,920
Units with female head	11,790	20.1	5,430	44.9	46	410	5,020	11,080	4,540
Unrelated individuals	6,910	11.8	3,450	28.5	50	240	3,210	3,450	.....
Under age 65	3,800	6.5	1,410	11.7	37	180	1,240	1,410	.....
Aged 65 or over	3,110	5.3	2,030	16.8	65	60	1,970	2,030	.....
Families	4,880	8.3	1,980	16.4	41	180	1,800	7,630	4,540
With no children	2,050	3.5	420	3.4	19	20	390	940	940
With children	2,830	4.8	1,570	13.0	55	160	1,410	6,690	4,540
1	1,030	1.8	390	3.3	38	30	360	910	390
2	750	1.2	360	3.0	48	40	320	1,210	720
3	490	.8	340	2.8	70	40	300	1,490	1,010
4	260	.4	190	1.6	74	20	170	1,040	770
5	140	.2	130	1.1	91	20	110	840	660
6 or more	160	.3	150	1.3	93	10	140	1,220	990

[1] For definition of poverty criteria, see text.

[2] See footnote 3, table 9.

designed especially for them. Because some families stay on the assistance rolls less than a full year, 4 million to 4½ million children received aid during 1963.

Many children receive benefits from other public programs, such as old-age, survivors, and disability insurance and veterans' programs. It is not known at this writing how many of them are numbered among the poor or how many are in families with total income from all sources below the public assistance standards for their State.

Children in poor families with a man at the head are less likely than others to receive help. Such children number more than 10 million, but today the number of children with a father in the home who receive assistance in the form of aid to families with dependent children is less than 1 million, a ratio of not even 1 in 10.

Many of the families with children receiving public assistance undoubtedly swell the ranks of our poorest poor, because even by the limited standards of assistance of their own States—almost all of which allow less than the economy level of income—nearly half of the recipients have some unmet need. For a fourth of the families, according to a recent study, the unmet need came to as much as $30 a month or more.[14]

As would be expected—the larger the family, the more likely it is to include children. Indeed, among families of five or more, almost all have some children, and three-fourths have at least three.* The fewer adults in the family, the less opportunity there will be for additional earnings.

The statistics on family income that are generally available do not show detail by both family size and number of children. The figures presented in table 8 do show such data for 1963 for nonfarm families. It is readily apparent that no matter what the family size, the income decreases with increasing number of children at a rate that is not likely to be offset by the fact that children have lower income needs.

Accordingly not only do poverty rates among families vary with family size, but among families of a given size the chances of being poor vary in accordance with the number of children under age 18. The percentages below show the incidence of poverty—as defined by the Social Security Administration criterion at the economy level— among nonfarm families with specified number of children.

The sorry plight of the families with female head and children

---

[14] Gerald Kahn and Ellen J. Perkins, "Families Receiving AFDC: What Do They Have To Live On?" *Welfare in Review* (Welfare Administration), October 1964.
    * Descriptive table omitted from original.

TABLE 12

Total number of family members	Children under age 18						
	None	1	2	3	4	5	6 or more
Families with male head:							
3	6	8	(1)	....	....	....	....
4	3	6	7	(1)	....	....	....
5	2	9	9	11	(1)	....	....
6	(1)	(1)	4	14	16	(1)	....
7 or more	(1)	(1)	(1)	10	22	30	42
Families with female head:							
2²	14	47	....	....	....	....	....
3	9	21	54	....	....	....	....
4	(1)	18	43	73	.....	....	....

¹ Percentage not shown for base less than 100,000.
² Head under age 65.

is also evident. It needs no poverty line to explain why two-thirds of the children in such families must be considered poor.

An earlier report cited evidence that women in families without a husband present had more children than in those where the husband was still present.[15] Some of the poor families with children and a female head may well, at an earlier stage, have been members of a large household with a male head and inadequate income.

Finally, since the data both on income and on incidence of poverty relate to the number now in the family, there is an understatement of the relationship between large families and low income: Some of the families currently listed as having only one or two children undoubtedly will have more in the future or have others who are now past age 18 and may no longer be in the home. It is not likely that family income adjusts in equal measure. If anything, it may decline rather than increase as the family grows because it will be more difficult for the mother to work, and many of the families can escape poverty only by having the wife as well as the head in the labor force (table 16).

Age and Poverty

The figures in table 9 summarize the number of individuals and family units judged to be in poverty status in accordance with the economy level.

The total number of aged persons among the 34.6 million poor is about 5.2 million, or 1 in 7. Perhaps the poorest of the aged are

---

[15] See Mollie Orshansky, "Children of the Poor," *Social Security Bulletin*, July 1963.

elderly relatives living in the home of a younger family. Such elderly persons living in a family of which they were neither the head nor the wife of the head in March 1964 numbered about 2.5 million. There probably were a variety of reasons for their choice of living arrangements, but that financial stringency was a major factor is obvious: four-fifths of these elderly relatives had less than $1,500 in income of their own during 1963, the minimum required for an aged person to live alone. The vast majority of elderly persons designated as "other relatives" were living in a family with income above the poverty level.

Every second person living alone (or with nonrelatives) and classified as poor was aged 65 or older, and four-fifths of the aged poor were women. The low resources generally prevailing among this group mean that those who, by choice or necessity, live independently are likely to do so only at the most meager level, even if allowance is made for their using up any savings.[16]

The present analysis indicates that more than 40 percent of all aged men and nearly two-thirds of the aged women living by themselves in 1963 had income below the economy level. Only 1 in 4 of the aged women living alone had income above the low-cost level.

In summary, if to the 2.5 million aged persons living alone in poverty and the 2.7 million living in poor families as aged head, spouse, or relative are added the 1.7 million aged relatives too poor to get by on their own, but not included in the current count of the poor because the families they live with are above the economy level of the poverty index, the number of impoverished aged would rise to almost 7 million. Two-fifths of the population aged 65 or older (not in institutions) are thus presently subject to poverty, or escaping it only by virtue of living with more fortunate relatives.

Among poor individuals under age 65, poverty for some undoubtedly represented only a stage through which they were passing. The poverty rate was high among persons under age 25, half having incomes below the economy level, and dropped to about 1 in 4 for those aged 25–34 (table 16).

Among 2-person families, 16 percent of whom were poor by the economy level criterion, there was also a difference between the situation of those units approaching the last stage in the family cycle and those who were younger. Of all 2-person units, a third had a head aged 65 or older, but of those 2-person units called poor, half had an aged

---

[16] See Lenore A. Epstein, "Income of the Aged in 1962: First Findings of the 1963 Survey of the Aged," *Social Security Bulletin*, March 1964, and Janet Murray, "Potential Income From Assets . . .," *Social Security Bulletin*, December 1964.

TABLE 13

Family type	Male head Total number of units (in thousands)	Per- cent poor	Female head Total number of units (in thousands)	Per- cent poor
Two adults	13,026	14	1,557	22
Head under age 65	8,769	10	876	14
Head aged 65 or older	4,257	22	681	32
One adult, one child	87	(¹)	618	50

¹ Percentage not shown for base less than 100,000.

head. Presumably, some of the other units who were currently poor represented young couples who had decided not to delay marriage until they attained the better job status—and income—that they one day hoped to enjoy. But others consisted of a mother with a child, who were suffering the poverty that is likely to be the lot of the family with no man to provide support. Table 13 shows the rates of poverty, according to the economy level, among the different types of 2-person families.

Work and Poverty

The greater overall vulnerability of families headed by a woman is evidenced by the fact that such families, who number only 1 in 10 of all families in the country, account for nearly 1 in 3 of the Nation's poor. Although the inadequate income of the poor families with a female head may be attributed to the fact that few of the family heads are employed, this is not the reason among the families headed by a man. A majority of the men are working, but at jobs that do not pay enough to provide for their family needs. Moreover, of those not at work, most report themselves as out of the labor force altogether rather than unemployed. Yet the rate of unemployment reported by the poor was more than three times that among the heads of families above the poverty level (table 8).*

Current Employment Status

The employment status of the family heads in March 1964, when the income data were collected, was recorded as shown in table 14.

Detailed analysis of the data for white and nonwhite families will be reserved for a subsequent report, but some highlights seem pertinent here.

Despite the fact that unemployment generally is more prevalent among the nonwhite population than the white, among families whose

---

* Descriptive table omitted.

TABLE 14

Employment status of head, March 1964	Male head		Female head	
	Poor family	Nonpoor family	Poor family	Nonpoor family
Total	100	100	100	100
In labor force	67	88	33	60
Employed	60	85	29	57
Unemployed	6	3	4	3
Not in labor force	33	12	67	40

income marked them as poor there was no difference by race in the total proportion of the men currently looking for work. Among white and nonwhite male heads alike, 6 percent said they were out of a job. Indeed, since fewer among the white heads of families who are poor were in the labor force than was true among nonwhite heads of poor families, the rate of unemployment among those actually available for work was noticeably higher for the former group. What is more significant is that 73 percent of the nonwhite male heads of poor families were currently employed, and more than half of them—42 percent of all the poor—had been employed full time throughout 1963. Among male heads in white families with incomes below the economy level, only 56 percent were currently working, and no more than a third had been year-round full-time workers in 1963.

Unemployment for nonwhite workers is undeniably serious. But the concentration of nonwhite men in low-paying jobs at which any worker—white or nonwhite—is apt to earn too little to support a large family may be even more crucial in consigning their families to poverty at a rate three times that of their white fellow citizens.

In point of fact, the family of a nonwhite male is somewhat worse off in relation to that of a white male when both are working than when both are not, as table 15 suggests.

This difference does not come as a complete surprise. Earlier analysis of the income life cycle of the nonwhite man suggested that it is only when he and his white counterpart exchange their weekly pay

TABLE 15

Employment status of head, March 1964	Percent of families with male head with income below the economy level	
	White	Non-white
All families	10	34
Not in labor force	25	50
Unemployed	22	47
Employed	7	31
Year-round, full-time in 1963...............	5	23

envelope for a check from a public income-maintenance program that they begin to approach economic equality.[17] For most white families, retirement or other type of withdrawal from the labor force brings with it a marked decline in income. Some nonwhite families, however, are then actually not much worse off than when working.

Work Experience in 1963

Since it was the annual income for 1963 that determined whether the family would be ranked as poor, the work experience of the head in 1963 is even more relevant to the poverty profile than the employment status at the time of the Current Population Survey.

Among the male heads, only 1 in 3 of those in poor families was a full-time worker all during the year, compared with 3 in 4 of the heads in nonpoor families. Among the female heads, as would be expected, the proportion working full time was much smaller—a tenth among poor families and not a full four-tenths among the nonpoor. All told, the poor families headed by a man fully employed throughout 1963 included 5.2 million children under age 18 and those headed by a fully employed woman worker had half a million. Thus 2 in 5 of all the children growing up in poverty were in a family of a worker with a regular full-time job.

It is difficult to say which is the more striking statistic: that 6 percent of the families headed by a male year-round full-time worker were nevertheless poor, or that 25 percent of the families with a male head who did not have a full-time job all year were poor.

That a man risks poverty for his family when he does not or cannot work all the time might be expected, but to end the year with so inadequate an income, even when he has worked all week every week, must make his efforts seem hopeless.

Yet, with minimum wage provisions guaranteeing an annual income of only $2,600, and many workers entitled to not even this amount, it should not be too surprising that in 1963 there were 2 million families in poverty despite the fact that the head never was out of a job, as shown below.

Almost all the male heads who had worked full-time all year in 1963 were also currently employed in March 1964 in poor and nonpoor families alike. Among the women year-round full-time workers, only 80 percent of those at the head of families who were poor in terms of their 1963 income were still employed in the spring of the following year, compared with 96 percent of those not poor. Among 1.8 million

---

[17] Mollie Orshansky, "The Aged Negro and His Income," *Social Security Bulletin,* February 1964.

TABLE 16

Incidence of poverty in 1963, according to SSA poverty index: Percent of families and unrelated individuals with 1963 income below specified level,[1] by specified characteristics and race of head

[Numbers in thousands; data are estimates derived from a survey of households and are therefore subject to sampling variability that may be relatively large where the size of the percentage or size of the total on which the percentage is based is small; as in all surveys, the figures are subject to errors of response and nonreporting]

Characteristic	All units			White			Nonwhite		
	Total number	Percent with incomes below—		Total number	Percent with incomes below—		Total number	Percent with incomes below—	
		Economy level	Low-cost level		Economy level	Low-cost level		Economy level	Low-cost level
Families									
Total	47,436	15.1	23.0	42,663	12.0	19.3	4,773	42.5	55.6
Residence:									
Nonfarm	44,343	14.6	22.4	39,854	11.6	18.7	4,489	41.2	54.3
Farm	3,093	23.0	31.8	2,809	18.9	27.2	284	62.3	75.5
Race of head:									
White	42,663	12.0	19.3	.....	....	....	....	....	....
Nonwhite	4,773	42.5	55.6	.....	....	....	....	....	....
Age of head:									
14-24	2,744	25.8	35.3	2,391	20.7	29.9	353	59.8	71.0
25-34	9,128	14.7	23.6	8,109	11.1	19.1	1,019	43.2	59.2
35-44	11,437	13.7	20.7	10,220	10.5	17.0	1,217	40.2	52.2
45-54	9,986	9.8	15.2	9,012	7.0	11.8	974	35.4	46.9
55-64	7,382	13.3	18.5	6,717	10.9	15.7	665	38.0	48.5
65 and over	6,759	23.5	36.9	6,214	20.9	33.9	545	52.6	70.4
Number of persons in family:									
2	15,287	16.1	24.3	13,917	14.4	22.3	1,370	33.0	44.7
3	9,808	10.6	16.5	8,906	8.7	13.6	902	29.0	44.8
4	9,435	10.3	15.9	8,678	7.6	12.6	757	41.9	53.9
5	6,268	14.5	22.1	5,718	11.4	18.2	550	45.2	59.9
6	3,324	19.1	30.9	2,908	14.2	26.1	416	53.8	65.0
7 or more	3,314	34.8	49.6	2,536	24.9	39.9	778	68.4	82.2

Number of related children under age 18:									
None	19,119	12.7	20.1	17,607	11.5	18.5	1,512	26.8	39.3
1	8,682	12.1	17.7	7,771	9.6	18.4	911	32.8	45.6
2	8,579	11.3	17.5	7,824	8.3	13.8	755	42.5	56.1
3	5,554	17.4	26.8	5,030	14.0	22.5	524	48.2	66.2
4	2,863	22.8	34.8	2,476	16.8	29.1	387	60.7	70.5
5	1,429	35.8	53.0	1,145	27.2	44.7	284	73.6	89.6
6 or more	1,210	49.3	63.5	810	35.3	51.2	400	77.3	87.7
Region:									
Northeast	11,902	9.8	16.5	11,017	8.4	14.6	885	26.6	39.5
North Central	13,358	11.5	18.7	12,472	10.3	17.0	886	29.7	43.5
South	14,389	24.6	34.6	12,005	17.9	27.1	2,384	58.3	71.9
West	7,787	11.7	18.5	7,169	11.0	17.4	618	20.7	31.4
Type of family:									
Male head	42,554	12.3	20.0	38,866	10.2	17.3	3,688	34.1	48.2
Married, wife present	41,310	12.1	19.9	37,799	10.1	17.2	3,511	34.3	48.5
Wife in paid labor force	13,398	6.8	11.9	11,851	4.3	8.7	1,547	25.5	36.5
Wife not in paid labor force	27,912	14.6	23.6	25,948	12.6	21.0	1,964	41.3	58.0
Other marital status	1,243	17.0	23.4	1,067	14.5	20.1	177	[2]31.2	[2]42.6
Female head	4,882	40.1	49.3	3,797	31.2	40.1	1,085	70.8	80.5
Number of earners:									
None	3,695	53.4	70.2	3,242	49.2	66.9	453	83.9	93.9
1	20,832	15.7	24.7	18,976	12.5	20.7	1,856	48.5	64.5
2	17,306	8.7	14.4	15,484	6.3	11.3	1,822	28.8	39.8
3 or more	5,603	7.4	12.3	4,961	3.9	7.7	642	34.8	48.0
Employment status and occupation of head:									
Not in labor force[3]	8,757	34.4	47.9	7,673	30.0	43.7	1,084	65.4	77.6
Unemployed	1,427	28.3	39.9	1,190	23.8	34.5	237	53.4	70.2
Employed	37,252	10.0	16.4	33,800	7.5	13.1	3,452	34.5	47.8
Professional and technical workers	4,688	2.8	5.5	4,479	2.4	5.1	209	10.9	14.7
Farmers and farm managers	1,846	29.3	37.3	1,739	26.5	34.1	107	[2]77.0	[2]93.2
Managers, officials, and proprietors (except farm)	5,981	5.4	9.9	5,860	5.0	9.5	121	[2]22.2	[2]30.0
Clerical and sales workers	4,865	4.3	9.1	4,637	3.7	8.1	228	16.6	28.7
Craftsmen and foremen	7,102	5.5	11.1	6,704	4.5	9.7	398	21.3	32.3
Operatives	7,430	11.2	19.1	6,572	8.9	15.9	858	29.8	44.8
Service workers, including private household	2,996	20.1	29.8	2,184	12.1	19.9	812	40.2	54.8
Private household workers	285	63.8	70.0	95	(4)	33.8	190	[2]77.5	[2]83.1
Laborers (except mine)	2,344	29.9	43.2	1,625	21.1	(4)	719	50.0	64.4

See footnotes at end of table.

TABLE 16 (cont'd)

Incidence of poverty in 1963, according to SSA poverty index: Percent of families and unrelated individuals with 1963 income below specified level,[1] by specified characteristics and race of head

[Numbers in thousands: data are estimates derived from a survey of households and are therefore subject to sampling variability that may be relatively large where the size of the percentage or size of the total on which the percentage is based is small; as in all surveys, the figures are subject to errors of response and nonreporting]

Characteristic	All units			White			Nonwhite		
	Total number	Percent with incomes below—		Total number	Percent with incomes below—		Total number	Percent with incomes below—	
		Economy level	Low-cost level		Economy level	Low-cost level		Economy level	Low-cost level
Families									
Work experience of head:[5]									
Worked in 1963	40,753	11.3	18.2	36,791	8.6	14.8	3,962	36.9	50.4
Worked at full-time jobs	37,913	9.5	16.0	34,505	7.2	13.1	3,408	31.7	45.7
50-52 weeks	30,689	6.6	12.2	28,210	4.9	9.8	2,479	25.8	38.7
40-49 weeks	3,515	14.2	23.5	3,128	10.9	19.4	387	39.4	55.8
39 weeks or less	3,709	28.6	40.3	3,167	24.5	35.4	542	52.9	69.8
Worked at part-time jobs	2,840	36.2	47.9	2,286	28.5	40.7	554	67.9	79.2
50-52 weeks	1,065	30.0	40.6	868	22.4	32.0	197	[2]63.6	[2]78.8
49 weeks or less	1,775	39.9	52.3	1,418	32.3	46.0	357	70.3	79.3
Did not work in 1963	6,683	38.3	51.9	5,872	33.9	47.7	811	69.8	81.1
Ill or disabled	1,745	46.5	59.9	1,441	41.4	54.4	304	68.2	83.7
Keeping house	1,603	49.7	57.8	1,329	42.8	51.7	274	83.2	86.5
Going to school	77	....	....	68	....	....	9	....	....
Could not find work	202	49.3	60.5	154	[2]41.9	[2]53.8	48	....	....
Other	3,056	26.8	43.7	2,880	25.3	42.0	176	[2]52.7	[2]70.5
Unrelated individuals									
Total	11,182	43.9	49.8	9,719	41.8	48.0	1,463	57.5	61.7
Residence:									
Nonfarm	10,820	44.0	49.8	9,379	42.0	48.0	1,441	57.4	61.7
Farm	362	40.4	49.3	340	38.6	48.0	22	(4)	(4)

Race:									
White	....	....	....	....	....	....	48.0	41.8	9,719
Nonwhite	....	....	....	....	....	....	61.8	57.6	1,463
Age:									
14-24	[2]65.9	[2]62.5	116	47.6	45.5	873	49.9	47.6	989
25-34	42.7	38.7	203	25.2	23.3	792	28.6	26.3	995
35-44	39.6	37.1	215	21.8	19.9	785	25.4	23.6	1,000
45-54	59.5	52.0	267	30.2	25.9	1,308	35.3	30.5	1,575
55-64	70.4	67.8	308	39.3	34.9	2,024	43.4	39.3	2,332
65 and over	78.3	73.8	354	68.3	58.0	3,937	69.2	59.3	4,291
Sex:									
Male	50.0	46.1	684	37.3	31.3	3,591	39.4	33.7	4,275
Female	72.1	67.6	779	54.3	48.1	6,128	56.3	50.3	6,907
Region:									
Northeast	46.5	44.1	341	47.8	41.8	2,778	47.7	42.1	3,119
North Central	64.7	58.9	254	51.6	44.3	2,720	52.7	45.5	2,974
South	75.7	72.5	666	51.9	46.6	2,164	57.5	52.7	2,830
West	37.3	28.7	202	39.3	33.8	2,057	39.1	33.3	2,259
Earner status:									
Earner	49.0	43.8	986	27.4	23.0	5,992	30.4	26.0	6,978
Nonearner	88.0	85.7	477	81.2	72.2	3,727	82.0	73.8	4,204
Employment status and occupation:									
Not in labor force[3]	85.3	82.0	520	74.4	65.0	4,289	75.5	66.9	4,809
Unemployed	66.2	60.6	93	45.3	40.5	367	49.4	44.5	460
Employed	46.8	42.2	850	25.9	22.3	5,063	28.9	25.2	5,913
Professional and technical workers	40.0	35.6	75	30.7	28.4	1,159	30.8	28.5	1,234
Farmers and farm managers	(4)	(4)	10	[2]44.0	[2]39.6	121	[2]46.9	[2]42.9	131
Managers, officials and proprietors (except farm)	50.0	50.0	20	21.5	17.0	425	23.1	18.9	445
Clerical and sales workers	17.1	17.1	97	14.4	11.2	1,270	14.6	11.6	1,367
Craftsmen and foremen	....	....	12	7.8	6.0	289	7.5	5.8	301
Operatives	36.5	29.8	139	14.0	11.4	727	17.6	14.4	866
Service workers, including private household	60.7	55.6	368	47.4	40.4	803	51.5	44.9	1,171
Private household workers	[2]78.2	[2]69.4	198	79.4	70.9	223	78.5	70.2	421
Laborers (except mine)	52.1	45.8	129	45.3	42.4	269	47.5	43.5	398

See footnotes at end of table.

TABLE 16 (cont'd)

Incidence of poverty in 1963, according to SSA poverty index: Percent of families and unrelated individuals with 1963 income below specified level,[1] by specified characteristics and race of head

[Numbers in thousands: data are estimates derived from a survey of households and are therefore subject to sampling variability that may be relatively large where the size of the percentage or size of the total on which the percentage is based is small; as in all surveys, the figures are subject to errors of response and nonreporting]

Characteristic	All units			White			Nonwhite		
	Total number	Percent with incomes below—		Total number	Percent with incomes below—		Total number	Percent with incomes below—	
		Economy level	Low-cost level		Economy level	Low-cost level		Economy level	Low-cost level
Work experience:[5]									
Worked in 1963	6,729	26.4	30.8	5,788	23.7	28.0	941	43.7	48.9
Worked at full-time jobs	5,564	20.8	23.9	4,864	19.2	22.1	700	32.4	38.0
50-52 weeks	3,719	12.8	15.6	3,294	11.5	13.9	425	22.3	29.1
40-49 weeks	744	22.9	25.9	650	21.6	24.5	94	(4)	(4)
39 weeks or less	1,101	46.1	50.6	920	44.9	50.0	181	53.9	55.3
Worked at part-time jobs	1,165	53.5	63.9	924	47.2	58.9	241	75.3	79.6
50-52 weeks	396	49.3	57.1	307	45.9	54.1	89	57.8	64.1
49 weeks or less	769	55.7	67.4	617	47.9	61.2	152	84.4	87.7
Did not work in 1963	4,453	70.4	78.5	3,931	68.7	77.5	522	82.7	85.0
Ill or disabled	974	79.8	86.4	747	76.6	84.9	227	87.2	88.4
Keeping house	2,076	71.5	79.8	1,941	70.8	79.5	135	84.8	84.8
Going to school	106	²88.6	²88.6	83	(4)	(4)	23	(4)	(4)
Could not find work	128	²83.3	²87.5	89	(4)	(4)	39	(4)	(4)
Other	1,169	57.6	68.0	1,071	56.8	67.0	98	...	...
Source of income:									
Earnings only	3,838	29.7	32.7	3,111	26.5	29.2	727	43.5	47.5
Earnings and other income	3,138	21.3	27.6	2,882	19.2	25.3	256	44.5	52.9
Other income only or no income	4,206	73.8	82.0	3,726	72.2	81.2	480	85.8	88.0

Unrelated individuals

[1] For definition of poverty criteria, see text.
[2] Base between 100,000 and 200,000.
[3] Includes members of the Armed Forces.
[4] Not shown for fewer than 100,000 units.
[5] All work-experience data, including data for year-round, full-time workers, limited to civilian workers.

Source: Derived from tabulation of the *Current Population Survey*, March 1964, by the Bureau of the Census for the Social Security Administration.

TABLE 17
(In millions)

Type of family	All families	Male head	Female head
Total number of poor families........	7.2	5.2	2.0
With head a year-round, full-time worker..	2.0	1.8	.2
White	1.4	1.3	.1
Nonwhite	.6	.5	.1
Other	5.2	3.4	1.8
White	2.7	2.6	1.1
Nonwhite	1.5	.8	.7

male heads of families who were poor despite their year-round full-time employment, more than a fifth gave their current occupation as farmers, an equal number were operatives, and nearly a fifth were laborers. Only 3 percent were professional or technical workers. By contrast, among the nonpoor, 1 in 7 of the male family heads working the year around at full-time jobs were currently employed as professional or technical workers and only 4 percent each were farmers or laborers.

Notwithstanding the current stress on more jobs, it is clear that at least for poor families headed by a full-time year-round worker—more than a fourth of the total—it is not so much that more jobs are required but better ones, if it is presumed that the head of the family will continue to be the main source of support and that there will continue to be as many large families. In less than a fifth of the poor families headed by a man working full time the year around was the wife in the paid labor force, and in only about two-fifths was there more than one earner. By contrast, in the corresponding group of nonpoor families, one-third of the wives were working or in the market for a job, and 55 percent of the families in all had at least one earner in addition to the head.*

Not even for the 5.2 million poor families with a head who worked less than a full year can jobs alone provide an answer. Among the poor, about two-thirds of the male heads who had worked part of the year or not at all in 1963 gave ill health or other reasons—including retirement—as the main reason, rather than an inability to find work. Of the female heads less than fully employed in 1963, about five-sixths gave household responsibilities as the reason; though fewer claimed ill health or disability, they nevertheless outnumbered those who said they

---

* Illustrative table omitted.

had been looking for work. Among the unrelated individuals, only 1 in 6 of the men and 1 in 14 of the women not working the year around gave unemployment as the chief reason. At best it will be difficult to find jobs that a large number of the underemployed heads of poor households can fill, as Table 18 indicates.

Occupation and Poverty

The chances of a family's being poor differ not only with the amount of employment of the head but also with the kind of work he does. This is a reflection of the different pay rates and lifetime earning patterns that workers at different trades can expect. It appears, however, that the association is compounded: Not only do certain occupations pay less well than others, but workers in those occupations tend to have larger families than the others. Thus an income unlikely to be high to begin with must be stretched to provide for more children rather than less.

Of families headed by a male year-round full-time worker and with income above the economy level, more than half had either no children under age 18 in the household or only one. Only 4 percent had more than four. By contrast, among the corresponding group of families with income less than the economy level, fewer than a third had no more than one child in the home and nearly a fourth had five or more.

The poverty rates for families with heads in different occupations (table 16) take on new meaning when ranked by a measure of

TABLE 18

	Percentage distribution of units with income below economy level			
	Families		Unrelated individuals	
Work experience of head in 1963	Male head	Female head	Male	Female
Total	100	100	100	100
Worked all year..............	39	15	21	11
Full-time job	35	9	17	7
Part-time job	4	6	4	4
Worked part of the year	33	28	28	20
Looking for work	19	7	11	4
Ill, disabled	6	4	4	3
Keeping house	. . .	15	. . .	6
All other	8	2	13	7
Didn't work at all	28	58	51	69
Ill, disabled	12	10	20	14
Keeping house	. . .	41	. . .	43
Couldn't find work	1	2	4	2
All other	15	5	27	10

earnings potential. There is a cycle in family income as well as in family size, although the two patterns are not generally in perfect correspondence. On the assumption that for the average family it is mainly the earning capacity of the husband that sets the scale at which the family must live, the poverty rates for families of employed male heads by occupation have been arrayed according to the median earnings (in 1959) of men aged 35–44. This is the age at which, on the basis of cross-

TABLE 19

Occupation group	Median earnings of male workers aged 35-44[1]	Incidence of poverty among families with employed male head[2]	Percent of wives aged 35-44 of employed workers, with specified number of children ever born[3]		
			0-2	3	4 or more
White males:					
Professional and technical workers	$8,015	2	56	23	20
Managers, officials, proprietors, (except farm)	7,465	5	57	23	20
Sales workers	6,325	3	60	22	19
Craftsmen and foremen	5,795	4	54	21	25
Clerical and kindred workers	5,505	2	61	20	19
Operatives	5,075	9	52	20	27
Service workers	4,610	8	57	20	23
Nonfarm laborers	4,095	15	49	19	33
Farmers and farm managers	2,945	26	42	22	36
Farm laborers	2,020	43	35	17	48
Nonwhite males:					
Professional and technical workers	5,485	12	65	16	19
Managers, officials, proprietors (except farm)	4,655	21	57	16	27
Clerical and kindred workers	4,630	13	61	14	25
Sales workers	4,010	(4)	57	16	27
Craftsmen and foremen	3,885	21	52	13	35
Operatives	3,495	27	51	12	37
Service workers	2,970	25	57	13	30
Nonfarm laborers	2,825	45	48	11	41
Farm laborers	975	70	34	9	57
Farmers and farm managers	945	78	27	9	65

[1] In 1959.

[2] Currently employed family heads in March 1964, with 1963 family money income below the economy level in 1963.

[3] Wives of currently employed men at time of 1960 Decennial Census.

[4] Not available.

Source: *U.S. Census of Population, 1960: Occupation by Earnings and Education,* PC(2)-7B; *Women by Number of Children Ever Born,* PC(2)-3A; and Social Security Administration.

sectional data, earnings for the average worker in most occupations are at their peak. Two things are abundantly clear.

In general, the poverty rates for families of men in different occupations are inversely related to the median peak earnings—that is, the lower the average earnings at age 35–44, the greater the risk of poverty for the family. (In some instances, as among families of some of the proprietors, work of the wife and other adults may count as unpaid family labor rather than add earnings to the family income.) The size of the average family with children seems also to vary inversely with earning capacity, in terms of the number of children ever born to the wives aged 35–44 of men employed in these occupations.

Table 19 illustrates the patterns separately for white and nonwhite families with male head.

For many families a critical point in financial status may be the arrival of the fourth or fifth child. At all occupational levels (except among wives of professional and technical employees) the nonwhite family tends to be larger than the white, but on the average nonwhite families are at a lower economic level than white families in the same occupational class. A more accurate, or at least a narrower, occupational grouping would probably show less difference between the sizes of white and nonwhite families at equivalent economic levels.

Some of the differences in number of children are related to different patterns of age at first marriage. But even among women who married at the same age there remains evidence of a difference in life style among occupational groups, in terms of number of children ever born.

The discussion here centers on children ever born rather than the more common statistic of children present in the home. Use of the latter figure results in serious understatement of the total number of children in large families who may be subject to the risk of poverty before they reach adulthood.

Differences in the two statistics are greater for the low-income occupations, such as nonfarm laborers with their large families, than for high-income occupations, such as professional and technical workers with their smaller families. It appears to be the families with less income to look forward to in the first place who have more children.[18]

The statistics by occupation may throw light on the intergeneration cycle of poverty. It is not necessary here to repeat the admonition that education for our youngsters is a long step up in the escape from poverty. It is of importance, however, that in these days, when children generally are receiving more education than those a generation ago,

[18] See also Bureau of the Census, *Current Population Reports*, "Socioeconomic Characteristics of the Population: 1960," Series P-23, No. 12, July 31, 1964.

the degree of upward mobility is affected by social environment as indicated by the occupation as well as by the education of the father. According to a recent report, among children of men with the same educational attainment, those with fathers in white-collar jobs are much more likely than children of fathers in manual and service jobs or in farm jobs to acquire more years of school training than their parents.[19]

The statistics on occupation and poverty may have even further import. The work history of aged persons currently receiving public assistance might well show that many of the recipients (or the persons on whom they had depended for support) used to work at the same kinds of jobs currently held by many of the employed poor. Earnings too little to support a growing family are not likely to leave much margin for saving for old age. Moreover, such low earnings will bring entitlement to only minimal O.A.S.D.I. benefits.

Implications

The causes of poverty are many and varied. Because some groups in the population are more vulnerable, however, a cross-section of the poor will differ from one of the nonpoor, measure for measure. The mothers bringing up children without a father, the aged or disabled who cannot earn, and the Negro who may not be allowed to earn will, more often than the rest of us, know the dreary privation that denies them the good living that has become the hallmark of America.

But there are others thus set apart, without the handicap of discrimination or disability, who cannot even regard their plight as the logical consequence of being unemployed. There are millions of children in "normal" as well as broken homes who will lose out on their chance ever to strive as equals in this competitive society because they are denied now even the basic needs that money can buy. And finally there are the children yet to come, whose encounter with poverty can be predicted unless the situation is changed for those currently poor.

Neither the present circumstances nor the reasons for them are alike for all our impoverished millions, and the measures that can help reduce their number must likewise be many and varied. No single program, placing its major emphasis on the needs of one special group alone, will succeed. Any complex of programs that does not allow for the diversity of the many groups among the poor will to that degree leave the task undone. The poor have been counted many times. It remains now to count the ways by which to help them gain a new identity.

---

[19] Bureau of the Census, *Current Population Reports,* "Educational Change in a Generation," Series P-20, No. 132, Sept. 22, 1964.

Selected Bibliography

1. Ben H. Bagdikian. *In the Midst of Plenty: A New Report on the Poor in America*. New York: Signet Books, 1964.

2. Robert H. Brenner. *From the Depths: The Discovery of Poverty in the United States*. New York: New York University Press, 1956.

3. Wilbur J. Cohen and Eugenia Sullivan. "Poverty in the United States," *Health, Education and Welfare Indicators*, February, 1964.

4. John Kenneth Galbraith. *The Affluent Society*. Boston: Houghton Mifflin Company, 1960.

5. Michael Harrington. *The Other America—Poverty in the United States*. New York: The Macmillan Co., 1962.

6. Nat Hentoff. *The New Equality*. New York: The Viking Press, 1964.

7. Leon H. Keyserling. *Progress or Poverty: The United States at the Crossroads*. Washington, D.C.: Conference on Economic Progress, December, 1964.

8. Helen H. Lamale and Margaret S. Strotz. "The Interim City Worker's Family Budget," *Monthly Labor Review*, August, 1960.

9. Robert J. Lampman. *The Low Income Population and Economic Growth*. United States Congress, Joint Economic Committee, Study Paper Number 12, 86th Congress, First Session, December, 1959.

10. Herman P. Miller. *Income of the American People*. New York: John Wiley and Sons, Inc., 1955.

11. Herman P. Miller. *Rich Man, Poor Man: A Study of Income Distribution in America*. New York: Crowell, 1964.

12. James N. Morgan, David H. Martin, Wilbur J. Cohen, and Harvey E. Brazer. *Income and Welfare in the United States*. New York: McGraw-Hill Book Co., Inc., 1962.

13. Mollie Orshansky. "Budget for an Elderly Couple. An Interim Revision by the Bureau of Labor Statistics," *Social Security Bulletin*, December, 1960.

14. Charles E. Silberman. *Crisis in Black and White*. New York: Random House, 1964.

15. *Economic Report of the President,* Transmitted to the Congress, January 1964 and 1965 together with *The Annual Report of the Council of Economic Advisors*.

16. *Manpower Report of the President,* and *A Report on Manpower Requirements, Resources, Utilization and Training by the United States Department of Labor,* Transmitted to Congress, March, 1964 and March, 1965.

Chapter 2

Who Are the Poor?

Poverty is costly not only to the individual but also to society. Physical and mental disease, delinquency and crime, loss of productive capacity—all of these are part of the environment of poverty. But the most fundamental reason for declaring war on poverty is a moral one. This Nation and its institutions are founded upon the belief that each individual should have the opportunity to develop his capacity to the fullest. Those who are born into the world of poverty are not only deprived of most of the material comforts of life, but are also stunted in their emotional, intellectual, and social development, and thus effectively prevented from realizing their human potentialities. Past accomplishments in reducing the extent of poverty have been the result of combined efforts of all levels of government and of private groups. Similarly, the eventual elimination of poverty will call for a national effort involving a wide range of public and private measures to stimulate economic growth, wipe out discrimination, and increase opportunities by raising the educational, skill, health, and living levels of those Americans who have heretofore failed to share in the fruits of economic progress.

In order to attack the problem of poverty, it is essential to know who are the poor and what causes their poverty.

—From "Poverty in the United States" by Wilbur J. Cohen and Eugenia Sullivan, *Health, Education, and Welfare Indicators*, February, 1964.

RECENT ESTIMATES have focused on thirty million, forty million and even fifty million persons in the United States who are "poor"—who do not have enough money to buy an adequate living and little opportunity to better themselves. Who are these people with inadequate incomes? The point has been made that most of them suffer from some handicapping characteristic. Two-thirds of the total are members of families of low-paid or unemployed workers. Women living alone or heading up families constitute one in three such units. Nonwhite persons make up or head one out of five such households. People over age 65 head up two out of five family units with insufficient income.

There are eleven million children among the thirty-five million people defined as poor in this country by the $3,000 "poverty-line" standard. The infants born in the post World War II baby boom have reached the critical 16 to 21 age group. In one month in 1963 over 730,000 of these young people neither held a job nor attended school. Government officials have predicted that by 1970 there will be a million young people age 16 to 21 without jobs and with no training unless the present trend is reversed.

Millions of workers constitute what has been called the "economic underworld of the by-passed." Many of them face the choice of a job at low level wages or no job at all. Many of them are not covered by the federal minimum wage and their poverty is due to the low rates of pay found most commonly in certain occupations. Others suffer irregular employment due to seasonal work, plant shutdowns, sickness or injury, discrimination and low bargaining power. Thousands have been bypassed by modern technological advances, unable because of outdated skills and meager education to get jobs. Some of these workers find that they are "too old" at age 40 or 50 to be reabsorbed in the labor force after their plant relocates or a machine takes over their old job. If they are lucky, they may find steady work, but in low paying, marginal industries at wage rates that are insufficient to meet their family needs.

Rural poverty has been described by Michael Harrington as "the poorest, lowest and meanest in the nation." The rural poor include farm laborers and migratory workers, ex-farmers, ex-coal miners, unemployed timber workers, reservation Indians. Migratory farm workers are among those rural workers having the most serious problems of income, health and education. One-and-a-half million rural farm families live on less than $250 a month; 2.8 million rural nonfarm families exist at the same income level. Over a million rural families have no more than $80 a month to pay for all their needs. A half-million rural youth between age 14 and 24 have never finished grade school. Their vision ends at the edge of a few acres of exhausted land.

The minority poor—Negroes, Puerto Ricans, Spanish-speaking Americans, American Indians—are hired last, paid less, and fired first. Nearly half the total Negro population in the United States—eight million—are poor. They number one-fifth of the country's total poverty stricken. Typically, wage rates for nonwhites are lower than for white workers, even when they work at the same jobs and have the same educational background. Negro college graduates can expect to earn only as much as white workers who leave school after the eighth grade, and white workers in their lifetime earn fifty percent more than Negroes and Puerto Ricans and one-third more than Spanish-speaking Americans. Fifty-three percent of New York City's Puerto Rican residents earned less than $4,000 in 1959; only eight percent earned more than $8,000. Three-fourths of Puerto Rican youth never enter high school. In the Southwest, three and a half million Spanish-speaking Americans face prejudice, inadequate education and language barriers. Of the half-million American Indians, among the hardest hit of this country's poverty stricken, 380,000 who live on or near reservations subsist on average family income one-fourth to one-third of the national average.

 — Death, desertion, divorce, and disability left almost five million fatherless families in the United States in 1962. Almost half live below the poverty-line. Many of the women heading multi-person households lack the education, training, and experience to get jobs with adequate incomes. Over eighty-five percent of the mothers receiving public assistance had not finished high school. They had worked as domestics, service workers and unskilled laborers; their chances of finding stable employment with adequate wage rates are remote.

But even among unattached individuals as distinct from multi-person households, sex is a factor in poverty. About thirty-eight percent of all women over age 14 are now in the labor force. Their median pay for full-time, year-round work is about sixty percent that of men. In addition, when jobs are scarce, they are more subject to unemployment. More than half of all single women live in poverty, contrasted to a little more than a third of all single men. Over a third of single women live on less than $1,000 a year, contrasted to slightly more than a fifth of the males.

Many of the aged poor have lived their lives in poverty and could not save enough throughout their working years to provide for independence after retirement. Half of the six and eight-tenths million heads of families over age 65 live on less than $3,000 a year. Half of these people support their families on less than $1,000 a year. Although the majority of older people are covered by Social Security, nearly two-thirds of the poorest aged—those living alone on incomes of less than $1,000 a year—are not covered by Social Security.

The people who live on incomes of under $3,000 a year are not a homogenous group. They include the young and the old, disabled and able-bodied, white and nonwhite, city and country dwellers. They include the employed, the underemployed, and the unemployed. They include those who were born in poverty and those who skidded into poverty through unemployment, sickness, disability, or advancing age.

The majority of persons with inadequate incomes, however, share one common characteristic. Sixty-seven percent of our poorest live in families headed by persons who left school before eighth grade. A recent University of Michigan study revealed that fewer than two-fifths of the heads of poor families had gone beyond the educational attainment of their fathers. Only forty-five percent of the children in poor families finished high school compared to sixty-five percent of the children of all families. One-third of the children of the poor have less than a grade school education.

The findings of the President's Task Force on Manpower Conservation attested to the fact that poverty breeds poverty. The report of the Task Force, issued in January, 1964, found that one-third of this country's young people would fail to meet the standards for military services set by the Selective Service System. Poverty was the principal reason for their falling below the minimum mental and physical standards needed to be a private in the United States Army. About one-fifth of the young men refused on educational grounds from the service came from families which had received public assistance in the previous five years. Almost half came from families with six or more children. The fathers of more than half of these rejectees never finished grade school and four out of five of the rejectees had themselves dropped out of school.

Poverty, which cuts across many groups in our country, also is found in many different areas. About half of the lowest income families in the United States live in urban centers. The remainder live on farms or in rural areas. A large concentration is found in the South. Three out of every ten low-income families live in the South compared with one in nine in the Northeast and one in eight in the West.

This chapter focuses on several groups of the poverty stricken in this country. Michael Harrington describes some of "the rejects" of our industrial society. Sar Levitan analyzes the socio-economic characteristics of urban depressed areas aided by the Area Redevelopment Administration. The characteristics and demography of the rural poor are discussed by Lee G. Burchinal and Hilda Siff. Alan Batchelder analyzes the economic condition of the Negro poor. The inadequacy of income for many of our aged citizens is focused on by Ellen Winston. Finally, the economic problems of low-paid workers are reviewed in a statement by the Research Department of the A.F.L.–C.I.O.

The Rejects

Michael Harrington

League for Industrial Democracy

[Reprinted from Chapter 2 of The Other America: Poverty in the United
States *(New York, 1963) by permission of The Macmillan Company. Copyright © 1962 Michael Harrington.]*

IN NEW YORK CITY, some of my friends call 80 Warren Street "the
slave market."

It is a big building in downtown Manhattan. Its corridors have the
littered, trampled air of a courthouse. They are lined with employment-
agency offices. Some of these places list good-paying and highly skilled
jobs. But many of them provide the work force for the economic underworld in the big city: the dishwashers and day workers, the fly-by-
night jobs.

Early every morning, there is a great press of human beings in
80 Warren Street. It is made up of Puerto Ricans and Negroes, alcoholics, drifters, and disturbed people. Some of them will pay a flat fee
(usually around 10 percent) for a day's work. They pay $0.50 for a
$5.00 job and they are given the address of a luncheonette. If all goes
well, they will make their wage. If not, they have a legal right to come
back and get their half-dollar. But many of them don't know that, for
they are people that are not familiar with laws and rights.

But perhaps the most depressing time at 80 Warren Street is in
the afternoon. The jobs have all been handed out, yet the people still
mill around. Some of them sit on benches in the larger offices. There
is no real point to their waiting, yet they have nothing else to do. For
some, it is probably a point of pride to be here, a feeling that they are
somehow still looking for a job even if they know that there is no chance
to get one until early in the morning.

Most of the people at 80 Warren Street were born poor. (The alcoholics are an exception.) They are incompetent as far as American society is concerned, lacking the education and the skills to get decent work.
If they find steady employment, it will be in a sweatshop or a kitchen.

In a Chicago factory, another group of people are working. A
year or so ago, they were in a union shop making good wages, with sick
leave, pension rights, and vacations. Now they are making artificial
Christmas trees at less than half the pay they had been receiving. They
have no contract rights, and the foreman is absolute monarch. Permission is required if a worker wants to go to the bathroom. A few are
fired every day for insubordination.

These are people who have become poor. They possess skills, and they once moved upward with the rest of the society. But now their jobs have been destroyed, and their skills have been rendered useless. In the process, they have been pushed down toward the poverty from whence they came. This particular group is Negro, and the chances of ever breaking through, of returning to the old conditions, are very slim. Yet their plight is not exclusively racial, for it is shared by all the semi-skilled and unskilled workers who are the victims of technological unemployment in the mass-production industries. They are involved in an interracial misery.

These people are the rejects of the affluent society. They never had the right skills in the first place, or they lost them when the rest of the economy advanced. They are the ones who make up a huge portion of the culture of poverty in the cities of America. They are to be counted in the millions.

* * *

Each big city in the United States has an economic underworld. And often enough this phrase is a literal description: it refers to the kitchens and furnace rooms that are under the city; it tells of the place where tens of thousands of hidden people labor at impossible wages. Like the underworld of crime, the economic underworld is out of sight, clandestine.

The workers in the economic underworld are concentrated among the urban section of the more than 16,000,000 Americans denied coverage by the Minimum-Wage Law of 1961. They are domestic workers, hotel employees, bus boys, and dishwashers, and some of the people working in small retail stores. In the most recent Government figures, for example, hotel workers averaged $47.44 a week, laundry workers $46.45, general-merchandise employees $48.37, and workers in factories making work clothing $45.58.

This sector of the American economy has proved itself immune to progress. And one of the main reasons is that it is almost impossible to organize the workers of the economic underworld in their self-defense. They are at the mercy of unscrupulous employers (and, in the case of hospital workers, management might well be a board composed of the "best" people of the city who, in pursuing a charitable bent, participate in a conspiracy to exploit the most helpless citizens). They are cheated by crooked unions; they are used by racketeers.

In the late fifties I talked to some hospital workers in Chicago. They were walking a picket line, seeking union recognition. (They lost.) Most of them made about $30 a week and were the main support of their families. The hospital deducted several dollars a week for food that they ate on the job. But then, they had no choice in this matter. If they didn't take the food, they had to pay for it anyway.

When the union came, it found a work force at the point of desperation. A majority of them had signed up as soon as they had the chance. But, like most of the workers in the economic underworld, these women were hard to keep organized. Their dues were miniscule, and in effect they were being subsidized by the better-paid workers in the union. Their skills were so low that supervisory personnel could take over many of their functions during a strike. It required an enormous effort to reach them and to help them, and in this case it failed.

An extreme instance of this institutional poverty took place in Atlanta, Georgia, among hospital workers in mid-1960. Men who worked the dishwashing machines received $0.68 an hour; women kitchen helpers got $0.56; and the maids $0.55 an hour. If these people all put in the regular two thousand hours of work a year, they would receive just over $1,000 for their services.

The restaurants of the economic underworld are somewhat like the hospitals. The "hidden help" in the kitchen are an unstable group. They shift jobs rapidly. As a result, a union will sign up all the employees in a place, but before a union certification election can occur half of those who had joined will have moved on to other work. This means that it is extremely expensive for the labor movement to try to organize these workers: they are dispersed in small groups; they cannot pay for themselves; and they require constant servicing, checking, and rechecking to be sure that the new workers are brought into the union structure. . . .

When the hotels, the restaurants, the hospitals, and the sweatshops are added up, one confronts a section of the economy that employs millions and millions of workers. In retailing alone, there are 6,000,000 or 7,000,000 employees who are unorganized, and many of them are not covered by minimum wage. For instance, in 1961 the general-merchandise stores (with an average weekly wage of $48.37) counted over 1,250,000 employees. Those who made work clothes, averaging just over $45.00 a week, totaled some 300,000 citizens, most of them living in the other America of the poor.

Thus, in the society of abundance and high standards of living there is an economically backward sector which is incredibly capable of being exploited; it is unorganized, and in many cases without the protection of Federal law. It is in this area that the disabled, the retarded, and the minorities toil. In Los Angeles they might be Mexican-Americans, in the runaway shops of West Virginia or Pennsylvania, white Anglo-Saxon Protestants. All of them are poor; regardless of race, creed, or color, all of them are victims.

In the spring of 1961, American society faced up to the problem of the economic underworld. It decided that it was not worth solving. Since these workers cannot organize to help themselves, their only real hope for aid must be directed toward the intervention of the Federal Government. After the election of President Kennedy, this issue was joined in terms of a minimum-wage bill. The A.F.L.–C.I.O. proposed that minimum-wage coverage should be extended to about 6,500,000 new workers; the Administration proposed new coverage for a little better than 3,000,000 workers; the conservatives of the Dixiecrat-Republican coalition wanted to hold the figure down to about 1,000,000.

There was tremendous logrolling in Congress over the issue. In order to win support for the Administration approach, concessions were made. It does not take much political acumen to guess which human beings were conceded: the poor. The laundry workers (there are over 300,000 of them, and according to the most recent Bureau of Labor statistics figures they averaged $47.72 a week) and the hospital workers were dropped from the extension of coverage. The papers announced that over 3,000,000 new workers had been granted coverage—but they failed to note that a good number of them were already in well-paid industries and didn't need help.

In power politics, organized strength tells. So it was that America turned its back on the rejects in the economic underworld. As one reporter put it, "We've got the people who make $26 a day safely covered; it's the people making $26 a week who are left out." Once again, there is the irony that the welfare state benefits least those who need help most.

Characteristics of Urban Depressed Areas

Sar A. Levitan

Upjohn Institute for Employment Research

[The following article from the Monthly Labor Review, *January, 1964, was excerpted from Chapter 3 of* Federal Aid to Depressed Areas *by Sar A. Levitan (Baltimore, 1964), by permission of the Johns Hopkins University Press.]*

A HIGH RATE OF CHRONIC UNEMPLOYMENT is only one of many socioeconomic characteristics signaling distress in an area. A stagnating population, deterioration in the quality of available labor resources, declining labor force participation rates, low wages and income, inadequate investment in capital outlays, and substandard housing are associated with chronic labor surplus areas.

In order to indicate the magnitude and evaluate the significance of these factors, the following discussion compares socioeconomic characteristics in nondesignated areas with the redevelopment areas eligible for ARA assistance.

Population in the ARA areas barely held its own between 1950–60, with the natural increase in population only slightly offsetting losses due to out-migration (table 1). The 30 selected areas[1] suffered even more severely from out-migration and population decline in the decade. In contrast, in the more prosperous nondesignated areas of the country, population increased by almost one-fourth. Net civilian migration alone accounted for a loss of more than one-tenth of the 1950 population in all designated areas and was much higher in the selected 5(a) areas. At the same time, the more prosperous areas were increasing their population—a rise of 5 percent because of the in-migration of civilians. Out-migration in designated areas is highly selective and is heavily concentrated among males in the primary working ages and those with the highest educational attainments. The impact of out-migration among the prime working age groups is very striking in the selected areas: in the 30 5(a) areas, the proportion of the population 18–44 years of age drops to 31.1 percent. Among those in the oldest age group, migration has an opposite effect; 8.5 percent of the U.S. male population was 65 years and over in 1960, but 10.6 percent in the 30 areas was in this age group (table 2). Much the same age pattern is found in the female population and would seem to imply that out-migration consists largely of married families under 45 years of age and tends to be permanent as long as economic activity is declining.

A significant feature about the labor force in chronic labor surplus areas is that the lack of job opportunities delays the entry of youths

---

[1] NOTE.—Total ARA designated areas were divided into two groups in accordance with the criteria for designating areas provided in sections 5(a) and 5(b) of the Area Redevelopment Act. Those 129 labor markets most of which in 1960 had a labor force of 15,000 or more including at least 8,000 nonagricultural workers were termed 5(a) areas while predominantly rural areas with a labor force of less than 15,000 were termed 5(b) areas. The 129 5(a) areas were further segregated to obtain 120 5(a) areas by excluding certain unrepresentative influences of six New England areas, Detroit and Flint, Mich., and Pittsburgh, Pa. A special tabulation of 30 chronic labor surplus areas was obtained from the Bureau of the Census selected to cover all geographical regions and to take into account factors which have contributed to economic stagnation and high unemployment in many urban areas. Of these 30 selected 5(a) areas, five labor markets which had lost more than 10 percent of their population between 1950 and 1960 were classified as representative of our most depressed areas. The 5(b) areas were also subdivided and discussed in the complete study, but except where the term "all designated areas" is used, this excerpt is limited to characteristics of 5(a) areas only.

TABLE 1

Population, Net Civilian Migration, Unemployment, and Female Labor Force Participation Rates in ARA Designated Areas,[1] 1950-60

Area[1]	Population 1960	Percent				Females as a percent of 1960	
		Change in population, 1950-60	Net civilian migration, 1950-60	Change in civilian labor force, 1950-60	Unemployment, April 1960	Civilian labor force	Unemployment
United States	179,323,175	18.5	2.0	15.8	5.1	32.8	34.5
Nondesignated areas	146,502,215	22.1	5.3	18.9	4.8	33.3	36.0
Total ARA areas	32,820,960	4.1	—10.9	1.8	7.0	30.8	29.6
Total 5(a) areas	21,073,650	8.4	—6.3	4.9	7.4	31.3	29.2
New England	2,455,175	10.5	—1.7	8.7	4.3	36.2	37.8
Detroit, Flint, and Pittsburgh	6,542,108	18.9	0.9	10.4	7.4	29.7	29.4
120 areas[2]	12,076,367	3.1	—9.7	1.1	8.0	31.1	27.9
30 areas	2,892,247	—3.4	—15.3	—6.4	8.2	31.1	27.2
5 areas	487,864	—16.3	—30.0	—22.3	14.2	25.5	14.8

[1] For definition of areas, see text footnote 1.
[2] Total 5(a) areas excluding 6 New England areas, Detroit, Mich., Flint, Mich., and Pittsburgh, Pa.

Source: *Statistical Profiles, Redeveloped Areas* (SP Series) (U.S. Bureau of the Census).

TABLE 2

Percent Distribution of Population in ARA Areas,[1] by Sex and Age Group, 1960

Area[1]	Males					Females				
	Less than 18	18-24	25-44	45-64	65 and over	Less than 18	18-24	25-44	45-64	65 and over
United States	36.9	8.6	26.0	20.0	8.5	34.7	8.7	26.3	20.3	10.0
Nondesignated areas	36.6	8.8	26.4	19.9	8.3	34.5	8.8	26.6	20.2	9.9
Total ARA areas	38.2	8.2	24.1	20.1	9.3	36.0	8.3	25.1	25.1	10.2
Total 5(a) areas	37.1	7.9	25.5	20.5	9.0	34.8	8.2	26.3	26.3	10.1
120 areas	37.4	8.4	24.2	20.3	9.7	35.1	8.3	25.2	20.6	10.7
30 areas	36.9	7.5	23.6	21.4	10.6	34.1	8.0	24.7	21.6	11.6
5 areas	41.3	6.9	22.3	20.0	9.5	38.7	7.8	25.0	19.7	8.8

[1] For definition of areas, see text footnote 1.
Note: Because of rounding, sums of individual items may not equal 100.
Source: *Statistical Profiles, Redeveloped Areas* (SP Series) (U.S. Bureau of the Census).

TABLE 3

Labor Force Participation Rates[1] in ARA Areas,[2] by Sex and Age Group, 1960

Area[1]	Total	Males						Females					
		Total	14-17	18-24	25-44	45-64	65 and over	Total	14-17	18-24	25-44	45-64	65 and over
Nondesignated areas	55.3	77.4	27.0	80.0	95.2	89.4	29.7	34.5	14.0	45.2	39.2	42.0	10.1
United States	56.2	78.2	27.8	80.7	95.3	89.9	30.7	35.4	14.6	46.1	39.9	43.2	10.6
Total ARA areas	51.5	73.7	23.9	76.8	94.4	87.4	25.8	30.3	11.9	40.8	35.6	36.6	8.3
Total 5(a) areas	52.7	75.6	23.2	78.5	95.4	88.8	25.2	31.3	12.7	44.3	35.2	37.8	8.6
120 areas	50.0	73.2	21.5	77.8	94.5	86.9	24.5	29.8	10.8	40.3	34.8	36.5	8.4
30 areas	50.0	71.1	20.9	74.5	94.1	86.8	23.1	29.9	11.5	42.6	35.3	36.3	8.3
5 areas	39.4	57.4	11.1	64.2	90.9	78.2	16.1	20.6	6.8	30.9	24.3	23.9	5.7

[1] Normally, only noninstitutional population is included in calculating labor force participation rate, but data on institutional population were not available for designated areas. Hence, total population in the respective age group was used to calculate labor force participation rates.

[2] For definition of areas, see text footnote 1.
Source: *Statistical Profiles, Redeveloped Areas* (SP Series) (U.S. Bureau of the Census).

into the labor force, drives older persons out of the labor force at an earlier age, and discourages women from entering the labor force (table 3). Exactly half of the persons aged 14 and over in the 120 5(a) areas were in the labor force when the 1960 Census was taken. In nondesignated areas, 56 of every 100 persons 14 and over were in the labor force.

The lack of job opportunities in designated areas seems to affect women relatively more than men as far as participation in the labor force is concerned. According to the 1960 Census, women constituted exactly one-third of the total labor force in nondesignated areas, compared with 31.1 percent in the 30 selected 5(a) areas.

The sharp difference in labor force participation rates therefore suggests that the reported unemployment rates in expanding economies and depressed areas are not entirely comparable. A significant proportion of the potential manpower resources in the latter areas is not counted in the labor force, and this tends to understate the rate of unemployment in depressed areas. Unemployment rates in depressed areas therefore cannot present the full implication of the lack of job opportunities and fail to measure the full impact of wasted human resources. If this hypothesis is correct, and the data seem to justify it, comparisons of unemployment rates for periods of full employment and high unemployment for the country as a whole lose some of their validity. During bad times many persons do not enter or withdraw from the labor force because jobs are not available and they are not counted as unemployed.

Unemployment and Employment

The rate of unemployment for all designated areas during April 1960, the date for the 1960 Census, was 7.0 percent, barely half again as much as the 4.8 percent in other areas. Unemployment in 5(a) areas was 46 percent higher than the national average during the Census month. In addition, preliminary unpublished data collected by the Census Bureau indicate that the average annual rate of unemployment in the 5(a) areas exceeded the national average by 44 percent in 1960 and 50 percent in 1961.

The 1960 Decennial Census and the preliminary annual data for 1960 and 1961 indicate that some areas which were certified for designation by the Bureau of Employment Security would not have qualified to receive ARA assistance on the basis of Census data. In order to qualify for assistance, unemployment in an area must exceed the national average by at least 50 percent during 3 of the preceding 4 years. The fact that during the 2 years unemployment in all the 5(a) areas did not exceed the national average by more than 50 percent would suggest

TABLE 4

Percent Change Between 1950 and 1960 in Employment in the United States and 30 5(a) ARA Areas,[1] by Major Industry Group

Industry	Percent change	
	United States	30 5(a) areas[1]
Total	11.8	—10.4
Agriculture, forestry, and fisheries	—38.2	—43.7
Mining	—29.8	—57.8
Construction	10.4	—3.5
Manufacturing	19.3	—.1
Transportation, communication, and public utilities...	2.1	—20.0
Wholesale and retail trade	12.2	—.4
Finance	40.4	20.7
Services	34.3	16.0
Public administration	27.4	13.4

[1] For definition of areas, see text footnote 1.

Source: *Statistical Profiles, Redevelopment Areas* (SP Series) (U.S. Bureau of the Census).

that some areas must have had, according to Census data, a rate of unemployment less than 50 percent above the national average.

An examination of shifts in employment distribution by industry between 1950 and 1960 reveals some of the major causes which have contributed to economic stagnation or decline of chronic labor surplus areas. These data were prepared only for the group of 30 areas. In 1950, 1 of every 9 employed persons in these areas was engaged in mining, but a decade later, almost two-thirds of the mining jobs were gone (table 4). This accounted for a loss of 67,300 jobs out of a total of 1,019,000 jobs that existed in these areas when the 1950 Census was taken. Decline of agricultural employment contributed to the loss of an additional 50,000 jobs, while employment in manufacturing remained virtually unchanged. As a result of stagnation or decline in primary industry, growth in services, trade, finances, and government employment, which accounted for the bulk of growth in U.S. employment during the fifties, was also arrested, and the relative employment gain in each of these sectors was less than half the gains made for the United States. Total employment in these areas declined by 10 percent between 1950 and 1960, compared with a gain of 12 percent for the United States.

A breakdown of the shifts in occupational distribution between 1950 and 1960 also shows wide variations in employment patterns for the United States and the sample of 30 areas. Employment in professional, clerical, and service occupations, which experienced the greatest expansion in the country during the fifties increased in the 30 areas but at a much slower rate than for the United States as a whole (table 5).

TABLE 5

Unemployment in 1960 and Employment Between 1950 and 1960 in the United States and ARA Areas,[1] by Major Occupational Group

| Occupation | United States | | | | | | ARA 5(a) areas | | | | |
| | Unemployment rate | Employment[2] | | | Unemployment rate | Unemployment as percent above U.S. level | 30 areas Employment[2] | | | 5 areas | |
		1960 distribution	1950 distribution	Percent change			1960 distribution	1950 distribution	Percent change	Unemployment rate	Unemployment as percent above U.S. level
Total	4.7	100.0	100.0	15.6	7.1	51	100.0	100.0	—14.3	13.1	179
Professional and managerial	1.4	21.1	18.9	29.0	1.8	29	17.2	14.2	3.8	2.1	50
Farmers and farm managers	.8	4.2	8.3	—41.9	0.9	12	4.3	6.8	—45.7	1.3	62
Clerical and sales	3.3	23.2	20.9	28.4	4.8	45	18.8	13.8	17.0	6.1	85
Service	5.5	11.9	10.4	32.8	6.6	20	10.7	7.9	16.3	8.7	58
Craftsmen and kindred	5.4	14.6	15.0	12.0	8.9	65	14.7	12.5	.7	15.0	178
Semiskilled	7.3	19.8	19.8	15.6	12.7	74	26.5	35.3	—37.5	20.0	174
Laborers, except farm and mine	12.0	5.2	6.6	—9.6	16.6	38	7.9	9.6	—29.5	35.3	194

[1] For definition of areas, see text footnote 1.
[2] Excludes farm laborers and farm foremen and persons with occupations not reported.

Note: Because of rounding, sums of individual items may not equal 100.
Source: *Statistical Profiles, Redevelopment Areas* (SP Series) (U.S. Bureau of the Census).

This is a result of the stagnation of secondary industries where the bulk of persons in the above occupations are employed.

Unemployment in almost every occupation in the sample areas was higher than the national pattern.[2] In the 30 5(a) areas, the occupations which had the highest unemployment relative to those for the Nation were craftsmen and semi-skilled workers. Unemployment in these occupations in the 30 areas was more than two-thirds higher than in the United States.

Education

Data on educational attainment in designated areas support the frequently stated assertion that the better educated are more prone to migrate from depressed areas than those with lesser educational achievements. For those in the school ages, the pattern of education does not differ in designated and more prosperous areas. Almost the same proportion of teenagers attend school in both types of areas. But the proportion of high school graduates was significantly lower in ARA areas than in other areas of the country, as shown below:

	Percent of population 25 years and over who completed high school	
	Male	*Female*
United States	39.5	42.5
Nondesignated areas	40.8	43.7
Total ARA areas	32.4	36.3
Total 5(a) areas	35.4	38.9
120 areas	32.1	35.9
30 areas	29.8	34.6
5 areas	22.0	25.7

Depressed areas allocate a higher proportion, but less per capita, of the total local expenditures to education than nondesignated areas. Apparently, the more prosperous areas are the beneficiaries of the depressed area investment in the development of human resources. Whatever the cause, the educational attainment of adults remaining in depressed areas is below that of adults in nondesignated areas.

Income

Declining employment opportunities and the associated economic influences of out-migration, the lower level of educational attainment, lack

---

[2] Unemployment data by occupation differ from total unemployment data discussed earlier because the former includes only persons who have had previous job experience.

of jobs for potential secondary family wage earners, differences of industry-mix, higher rates of unemployment, larger proportion of farm population and generally undeveloped state of some designated areas account for a lower level of income in these areas than in nondesignated areas. As shown in table 6, per capita income in the latter areas was more than a fourth higher than in ARA areas.

By any standards, an annual family income of less than $3,000 in the United States connotes poverty. Based on this criterion, more than 1 of every 5 families in the United States was impoverished during 1959, but in designated areas the comparable ratio was 3 of every 10 families. As a result of lower labor force participation and higher unemployment rates, there are more dependents per gainfully employed person in chronic labor surplus areas than in the balance of the country. Low income level accounts for the larger number of families in designated areas depending upon public assistance for a livelihood. Three percent of the population depended upon public assistance for support in nondesignated areas in 1961, compared with 4.6 percent in this category in all ARA areas.

Wages

Wages are lower in chronic labor surplus areas than in other parts of the United States (table 7). However, the extent to which the differentials are due to industry-mix or lower level of earnings that prevail in

TABLE 6

Income[1] and Percent of Population Receiving Public Assistance in ARA Areas,[2] 1959 and 1961

Area[1]	Per capita income 1959[1]		Percent families with 1959 income		Percent of population receiving public assistance, 1961
	Amount	Percent of United States	$3,000 or less	$2,000 or less	
United States ...	$1,850	100.0	21.4	13.0	3.3
Nondesignated areas....	1,925	104.0	19.6	11.6	3.0
Total ARA areas	1,512	81.7	29.6	19.5	4.6
Total 5(a) areas	1,733	93.7	21.8	13.5	3.5
120 areas.........	1,498	81.0	27.9	17.6	4.2
30 areas	1,466	79.2	29.2	(3)	4.6

[1] Total money income (1959) divided by population (1960).

[2] For definition of areas, see text footnote 1.

[3] Data not available.

Source: *Statistical Profiles, Redevelopment Areas* (SP Series) (U.S. Bureau of the Census).

TABLE 7

Average Annual Wages and Salaries per Employee in the United States and
30 5(a)[1] ARA Areas, by Industry, 1958

Industry	United States	30[1] 5(a) areas
Average annual wage per full-time employee, 1958:		
Manufacturing	$4,789	$4,189
Retail trade	2,720	2,499
Wholesale trade	4,717	4,044
Services	3,115	2,413
Increase in average annual wage, 1948-58:		
Manufacturing[2]	72.5	67.2
Retail trade	35.7	42.6
Wholesale trade	40.6	45.4
Services	57.0	47.4
Manufacturing payroll as percent of value added, 1958 . .	52.2	53.4
Value added per employee, 1958	$9,175	$7,843

[1] For definitions of areas, see text footnote 1.
[2] 1947 to 1958.
Source: *Statistical Profiles, Redevelopment Areas* (SP Series) (U.S. Bureau of the Census).

these areas is unknown and cannot be judged from the limited data prepared for this study.

Between 1947 and 1958, annual manufacturing wages rose less in the chronic labor surplus areas than in the rest of the Nation. This lag may have been due to a surplus supply of labor, relatively longer lay-offs, and a shorter workweek. However, in retail and wholesale trade, although the wage levels were lower, the percentage increase in annual wages was more rapid in chronic labor surplus areas. This phenomenon might have been due to a greater expansion in the Nation as a whole of part-time employment of women. In chronic labor surplus areas the ample labor supply might have made it unnecessary for employers to require part-time help.

Housing

Housing conditions also reflect the economic stagnation that prevails in chronic labor surplus areas. The proportion of dwellings built within the decade prior to the 1960 Census accounted for almost 28 percent of total housing units; the comparable proportion of newer housing units in chronic labor surplus areas was about 17 percent.

Home ownership is somewhat more prevalent in the chronic labor surplus areas than in the balance of the United States; more than 3 of every 5 U.S. families reside in their own homes. However, there is a considerable difference in the condition of the occupied housing units; less than a seventh of the 1960 housing units in the country were classified as substandard; in the sample of 30 5(a) areas, 3 of every 10 houses were so classified.[3]

Since there are relatively more substandard housing units in depressed areas than in the rest of the country, the median cost of housing and rental is appreciably lower in depressed areas than for the country as a whole. However, the ratio of the value of the housing units in depressed areas to the U.S. median is somewhat lower than the comparable cost of rent; this may be due to the fact that depressed economic conditions may tend to reduce the value of houses more than the cost of rent because of the difficulty in selling homes due to the high rate of out-migration. But the statistics do not support the claim that out-migration leaves many housing units in depressed areas vacant. The proportion of vacant housing was lower in the chronic labor surplus areas than for the country as a whole; even in the five most depressed areas, the proportion of vacant units hardly exceeded the national average. Depressed economic conditions and out-migration tend to discourage the construction of new homes, but older structures, though in poor condition, apparently continue to be utilized longer in depressed areas.

Rural Poverty

Lee G. Burchinal and Hilda Siff
U. S. Department of Health, Education, and Welfare

[*Reprinted by permission from the* Journal of Marriage and the Family, *November 1964.*]

SINCE THE DARK DAYS OF THE DEPRESSION when poverty struck at least one in every three Americans, great social and economic progress has occurred in the United States. Indicators of national economic growth and development abound. While the total number of families in the United States increased by ten million in the last 15 years, the number with incomes of less than $3,000 (in 1962 dollars) dropped by 2.6 million. In 1963, for the first time in history:

---

[3] The Public Housing Administration classifies a housing unit as substandard if it lacks hot and cold piped water and flush toilet and bathtub or shower for the exclusive use of the occupants of the unit.

The gross national product passed a $600 billion mark;

Civilian employment exceeded 70 million;

Personal income (before taxes) reached an average rate of some $2,500 per capita.

These developments document the elimination of mass poverty in the United States, but averages do not describe the whole story. Other data demonstrate that poverty, no matter how defined, is widespread in the United States, and that some groups suffer more than others. Poverty is linked with many characteristics, among which is living in a rural area, especially on a farm.

It would be easy, although a serious mistake, to omit special consideration of rural poverty. American society is now urban-oriented and increasingly urban-dominated, but problems of rural poverty remain to plague both rural and urban communities.

While the total population has been increasing sharply, the rural population has remained relatively the same, and the farm population has been decreasing rapidly. Daily headlines remind us of the conflicts and crises generated by slums and urban poverty. By way of contrast, equally serious, though less dramatic and visible, social problems remain in rural communities—at least until the youth from impoverished rural families and communities attempt to find jobs and adapt to urban ways of life. Then the results of intergenerational poverty, poor schools, and lack of community opportunities for work or play become visible, but now as urban social problems. In reality, however, their roots go back to the hills, hollows, and other backstream eddies of modern society.

In yet another way, the contributions of rural poverty to massive urban problems, including unemployment, limited national economic growth and development, disruption of family life, and social and cultural deprivation of children and youth, demonstrates again the dynamic but imperfect interrelationships between rural and urban society.[1] So too, an understanding of poverty in our affluent society must include an analysis of rural as well as urban poverty.

The present discussion focuses on rural poverty. Two interrelated sets of conditions which need to be considered in any discussion of rural poverty are: (1) some salient characteristics of the rural population; and (2) prevalence of poverty among groups in the rural population.

---

[1] For a comprehensive and varied treatment of rural-urban interrelations, see *Our Changing Rural Society: Perspectives and Trends*, ed. by James H. Copp, Ames, Iowa: Iowa State University Press, 1964. Chapter 5, "The Rural Family of the Future," by Lee G. Burchinal, contains ten interrelated propositions for analyzing rural-urban interrelations which affect changes in rural family patterns.

Rural Population

By definition, the rural population is a residual category, that which remains after the urban population has been counted. The urban population includes all persons living in places of 2,500 population or more. Unfortunately, this dichotomy, standardized by the Bureau of Census, is no longer a viable conceptualization, but it must be used because data are available on the basis of this definition.

The size of the rural population has not changed greatly in recent years. In 1960, there were slightly over 54 million residents, essentially the same number as in 1950, and projections call for an estimated rural population of 60 million persons in 1980. By 1980, the rural population is expected to include 25 percent of the national total, compared with almost 30 percent as of 1960. The composition and regional distribution of the rural population, however, is changing greatly.

First, the rural population is no longer predominantly a farm population. In 1910, two of every three rural residents lived on farms; today only one-fourth of the rural population are farm residents, and this population continues to decline. Currently, the farm population stands at about 13.4 million persons; by 1980, there will be only approximately nine million farm residents. In 1960, one-fifth of the rural labor force was engaged in agricultural employment, down from one-half in 1940. Continued expansion of farm size and increased efficiency in agricultural production combine to reduce the demand for agriculture workers by approximately 200,000 workers per year. On the other hand, as in nonfarm employment, skills required for farm work and management are constantly rising.

The decline in dependency on farm work also is shown by increased nonfarm employment among farm residents. In 1959, three out of ten farm workers worked off the farm 100 days or more. Meanwhile, between 1950 and 1960, the proportion of rural residents employed at white collar and semiskilled jobs increased by more than 40 percent. During the 1950's, in fact, blue collar workers replaced farm workers as the largest rural occupational group.

Changes in employment are only one facet of changes in rural life: outmigration and internal redistribution of rural population also point to developments which must be taken into account in developing programs to reduce rural poverty.

Outmigration is typical of most rural communities, especially in the South. During the last decade, the South and Plains states experienced substantial losses of rural population. In contrast, increases in rural population occurred in the Northeastern states, Southern Great Lakes states, Florida, and the Pacific states. Still, in 1960, the rural population remained concentrated in the South (42.3 percent of the total) and in the North Central states (29.8 percent), with the Northeast having only 16.3 percent and the West, 11.6 percent of the total rural population. The majority of nonwhite rural residents (almost 86 percent), practically all of whom are Negroes, live in the South.

Outmigration runs into large figures. Between 1940 and 1962, the net loss to the rural population amounted to 23 million persons, most of whom were youth and young adults. High rural birth rates point to continued outmigration. In the 1960's, for every 100 rural males who will die or retire, 177 males will reach 20 years of age. It is extremely unlikely that most of these additional men will be absorbed into the rural labor force. Most will migrate to urban areas either from choice or necessity. Many will move from one region of the country to another. Their occupational and economic achievement and social integration in urban areas will depend in large part upon their level and adequacy of education, skills, work habits, general social awareness, attitudes, and aspirations. Even though migration opens opportunities to rural youth, considerable data indicate that rural-reared youth in general, not just those from depressed communities, are at a disadvantage relative to urban youth in competition for jobs in the urban labor market.[2]

Size of population losses generally is inversely related to the size of population centers in rural areas. The more than 1,500 counties which lost population between 1950 and 1960 typically lacked an urban center or had as their largest center a place with under 10,000 population. Counties showing an increase in population generally were those which included a city of at least 10,000 persons or were near metropolitan areas. This demographic fact provides a basis for plans to combat rural poverty—a point which is developed later in the discussion.

One other important demographic fact should be noted. In contrast to broad generalizations that rural-urban differences have greatly declined or virtually disappeared are hard data which show that important rural-urban differences still exist. Such generalizations divert attention from glaring differences between rural and urban levels of education and income and the availability and adequacy of services required for reasonably competent functioning in our urban dominated society. Moreover, aside from the effects of national mass media, whose

---

[2]Considerable documentation for this generalization is found in: Lee G. Burchinal, with Archibald O. Haller and Marvin J. Taves, *Career Choices of Rural Youth in a Changing Society*, North Central Regional Publication No. 142, University of Minnesota, Agricultural Experiment Station, November 1962; and in Lee G. Burchinal and James D. Cowhig, "Rural Youth in Urban Society," *Children*, 10 (September–October 1963), pp. 167–172.

impact on personality, skills, values, attitudes, and information is not well established, direct influences of metropolitan centers extend to only a minority of rural residents. In 1960, the 512 counties that contained a standard metropolitan area included only 35 percent of the rural population and 25 percent of the farm population. Such persons could be included among those directly open to city influences and corresponding employment, educational, and service opportunities. While an undetermined additional number of rural residents lived in counties adjacent to those containing metropolitan centers, it is clear that much of the rural population still lives under more isolated circumstances than is commonly believed.

In summary to this point, the rural population is more varied today than previously, is becoming more urban, will increase only slightly in the near future, and will continue to become a smaller proportion of the total population. Rural inhabitants are still largely concentrated in the South, which also is the region with the greatest dependence upon agricultural employment and with a majority of rural nonwhite residents. Outmigration continues to be a common characteristic of rural communities and consists mainly of youth and young adults. A sizable, though precisely unknown, proportion of the rural population still lacks integration with centers of urban growth—what has been called the mainstream of American society. Efforts to prevent or reduce rural poverty must take cognizance of these facts. Also, development of programs must vary with characteristics of the poor.

Rural Poverty

To some extent, poverty is a relative concept, reflecting societal standards of living. Shades of gray obscure any fine line between being "really poor," being "deprived," or simply being less well off than most. Still, there are absolute limits below which it is difficult or impossible to maintain or foster human health, growth, and dignity. In the search for these limits, several sets of income figures have been advanced.

One commonly used definition of poverty is family income below $3,000. By this definition, poverty is more prevalent, comparatively speaking, in rural than in urban America. Of the 13.2 million rural families in the United States in 1962, some 4.2 million or 22 percent of these families—containing more than 16 million persons—had total money incomes below $3,000.

While farm families make up seven percent of the total number of families in the country, they include 16 percent of the poor families; rural nonfarm families comprise 22 percent of the total and 30 percent of the poor families; in contrast, urban families represent 71 percent of the total of all families and 54 percent of all poor families.

Clearly, then, poverty and deprivation are not only widespread among rural residents, but are more characteristic of rural areas than cities, notwithstanding the conditions of urban slums. Rural slums, less dramatic and less visible, are nevertheless inhabited by millions of Americans, including large numbers of children and youth. Unless these children and youth receive greater assistance than now generally is available to them, they will add further to both rural and urban poverty.

Of the more than 16 million rural persons in poor families, using the $3,000 figure, three-fourths (11.25 million) are white, and over half of these live in the South; one-fourth are nonwhite (3.25 million), the majority of whom are Negroes and who also live in the South, mainly as rural nonfarm residents. Farm Negroes are a rapidly diminishing group.

Being a rural resident and being a Negro greatly increases the risk of being poor. Typically, nonwhites earn less than whites with the same education even when they have the same occupation, and especially when employed in agriculture. For instance, among workers having only an elementary school education, nonwhite craftsmen, foremen, and kindred workers earned 72 percent as much as whites in 1959; nonwhite operators and kindred workers or service workers earned 75 percent as much as corresponding white workers; whereas nonwhite farm laborers and foremen earned only 62 percent as much as corresponding white workers. Moreover, incomes of nonwhites, relatively speaking, are falling behind those of whites. In 24 of the 26 states with large Negro populations, the Negro share of per capita income has been falling behind that of whites, rural and urban combined. In Michigan, for instance, in 1949, Negroes earned 87 percent as much as whites, whereas in 1959, they earned only 76 percent as much; in North Carolina, the proportion fell from 54 percent to 43 percent in the same period of time; and in Arkansas, the drop was from 53 percent to 39 percent.[3] Obviously, efforts to reduce rural poverty must include removal of racial barriers to education and employment.

The remaining rural poor include approximately 400,000 Spanish-Americans, mainly in Arizona, California, Colorado, New Mexico, and Texas; and 200,000 American Indians, mostly in the West and Southwest. Contrary to earlier expectations, American Indians are not a vanishing group. Their numbers are increasing, although health problems, including infant death rates and high rates of infectious diseases, continue to prevail among them.

---

[3] "The War on Poverty: The Economic Opportunity Act of 1964," a compilation of materials relevant to S. 2642, prepared for the Select Subcommittee on Poverty of the Committee on Labor and Public Welfare, United States Senate, 88th Congress, Second Session, U. S. Government Printing Office, Washington, D.C., p. 38.

Domestic migratory workers, including Negroes, Spanish-Americans, and other white persons, are an especially disadvantaged though diminishing group. In 1962, this work force declined in size for the third straight year, numbering 380,000 workers or ten percent of the agricultural work force. But one thing has not changed: their incomes remain low. The average migratory worker who worked at least 25 days or more at farm wage work worked 141 days in 1962, of which 116 days were at farm work. His average total earnings were $1,123, with $874 coming from farm wage work and $249 from nonfarm wage work.

Besides being nonwhite, additional characteristics of the rural poor, as with the urban poor, include being poorly educated, being elderly, lacking employment, and living in a large family or one headed by a female or a person under 20 years of age. The risk of poverty varies with each of these factors but increases markedly when two or more of these factors are present.

Dr. Ornati has prepared some dramatic data showing differential risks of poverty for families with these characteristics.[4] The three levels of income used in his analyses are up to $2,500 for less than subsistence, up to $4,500 for minimum adequacy, and up to $5,500 for minimum comfort, based on 1960 data for a family of four persons. Poverty-linked factors such as farm residence, female or aged head of household, and nonwhite racial status are related separately and jointly with each of the three income levels. Data for the complex analysis are sufficient to document the extent of poverty among the several categories studied.

When three of these factors are combined, as represented by nonwhite farm families headed by either an elderly person or female, for instance, percentages for being below subsistence levels are 81 and 87; for below minimum adequacy, 92 and 95; and for below minimum comfort, 95 and 98. In contrast, for single factors, corresponding percentages ranged from 30 to 70 percent.

Although data are not available, it is likely that comparable patterns, although not necessarily the same rates, exist among rural nonfarm groups. Table 1, for instance, presents 1960 median incomes for four-person families, husband-wife and two children, by race and residence categories. In all three residential categories, nonwhite family incomes were substantially below those of whites, but the correspondence of white-to-nonwhite incomes was greatest among urban families and least among farm families. While the median income for nonwhite urban families was 70 percent of that for white urban families, it was

---

[4] See Chapter 1.

TABLE 1

Median Income in 1959 of Husband-Wife Families with Head an Earner and two Children Under Age 18, by Color, for the United States, Urban and Rural: 1960

Residence	Total	White	Nonwhite
Urban	$6,580	$6,678	$4,469
Rural Nonfarm	5,486	5,549	2,645
Rural Farm	3,779	3,863	1,323
United States	6,206	6,297	4,096

Source: U.S. Bureau of the Census, *U.S. Census of Population: 1960,* Final Report PC(1)-1C, Table 95.

only 48 percent for rural nonfarm families and 34 percent for farm families. Also, within each racial group, incomes declined consistently from urban to rural nonfarm and to farm residential categories. Urban white families earned the most, and Negro farm families earned the least.

Levels of income do not tell the whole story.[5] Social characteristics of the rural population also help to explain the existence of rural poverty.

First, education levels of rural residents still lag far behind those of city dwellers. In 1960, the median educational level achieved by white urban males 25 years of age or older was 11.3, as compared with 9.4 for white rural nonfarm males. Education levels for nonwhite males were considerably lower: urban, 8.5; rural nonfarm, 5.8; and farm, 4.8 years of education. Similar differences existed among women.

Education levels are less disparate for younger groups, though rural youth still lags behind youth in urban areas. Among persons 25 to 29 years old, 51 percent of the rural farm residents compared with 53 percent of the rural nonfarm and 64 percent of urban residents had at least four years of high school education.

School dropout rates are not substantially different between rural and urban populations, but considerably greater proportions of urban than rural youth, particularly farm youth, continue their education beyond high school. Only one-third of all rural high school graduates in 1959 enrolled in college in 1960 as compared with almost half of urban graduates.[6] Among those who do attend college, some studies indicate

---

[5] Some readers may object to direct comparisons of farm and nonfarm incomes. Allowances for the absence of rent or lower costs for housing for many farm families and their greater consumption of homegrown or produced foodstuffs, while not included in farm incomes, would not be sufficient even if included to narrow income differences substantially between the two populations.

[6] Charles B. Nam and James D. Cowhig, "Factors Related to College Attendance of Farm and Nonfarm High School Graduates: 1960," Service Census—ERS, *Farm Population,* 32 (July 15, 1962), p. 27.

that students from rural schools are less well prepared than those from urban schools. Underachievement in college has also been linked to rural backgrounds.[7]

In addition to differences in education, sharp rural-urban differences exist in quality of housing. In 1960, 95 percent of urban dwellings had hot and cold water piped into the structure, but only 70 percent of rural nonfarm houses and 65 percent of farm houses had such arrangements. Also, a comparatively higher proportion of farm (30 percent) than of rural nonfarm (26 percent) or urban (14 percent) housing units were deteriorated or dilapidated in 1960.

With less adequate resources and poorer housing, rural families struggle to raise more children than urban families. The birth rate for farm women, aged 35 to 39 in 1960, was about 3.5. This is 14 percent higher than that for comparable rural nonfarm women and 38 percent higher than that for comparable urban women. Correspondingly, rural farm and nonfarm families have remained larger than urban families.

Most health standards and practices point to greater ill health among rural residents. According to the National Health Survey, in comparison with urban persons, rural residents suffer more frequently from chronic illnesses and yet less frequently have sought medical services, have lower expenditures for health practices, and to a much greater degree are without any form of health insurance. In particular, the rural aged most frequently must rely upon whatever resources they possess, and generally these are meager, to pay for whatever health services they need.[8] Although infant mortality rates do not differ greatly between rural and urban populations, large differences exist between counties having a metropolitan center and those not having such a center, with nonmetropolitan counties having higher infant mortality rates. Also, nonwhite infant mortality rates lead white rates by a substantial margin, and rates for rural nonwhites living in nonmetropolitan counties were twice the national average in 1959.[9]

Further data for documenting rural poverty and deprivation hardly seem necessary. Discussion of rural poverty, however, must include an analysis of community institutions needed to prevent and

---

[7] Louis A. Fliegler and Charles E. Bish, "The Gifted and Talented," *Review of Educational Research*, 29 (December 1959), pp. 408–450; and William S. Folkman, *Progress of Rural and Urban Students Entering Iowa State University, Fall 1955*, Economic Research Service, U. S. Department of Agriculture, Agricultural Economic Report No. 12, July 1962.

[8] Helen L. Johnston, "Health Trends in Rural America," *A Place to Live: The Yearbook of Agriculture 1963*, U. S. Department of Agriculture, Washington, D.C., pp. 191–195.

[9] *Ibid.*, p. 191.

reduce poverty—both in rural areas and in urban centers to which rural-reared persons migrate.

Rural Community Development

Wide variations exist among rural families and communities. Some rural communities are composed mainly of families with adequate incomes, others of families of more modest means, and still other rural communities have a predominance of poor people. Most rural communities, though, include families with incomes considerably below those of most urban communities. Similarly, the adequacy of community institutions varies greatly among rural areas. Community facilities are lacking or are badly impoverished in the poorest ones. Space allows only brief examination of several systems of community services.

Despite great progress in many areas, rural education continues to lag behind national standards. According to a recent report of the National Education Association, in contrast to urban school systems, teachers in rural schools have less education, generally receive lower salaries, are not so often members of professional organizations, and have more complicated teaching responsibilities—about twice as large a proportion of rural as urban teachers teach more than one subject. Furthermore, current expenses, instructional costs, and current value of school property—all based on per pupil in average daily attendance—are much lower in rural than in urban systems.[10] Other limitations of rural schools have been noted by the Panel of Consultants on Vocational Education. In November 1962, they reported: "Youth in small towns have relatively little opportunity to get proper training for industrial occupations, and where they have such opportunities their choices are greatly restricted. The rural high schools have given little attention to the training of the large number of youth who must migrate to urban areas to obtain employment and have concentrated their efforts on agriculture and home economics programs."[11]

Health services are less available to rural than to urban residents. For example, in mid-1959, metropolitan counties had 146 physicians per 100,000 persons; bordering counties, 77; and isolated counties, 75. Services for rural groups having special needs because of age, health conditions, or low income are minimal in most small communities.[12]

---

[10] *Handbook on Rural Education,* National Educational Association, Department of Rural Education, Washington, D.C.

[11] U.S. Panel of Consultants on Vocational Education, *Education for a Changing World of Work,* Office of Education, U. S. Department of Health, Education, and Welfare, Washington, D.C., 1963, p. 116.

[12] Johnston, *op. cit.,* p. 193.

Welfare services too frequently are inadequate to help families bridge the gap between their starkest needs and minimal subsistence levels. Recent data from the Bureau of Family Services, Welfare Administration, shows that not more than one in every six impoverished children—a term covering an estimated 17 to 23 million youngsters in families with incomes so low that they must choose between an adequate diet and other necessities, but cannot afford both—was reached by Aid to Families with Dependent Children in September 1962. Moreover, the AFDC program reached about one-half of the poor families headed by women. Furthermore, while the highest proportion of persons assisted are in declining rural areas, especially in the South and border states, these also are the areas of lowest assistance payments.[13]

Solutions to rural poverty obviously must begin by adapting the major community programs serving rural areas to the demands of our urban economy and society. Solutions will be varied and complex and will involve all levels of Government working with private enterprise and voluntary or private agencies.

In special need are an estimated 2.6 million farm and rural non-farm families, of which about 59 percent are headed by individuals too old, poorly educated, or physically handicapped to transfer into other occupations. Given the requirements of the present-day employment market, it is impractical to attempt to retrain the majority of these for other occupations. Among the most practical aids for increasing incomes among over one-third of these families which are headed by an aged person are increased old age, disability, or retirement benefits. Programs now under way by the Area Redevelopment Administration and the Rural Areas Development Program, and those which will be begun under provisions included in Title IV, "Special Programs to Combat Poverty in Rural Areas," of the Economic Opportunity Act of 1964 will aid some of these boxed-in families as well.[14]

The remaining 41 percent of heads of rural families may be considered as opportunity-oriented. They are younger and, even if they lack a formal education, probably would be more likely to take advantage of training or educational programs when offered and probably would be more willing to move to improve their economic chances. For the millions of rural children, youth, and young adults, comprehen-

---

[13] *Public Assistance in the Counties of the United States*, Bureau of Family Services, Welfare Administration, U. S. Department of Health, Education, and Welfare, Washington, D.C., June 1960.

[14] Economic Opportunity Act of 1964, 88th Congress, Second Session, Report No. 1458 to accompany H. R. 11377.

sive and diversified education, at least through high school, is critically necessary.

Further modernization of rural education, however, is only a facet of needed programs of rural community development. The starting point for most rural community development efforts can well be the development of viable community services in urban centers which provide the bulk of services and employment opportunities for surrounding rural areas. Generally, rural programs do not exist as such; instead, rural families increasingly use facilities and services located in small towns and cities. From a sociological perspective, rural persons and families will benefit as well as town or city residents by various measures which improve the educational, economic, governmental, religious, and community systems of the small towns and cities to which residents in rural areas turn for satisfaction of various needs. Development efforts in the larger towns which are scattered through rural areas (the lower limit suggested here is 10,000 persons) may well provide the greatest long-term returns to rural residents.

Along with the development of adequate educational, remedial, and retraining programs for all children, youth, and adults who can benefit from them goes the development of more effective health, housing, and welfare services and facilities. Expansion of the national labor market through increased economic growth will directly benefit low-income rural residents. Migration from rural to urban areas ebbs and flows in direct relation to the conditions of the urban labor market. Expanded occupational counseling and greater assistance to rural youth and young adults in making occupational choices will further increase their contributions to national economic growth and development and help alleviate rural poverty.

Attainment of these objectives will require concerted action by local, state, and federal agencies. Local resources typically are not adequate: tax bases frequently are extremely limited and migration too often has siphoned off much local leadership and talent. State and federal contributions of capital, talent, and leadership, teamed with local resources, will be necessary to build programs rural people need. Steady progress is being made in modernizing rural community services and facilities. The war on poverty provides further impetus. Much, however, remains to be done and will require funds, talent, and reorganization of community services and facilities far beyond those presently contemplated.

Being poor is an index of a complex set of interrelated problems and processes. Simply having steady employment of the family head with an income to meet minimum subsistence or comfort needs will not, by itself, resolve all family and personal problems of the poor. Additional assistance beyond income maintenance, such as informal education and counseling and expanded health and welfare services, is necessary as well.

Poor and marginally self-sufficient families need help in resolving persistent personal family crises and in providing encouragement for children to stay in school, to take advantage of educational opportunities, and to plan for education or training beyond high school. Children in these families need to be prepared not only for geographical mobility, especially the rural children from more isolated areas, but also for social mobility and for satisfying and constructive adult lives in cities. Families need assistance in budgeting; in developing consumption patterns within their income limits; in bargaining for housing; in refurnishing their homes; in food preparation and planning for low-cost, nutritious meals; and in enriching their lives and those of their children. Programs from pre-school day care through adult socialization and retirement are needed. Attainment of these goals can come about through personal interaction between persons who need help and teachers, agricultural extension specialists, health and welfare workers, and other professionals and lay persons who are equipped and motivated to assist poor families.

Poverty: the Special Case of the Negro

Alan Batchelder*
Kenyon College

[Excerpted, with permission of the American Economic Association, from "Poverty: The Special Case of the Negro," in the American Economic Review, *May 1965.]*

PRESUMABLY, a Negro family receiving $2,400 annually would experience, because of such low income, discomfort identical with that experienced by a white family in exactly the same circumstances. Why, then, a special *economics* paper on Negro poverty? Because at least four economic considerations distinguish Negro from white poverty. As Wordsworth observed of the echo, "Like,—but oh how different."

----
* I wish to thank P. M. Titus, P. B. Trescott, W. G. Grigsby, and Yung Ping Chen for their many helpful comments.

First, $1,000 buys less for a poor Negro than for a poor white. Second, the demographic cross section of the Negro poor is unlike that of the white poor. Third, poor Negroes suffer though the general weal and poor whites benefit from secular changes in urban renewal, education medians, agriculture, manufacturing location, technology, and social minimum wages. Fourth, discrimination operates against Negroes to restrict access to education and to the jobs that can provide an escape from poverty. These considerations will be discussed in turn.

First, Some Historical Perspective

When considering American Negro affairs, one must remember that social and economic conditions of Negroes are most responsive to changes in unemployment rates. In 1900, 90 percent of American Negroes lived in the South, most on farms. The few urban Negroes were totally excluded from manufacturing and from all but menial and laborious jobs. The situation changed to the Negro's advantage only during German nationalism's wars. Wartime labor shortages induced managers of large manufacturing corporations to admit Negroes to the production jobs that permitted Negroes to make relative income gains.

During peacetime, the Negro position remained the same or deteriorated. When labor markets softened between 1949 and 1959, the income position of Negro men relative to that of white men fell in every section of the country. Rising productivity cut the number of whites and Negroes living in poverty, but the incidence of poverty among Negroes rose between 1950 and 1962 from 2 to 2½ times the white rate.

The past decade's many admonitions and laws opposing discrimination could, by themselves, not raise the Negro's relative economic position in the face of rising unemployment. If Negroes are to approach economic and civil equality in the future, unemployment rates must fall.

Full employment affects all Negroes. Attention now turns to the characteristics distinguishing poor Negro from poor white Americans.

The Negro Dollar, Second Class Money

When citing statistics of poverty, the portion of Negro families receiving incomes below a particular figure, e.g. $3,000, is often compared with the portion of white families receiving incomes below $3,000. Such comparisons implicitly assume the Negro's $3,000 buys as much as the white's $3,000. It does not.

American cities have two housing markets: the city-wide white market and the circumscribed Negro market. Because supply is restricted, Negroes "receive less housing value for their dollars spent than do white. . . . Census statistics indicate that . . . non-white renters and home owners obtain fewer standard quality dwellings and frequently less space than do whites paying the same amounts."

Landlords are sometimes judged greedy extortionists for charging Negro tenants higher rents than whites. But they are operating in a market of restricted supply; high Negro rents reflect supply and demand relationships, not conspiratorial landlord greed. Since 15 percent of the consumption expenditures of urban Negro families is for shelter, real income is significantly reduced by relatively high rents.

Poor urban Negroes also pay more than whites for identical consumer durables bought on credit. The difference may be due to white reluctance to sell to Negroes (Becker's discrimination), to Negro immobility, or to the sellers' assumption that poor Negroes are poorer risks than poor whites. Whatever the cause, real income suffers.

Poor Negro families average a half person larger than poor white families. Consequently, per capita real income of poor Negroes is even farther below per capita real income of poor whites with the same money income.

If, then, $3,000 in Negro money buys only as much as $2,800 or even $2,500 in white money and is distributed over more people, one should keep in mind appropriate reservations when comparing percentage of whites with percentage of Negroes below some income level.

Differences in Demographic Characteristics

The Negro poor differ secondly from the white poor in demographic characteristics. Remembering that Negro numbers will be understated, uniform dollar incomes can be used to identify non-white (not Negro) and white poor. Defining as poor, families with incomes under $3,000 and individuals living independently with incomes under $1,500 in 1959, four social-economic variables distinguish the non-white from the white poor.

First, the non-white poor are concentrated in the South. In 1960, 72 percent (52%)[1] of poor non-white families; only four of ten (27%) poor white families lived in the South.[2] The 32 point difference in Southern concentration resulted because, in 1960, the proportion of non-whites was double the proportion of whites living in the South.

Second, low-income is more of a rural phenomenon for whites than for non-whites; 18 of every 100 (4%) poor white families, 12 of every 100 (3%) poor non-white families lived on farms in 1960. Most

---

[1] The figures in parentheses refer to individuals living independently.

[2] See U.S. Bureau of the Census. U.S. Census of Population: 1960, Supplementary Reports, Low Income Families: 1960, PC(S1)-43, February 24, 1964.

rural non-whites are poor. Fully 84 percent (79%) of non-white, only 44 percent (65%) of white, farm families were poor in 1959, but non-whites have withdrawn from farming more completely than have whites.

Third, the aging of husbands is a much more important cause of white than of non-white poverty. In 1959, 29 percent of poor white families but only 13 percent of poor non-white families were headed by a man older than 64 years. Among unrelated individuals, 40 percent of the white poor, only 26 percent of the non-white poor were past 64.

Fourth, non-white poverty, far more than white, is associated with families headed by women. American Negro women have always borne exceptionally heavy family responsibility. In 1910, for every 100 employed white men, there were 20 gainfully employed white women; for every 100 employed Negro men, there were 67 employed Negro women. Even in 1959, only eight percent of white families but 21 percent of non-white families were headed by women, and three-fourths of these non-white families were poor in 1959. Consequently, 32 percent of all poor non-white families, only 19 percent of all poor white families, were headed by women in 1959. So much for demographic differences involving regional residence, urban residence, age of men, and female heads of families.

Urban Renewal, Shrinking the Supply of Dwellings

The third difference between the Negro poor and the white poor is the collection of some six forces afoot today that enrich the affluent members of society and even poor whites while injuring poor Negroes. One of these forces is urban renewal. It replaces slums with aesthetically attractive, commercially profitable structures, some of which provide low-income housing superior to that which the private market could provide.

Yet urban renewal seems to effect a net reduction in housing supply for poor Negroes. L. K. Northwood found "The supply of housing has been reduced in areas formerly occupied by Negro families . . . 115,000 housing units were . . . planned to replace 190,500 . . . *a net loss of 75,000.*" Because many urban Negroes live in slums, 60 percent of the persons dispossessed by urban renewal demolition have been Negroes.

The long run tendency to reduce the supply of low-cost housing is aggravated in the short run because time must elapse between demolition of old and dedication of new buildings. During short runs as long as five years urban renewal reduces housing supply by demolition uncompensated by new construction.

Poor whites may move elsewhere; poor Negroes must face reduced supply. Reduced supply should raise prices, and there is evidence that Negroes displaced by urban renewal pay rent ten percent higher after relocation than before.

Education: The Illiterate Fall Farther Behind

The second force benefitting the rest of society but injuring poor Negroes is rising education norms. Improved education is manifested in rising median school years completed. 1950 Negro medians for men and for women, past age 24, lagged white medians by 2.8 years. By 1960, Negro medians had pushed up a year and a third. So had white medians. Average Negroes remained in the same relative position, but rising educational medians increased the comparative disadvantage of the 2,265,000 non-white functional illiterates (less than five years of school) making up 23.5 percent of the 1960 non-white population past age 24.

Many poor whites are illiterate, but figures on school years completed understate the number of illiterate Negroes and the size of their educational disadvantage. Understatements result for Negroes because so many attended inefficient segregated Southern schools. Testing poor Negro literacy, Illinois departments of public aid recently sampled able-bodied Negroes aged 16–64 receiving public assistance (*not* a random sample of all Negroes). Each person was asked his school attainment; each took the *New Stanford Reading Test*. Of persons educated in Illinois, three percent were functionally illiterate; 35 percent tested as illiterate. Of persons educated in Mississippi, 23 percent were functionally illiterate; 81 percent, four of five adults, tested as illiterate.

Of non-whites living North or West in 1960, 41 percent had been born in the South. These educationally deprived poor Southern Negroes are increasingly disadvantaged in regions where the median education of the local labor force and the quality of local schools rise each year.

Left ever farther behind rising national educational norms, poor Negro families are ever less qualified to compete for jobs or to help their children acquire the education required to escape poverty. Improving education benefits the general public but injures poor Negroes moving from the South to the North and West.

Agriculture: End of an Exodus

The third force benefitting most Americans but particularly injuring poor Negroes has been agricultural change. Since 1945, the mechanization of cotton culture has revolutionized Southern agriculture. There has also been persistent change in crops grown and livestock raised. These changes raised agricultural productivity and expelled hand labor from Southern farms. In 1930, there were 882,000 Negro farms (with 4,680,500 residents). In 1950, there were 559,000 (with 3,167,000 residents); in 1959, only 265,000 (with 1,482,000 residents).

The economy benefits as productivity rises. The effect on Negroes is less favorable. As whites left, the white farms that averaged 130 acres in 1930 grew to average 249 acres in 1959. But Negro farms showed little growth. They averaged 43 acres in 1930, 52 acres in 1960; the remaining Negro farmers remained poor.

Change has not resulted in larger, more prosperous Negro farms. Change has expelled from Southern farms the most ill-educated Americans.

Looking ahead, the Negro reservoir is nearly exhausted. The number of rural farm Negroes in 1960 was only 47 percent the number in 1950. The Negro exodus can never again approach the scale reached during the 1950's. Poor Negroes are already committed to the city.

Manufacturing Migration: Jobs Out of Reach

The fourth change benefitting the general public and injuring poor Negroes has been manufacturing migration. Since 1950, Southern manufacturing has expanded more rapidly than Northern. From 1950 to 1960, the number of manufacturing jobs grew 28 percent in the South, only 12 percent in the North. Because most poor Negroes live in the South, and because Negroes' wartime income gains were based on accession of Negroes to production jobs in manufacturing, Negroes are particularly affected by shifts in manufacturing employment.

Manufacturing's Southern migration to new markets and new sources of raw material has distributed American resources more efficiently. It has taken jobs to poor whites but not to poor Negro men. Between 1950 and 1960, the number of jobs in Southern manufacturing rose by 944,000. Of these 944,000 jobs, 12,000 went to Negro women (proportionately fewer than to white women); none went to Negro men.

Manufacturing: Technological Change Blocks the Exits

During wartime, rural Southern Negroes proved themselves in manufacturing and developed vested interests in the growth of unskilled and semi-skilled manufacturing jobs.

Today, technological change benefits all by raising productivity. It also changes America's occupational cross section. In 1880 textile mechanization replaced skilled workers with unskilled rural immigrants. Negroes would prefer such changes today, but in 1964 skilled workers replaced unskilled.

In recent years, the occupations that during war gave Negroes a chance to get ahead have not grown as rapidly as the number of Negroes seeking work. Between 1947 and 1964, as male employment rose 10 percent, the number of manufacturing production jobs rose only 5½ percent. Between 1950 and 1960, male employment rose 6.9 percent;

the number of semi-skilled jobs in manufacturing rose only 4.1 percent.

Most unfavorable for aspiring unskilled poor Negroes, the number of men's laboring jobs in manufacturing fell twenty percent (by 200,000) between 1950 and 1960.

These changes in America's occupational cross section result from technological developments that raise society's affluence. Poor whites are relatively free to enter other occupations, but, as present trends continue, manufacturing, the Negro's past ladder to escape from poverty, will offer fewer exits from poverty for Negroes handicapped by rural Southern origins.

The Rising Social Minimum Wage and the Able-Bodied Unemployed

Many Negroes transplanted from farms to cities are unable to obtain steady work. Long's argument that America's social minimum wage rises above the marginal revenue product of society's least productive members applies especially to urban Negroes with rural Southern antecedents. Law and respectable custom press upward on the social minimum wage. The general welfare benefits as many low income persons receive more money and employers increase efficiency to offset higher costs. But the first increase in the minimum causes the discharge of the least able persons employed. Successive increases cause the discharge of successively more able persons among the less able employed.

It is the function of the market to choose technology appropriate to available resources as reflected in flexible resource prices. But the market does not operate below the social minimum. Weighed down with their heritage from the Southern Way of Life, able-bodied Negroes with marginal revenue products below the social minimum wage must either find employers paying below the minimum or depend on transfers.

So much for six forces benefitting the general public but especially hurting poor Negroes.

Peroration

Because of discrimination in education and employment, there is one last important difference between the Negro and white poor. Logic rather than statistics suggests its existence and its implications. To begin, assume the innate ability distribution of Negroes is identical with that of whites. Next assume the inexorable winnowing out of those least able to earn is the dominant cause of white poverty, but is only a partial cause of Negro poverty. It follows that poor whites are the least able whites, but that poor Negroes include those least able as well as many of middling to superior ability. These able Negroes are poor because of racial discrimination; society denied them access to the channels in which their earning ability could be developed and used.

The economist then concludes that the marginal efficiency of social capital invested in educating and finding work for the Negro poor could be much higher than the marginal efficiency of social capital similarly invested in the white poor. However, we know that the conversion of the poor Negro's potential into dollar product is very difficult in American society. The potential is latent in the Negro poor. Since Southern segregated Negro schools have placed poor Negroes at a greater disadvantage than poor whites, since racial discrimination keeps qualified Negroes from demanding jobs, since weak labor markets remove the inducement that historically has been most important in helping Negroes score economic gains, it follows that improved education, reduced discrimination, or a three percent unemployment level would bring the Negro poor nearer the realization of their latent potential.

Dimensions of Poverty Among the Aged

Ellen Winston
U. S. Department of Health, Education, and Welfare

MUCH OF THE DISCUSSION of the war on poverty has related to youth—education, youth employment and other measures to break the cycle of poverty. Ten or twenty years from now, we will be able to see the benefits of such measures. While there is youth, there is hope for the future and we must make every effort to see that the millions of children now growing up in deprivation have the new and additional services required for full development of their capacities. However, the aged must live in the present, and for most their hopes can only be for the amelioration of their poverty. Most cannot, through their own efforts, greatly increase their income or replace savings once spent. Therefore, although we should give consideration to measures which will *prevent* poverty among those who become aged in future years, we cannot devote our attention exclusively to long-range plans. We should seek recommendations which are practical and feasible to initiate within the immediate future.

In a volume by Oscar Lewis entitled the *Children of Sanchez*, a study of the culture of poverty in Mexico, it is interesting to note that when the older children of Sanchez tell the story of their early lives they do not talk about their poverty or hunger. They do not seem to be aware that they are poor, despite the fact that the family has a cash income of about $300 and lives in one room, with three in a bed and the sons sleeping on the floor, without sanitary facilities, etc. This would describe extreme poverty in this country. What the children do dwell upon are their relationships within the family and with their kinfolks and neighbors. These supply warmth and support. For example, a recording machine is rented for dances in the street and the public bathhouse is a social center.

It is precisely this human aspect that is all too often neglected and distorted when we organize to provide income and the services related to sheer physical survival. In Jules Henry's *Culture Against Man,* there is a chapter on human obsolescence which deals with three homes for the aged. I should like to quote briefly one paragraph. "The social definition of the inmates is that of near paupers who are mixture of dog, child, and lunatic; and the social definition makes it possible for the help to treat them like creatures without personality. On the other hand, the powerlessness of the inmates makes it necessary for them to accept the definition and the treatment that goes along with it." For example, Henry observes that in an institution for "obsolete social security paupers, the supervisor can tell whether or not a patient has been bathed but not whether the aide who did it, spent a little extra time with the patient as if he were a human being rather than something inanimate." Since time devoted to being human will make an aide late in getting her quota of patients "done," they are washed "like a row of sinks."

The Council of Economic Advisors, using the criterion of $3,000 of annual income, finds that there are 9.3 million poor families of whom one-third are headed by persons 65 and over. Of all families whose heads are aged 65 and over about half fall under this definition of poverty. The use of a single touchstone of $3,000 counts as poor proportionately more families with head aged 65 and over than younger families (although the younger families may be larger). On the other hand, many aged people living with a younger family whose income exceeds $3,000 are poor by almost any standard.

For retired couples the budget developed by the Bureau of Labor Statistics to gauge a "modest but adequate" level of living has been widely accepted as a meaningful benchmark. The BLS estimated for this "modest but adequate" level, a median cost of $3,000 in 20 large cities in 1959. These estimates have recently been revised to roughly $2,500 to allow for lower costs for home owners and in smaller communities. Adapted to take account of the differential cost of living alone, the corresponding cost for one person was estimated at $1,800. Using these amounts, at least 1.9 million aged couples and at least 5.7 million nonmarried persons had less income than is required for "modest but adequate" living.

If we use cost standards for basic needs developed by State public assistance agencies instead of the "modest but adequate" level, we might take about $1,800 as a poverty level for an aged couple. For basic needs, not including any allowance for medical care, the cost standards when last summarized ranged from just over $900 in West Virginia to about $2,500 in Colorado and Alaska, the States with the highest standards. The median for the 50 States was $1,720 in January 1961, and would probably be higher now. More than 1.2 million couples had money incomes, including public assistance below this level. At least 4½ million aged persons not living with husband or wife had total cash incomes of their own too low (under $1,300) to allow them to live independently at a similar level.

Both measures assume retirement, but a considerable proportion of the aged have some earnings or other resources. For many purposes it may be more useful, therefore, to compare the cost standards with some measure of reasonably permanent income. The Social Security Administration has prepared a special analysis of the number of couples receiving Social Security retirement benefits with incomes (excluding earnings and public assistance) below the two levels we have considered.

The annual amounts of $1,720 for a couple and $1,300 for an individual are more meaningful when translated to $33 a week for a couple and $25 for an individual for all living expenses. Few would deny that these levels at which about 6 million older persons live—are real poverty.

To give you some idea of what such budgets mean, the "modest but adequate" budget would allow a couple not quite an egg a day per person and two small servings per day of meat, poultry or fish, replacement of the man's topcoat every ninth year (or once during his remaining life expectancy), four bus or trolley fares a week. The economy plan would mean an egg a day for two and a small serving of meat or fish every other day.

Why are so many of the aged living in poverty? Are they poor because they are old? Or are they poor because they have always been poor, or because they are members of minority groups, or because they live in rural, non-industrialized areas, or because they are unemployed or have never been employed or were employed at very low earnings in the past? An analysis of State variations in the income of the aged for 1959 sheds some light.

The lowest median income of aged couples occurs in Southern States, which, until fairly recently, have been largely non-industrialized and non-urban. Present income reflects the type of employment available and the level of income during the working years. By any measure, both farm and industrial earnings have consistently been well below national averages.

Another significant factor, as was indicated earlier, relates to the State standards for old-age assistance, especially for non-married individuals. This is only part of the story, however, as States use the devices of ceilings, percent of need, and failure to include essential items in the budget to hold grants down. This unfortunate situation results from the necessity to stay within appropriations by State and local appropriating bodies.

The proportions of non-white aged families and rural aged families who are poor are higher than average. In 1959 one out of four husband-wife families who lived in *urban* areas and who were white had incomes of less than $2,000, but four out of ten such families living in *rural* areas had incomes below $2,000.

More than four out of ten *urban non-whites* and three out of four *rural non-whites* had incomes of less than $2,000. But a family does not escape poverty because it is white. There are, reflecting the distribution of the total population, far more white than non-white elderly couples living in poverty—1,380,000 white couples as compared to 187,000 Negro couples had incomes of less than $2,000 in 1959.

For unrelated aged individuals the chances of being desperately poor are greatest for *rural, non-white females;* for them the median income in 1959 was $548, nine out of ten had incomes of less than $1,000, whereas for the *urban white male* the median income was over $1,500, and three out of ten had less than $1,000. People who have three characteristics—rural, non-white female—are above all others, likely to be very poor. But poverty is not a non-white or rural phenomenon. Almost one million urban white women 65 and over living alone or with nonrelatives had incomes of less than $1,000. This constituted about one-half of all women in this category.

Of course, employment has significant effects on income levels. In 1959, half of the elderly couples had no earners in the family and half had an earner. When there were no earners, six out of ten couples had incomes of less than $2,000; for those couples with one earner—only two out of ten; and for those with two earners—only one out of ten had less than $2,000 in income.

Obviously, the increased income made possible by earnings from employment makes it desirable for older persons to continue in employment. There are about 3 million older persons still employed full-time or part-time. Quite obviously, the replacement of income now earned by these employed older men and women would necessitate large additional public expenditures.

However, the long-term trend in labor force participation of men 65 and over has been downward, and more and more of these employed work only part-time or seasonally. Only one out of ten women and a little more than a fourth of the men in the age group 65 and over are still working, and they are mainly the younger aged. After 65, rates of labor force participation decrease rapidly with age. Forty-four percent of men 65 to 69 are in the labor force; 29 percent of those between 70 and 74; 19 percent of those between 75 and 79; 11 percent between 80 and 84. Among women aged 65 to 69, 17 percent are in the labor force; between 70 and 74, 10 percent; between 75 and 79, 6 percent.

Of those who do work, the proportion who work only part-time steadily increases with age—from approximately one out of four employed men between age 65 and 69 to one out of three men between 70 and 74; and to one out of two employed men aged 75 to 79.

Of course, when we are talking about the employed, we are talking about the more prosperous of the aged. Amongst the very poor there is less employment. Unfortunately we do not have breakdowns of employment and income for five year age groups of those age 65 and over. We may, however, consider data on Old Age Assistance recipients as they constitute about 2 million of the poverty-stricken aged. An analysis in 1960 showed that the median age was 76.4 years. Women comprise two out of three of the persons receiving OAA. In view of these age and sex characteristics, it is quite apparent that for most of our very poor aged the hope of finding employment is pure fantasy. Further, in this survey of old age assistance recipients it was found that 20 percent were confined to their homes and almost 8 percent were bedfast or chairfast. Of recipients not confined to their homes, a substantial proportion needed help to get around outside the home.

Under one of the 1962 public welfare amendments, States were permitted to allow OAA recipients to earn up to $50 monthly and give them the benefit without a reduction in the grant of the first $10 and of half the balance for a total of $30. So far 22 States were using this provision. Our next comprehensive survey will assess the effect of this provision.

Figured by any standard, many elderly citizens of this affluent nation are miserably poor. Before we can count the war against poverty won, we must find ways of assuring them of incomes on which they can live in dignity and decency.

The Low-Paid Worker

A.F.L.–C.I.O. Department of Research

[Reprinted by permission from "The Wage-Hour Law—A Lift Out of Poverty" in the A.F.L.–C.I.O. American Federationist, August 1964.]

MASS POVERTY, one of the most serious domestic problems of the 1930s, has been greatly reduced with the help of federal minimum wage and hour protection. On January 8, 1964, President Lyndon B. Johnson called the nation to a renewed war against poverty, pointing out that in the 1960s, one-fifth of all American families had incomes too small to meet their basic needs. To be meaningful, this new war on poverty also must include an attack on low wages and long hours through improvements in the Fair Labor Standards Act.

The fall in worker purchasing power, which led to lower demand for goods and services and reduced employment opportunities, was of great concern during the depression of the 1930s. Passage of the Fair Labor Standards Act was aimed at maintaining worker purchasing power and curbing the vicious downward spiral of wage cuts which bred unemployment.

In the 25 years since passage of the Act, it has proved to be an important stabilizing factor in maintaining the purchasing power of those workers covered by the Act. To maintain this safeguard, the gap between average wages and the minimum wage must now be narrowed.

The Act placed a floor under wages. This wage floor has needed periodic adjustment to reflect changing economic conditions and increased living costs. Such improvements were made in 1949, 1955 and 1961. Today, the Act again needs to be adjusted upward to reflect current conditions.

FLSA Coverage Incomplete

There is a total of approximately 69 million people at work in the United States. Of these 69 million people, 25 million are in such groups as the self-employed, government workers, executives, professionals or outside salesmen. That leaves 44 million other wage and salary earners.

The Fair Labor Standards Act at present, however, applies to only 29 million of the 44 million workers. About 15 million wage and salary earners are excluded from the law's protection by special exemptions and by an unduly narrow definition of covered interstate commerce. Many of these excluded wage earners suffer very low wages and poor working conditions. The Act excludes 3.3 million retail trade workers, more than 4 million employes in the services, particularly hotels, laundries and hospitals; approximately 2.5 million domestic service workers and about 2 million in agriculture.

In addition, there are special groups of workers still excluded from the minimum wage law—workers in small logging operations, some processing of farm products, cotton ginning and theaters.

Most of the exclusions date from the Act's original adoption in 1938.

Restaurants

Over 1.5 million non-supervisory workers in restaurants and other food service enterprises are excluded from the minimum wage and overtime provisions of the Fair Labor Standards Act. The June 1963 U. S. Labor Department survey of wages paid these workers reported average hourly earnings of $1.14. In the South, the average was only 80 cents an hour—half of the $1.58 average paid in the West.

The average wage hides the even lower wages paid to tens of thousands of these workers. Nearly one-fourth of these workers—300,000 —were paid less than 75 cents an hour.

Contrary to popular belief, a large majority of employes in restaurants do not receive tips.

Of more than 1 million people surveyed in the restaurant field by the Labor Department, only one-third were waiters and waitresses. Others were chefs, cooks, bakers, dishwashers, porters, cashiers, hostesses and others. These workers received no supplement to their low wage scales and tipped employes, too, should be guaranteed a minimum wage and decent workweek.

The fact that many union contracts provide minimums substantially above $1.25 shows the industry could adjust to coverage.

Nearly a fifth of all restaurant employes are already guaranteed a minimum wage of $1.15 or more an hour by state minimum wage laws. Thus the industry plainly is able to adjust to a legal minimum wage level.

The impact on the total wage bill of bringing workers up to the present $1.25 minimum wage would be nearly 25 percent. However, since labor costs are only 22 percent of total sales, the maximum impact would amount to only 5 percent of the sales dollar or a little more than many existing state sales taxes.

Long working hours are another problem in this industry. One-third of all restaurant workers now work 48 or more hours each week. Thousands of additional fulltime jobs could be made available by extending maximum hours coverage to restaurant workers. Elimination

THE LABOR FORCE AND FEDERAL WAGE-HOUR COVERAGE

Each complete symbol equals 1,000,000 workers.

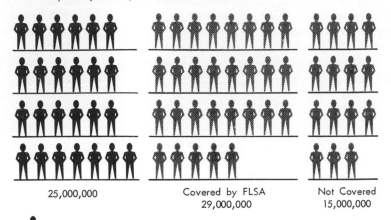

| 25,000,000 | Covered by FLSA 29,000,000 | Not Covered 15,000,000 |

 Self-Employed, Government Workers, Executives, Professionals and Outside Salesmen

Wage and Salary Workers Excluding Supervisory and Others

Source: Based on 1962 estimates of W.H. & P.C.
U.S. Department of Labor

of excessive hours worked in these establishments would be sufficient to provide as many as 30,000 additional fulltime job opportunities.

Hotels

There are 489,000 non-supervisory workers in hotels and motels excluded from minimum wage and overtime provisions of the Fair Labor Standards Act. Average hourly earnings of these workers are $1.17, according to the June 1963 Labor Department survey. Again, southern wages were much lower—with an average of only 85 cents an hour.

The average doesn't tell us about the very low wages in this industry. Nearly 10 percent—34,000—are paid less than 50 cents an hour. Other surveys made by the Labor Department show who some of these workers are. For example, chambermaids in New Orleans averaged only 50 cents an hour in July 1961. In 1948, these chambermaids had an average of 29 cents an hour, so their wages had increased 21 cents over this 13-year period while the federal minimum wage increased 60 cents during the same time period.

Those earning less than $1.25 in hotels and motels in 1963 comprised 61 percent of the non-supervisory employes. Raising the earnings of these workers to $1.25 would have a 22 percent impact upon the hourly wage bill. Since labor costs account for only 20 percent of hotel receipts, the maximum total impact on the sales price would be about 4 to 8 percent.

This industry, with $3 billion in annual sales, also has shown it can accommodate itself to decent minimum wages. Union contracts in various parts of the country provide for conditions substantially above the federal minimum. Approximately 20 percent of all hotel and motel employes are now protected by state minimum wage rates of $1.15 or more.

Long hours are also an unwholesome feature of the hotel and motel industry. Thirty percent of the employes work 48 hours or more a week. By extending the Fair Labor Standards Act to the 489,000 workers in this industry and curtailing their hours to 40, as many as 25,000 additional fulltime jobs could be made available.

Laundries

The 513,000 non-supervisory laundry and cleaning workers need the protection of the federal minimum wage and hour law. This is another low-wage industry, with average hourly earnings of $1.26, according to the June 1963 Labor Department survey. In the South, the average hourly earnings were only 95 cents.

Wages paid laundry workers are particularly oppressive. More than half the workers are paid less than $1.25 an hour. About 40,000 of these workers earn less than 75 cents an hour. The hundred lowest-paid employes, according to the survey, all of whom were in large establishments with annual sales of $250,000 or more, were paid less than 35 cents an hour—an outrageous condition in the 1960s.

Other Labor Department studies show that average hourly earnings for bundle wrappers in Memphis increased only 11 cents—from 47 to 58 cents an hour—between 1951 and 1963. During the same time period, the federal minimum wage rose 50 cents an hour.

Raising of laundry and cleaning worker wages to $1.25 an hour would mean a 13 percent increase in the hourly wage bill. The labor costs in this industry are about 46 percent, meaning the maximum impact would be no more than 6 percent on the sales dollar. A few workers in this industry have already gained substantial increases in recent years—indicating the country's ability to adjust to higher wages.

In Newark, N. J., average hourly earnings rose from $1.31 to $1.48 between 1961 and 1963, an increase of 13 percent.

Coverage of laundry workers by the Fair Labor Standards Act is feasible. Already 17,000 non-supervisory laundry workers are protected by the Act since they are employed in laundries selling across state lines or servicing primarily manufacturing plants. Most union contracts also have minimums of at least $1.25 an hour. Eight states have minimum wage rates for laundry and cleaning workers of at least $1.25 an hour.

Overtime protection is also needed by laundry workers. One-fourth of them work more than 44 hours a week.

Hospitals

About 700,000 non-supervisory, non-professional workers are employed in non-governmental hospitals. In 1963, the Labor Department surveys showed that one-fourth of the non-supervisory non-professional employes studied were paid less than $1.25 an hour.

Many of these workers are engaged in the same type work as employes unprotected in some of these previously mentioned industries. Among the lowest-paid hospital employes are kitchen helpers, dishwashers, porters, maids and laundry workers. The earnings of some of these hospital employes are as low as those found in surveys of restaurants, hotels and laundries.

Retail Workers

About 3.3 million retail employes, in addition to restaurant workers, are still excluded from protection because of the high dollar volume standards established for coverage of retail employes. In 1961, minimum wage protection was extended to about 2 million retail workers employed by firms with annual gross sales of $1 million or more, provided the particular store at which they worked had sales of $250,000 or more.

The 1962 Labor Department surveys showed that, whereas the newly-protected workers had a floor placed under their earnings and a ceiling on their hours, conditions of the unprotected workers did not substantially improve. Tens of thousands of these workers, excluded from FLSA coverage, still were paid less than $1 an hour.

Farm Workers

The nearly 2 million Americans who work for wages in agriculture are among the most oppressed workers excluded from coverage. Average hourly earnings of farm workers were 89 cents an hour in May 1963 and the majority of these workers were employed much less than a full year. Nearly half of the farm workers earned less than 75 cents an hour. For some 75,000 workers, their earnings were less than 30 cents an hour.

Congressional studies of the plight of migratory farm laborers

FEDERAL WAGE-HOUR COVERAGE BY INDUSTRY

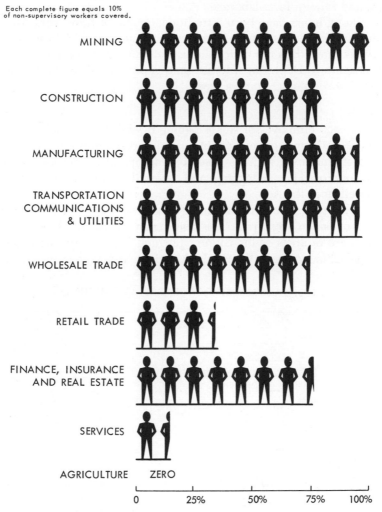

Each complete figure equals 10% of non-supervisory workers covered.

MINING

CONSTRUCTION

MANUFACTURING

TRANSPORTATION COMMUNICATIONS & UTILITIES

WHOLESALE TRADE

RETAIL TRADE

FINANCE, INSURANCE AND REAL ESTATE

SERVICES

AGRICULTURE   ZERO

0   25%   50%   75%   100%

Source: Based on 1962 estimates of Wage-Hour and Public Contracts Divisions, U.S. Department of Labor.

has shown the need and destitution of these workers who toil in an industry heavily subsidized by the federal government. In addition, their low wages undermine the standards of family farms.

Minimum wages of $1.25 an hour have been set in a number of union contracts. Two states also have placed farmworkers under their minimum wage laws. Even the federal government has established minimum wages for some farm workers—such as those in the sugar fields and foreign farm laborers.

Long hours have been a traditional curse of farm work. In spite of the vast increase of mechanization, large numbers of farm workers still work more than the typical industrial workweek. In a 1962 survey, the Agriculture Department found that 45 percent of the farm laborers worked more than 44 hours a week.

Logging

About 87,000 employes of small logging operations are now excluded from the Act's protection. Logging camp and sawmill employes working for an employer with less than 13 employes are unprotected. Thus 87,000 out of 340,000 logging and sawmill employes are presently exempted from the Act.

The 1963 Labor Department survey showed that thousands of these woodsmen were paid less than $1.25 an hour. Many of these workers are in areas of the country plagued by poverty, such as parts of Appalachia, northern Wisconsin, Michigan and Minnesota.

MILLIONS UNPROTECTED BY FEDERAL WAGE-HOUR LAW

*Not covered by 1961 extension of coverage to giant retail and department stores.
Source: Based on estimates of Wage-Hour and Public Contracts Divisions, U.S. Department of Labor.

According to the government survey, 52 percent of the workers in small non-integrated logging establishments in the South were earning less than $1.25 an hour in 1963. Raising their wages to $1.25 would have a 6.6 percent impact on the hourly wage bill. Labor costs represent about one-fourth of the total value of the industry's shipments. Thus the maximum impact in the lowest wage areas would only be about 1.5 percent on the sales dollar.

When the $1.25 minimum wage went into effect for sawmill and planing mill workers in larger operations covered by FLSA, 73 percent of those working in the South received wage increases to $1.25. The industry met this requirement and continued to prosper. Certainly the industry can adjust to covering those workers now excluded.

Overtime protection is also needed for workers in this industry. The Labor Department survey showed that 15 percent of the employes in small logging operations worked more than 40 hours a week.

Agricultural Processing Workers

Agricultural processing workers and cotton ginning employes are enmeshed in a hodgepodge of exemptions. The minimum wage and maximum hours exemptions applying to such workers should be eliminated. The great majority of agricultural processing workers are already covered without any serious problems and the exclusions should be dropped.

An example of the hodgepodge of exemptions is a worker at a grain elevator that (a) is not located in a place of 2,500 or more population or within a mile of such place and (b) has not received 95 percent of the grain from within 50 miles of the elevator. However, for the storing of commodities other than grain and soybeans, a 20-mile test applies. For cotton ginning, a 10-mile test applies. A tobacco warehouse has to be within 50 miles of its source to be exempt.

Miscellaneous

About 130,000 motion picture theatre employes are presently excluded. The 1962 Labor Department survey of wages in Washington, D. C., showed that 40 percent of the men who work in theatres were paid less than $1 an hour. Other amusement and service workers are similarly ill-paid.

Extension of Hours Protection

Many workers who are covered by the federal minimum wage provisions are still exempt from the overtime provisions of the Fair Labor Standards Act.

Local transit employes and gas station attendants at stations with annual sales of $250,000 were covered by the 1961 amendments, but only by the minimum wage provisions. Also, the 1961 amendments continued the hours exemption for truck drivers and railroad employes under the nominal jurisdiction of the Interstate Commerce Commission.

There is no rational reason for continuing these exemptions. High unemployment calls for a reduction in hours so more workers can share in the available employment opportunities.

Agricultural processing employes have been plagued with duplicating and overlapping overtime exemptions, all applying to the same industry. The Labor Department reported that "differences in the extent of the exemption period available for the various industries are not related to length of season or length of workweek." These unjustified exemptions should be removed.

Selected Bibliography

1. Sydney E. Bernard. "Poverty, Public Assistance and the Low Income," in *The One Parent Family in the United States* (Robert Bell, Ed.) (forthcoming).

2. Donald J. Bogue. *Skid Row in American Cities.* Chicago: Community and Family Study Center at the University of Chicago, 1963.

3. M. Elaine Burgess and Daniel O. Price. *An American Dependency Challenge.* Chicago: American Public Welfare Association, 1963.

4. Harry M. Caudill. *Night Comes to the Cumberlands: A Biography of a Depressed Area.* Boston: Little Brown and Company, 1963.

5. Lenore A. Epstein. "Income of the Aged in 1962: First Findings of the 1963 Survey of the Aged," *Social Security Bulletin,* March, 1964.

6. Richard Greenberg. *Problems Related to Unemployment in the Vicinity of Hazard, Kentucky.* New York: Committee of Miners, 1963.

7. Vivian W. Henderson. *The Economic Status of Negroes: in the Nation and in the South.* Atlanta, Georgia: Southern Regional Council, 1963.

8. Herbert Hill. *No Harvest for the Reaper.* New York: National Association for the Advancement of Colored People, 1960.

9. Sar A. Levitan. *Federal Aid to Depressed Areas: An Evaluation of the Area Redevelopment Administration.* Baltimore: Johns Hopkins Press, 1964.

10. Edgar May. *The Wasted Americans.* New York: Harper and Row, 1963.

11. Mollie Orshansky and Thomas Karter. *Economic and Social Status of the Negro in the United States.* New York: National Urban League, 1961.

12. President's Task Force on Manpower Conservation. *One-Third of a Nation: A Report on Young Men Found Unqualified for Military Service,* 1964.

13. United States Congress, Senate Subcommittee on Migratory Labor of the Committee on Labor and Public Welfare. *The Migrant Farm Worker in America: Background Data in the United States Today.* Washington: Government Printing Office, 1963.

14. United States Department of Agriculture, Economic Research Service. *Economic, Social, and Demographic Characteristics of Spanish-American Wage Workers on U. S. Farms,* Agricultural Economic Report Number 27, March, 1963.

Chapter 3

Poverty and the Political Economy

The growth of a "Pressure Group State," generated by more massive concentrations of interlocking economic, managerial and self-regarding professional power, points . . . towards more inequality; towards the restriction of social rights and liberties and the muffling of social protest among a large section of the population. The growing conservatism of professionalism, of the imposed inequalities resulting from the decisions of congeries of social power . . . [raises] the fundamental problem of reinterpreting social equality and personal liberty in the conditions of a new age and a changed society.

—Richard M. Titmuss. *Essays on "The Welfare State,"* London: Unwin University Books, 1963.

SOCIOLOGICAL AND ECONOMIC DESCRIPTIONS of the poor identify a variety of "negative risk factors" associated with poverty: low education, mental deficiency, colored skin, old age, poor health, large or unstable families, and rural background. These in turn are related to "negative personality characteristics": apathy, hopelessness, rejection of the work ethic and chronic dependency. It is easy to jump from this descriptive accumulation of negative characteristics to the notion that the *cause* of poverty therefore lies with the poor themselves. The next "logical" step is to see the remedy to poverty in "correcting" the poor, particularly improving their education and providing special social services to enable better social adjustment.

The problem of causation must be approached differently. It is true that the situation of economic marginality and deprivation is, in some cases, associated with personal attributes which limit an individual's ability to take advantage of social opportunity. And, in a clinical sense, these personal attributes—the so-called "culture of poverty"—must be altered if an individual's full potential is to be released. However:

(1) For most poor people, the attribution of these negative per-

sonality factors is totally inappropriate. Far from being slothful and hopeless and chronically dependent, they work harder, longer and under more trying conditions than do most Americans. They have aspirations for their families, if no longer for themselves, further above their present status than do most Americans; and they are bitterly resistant to charity, paternalistic social services and imputations of inferior social worth.

(2) These negative characteristics, even where they do apply, do not have functional autonomy. They derive from a restricted environment and are largely a defensive adaptation to environmental stress, powerlessness and objective deprivation. When hard experience undercuts expectations, aspirations are soon brought down into line.

(3) Negative personal characteristics rarely produce poverty. People who start poor tend to stay poor; poverty produces poverty. Poor people who do not start poor become poor only rarely because of low motivation, a preference for the dole, mental illness or the like. They become poor because they are subjected to the action of external forces which deprive them of adequate income: job shortages, enforced retirement, accidental disability, or obligation to care for dependent children.

In each case, the lack of opportunities, and not the ability of the poor to take advantage of opportunities, is the factor limiting mobility. The question of causation must focus on those forces outside the control of the poor which limit their opportunity for economic well-being. These are the forces which determine the availability of jobs and skill training, wage scales, size of transfer payments, availability of credit, race discrimination, etc. They are part of the total functioning of the American political economy.

Political economy concerns the allocation of economic and community resources. It involves both impersonal social and economic processes and the conscious decisions of political and economic units. The poor in America are groups which, by and large, receive the smallest share of the nation's economic resources and the least adequate community resources. They have the weakest voice in the decision-making processes which govern resource allocation.

Furthermore, the poor are excluded from the main institutions of the political economy: they do not have organized lobbies; they are low political participators; and in urban areas, their neighborhoods tend to be dominated by patronage machines. They are not organized in labor unions and usually their jobs are not even protected by the legislative minimums of wages and working conditions won by more strongly organized workers. They are rarely represented on public bodies: school boards, welfare departments, urban renewal planning committees, utility regulatory commissions and even antipoverty program boards. The dictum of democracy—that the people should have voice in the decisions which affect their lives—is imperfectly realized for affluent America, but for the poor it is so much empty rhetoric.

This chapter will explore several aspects of the political economy of poverty: trends in automation which decrease the availability of low-skill jobs and increase the required investment in the labor force (Killingsworth); the interaction of race discrimination and changing labor demands to create a virtual class exclusion of the mass of Negroes from the economy (Kahn); the wage-depressing effects of high competition in labor intensive, low-skill industries (Tyler); and the conditions of automation and concentration which are eroding the economic position of the small farmer (Bennett).

While these topics highlight certain key factors in the social causation of poverty, by no means do they cover all aspects of the relation between poverty and the ongoing processes of the affluent society. There are at least five additional features of the American political economy that have relevance to the political economy of poverty.

One: Defense Spending and Poverty

The massive defense budget preempts fifty to sixty percent of federal funds for nonconsumable goods thereby imposing sharp limits on resources available for social investment. The budget concentrates job demands in high skill areas, creating a skilled technician group. It subsidizes extensive research and development by universities and corporations thereby accelerating technological change and eroding the existing occupational structure. It creates community dependency on defense production and consequent community disruption and social hardship with changes in procurement patterns. It concentrates defense profits in relatively few business units, giving them an inordinate investment in the status quo. Such effects of a massive defense budget have certain consequences for the political economy of poverty. The engineer in an affluent defense industry in San Diego has a vested interest in the perseverance of current resource allocation. The career military officer and the company that has a heavy investment in defense work will also favor the current resource allocation. These people will not favor change in resource allocation at the expense of their own interests but may use social and political power at their command to retain the status quo.

Two: Cold War Ideology and Poverty

The prevailing political posture of "domestic unity in the face of communist threat" generates and reinforces a social and political climate where there is a distrust of social experimentation, innovation, and planning. A strong reactionary current in this country, partly generated by the Cold War and partly by historical process, has made a mystique of free enterpise, individualism, private property, states rights and profits and rendered as virtually un-American any discussion of major economic reform (e.g. national economic planning, some regulation of private economic power or the development of a comprehensive base of income, medical and welfare benefits). In this climate, the fundamental changes needed for a concerted attack on the roots of poverty are apt to be opposed by national, state and local interest groups. The range of alternatives for action are, thus, severely restricted and considerable effort must be expended for small social gains. It is this climate also that generates a distrust of the social reformer or the dissenter and his voice is muted by the threatened or real pressures that these interest groups can bring to play on him.

Three: Corporate Power and Poverty

Competition among large corporate structures with new patterns of corporate consolidation, product change, scientific management and market domination have resulted in increased pressures to reduce operating costs. This pressure manifests itself in an acceleration of technological change and a twist in labor demand away from the low-skilled and manual worker toward higher skilled, service and professional workers. These patterns concentrate the gains from governmental demand stimulating policies in highly capitalized markets, with relatively little job-creating benefit for low-skilled workers. They also invest some corporate structures with an inordinate degree of influence in establishing market conditions that are detrimental to the reduction of poverty. Such influence usually is exerted in a climate where the prime consideration is profit motivated actions with substantial social costs and consequences. The end result is to create major concentrations of political influence which have effective veto power over tax reform measures that can be used as a means of financing federal or local social investment programs.

Four: Community Power Structure and Poverty

In most communities the limits on policy alternatives and political action are effectively set by an informal coalition of economic leaders and some segment of the formal political leadership. This group usually exerts some control over the mass media of the community through direct business pressures and informal protest measures. At the day-to-day "grass roots" level, there usually exist mechanisms to maintain social stability and protect property and financial interests. These tend to involve a close working relationship between public officials, local merchants, real estate interests and other forms of organized community power. Groups pressing disruptive demands, whether for redress of individual grievances or broad social betterment are faced with the organized power of the community—power which is wielded in the name of the public welfare but which serves to protect the private interests of the privileged. In some cases this power is used subtly and only the community intimate can recognize its form of expression. In other cases, as in Selma, Alabama, the power is used overtly and its form of expression is easily recognizable.

Five: Conservative Coalition and Poverty

The Congress for the last twenty-five years has been dominated by a working coalition of Southern Democrats and Conservative Republicans which has blocked or forced major revision in nearly every item of proposed social welfare legislation and has exerted major influence in the structure and staffing of regulatory agencies. This coalition, in turn, serves as the congressional voice for the major lobbies of conservative economic and social policy: the National Association of Manufacturers, the Chamber of Commerce, the American Medical Association, the National Farm Bureau Federation and other economic interest groups. In turn, they find their public platform through heavily financed campaigns in the major mass media and in professional-business associations which share their political and social views.

This range of topics has not been subject to systematic research, at least in terms of their effects on the generation and possible elimination of poverty. They involve, needless to say, issues of great scope and high controversy. It is a mark of our intellectual deficit that these unresearched topics will probably have far greater consequences in the war on poverty than many of the issues to which social science has given its most careful attention.

Automation, Jobs, and Manpower

Charles C. Killingsworth

Michigan State University

[Excerpted, by permission, from testimony given before the Senate Subcommittee on Employment and Manpower, September 20, 1963.]

ON THE SAME DAY the *New York Times* carried two news stories which seem to typify the continuing discussion of automation. The headline over one story read, "Automation Hailed as Creator of Jobs." The headline over the other story read, "Electronic 'Brains' Already Setting Type and Keeping Books on Three Newspapers—Employees Uneasy Over Jobs."

Does automation create jobs or does it destroy them? In the view of a great many people, that important question has been conclusively answered, and it is a waste of time to debate it further. Unfortunately, however, there is still strong disagreement as to what that conclusive answer is. The great majority of professional economists today agree that we simply cannot have any such thing as permanent technological unemployment. A prominent economist recently remarked that those who dispute that proposition are simply challenging the main stream of economic thought. On the other hand, voices are heard in the land disputing the proposition that automation creates jobs. Labor leaders, among others, point to such examples as the elimination of tens of thousands of elevator operator jobs in New York City alone as a concrete result of automation, and they view with alarm the appearance of such revolutionary innovations as automatic typesetting.

This sharp conflict between the excessively general assertion and the excessively specific example has seriously hampered the search for solutions to problems of automation and employment. It is hard to agree on solutions when there is no agreement on what the problems are.

(I)   What is automation?

(II) How is automation different from earlier kinds of technological changes?

(III) What are the effects of automation on jobs?

I. What Is Automation?

So many definitions of automation have been offered that a number of thoughtful people have concluded that the word has no fixed meaning— that it is simply an emotion-laden slogan which responsible discussion should avoid. Undoubtedly the term is frequently used very loosely, and misused, in popular discussion. But I insist that the word, "automation," is a useful and necessary addition to the language because—in careful usage—it identifies a distinguishable and significant development in modern technology.

The word was originally coined, I believe, simply as a short-cut way of saying, "automatic operation." And that is still an acceptable way to define the word. Many of the more elaborate definitions that have been offered have really attempted to describe particular applications, or particular techniques used to achieve automatic operation. An examination of the fundamental concepts involved in modern automatic systems will, I believe, provide the basis for a more comprehensive and illuminating definition of the term.

Let us take as an example a complex petroleum refining unit which is completely controlled by an electronic computer. One such unit is located at Port Arthur, Texas. This unit is a multi-million dollar installation, several stories tall and with miles of pipes and wires connecting a great variety of vessels and other equipment. It processes several million gallons of raw material daily. Although human operators are still assigned to the control room, they are little more than "witnesses." The entire operation is constantly monitored, and the necessary adjustments are made by the computer without human assistance.

The basic elements required for automatic operation are by no means new. And examples of automatic systems of various kinds can be found even in the ancient world. But the explosive growth of scientific knowledge in the last two decades and our successes in applying this new knowledge have greatly affected the elements of automation. Measuring instruments have multiplied in numbers and kinds and they have become incredibly sensitive and reliable. Powered controls have become more versatile and powerful. We have a burgeoning young science of communication and control, called cybernetics, which makes it possible to rig up the measuring instruments to transmit great quantities of information in the form of electric pulses, and to rig up the computer to generate instructions which produce the desired response in the controls. Most significant of all is the development of the computer, which has an infallible memory and the capability to duplicate at lightning speed some kinds of human thought processes.

"Automation is the mechanization of sensory, control, and thought processes."

Not all applications of automation techniques involve all three of these elements; i.e., sensory, control, and thought processes. As I will develop further at a later point, automation is a matter of degree.

But even the completely automatic refining unit is by no means a unique example. There are several such units in the petroleum industry. The same basic technique is employed in the construction of several automatic chemical plants which are now in operation; in automatic power-plants; and in computer-controlled steel rolling mills, to cite a few other examples. Some important kinds of automation do not include a computer in the system. For example, "Detroit automation" involves huge compound metalworking machines which have their instructions designed into them; the raw material on which they work is fairly uniform, and they are used for long production runs, so that the kind of flexibility and adaptability which a computer provides are not needed. But the transfer machines do incorporate measuring instruments and powered controls, and they utilize some of the principles of cybernetics to achieve a high degree of self-regulation.

II. How Is Automation Different from Earlier Technological Changes?

I now turn to my second basic question. A great many people today argue that automation is essentially no different from earlier technological developments like the assembly line. In my opinion, this argument is a source of error. The magnitude of the error is revealed, I believe, by a consideration, first, of the changed economic environment of today, and second, of some intrinsic characteristics of automation which make it different from such developments as the assembly line.

The economic environment in the United States today is far different from what it was when the steam engine, electric power, the assembly line and other major technological changes of the past appeared. Today, we live in a rather fully developed mass-consumption society. Let me illustrate the point by reference to data on one important economic barometer: automobile registrations.* The year when Henry Ford introduced his revolutionary idea of a moving assembly line was 1913. In that year, the automobile industry was in its early adolescence—a period of explosive growth and great potential for further growth. The country had only about a million automobiles registered in that year, which was 1 car for every 100 people in the country. The assembly line greatly increased productivity in Ford's factory; direct labor requirements were cut by 90 percent on the assembly line. But sales increased enormously: the number of cars registered increased tenfold in the 10 years following 1913, and most of them were Fords. By 1923, there was 1 car for every 10 people. So the rapidly growing

---

* Illustrative chart omitted.

market for cars enabled Ford to employ more workers despite his labor-saving inventions. It should be added that the growth of the market was stimulated by Ford's big price cuts.

Compare that 1913 situation with the situation in the 1950's, when the transfer machine—"Detroit automation"—made its appearance. This new device in some major installations typically achieved direct labor savings of about 90 percent—about the same as the assembly line. But in the 1950's we had an automobile industry which had completed the rapid growth phase of its development. There were already 40 million cars registered in the United States, which was 1 car for every 4 persons. The market was not completely saturated, but the growth potential was much more limited than it was in 1913. In the decade of the fifties (the most prosperous period this country had seen up to that time), the total number of automobile registrations continued to climb. But the growth in 10 years was 50 percent, compared with the increase of 1,000 percent in the 10 years following 1913. We moved from one car for each four persons in 1950 to one for three in 1960.

I think that this comparison illustrates a point of fundamental importance. When a major laborsaving invention is introduced in an industry which is in its rapid growth stage—its adolescence—the invention may help to spur further rapid growth, especially through price cuts, and total employment in the industry may increase substantially. This is the historical pattern which prompts many people to argue that "machines make jobs." But the fact is that when an industry has reached maturity—for example, when there is already one car for each three people—it just is not possible to achieve further dramatic increases in sales, even with the largest price cuts within the realm of reason. The improved productivity made possible by laborsaving machines simply enables the industry to keep up with the normal growth of the market while employing fewer production workers. This is what happened in a number of our major industries in the 1950's.

Look across the whole range of consumer goods and you will see that our mass consumption society has done a highly effective job of supplying the wants of the great majority of consumers.[1] About 99.5

---

[1] I am not unaware of the "vast unmet needs" (to use the familiar phrase) in such fields as education and housing. I have more to say about education below. The housing needs are found almost entirely in "the other America"—the 20 or 30 percent of the population with incomes so low that these people do not realistically provide a market for anything more than the barest essentials. Unless their incomes rise dramatically—and there is no apparent reason to expect this to happen—their housing and other needs will remain unmet. This is not, of course, a situation which we should complacently accept; but we are not doing very much about it.

percent of the homes that are wired for electricity have electric refrigerators; 93 percent have television sets; 83 percent have electric washing machines; and we have even more radios than homes. The only sharply rising sales curve in the consumer durables field today is that of the electric can opener industry. The electric toothbrush and electric hairbrush industries are starting to grow rapidly, too. But the growth of employment in these new "industries" will not offset the declines in the older, larger consumer goods industries.

The doctrine that "machines make jobs," to the extent that it rests on research rather than faith, is drawn primarily from studies of the periods 1899–1937 and 1899–1953. These were mainly years when the growth potential of most markets for goods was still very great. I think that it is a major source of error to assume that the markets of our great mass-production industries will grow at the same prodigious rate in the 2d half of the 20th century that they achieved in the 1st half. Without that kind of growth rate, the doctrine that "machines make jobs" will surely be as obsolete as the model T.

We can get some perspective on our present situation by considering the basic causes for the booming prosperity which most of Western Europe and Japan are now enjoying. Those countries are in the early growth stages of the mass-consumption society. Their ratios of automobiles to population, electric refrigerators to houses, and so on, are generally comparable to our ratios in the 1920's (or earlier). At their present rates of growth, it will be several decades before they achieve our degree of saturation of markets. So automation is having a different impact there.

I do not mean to suggest that all consumer markets in the United States are approaching saturation and that consumers will soon be buying only replacements for what they already have. One of the few things that we can predict with reasonable certainty in economics is that as consumers' incomes rise, their spending will rise, too. But our history reveals some longrun changes in the patterns of consumer spending. These changes have an important effect on patterns of employment. The recent decline of employment in the goods-producing industries accompanies the long-term rise in employment in the service-producing industries—banking, trade, health care, education, and Government. This slow shift in emphasis from the production of goods to the production of services appears to be characteristic of the mature

---

The point here is the elementary one that in our society "vast unmet needs" do not equal vast markets without purchasing power in the hands of those who have the needs.

stage of a mass-consumption society. The United States is the only country in the world in which the jobs in services outnumber the jobs in goods industries.

Will the growth of jobs in the services offset the loss of jobs in goods industries? This kind of offset is possible, but by no means inevitable. We cannot safely accept the convenient assumption of economic theory that all labor is homogeneous, and the conclusion that only inertia or ignorance can impede the free flow of laborers from one industry to another as the patterns of consumer spending change. The displaced assembly line worker may be readily adaptable to work in a filling station; he may be much less acceptable as a clerk in a department store; and, without years of training, he cannot qualify as a teacher or a nurse. Adapting the labor force to changes in the supply of jobs is a matter of crucial importance in our society today. I will return to this point shortly.

The economic environment today is so different from that of 40 or 50 years ago that simply more of the same kinds of technological change that we experienced in the first half of the century would have a different impact now. But automation differs in some respects from most of the earlier technological changes.

One major difference is the much broader applicability of automation. Computer technology in particular seems likely to invade almost every area of industrial activity.

A related difference is that automation appears to be spreading more rapidly than most major technological changes of the past.[2]

A third characteristic of automation techniques is that, to a much greater extent than past technologies, they are the product of the laboratory scientist rather than the production man. In other words, the importance of pure science as a source of invention has greatly increased. In the Nation as a whole, about 20 percent of our productive capacity is idle. The automatic refining unit and the automatic steel mill were not invented because of an urgent demand for vastly larger quantities of oil and steel. These inventions were the byproduct

---

[2] If automation is spreading as rapidly as I think, why don't our productivity figures show substantial increase? In the first place, the rate of improvement in output per man-hour has been somewhat higher in recent years than the long-run trend (about at the level of the 1920's, in fact). In the second place, as I have already suggested, most automation installations require a very large investment of man-hours in preparatory work; charging these man-hours against current output undoubtedly results in an understatement of the current rate of productivity improvement. The operation of the economy at considerably less than optimum levels of output has also helped to hold down the productivity figures.

of the very rapid growth of scientific knowledge in our generation. In the last half of the century, we are often finding that "invention is the mother of necessity."

Last, automation has effects on the structure of demand for labor which are different from those of earlier technological developments.

III.   What Are the Effects of Automation on Jobs?

Automation, especially in its advanced forms, fundamentally changes the man-machine relation. There are two major results. One is a great reduction in the number of simple, repetitive jobs where all you need is your five senses and an untrained mind. The other result is a great increase in the number of jobs involved in designing, engineering, programing and administering these automatic production systems. Industry needs many more scientists, engineers, mathematicians, and other highly trained people, and many fewer blue-collar workers.

Between 1957 and 1962 in manufacturing, production workers declined by nearly a million, while nonproduction workers increased by about a third of a million. Moreover, what happened from 1957 to 1962 was the continuation of a postwar trend. Throughout the 1920's, the ratio between production and nonproduction workers in manufacturing fluctuated between narrow limits at around 19 or 20 percent. The great depression and World War II temporarily affected the ratio; at the outset of the depression, the blue-collar workers were laid off before the white-collar workers were, and in the war salesmen and clerks were drafted while blue-collar workers were added. By about 1951, the prewar ratio of about one white-collar worker to four blue-collar workers had been reestablished. But as automation gathered momentum during the 1950's, the ratio continued to change. It is now at about 26 percent and the trend is still strongly upward. Generally, the most highly automated industries have the highest ratio of white-collar workers. In chemicals and petroleum, for example, the ratio is 40 percent.

In an economy in which so many patterns are changing rapidly, broad averages and grand totals may conceal more than they reveal. I think that this is especially true of the effects of automation and the concomitant changes of today. Let us take as an example the figures showing total civilian employment since 1949. Those figures clearly reveal the persistent upward trend in total employment—from 58 million jobs in 1949 to more than 68 million in 1963. This great increase is another piece of evidence often cited by those who claim that "machines make jobs." But there is another side to this coin. Unemployment crept upward during the latter part of this period—first two notches up, then one notch down, and then another two notches up. In 1951–53, the average was about a 3 percent rate of unemployment. In 1962–63, the average has been almost double that, or between 5½ and 6 percent.

It is not self-evident from these figures that any part of this creeping unemployment problem is due to automation or other basic changes in the patterns of the economy. There is eminent authority to the contrary. The President's Council of Economic Advisers has repeatedly declared that automation and "structural unemployment" are not responsible for the gradual creep of unemployment above the 4-percent level of 1957. For example, the 1963 report of the Council includes the following passage (p. 25):

"The problems of structural unemployment—of imperfect adaptation of jobs and workers—are persistent and serious, and they are thrown into bold relief by the prolonged lack of sufficient job opportunities over the past 5 years. *But these problems of adaptation have not constituted a greater cause of unemployment in recent years than in earlier periods.* The source of the higher employment rates in recent years, even in periods of cyclical expansion, lies not in labor market imbalance, but in the markets for goods and services." [Emphasis not in original.]

I think that it can be demonstrated that the Council is the victim of a half-truth. The lagging growth rate is only a part of the problem, and it may not be the most important part. It gives woefully inadequate attention to what I regard as a key aspect of the unemployment problem of the 1960's; namely, labor market imbalance.

Let me preface my analysis with a brief restatement of my argument to this point. The fundamental effect of automation on the labor market is to "twist" the pattern of demand—that is, it pushes down the demand for workers with little training while pushing up the demand for workers with large amounts of training. The shift from goods to services is a second major factor which twists the labor market in the same way. There are some low-skilled, blue-collar jobs in service-producing industries; but the most rapidly growing parts of the service sector are health care and education, both of which require a heavy preponderance of highly trained people.

These changing patterns of demand for labor would not create labor market imbalance, however, unless changes in the supply of labor lagged behind. We turn now to the figures which show that such a lag has in fact developed.

Table 1 shows the relationship between rates of unemployment and levels of education of males 18 and over in 2 years—1950 and 1962.

The overall unemployment rate was substantially the same in both years—6.2 in 1950, and 6.0 in 1962. But there was a redistribution

TABLE 1

Education and unemployment, April 1950 and March 1962
(males, 18 and over)

Years of school completed	Unemployment rates		Percentage change,
	1950	1962	1950 to 1962
0 to 7	8.4	9.2	+9.5
8	6.6	7.5	+13.6
9 to 11	6.9	7.8	+13.0
12	4.6	4.8	+4.3
13 to 15	4.1	4.0	−2.4
16 or more	2.2	1.4	−36.4
All groups	6.2	6.0	−3.2

of unemployment between these 2 years. The unemployment rates at
the top of the educational attainment ladder went down, while the
rates at the middle and lower rungs of the ladder went up substantially. The most significant figure in this table, I think, is the one showing
the very large decrease in the unemployment rate of college graduates.

In a sense, these unemployment figures are only the part of the
iceberg that is above the water. For a better understanding of their
significance, we must consider also the changes in demand and supply
that took place at the various educational levels between 1950 and
1962. Chart 1 shows (for males 18 and over) the percentage changes

CHART 1

THE CHANGING STRUCTURE OF LABOR FORCE,
EMPLOYMENT AND UNEMPLOYMENT, 1950 TO 1962
(males, 18 and older)

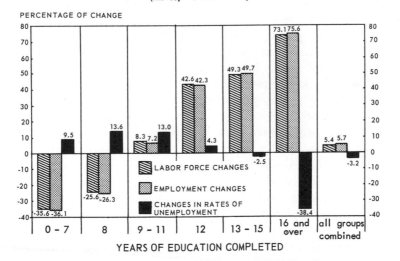

in the supply of labor (labor force), in the demand for labor (employment), and in unemployment rates at various levels of educational attainment between 1950 and 1962. The left-hand bars show labor force changes, the center bars show employment changes, and the right-hand bars show unemployment rate changes. The three bars at the far right of the chart show these changes for all groups combined; these aggregates obviously conceal some differences between educational levels which are of cardinal importance.

The bars for the 0 to 7 years of education group show that the number of this group in the labor force declined very greatly from 1950 to 1962; but the jobs held by this group declined even more, so that its unemployment rate went up. The experience of the group with 16 or more years of education was particularly striking. The supply of men in this group increased by 75 percent, but the jobs for them increased even more than that, so that their unemployment rate went down by more than a third.

It is important to note that all of the improvement in the unemployment situation in 1962, as compared with 1950, was concentrated in the elite group of our labor force—the approximately 20 percent with college training. In all of the other categories, which have about 80 percent of the labor force, unemployment rates were substantially higher in 1962 than in 1950. These figures, I contend, substantiate the thesis that the patterns of demand for labor have been twisted faster than the patterns of supply have changed, and that as a result we had a substantially greater degree of labor market imbalance in 1962 than in 1950.

But these figures do not fully reveal the power of the labor market twist. The "labor force" enumeration includes (with minor exceptions) only those who say that they have jobs or that they have actively sought work in the week preceding the survey. Those who have been out of work so long that they have given up hope and are no longer "actively seeking" work—but who would take a job if one were available—are simply not counted either as unemployed or as a member of the labor force. The percentage of a given category of the total population that is "in the labor force" (under the foregoing definition) is expressed as the "labor force participation rate." It seems probable that worsening employment prospects for a particular group over a long period would force down the labor force participation rate—i.e., would squeeze a number of people out of the labor market altogether, in the sense that they would give up the continuing, active search for jobs. Conversely, it seems probable that improving employment prospects would tend to pull more people into the labor market and thus to raise the labor force participation rate. These two trends are indeed observable

TABLE 2

Labor Force Participation Rates and Educational Attainment,
April 1950 and March 1962 (males, 18 and over)

Years of school completed	Labor force participation rates		Percentage change in rate, 1950 to 1962
	1950	1962	
0 to 4	74.6	58.2	−22.0
5 to 7	85.0	74.6	−14.4
8	88.1	78.2	−12.7
9 to 11	92.1	88.8	−3.9
12	94.0	90.7	−3.7
13 to 15	79.6	83.0	+5.4
16 or more	92.1	92.3	+0.2
All groups	87.6	83.5	−4.7

Source: The 1950 population data are taken from the 1950 census. The 1962
figures are from unpublished data supplied by the U.S. Bureau of Labor Statistics.

since 1950. The squeezing out of people at the lower end of the educational ladder and the pulling in of people at the upper end is another manifestation of the labor market twist. Table 2 presents the pertinent figures for males.

This table tells us that the participation rates at the lower end of the educational scale, which were already relatively low in 1950, had gone much lower by 1962. At the other end of the scale, participation rates had gone up by 1962. Some of the decline in participation rates at the lower end of the scale is due to higher average ages, with a larger proportion in this group (as compared with upper groups) attaining age 65 and voluntarily retiring. But that is by no means the whole story. A detailed comparison by age group as well as by educational level shows that declines occurred at almost every age level in the noncollege category, while there was a rise in participation rates for a majority of the age groups of men with college training.

The important point that I want to make with these figures is that in all likelihood the official unemployment statistics substantially understate the size of the labor surplus of men with limited education. If we found jobs for most of those now officially reported as unemployed, the news of improving opportunities would undoubtedly bring back into the labor force many men who are not now counted as members of it. Unfortunately, we cannot count on the same flexibility of supply at the top of the educational scale. Even the most extreme pressures of demand cannot pull the participation rate much above 98 or 99 percent, which is the current rate in some college-trained age groups.

Our overall unemployment rate has now been above 5 percent

for more than 5 years, and we cannot be sure what effects a substantial increase in spending by consumers, businesses and Government (i.e., an increase in aggregate demand) would have on the patterns of employment, unemployment, and labor force participation just discussed. Many respected economists believe, as one of them once put it, that the hard core of unemployment is made of ice, not rock, and that it would melt away if overall demand rose high enough. This line of reasoning assumes (either implicitly or sometimes explicitly) that no serious bottlenecks of labor supply would appear before the achievement of the overall unemployment rate of 4 percent. I seriously question the validity of this critically important assumption under the labor market conditions of today and the foreseeable future.

The benefits of a decline in the overall rate of unemployment appear to be quite unevenly distributed among the educational attainment groups that we have been considering. The year 1957 was the last one in which we had an unemployment rate as low as 4 percent. It is instructive to see how the patterns of unemployment changed from 1950, when the overall rate was above 6 percent, to 1957, and then again to 1962, which had about the same overall rate as 1950. This comparison is made in two forms in Table 3. This table shows the actual unemployment rates for the various educational attainment groups in those 3 years, and it also expresses the unemployment rate for each group in each of the 3 years as a ratio of the rate for all of the other groups combined. (Thus, the 0 to 7 years of education group had an unemployment rate about 50 percent higher than all other groups combined in 1950; its rate was more than double the rate for all other groups in 1957; and its rate was 70 percent higher in 1962.)

TABLE 3

Actual and Relative Unemployment Rates by Educational Attainment, April 1950, March 1957, and March 1962 (males, 18 and over)

| Years of school completed | Unemployment rates | | | | | |
| | Actual percentages | | | Relative[1] | | |
	1950	1957	1962	1950	1957	1962
0 to 7	8.4	6.9	9.2	154	203	170
8	6.6	4.4	7.5	108	110	132
9 to 11	6.9	4.7	7.3	115	120	142
12	4.6	3.0	4.8	70	67	75
13 to 15	4.1	2.7	4.0	64	64	65
16 or more	2.2	.6	1.4	34	14	21
All groups . . . . . . : . .	6.2	4.1	6.0	(1)	(1)	(1)

[1] The relative unemployment rate is the ratio between the percentage unemployment rate for a given educational attainment group and the percentage unemployment rate for all other groups at the same point in time.

Clearly, unemployment at the bottom of the educational scale was relatively unresponsive to general increases in the demand for labor, while there was very strong responsiveness at the top of the educational scale. The percentage unemployment rate for college graduates in 1957 merits close attention. It was an almost incredible 0.6 percent. I have queried the experts in the Bureau of Labor Statistics on this figure, and they assure me that they have no less confidence in it than in the other 1957 figures. Surely a figure as low as that represents what is sometimes called "overfull" employment—i.e., demand which seriously exceeds supply.

Bear in mind that the unemployment rates for the lower educational attainment groups (those with 80 percent of the men) are now higher than in 1950, and that the unemployment rate for college graduates is now substantially lower than in 1950. Also bear in mind that the labor force participation rate figures strongly suggest a large and growing "reserve army"—which is not counted among the unemployed—at the lower educational levels, and that there is no evidence of any such reserve of college-trained men. Finally, bear in mind the differences between the lower end of the educational scale and the upper end in responsiveness to overall decreases in the unemployment rate.

When you put all of these considerations together, I believe that you are ineluctably led to the conclusion that long before we could get down to an overall unemployment rate as low as 4 percent, we would have a severe shortage of workers at the top of the educational ladder. This shortage would be a bottleneck to further expansion of employment. I cannot pinpoint the level at which the bottleneck would begin to seriously impede expansion; but, on the basis of the relationships revealed by Table 3, it seems reasonable to believe that we could not get very far below a 5-percent overall unemployment level without hitting that bottleneck.

IV. Conclusion

The most fundamental conclusion that emerges from my analysis is that automation and the changing pattern of consumer wants have greatly increased the importance of investment in human beings as a factor in economic growth. More investment in plant and equipment, without very large increases in our investment in human beings, seems certain to enlarge the surplus of underdeveloped manpower and to create a shortage of the highly developed manpower needed to design, install, and man modern production facilities.

The Manpower Development and Training Act is aptly named, soundly conceived, and well administered. This program was not originally intended to provide general literacy training as such. Experience under the Act has shown how essential literacy training is as a prerequisite for specific occupational training. But I doubt that even the most enthusiastic supporters of the Manpower Development and Training Act program (and I count myself among them) would argue that its present or projected size is really commensurate with the size of the job to be done. We ought to be thinking in terms of helping two or three times as many people as this program is now expected to reach. Money is not the limiting factor in the development of the Manpower Development and Training Act program. The real shortage in most areas, I believe, is trained manpower—specifically, qualified instructors and program administrators. It would be pointless to double or triple the appropriations for the program if the extra money could not be spent, and I doubt that it could be. Here we have an example of a present shortage of highly trained manpower, a shortage that limits the possibility of investment to remedy the educational deficiencies of the past.

Let us consider another, somewhat similar example. As we have all heard over and over again, the outlook for high school dropouts is bleak indeed. But here again dollars alone are not the answer. We need many more highly skilled teachers, counselors, and social workers. These, too, are in very short supply. Many other present shortages of highly trained manpower, in the private sector of the economy as well as in the public, could be cited. Unquestionably these shortages would be intensified and new ones would appear if we moved closer to full utilization of our economic potential.

To my mind, the greatest shortcoming of the administration's program for reducing unemployment is the failure to recognize the crucial need to break the trained manpower bottleneck. More important, even the largest appropriations for higher education within the realm of remote possibility would leave virtually untouched the most difficult aspect of the financing of higher education. That is the investment that the student, or his parents, must make in his subsistence costs during 4 or more years of training. For most students today, the minimum cost is $5,000.

To put a complex matter briefly, we must find a fundamentally new approach to the financing of at least this important part of the cost of higher education. We must make it as easy for an individual to finance his own investment in higher education as it is for him to finance the purchase of a home.

And we don't have all the time in the world. Human history has been described as a race between education and catastrophe. In the past dozen years, education has been falling behind in that race.

The Economics of Equality

Tom Kahn

League for Industrial Democracy

[Excerpted from the monograph, The Economics of Equality *by Tom Kahn (New York, 1964) by permission from the League for Industrial Democracy.]*

The relative economic position of the Negro is declining. In part this is due to overt racial discrimination, but mainly to his membership in an economic class to which he has been bound by centuries of exploitation. The position of this class is deteriorating because of technological developments which are revolutionizing the structure of the labor force. More precisely, it results from the failure to evolve sweeping national policies to meet the economic and social problems thrown up by the technological revolution. Since the economic future of the Negro is inseparable from that of his economic class, the civil rights movement must mobilize behind radical programs for the abolition of poverty and unemployment, thus infusing "the other America" with the dynamic and spirit of the Negro revolt. Failing this, persistent economic inequalities will undermine the drive toward legal and social equality.

The Treadmill

Running fast to stand still is essentially the position in which the Negro finds himself today. If the segregated lunch-counter is a hollow relic of the *ancient régime*, one which would inevitably topple at an early stage in the civil rights revolution, the more fundamental, institutional forms of discrimination are more securely rooted in our economic system. And current trends in that system imperil the Negro's economic future.

What emerges from the statistics on jobs and income are the following trends:

1. There is a widening *dollar gap* between Negroes and whites.

2. The *relative* income gap between Negroes and whites has remained virtually constant over the past decade.

3. The unemployment gap between Negroes and whites has been widening.

4. The industries and occupations where the Negro made his greatest gains have either declined or shown relatively little growth over the past decade.

5. Negroes constitute a growing percentage of all workers in most of the declining job categories.

Widening Dollar Gap

The median Negro family income is $3,233, or 54% of the white family's $5,835. Approximately two out of every three Negro families subsist on less than $4,000 annually—and are therefore poor or deprived—as compared with 27.7% of the white families. Only one out of five Negro families earns $6,000 or more, as compared with one out of two white families. In the whole country there are only 6,000 Negro families that can boast of incomes of $25,000 or more.

These figures tell us where the Negro is today, but they become more meaningful when compared to the 1945 figures, as Table 1 shows.

TABLE 1

Percent Distribution of Income of Families by Color for United States, 1945-1961

Total Money Income Level	1945		1961		Percent Change in Ratio Over 1945	
	White	Nonwhite	White	Nonwhite	White	Nonwhite
Under $4,000	75.5	90.1	27.7	60.2	− 63.3	− 33.1
$4,000-$5,999	16.8	6.1	22.4	19.7	+ 33.3	+223.0
$6,000 and over....	7.7	3.8	49.9	20.1	+548.0	+429.0
Total	100.0	100.0	100.0	100.0		

Source: U.S. Department of Commerce, *Current Population Reports,* Consumers Income, Series P-60, No. 2, March 2, 1948 and No. 38, August 28, 1962.

Notice that between 1945 and 1961, the percentage ratio of whites who escaped from the below $4,000 category (63.3%) is almost double that for Negroes (33.1%), despite the fact that a larger percentage of Negroes were in that category in 1945 (90.1% as against 75.5% of white families). Similarly, whites entered the $6,000-and-over category at a faster rate than Negroes.

On the other hand, the percentage increase of Negro families entering the $4,000–$5,999 category seems very impressive when compared with the figures for whites. But the percentage gain is great only because the starting figure was so low.

Fisk economist Vivian Henderson emphasizes that while

relative growth in wage and salary income of Negroes since 1940 has been greater than that of whites . . . the absolute, or *dollar,* difference has widened considerably. . . . People spend and save dollars. It is this dollar difference that counts. Pronouncements regarding economic progress which are confined to acceleration concepts and percentage change obscure the real predicament—*Negroes are losing ground rapidly in gaining dollar parity with whites*. The "dollar gap" trend . . . means very simply that earnings are increasing for whites at a faster pace than for Negroes. [*The Economic Status of Negroes,* Southern Regional Council, pp. 12–13.]

One aspect of the earning gap is particularly astonishing. When we compare the lifetime earnings of Negro and white males by education (Table 2), we find that the Negro who finishes four years of college will earn less than a white with only eight years of elementary school.

TABLE 2

Male Lifetime Earnings by Race and Education
(in thousands)

Highest Grade Completed	White	Negro	Negro As % of White
Elementary School			
Less Than 8 Years	$157	$ 95	61
8 Years	191	123	64
High School			
1 to 3 Years	221	132	60
4 Years	253	151	60
College			
1 to 3 Years	301	162	54
4 Years	395	185	47
5 Years or More	466	246	53
Average	241	122	51

Source: Employment and Earnings, Bureau of Labor Statistics, Feb. 1964.

Relative Income Gap

Not only is the dollar gap widening, but the *relative* income gap has remained virtually constant for almost a decade. While the figures reported by statisticians vary slightly, they point to the conclusion of Herman P. Miller of the Census Bureau:

In the last decade . . . there has been no change in income differential between [Negroes and whites]. The median pay of the Negro worker has remained stuck at about 55% of the white [*N.Y. Times,* Aug. 12, 1963].

The Negro's *relative* income gains were actually registered between 1940 and 1954, when Negro family median income jumped from 37% to 56% of the white figure.

Behind this gain was World War II (not the New Deal, after eight years of which 25% of the Negro work force was still unemployed as against 13% of the white). War production created a shortage not only of skilled workers, but of semiskilled and unskilled workers as well.

Consequently, thousands of Negroes left the rural South and poured into the factories. Protected by a federal FEPC, needed by an expanding economy, and absorbed in large numbers into the CIO, they won higher wages than the farms could offer. Many acquired new skills. The base of the Negro lower middle class was considerably expanded.

After Congress killed FEPC in 1946, job discrimination surged up and many of the newly acquired skills were lost to the Negro community through lack of use. Still, in the relatively prosperous post-war years, the unemployment rate among Negroes was only about 60% higher than the white rate. *Since 1954 it has been at least 200% higher.*

The point to be stressed here is that the Negro's income gains were the result of peculiar employment opportunities that no longer exist. In part, as Michael Harrington has observed, these gains were due to "economic geography rather than the workings of the society." They reflect the shift of rural Negroes to cities and Southern Negroes to the North. In these cases, the people involved increased their income by going into a more prosperous section of the economy as a whole. But within each area—Northern city, Southern city, agriculture —*their relative position remained the same: at the bottom.*

Thus, masses of Negroes entered industrial production but were concentrated in unskilled and semiskilled jobs. And these are precisely the jobs now being destroyed by automation. The "bottom" is falling out of society; it is no longer needed.

"Invisible Army of the Unemployed"

Just as the dollar gap between Negroes and whites has been widening, so has the unemployment gap, as Figure 1 indicates. Whereas the unemployment rate from 1947 to 1953 never exceeded 8.5% for Negroes and 4.6% for whites, now it stands at 12.4% and 5.9% respectively. Not only have there been rising levels of unemployment since 1954, but— and this is of strategic importance—the Negro-white unemployment gap has tended to widen in times of high unemployment and narrow in times of low unemployment. Historically the Negro fares better, absolutely and relatively, the closer the economy is to full employment.

Both tendencies—rising unemployment and a widening unemployment gap—come into sharper focus if we replace the official figures with more realistic ones which take into account what Professor Killingsworth (see preceding article) has called the "invisible army of unemployed"—"people forced out of the labor market some time ago who are willing and able to work, but have become too discouraged to search for jobs" and are therefore not counted as part of the labor force by the government. Professor Killingsworth carefully calculated the size

FIGURE 1: NEGRO AND OVER-ALL UNEMPLOYMENT RATES, 1947–1963

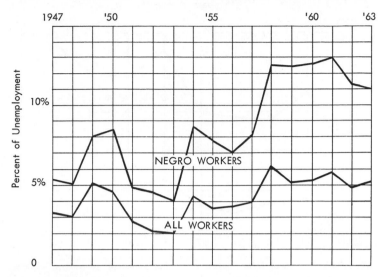

Estimates based on statistics of U. S. Department of Commerce, Bureau of the Census, and other sources.

of this "invisible army" at 1½ million. They would raise the national unemployment rate to 8.8%. Gunnar Myrdal, the eminent Swedish economist, likewise taking into account the number of persons who would re-enter the labor force if jobs opened up, put the figure at 9%.

While Killingsworth has not made a racial breakdown of the "invisible army," he emphasized that its members are educationally disadvantaged. A disproportionate number are undoubtedly Negroes, many of whom support themselves in the ghettos by means they are not likely to report to census takers. Labor economists believe the real Negro unemployment rate is probably close to 20%. In the words of the *New York Times*, "Unemployment of these proportions, were it general, would be a national catastrophe."

The Under-class

Especially ominous is the long-term unemployment rate among Negroes. For the long-term unemployed tend also to be the most frequently hit by unemployment, and the longer they are unemployed the less chance they have of ever finding jobs. They make up a swelling "under-class" that is daily becoming economically more obsolete. This "under-class" is composed mainly of Negroes, males 65 and over, young men, farm laborers, those in unskilled occupations and those with less

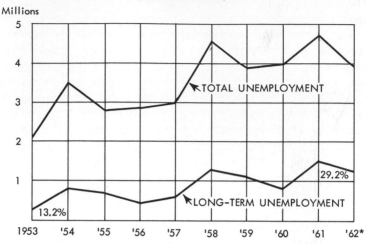

FIGURE 2: LONG-TERM UNEMPLOYMENT, 1953—1962
(15 weeks or more)

Source: U.S. Bureau of Labor Statistics   *January–June, seasonally adjusted.

than 12 years of schooling. For all of them, unemployment is worsening in frequency and duration. The mass unemployment of the thirties has yielded to a new "under-class" unemployment.

The seriousness of the problem is illustrated in Figure 2, which shows that since 1953 the long-term unemployed have been constituting *an increasing percentage of the total unemployed.* This means that a growing section of the work force is being more or less permanently detached from the economy and sinking into the "under-class."

Within this "under-class," Negro representation is mounting. Vivian Henderson reports that

in September, 1958, the average duration of unemployment for Negroes was 17.8 weeks and for white workers 13.3 weeks. The average length of unemployment in September, 1962, for Negroes was 18 weeks while that for whites had dropped to 13 weeks. Negroes accounted for about 25% of all the long-term unemployed, but for only about 11% of the labor force. About 29% of the very long term unemployed in September, 1962, were Negroes compared with 21% in September, 1961. Long-term joblessness among Negroes results from discrimination in hiring and inadequate training and inadequate manpower development. [*op. cit.,* p. 16.]

Generally, the long-term unemployed are more likely to be the victims of technological change, while the short-term unemployed may be seasonal lay-offs, retrainees, or seekers of better jobs. What percentage of long-term joblessness among Negroes is attributable to discrimination *per se* and what percentage to inadequate training is difficult to state with precision.

The role of discrimination is clearest in the areas of income and occupational distribution of Negro college graduates. Lack of training certainly cannot explain the figures in Table 2. Nor can it satisfactorily explain why only 5% of Negro college men become proprietors, managers, or officials as compared with 22% of white college men; or why Negroes with some college training are found in service and laborer jobs in numbers five times greater than whites with similar training. It absolutely cannot explain why 10% of Negro women who finish college end up as domestics! Here is an obvious waste of skills that can be ascribed only to blatant discrimination and segregation.

On the other hand, college graduates constitute only 3.5% of the non-white population, and they are not usually to be found in the ranks of the long-term unemployed. In fact, because of skilled manpower shortages, educated Negroes are likely to make the most rapid progress in the period ahead.

For the vast majority of Negroes, however, an economic crisis is in the offing. And overt discrimination seems less a part of it than the weight of centuries of past discrimination combining with portentous economic forces that are themselves color-blind. *It is as if racism, having put the Negro in his economic "place," stepped aside to watch technology destroy that place.*

Changing Labor Force

As indicated above, most of the Negroes' economic gains in recent years were made in the period 1940–1953 and reflect their movement out of agriculture into mining, manufacturing, and construction, where they took up unskilled and semiskilled jobs. These blue-collar jobs in the goods-producing industries paid better than the unskilled and semiskilled jobs in the service-producing industries. But they were also the jobs most hit by automation and technological change.

As Table 3 shows, the past decade has witnessed a decline of 339,000 jobs in the goods-producing industries and an increase of 7.3 million jobs in the service-producing industries.

But these figures reveal only part of the impact of the technological revolution on the work force. Customarily, goods-producing jobs are considered blue-collar and service-producing jobs are considered white-collar. The fact is that *within* the goods-producing industries there has been a dramatic increase in the number of white-collar jobs and an even more dramatic loss of blue-collar jobs.

TABLE 3

The Shift in Non-Farm Jobs 1953-1963
(in thousands)

	1953	1963	Gain	Loss
Goods-Producing				
Mining	866	634		232
Construction	2,623	3,030	407[1]	
Manufacturing	17,549	17,035		514
	21,038	20,699		339
Service-Producing				
Transportation, Public Utilities	4,290	3,913		377
Wholesale Trade	2,727	3,143	416	
Retail Trade	7,520	8,721	1,201	
Finance, Insurance, & Real Estate ..	2,146	2,866	720	
Miscellaneous Services	5,867	8,297	2,430[2]	
Federal Government	2,305	2,358	53	
State, Local	4,340	7,177	2,837	
	29,195	36,475	7,280	

[1] Most of this increase was made by 1957; since then the number of construction jobs has remained fairly static.

[2] A high proportion of these jobs is part-time.

Source: *Employment and Earnings*, U.S. Bureau of Labor Statistics, Feb. 1964.

In manufacturing, for example, 1.6 million blue-collar (production and maintenance) jobs have been obliterated in this decade while more than one million white-collar (non-production) jobs have been added. The blue-collar decline is also evident in the service-producing industries. Note that the only service-producing jobs that declined since 1953 were in transportation and utilities (especially in railroading).

Thus the growth in white-collar jobs resulted not only from the expansion of the service industries, but also from the application of technology to the productive process itself. The economic revolution wrought by these developments became fully evident in the mid-1950s when the number of white-collar workers exceeded the number of blue-collar workers for the first time in history.* The decrease in the agricultural work force is also evident. As a consequence of agricultural mechanization, more than 1.5 million farm jobs have been wiped out since 1953.

It is against this background that the economic position of the Negro must be viewed. Figure 3 shows the percentage of whites and non-whites in each of the occupational categories. Notice the disproportionate concentration of Negroes in blue-collar and service jobs. (These service jobs are not to be confused with white-collar jobs in *service-producing* industries.)

* Illustrative table omitted.

FIGURE 3: OCCUPATIONAL BREAKDOWN BY RACE

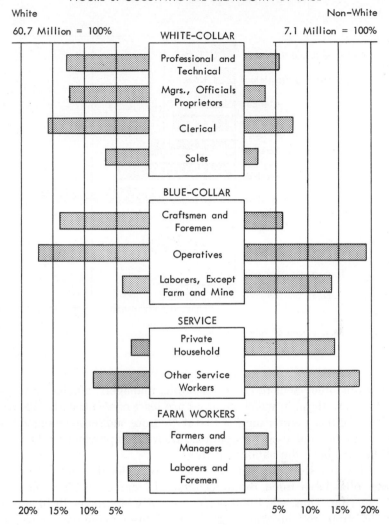

Source: U.S. Bureau of Labor Statistics

That these jobs are becoming increasingly marginal to the economy becomes clear when we examine Figure 4, which shows the rate of unemployment in each occupation. Note that the occupations in which unemployment is highest—for example, laborers, operatives, and "other service workers"—are precisely the occupations in which Negroes are most heavily concentrated. Conversely, the occupations with the

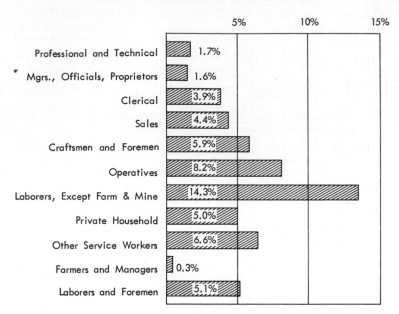

FIGURE 4: UNEMPLOYMENT BY OCCUPATION

Source: U.S. Bureau of Labor Statistics

lowest unemployment rates—for example, managers, officials, and proprietors—are those in which Negroes are least concentrated. Taken together, Figures 3 and 4 suggest that if Negroes suddenly changed their skin color but not their occupations, their unemployment rate would still be far above the national average.

Further study reveals that while the national trend is toward a white-collar labor force, the percentage of Negroes in blue-collar jobs is increasing. Thus, while the percentage of white males in blue-collar jobs *fell* from 53% in 1950 to 50% in 1960, the percentage for Negroes rose from 64% to 67%. And the greater part of this increase was in the "laborer" category. These are the figures for Negro *males*. More shocking are those for Negro females, an increasing percentage of whom are now in *blue-collar* jobs (15% in 1950, 17.2% in 1962; corresponding figures for white women are 22.3% and 17.3%).

The percentage of Negroes in white-collar jobs is also increasing, though in percentage points whites gained more than Negroes in professional and technical jobs. Most of the Negroes' gains were in clerical jobs where wages are generally lower than in manufacturing. It is precisely in the professional and technical field that the job market is expanding most rapidly. Herman Miller concludes, "In most states, the nonwhite male now has about the same occupational distribution relative to whites that he had in 1940 and 1950."

But unless this occupational distribution is radically altered, disaster looms for the Negro. Not only will the unemployment gap widen because of increasing automation in categories where Negroes are concentrated, but so will the dollar gap. As Henderson summarizes,

> Whites are acquiring the highest paying jobs in the higher occupational classifications. The benefits of general economic expansion and technology, therefore, have only trickled down to the Negroes, putting more of them into wage and salary jobs. These benefits automatically produced high acceleration in income change, but were restricted tightly to lower occupational classifications. Thus, despite the unprecedented growth of income among Negroes and the percentage gains made, the fact remains that *income progress of Negroes has leveled off*. The percentage of Negro families in lower income brackets is twice as high as whites, and *the differential in earnings of whites and Negroes continues to widen,* largely offsetting percentage gains. Accordingly, it is still difficult for Negroes to purchase health, education and the amenities of life on the same level as other members of the population. [*op. cit.,* pp. 12–13. Italics added.]

Not only are Negroes trapped in declining and stagnant job categories; *they constitute a growing percentage of the total workers in these categories.* Of all laborers (except farm and mine), Negroes were 27.6% in 1960 as against 21.2% in 1940; among operatives and kindred workers, Negroes constituted 11.6% as against 6.1%; among clerical workers, 6.7% as against 1.6%. While Negroes constituted a larger percentage of farm laborers and foremen in 1960 (23.6%) than in 1940 (22.5%), they make up a decreasing percentage of farmers and farm managers (8.6% as against 13.1%). The reason for this, of course, is agricultural mechanization, which has hit Negroes hardest. Between 1940 and 1959, the drop in the number of American farms was 39%, but the number of farms owned or operated by Negroes was cut more than one-half, from over 700,000 to less than 300,000. (Only 23% of Southern Negro farm workers own their own farms as contrasted with 60% of white farm workers. On the other hand, almost half of all tenant farmers and over 65% of all sharecroppers are Negroes.)

The Talk of Progress

To sum up, then, the decline in the relative economic position of the Negro is evident in the widening dollar and unemployment gaps between Negroes and whites, stagnation of the relative income gap, erosion of the job categories in which Negroes are concentrated, and the increasing segregation of Negroes in the declining job categories.

Underlying these trends are basic changes in the structure of the total labor force. The rising productivity caused by technological advances has reduced the number of workers required to produce the goods and services we need. While the effect of automation will become increasingly widespread, the blue-collar production and maintenance jobs are hardest hit. Paralleling the erosion of unskilled and semiskilled jobs is the growth of white-collar jobs and a mounting demand for skilled labor, where manpower shortages already exist. Because of centuries of discrimination and exploitation Negroes have been disproportionately concentrated in the unskilled and semiskilled jobs now being obliterated and lack the training demanded by the new skilled jobs. Even if every racial barrier were immediately torn down, the mass of Negroes would still face a disastrous economic future.

> *Nothing even vaguely resembling a "master plan" has been set in motion to eliminate the twin problems of racial inequality and technological unemployment. Because current government programs do not cope with the economic revolution, deepening structural unemployment frustrates the efforts of Negroes to enter the job market even when discriminatory barriers are eliminated. Thus, even if existing apprenticeship openings were fully integrated, Negro unemployment rates would remain intolerably high. Neither "equal opportunity" nor "preferential treatment" can solve the problems of Negro unemployment within the framework of a private economy which has failed to generate jobs over the past decade. To accept this framework is necessarily to accept a form of economic tokenism which benefits relatively few Negroes, and not those most in need.*

Causes and Cures

In an article against "discrimination in reverse," Secretary of Labor Wirtz cited the "three causes of minority group unemployment":

1.   "The present shortage of jobs in the economy as a whole for *all* workers."

2.   "Unquestionably the fact of lesser qualifications" among minority groups.

3.   "The harsh ugly fact of discrimination." ["Toward Equal Opportunity," *American Child*, Nov., 1963.]

These remarks are an excellent point of departure for an evaluation of government programs in the field.

Federal Training and Education Programs

The Manpower Development and Training Act of 1962 sought to retrain 400,000 workers within three years. A bill extending the program and adding 93,000 workers was signed by President Johnson in December, 1963. As Dan Schulder, of the Manpower Development and Training Agency, told a Washington Conference in November, 1963,

> MDTA programs in the South in the first 8 months of operation have trained only 234 Negroes, according to the report of the Civil Rights Commission. That figure represents only 11% of the total MDTA trainees, while Negro unemployment in the South is 30%. Further, training has been offered to Negroes in only a few of the occupations provided by the Commission. In the clerical and sales categories, 90% of the Negroes were trained as stenograph-typists. In the service category, such jobs as tailoring, typewriter-repairing were available to most of the Negroes. Others were trained as waiters and waitresses. [!]

Under the original terms of the Act, one-third of the applicants under 25 were rejected on grounds of illiteracy—an added handicap for Southern Negroes, who have a disproportionately high illiteracy rate.* Racist state officials are a stumbling block, since the states are responsible for approving the training programs. Mississippi has no program under way because the state refuses to offer assurances that the program would be administered on a nonracial basis. Finally,

> the Act states that people cannot be accepted for training without "reasonable expectation of employment"; in the South this provision can be interpreted to mean that since a white man will not want to hire a Negro for any job but a "Negro job" (cleaning, digging), there is not reasonable expectation of employment.

In short, the Federal retraining program is not only inadequate to begin with, but it is also forced to accommodate to the dominant political and economic patterns within the states.

Apprenticeships

NAACP Labor Secretary Herbert Hill estimated in 1960 that Negroes make up only 1.69% of the total number of apprentices in the economy. This is the result of generations of systematic exclusions of Negroes

---

* There are 8 million "functional illiterates" in the U.S., i.e., persons who have completed fewer than 4 years of school. The illiteracy rate among Negroes is four times that of whites. It has been estimated that one out of every 10 Negro men in the U.S. is completely illiterate.

from skilled trades. The segregationist practices of the craft unions are well-known and among the ugliest chapters in labor history. They are now under fire from the AFL–CIO itself.

However, the struggle against discrimination in apprenticeship programs, though vital, cannot solve the problem of Negro employment. Such discrimination is not a major cause of the present high levels of Negro unemployment. As A. Philip Randolph has pointed out,

> We complain because the building trades have no room for Negroes; but the real trouble now is that these unions are designed for profit through scarcity. If the crafts were open to us, that could not, in the present economy, create more than 40,000 jobs. (*Testimony before the Committee on Employment and Manpower*, July 25, 1963.)

From California the note is echoed by William Becker of the Jewish Labor Committee:

> It is not enough to prohibit discrimination in the apprenticeship programs which receive government assistance. It is important to take steps to provide for *more* apprenticeship training programs and *more* opportunities for the employment of apprentices. Equal opportunity is important.

The point here is that the effort to secure apprenticeship openings for Negroes is inevitably conditioned by the total number of apprenticeship openings available. When that number is relatively small, proportional representation for Negroes in the entire population of apprentices can be achieved only at the expense of white workers. It requires an idealized faith in the altruism of insecure white workers to believe for a moment that Negro workers could win their objectives under such circumstances. Labor unions must share the blame for the historical development of discrimination in apprenticeship programs, but the scarcity of apprenticeships results from the state of the national economy—from the changing structure of the work force. For this the labor movement bears little responsibility. Business and government must carry the brunt. FEPC's effectiveness depends on how much room it has to operate in. If the job market is expanding, then FEPC can bring widespread results. In itself, however, FEPC does not affect the job market. Moreover, FEPC outlaws discrimination at the *point of hiring*. It cannot deal with past discrimination which has impeded the acquisition of the skills required for the most rapidly expanding job opportunities. Thus the "equal opportunity" principle is only a principle and not a formula for jobs. Even the most rigorously enforced FEPC would be inadequate to this end, as inadequate as "equal opportunity" in apprenticeship programs.

The operational sterility of the "equal opportunity" principle has given rise to the "preferential treatment" slogan. Other terms have been coined—"compensatory hiring," "positive discrimination," the "doctrine of the debt," etc.—all meaning essentially the same thing.

Corporate Orientation

The moral objections to "preferential treatment" have on the whole been flabby and pious. The real deficiencies in "preferential treatment" are on another level.

The real question is, what are the limitations on private economic action, to reduce the differentials in Negro employment, education, and housing? Who will benefit from "preferential treatment" in the absence of basic, government-spearheaded economic reform? Without such reform, can there be full employment—and can there be fair employment without full employment?

So long as we have class unemployment and Negroes are disproportionately concentrated in the lower job categories, only full employment can keep them engaged in the economy. This is not a notion to which one either subscribes or doesn't subscribe. It's an implacable economic reality which would not obtain if Negroes had the same job distribution as whites. Preferential treatment cannot substantially alter this distribution in the context of a stagnant economy.

But If No Job Exists?

A Negro cannot be given preference over a white if no jobs exist for either of them. The demand for preferential treatment has been unsuccessful where labor supply exceeds labor demand (as in the New York construction industry). This is the situation confronted by workers with the least education because of the inadequate expansion of the unskilled and semiskilled occupations for which they are qualified.

Preferential treatment has benefited those Negroes who can qualify for the more skilled occupations. These are the occupations that are expanding most rapidly. The more education and training they require, the more they are characterized by an excess of labor demand over labor supply. Professional and technical occupations—the fastest growing part of the labor force—will expand 40% in the '60's, as compared with 15% for semiskilled jobs and no growth at all in unskilled jobs.

To list the companies most commonly associated with "preferential treatment" policies is to indicate expanding industries in need of skilled manpower.

For the 3.5% of the adult Negro population with college degrees, for the 240,000 Negroes presently enrolled in colleges and professional schools, and for numbers of Negro high-school graduates, preferential treatment could quicken the pace of their absorption into the occupations that are expanding with technological progress.

Not only do these Negroes constitute a relatively small portion of the Negro population; they are also the least disadvantaged. Their incomes are higher, their unemployment rates lower. Preferential treatment is the most militant demand of the "black bourgeoisie."

Meanwhile, there is the danger that the emphasis on preferential treatment sows the illusion that Negroes can make progress in a declining economy, and diverts attention from the real nature of the unemployment problem. Moreover, while one may scoff at the abstract arguments against preferential treatment used by middle-class liberals, one cannot dismiss the fears it arouses among white workers, especially those whose own economic positions are marginal.

Preferential treatment, at least in the context of the present economic order, does not go to the root of the Negro's job problem. The great majority of the Negro population is trapped in the lower educational categories. As the figure below indicates, members of these categories have the highest unemployment rates and these rates will increase even more as cybernation's conquest of our economy places mounting premiums on skilled labor.

Thus Daniel Bell predicts that:

> By 1970 with the demand for unskilled labor shrinking, relative to the total labor force, and the substantial majority of workers in white-collar or highly skilled blue-collar jobs, the relative disproportion between whites and Negroes in the low-skilled and service jobs—despite a rise in the levels of Negro education—may be even greater. For while the levels of Negro education are rising they are not rising fast enough.

Failure of the Private Economy

There are three possible—but not mutually exclusive—solutions:

1. Massive education and training to qualify Negroes for the expanding occupations;

2. Planned creation of unskilled and semiskilled jobs for which Negroes are already qualified;

3. Direct financial relief.

None of these approaches, taken singly or in combination, can be seriously entrusted to the private economy; they are simply not natural functions of the profit motive.

Whichever approach is taken, the private economy has little to offer. Take education, for example. Corporations may contribute to higher education, from which they reap the most immediate rewards. Elementary and secondary education, however, depend on real estate taxes for their basic revenue. These generally regressive taxes are among the costs which business enterprises seek to *reduce* when selecting sites. Yet expansion and reform of the elementary and secondary school systems is indispensable for raising the educational status of the general Negro community.

Moreover, while expanding sections of the private economy may apply preferential treatment in the acquisition and training of needed white-collar workers, they are not concerned with *creating* jobs of the kind that the mass of Negro workers could readily assume. These jobs can be performed more profitably by machines.

The purpose of business, if we need to be reminded, is to make profit, not jobs. The two don't necessarily go together.

The fact is that the demand for labor in the total private economy has remained virtually constant in recent years. Between World War II and 1957, nearly a million new jobs were created each year. Since then, fewer then 500,000 have been generated. But even these figures do not tell the full story. In the past ten years, most of the net jobs-increase in private industries was in part-time work. By contrast, state and local government jobs have risen by more than 2.5 million. There could be no more devastating answer to the champions of "free enterprise" who flail against "big government."

The failure of the private economy to generate jobs must be measured against future needs. It has been estimated that 30 million jobs must be created by 1970 to offset technological displacement and to absorb the 26 million young workers who will be added to the labor force. If the total economy continues to open new jobs at the present rate, unemployment will reach eleven million in 1970.

Corporate Profits

Side by side with rising unemployment are rising corporate profits. Largely because of automation, *productivity* (output per man-hour) increased 20.2% between 1956 and 1962. This means that private industry could produce more with fewer workers, thereby saving on labor costs. But the increase in workers' purchasing power in this period was only 15.2%. As Figure 5 shows, the disparity is even greater for manufacturing workers, many of whom are Negroes.

Thus the cost savings resulting from higher productivity have not been passed on to the consumer through lower prices or to workers through commensurately higher wages. They have gone into corporate profits, which reached a record $26.8 billion after taxes in the second quarter of last year.

FIGURE 5: LAG OF REAL WAGES BEHIND ADVANCING PRODUCTIVITY

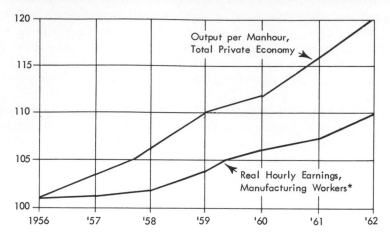

*Hourly earnings, including payroll fringe benefits, adjusted for changes in the Consumer Price Index. Earnings figures exclude non-payroll fringes, such as pension and health-welfare plans.
Source: U.S. Bureau of Labor Statistics.

This imbalance in our economy is revealed even more dramatically in Figure 6. In the past ten years, the rise of personal income has lagged far behind the cash-flow to corporations.

One result of this trend is the growing concentration of the nation's wealth in fewer hands. The share held by the richest 1% grew from 24.2% in 1953 to 28% in 1961; the number of millionaires leaped from 27,000 to 100,000. Meanwhile, the share of the 60% of all families at the bottom of the economic ladder has gone down.

FIGURE 6: LAG IN RISE OF PERSONAL INCOME BEHIND
CASH FLOW TO CORPORATIONS 1953-1963.

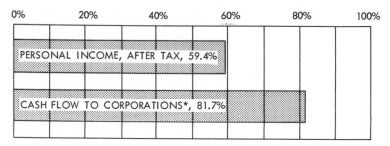

* Corporate profits and depreciation allowances after payment of all costs, taxes, and rising dividends to stockholders.
Source: U.S. Department of Commerce

Production Lag

Because real wages have not kept pace with productivity and profit, the ability of consumers to purchase goods and services has fallen behind our capacity to produce those goods and services. One way to prevent inadequate purchasing power from putting the brakes on production would be to produce at maximum capacity and distribute goods and services on the basis of need. Our economic system is based on production for profit, however, and production has therefore been limited to the demands of the market. Corporate profits keep soaring because many large corporations can do better by maintaining high profit margins on a smaller volume of production than by lowering margins in hopes of raising volume.

The overall result, as Figure 7 shows, is a growing gap between actual and potential national production. This gap between the economy's actual performance and its growing potential to produce amounted to $63 billion in 1963. Were it not for our "permanent war economy"—which does not produce goods for use—the gap would be even greater. In any case, this untapped reservoir of wealth, if exploited in the interest of the society at large, could go a long way toward lifting living standards, improving education and health facilities, clearing slums, and reducing poverty.

There is every reason to believe that the gap between actual and potential production will widen in the years ahead as automation boosts

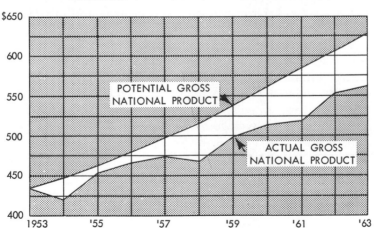

FIGURE 7: GROWING GAP BETWEEN ACTUAL AND POTENTIAL NATIONAL PRODUCTION (in billions of 1962 dollars)

AFL–CIO Estimate
Source: Council of Economic Affairs and AFL–CIO Research Department

productivity. Furthermore, it is unlikely that social altruism will dethrone the profit motive in the private economy and prompt decisions to close the gap by increasing production for the purpose of waging war on poverty. It is equally unlikely that a private economy characterized by high profits and high unemployment can undertake a "Marshall Plan" that would substantially improve the living conditions of the majority of Negroes. This is a social responsibility. It rests with government, which is ultimately entrusted with the national welfare. The exercise of this responsibility is therefore a political, not a private, decision.*

Marginal Industries, Low Wages, and High Risks
Gus Tyler
International Ladies' Garment Workers Union

[Reprinted with permission from Dissent, *Summer 1961.]*

THE SOURCES OF POVERTY are generally sought among the unemployed and the low-income unorganized. Virtually no attention is paid to the poor who are employed and who are members of unions. The assumption is that if you have a job and are covered by a union contract, you are a part of the affluent society. Yet there are several million workers in America who, though the beneficiaries of union contracts, should be counted among the poor; indeed, many of them are fully employed yet "on relief."

Attention has been diverted from these "unionized" poor by a normal public interest in the titans of our economy: steel, auto, rubber, transportation, oil. In these basic industries, the hourly wage—especially the union wage—runs high. (The term "high" here does not compare these "wages" with those in professional and administrative categories but with the average blue or white collar worker.) Much of the public knows very little, if anything, about the millions of workers in light industry, service trades, small retail establishments and offices; the news stories about steel and auto contracts create an impression about how every union worker lives. This mis-impression is height-

---

* This does not mean that private enterprise can play no role in a domestic "Marshall Plan." It can play an important role in housing, for example. But government priming and leadership in setting goals is essential.

ened by constant reference to how the contracts in these basic industries "set the pattern" for American labor.

The truth is there is no such pattern. Nor can there be. Two unions, like those in steel and auto, may vie with and copy one another because they operate in two industries that are of the same genre. But it would be impossible for a union of restaurant workers to win a General Motors contract or a union of lampshade workers to win a United States Can Corporation contract. The economics of the differing industries prohibits imitation. Hence, the notion that steel, auto or communications workers—the employees of Midas-like oligopolies such as United States Steel, General Motors or American Telephone and Telegraph—set the format for life among the unionized workers of America is totally false.

While the nature of union leadership in the different industries—militancy, bargaining skill, degree of organization—has considerable meaning, a major determinant in deciding what a union gets for employees from an industry depends upon the economics of the industry. Three high-wage unions—auto, steel, and the International Brotherhood of Electrical Workers—have leadership of divergent, sometimes contrary, style; but they all get good cash results—largely, because of the character of their industries. On the other hand, there are unions with aggressive, shrewd, knowledgeable leadership operating in industries with a high percentage of organization whose "wage package" to their members is often embarrassingly modest. And again, a major determinant is the state of the trade.

In an economy where at the commanding heights "free trade" has had to yield to consideration of capital and administered prices, there still are large sectors—probably employing a majority of the wage earners in the private portion of America's economy—that run as Adam Smith thought a system of free enterprise should or does run. Twenty-five per cent of the workers in the United States are in manufacturing establishments employing less than one hundred workers and a majority in establishments with less than five hundred. These are the sectors where competition flourishes, where entry into business is easy, where work is relatively simple, where industry profit margins are tiny, but where the workers—attached to the same employer for many years and covered by a union contract—must turn to the Department of Public Welfare to feed their families.

Where there is a concentration of such competitive industry in any one spot—such as New York—we discover an industrial Appalachia, a sector of poverty in the richest city in the world. Why do certain products and certain stages of production gravitate into the metropolitan region? If you view manufacture as part art and part muscle, part inspiration and part perspiration, part invention and part repetition, part diversity and part uniformity, then those portions of manufacture that are arty, inspirational, inventive and diverse, tend to seek out and stick to the cities. And those portions that are muscular, sweaty, repetitious and uniform, tend to locate outside the metropolitan region. Put differently, the unstandardized products and operations are city dwellers; the standardized work seeks the wider open spaces.

A summary statement of *Made in New York*, a study of the garment, printing publications and electronics industries in the metropolitan area, states this central thesis:

> In all three (industries), the activities which took most readily to the Region tended to be activities resulting in products whose characteristics could not be accurately anticipated—products, that is, which were unstandardized. . . . The making of [such] products required materials and labor and services that were not easily determined in advance. . . . Dresses subject to style changes, for example, have changing inputs of design, fabrics, dyes, tailorwork, buttons and finishing touches. . . . Uncertainty over the product and the inputs causes a manufacturing establishment to need flexibility. Uncertainty over the "volume" of output has a similar effect. Establishments for which uncertainty is a normal part of life cannot generally achieve a high degree of self-sufficiency. Rubbing elbows with others of their kind and with ancillary firms that exist to serve them, they can satisfy their variable wants by drawing upon common pools of space-labor, materials and services. In more concise language, they can take advantage of "external" economies.[1]

This thesis contains a large grain of truth. A "schmooes" at lunch time on the corner of 7th Avenue and 38th Street is as vital to a cloak and suiter as a Madison Avenue address to an ad agency. Styles to steal are as vital to the dress house as voluminous photo agencies to the huckster. Talent and taste, brains and brass, services and servicemen, gossip and gospel, museums and libraries and schools, speed and spark and specialists are at the core of these industries. These compose the external economies, the big come-ons for New York.

But the argument of *Made in New York* is *not* the whole truth. New York has "internal" economies to offer: space and—sadly—cheap labor. This tawdry aspect of the New York economy is somewhat obscured by the book's emphasis on the city as a high-wage center. Actu-

---

[1] *Made in New York:* Case Studies in Metropolitan Manufacturing, by Roy B. Helfgott, W. Eric Gustafson, James M. Hund. Edited by Max Hall. Cambridge, Mass.: Harvard University Press, 1959.

ally, it ranks 19th among America's cities in terms of wages. Alongside the men of talent and taste, the hucksters and the artists, there is in the metropolitan area a great reservoir of low-paid, unskilled laborers—and for this there are many reasons.

First, New York is still a port of entry for migrants and immigrants. The greatest waves in recent decades have been the Negro and Puerto Rican. While few of these have found their way into the skilled trades of printing and publishing, great hordes have come to garment manufacture and electronics. Thousands have turned to the service trades, culinary trades, hotels, hospitals, etc. And, like all other newcomers, they compose a low-wage group until such time as they learn skills, the language, and the cultural ropes.

Second, these newcomers tend to settle in ghettoes—by choice or necessity—and to create pockets of cheap labor. Light industry entrepreneurs (and New York City manufacture is predominantly light industry) tend to set up shop in the midst of or within walking distance of these newcomer communities. They reach out for unskilled, often female, labor—offering a special inducement in the form of proximity, late arrival, early departure, and minimal penalties for days off when family life becomes demanding. In exchange, these women work for sub-standard wages.

Third, these light industries producing easily transportable commodities face national—and international—competition. Low wages are paralleled by narrow profit margins, high seasonality, recurrent bankruptcies. These industries are marginal, living on marginal populations, constantly threatened by the even more marginal sectors of the same trade living in even more marginal cultures. The marginal and savagely competitive character of these trades places self-executing limits on union contracts. A high-wage contract, strictly enforced, sometimes means automatic bankruptcy.

Fourth, New York City is not a center of basic industry in which wage levels are relatively high even for unskilled and semiskilled labor. Hence, these industries do not offer competition in New York for the available labor supply. In basic industries, wages tend to be higher for three reasons: (a) management can establish "administered" prices; (b) the labor factor is relatively small as part of total cost because operations tend to be highly mechanized and automated; (c) the plant cannot duck and dodge and disappear and reappear to play an endless game of cat and mouse with union organizers. In a city such as Cleveland, with its huge heavy industry plants, light industry of a highly competitive character with a high labor ingredient in its ultimate cost finds it almost impossible to flourish.

The problem of the *marginal* worker arises in no small part from the fact that his marginal industry exists in an economy alongside of oligopolies. These latter can administer prices; the former cannot. The latter can guarantee or enlarge their share of the consumer dollar; the former cannot. The latter can afford higher wages because the basic cost is in equipment, plant and materials rather than in labor; the former cannot afford the same high wages because the profit margin is close, because labor is often a major cost factor, and because the end product is in fierce national and international competition. Finally, the basic industry, highly automated with its uniformity of product, can rapidly increase its productivity year after year, while the smaller industries are often compelled to operate for decades under a compromised economy precisely because they turn out small lots of diversified goods.

Just as small industry must lose out to oligopoly in the struggle for the market so, too, must the worker in the competitive, mobile, low-profit trades lose his standing relative to the worker in the mechanized, immobile, high-profit industries. An understanding of the differing positions of competitive and non-competitive industries, of non-automated and automated industries in our economy, explains the curious wage paradox of New York: *a high-wage city that ranks nineteenth among cities in the nation.*

In a given industry, such as dresses, coats, toys, novelties, dolls, plastics, the New York wage generally tops the national wage, thanks to the work of unions in these nationally competitive, traditionally sweatshop trades. But the vast number of service trades in New York lower the wage level first because these sectors of the economy generally lag behind manufacturing and secondly, because a sizable portion of income in these trades consists of tips and meals rather than wages. Even where the New York wage in services tops other parts of the country, again because of unionization, the high proportion of workers in such trades in the metropolitan region tends to depress the city average.

Thus New York represents a high-wage sector of certain national industries and trades, but because of the metropolitan "mix," the relatively light sprinkling of heavy, automated, non-competitive industry, New York appears to rank low. This explains the continuing debate as to whether the metropolis is a high-wage or a low-wage area. The answer is that New York is both—the high-wage *end* of *low-wage industries and trades.*

In most discussions of wages in America, only the average earnings of workers are considered. A more realistic approach, however, must differentiate between the wages of workers in mechanized monopoly industries and in wage-oriented competitive industries. It is the workers in these latter industries who pose the problem of indigence even in the midst of an "affluent society" and who make up a major part of that one-fifth of the nation that is still ill-fed, ill-clothed, and ill-housed.

A primary step in relieving the oppressive poverty of this one-fifth of the nation (not confined to the South but all too present in the streets of our greatest metropolis) is to raise the Federal minimum wage and to extend its coverage to the millions of workers who are not included under the present provisions. A national statute would establish a firm base on which to erect a higher wage in areas that offer "external economies" to the manufacturer. Unions could then negotiate more rewarding contracts because the wage differential between union and non-union areas would be offset by the advantages of the metropolitan climate.

A second step is to encourage rather than discourage unionization outside the already well organized areas like New York. Federal (or state) legislation or court actions which hinder union organizing efforts in the generally unorganized sectors of the nation not only keep wage levels low in these sectors but depress wage levels nationally. Lack of unionization in Mississippi or Georgia directly affects earnings in Brooklyn and the Bronx. Actually, the South is merely the most militant and effective spokesman for a "rural" point of view that acts as a nineteenth-century drag on a twentieth-century civilization, as an agrarian weight around the neck of the metropolis.

A third step is to use governmental power to tax the more affluent sector of the society to care for the needs of the less affluent. The twenty-five percent profit return on original investment not uncommon in steel and autos as contrasted with the one percent profit in garments does not derive from an inherent virtue of metal over fabrics, but from the monopoly character of the former and the competitive character of the latter. The workers in the latter industries suffer although many of them possess skills as great or even greater than those required in the basic industries. If the products created by low-paid workers are vital to our society—such commodities, for example, as food, fibres, wood, tubes, bulbs, transistors, dresses, overalls, shoes, gloves, and diapers—then society has no right to victimize these workers because their industries are competitive and defy automation.

While part of this redistribution of wealth can be accomplished locally or regionally—through local minimum wage laws, housing, medical services—the ultimate solution must be national, because the root of the problem is not local but national. This will help the forgotten men, a good many of them in New York City, of our allegedly affluent society.

The Condition of Farm Workers

Fay Bennett

National Sharecroppers Fund

[Excerpted from the 1963, 1964 Annual Reports of the National Sharecroppers Fund with permission from the Fund.]

AMERICAN AGRICULTURE ought to be the greatest success story in the whole historical saga of the United States as a land of wealth and opportunity. In 1910, one American farm worker could produce enough food and fiber to meet the needs of seven people. The next half-century saw a continuous rise in the national standard of living, and by 1963, when the average American was consuming a great deal more, a single farm worker could produce enough for nearly 28 persons.

Yet when pockets of poverty in our affluent society are uncovered, the largest single area of distress turns out to be the farm economy. Nearly half of the nation's 3,300,000 farm families have incomes below $3,000. Probably three-fourths of the 800,000 rural families whose chief income is from wages live below the poverty level.

As productivity per worker has soared, two things have happened: First, far fewer workers are needed. Second, the capitalization costs of these technical productive miracles are rising beyond the reach of many present and potential farm owners. Farm workers and working farmers alike are being displaced.

Concentration of Control: Wealth vs. Poverty

There were 5.4 million farms in 1950. These were reduced to 4.8 million in 1954; to 3.7 million in 1959. Between 1959 and 1960 an estimated 370,000 more, involving over a million people, have given up. Two-thirds (about two million) of the families who stayed on their farms earned less than $1,000 a year from both farm and nonfarm work.

Only 21.5% of U. S. farms have sales of $10,000 or more, which the Department of Agriculture estimates will return a minimum family income of $2,500. But it takes $4,000 "to place the multi-person family above poverty in the American context today," according to the Conference on Economic Progress and other authorities. At the other end, only 2.7% of the farms have sales of $40,000 or more. They control 20% of all farm land and 14% of all cropland harvested, and profit from more than 30% of all farm products sold.

Greatest Poverty in the South

About one out of every six Southern farm operators is Negro. Less than one-third own or even rent their own farms; about 40% are sharecroppers, and the rest are tenant farmers.

The average size white-operated commercial farm in the South is about 382 acres; the average non-white commercial farm, 56 acres. The average value of land and buildings is $37,816 for whites, and $7,328 for non-whites. The average value of products sold is $10,396 for whites and $3,029 for non-whites. Displacement, greater in the South than elsewhere, is proportionately greater among Negro farmers. In the last decade the South has lost half its Negro-operated farms. The number of tenants, both Negro and white, dropped about 45% and the number of sharecroppers about 55 per cent.

Declining Work Opportunities

The decline in the number of farms in this century has been continuous. In the decade 1950–60 alone, the number dropped from 5.4 million to 3.7 million. A third of those who made their living on the land had to turn elsewhere. The decline in the number of hired workers tells a different story. While their number dropped from 3.4 million in 1910 to 1.8 in 1962, their role in the total farm work force rose from 24.9 to 27.3 per cent, as independent farmers, tenants, and sharecroppers became hired workers on the large corporate farms that have developed.

The number of migrants is never known with exactness, but it is declining each year. The official 1962 estimate (probably much too low) was about 380,000, plus half that many foreign contract workers. How many children travel with the recognized workers is not known either, but it may be double their number. Somewhere between a million and a million and a half people still follow the crops each year.

Income

Hired farm laborers, excluding casual workers and those who worked less than 25 days, averaged 137 days of work. Their average annual cash wage from farm and nonfarm work together was only $1,164 in 1962, the last year for which figures are available. If all farm wage workers are included, the average—even including nonfarm work—drops to $896. Migrants averaged 116 days of work, and their average annual earnings from both farm and nonfarm work were $1,123.

The one worker in eight who found full-time work (250 days or more) averaged $2,094 in earnings, while the average annual income of the factory worker was $5,021. While manufacturing wages have increased about 50 per cent and farm wage rates about 30 per cent in the last ten years, the cash increase for factory workers has been just over 75 cents an hour, that of farm workers just under 25 cents.

The farm worker's security is depressed further by the fact that he has no unemployment insurance and usually no accident or disability insurance, and he is often denied local social services because of insufficient residence time.

Mechanization and Unemployment

The greatest decline in work opportunities last year was again in cotton. It is hard to distinguish between underemployment and unemployment, but the manpower of between one-quarter and one-half million persons is being replaced. In cotton, as in many other crops, this is due not only to the mechanization of harvesting, when the peak number of workers is used. It also includes use of chemicals and other agents (such as geese) to destroy weeds; this cuts off work in another part of the year.

The very size and shape of our fruits and vegetables is under continuous adaptation to meet the needs of the developing harvest machines. The list seems endless. Cranberries are now 95 per cent mechanized and so are snap beans in most states. Tomatoes and cucumbers are two or three years away from complete mechanization. An electric fan which blows grapefruit from trees was 99 per cent successful in tests; if leaf damage does not hurt next year's crop, grapefruit will be almost entirely mechanically picked within two years. In every part of the country and in nearly every crop, the advance is steady.

Each change eliminates some farm jobs. In 1962, 271,000 farm workers reported their major occupation as "unemployment." Many of these displaced workers are settling in sprawling rural fringes of the cities to seek nonfarm work, which becomes more scarce all the time. The number of unskilled jobs in the national economy is steadily declining, and farm workers have less of the educational qualifications necessary for acquiring new skills than any other group in the country. The median years of school completed by male farm workers 18 years and older was 7.7 in 1959, not significantly more than the 7.6 it had been twenty years before. Of adult migrants 25 years and older, 34 per cent have had less than five years' schooling, and their children are repeating the cycle.

Migrant Children

The most neglected children of America, it was reported at April, 1963, hearings on farm worker legislation, are those 50,000 migrant children who are six years old and less. Too young to work in the fields (although some are so employed at the age of 5 or 6), they are either left locked up in the shack that serves as home, perhaps in the care of a scarcely older child, or taken to the fields to sleep in trucks or play in the dust under a blazing sun.

At least another hundred thousand children of school age follow the crops with their parents. The Fair Labor Standards Act provides a 16-year minimum age for their employment in agriculture during school hours but no minimum age outside of school hours. Local crop and harvest "vacations" make it legal to bring them out of the classroom at peak seasons. Yet the Department of Labor, with limited inspection facilities, found 6,712 children illegally employed in the fields in 1962. Of those who were migrants, 72 per cent were below their normal school grade.

Housing and Health

Rural America has almost three times the proportion of dilapidated houses as urban America. Shelter for seasonal workers often does not approach the classification "houses." While 39 states have a peak employment of more than 1,000 seasonal farm workers, only 29 states have laws setting any standards for labor camps or similar farm housing. These range from limited to comprehensive coverage of sanitation, housing, location, and construction. The degree of inspection and enforcement also leaves much to be desired.

Testimony submitted in October, 1963, as the result of investigations by the Bureau of Labor Standards, indicated that many farm workers still must work and live in shocking conditions. In a midwestern state,

> The first camp visited consisted of a group of six city buses and a trailer located in the middle of a field in the hot sun with no shade . . . no water of any kind was available in the camp itself. Water was hauled in a large garbage-type can from a long distance; garbage and waste were collected in uncovered cans within 15 feet of the bus, which had no screens of any kind.

In a southwestern state,

> The camp was found to have no hot water for bathing, improper drainage, and fire hazards. In other camps the investigator found stagnant water around outside spigots, bath water seeping into a nearby well, screens in need of repair, and doors, floors, and seats from outside toilets missing.

The American Public Health Association has testified:

Crowded, unsanitary, and insect- and rodent-infested housing accommodations increase the likelihood of enteric and communicable diseases. Crowded living quarters are conducive to the spread of tuberculosis, a disease found in inordinate amount among migrants and their families. Unscreened, filthy housing brings an automatic toll of debilitating and disabling illness. To this can be added the complication and attendant problems borne by lack of water and sanitation facilities; namely, acute dysentery and dehydration.

Not enough attention has yet been given to the dangers involved in the increasing use of chemicals for weed and crop-disease control. Reports to the California State Health Department indicate that between 1950 and 1961, 3,040 farm workers in that state were poisoned by pesticides and other farm chemicals; 22 workers and 63 children died from this cause.

Accidents

In the latest report of the National Safety Council, agriculture is still third, after mining and construction, in death rates per 100,000 workers in work-related accidents. The rate is 60 per 100,000, up from 54 in 1952. The actual figure for agriculture is higher: 3,100 deaths compared with 2,400 in construction and 700 in mining. Despite this record of mechanized agriculture as one of the most hazardous of occupations, only seven states require workmen's compensation for agricultural, as for industrial, workers.

Legislation

A primary reason for deplorable conditions among farm workers is their continued exclusion from the benefits of social legislation that most American workers enjoy. Some of them are now covered by Old Age Assistance and Survivors Insurance; and the Migrant Health Act is the beginning of the extension of health services to them.

Eleven farm labor bills were introduced in the first session of the 88th Congress. Six were passed by the Senate but not by the House. They dealt with assistance to states for education of migrant children; day-care services for migrant children; regulation of child labor outside of school hours; registration of crew leaders; aid to employers for construction of sanitary facilities; and establishment of a national advisory council on migratory labor. Neither House has completed action on three other bills: two would aid in farm labor housing; the third would provide a Voluntary Farm Employment Service for recruiting, training, placing, and transporting agricultural workers.

Two urgently needed measures, extending to farm workers the minimum wage and the right to collective bargaining, are buried in Congressional committees with no hearings scheduled.

Federal Farm Benefits

The claim that extension of protective labor legislation to cover farm workers would be ruinous to the nation's small farmers falls before an examination of who hires farm labor and who benefits now under federal programs. In fact, only 5 per cent of the nation's farmers pay $2,000 a year or more in farm wages. Small farmers have to compete in the market with the produce of the agricultural giants, and their incomes are depressed by the low wages of the corporation farms.

The agricultural giants benefit disproportionately from federal farm subsidies. Seventy per cent of all cotton farmers are small farmers whose allotment is 10 acres or less; the average subsidy they received in 1961 amounted to about $60 for the year. At the same time, 322 farmers had allotments of 1,000 acres or more; their average subsidy was $133,657 each. Two great corporations received more than $2,000,000 each; and the 13 farms with allotments above 5,000 acres averaged $649,753 in subsidy. Small farmers cannot afford to cut their acreage; large farmers profit exorbitantly by doing so.

Despite increasing public awareness of the problem of poverty in America, the needs of the sharecropper, the small farmer, the migrant, and other farm workers and low-income rural people continue to be neglected. The job of speaking out for them remains urgent.

Selected Bibliography

1. A. A. Berle. *American Economic Republic.* New York: Harcourt, Brace and World, 1963.

2. Conference on Economic Progress. *The Toll of Rising Interest Rates: The One Great Waste in the Federal Budget.* Washington: The Conference, 1964.

3. Herbert Hill. "Racial Inequality in Employment: The Patterns of Discrimination," *Annals of the American Academy of Political and Social Science,* February, 1965.

4. Gabriel Kolko. *Wealth and Power in America: An Analysis of Social Class and Income Distribution.* New York: Praeger, 1962.

5. Donald Michael. *Cybernation: The Silent Conquest.* Santa Barbara: Center for the Study of Democratic Institutions, 1962.

6. S. M. Miller. "The Politics of Poverty," *Dissent,* Spring, 1964.

7. Gunnar Myrdal. *Challenge to Affluence.* New York: Pantheon, 1962.

8. Bernard Nossiter. *The Mythmakers: An Essay in Power and Wealth.* Boston: Houghton-Mifflin, 1964.

9. *Nation's Manpower Revolution.* Hearings Before the Subcommittee on Manpower and Employment of the Committee on Labor and Public Welfare, United States Senate, Pts. I–X and Subcommittee Report, 1963–64.

10. National Advisory Committee on Farm Labor. *Agribusiness and Its Workers.* New York: The Committee, 1964.

11. Arthur M. Ross. *Unemployment and the American Economy.* New York: Wiley, 1964.

12. Tax Foundation. *Allocation of the Tax Burden by Income Class.* New York: The Foundation, 1960.

13. Richard M. Titmuss. *Income Distribution and Social Change.* George Allen and Unwin, London, 1962.

14. Don Villarejo. "Stock Ownership and Control of American Corporations," *New University Thought,* Pts. I, II, III, 1961.

15. Arnold R. Weber. "The Rich and the Poor: Employment in An Age of Automation," *Social Service Review,* 37 (September, 1963).

16. William Appelman Williams. *The Great Evasion.* Chicago: Quadrangle Press, 1964.

17. Carl Wittman and Tom Hayden. *An Interracial Movement of the Poor.* Ann Arbor, Mich.: Economic Research and Action Project, 1964.

Chapter 4

Sustaining Conditions of Poverty

There remains an unseen America, a land of limited opportunity and restricted choice. In it live nearly 10 million families who try to find shelter, feed and clothe their children, stave off disease and malnutrition, and somehow build a better life on less than $60 a week. Almost two-thirds of these families struggle to get along on less than $40 a week.

These are the people behind the American looking glass. There are nearly 35 million of them. Being poor is not a choice for these millions; it is a rigid way of life. It is handed down from generation to generation in a cycle of inadequate education, inadequate homes, inadequate jobs, and stunted ambitions. It is a peculiar axiom of poverty that the poor are poor because they earn little, and they also earn little because they are poor. For the rebel who seeks a way out of this closed cycle, there is little help. The communities of the poor generally have the poorest schools, the scarcest opportunities for training. The poor citizen lacks organization, endures sometimes arbitrary impingement on his rights by courts and law enforcement agencies; cannot make his protest heard or has stopped protesting. A spirit of defeatism often pervades his life and remains the only legacy for his children.

If the American economy can be compared to a 20-story luxury apartment house where even the ground floor tenants share the comforts, then this one-fifth of our population inhabits a sub-basement, out of sight, and almost out of mind.

—From "The War on Poverty," A Congressional Presentation, March 17, 1964, prepared under the direction of Sargent Shriver, special assistant to the President.

THE POOR ARE CAUGHT UP in what Alvin Schorr, in *Slums and Social Insecurity*, has called "a syndrome of mutually reinforcing handicaps." On a day-to-day basis a poor person faces a vicious cycle of disabling circumstances in the way social and economic institutions are conceived, developed, and operated.

By the sustaining conditions of poverty, we are referring to the institutional structures and social relationships in American society that prevent the poor from gaining access to adequate financial resources and social rewards. There are at least five such factors in our society that act to sustain poverty: (1) ecological and demographic trends; (2) the limited opportunity structure for the poor; (3) patterns of racial discrimination; (4) deficiencies in community resources for the poor; and (5) agency-client relationships.

One: Ecological and Demographic Trends

One of the most pronounced trends in the last twenty years has been the "suburban drift." The affluent have fled the cities in ever greater numbers to live in the suburbs. The results of this movement have been deeply felt by the poor who remain in the core of urban areas. First, a reduced tax base limits the educational investment of the community. Deteriorated school facilities, inadequate supplies, ill-equipped or unqualified teaching staffs handicap the children who need special educational resources.

The spatial ghettoization of the poor is a second consequence of this suburban drift. Indeed, the poor may be so physically and socially distant that for all practical purposes they are invisible. Their social participation patterns are sharply limited. Their children grow up in a social environment lacking the educational, recreational, and social advantages offered to children of higher income families.

Urban renewal patterns also help reinforce the financial problems of the poor. Slum clearance programs have replaced the slum dwellings of the poor with higher-cost housing which low-income families can't afford. The poor are concentrated in ever-shrinking land areas of slum housing. Urban renewal may also mean an uprooting of the poverty-stricken from their familiar social and physical environment into new neighborhoods among strangers where housing may be more expensive and where living conditions may be more crowded and disorganized than ever before.

Two: the Opportunity Structure for the Poor

Poverty is also sustained by a limited opportunity structure for those persons who have inadequate incomes. The undereducated, the under-skilled, the Negro and the aged worker are at a competitive disadvantage in the labor market. They must accept the job opportunities that have been rejected by others—unstable, low-paying work which is generally unprotected by the institutional safeguards of better paying jobs. Many of these jobs are economically exploitive; some of them easily lend themselves to mechanization or automation with the result that even this meager opportunity structure for the marginal worker in low-paid employment is shrinking, making predictability in economic and social life difficult, if not impossible.

Three: Patterns of Racial Discrimination

About twenty-five percent of the poverty-stricken are members of minority groups. Their exclusion from the economic and social opportunities of the society needs no documentation. The Negro, for example, may be denied entrance to the job, or training for the job, or residence in an area where jobs are available. The opening of new plants with job opportunities in a suburban area does the Negro, or Spanish-American, or Puerto Rican little good if he is residentially chained to the center city ghetto where travel to a distant job involves heavy costs in transportation time and money. The perseverance of these patterns of discriminatory practices reinforces the poverty of the minority group member and hampers his movement toward full participation in the society.

Four: Deficiencies in Community Resources for the Poor

The poor are not only deficient in money, but also in obtaining the special resources of the community. This process is most strikingly seen in their lack of access to adequate medical care, housing, credit, and legal aid.

Health: United States National Health Survey statistics have shown that the poor get sick more frequently, take longer to recover, seek and receive less medical, dental, and hospital treatment, and suffer far more disabling consequences than persons with higher incomes. One reason is that persons with incomes under $4,000 spend half as much money on medical care than those in the higher income brackets. Yet, four times the number of people in the lower income group find their major activities limited by chronic ailments than do persons with family incomes over $7,000.

The poor can't afford adequate health protection. Only one-third of families with incomes under $2,000 have health insurance compared with three-quarters of all American families. The hospitalization rate for poor Negroes is twenty times lower than for the population as a whole. Unequal access to medical care is reflected in the higher morbidity and mortality rates in low-income states and in low-income neighborhoods of major cities. For example, one-third of the pregnant women in cities with populations over 100,000 are medically indigent, a 1962 United States Health, Education and Welfare study revealed. Increasing numbers receive little or no prenatal care although prenatal care is a major preventable cause of premature births and mental retardation. Reflecting the high concentration of poverty, four times as many Negro as white women die in childbirth.

Recent studies have also shown that mental illness is often a product of the strains and stresses of poverty. Robert E. Clark found in 1949 that unskilled and semi-skilled workers were six times more likely to be hospitalized for psychoses than professional or managerial personnel. In *Social Class and Mental Illness* (New York: John Wiley & Sons, Inc., 1958), Hollingshead and Redlich found that three times as many persons in the poorest group studied in New Haven, Connecticut, had psychiatric illnesses than did persons in upper income groups. Yet three times as much money had been spent on the mentally ill at the top of the income ladder than on those at the bottom rung.

Overcrowded and inefficient public clinics, vast and impersonal city hospitals, understaffed and overpopulated mental institutions—all of these compound the suffering of the low-income ill. Having the breadwinner become sick or disabled is a tragedy in any family, but for the poor, unprotected by savings and medical insurance, it may be a disaster.

Housing: Lack of access to good housing also sustains poverty. In *The Other America,* Michael Harrington has written, "The slum, with its dense life, hammers away at the individual. . . . It is as if human beings dilapidate along with the tenements in which they live." Rentals for slum housing are frequently higher than the rent paid by higher income groups for better housing. But beyond that, better housing may be closed to the poor because of discrimination—racial discrimination against non-whites and, in addition, social discrimination against the life styles of the poor, black or white.

Slum housing problems are also aggravated by the problems of absentee ownership. The slum landlord reaps a high return on his property due to the high demand for his facilities and his low investment in maintaining even adequate living conditions. Few of the poor ever get to see the owners of their homes; the insensitivity of the rental agent to their problems is widely known.

The poor may pay for their housing by sacrificing quality and accepting minimum living standards, or by living with other family units to extend their housing budgets, or by borrowing money from other budget items. The end result is the same: the development of a complex web that makes it increasingly difficult for the poor to leave not only the slums, but the complex net of poverty in which they are caught.

Credit: Failure to gain access to reliable commercial credit sources may also keep the poor in a state of financial crisis. In the area of purchasing power, people with inadequate incomes face formidable obstacles in getting even normal value out of the little money they have. They become poorer for the ironic reason that they don't have ~nough money.

Lacking the ready cash to shop at discount stores, and lacking the stable employment records to open charge accounts at large downtown stores, most low-income families buy their durables from neighborhood dealers and door-to-door peddlers. These merchants frequently cover their risk of extending credit to low-income families by exorbitant markups on low-quality merchandise.

Dependent on credit, lacking shopping sophistication, the poor are more vulnerable to high pressure salesmen who attempt to convert them from cash to credit customers. Their shopping difficulties are compounded by other merchandising practices: bait advertising, erroneous information about costs or credit charges, faulty or repossessed merchandise sold to them as new. As a result, many low-income families encounter serious consumer difficulties: legal pressures because of missed payments, repossession of goods, garnishment of salary or threats of garnishment. Their heavy credit obligations may reach crisis proportions when their income is suddenly reduced through unemployment or ill health. Certainly, the failure to establish reliable commercial credit prevents the poverty-stricken from obtaining adequate goods and services.

Legal aid: The poor are also disadvantaged in their access to legal services. As United States Attorney General Nicholas Katzenbach stated in a recent government conference on legal aid for the poor, "For a poor person to hold rights in theory satisfies only the theory. . . . Unknown, unasserted rights are no rights at all."

Yet from the attitude of the corner policeman to the institutional maze of legal technicalities and details, the poor face a network of legal problems which frequently leads to unequal protection of their individual freedom, curtailment of their social entitlements, and unequal access to the protection of law. Lack of knowledge of their legal prerogatives and lack of legal aid compound their legal problems. In turn, this increases their vulnerability to fines, garnishments, jailings, and other sanctions of the law which further reduces their income through suspensions, firings, and even blacklisting from the chances of getting a steady job.

Thousands whose public assistance is revoked or reduced have no ideas of their legal rights of appeal. Large numbers must honor contract obligations with finance companies even though the merchandise for which they pay has never been delivered or fails to work. Many have their purchases repossessed after months of payment with no idea that they are entitled to get their equity returned.

It has been pointed out that there are two legal systems in family law—one for those with money, and one for those without. A poor person who applies to a legal aid society for help in obtaining a divorce must frequently follow the agency's prescribed procedures to attempt a marital reconciliation. Persons who have money may just hire a lawyer and get a divorce.

Professor Monroe G. Paulsen of Columbia University Law School told a recent government conference on legal aid to the poor, "It seems rather too bad to require something of indigents that is not required of those with means. . . . This kind of notion, I believe, runs through a great many of the legal institutions which the poor must use. . . . To me, however, it is an unhappy thought because it contributes to what I believe to be one of the most difficult aspects of dealing with poverty: the existence of an attitude on the part of the poor that they are clients rather than citizens, an attitude unhappily reflected in the minds of many who deal with them."

Thus there are many deficiencies in access to community services. The very access that the higher income groups take for granted may involve either a closed door or a long wait for the poor. Invariably, the poor may have to accept inferior substitutes for these services, or go without.

Five: Agency-Client Relationships

The poverty-stricken are related to the society through a network of contacts with social agencies that offer specialized services to the poor (e.g., child care centers, family service agencies, legal aid societies, and public welfare agencies). There are two apparent handicaps to these agency-client relationships which block avenues of aid to the poor in their efforts to cope with problems of poverty. First, inadequate financial resources and personnel limit the amount of resources an agency can offer to its clients. Social work agencies compete with a network of other interest groups for a share of the charity dollar. All too often, the formula for distributing community charity money is outdated; frequently, agencies that are *relatively* unimportant in poverty reduction obtain the lion's share of community financial resources. In addition, the resources needed to meet the complex and heterogeneous needs of the poverty problem are not easily understood. The result is that funding for agency services to the poor tends to fall ,short of that needed for adequate personnel and programs.

A second handicap to good agency-client relationships is the pessimism and bureaucratic rigidity that overwhelms many of these social agencies. For example, the case worker in a welfare agency is frequently overworked, underpaid, and undertrained. His case load, which may range from two hundred to three hundred clients, may include a mixture of the indigent, the aged, ADC mothers, and special problem cases. As a result, the agency may indirectly foster the development of *structured dependency* from their clients. Activities of the poor may be controlled and monitored for more efficient record-keeping purposes and these efforts may take precedence over other service and rehabilitation activities that could help the client to more effectively handle his problems. In such a climate, the client is intentionally or unintentionally encouraged to be dependent on the agency worker and to accept his judgment of the situation. Consequently, the poor may develop an attitude of pessimism or even hostility to the agency worker who may come to symbolize his frustrations and bitterness rather than to represent an avenue of help or the alleviation of basic problems.

These, then, are some of the major sustaining causes of poverty. There are others that could be briefly mentioned: the lag that inevitably occurs between the social needs of the poor and the legislation that develops to serve these needs; the lack of socially developed mechanisms to provide services to families or individuals making the transition from rural to urban areas; and finally, the perseverance of old social, economic, and educational institutions in the face of change. An elimination of the sustaining conditions of poverty will require a critical self-examination of American life, particularly those institutional structures and social relationships that directly and indirectly affect the poor.

In this chapter, Edwin J. Lukas explores the defaults of the society in safeguarding the civil rights of the poor and insuring their freedom from discrimination. David Caplovitz describes the many consumer problems faced by low-income customers in dealing with the marketing system in low-income areas. The relationship between housing codes, taxes, and substandard housing is analyzed by Alvin L. Schorr who also discusses the public and private dimensions in how the poor pay for their housing. Major urban school issues and some suggestions for their possible solution are reviewed by Patricia C. Sexton, and Samuel Mencher reassesses some of the basic issues in welfare philosophy, policies, and programs.

Social Welfare and the Rights of the Poor

Edwin J. Lukas

American Jewish Committee

[Reprinted from the monograph Social Welfare and the Rights of the Poor *by Edwin J. Lukas (New York, 1964) by permission of the American Jewish Committee.]*

THIS IS AN EFFORT to explore how we default in safeguarding the civil rights of the poor, and in insuring their freedom from discrimination. If all that results from such an exploration is an increased sense of out-rage among us, the effort will have been justified.

I begin with two basic assumptions: First, that the poor are entitled to enjoy precisely the same civil rights and liberties as others; and second, that the social-work profession is especially interested in, and concerned with, their protection. Those who quarrel with these assumptions will, of course, disagree with my conclusions. . . .

What we are discussing now is the economic underworld—that portion of our population whose more-or-less chronic status is that of the slum and ghetto dweller: the unskilled, the unemployed, the relief recipients, the out-of-wedlock mothers, the deserted families—in short, those millions of Americans who, for a host of reasons, depend on our society for life-giving aid.

It is my contention, and certainly not mine alone, that in addition to the plaguing, gnawing inability to push their individual or family incomes to the point of mere subsistence, these disadvantaged citizens are also shackled by the woefully inadequate protection of their civil rights.

I shall not attempt to catalogue all the urgent problems which confront the poor in their struggle to protect themselves from assaults upon their civil rights and political freedoms. Elizabeth Wickenden, Technical Consultant on Public Social Policy of the National Social Welfare Assembly, identifies primary constitutional guarantees which are often denied to persons distinguished from their fellows merely by their poverty. One is equal treatment under the law; another is free-dom of movement among the states; still another is the right of privacy. Then there are the more subtle discriminations: the charge of neglect which is applied far more rigidly to mothers whose children receive public assistance than to parents of children not receiving aid; and the special criminal or civil penalties applicable to mothers on welfare because of so-called "mismanagement" of their grants, quite aside from alleged fraud or neglect.

I should like to address myself particularly to several of these points. It is axiomatic by now that the indigent suffer more at the hands of our criminal courts than do the rich or the middle class. The vast majority of those who face long prison terms or even capital punishment, are impoverished defendants. The economically secure usually can avail themselves of experienced legal counsel to help them avoid harsh penalties. This advantage is nearly always denied the poor. Such a disparity in the administration of criminal justice is notorious, and cries out desperately for drastic remedial action. The U. S. Supreme Court ruled only recently, in the *Gideon* case, that every defendant charged with a criminal offense is entitled to the services of counsel.

Some people have advocated an extension of the public-defender system to give lawyers who defend the poor the funds and other facilities to match the facilities at the command of the prosecutor. Before the "equal protection of the law" and "due process" guaranteed to all in our Constitution can have real meaning, every defendant, regardless of his economic status, should be assured of equal accessibility to vital witnesses and other evidence, adequate medical and psychiatric advice, and other aids essential to a proper defense. It is my melancholy view that the public has been totally indifferent to the absence of these safeguards for impoverished defendants who brush with the law—even though many, if not most, of the individuals in question and their families are known to one or more public or private social agencies.

Nor is the defendant without means disadvantaged only with respect to major crime. As Supreme Court Justice Arthur J. Goldberg recently pointed out, the choice of a $100 fine or 30 days in jail is really no choice at all to the person who cannot raise $100. Moreover, thousands of persons languish in jail for months awaiting trial because they cannot post even modest bail. A society which continues to ignore these conditions cannot lay claim to the even-handed administration of criminal justice.

We come next to administrative assaults on the rights of the poor—frequently encountered by social workers in the course of their daily chores, particularly in the area of public welfare. The examples that follow were selected from many more that could be cited.

The progressively administered New York City Housing Authority, for example, has promulgated elaborate procedures concerning "non-desirability" of tenants, and methods of terminating such tenancies. Although an effort is made to provide the tenant with adequate rights of appeal, the criteria of "non-desirability" are subject to serious challenge.

According to the standards established by the Housing Authority, certain tenants may be classified as "clear and present danger cases," or they may be considered to represent "conditions indicative of potential problems." Tenants in the latter category may be asked to vacate because one or more members of the family have given birth to out-of-wedlock children, or maintain a "common-law relationship where there is no impediment to marriage." Thus we have an administrative ruling which says, in effect, that children in need of decent housing whose mothers do not possess a marriage certificate may be denied a low-rent dwelling, while those whose mothers are legally married may remain in such housing. Has there been an effective outcry against these standards by social-work practitioners?

Consider the criterion of the "suitable home," often used to strike at minority groups. The Aid to Dependent Children title of the Social Security Act was adopted for purposes of encouraging the care of dependent children in their own homes, or in the homes of relatives. But Federal grants enable the states to deny financial and other assistance on the ground that the homes in which the children reside are not suitable. In New Orleans, during the school desegregation struggle in recent years, this power was used to strike at thousands of Negro mothers and children receiving ADC grants, on the grounds of doubtful morality, or improper home settings.

Ponder for a moment the issue of confidentiality of agency records. In an effort to discourage needy persons from either applying for assistance or remaining on relief rolls, many states and governmental departments have publicized the names of relief recipients. In some cases, state legislatures have encouraged this. In Newburgh, New York, where violation of decent welfare standards attracted nationwide attention, relief recipients were photographed, without consent, when they arrived to pick up their checks.

In Alameda County, California, a midnight raid was conducted on 500 mothers receiving assistance, to determine whether or not there was a man in the house. A social worker who refused to participate in such raids was discharged for insubordination. Did this professional receive the timely and effective support of his fellows? Is it not curious that so many of his colleagues in California and elsewhere have participated without protest in such raids?

In Cook County, Illinois, one mother under the Aid to Dependent Children program was refused further aid because the caseworker found a man's jacket in the closet of her apartment. The mother maintained that it was the dead father's jacket, but she could not convince the caseworker. Which legal authority sanctioned that search? What was the caseworker doing looking through closets?

The practice of unannounced inspections of the homes of relief recipients and others receiving public assistance is a shocking invasion of privacy and violation of civil liberties. In most instances, these searches are made without search warrants, at or near midnight, with the ostensible purpose of conducting a surprise check on the individual's eligibility for continued assistance: Is the child for whom public support is being given actually living with the mother? Is there an adult man in the house capable of supporting the family? Are the children receiving aid residing in a "suitable home"? Should the relief recipients refuse entry, the implication is that public assistance will be discontinued; thus the threat is a substitute for the warrant.

Apart from the highly questionable permissibility of such midnight welfare searches, it should be noted that they are conducted not only under the auspices of the welfare department of the municipality or state, but with the indirect—and perhaps, unintended—participation of the U. S. Department of Health, Education and Welfare. The Social Security Act provides for Federal-state cooperation in welfare programs. The Secretary of the Department could, if he would, issue a regulation which would deny further Federal funds to states engaging in such nocturnal visits, or provide for direct payments to the relief recipients in such instances. The failure to issue and enforce such a regulation has made persons on public assistance the victims of grossly unconstitutional behavior.

In most instances these victims, already "clients" of a social agency, are in no position to enforce their vouchsafed right of privacy; they lack both the means and knowledge to litigate such questions. Hence the role of the social worker is clearly central in these situations. Where else can these people turn for help, or referral to legal aid, to resist the assumption that those supported by public agencies must open their homes to summary inspection?

A corollary problem is the use of non-social workers to determine relief eligibility. Washington, D. C., where the plight of the poor has been characterized by Senator Humphrey as "unbelievable," is a prime example. The District is said to have an investigative force trained in police methods, not social work, that is larger than the investigative force of any other city. Relief applicants are subjected to police-type investigations, which have resulted in the denial of aid to a greater percentage of applicants than in any other city. Has the social-work fraternity protested this practice effectively?

State requirements which designate "maximum grants" for welfare payments, regardless of the size of the family, discriminate against children in large families. One interesting case, which subsequently came to the Supreme Court of Iowa, concerned a family whose relief allowance was reduced from $291 a month to $175 after the state adopted a "maximum grant" regulation. In its decision, the court said: "It is as though the legislature had written, 'children in small families shall receive full needs. Others shall receive two-thirds.'" I have wondered whether any social agencies sought to file a brief *amicus* in that case.

Someone recently remarked—quite pertinently—that the problem of the poor will never be solved until we deal with the problems posed by our rapidly growing population—here and throughout the world. Yet, the issue of supplying birth-control information to relief recipients has aroused a great deal of public controversy.

In 1962, in the Virginia legislature, a bill was introduced providing for compulsory sterilization of welfare recipients with more than a certain number of children. This was later amended to make such action voluntary. But in many other communities, there is opposition to giving birth-control information to relief recipients on religious grounds. This means that women with money for private doctors can acquire such information while relief recipients are deprived of the right to seek birth-control aid. This particular controversy may be resolved if, as recent press reports indicate, the 1964 session of the Vatican's Ecumenical Council should consider a declaration to the effect that family limitation may be desirable in the modern world.

Let me summarize by saying that official condescension and prying on the one hand, and indifference on the part of the community on the other, is a heavy price to pay for the inability to support one's self. It is a price that includes not only the original humiliation on the part of most, I believe, of those applying for assistance, but also the subsequent erosion of self-respect and the violation of the sanctity of the home.

To be sure, the foregoing examples—merely a few of the many that could be cited—reflect infringements and violations arising out of public, rather than private welfare programs. But this does not necessarily exonerate the social worker on the staff of a private welfare institution to which, for example, a relief recipient, an out-of-wedlock mother, or any other person receiving public assistance, might turn for auxiliary services. The crucial question remains whether social-work practices do not include an affirmative obligation to offer protection against excesses of authority even when the law does not require the social worker to supply such aid.

The Merchant and the Low-Income Consumer

David Caplovitz

Columbia University

[Reprinted from Chapter 2* of The Poor Pay More: Consumer Practices of Low-Income Families *by David Caplovitz (New York, 1963) by permission of The Free Press of Glencoe, A Division of The Macmillan Company. Copyright © 1963.]*

THE VISITOR TO EAST HARLEM cannot fail to notice the sixty or so furniture and appliance stores that mark the area, mostly around Third Avenue and 125th Street. At first this may seem surprising. After all, this is obviously a low-income area. Many of the residents are on relief. Many are employed in seasonal work and in marginal industries, such as the garment industry, which are the first to feel the effects of a recession in the economy. On the face of it, residents of the area would seem unable to afford the merchandise offered for sale in these stores.

That merchants nevertheless find it profitable to locate in these areas attests to a commonly overlooked fact: low-income families, like those of higher income, are consumers of many major durables. The popular image of the American as striving for the material possessions which bestow upon him both comfort and prestige in the eyes of his fellows does not hold only for the ever-increasing middle class. The cultural pressures to buy major durables reach low- as well as middle-income families. In some ways, consumption may take on even more significance for low-income families than for those in higher classes. Since many have small prospect of greatly improving their low social standing through occupational mobility, they are apt to turn to consumption as at least one sphere in which they can make some progress toward the American dream of success. If the upper strata that were observed by Veblen engaged in conspicuous consumption to symbolize their social superiority, it might be said that the lower classes today are apt to engage in *compensatory consumption*. Appliances, automobiles, and the dream of a home of their own can become compensations for blocked social mobility.[1]

---

* This chapter is based in part on an unpublished research report by Wolfram Arendt and Murray Caylay.

[1] I am indebted to Robert K. Merton for suggesting the apt phrase "compensatory consumption." The idea expressed by this term figures prominently in the writings of Robert S. Lynd. Observing the workers in Middletown, Lynd noted that their declining opportunities for occupational advancement and even

The dilemma of the low-income consumer lies in these facts. He is trained by society (and his position in it) to want the symbols and appurtenances of the "good life" at the same time that he lacks the means needed to fulfill these socially induced wants. People with small incomes lack not only the ready cash for consuming major durables but are also poorly qualified for that growing substitute for available cash—credit. Their low income, their negligible savings, their job insecurity all contribute to their being poor credit risks. Moreover, many low-income families in New York City are fairly recent migrants from the South or from Puerto Rico and so do not have other requisites of good credit, such as long-term residence at the same address and friends who meet the credit requirements and are willing to vouch for them.[2]

Not having enough cash and credit would seem to create a sufficient problem for low-income consumers. But they have other limitations as well. They tend to lack the information and training needed

---

the depression did not make them class-conscious. Instead, their aspirations shifted to the realm of consumption.

> Fascinated by a rising standard of living offered them on every hand on the installment plan, they [the working class] do not readily segregate themselves from the rest of the city. They want what Middletown wants, so long as it gives them their great symbol of advancement—an automobile. Car ownership stands to them for a large share of the "American dream"; they cling to it as they cling to self respect, and it was not unusual to see a family drive up to the relief commissary in 1935 to stand in line for its four or five dollar weekly food dole. [The Lynds go on to quote a union official:] It's easy to see why our workers don't think much about joining unions. So long as they have a car and can borrow or steal a gallon of gas, they'll ride around and pay no attention to labor organization. . . . [Robert S. Lynd and Helen Merrill Lynd, *Middletown in Transition* (New York: Harcourt, Brace and Co., 1937), p. 26. See also pp. 447–448.]

It should be noted that the Lynds identify the installment plan as the mechanism through which workers are able to realize their consumption aspirations. Similar observations are to be found in *Knowledge for What?* (Princeton University Press: 1939), pp. 91, 198. Lynd's student, Eli Chinoy, also makes use of the idea of compensatory consumption in his study of automobile workers. He found that when confronted with the impossibility of rising to the ranks of management, workers shifted their aspirations from the occupational to the consumption sphere. "With their wants constantly stimulated by high powered advertising, they measure their success by what they are able to buy." Eli Chinoy, "Aspirations of Automobile Workers," *American Journal of Sociology*, 57 (1952), 453–459. For further discussion of the political implications of this process, see Daniel Bell, "Work and Its Discontents" in *The End of Ideology* (New York: The Free Press of Glencoe, 1960), pp. 246 ff.

[2] A frequent practice in extending credit to poor risks is to have cosigners who will make good the debt should the original borrower default. The new arrivals are apt to be disadvantaged by their greater difficulty in finding cosigners.

to be effective consumers in a bureaucratic society. Partly because of their limited education and partly because as migrants from more traditional societies they are unfamiliar with urban culture, they are not apt to follow the announcements of sales in the newspapers, to engage in comparative shopping, to know their way around the major department stores and bargain centers, to know how to evaluate the advice of salesmen—practices necessary for some degree of sophistication in the realm of consumption. The institution of credit introduces special complex requirements for intelligent consumption. Because of the diverse and frequently misleading ways in which charges for credit are stated, even the highly-educated consumer has difficulty knowing which set of terms is most economical.[3]

These characteristics of the low-income consumer—his socially supported want for major durables, his small funds, his poor credit position, his lack of shopping sophistication—constitute the conditions under which durables are marketed in low-income areas. To understand the paradox set by the many stores selling high-cost durables in these areas it is necessary to know how the merchants adapt to these conditions. Clearly the normal marketing arrangements, based on a model of the "adequate" consumer (the consumer with funds, credit, and shopping sophistication), cannot prevail if these merchants are to stay in business.

On the basis of interviews with fourteen of these merchants, the broad outlines of this marketing system can be described. This picture, in turn, provides a backdrop for the more detailed examination in later chapters of the marketing relationship from the viewpoint of the consumer.

Merchandising in a Low-Income Area

The key to the marketing system in low-income areas lies in special adaptations of the institution of credit. The many merchants who locate

---

[3] Professor Samuel S. Myers of Morgan State College has studied the credit terms of major department stores and appliance outlets in Baltimore. Visiting the ten most popular stores, he priced the same model of TV set and gathered information on down-payments and credit terms. He found that the cash price was practically the same in the various stores, but that there were wide variations in the credit terms leading to sizeable differences in the final cost to the consumer. (Based on personal communication with Professor Myers.)

In his statement to the Douglas Committee considering the "Truth in Interest" bill, George Katona presented findings from the consumer surveys carried out by the Survey Research Center of The University of Michigan. These studies show that people with high income and substantial education are no better informed about the costs of credit than people of low income and little education.

in these areas and find it profitable to do so are prepared to offer credit in spite of the high risks involved. Moreover, their credit is tailored to the particular needs of the low-income consumer. All kinds of durable goods can be obtained in this market at terms not too different from the slogan, "a dollar down, a dollar a week." The consumer can buy furniture, a TV set, a stereophonic phonograph, or, if he is so minded, a combination phonograph-TV set, if not for a dollar a week then for only a few dollars a week. In practically every one of these stores, the availability of "easy credit" is announced to the customer in both English and Spanish by large signs in the windows and sometimes by neon signs over the doorways. Of the fourteen merchants interviewed, twelve claimed that from 75 to 90 percent of their business consisted of credit and the other two said that credit made up half their business. That these merchants extend credit to their customers does not, of course, explain how they stay in business. They still face the problem of dealing with their risks.

The Markup and Quality of Goods

It might at first seem that the merchant would solve his problem by charging high rates of interest on the credit he extends. But the law in New York State now regulates the amount that can be charged for credit, and most of these merchants claim they use installment contracts which conform to the law. The fact is that they do not always use these contracts. Some merchants will give customers only a card on which payments are noted. In these transactions the cost of credit and the cash price are not specified as the law requires. The customer peddlers, whom we shall soon meet, seldom use installment contracts. In all these cases the consumer has no idea of how much he is paying for credit, for the cost of credit is not differentiated from the cost of the product.

Although credit charges are now regulated by law, no law regulates the merchant's markup on his goods. East Harlem is known to the merchants of furniture and appliances in New York City as the area in which pricing is done by "numbers." We first heard of the "number" system from a woman who had been employed as a bookkeeper in such a store. She illustrated a "one number" item by writing down a hypothetical wholesale price and then adding the same figure to it, a 100 percent markup. Her frequent references to "two number" and "three number" prices indicated that prices are never less than "one number," and are often more.

The system of pricing in the low-income market differs from that in the bureaucratic market of the downtown stores in another respect:

in East Harlem there are hardly any "one price" stores. In keeping with a multi-price policy, price tags are conspicuously absent from the merchandise. The customer has to ask, "how much?," and the answer he gets will depend on several things. If the merchant considers him a poor risk, if he thinks the customer is naïve, or if the customer was referred to him by another merchant or a peddler to whom he must pay a comission, the price will be higher. The fact that prices can be affected by "referrals" calls attention to another peculiarity of the low-income market, what the merchants call the "T.O." system.

Anyone closely familiar with sales practices in a large retailing establishment probably understands the meaning of "T.O." When a salesman is confronted with a customer who is not responding to the "sales pitch," he will call over another salesman, signal the nature of the situation by whispering, "this is a T.O.," and then introduce him to the customer as the "assistant manager."[4] In East Harlem, as the interviewers learned, T.O.'s extend beyond the store. When a merchant finds himself with a customer who seems to be a greater risk than he is prepared to accept, he does not send the customer away. Instead, he will tell the customer that he happens to be out of the item he wants, but that it can be obtained at the store of his "friend" or "cousin," just a few blocks away. The merchant will then take the customer to a storekeeper with a less conservative credit policy.[5] The second merchant fully understands that his colleague expects a commission and takes this into account in fixing the price.[6] As a result, the customer who happens to walk into the "wrong" store ends up paying more. In essence, he is being charged for the service of having his credit potential matched with the risk policy of a merchant.

---

[4] The initials stand for "turn over." The "assistant manager" is ready to make a small concession to the customer, who is usually so flattered by this gesture that he offers no further resistance to the sale. For further descriptions of the "T.O.," see Cecil L. French, "Correlates of Success in Retail Selling," *American Journal of Sociology*, 66 (September, 1960), 128–134; and Erving Goffman, *Presentation of Self in Everyday Life* (New York: Doubleday, Anchor Books, 1959), pp. 178–180.

[5] The interviewers found that the stores closer to the main shopping area of 125th Street generally had more conservative credit policies than those somewhat farther away. This was indicated by the percentage of credit sales the merchants reported as defaults. The higher-rental stores near 125th Street reported default rates of 5 and 6 percent, those six or seven blocks away, as high as 20 percent.

[6] The referring merchant does not receive his commission right away. Whether he gets it at all depends upon the customer's payment record. He will keep a record of his referrals and check on them after several months. When the merchant who has made the sale has received a certain percentage of the payments, he will give the referring merchant his commission.

As for the merchandise sold in these stores, the interviewers noticed that the furniture on display was of obviously poor quality. Most of all, they were struck by the absence of well-known brands of appliances in most of the stores. To find out about the sales of better-known brands, they initially asked about the volume of sales of "high-price lines." But this question had little meaning for the merchants, because high prices were being charged for the low-quality goods in evidence. The question had to be rephrased in terms of "high *quality*" merchandise or, as the merchants themselves refer to such goods, "custom lines." To quote from the report of these interviews:

> It became apparent that the question raised a problem of communication. We were familiar with the prices generally charged for high quality lines and began to notice that the same prices were charged for much lower quality merchandise. The markup was obviously quite different from that in other areas. The local merchants said that the sale of "custom" merchandise was limited by a slow turnover. In fact, a comparable markup on the higher quality lines would make the final price so prohibitively high that they could not be moved at all. A lower markup would be inconsistent with the risk and would result in such small profits that the business could not be continued.

The high markup on low-quality goods is thus a major device used by the merchants to protect themselves against the risks of their credit business. This policy represents a marked departure from the "normal" marketing situation. In the "normal" market, competition between merchants results in a pricing policy roughly commensurate with the quality of the goods. It is apparent, then, that these merchants do not see themselves competing with stores outside the neighborhood. This results in the irony that the people who can least afford the goods they buy are required to pay high prices relative to quality, thus receiving a comparatively low return for their consumer dollar.

In large part, these merchants have a "captive" market because their customers do not meet the economic requirements of consumers in the larger, bureaucratic marketplace. But also, they can sell inferior goods at high prices because, in their own words, the customers are not "price and quality conscious." Interviewers found that the merchants perceive their customers as unsophisticated shoppers. One merchant rather cynically explained that the amount of goods sold a customer depends not on the customer but on the merchant's willingness to extend him credit. If the merchant is willing to accept great risk, he can sell the customer almost as much as he cares to. Another merchant, commenting on the buying habits of the customer, said, "People do not shop in this area. Each person who comes into the store wants to buy something and is a potential customer. It is just up to who catches him."

The notion of "who catches him" is rather important in this economy. Merchants compete not so much in price or quality, but in getting customers to the store on other grounds. (Some of these gathering techniques will shortly be described.)

Another merchant commented rather grudgingly that the Negroes were beginning to show signs of greater sophistication by "shopping around." Presumably this practice is not followed by the newer migrants to the area.

But although the merchants are ready to exploit the naïveté of their traditionalistic customers, it is important to point out that they also cater to the customer's traditionalism. As a result of the heavy influx of Puerto Ricans into the area, many of these stores now employ Puerto Rican salesmen. The customers who enter these stores need not be concerned about possible embarrassment because of their broken English or their poor dress. On the contrary, these merchants are adept at making the customer feel at ease, as a personal experience will testify.

> Visiting the area and stopping occasionally to read the ads in the windows, I happened to pause before an appliance store. A salesman promptly emerged and said, "I know, I bet you're looking for a nice TV set. Come inside. We've got lots of nice ones." Finding myself thrust into the role of customer, I followed him into the store and listened to his sales-pitch. Part way through his talk, he asked my name. I hesitated a moment and then provided him with a fictitious last name, at which point he said, "No, no—no last names. What's your first name? . . . Ah, Dave; I'm Irv. We only care about first names here." When I was ready to leave after making some excuse about having to think things over, he handed me his card. Like most business cards of employees, this one had the name and address of the enterprise in large type and in small type the name of the salesman. But instead of his full name, there appeared only the amiable, "Irv."

As this episode indicates, the merchants in this low-income area are ready to personalize their services. To consumers from a more traditional society, unaccustomed to the impersonality of the bureaucratic market, this may be no small matter.

So far, we have reviewed the elements of the system of exchange that comprise the low-income market. For the consumer, these are the availability of merchandise, the "easy" installments, and the reassurance of dealing with merchants who make them feel at home. In return, the merchant reserves for himself the right to sell low-quality merchandise at exorbitant prices.

But the high markup on goods does not insure that the business will be profitable. No matter what he charges, the merchant can remain in business only if customers actually pay. In this market, the customer's intention and ability to pay—the assumptions underlying any credit system—cannot be taken for granted. Techniques for insuring continuity of payments are a fundamental part of this distinctive economy.

Formal Controls

When the merchant uses an installment contract, he has recourse to legal controls over his customers. But as we shall see, legal controls are not sufficient to cope with the merchant's problem and they are seldom used.

Liens Against Property and Wages.—The merchant can, of course, sue the defaulting customer. By winning a court judgment, he can have the customer's property attached. Should this fail to satisfy the debt, he can take the further step of having the customer's salary garnisheed.[7] But these devices are not fully adequate for several reasons. Not all customers have property of value or regular jobs. Furthermore, their employers will not hesitate to fire them rather than submit to the nuisance of a garnishment. But since the customer knows he may lose his job if he is garnisheed, the mere threat of garnishment is sometimes enough to insure regularity of payments.[8] The main limitation with legal controls, however, is that the merchant who uses them repeatedly runs the risk of forfeiting good will in the neighborhood.

Repossession.—Under the law, the merchant can, of course, repossess his merchandise, should the customer default on payments. But repossession, according to the merchants, is rare. They claim that the merchandise receives such heavy use as to become practically worthless in a short time. And no doubt the shoddy merchandise will not stand much use, heavy or light. One merchant said that he will occasionally repossess an item, not to regain his equity, but to punish a customer he feels is trying to cheat him.

Discounting Paper.—The concern with good will places a limitation on the use of another legal practice open to merchants for minimizing their risk: the sale of their contracts to a credit agency at a discount. By selling his contracts to one of the licensed finance companies, the merchant can realize an immediate return on his investment.

---

[7] It is of some interest that the low-income families we interviewed were all familiar with the word "garnishee." This may well be one word in the language that the poorly educated are more likely to know than the better educated.

[8] Welfare families cannot, of course, be garnisheed, and more than half the merchants reported that they sell to them. But the merchants can threaten to disclose the credit purchase to the welfare authorities. Since recipients of welfare funds are not supposed to buy on credit, this threat exerts powerful pressure on the family.

The problem with this technique is that the merchant loses control over his customer. As an impersonal, bureaucratic organization, the credit agency has recourse only to legal controls. Should the customer miss a payment, the credit agency will take the matter to court. But in the customer's mind, his contract exists with the merchant, not with the credit agency. Consequently, the legal actions taken against him reflect upon the merchant, and so good will is not preserved after all.

For this reason, the merchant is reluctant to "sell his paper," particularly if he has reason to believe that the customer will miss some payments. When he does sell some of his contracts at a discount, his motive is not to reduce risk, but rather to obtain working capital. Since so much of his capital is tied up in credit transactions, he frequently finds it necessary to make such sales. Oddly enough, he is apt to sell his better "paper," that is, the contracts of customers who pay regularly, for he wants to avoid incurring the ill will of customers. This practice also has its drawbacks for the merchant. Competitors can find out from the credit agencies which customers pay regularly and then try to lure them away from the original merchant. Some merchants reported that in order to retain control over their customers, they will buy back contracts from credit agencies they suspect are giving information to competitors.[9]

Credit Association Ratings.—All credit merchants report their bad debtors to the credit association to which they belong. The merchants interviewed said that they always consult the "skip lists" of their association before extending credit to a new customer.[10] In this way they can avoid at least the customers known to be bad risks. This form of control tends to be effective in the long run because the customers find that they are unable to obtain credit until they have made good on their past debts. During the interviews with them, some consumers mentioned this need to restore their credit rating as the reason why they were paying off debts in spite of their belief that they had been cheated.

---

[9] Not all merchants are particularly concerned with good will. A few specialize in extending credit to the worst risks, customers turned away by most other merchants. These men will try to collect as much as they can on their accounts during the year and then will sell all their outstanding accounts to a finance company. As a result, the most inadequate consumers are apt to meet with the bureaucratic controls employed by the finance company. For a description of how bill collectors operate, see Hillel Black, *Buy Now, Pay Later* (New York: William Morrow and Co., 1961), chap. 4.

[10] See *Ibid.*, chap. 3, for a description of the world's largest credit association, the one serving most of the stores in the New York City area.

But these various formal techniques of control are not sufficient to cope with the merchant's problem of risk. He also depends heavily on informal and personal techniques of control.

Informal Controls

The merchant starts from the premise that most of his customers are honest people who intend to pay but have difficulty managing their money. Missed payments are seen as more often due to poor management and to emergencies than to dishonesty. The merchants anticipate that their customers will miss some payments and they rely on informal controls to insure that payments are eventually made.

All the merchants described their credit business as operating on a "fifteen-month year." This means that they expect the customer to miss about one of every four payments and they compute the markup accordingly. Unlike the credit companies, which insist upon regular payments and add service charges for late payments, the neighborhood merchant is prepared to extend "flexible" credit. Should the customer miss an occasional payment or should he be short on another, the merchant considers this a normal part of his business.

To insure the close personal control necessary for this system of credit, the merchant frequently draws up a contract calling for weekly payments which the customer usually brings to the store. This serves several functions for the merchant. To begin with, the sum of money represented by a weekly payment is relatively small and so helps to create the illusion of "easy credit." Customers are apt to think more of the size of the payments than of the cost of the item or the length of the contract.

More importantly, the frequent contact of a weekly-payment system enables the merchant to get to know his customer. He learns when the customer receives his pay check, when his rent is due, who his friends are, when job layoffs, illnesses, and other emergencies occur—in short, all sorts of information which allow him to interpret the reason for a missed payment. Some merchants reported that when they know the customer has missed a payment for a legitimate reason such as illness or a job layoff, they will send a sympathetic note and offer the customer a gift (an inexpensive lamp or wall picture) when payments are resumed. This procedure, they say, frequently brings the customer back with his missed payments.

The short interval between payments also functions to give the merchant an early warning when something is amiss. His chances of locating the delinquent customer are that much greater. Furthermore, the merchant can keep tabs on a delinquent customer through his knowledge of the latter's friends, relatives, neighbors, and associates, who are also apt to be customers of his. In this way, still another informal device, the existing network of social relations, is utilized by the neighborhood merchant in conducting his business.[11]

The weekly-payment system also provides the merchant with the opportunity to sell other items to the customer. When the first purchase is almost paid for, the merchant will try to persuade the customer to make another. Having the customer in the store, where he can look at the merchandise, makes the next sale that much easier. This system of successive sales is, of course, an ideal arrangement—for the merchant. As a result, the customer remains continuously in debt to him. The pattern is somewhat reminiscent of the Southern sharecropper's relation to the company store. And since a number of customers grew up in more traditional environments with just such economies, they may find the arrangement acceptable. The practice of buying from peddlers, found to be common in these low-income areas, also involves the principle of continuous indebtedness. The urban low-income economy, then, is in some respects like the sharecropper system; it might almost be called an "urban sharecropper system."[12]

The Customer Peddlers

Characteristic of the comparatively traditional and personal form of the low-income economy is the important role played in it by the door-to-door credit salesman, the customer peddler. The study of merchants found that these peddlers are not necessarily competitors of the store-owners. Almost all merchants make use of peddlers in the great competition for customers. The merchants tend to regard peddlers as necessary evils who add greatly to the final cost of purchases. But they need them because in their view, customers are too ignorant, frightened, or lazy to come to the stores themselves. Thus, the merchants' apparent contempt for peddlers does not bar them from employing outdoor sales-

---

[11] The merchant's access to these networks of social relations is not entirely independent of economic considerations. Just as merchants who refer customers receive commissions, so customers who recommend others are often given commissions. Frequently, this is why a customer will urge his friends to deal with a particular merchant.

[12] The local merchants are not the only ones promoting continuous debt. The coupon books issued by banks and finance companies which underwrite installment contracts contain notices in the middle announcing that the consumer can, if he wishes, refinance the loan. The consumer is told, in effect, that he is a good risk because presumably he has regularly paid half the installments and that he need not wait until he has made the last payment before borrowing more money.

men (or "canvassers," as they describe the peddlers who work for one store or another). Even the merchants who are themselves reluctant to hire canvassers find they must do so in order to meet the competition. The peddler's main function for the merchant, then, is getting the customer to the store, and if he will not come, getting the store to the customer. But this is not his only function.

Much more than the storekeeper, the peddler operates on the basis of a personal relationship with the customer. By going to the customer's home, he gets to know the entire family; he sees the condition of the home and he comes to know the family's habits and wants. From this vantage point he is better able than the merchant to evaluate the customer as a credit risk. Since many of the merchant's potential customers lack the standard credentials of credit, such as having a permanent job, the merchant needs some other basis for discriminating between good and bad risks. If the peddler, who has come to know the family, is ready to vouch for the customer, the merchant will be ready to make the transaction. In short, the peddler acts as a fiduciary agent, a Dun and Bradstreet for the poor, telling the merchant which family is likely to meet its obligations and which is not.

Not all peddlers are employed by stores. Many are independent enterprisers (who may have started as canvassers for stores).[13] A number of the independent peddlers have accumulated enough capital to supply their customers with major durables. These are the elite peddlers, known as "dealers," who buy appliances and furniture from local merchants at a "wholesale" price, and then sell them on credit to their customers. In these transactions, the peddler either takes the customer to the store or sends the customer to the store with his card on which he has written some such message as "Please give Mr. Jones a TV set."[14] The merchant then sells the customer the TV set at a price much higher than he would ordinarily charge. The "dealer" is generally given two months to pay the merchant the "wholesale" price, and meanwhile he

---

[13] A systematic study of local merchants and peddlers would probably find that a typical career pattern is to start as a canvasser, become a self-employed peddler, and finally a storekeeper.

[14] According to a former customer peddler, now in the furniture business, the peddlers' message will either read "Please *give* Mr. Jones . . ." or "Please let Mr. Jones *pick out* . . ." In the former case, the customer is given the merchandise right away; in the latter, it is set aside for him until the peddler says that it is all right to let the customer have it. The peddler uses the second form when his customer is already heavily in debt to him and he wants to be certain that the customer will agree to the higher weekly payments that will be necessary.

takes over the responsibility of collecting from his customer. Some "dealers" are so successful that they employ canvassers in their own right.[15] And some merchants do so much business with "dealers" that they come to think of themselves as "wholesalers" even though they are fully prepared to do their own retail business.

Independent peddlers without much capital also have economic relations with local merchants. They act as brokers, directing their customers to neighborhood stores that will extend them credit. And for this service they of course receive a commission. In these transactions, it is the merchant who accepts the risks and assumes the responsibility for collecting payments. The peddler who acts as a broker performs the same function as the merchant in the T.O. system. He knows which merchants will accept great risk and which will not, and directs his customers accordingly.

There are, then, three kinds of customer peddlers operating in these low-income neighborhoods who cooperate with local merchants: the canvassers who are employed directly by the stores; the small entrepreneurs who act as brokers; and the more successful entrepreneurs who operate as "dealers." A fourth type of peddler consists of salesmen representing large companies not necessarily located in the neighborhood. These men are, for the most part, canvassers for firms specializing in a particular commodity, e.g., encyclopedias, vacuum cleaners, or pots and pans. They differ from the other peddlers by specializing in what they sell and by depending more on contracts and legal controls. This type of peddler, in particular, can cause a good deal of trouble for the low-income consumer.

Peddlers thus aid the local merchants by finding customers, evaluating them as credit risks, and helping in the collection of payments. And as the merchants themselves point out, these services add greatly to the cost of the goods. One storekeeper said that peddlers are apt to charge five and six times the amount the store charges for relatively inexpensive purchases. Pointing to a religious picture which he sells for $5, he maintained that peddlers sell it for as much as $30. And he estimated that the peddler adds 30 to 50 percent to the final sales price of appliances and furniture.

---

[15] One tiny store in the area, with little merchandise in evidence, is reported to employ over a hundred canvassers. The owner would not consent to an interview, but the student-observers did notice that this apparently small merchant kept some four or five bookkeepers at work in a back room. The owner is obviously a "dealer" whose store is his office. As a "dealer," he has no interest in maintaining stock and displays for street trade.

Unethical and Illegal Practices

The interviewers uncovered some evidence that some local merchants engage in the illegal practice of selling reconditioned furniture and appliances as new. Of course, no merchant would admit that he did this himself, but five of them hinted that their competitors engaged in this practice.[16] Several of the consumers we interviewed were quite certain that they had been victimized in this way.

One unethical, if not illegal, activity widely practiced by stores is "bait" advertising with its concomitant, the "switch sale." In the competition for customers, merchants depend heavily upon advertising displays in their windows which announce furniture or appliances at unusually low prices. The customer may enter the store assuming that the low offer in the window signifies a reasonably low price line. Under severe pressure, the storekeeper may even be prepared to sell the merchandise at the advertised price, for not to do so would be against the law. What most often happens, however, is that the unsuspecting customer is convinced by the salesman that he doesn't really want the goods advertised in the window and is then persuaded to buy a smaller amount of more expensive goods. Generally, not much persuasion is necessary. The most popular "bait ad" is the announcement of three rooms of furniture for "only $149" or "only $199." The customer who inquires about this bargain is shown a bedroom set consisting of two cheap and (sometimes deliberately) chipped bureaus and one bed frame. He learns that the spring and mattress are not included in the advertised price, but can be had for another $75 or $100. The living-room set in these "specials" consists of a fragile-looking sofa and one unmatching chair.[17]

The frequent success of this kind of exploitation, known in the trade as the "switch sale," is reflected in this comment by one merchant: "I don't know how they do it. They advertise three rooms of furniture for $149 and the customers swarm in. *They end up buying a $400 bedroom set for $600 and none of us can believe how easy it is to make these sales.*"

In sum, a fairly intricate system of sales-and-credit has evolved in response to the distinctive situation of the low-income consumer and the local merchant. It is a system heavily slanted in the direction

---

[16] Events are sometimes more telling than words. During an interview with a merchant, the interviewer volunteered to help several men who were carrying bed frames into the store. The owner excitedly told him not to help because he might get paint on his hands.

[17] In one store in which I inspected this special offer, I was told by the salesman that he would find a chair that was a "fairly close match."

of a traditional economy in which informal, personal ties play a major part in the transaction. At the same time it is connected to impersonal bureaucratic agencies through the instrument of the installment contract. Should the informal system break down, credit companies, courts of law, and agencies of law enforcement come to play a part.

The system is not only different from the larger, more formal economy; in some respects it is a *deviant* system in which practices that violate prevailing moral standards are commonplace. As Merton has pointed out in his analysis of the political machine, the persistence of deviant social structures can only be understood when their social functions (as well as dysfunctions) are taken into account.[18] The basic function of the low-income marketing system is to provide consumer goods to people who fail to meet the requirements of the more legitimate, bureaucratic market, or who choose to exclude themselves from the larger market because they do not feel comfortable in it. As we have seen, the system is extraordinarily flexible. Almost no one—however great a risk—is turned away. Various mechanisms sift and sort customers according to their credit risk and match them with merchants ready to sell them the goods they want. Even the family on welfare is permitted to maintain its self-respect by consuming in much the same way as do its social peers who happen not to be on welfare. Whether the system, with its patently exploitative features, can be seriously altered without the emergence of more legitimate institutions to perform its functions, is a question to be considered at length.

Housing Codes, Taxes, and Slums*

Alvin L. Schorr

U. S. Department of Health, Education, and Welfare

[Reprinted from Chapter 4 of Slums and Social Insecurity *by Alvin L. Schorr (Washington, D.C., 1963).]*

WIDESPREAD FAILURE to attempt to enforce housing codes is one of the reasons that so much housing is now substandard. Housing codes are a key element of successful rehabilitation programs. Yet, in current circumstances, it is not at all certain that they can be or will be broadly enforced. When violations become a public scandal, the laws may be

---

[18] Robert K. Merton, *Social Theory and Social Structure*, rev. ed. (New York: The Free Press of Glencoe, 1957), pp. 71–82.

* Biographical footnotes have been omitted.

enforced with some effect. (In the past decade, slum fires in Baltimore, Brooklyn, Chicago, and Cleveland, killing 15, touched off, respectively, a new ordinance, a grand jury investigation, an angry article in a national magazine, and an enforcement campaign.) But where public attention is not engaged, violations are endemic.

Why is it so difficult to enforce codes? Why do they not work effectively? These questions have many overlapping answers. Codes are antiquated and unclear. Penalties embodied in the law are slight. Owners find it cheaper to pay occasional fines than to make repairs. Municipal enforcement staff is likely to be undermanned. Political interests may not support or may actively sabotage enforcement efforts. Those who must move because of crowding or because buildings are condemned cannot find even equivalent housing. Absentee owners cannot, without a good deal of trouble, be put under sufficient pressure to produce results. Resident owners may not have the resources to make improvements. Tenants may resist enforcement because it means rent rises or that some must move. Even with momentarily successful enforcement, in the long run industry, highways, and other blighting influences take their toll.

Some of the remedies for these difficulties are obvious; some that are less obvious are being developed. A sustained, effective enforcement program requires a clear law, an adequately manned enforcement body with defined responsibility and support from city hall. In addition, Baltimore has pioneered the use of a housing court, a court thoroughly familiar with housing practices that has special counseling services at its disposal. It has been suggested that there should be special organizations to take over and rehabilitate properties that a city forces onto the market. Attention has focused on methods for dealing with recalcitrant landlords. It has been suggested that any building should be condemned and torn down if the cost of repairs is equivalent to 50 percent of its "true" value. New York City now has the power to seize buildings, make repairs that are necessary to meet minimum requirements, and recapture the cost out of rent collections.[1]

---

[1] Prior to this, the statute permitted "the Department of Buildings to declare a building a public nuisance; let out contracts for repairs to be made and . . . maintain a suit against the owner to recover the amount of the expense. Such a procedure is so unsatisfactory as to preclude its use. . . . It is . . . an open invitation to the unscrupulous owner to milk the profits from the property, have the city make necessary repairs, and through legal maneuvering make it exceedingly difficult for the city to recoup expenditures." Letter from Peter J. Reidy, Commissioner of the Department of Buildings, the City of New York, to Frank P. Zeidler, Mar. 2, 1961.

For thoughtful descriptions of the problems that interfere with enforcement and for proposals for remedies, see *Guiding Metropolitan Growth, Residential Re-*

One cannot review the problems of code enforcement and the solutions that are proposed without concluding that they are superficial, if grave, symptoms of a deeper maladjustment. The hard fact is that profitmaking incentives run counter—so far as the maintenance of housing is concerned—to the best interests of the poor. Tax laws and condemnation procedures combine with the peculiarly vulnerable situation of those who are poor to pay the most profit for the worst housing. Where enforcement is pitted day by day against the businessman's incentive to make profit, enforcement is bound to be in trouble.

Factors that operate in this fashion are the municipal property tax, the capital gains tax, the basis for calculating value in condemnation, and the depreciation allowance. The property tax, as it is based upon valuation, increases as property is improved. Any number of observers and some studies testify that such a basis for a tax leads to neglect of property. A more touching bit of testimony is an information bulletin offered to homeowners by the government of Dayton, Ohio. "Protect your home!" it reads. "Home Maintenance Does Not Increase Your Taxes." Obviously, the possibility of a tax rise deters not only those who are interested in profit, but some who might be improving their own homes as well.

The capital gains tax may have a somewhat similar effect. If the owner's income tax bracket is high, his interest centers on ultimate resale value. Though resale value in other property may depend on maintenance, in low-income neighborhoods it is likely to depend on the value of the land and on the net income that is being produced. Thus, the profit lies in holding on while the land becomes valuable and, secondarily, in current income. Neither of these incentives need involve maintenance of a building. Condemnation procedures provide one of the reasons that income production determines resale value. Even though income is not a consideration in setting the property tax, it is recognized as a factor in negotiating payment upon condemnation. Thus, for this reason too, money spent on maintenance brings little cash benefit. The most deteriorated property may eventually be disposed of to the city at a profit.[2]

The depreciation allowance provides a further element that influences the maintenance of housing. In Federal income tax the depreciation allowance treats real estate like machinery and equipment. A

---

habilitation: Private Profits and Public Purposes, The Human Side of Urban Renewal, and *Making Urban Renewal More Effective.*

[2] Summarizing the opinions of "outstanding authorities" in the investment field, Arthur M. Weimer writes: "Most investors . . . recognize that renewal programs . . . have the effect of bailing out the owners of various properties and of shoring up the expectations of the owners of many near-in properties."

high percentage may be written off in early years and declining percentages subsequently. Though a single owner may not receive credit
for more than his own cost, upon resale the property may be depreciated all over again. The point of largest profit, therefore, is in the
early years. After 6 or 8 years, if tax cost is a consideration for the
owner, it becomes profitable to sell and purchase a new property.[3] This
effect may seem to operate in the opposite direction from the effect,
just cited, of the capital gains tax, which leads to holding on to property for increase in value. The two provisions have in common, however,
that they return no profit for the cost of maintaining or improving center-
city property. Maximum profit lies in manipulating tax and financial
matters quite unrelated to building maintenance. It lies also in securing
high short-term profit: this translates into securing the most tenants that
are feasible in the space available, with the lowest possible expenditure.

In practice, the effect of these financial incentives turns out
approximately as follows:

> One of the great problems of slum ownership is the fact that slum
> properties have changed hands many times during their life and each
> person has expected to make a profit from the sale. The tendency
> therefore is to raise the price of the building and to seek ever-increasing
> rents at the same time the physical value of the building is deteriorat-
> ing. As a building gets older and the price the latest owner pays for
> it represents more and more profit taking in successive sales, the latest
> owner must crowd more and more tenants in a dying building to meet
> his costs, thus hastening its dilapidation. . . . The latest owner may
> possess what is little or more than a pile of bricks and kindling wood,
> but he presumes the building has a high residual value. If he is lucky,

---

[3] That rapid turnover of real estate is one result of the depreciation allowance was, in effect, agreed upon in hearings before the House Ways and Means
Committee. The administration had proposed that profit on the sale of real estate
be treated as ordinary (not capital gains) income to the extent of past depreciation.
Speaking for the proposal, Dan Throop Smith, professor of finance at Harvard University, asked that it apply especially to real estate. "The opportunities for manipulation," he said, "are particularly great in buildings, where properties can be and
are bought, depreciated and sold by a succession of owners in a way that is not
feasible for most machinery and equipment." Speaking against the administration
proposal, Richard H. Swesnick, of the National Association of Real Estate Boards,
said: ". . . Owners would be unwilling to sell real estate except in distress or
other highly unusual circumstances, and purchasers would be unwilling to acquire
new real property which, as a practical matter, they would have to treat as a permanent investment." Obviously other issues are involved, but the point here is that
there is agreement from diverse sources that the depreciation allowance produces
rapid turnover.

the local government will come along and buy him out at an inflated price for some public work or a slum clearance project.[4]

As buildings are subdivided, crowded, and more deteriorated, they become well nigh impossible to maintain. Moreover, it becomes impractical to try to maintain neighboring houses. They too become a profitable investment and slum development spirals. If the city steps in and tries to enforce codes strictly, some owners will be able to make no profit at all. They paid too high a price and counted on overcrowding. If it is suggested that the municipality take the houses over, paying for their reasonable value, it develops that this is less than the current owner paid for it. Why pick on him? Once begun, the cycle is not readily interrupted.

The significance of these forces cannot be overestimated. The maintenance of existing housing is far more important to poor families than the building of new housing. Programs to rehabilitate existing housing will be token remedies unless the underlying processes can be made healthy. There are not enough, and there cannot be enough, housing inspectors in the country to assure code enforcement against the tidal forces that present public policies establish.

How the Poor Are Housed*

Alvin L. Schorr

U. S. Department of Health, Education, and Welfare

[Reprinted from Chapter 5 of Slums and Social Insecurity *by Alvin L. Schorr (Washington, D.C., 1963).]*

How do poor families pay for housing? The question has dimensions that are private and public. As a private matter, the question is answerable in terms of budget management and family arrangements. As a public matter, one answers in terms of specific public programs or of the concept that housing filters down to the poor as those who are better off move on to better housing. All national programs intended

---

[4] Zeidler, Frank P. *Making Urban Renewal More Effective.* A series of twelve reports dated August 1, 1960 to July 1, 1961, to the American Institute for Municipal Research, Education, and Training, Inc., Washington, D.C., p. 32.

* Biographical footnotes have been omitted.

to sustain income and insure against such risks as old age are, in a certain sense, devices to provide housing (et cetera) to those who might otherwise be poor. However, most of these programs place in the beneficiary's hand money which he has, in one manner or another, earned. He is in the same situation as any wage earner, so far as housing is concerned. (If his benefits are inadequate, he is in the same situation as other people.) Two national programs, public assistance and public housing, incorporate a means test and intervene directly in the housing of the poor. They will merit special attention when we come to the public dimension of the provision of housing to the poor.

The Private Dimension

The poor pay for housing, first, in its poor quality. Reflection will show that this is a theme that lies just under the surface of most of our discussion. Whether they own or rent, it is the poor families who tend to occupy the country's substandard housing. In 1956 half of those with income less than $2,000 lived in housing that was dilapidated or lacked plumbing.

This is a rough measure. We have not taken into account size of family. Moreover, current income counts several kinds of people as if they were the same: the rich man who has taken a temporary loss, the retired man who once had more income, and the man who is chronically poor. The first man is likely to be able to spend out of savings and conceivably the retired man too, but hardly the man who has never had a decent income. Nevertheless, the rough measure makes it clear that some who are poor acquire standard housing. They do not acquire it by accident. Analysis of the Chicago population shows that the poor in standard dwellings "typically" pay more rent than those in substandard dwellings. Even those who do not manage standard housing make sacrifices for the quality that they do achieve.

One step that poor families take is to allocate a high percentage of their income to housing. We have already noted a tendency for those who relocate from cleared areas to spend more for improved housing. In 1956 the great majority of families with incomes under $2,000 spent 30 percent or more of their income on rent. On the other hand, of families with incomes between $8,000 and $10,000 the great majority spent less than 15 percent. We have suggested that current income is not always a good indication of a family's financial circumstances. However, relating the amount a family spends to the cost of its housing gives a similar picture. In 1950 urban families with incomes under $1,000 a year spent 26 percent of their total outlay for housing. Families from $1,000 to $2,000 spent 22 percent; from $2,000 to $3,000, 18 percent; and so on.

What would a suitable yardstick be? For most cities the BLS city worker's family budget allocates to housing something less than 20 percent of the total.[1] Moreover, the BLS budget totals are over twice as high as the level of poverty. One would assume that if, out of incomes already lower than adequate, more than 20 percent is allocated to housing, increased deprivation will be felt in other areas of the budget. A depression study in Stockton, England, concluded that higher rents had led to malnutrition. A study reported by Elizabeth Wood came to a more refined conclusion. The study addressed itself to the question, "Can a family pay one-third of its income for rent and yet have enough left to nourish the family?" The conclusion: ". . . under such conditions fathers and children were sufficiently well-nourished, but mothers tended to be undernourished." The same point is made in reverse by a District of Columbia study of 81 families living in public housing who presented rent payment problems. Of the families who presented rent problems, "28 percent had spent their rent money for clothing and other unmet needs of their children."[2]

One possibility is clear—to pay for adequate shelter by settling for inadequate food and clothing. In many cases, the family must be governed not by a deliberate choice to favor housing but by the way inadequate money gets spent. Under sustained pressure, costs that are fixed and regular are met and those that seem stretchable or postponable—food, clothing, recreation, medical care—are not met. In any case, the consequences of spending more than 20 percent for housing do not seem healthy. It is anybody's guess how much lower than 20 percent a rule of thumb for poor families ought to be. Certainly, so far as public decisions are concerned, 20 percent should be regarded as a maximum rather than an average housing expenditure for poor families.

Income for income, naturally, the pressure to make some adjustment to housing needs is felt most by large families. If figures can reflect a sense of strain, perhaps those that follow suggest the financial pressure that builds up in the budget management of a large, low-income family. The table is based on the rents paid by families of varying size before and after relocation. The report covers 1,373 families in 9 cities that did not substantially assist with relocation; rentals reported for 5 cities that did assist show a similar pattern.

---

[1] One city, 15 percent; 2 cities, 16 percent; 6 cities, 17 percent; 4 cities, 19 percent; 5 cities, 20 percent; and 2 cities, 21 percent. The BLS budget includes the cost of rent and heat. The *1956 National Housing Inventory* figures above and the 1950 figures based on the *Survey of Consumer Expenditures* also represent the "gross" cost of housing.

[2] 21 percent had failed to receive support money due them; 18 percent presented budget management problems; 33 percent failed for miscellaneous reasons.

Average Monthly Rentals Before and After Relocation
[By family size, 9 cities, 1955–58]

Number of persons in family	Rent before relocation	Rent after relocation	Rent increase
2	$30.35	$34.81	$4.46
3	32.35	36.23	3.88
4	34.45	37.96	3.51
5	36.50	39.07	2.57

Does it force these data to suggest that these small but consistent differences indicate the degree to which any increased cost must be resisted? Relocation means that all the families must pay more. The larger the family, the less, by a matter of pennies, it can accede to the pressure for higher cost.

What steps do the large families take? Reviewing the *1950 Survey of Consumer Expenditures,* Louis Winnick concludes about the average large family: "They obtain more housing space and, at the same time, maintain or even increase the budgets devoted to other consumer goods." However, poor large families are not able to bring this off. They spend more in total for food and for clothing. To balance the increase, they spend less in total for housing, household operation, and medical care. (This confirms a conclusion we had already reached.) How do the higher income families manage to maintain their spending for other items while obtaining more space? Apparently they do it by sacrificing the physical quality of the housing. (We have seen that poor families are familiar with this tactic too.) So far as ownership is concerned, for example, small families tend to have houses that are worth more, compared to their incomes, than large families. Thus, relative values are lower for the larger families despite the fact that they have more space. Larger families generally try to gain some advantage by purchasing rather than renting, but lower incomes tend to close off this possibility. Poor large families do not, like other large families, show a markedly higher tendency to own than smaller families.

To return to speaking of poor families in general, an additional strategy has now been suggested. Any family, large or small, may think of purchase as a way to secure more housing for its money.[3] Obviously, however, low income restricts the opportunity to buy. Almost 60 percent of the dwellings in metropolitan areas are now owned by the families in them. But in the lowest fifth of the income distribution, in Chicago, 20 percent of the families owned homes. Of urban families

---

[3] The question of ownership versus rental is not determined simply on financial grounds.

receiving aid to families with dependent children, predominantly with incomes under $2,000 a year, 17 percent own homes. For those families that manage it, buying a house involves them in the same tactic as committing a high percentage of income to housing. When a poor family buys a house, it is almost always valued at three times or more the family's income. By contrast, families with incomes over $6,000 tend to pay 1.5 to 2 times their income.[4] Further, buying reduces the flexibility with which a family can meet other contingencies—illness, unemployment, and so forth.

The purchase of housing, though it is not usually thought of in the same terms, is a form of going into debt. Poor families may not receive more short-term credit than families with more income (because it will be refused), but the struggle to buy on credit or borrow money is an everyday fact of life. Borrowed money may be applied directly to rent or it may buy clothing because clothing money went for rent—the effect is the same. The use of credit to pay for housing produces the problems that have just been noted—a future commitment to sacrifice something tomorrow to pay for today's housing and limited flexibility in the face of emergencies. Moreover, the poor family pays a premium for credit. A study of the buying patterns of families in several public housing projects notes some of the problems associated with credit:

> Because of their poor credit potential, many of these families are restricted in where they can shop for durables. . . . They do not shop in department stores and discount houses. Instead they depend upon chain stores, neighborhood merchants and door-to-door peddlers—in short, merchants who are prepared to extend credit to poor risks. The dependence upon such credit means that they pay high prices for appliances.

----

[4] These observations are based on the relation of current income to value, and may be somewhat influenced by families who had purchased homes some time before and whose incomes had declined. However, figures taken at the point of purchase of FHA-insured homes show a similar trend. In 1959 those with incomes under $3,600 bought new homes valued at over 3 times their income or existing homes valued at 2.5 times their income. The ratio of value to income in 1959 shows a steady fall as family income rises.

The values cited in relation to income may understate the poor family's disadvantage in buying a house. If a family with larger income has made a larger downpayment, their monthly payment is reduced even more. Moreover, the owner with more income is likely to secure better lending terms. Some low-income families, at the other extreme, find themselves buying under lease-purchase, with inflated monthly payments and very little chance indeed of eventually obtaining title to the property.

. . . Because of their poor education and relatively young age, and because many are recent migrants to the city, they tend to be naïve shoppers, vulnerable to the lure of "easy credit." . . . Perhaps as many as a third of the families have suffered at the hands of unscrupulous salesmen.[5]

The strategies that are open to poor families are not limited to trying to shift about small sums of money. Analysis of the living arrangements of the aged in the United States indicates that, when help for the old person is needed, the poor tend to pool living arrangements. The plight of the poor "is so difficult that they must select the most efficient way of sharing, which is living together." An attempt to understand crowding among Negroes in Chicago produces a somewhat similar observation:

> Doubling-up of families and sharing the dwelling with nonrelatives probably account for the relatively large household size in the nonwhite population; and such doubling-up and sharing of dwellings are themselves probably means by which nonwhites pool incomes in order to compete for housing.

Smaller studies produce supporting evidence. In sum, one tactic for providing housing is to share space beyond the immediate family and to pool available money.

On the other hand, apparently there is a point of surrender, when adequate housing comes to seem impossible and families break apart. Studying a group of families who were being required to relocate, the Department of Public Welfare of the District of Columbia reported:

> . . . We found some who had already accepted separation as a partial answer. Other families were on the verge of breaking up when it appeared that it would no longer be possible to maintain a common home.[6]

This strategy, if one can call it that, has been of special concern to child welfare agencies. Of 11,500 children in foster care in New York City at one point, 750 could have gone home "at once" if adequate low-cost housing had been available. ". . . 112 children might not have been placed at all had adequate housing with supportive services been available at the point of placement." A study of women committed to the

---

[5] Caplovitz, David, with the assistance of Louis Lieberman. *The Consumer Behavior of Low Income Families.* Columbia University Bureau of Applied Social Research, New York, 1961, pp. 197–98.

[6] Department of Public Welfare, Public Assistance Division. "Report of the Advisory Committee of the Service to Displaced Families to the Director of Public Welfare at the Expiration of the Six Months Trial Period," March 21, 1960 to September 20, 1960. Washington, D.C., November 1, 1960, mimeographed.

New Jersey Reformatory for Women on charges of child neglect found that close to 50 percent "had been living in housing that could only be described as dangerous and not fit for human habitation. . . . Mother after mother described the feeling of discouragement and frustration that came after hours of house-hunting with no success." Says this study in conclusion:

> Grossly inadequate housing was a serious problem to more than 60 percent of these families. This factor was particularly pertinent to the large family groups. A community that cannot provide decent housing and does not exercise adequate control to protect families from exploitation and from living in dangerous situations certainly runs the risk of increasing the neglect problem.[7]

The figures vary from study to study, but all make a similar point. Despite a national policy that is, perhaps, 50 years old,[8] economic need is still an effective force in separating children from their families. Chief among the specific mechanisms that operate in financial need is inability to find adequate housing.

Obviously, families also seek in a variety of ways to *improve* their income. One device that has consequences for family arrangements is to send an additional member of the family to work. Of the group of families cited earlier who left public housing to purchase homes, 7 percent had originally had more than one member of the family working. When interviewed in their own homes not long afterward, 32 percent had more than one worker. The rate at which married women work appears to confirm this finding. On the whole, women tend not to work when they have preschool children in the home. But couples with less than $2,000 income show a marked tendency for the wife to work, if they have preschool children and if they do not. Presumably the wife's income is the only income or it is a necessary supplement to bring family income even to this low level. . . .

Public Housing.—Public housing is not a single program, historically; it is a single vessel that has been used for diverse public purposes.

---

[7] Hancock, Claire R. *A Study of Protective Services and the Problem of Neglect of Children in New Jersey, 1958*. Report of project sponsored by the New Jersey State Board of Child Welfare, Department of Institutions and Agencies, conducted June 1957–January 1958.

[8] Among the conclusions of the White House Conference on Children in 1909: "Home life is the highest and finest product of civilization. It is the great molding force of mind and of character. Children should not be deprived of it except for urgent and compelling reasons. . . . Except in unusual circumstances, the home should not be broken up for reasons of poverty, but only for consideration of inefficiency or immorality."

In the 1930's, public housing was intended for families who voluntarily sought to improve their housing but could not afford private rentals. This group was not regarded as dependent. Indeed, some housing authorities limited the number of public assistance recipients they would accept and others would not admit any. In the 1940's, the program was redirected to provide housing for war workers. Following the Housing Act of 1949, public housing was oriented again to poor families—with a difference. Partly because postwar amendments gave priority to families having the most urgent housing need, to the aged, and to those displaced by urban renewal, this third generation in public housing contains a high concentration of depressed, untutored, and dependent families.

It would be misleading to speak of the development of the program as if all the crucial changes were made by Congress. If public housing is the vessel, perhaps Congress is the vintner, but one must ask about the grape and the palate of the taster. The recipe for populating a city, of which we have spoken, concentrates Negroes in public housing as in slums. Segregation is not entirely new, of course, but since 1954 it has become a more open insult. To the extent that public housing found its sites chiefly in land cleared for renewal, large areas were devoted exclusively to public housing (St. Louis is an example). To the extent that the growing suburbs successfully resisted public housing, they confined it to the city core. Meanwhile, as between 1935 and 1960, there was a greater proportion of Americans who had never experienced poverty personally or were trying to forget it. They contributed to a more critical, if not pious, public view of public housing. Thus, a conjunction of social and economic trends leads to the setting apart of families in public housing.

As is so often the case, internal problems of policy and administration aggravate a difficult situation. Authorities have been widely criticized for poor housing design—too much standardization, too high densities, lack of imagination, and disregard of informal social patterns. The Commissioner of Public Housing took note of the criticism in a letter to local authorities.

> What the localities need [she said in part] is a loosening of regulations by Washington, and that we will do. There are so many regulations about square footage and the space between buildings, for example, that the result is the same housing in Maine and in southern California.[9]

---

[9] *New York Times.* "New Ideas Sought in Public Housing," November 26, 1961.

Housing that was tending to be concentrated in terms of people had taken on, as well, an institutional appearance. Further, tenants must leave public housing if their income exceeds a permissible maximum.[10] In effect, those families must leave who achieve at least limited success and who might provide variety and leadership in the housing developments. The struggle of housing authorities to find remedies may itself create a problem. As a number of tenants have the most primitive understanding of housing, regulations and penalties proliferate: Windows must be shut in the winter . . . a fine if drains are plugged without good reason . . . eviction for an illegitimate pregnancy . . . and so forth. Some tenants find this to be precisely a confirmation of their greatest anxiety, that they were being offered decent housing in exchange for their independence. The stage is set for mutual suspicion between tenant and manager, with relationships inside a housing development diverging increasingly from those that are typical in private housing.[11]

The alteration in its population also leads to a financial problem for public housing. Tenants' income (in constant dollars) has remained level in the past decade, but each year the tenants' income falls further below the median for the country. That is, in 1955 the median net income of families admitted to public housing was 46.5 percent of the median income of all families in the United States. In 1961, it was less than 40 percent. Consequently, the rents that may be collected from tenants do not rise as rapidly as maintenance costs. Between 1950 and 1958 monthly receipts from rent increased by 25 percent (from $28.93 to $36.50 per unit per month), but expenditures increased by 52 percent (from $21.32 to $32.50). Not unexpectedly, then, the Federal contribution to local housing authorities has been moving steadily toward its permissible maximum. With the overall Federal contribution reaching 87 percent of the maximum in fiscal year 1961, some local housing authorities would find themselves still with substantial leeway and others with rather little.

Public housing is faced with grave problems which go to the heart of its ability to remain solvent and shape the kind of housing, in the sense of total social and physical environment, that it is able to

---

[10] The Housing Act of 1961 permits local housing authorities to retain over-income families for a limited period if it can be shown that standard private housing is not available to them.

[11] A study of management policies in public housing concludes that ". . . the imposing of numerous controls on tenant behavior has tended to intensify the misunderstandings which arise between tenants and managers."

TABLE 1

Percentage of 3- and 4-Person Families in Total Population and
Moving Into Public Housing, 1960

Income for year	Percentage of total population	Percentage of all families moving into public housing
Under $1,500	5.8	11.7
$1,500 to $4,000	18.7	83.7

Sources: *Current Population Reports*, table 5, and *Families Moving Into Low-Rent Housing, Calendar Year 1960*, table 6.

provide.[12] What are the consequences for tenants? The first and perhaps the most serious consequence is that public housing is not available to more than a small proportion of the low-income families. Though the Housing Act of 1949 authorized 810,000 units, that authorization is as yet far from exhausted. There are in all something over half a million units—roughly 1 percent of the housing supply. If public housing were limited to the lowest incomes, with current resources it could house 2 million of the 32 million we have defined as poor. As it reaches above the very lowest incomes, it houses even a smaller percentage of the poor than these figures indicate. Consequently there are waiting lists of people eligible for public housing. In the District of Columbia, the number of families awaiting admission has at times exceeded the total number of housing units.

Since public housing must look to its receipts, it tends to exclude families with the lowest incomes who cannot pay minimum rents. Table 1 sets numbers to this observation. That is, the bulk of families entering public housing have incomes under $4,000 a year. Among the families having less than $4,000, in the total population roughly one in four has under $1,500 income. But only one in eight of those who move into public housing has less than $1,500.[13] Families may be excluded as undesirable, too. Though such exclusions would doubtless diminish if there were more public housing, they represent an effort to maintain a degree of acceptability among tenants. On the other hand, when

---

[12] Not all of the problems have been touched on here. For a careful description of policy and financial developments, see the "working paper" by Warren Jay Vinton for the Conference on Housing the Economically and Socially Disadvantaged Groups in the Population. For a development of the meaning of the change in tenant population, see "Public Housing and Mrs. McGee."

[13] Perhaps half of the families with less than $1,500 income who move into public housing are public assistance recipients. The non-recipient with very low income is therefore represented in a very small proportion indeed.

careful study was made of 82 families excluded as undesirables in New York City, the decision was reversed for 33 of the families. Other reviews have produced higher percentages of reversal. In addition to the limited capacity of the program, we have already noted that many presumably eligible families are not willing to live in public housing. Their reluctance must arise, to some degree, from the program's current difficulties, but it also represents a feeling about living in a managed—particularly, in a Government-managed—community. As early as 1946, a local study reported that only a third of those eligible were willing to live in public housing. In sum, public housing is limited by its quantity, its fixity upon the middle range of low incomes, and by management and tenant views of acceptability.

Americans are often more attentive to the tempo and direction of a trend than to the underlying facts. Because we are preoccupied with the problems and movement of public housing, we may conceivably overlook the function it is performing. When they are asked, the majority of families who live in public housing say that they like it. They appreciate its facilities; their general morale is higher than it was in substandard housing. One must, of course, take into account that those who would object most to public housing never enter it, or they leave.[14] Nevertheless, for those who take up tenancy, public housing represents a considerable improvement in physical surroundings. Moreover, the aspects of the environment which are offensive to some families may be secondary or even functional for others. Kurt W. Back finds that two types of people move into public housing, those who seek to use it as a vehicle for change and those who see it as an end in itself. Of the latter, he writes:

> In general, the tenants form the weaker and more vulnerable part of the [public housing] population. They have less income, less secure income, and are more likely to represent broken homes. In a very real way they need the protection afforded by government action, and many of them received some government aid. These people apparently look on government housing as a type of institutional support, which they need.[15]

Thus, public housing performs at least acceptably for those poor families who see it as an improved, somewhat protected environment. Presumably, it offers their children a better start than they might otherwise

---

[14] The rate of moveouts, though it signals difficulty in some places, is not strikingly high compared with general population mobility. It is lower overall than the moveout rate for rental housing insured by FHA.

[15] Back, Kurt W. *Slums, Projects, and People: Social Psychological Problems of Relocation in Puerto Rico.* Durham, N.C.: Duke University Press, 1962, p. 102.

have had. Analysis of turnover statistics suggests that others use public housing as a way station to improved housing. In this sense, too, public housing serves the prevention of poverty.

Thus, strictly managed housing may suit one family—or at least not trouble it—and trouble others very much. Public housing is pressed, if it is going to serve families with any precision, to define its objectives and to alter policies to further these objectives. At least three choices are open: (1) A real estate operation for the respectable poor—the purely poor. (2) A rehabilitative program for the seriously dependent and troubled poor. (3) A greatly enlarged and altered program, at least in part deinstitutionalized, with a variety of kinds of housing opportunities. In the absence of a settled decision to seek the third course and of the legislation that would make it possible, local housing authorities are moving slowly, in most cases with pronounced reluctance, toward rehabilitative programs. Under present circumstances the families who are entering public housing make such a course inevitable. Not only are the families isolated and segregated; increasing numbers are aged, many receive public assistance, and many are in broken families. They cannot be abandoned to their problems; they must be served. Moreover, when they are not served, buildings deteriorate, delinquencies occur, and deprived youngsters grow into disabled adults. It becomes plain that neglect is expensive. . . .

How does public housing serve the poor? It serves some of them, a small minority of them. Those it serves, does it serve them well? Some of them, only some of them.

Public Assistance.—People who do not have enough money for decent living may be helped by public assistance. Major assistance programs, representing a partnership of Federal and State Governments, are addressed to children in family homes, to the aged, the blind, and the disabled. Some States and localities also provide general assistance for needy people not eligible under the categorical programs. In accordance with the Social Security Act, assistance in the Federal-State programs is given to recipients in money, without stipulating how it must be spent.[16] As this practice suggests, the intent of the legislation was to provide funds for subsistence, without public intrusion into the choices that must be made in family management. Public assistance agencies have, therefore, tended to refrain from dealing directly with

---

[16] However, payments may be made on behalf of a recipient to a person or organization providing medical or other remedial care. In aid to families with dependent children, in a limited number of cases where it is in the children's interest, the entire payment may be turned over to a third party to spend on behalf of the recipient family.

landlords. But assistance provides the means for securing housing. When recipients have difficulty in securing adequate housing, assistance agencies are perforce involved in their clients' problems. At the beginning of 1962, over 7 million people were receiving assistance. Though less directly than public housing, to be sure, public assistance is the largest national program concerned with the housing needs of the poor. It is important, therefore, to ask about the quality of housing that assistance recipients secure and about the welfare department's influence upon it.

⟶   Although information about the quality of recipients' housing has not been systematically collected, it is clear that the quality is poor. Data about plumbing facilities in Table 2 suggest how the housing of recipients compares with that of the general population. It may not be surprising that assistance recipients, having the lowest incomes, are worse off than the average. However, it is an impressive figure that 4 out of 10 aged recipients and 3 out of 10 recipient families with dependent children manage without each of these basic facilities. One can guess at the proportions of their dwellings that are dilapidated and deteriorated. Measures of crowding suggest that over time assistance recipients are not improving their housing at the same rate as the general population. In the decade from 1950 to 1960, the median number of persons per room in the AFDC household declined from 1.0 to 0.94. In the same period, the national median declined from 0.75 to 0.59. That the median number of persons per room in the AFDC household is now 0.94 means that almost half the families are crowded. One in five of the AFDC families are "critically overcrowded," living in households in which there are 1.5 persons or more per room.

TABLE 2

Plumbing Facilities Available in 1960, to Total U.S. Population, to Recipients of Aid to Families With Dependent Children, and of Old Age Assistance

	Total U.S. population, percent having	Aid to families with dependent children, percent of recipients having	Old-age assistance, percent of recipients having
Hot and cold running water inside structure	87	70	60
Exclusive use of a flush toilet	87	72[1]	59

[1] Includes a small number having a bath or shower but no flush toilet.

Sources: *1960 Census of Housing, Characteristics and Financial Circumstances of Recipients of Old-Age Assistance 1960,* and a national study of aid to families with dependent children.

Special State and city studies provide a more intimate appraisal of the housing of public assistance recipients. Florida reviewed 13,000 cases of aid to families with dependent children to determine whether the homes were suitable for children. The study noted "excessively high rents for unspeakably inadequate slum homes." A survey of recipient families with dependent children in the State of Maine found that four out of five did not have central heating. The report concludes:

> Over half [of AFDC families] do not have what most Americans take for granted: central heating and all three of the essential plumbing facilities, running water, bath, and exclusive use of a toilet. About a third . . . are overcrowded and many others lack privacy because of a need to share a living arrangement with relatives and non-relatives.[17]

There are variations in the numbers and the degree of detachment with which other studies report. But the same basic situation has been documented for Chicago; Atlanta; Baltimore; Washington, D.C.; Philadelphia; Westchester County, N.Y.; and Alexandria, Va. Occasionally a study inquires specifically into the housing of recipients who would have special difficulty in finding housing—for example, families with unmarried mothers. The findings are predictable. Of over 3,000 illegitimate children who were receiving AFDC, Cleveland reported that 10 percent were living in public housing. The remaining 90 percent lived in housing that was "overcrowded and substandard. . . . The majority live in neighborhoods that are rooming house areas and slums." A similar study in New York City found a quarter of the married mothers and half of the unmarried mothers living in "rooming houses considered undesirable for family living."

The repetition of percentages about crowding and sanitary facilities may fail to convey what caseworkers see and recipients experience. The Commissioner of Welfare in New York City quotes a caseworker as follows:

> In this six-story building, converted into furnished rooms, filth prevails throughout—filled garbage cans without covers line the hallways with the surplus refuse spilling over; roaches and rats abound; broken flooring, plumbing, windows, lighting fixtures and plaster are observable throughout. The average room size [occupied by a family] is 13x15 with two beds, a dresser, two chairs, a table, a refrigerator and a closet, as the standard equipment supplied by the landlord. One community kitchen is used by seven families. Twelve toilets are intermittently in service on six floors. There is no lock on the door from the street and

---

[17] Romanyshyn, John M. *Aid to Dependent Children in Maine*. State of Maine Department of Health and Welfare, June 1960, p. 10.

vagrants, including drug addicts and alcoholics, often wander in to sleep in the unlocked kitchens and bathrooms. This is the abode of thirty families and 105 children. . . .[18]

One has to ask how such conditions occur for so many people in programs intended to maintain health and decency and to strengthen family life. It goes without saying that, by the nature of the problem that makes recipients of them, some families are handicapped in finding and maintaining decent housing. Old age, physical disability, and a broken marriage or no marriage may each, in its own way, make a family poor tenants. But there are simpler, more powerful causes of the problem.

Fundamentally, the amount of money paid to recipients of public assistance in most places is not enough to pay for proper housing and the other elements of a healthful and decent budget. Payments under the Federal-State programs are, in all cases, based on an assessment of actual need. In making the assessment and determining the payment, however, a number of policies and practices are interposed to reduce the amount of assistance that is paid to a family. First, the basic amounts allowed for budget items are likely not to be realistically related to costs. The cost of rent or mortgage payments is not estimated in standard amounts by States; it is budgeted in relation to the actual payment. Seventeen States budget rentals "as paid" by the client or as paid for reasonable or modest housing. But 35 States budget rentals only "as paid *to a maximum.*" In an attempt to assess the realism of other budget items, in 1958 State standard allowances for food for a single man (OAA) and for a family of four (AFDC) were compared with the U.S. Department of Agriculture low-cost food plan. For the old-age assistance case, only Arizona budgeted an amount for food as great as the U.S. Department of Agriculture standard. For the family with dependent children, only Florida and Michigan matched the Department of Agriculture standard. Thus, it is clear in the initial calculation of need that real minimum costs will not be met.

Second, regardless of the amount of money that States determine to be needed, they may apply a maximum to the overall amount of the payment. About two-thirds of the States apply a maximum of some sort to payments in each of the Federal-State programs. In consequence, 29 percent of OAA recipients in 1960 received less than they had been determined to need by the State's own standards. The median amount of the deficit was over $9 a month. Forty-eight percent of AFDC families in

---

[18] Dumpson, James R. "The Human Side of Urban Renewal," *The Welfarer,* Vol. XIII, No. 10, October 1960, pp. 1, 4.

1958 received less than they had been determined to need. The average amount of the deficit was nearly $39 a month. A third practice that reduces the assistance payment is to impute income to a client, whether or not he receives it. Twenty-four States impute income—when there is a relative who is responsible to help, when a court orders a support payment to a family, or if a parent has refused available employment. Such policies are intended to encourage client or family responsibility but, as there may never actually be payment or earnings, the effect is frequently confined to reducing the amount of assistance. Finally, payments may be reduced simply because of human error. It is a curious fact, turned up by regular audits, that the majority of errors that are evident in public assistance records result in *under*payments to recipients. It is difficult to account for this, except to suppose that in administering complicated regulations some caseworkers are leaning far over backwards indeed to avoid overpayment. In simplest outline, these are the steps by which payments which are in principal minimally adequate become something less—or a great deal less—than adequate.

We have already looked at the dilemma in which the family with less than enough money finds itself. In addition, recipients are more than ordinarily likely to suffer [for housing purposes] from being Negro, in broken families, and having several children. The fact of being a recipient may itself lead landlords to refuse to rent. Less than enough money is, one might say, sufficient handicap. The compounding of the problem by other handicaps means that most recipients will not find decent housing unless they are somehow protected or aided. In fact, welfare departments are moving to assist with housing. Their motivations are several: the desperate circumstances of some recipients, the patent exploitation of others, and the cost of paying for hotels or institutional care simply because reasonable housing cannot be found. In general, three courses are open to welfare departments. They may provide counsel and other aids to clients. They may turn to public housing for their recipients. They may ally themselves with other community forces to eliminate substandard housing and superstandard charges for it. . . .

The issues that exist between public housing and public assistance are predictable byproducts of the convergence of two independent programs. The provision of more effective service by public assistance to its clients in public housing should assist in resolving these issues. But with or without issues, public housing is the one dependable resource to which public assistance may turn for acceptable housing for recipients. The help that it finds is limited chiefly because the quantity of public housing is limited.

The final course open in attempting to assist recipients is for welfare departments to ally themselves with other community forces to eliminate substandard housing and exorbitant rents. Though welfare departments are widely privy to violations of housing codes, they do not routinely press the appropriate municipal departments for enforcement. The studies of housing codes in Philadelphia and New York State that were touched upon earlier criticize welfare departments for failing to offer cooperation. It is unlikely that the failure arises from a lack of concern. Whether they have wished to be involved in providing decent housing or not, it looms up as a major problem confronting welfare administrators. Moreover, with funds for assistance chronically short, it nags at one's nerves to know that a portion of the money that is available goes into the exchequers of profiteers. In their experience in reporting violations, however, welfare departments have discovered how little they can expect in the way of result. They discover, with a certain immediacy, the powerful forces that operate against code enforcement. Depending upon the local situation, they may abandon reporting violations entirely or report the more dramatic ones—but without hope or followup.

From time to time, welfare administrators make ceremonial statements urging enforcement upon other executive officials and legislatures. For practical results, however, some appear to be looking to their own ability to put pressure on landlords. When negotiations with a landlord fail, they may assist the recipient to move. This constitutes effective pressure only in the comparatively few communities where housing is readily available. In 1962 New York State passed a law permitting public welfare officials to withhold welfare rent payments from seriously substandard dwellings. About the same time, welfare workers in Chicago were advising their clients to withhold rent payments in such dwellings.[19] Recipients were, in due course, evicted by their landlords but were able to find other housing. Since the welfare department does not pay rent in arrears, the cost to slum landlords was substantial. Moreover, the city corporation counsel filed suit against landlords at the same time to force them to correct code violations. An "sro" program in New York City was even more forceful. The housing authority and welfare and real estate departments collaborated in the enforcement of an ordinance prohibiting family occupancy of single rooms. (sro stands for "single room occupancy" as well as its more customary,

---

[19] In turn, the welfare department withholds rent money from the client. Where Federal money is involved, regulations would require clarity that the recipient was acting on his own behalf, not under compulsion by the welfare department.

entirely relevant meaning.) The city took legal possession of a number of houses that were conspicuous offenders and were largely tenanted by assistance recipients. The houses were cleared and adequate dwellings located for the tenants. . . .

How does public assistance serve in providing housing for poor people? It leaves many in poor housing and some in desperately poor housing. Basically, its failure is a failure to provide recipients with enough money to pay for decent housing. Because of this failure, public assistance is pressed to offer special aids and protection for its clients. These help, to some degree, but to larger degree are frustrated by limitations of available housing and inability to force legal maintenance of housing. Because public assistance has not historically regarded itself as a provider of housing, agencies may also fail to invest their fullest energies in the securing of housing.

Two old studies suggest the direction and pace with which public assistance has moved in relation to housing. A U.S. Children's Bureau study of Mothers' Aid (a predecessor to AFDC) in 10 representative communities in 1928 reports:

> Except in one large city, where housing conditions left much to be desired, the families were for the most part in decent, sanitary dwellings or flats in respectable neighborhoods; many were in comfortable one-family houses, and a considerable number had flower gardens. If families were found living in too congested quarters, under insanitary conditions, or in neighborhoods where morality was questionable, the courts required them—or the agencies persuaded them—to move to better locations.[20]

In 1940, the U.S. Housing Authority and the Social Security Board reviewed common areas of their programs. Among their conclusions:

> . . . it is apparent that relief and public assistance families are inadequately housed. . . . It is estimated that 50 to 90 percent of such families occupy the *worst* kind of shelter.
>
> . . . Inadequate housing is related to inadequate income with but few exceptions.
>
> . . . There are no *generally accepted* basic standards of the quantity and quality of housing considered a minimum essential for every family.[21]

---

[20] Bogue, Mary F. *Administration of Mothers' Aid in Ten Localities*, U.S. Department of Labor, Children's Bureau, Publication No. 184, 1928, p. 15.

[21] U.S. Housing Authority in Cooperation with the Social Security Board. *Housing and Welfare*, Federal Works Agency, Washington, D.C., May, 1940, pp. 6 and 7.

So far as the housing of public assistance recipients is concerned, the direction between 1928 and 1940 was downward. The recommendations that followed from the findings of the 1940 study are obvious: adequate payments, applying objective standards to recipients' housing, regular reporting of the quality of recipients' housing, more public housing to use for assistance recipients. Prescriptions that were plain when the Social Security Act was new have yet to be acted upon.

Can Poor Families Be Housed?

If one reflects upon the ways in which poor families pay for housing in their private lives and upon the ways in which public policies assist them, it is possible to perceive a discrepancy. The private and the public dimensions are out of balance. Poor people pay for housing as a total effort, out of their food and out of the fabric of their lives together. The effects of the struggle are experienced without Sabbath and without holiday. But public efforts to assist them are directed only to a minority. Out of those who are reached, many are helped meagerly, subject to conditions that may be relevant, irrelevant, or even self-defeating.

In public efforts to provide housing we have so far relied chiefly upon stimulation and subsidy of private industry. The results, for those with incomes over $5,000 or $6,000, have been respectable. Recent legislation attempts to extend the impact of such activity to lower incomes. The problem has so far appeared to be one of interesting builders and developers in such a market. It appears likely that some gains will be made. But it must be evident that the problem of the poor will not be met in this manner. We have referred to the reasons; they require only to be brought together.

First, though special incentives for low-income building and contraction of demand in the middle-income market may lead to more builder interest in low-cost housing than heretofore, it is unlikely that interest will reach down to the families with $2,500 incomes. High risks, limited profits, and other difficulties that have discouraged business from building for families with $5,000 incomes will seem insuperable at half those incomes.

Second, it is not unreasonable that builders and banks should take pause. A family of four with less than $2,500 income is not able to buy a house or pay a rent that provides a profit on it, no matter how low the interest rate on the mortgage. The family's income is not adequate to its need for food, clothing, and other necessary items—even if it were paying no rent at all.

Third, inducing low-income families to pay 25 or 30 percent of their incomes carries a heavy risk of its own and is not sound public policy. The housing that is bought at the expense of food or medical care is dearly bought.

This is not to say that we are unable to provide decent housing for all American families. Public housing and public assistance provide avenues for decent housing, providing that the serious limitations of these programs are corrected. Small-scale experiments of other sorts are being tried. A number involve public subsidy to those who provide housing for low-income families, with purchasers or tenants making such payments as they can afford. There has been recurrent consideration of the possibility of providing a direct subsidy to low-income families to be used for purchasing or renting standard housing. Such a proposal was considered by the Senate Subcommittee on Housing and Urban Redevelopment headed by Senator Robert A. Taft. Reporting in 1945, the subcommittee rejected direct subsidies, mainly because they might flow to substandard housing. There was also objection to channeling such funds through public assistance agencies. After more than a decade of experience with urban renewal, attention has been turning again to the possibility of providing a direct subsidy to poor families. A number of schemes have been put forward that provide protections against misuse; nor would subsidies necessarily be furnished through public assistance agencies.

We can indeed shape a program that will provide "a decent home and a suitable living environment for every American family." Such a program need not appear to be favoritism. On the contrary, aids that have so far been devised (income tax advantages, mortgage insurance) reach middle- and upper-income families with special effect. Resources and techniques are available to right the balance.

City Schools

Patricia Cayo Sexton

New York University

[Reprinted with permission from The Annals of the American Academy of Political and Social Science, March 1964.]

To TALK ABOUT URBAN EDUCATION is to talk about an old fallen phrase in such disrepute during two postwar decades that it has hidden out from scholarly journals like a furtive sex criminal. The phrase "class struggle" now appears in black tie and softened aliases as "slum and suburb," "inequalities," problems of the "disadvantaged," of the "culturally deprived," of "integration." However Americanized or blurred the new image may appear, the basic fact seems simple enough: a remarkable "class struggle" now rattles our nation's schools and the scene of sharpest conflict is the city. Southern cities—and New York—were the scenes of first eruptions, but now almost every northern city, and many suburbs, are feeling the new tremors.

A high-ranking official in New Rochelle, New York, put it in these words: "It's not just race in our schools . . . it's class warfare!" Class conflict, of course, is not the only issue in city schools. There is ethnic conflict and the special status of Negroes—and of Puerto Ricans and other identifiable groups—at the bottom end of the ladder and the special Rickover pressure-cooked conformism and prestige-college frenzy at the upper end.[1] Nor are the sides in the conflict always clearly formed. But, usually, when the chaff and wheat are separated, what is left is the "haves" in one pile and "have-nots" in another, with some impurities in each—middle-class white "liberals," for example, who support some Negro demands and white have-nots who oppose them. Banfield and Wilson claim four important cleavages in city politics: (1) haves and have-nots, (2) suburbanites and the central city, (3) ethnic and racial groups, (4) political parties.[2] A reduction to more basic outlines might show that the first category would, with some slippage, cover the other three. Indeed, the authors acknowledge as much when they say: "These tend to cut across each other and, in general, to become one fundamental cleavage separating two opposed conceptions of the public interest."[3] When they refer to ". . . The fundamental cleavage between the public-regarding Anglo-Saxon Protestant, middle-class ethos and the private-regarding lower-class, immigrant ethos," they seem to refer, though the phrase is unspoken, to one aspect of the class struggle.[4]

---

[1] Rickover supporters in the Council on Basic Education voice some misgivings about the Admiral's program to restrict higher education to an elite.

[2] Edward C. Banfield and James Q. Wilson, *City Politics* (Cambridge, Mass.: Harvard University Press and MIT Press, 1963).

[3] *Ibid.*, p. 35.

[4] *Ibid.*, p. 329. Their ascription of a "public-regarding" ethos to the middle class and a "private-regarding" one to the "lower class" seems an extraordinary and questionable reversal of the usual association of the middle class with private efforts and the lower class with public efforts. It is most puzzling when contrasted with their summary statement: "If in the old days [of lower class ward politics] specific material inducements were illegally given as bribes to favored individuals, now much bigger ones are legally given to a different class of favored individuals . . ." (p. 340).

Other major urban school issues exist—finances, bureaucracy, and the unionization of teachers, among others—and may seem, on the surface, unrelated to class conflict. At second glance, the shortage of school funds can be seen as a product of the antitax ideology of haves. The behemoth bureaucracies may be seen everywhere as more accessible to and influenced by haves, and the decentralization of administration—to which New York's Superintendent Gross and others have devoted themselves—may be seen as a partial response to the growing arousal of have-not groups. The unionization of city teachers may be seen as a response to the hitherto rather rigid conservative control of school systems and the new thrust of liberalism in the cities and the schools, released by have-not votes and agitation, as well as a defense against the difficult conditions in have-not schools.[5]

Levels of Conflict

The class struggle in the schools and the struggle for power which is part of it are carried on at many levels. In some cases, it seems least visible under the spotlight—on the school boards. Through liberal and have-not activity, some city school boards are now composed of middle-class moderates who are more inclined to represent the educational interests of have-nots than were their more conservative predecessors. Some big-city boards, as New York's, seem exemplary public servants, superior in purpose and competence to higher political bodies. Their efforts on behalf of have-nots are limited by several personal as well as external characteristics: they are haves, a quality that usually though not invariably limits zeal and identity with have-nots; they are moderates in contrast to those leading the more militant have-not groups. Among the limits set by school systems are: (1) the traditional conservative reluctance of boards to interfere in the operations of the bureaucracy; (2) the inertia and resistance of the bureaucracy to pressure from the board; (3) the usual tendency to become defensive of "their system" and to take criticisms of the system as personal affronts; (4) influences from middle-class interests which are usually more insistent and weighty than have-not pressure; (5) interference from outside groups—such as the unprecedented threat of the Northcentral Associa-

---

[5] In New York and Chicago especially, the popular political issues of "bossism" and "machine politics" have been referred to the school arena. In New York, 110 Livingston Street (the Board of Education headquarters) has appeared to many as the school equivalent of "city hall," the one place you "can't beat" and with which you often cannot even communicate. Now a proposal is being considered to divide the city schools into several fairly autonomous geographic units in order to scatter the shots at "city hall" and provide easier access.

tion to withdraw accreditation from the Chicago schools if the school board insisted on a step which forced Superintendent Willis into further desegregation. The external limits on the situation, however, seem more determining: (1) the difficulty of the job to be done, (2) the lack of sufficient money to do the job.

Services to have-nots within the city system, therefore, are limited by these conservative factors: (1) the moderate position of most liberal board members and the insufficiency of zeal or identification to drive home the grievances of have-nots; (2) conservatism and resistance within the bureaucracy; (3) conservative influence which acts to shut off funds to the schools.

In the movement of the class struggle from one end of the continuum, where a small elite holds total power, to the other extreme, where have-nots share proportionate influence, there are many points of compromise, and public officials tend to pursue ever more liberal ends and means. The white liberals who sit on some city boards may begin to push for more rapid change or may be replaced soon by representatives who will.

The claim that the city and its school system are so constrained by outside conservatism, especially at the state level, that they can do little seems largely true, though partially exaggerated. Too often outside interference is made an excuse for inertia. City schools have not given adequate service to have-nots largely because the have-nots were underrepresented in decision-making positions. As cities go, New York's school board seems unusually enlightened, appointed as it is by a relatively responsive mayor and served by two unusually alert citizen groups—the Public Education Association and the United Parents Association. Yet a nine-member board includes only one Negro and no Puerto Rican, although these groups together compose 40 percent of the city's public school enrollment. Nor is there any blue-collar worker or person of modest means or position on the board, but, then, such individuals are rare specimens on city boards. One trade unionist, himself a university graduate and member of a professional union, sits on the board. Of some 777 top officials in the system—board members, superintendents, and principals—it appears that only six are Negroes, 0.8 per cent of the total.[6]

Although it is sometimes asserted that the interest-group identity of board members does not affect their decision-making, what may be more nearly the case, given present knowledge of group dynamics,

---

[6] Daniel Griffiths and Others, *Teacher Mobility in New York City* (New York, 1963).

is that the group interests of the lone have-not representative may be submerged in a board's moderate consensus.

Perhaps the "equality lag" within city systems may be more directly attributable to deficiencies in have-not organization than to lack of good faith among liberals and board members. Many cities could nearly be "possessed" by Negroes who approach a majority in some cases, but Negroes do not vote their numerical strength and may be evicted from the city limits by urban renewal before they catch up with their potential. Nor do labor unions use their full authority in school affairs. A major weakness of have-nots is their limited understanding of power, who has it and how to get it; they also lack the time, money, and organization often needed to purchase it.[7]

Beyond the City Limits

Local class conflict seems only a dim reflection of a larger conflict. The main drama of class conflict and thrust of conservatism are seen in full dimension in a larger arena—at the federal and state levels. The national scene cannot be ignored in any consideration of the city school situation. Only at this level does there appear a possibility of releasing the funds needed to support high-quality education and the high-level job opportunity that goes with it. The claim that federal aid to education is the *only* school issue and that other concerns are simply distractions is given substantial support by any cursory study of city school budgets and revenue limitations.[8]

Nationally, the conflict seems shaped by at least two major factors:

(1) The congressional system is biased against have-nots and their representatives. The bias results from at least two forms of conservative manipulation: (a) manipulation of rural and small-town interests, North and South, and, through them, congressional apportionment

---

[7] Banfield and Wilson, *op. cit.*, p. 282: "Organized labor—even if it includes in its ranks the majority of all the adult citizens in the community—is generally regarded as a 'special interest' which must be 'represented'; businessmen, on the other hand, are often regarded, not as 'representing business' as a 'special interest,' but as serving the community as a whole. Businessmen, in Peter Clark's term, often are viewed as 'symbols of civic legitimacy.' Labor leaders rarely have this symbolic quality, but must contend with whatever stigma attaches to being from a lower-class background and associated with a special-interest group. . . . Labor is handicapped not only by having imputed to it less civic virtue but also by a shortage of money and organizational skills."

[8] This seems to suggest that social scientists could much more profitably study the political mechanisms by which such aid could be released rather than the often esoteric and "academic" studies of culture, personality, and the like which now tend overly to occupy many who are concerned with have-nots.

and votes; (b) the additional manipulation of southern rural conserva-tism—which is given unusual congressional power by the committee seniority system—through the exchange of votes on the race issue.

The superior effective power of haves at this top level serves to block federal legislation in general but specifically those measures that might ensure rapid economic growth through federal expenditures, full employment, and the extension of power to have-nots—measures that would give significant relief to the city's distress. More directly rele-vant, it has blocked any substantial aid to urban areas and held up the transfer of political power from rural to urban areas.[9]

Moreover, largely by the manipulation of conflicting religious interests, this coalition has prevented the passage of the federal aid that seems indispensable to urban schools. At the same time, it has continued, through extension programs, copious aid to rural education.

(2) Seriously deprived have-nots have failed to enter their full power into the political arena.

The State

If direct federal aid seems distant and the aid formula unlikely to provide much assistance to the cities, fiscal aid from the state may be closer at hand, depending upon how quickly reapportionment will be enforced in the states. New York City received $197 in school aid for each student in its public schools in 1961–1962, while the average in the rest of the state was $314. Miami, Florida paid $47 million in state taxes in one recent year and got back only $1.5 million in grants-in-aid. With sympathetic legislatures, cities may be able to call on other revenues, including an income tax on suburbanites working in the city such as has been adopted in Philadelphia and Detroit.

Inequalities

The consequences of local, state, and national class conflict are seen in the school inequalities and class-biased training given to children even within the most liberal city systems. Only in the past few years has the concern of some unionists, academicians, liberals, and many Negroes brought the full range of inequities to public attention. The "spoils" of the city school, limited as they are by outside controls, are usually divided according to the crude formula "them as has gets." Only now

---

[9] The assumption that a proper apportioning of representatives, giving a proper share to the city's suburban areas, will result in an accretion of power to haves may not be warranted inasmuch as have-nots are also being rapidly subur-banized yet, contrary to expectation, seem to be maintaining their political identity.

in some cities is there any insistence on the more radical "compensatory" formula—"to each according to need."

Documentary evidence about class inequalities, past and present, is now weighty. My own study of one large city school system, *Education and Income*, describes the various forms of class inequities within one system.[10] I will refer here only to a few facts about Chicago and New York (not the cities of my study). In 1955, following Dr. Kenneth Clark's demand for attention to Negro schools, an "outside" study found that Negro and Puerto Rican schools in New York City were generally inferior to "Other" schools.[11] In a group of Negro and Puerto Rican schools (the X Group), 50.3 percent of teachers were on tenure, compared to 78.2 percent in the "Other" group (the Y Group); 18.1 percent in the X group and only 8.3 percent in the Y group were "permanent substitutes." On the average, facilities in Group X schools were older, less adequate, and more poorly maintained than Y schools. The costs of operating Y schools were higher than costs in X schools. Though the New York Board of Education now claims that Negro and Puerto Rican schools are equal or superior to "Other" schools, Dr. Kenneth Clark still says Harlem schools reflect "a consistent pattern of criminal neglect."

In the absence of cost-accounting, comparative expenditures in have and have-not schools in New York cannot be checked. Certainly efforts are being made by New York schools to provide better education for deprived minorities, especially in "certain" schools where extra services tend to be over-concentrated, but the schools still do not seem to approach full equality, and the cost estimates do not measure the *full* cost of education—the differences in nursery and kindergarten education, the last two years of high school missed by the low-income dropout, and the costs of higher education—not to mention the low-quality and segregated "ability" tracks into which have-not children are often placed.

Though New York permitted an outside study of school inequalities in 1954, the Chicago Superintendent of Schools, Benjamin Willis, has only in the past year agreed to a three-man study committee of which he will be a member. In 1962 John E. Coons, Northwestern University law professor, prepared for the United States Commission on Civil Rights a report on segregated schools in Chicago.[12] Ten schools

[10] Patricia Cayo Sexton, *Education and Income* (New York: Viking Press, 1961).

[11] *The Status of the Public School Education of Negro and Puerto Rican Children in New York City*, October, 1955.

[12] John E. Coons, *Civil Rights USA, Chicago, 1962*, A Report to the United States Commission on Civil Rights.

in each of three groups were selected—white, integrated, Negro—and the findings were as follows:

1961–1962	*White*	*Integrated*	*Negro*
Number of pupils per classrooms	30.95	34.95	46.8
Appropriation per pupil	$342	$320	$269
Number of uncertified teachers	12%	23%	27%
Average number of books per pupil	5.0	3.5	2.5

In 1963 a *Handbook of Chicago School Segregation* claimed that 1961 appropriations for school operating expenses were almost 25 percent greater per pupil in white than in Negro schools, that teacher salaries were 18 percent higher, that nonteaching operating expenses—clerical and maintenance, salaries, supplies, textbooks—were 50 percent higher, and that only 3 percent of Chicago's Negro population finishes college.[13]

The reluctance of Chicago schools to move as far as New York on the race issue seems to derive from at least these sources: (1) the centralization of power in the Chicago system, parallel to the centralization of civic power in the person of the mayor; (2) the praise of Dr. Conant—probably the most influential person in American education—for Mr. Willis and the Chicago method and his concurrent criticism of the New York method; (3) the presence in New York of large numbers of unusually concerned and articulate white middle-class liberals; (4) the inordinate influence in Chicago schools and civic affairs of State Street, tax-conscious financial interests; (5) the past failures of have-not organization in Chicago.

An example of influential conservatism in relation to have-nots and the schools is seen in this passage from the Chicago *Tribune:* "Let's Throw the Slobs out of School":[14]

> The ignoramuses have had their chance. It is time to make them responsible for their actions. . . . Sweep through the school house with a fiery broom. Remove the deadwood, the troublemakers, the no-goods, the thugs. . . .
> [The teacher can tell on the first day] which students are the dis-

---

[13] *Handbook of Chicago School Segregation, 1963,* compiled and edited by the Education Committee, Coordinating Council of Community Organizations, August 1963.

[14] Reprint from *Chicago Tribune Magazine,* "Let's Throw the Slobs out of School," as it appears in *Human Events,* September 21, 1963, a weekly magazine distributed to social-studies classes in schools throughout the nation.

satisfied, the misfits, the illitearate [*sic*], undeserving, *non compos* nincompoops.

We have become the victims of the great transcendental fraud, a deceit put upon us by a generation of psychiatrists, guidance counselors, and psychologists, none of whom spends any more time in the classroom dealing with these apes than he has to.

Despite the fact that median income in Chicago is higher than in New York, Chicago in one recent year spent $410 per pupil while New York spent $761.52.[15]

Inequalities and the compensatory formula now being advocated —reverse inequality—produce only one kind of conflict, one which may be more easily resolved than other disputes because it involves simply the redistribution of money. The "concept" of equality itself seems far less susceptible to change—the notion that, with proper attention, the abilities of have-not children may prove roughly equal to those of haves and that, therefore, they should not be separated, sent off at an early age on different tracks, or given disproportionate access to higher education.

In New York City, fiscal inequality, segregation, and the "concept" of inequality resulted in the following racial distribution of recent graduating classes in New York's special high schools for "gifted children" drawn from the whole city:

	Negroes	Puerto Ricans	Others
Bronx High School of Science	14	2	863
Stuyvesant High School	23	2	629
High School of Music and Art	45	12	638
Brooklyn Technical School	22	6	907

In one recent year, Negroes and Puerto Ricans were about 14 percent of the graduating class in the city's academic high schools and about 50 percent in the city's vocational high schools. In the vocational schools, Negroes and Puerto Ricans tend to be heavily concentrated in inferior manual trade schools and seriously underrepresented in the technical schools. For example, in a class of 361 in the aviation school (a high-level technical school), 26 were Negroes, 51 were Puerto Ricans, 284 were "Others." In the class at the New York printing school, 4 were

---

[15] While 21.3 percent of Chicago's population have incomes over $10,000 annually, only 18.5 percent of New Yorkers are in this category. In Chicago, 26.3 percent of whites are in this bracket and only 8.7 percent of Negroes; at the same time, 9.9 percent of whites and 28.4 percent of Negroes have incomes less than $3,000 per year.

Negroes, 16 were Puerto Ricans, and 183 were "Others." At the Clara
Barton school for hospital workers, Negroes were a clear majority. Vocational schools have been "tightening standards" recently and sending
minorities to "academic" schools where, if neglected, they may be no
better off.

Higher Education

A developing conflict centers on higher education. Though ethnic records are not kept, one expert estimate is that about 2 percent of students at the University of the City of New York (formerly the city's
free colleges) are Negro. One branch of the University is located at
the edge of Harlem and is more integrated and accessible to Negroes
than other branches, yet less than 5 percent Negro enrollment is reported there.

In New York, Negroes tend to fall between the free city colleges
and the dominant and expensive private universities (New York University, Columbia, and their like). They can neither qualify for the
former nor afford the latter. Needs tests are not applied to city-college
admissions, and free tuition is extended to the affluent with an 85 high
school average and denied the impoverished with an 84 average; enrollments are reported to be now predominantly middle class.[16]

Some critics now say that the only equitable system of tuition
charges, in all types of institutions, is a sliding scale based on ability to
pay. New York does not have a single state university; what is called
the University of the State of New York is simply a scattered collection,
mainly in nonurban areas, of teachers colleges, agricultural schools, a
few technical schools.[17] Recently, the state gave a 40 percent subsidy
to New York's city colleges, converted by some graduate offerings into
the University of the City of New York. The importance of federal
funds to education is seen in federal research and development investments in California and the pervading effect such funds have had in
underwriting and stimulating growth of educational institutions there.

---

[16] A recent admissions change at the city university from sole reliance on
high school averages to inclusion of college boards scores is expected further to
lighten the skin of enrollees. The Board of Higher Education, however, is now discussing a change of admissions standards to accommodate more Negroes.

[17] California spent $33 million on community and junior colleges in 1961–
1962 and $214 million on other types of higher education. New York State spent
$5.7 million on community and junior colleges and $111 million on other types of
higher education. M. M. Chambers, Joint Office of Institutional Research, "Appropriations of State Funds for Operating Expenses of Higher Education, 1961–62,"
Washington, D. C., January 1962.

New York City's effort through the years to provide free college education and to compensate for the void at the state level has been extraordinary. No other city appears to have made any comparable effort. Still the city seems not to have deployed its college resources equitably, and the gathering debate over the city colleges suggests a conflict of view—or interest—between the city's have-nots and its numerous liberal middle class.[18]

The compilation and release of information about ethnic and social class enrollments in institutions of higher education, as well as the postsecondary experiences of students, appear to be the first step out of the college inequities which have, in turn, imposed inequities on lower educational levels. Equality of opportunity in higher education will probably come only through a national network of community colleges—low in cost and located within easy commuting distance—and available to all "average"-or-above students who want further education.[19] Perhaps Britain's proposed experiment with televised university instruction will provide an alternative, or supplementary model, to the community college.

Class and Ethnic Roles

Within the city itself, at least these elements seem to have some separate, though often overlapping, identity: (1) Negroes; (2) labor unions; (3) white have-nots; (4) white liberals; (5) the Jewish community; (6) the Catholic community; (7) business organizations and their allies in city silk-stocking areas.

The roles and activities of these groups in relation to the schools have never been adequately defined, but impressionistic observation seems to indicate the following outlines: The main white support for civil rights in the past several decades has unquestionably come from the leadership within the labor and Jewish communities—with some major assists from middle-class liberal and church groups, particularly in the last several years. The rank-and-file within the labor-union and

---

[18] None of the New York Board of Education's three community colleges (where admissions standards are such that Negroes can, and often do, qualify) are located in Negro areas. One is now scheduled for Manhattan, but the tentative location is between 23rd and 42nd streets, a white area—one of the few in Manhattan. One high ranking public-school official is quoted as saying "the municipal colleges are not equipped to operate vestibule courses for students who have to be civilized."

[19] The so-called "Russell Report" (Columbia Teachers College) to the Michigan legislature reported that the college enrollments by area rose and fell in proportion to the distance from the state's colleges.

Jewish communities, more personally threatened by Negroes, have tended to lag some distance behind on civil rights.[20]

In the schools, the class and ethnic lines are distinct, even though less clearly drawn than in the larger community. Some political allies of Negroes have been largely outside the school conflict: unions and large numbers of white have-nots, notably the Poles, Italians, and Irish who have tended to use parochial schools. Some feel it is fortunate that these have-not groups have tended to be outside the public school controversy; others feel that the parochial-public school separation has worked hardships on the public schools and delayed a crisis that would, in the long run, be beneficial to the public schools. Union leaders have been less involved in the schools than in other political affairs because of what seems to be a rather basic alienation from the schools and frequently because of their own parochial background. They have, however, supported school expansion, improvement, financing, and their organized political power, as in New York, has given important direct assistance to the schools and to the claims of Negroes on the schools.

The organized business community has traditionally opposed tax increases for public education, the leadership in these groups usually residing in the suburbs where they have provided ample funds for good schools. Powerful real-estate groups have opposed property taxes as well as school and housing integration. The "swing" group has been the Jewish community and, to some extent, the white liberal. The Jewish community, even middle and upper income, has consistently given solid support to the public schools,[21] but its own heavy stress on education and the fact that it is one of the largest remaining white middle-class groups within many cities have produced some ambivalence in its role and some conflict in unexpected places. The confrontation of these two allies in the city public schools is a source of growing distress to both groups. Because the Jewish community has tended to remain in the city and to use the public schools, it is generally contiguous, geographically

---

[20] On general political and economic issues, class lines seem quite clearly drawn: Negroes, unions, white have-nots, and a preponderance of the Jewish community appear on the have-not side, and the organized business, middle-class, and upper-class groups on the have side. Strangely, perhaps, and to some large extent understandably, Negroes chose two groups closest to them politically for their first-line offense: unions and the Jewish community. Both were vulnerable, having made continuing proclamations, accompanied by considerable effort, on behalf of equality and brotherhood, yet having done much less than their best to provide equality for Negroes within their own jurisdictions.

[21] In Detroit, a recent school-tax election was won, informed observers report, by majorities rolled up in the Negro and Jewish precincts.

and emphatically, with the Negro community and located in the middle of the integration cross fire.[22] Negroes point to Jewish predominance in the "better" high schools, the top "ability" groups, the free city colleges, and in public school administration. In many of the "integrating" areas of the city, the two groups have joined in open conflict, though in other areas they have integrated without friction. Thus, the Jewish community, because it has not fled like others from the city, often finds itself in the same situation as the labor movement with regard to Negroes: competition within a family of mutual interest for a scarcity of opportunities—in the schools in one case and in the job market in the other.[23] Perhaps for this reason, among others, the International Ladies Garment Workers Union has been a particularly sensitive target.[24]

Acculturation and Integration

The urban schools now confront the most difficult task they have attempted. Never before has a major *racial* minority been integrated into a nation's school or society. In fact, such integration within a dominantly non-Latin European population is unprecedented in history, the Soviets having settled their racial affairs by geographic separation.

The urban school, whose heavy job has always been the acculturation of immigrant and foreign-speaking ethnic groups, is now taking its first large bite of racial acculturation, as a giant reptile tries to swallow a whole animal. The city is accustomed to educating the immigrant:

---

[22] If the Jewish community is represented in the schools in proportion to its numbers in the population (one quarter of the New York population), then together with Negroes and Puerto Ricans (40 percent) it would represent at least 65 percent of public school enrollments.

[23] On the nine-man New York City school board, three representatives are traditionally selected for each of the three religious communities: Catholic, Protestant, Jewish. Though the Jewish community is represented by three board members, plus a Jewish-Unitarian superintendent of schools, the Negro and Puerto Rican communities, who constitute 40 percent of the public school population, have only one representative (a Negro) on the board.

[24] The Negro struggle seems to have an interacting effect on other have-not groups. In Detroit, the civil-rights movement is supported by the auto workers' union. In battle-torn Chicago, where the class struggle appears in its more primitive form, unembellished by righteous platitudes, the school board seems to have had two lone dissenters on equality and class issues: a steelworker representative (the only unionist on the board) and a Negro (another Negro member has consistently voted with the more conservative majority). The civil-rights drive, however, comes at a time when white workers feel insecure about jobs and their place in society and fear Negro competition in an already glutted job market. In areas of the nation where white have-nots are not organized (as in the South) and therefore do not have this broad view, racial conflict among have-nots is maximum.

In New York City in 1960, 48.6 percent of the population was either foreign-born or had at least one foreign-born parent; in Chicago, the figure was 35.9; in Detroit, 32.2; in San Francisco, 43.5. But the Negro group is unique in these respects: (1) it is the largest "immigrant" group of low-income, public-school-using Protestants (many other recent immigrations having skirted the public schools); (2) it is the first large racial minority to come to the city schools and the first large group with non-Western origins; (3) it has had a unique history of educational and social deprivation.

The active demand of Negro parents for integration perhaps cannot be fully appeased. Negro—and Puerto Rican—students are approaching a majority in many city public schools and any demand for total, one-for-one integration—which few would make—may be impossible in view of the increasing shortage of white public school students. Rather large-scale integration seems possible, however, as New York City is now beginning to demonstrate. Perhaps the issue will finally be settled by integrated urban renewal, or by setting up superschools and superservices in Negro areas—such as the Amidon school in Washington, D. C.—that will attract white students into Negro areas. Mainly, the urban school integration movement has served the latent function of calling attention to Negro education and arousing concern over the quality of Negro schools. The hope is held by many that, if Negro schools are improved, Negroes will not be so eager to integrate.

Among the newer racial demands in urban schools are: (1) compensatory treatment to balance past inequities; (2) "reverse" integration of schools and the busing of whites into Negro schools in order to "equalize" sacrifice (in New York, the demand has been for compulsory busing of both groups; on this most controversial point, Dr. Kenneth Clark has objected that Harlem schools are not fit either for Negroes or for whites and that busing should be "out" only); (3) heterogeneous grouping to scatter Negroes throughout the school population in any given school, rather than segregating them into slow-moving, homogeneous "ability" groups. In New York City and elsewhere, homogeneous grouping has proceeded so far that children in some places are "ability grouped" in kindergarten, based on whether or not they have been to nursery school; these groups, starting almost in the cradle, tend to perpetuate themselves throughout the child's school life.

Some Ways Out

In this author's view, major breakthroughs in urban education may come via any or all of the numerous possible routes.

Outside the school, the possibilities include: (1) a political breakthrough of have-nots at the congressional and state legislative levels; (2) increasing civil-rights activity and pressure; (3) organization of have-nots at the following levels: political community, ethnic (civil rights), on the job (union), out of a job (unemployed); (4) federal aid programs—either through direct federal aid or around this bottleneck and through special funds, job retraining, Health, Education, and Welfare funds, urban-renewal domestic peace corps, vocational education; (5) massive infusions of voluntary aid to the schools and assistance from private foundations.

Inside the schools, the break-through might come from such sources as: (1) massive enlargement of college opportunities through the introduction of new funds or new methods of teaching; (2) technological innovation in public school, especially educational television; (3) the unionization of teachers and the arousal of the professional group with the greatest stake in improved schools (organized teachers, it has been demonstrated in New York City, can have an electric effect on the schools, attracting qualified teachers through improved salaries and working conditions, reduced class size, improved curriculum, and quality of school administration and instruction); (4) decentralization of city school systems to encourage greater participation of have-nots and clearer and closer channels of communication.[25]

Recent months have seen a spectacular burst of citizen interest in the schools, perhaps unparalleled by anything in the history of public education. Women's clubs, youth groups, civil-rights organizations, settlement houses, churches, local government, private funds, and foundations have taken up "tutorials" in deprived areas, and the more imaginative and energetic groups have moved out from there into community organization. The intrusion of nonschool groups into the learning process has injected some new excited spirit into the institutional drabness.

Accompanying this new citizen concern with the "disadvantaged" is a new wave of interest among educators, writers, and scholars in the problems of poverty and equality, a current that has in recent months washed over previous concentration on the "gifted" and almost swept the word out of the educator's vocabulary.

Another source of backdoor assistance to the schools will be the decongestion of cities—a desperate need of New York especially—by: (1) the natural attrition of a suburban-bound, affluent population, and a Negro population pushing ever outward; (2) the forced decentraliza-

---

[25] In New York, the new community school boards, serving as advisory groups, have already geometrically increased the flow of new ideas, spirit, and activity into the schools from the local communities and cleared the clogged lines of communication.

tion of urban renewal, thinning out populations and bringing back into central areas a more taxable balance of middle and lower income groups. Renewal, intelligently, humanely, and artfully carried on, has the potential, of course to remake urban life—by decentralizing, rebuilding, rehabilitating, and creating a truly heterogeneous class and ethnic community.

Perspectives on Recent Welfare Legislation, Fore and Aft

Samuel Mencher

University of Pittsburgh Graduate School of Social Work

[Reprinted with permission of the National Association of Social Workers from Social Work, *Vol. 8, No. 5, (July 1963), pp. 59–64.]*

THIS IS A PERIOD of stock-taking for the field of public welfare. It is a time to re-examine the direction of welfare policy. The New Frontier symbolizes a new era for welfare, as it does for other areas of public policy. To what extent has there been a genuine reassessment of welfare programs? To what extent do the public welfare policies of the Kennedy administration only represent a cashing-in of old debts incurred during former eras of welfare innovation? Are the amendments of 1962 only catching up with the accounts left over from the New Deal of the 1930's, or are they projecting welfare policy for the decades ahead?

The history of public welfare, except in time of crucial emergencies such as in the thirties has more often been patchwork stitched onto outworn garments than a thoroughgoing policy of reform relevant to current needs and future requirements. There seems to be a compulsion among public welfare reformers and administrators to concentrate on the major inequities of previous decades rather than to plan policies for the future. This is not to deny the pressing need for such changes, but these may hardly be considered the symptoms of the "forward look" in welfare policy. Frequently, when these reforms do occur they may even be ill-suited to present conditions. For example, the great crusade against child labor has now been reflected in an abnormal number of school dropouts and the expansion of programs extending opportunities to youth. Early retirement of the aged, considered progressive in the thirties, has now exacerbated the psychological and physical difficulties of increasing longevity.

Underlying Philosophy

What has been the total contribution of the 1962 Public Welfare Amendments to the American welfare scene? A great part of these measures and their underlying philosophy are reforms of the original social security legislation or of more recent changes in the original act.

1. *Increased federal participation in present welfare programs—* increased grants to assistance programs of the states, for child welfare, and for the administration of public assistance.

2. *Efforts to make present programs more effective—*encouragement, albeit gentle, of combining the categorical or specific assistance programs—aid to the blind, aged, disabled; exemptions of small amounts of income from means test, particularly in old age assistance and AFDC; enlargement of responsibility for families with dependent children.

These are positive and praiseworthy, although hardly major, shifts in program. Yet, however much one might believe such changes inevitable, they were not undertaken previously and their contribution should not be minimized.

They are balanced, however, by other changes, and while in the long run these other measures may not be significant, they are important as indicators of an underlying philosophy among the present welfare leadership. There has been a retreat along the lines of work relief and controlled payments to assistance recipients. These are old sores of public assistance, and it was to be hoped that they would not be reopened. They must, of course, be handled gingerly, but no matter what the euphemisms employed they cannot but recall to us the earlier days of repressive poor relief policy. And there is no reason why they should not. One of the unpleasant facts of public welfare history is that it has a tendency to repeat itself, and very little of it bears repeating. Why work relief in a society less attuned to its success should be a valid policy today when it was found wanting from the seventeenth century onward is an interesting question. It is and has always been a sterile policy, and no new rationales have been found to explain away its 300-year failure.

It must be recognized frankly that controls placed upon economically dependent groups are discriminatory practices. While the sophisticated, the trained, the expert always find facile rationalizations for intervention, the intervention of the well-meaning specialist deprives the patient, the client, the citizen of his freedom as does any other kind of intervention. From an objective point of view the "Big Brother" of Orwell's *1984* is no more pleasant in the guise of a social practitioner than in the armband of an agent of political thought control. Almost a half-century ago Austin Chamberlain, the well-known British politician, made clear that although the Webbs' prescription for reform might be socially therapeutic it was psychologically unpalatable.[1]

Similarly we must be constantly on guard that merely because some citizens are dependent for economic support on the community's treasury, they must perforce accept the community's prescription for their way of life. It would be better to be part of a society that gives the same freedom to its dependent members, whatever the consequences, than rely on the good will of a society willing to intervene in the lives of those of its members whose economic and social failures make them amenable to social control. The principle of assistance should be that the recipient of public aid will be subjected to no greater controls than other citizens. Why should the assistance recipient be deprived of discretion about the use of his income by administrative fiat and for more stringent reasons than apply to the great body of his neighbors? Why are Americans so generous and sensitive in their foreign aid program and so picayune and miserly in helping their less fortunate fellow citizens?

Unpleasant as they are, these measures might be considered political hostages for really significant advances on the welfare scene. However, one must look sharply to recognize important constructive and compensatory action. There is a general emphasis on prevention and rehabilitation, but specific or concrete examples are few. The references to day care and the provision of welfare services to persons not actually on relief, but who have been or might be, are heartening. However, the combination of the administration of child welfare with financial aid to dependent children and the broad emphasis on services and control as an integral part of assistance-giving overshadow these beginning attempts at making public welfare a rational and humane system. A recent study of child welfare services in the United States and England concluded that "administrative submergence of child welfare services under the massive weight of public assistance is a severe deterrent to program development of child welfare services." This conclusion was bolstered not only by American data but by the advances made in England's child care services since their divorce from "departments otherwise fully occupied with markedly different programs and philosophies."[2]

Even the laudatory attention given to the training of professional

---

[1] Beatrice Webb, *Our Partnership* (London: Longmans, Green & Co., 1948), p. 450.

[2] Gladys M. Kammerer, *British and American Child Welfare Services* (Detroit: Wayne State University Press, 1962), pp. 414–417.

personnel in the 1962 amendments must be viewed in the light of the larger policy issues involved. As a professional group, social workers have prized self-criticism and placed even more emphasis than other groups on the upgrading of their profession. There has, however, been a tendency to identify with any program that provides for professional training or the expansion of professional personnel. Yet it is incumbent upon us neither to be so self-concerned nor so blind objectively as to judge the value of programs only from the vantage of our own professional interest or involvement. We are quick to criticize the AMA and other professional groups who maintain that what is good for them is good for the national welfare. In a most arresting essay, Richard M. Titmuss, a leading British welfare authority and educator, points out that health and welfare bureaucracies may threaten the general welfare as much as bureaucracies devoted to other less humanitarian ends.[3] Any professional group whose practice or program is determined by the attention given it or the respect paid it should seriously reconsider its devotion to the ethic of disinterested service.

Major Issues

The major issues in regard to contemporary public welfare revolve around the provision of economic security and of other welfare services essential for the psychological, social, and physical health of this country's citizenry. The question is strategically different from those pointed up by the 1962 American welfare amendments.

Underlying the structure of the present program and its reforms are problems that concerned the charity organization movement and the English Fabian reformers in the latter quarter of the nineteenth century and culminated in the Majority Report of the Royal Commission on the Poor Laws of 1905–1909. The report of this famous commission, influenced by Charity Organization Society thinking, espoused a philosophy of welfare not far different from that current in this country. However, the sea of circumstances and popular opinion had already swept past the Majority's barrier to fundamental poor law reform. British society clearly pressed toward both a sound system of economic assistance and a system of universal social and health services that culminated in the great acts immediately following World War II.

American welfare policy, nevertheless, seems to regress to the level of the early 1900's. True, contemporary American programs are, on the whole, more liberal than those conceived by the COS in 1900.

---

[3] *Essays on "The Welfare State"* (New Haven: Yale University Press, 1959), p. 202.

There is certainly less emphasis on institutional care and greater support of community care, but these differences are hardly sufficient to represent a half-century of major social and economic change. The major issues of welfare policy since the great industrial and urban expansion have been related to (1) the function of the welfare system, (2) the attitudes and beliefs as to the causes of the need for societal help or support and particularly the extent to which social or extra-individual factors may be held accountable and responsible for economic dependency, and (3) the development of an effective organization of socio-economic supports.

The basic welfare program of the United States, including its current amendments, has been guided by principles whose formulation both in the United States and Great Britain goes back *not* to the English Poor Law of 1601 (as is frequently stated) but to the poor law reforms of the first third of the nineteenth century. The original English act was a progressive measure solidifying the formulation of public responsibility. The reforms of the 1820's and 1830's in the United States and England were formulated at the height of *laissez-faire* influence and aimed to revoke the original commitment to social responsibility as well as the liberalization of earlier welfare practices. The present United States welfare program is in keeping with the philosophy of 1830 as revitalized by the Majority Report of the Royal Commission of 1905–1909 and the charity organization movement in the United States and England. In the contemporary American program the function of public welfare is viewed almost exclusively in relation to economic dependency, economic dependency is interpreted as much as possible from an individual or personal context rather than a social and environmental context, welfare services are elaborated almost entirely with regard to the groups receiving economic aid, and economic assistance programs are kept separate from other important economic measures.

This is an outmoded and anachronistic view of the welfare function. In addition, whatever the philosophy, the history of public welfare has demonstrated the sterility and the failure of such an approach. Philosophical rigidity has caused welfare leadership for some 150 years to focus on the technical aspects of problems rather than on the basic functional relationship to society of the welfare system. For 150 years the same philosophy, except for brief periods such as the early years of the Roosevelt administration, has dominated American policy. Tacking with the times, changes in the specifics of techniques or institutions have taken place, all in the hope that these measures would corroborate a basic *laissez-faire* philosophy. Indoor relief gave way to outdoor relief, local control to state and federal participation. Social insurance programs were introduced. At times, of course, society reverts to more primitive practices, e.g., work relief or protective payments and payments in kind. But the goal has always been the reduction and eventual dissolution of public support for the economically deprived rather than the establishment of a sound system of economic security.

There has been a continuous belief that it is somewhat immoral for a society to have, let alone recognize the existence of, an economically dependent population. While the presence of an economically dependent population is a problem not to be overlooked and hopefully to be remedied, the onus of its existence does not fall upon the public assistance mechanism. Nor can public assistance solve the great and complex social and economic maladjustments resulting, for example, in this country's continuing 6 percent unemployment rate during the past several years. Automation, mobility, depressed communities, changing family mores, the growing aged population, and the lack of opportunity for youth are not caused by, nor can they be cured by, an economic assistance program—no matter how well buttressed by psychosocial know-how!

The value of Galbraith's *Affluent Society* was that it stimulated a reassessment of the distribution of wealth in America. A variety of recent statistical analyses has shown that there are still large pockets of impoverished citizens, varying between 25 and 40 percent of the total population according to the criteria used. This is a social, not individual, phenomenon, as are the great number of the unemployed dependent on unemployment insurance and public assistance. In addition, there are several million persons on public assistance who are not employable according to contemporary principles and practices affecting employment—children, aged, blind, and disabled.

Dependency and poverty are part of the economic realities of America; it is not a question of a group of psychosocial misfits. Even Community Research Associates, who justify their existence by their ability to turn assistance recipients into self-supporting citizens, have found only a minor proportion of assistance clients to be employable. Thus there is a clear-cut problem of economic need responsive to the continuing and fluctuating conditions of the market economy of our society. It would seem overly euphoric, if not fatuous, to have this problem dominate the total pattern of welfare services when it only concerns a minority of the population. Economic problems will be solved more rationally if they are linked to the vast and complex network of programs related to the economic stability of the nation. There will be further consideration of this later.

Distinct from the problem of economic need are the many psychological and social problems indigenous to our society. Whatever the economic condition, whatever the occasion of their occurrence there is a broad and general need for programs aimed at the promotion of maximum psychosocial health. The prevalence of such problems is widespread, not limited to one economic group or to any particular element of the population. The children, the aged, the handicapped are society's concern wherever they are found. Their treatment is as necessary for the growth of a healthy society and for the fulfillment of our traditional humanitarian values as is maintenance of a sound economic structure. Many have been critical of the Marxist emphasis on the primacy of economic and material factors, yet our concentration on the centrality of economic dependence in welfare suggests that we are, in effect, victims of an overly simplified philosophy of economic determinism.

Separate the Economic from the Social

At this juncture, then, it is appropriate to accept responsibility and determine rational programs for two distinct functions whose prior symbiosis should not prevent future farsighted planning. There is as little or as much logic in combining the economic with the social in welfare agencies as maintaining that surgical wards should be in barber shops because they started out that way and frequently people are served by both. It is significant that Gordon Hamilton and Eveline Burns, approaching the issue from different vantage points, reached similar conclusions—the advisability of separating the income maintenance and service functions.[4]

Our society can afford to invest in the social and psychological welfare of its citizenry without maintaining a double bookkeeping account against which their economic return must be weighed. To a large degree this was the rationale of earlier relief programs and whatever their effectiveness they had the logic of a society of scarcity. Such efforts were not successful, but sometimes had momentary and spectacular results that still entice emphasis on, and investment in, programs aimed solely at rehabilitation of the economically dependent. The history of public welfare from the time of the famous houses of industry in late seventeenth-century Restoration England is replete with experiments and crusades to make the poor self-supporting. However, as Daniel Defoe, the author of *Robinson Crusoe,* pointed out in the early eighteenth

---

[4] *See* Gordon Hamilton, "Editor's Page," *Social Work,* Vol. 7, No. 1 (January 1962); and Eveline M. Burns, "What's Wrong with Public Welfare?" *Social Service Review,* Vol. 36, No. 2 (June 1962).

century, if the means of economic support had been available to the poor, few would have been on relief.[5] The problem of economic assistance is linked to the economic organization of society, not to the welfare system.

American society must break away from this unholy alliance of welfare and economic security. Perhaps, as the British did, we must establish a national system of economic security unrelated to, and unencumbered by, functions of social and psychological prevention and rehabilitation. We may even go further by unifying and rationalizing the total mechanism for economic security through creating a federation of the various agencies dealing with the problems of economic security for our citizens. Such a system might incorporate assistance programs, insurance programs for the aged and unemployed, and the various economic planning efforts related to retraining, job-finding, job-placement, and employment-creation, such as public works. These agencies could develop an approach to their problems fully as oriented to human values as are present programs. Hopefully, by working directly and effectively toward the practical solution of economic dependency and poverty, they will not require the compensating mechanism of the personalized treatment so heavily emphasized at present. Rather than needing social work to make palatable the bitter medicine of economic deprivation, they will provide dignified and realistic solutions to economic problems.

On the other side of the ledger, let us be free to develop a broad panorama of social services geared to the psychosocial development of our total citizenry. Serving the problems of marital discord, personal confusion, delinquency, and others should not be limited to the economically dependent. Many of these problems, in fact, affect economic potential and should be treated before they too greatly handicap the individual's contribution to his own and society's well-being. Those who see public assistance as a significant contribution to psychosocial health may be interested in the findings of the recently published study of the Survey Research Center of the University of Michigan. This research concluded that less than one-quarter of those families defined as "poor" had received any public assistance.[6] The public assistance system thus cannot even be considered a reliable mechanism for case-finding among those suffering from poverty alone.

---

[5] Dorothy Marshall, *The English Poor in the Eighteenth Century* (London: George Routledge & Sons, 1926), p. 50.

[6] James N. Morgan et al., *Income and Welfare in the United States* (New York: McGraw-Hill Book Co., 1962), pp. 216–217.

A full-scale program to aid children and parents, adolescents and the aged, that will neither be impeded by their tie to the public assistance mechanism nor psychologically weakened by the traditional stigma of economic dependency would be a major advance. Perhaps we might ask ourselves why we are among the few western countries without a family allowance system and at the same time find aid to dependent children our most controversial program. Are we really concerned with child and family welfare, or do we enjoy the inquisitorial satisfactions of puritan morality?

Are these criticisms of current welfare policy faint quibblings? Are they the resonant chords of a never-to-be-stilled compulsive and unnatural perfectionism? The author thinks not. Today the core of internal democratic policy is social welfare, which is the economic and social counterpart of the political democracy achieved almost two centuries ago in this country. It is the fruition of the political in the social and economic fields that will decide the future of this nation and much of this world. Failure in exporting political democracy without its social and economic equivalents has been illustrated in Latin America and in a great number of so-called underdeveloped regions. It is this country that is still undecided about its commitment to social and economic democracy. How far are we willing to go in guaranteeing equality of opportunity in health, education, and welfare?

The issue at this time is not the *size* of case loads in public assistance, but whether *we shall have* case loads in public assistance. The issue is whether we shall have a sound health program for all our citizenry, not whether a minority of the most and least fortunate shall enjoy the privileges of modern scientific medicine. The issue is whether education will be recognized as the social heritage of a civilized people, not solely as the vocational necessity of a cold war.

Selected Bibliography

1. Junius L. Allison. "Poverty and the Administration of Justice in the Criminal Courts," *Journal of Criminal Law, Criminology, and Police Science,* 55 (June, 1964).

2. Odin W. Anderson, Patricia Collette, and Jacob J. Feldman. *Changes in Family Medical Care Expenditures and Voluntary Health Insurance: A Five Year Resurvey.* Cambridge: Harvard University Press, 1963.

3. Edgar S. and Jean C. Cahn. "The War on Poverty: A Civilian Perspective." *Yale Law Journal,* 73 (July, 1964).

4. David Caplovitz. *The Poor Pay More.* New York: The Free Press of Glencoe, A Division of the Macmillan Company, 1963.

5. James B. Conant. *Slums and Suburbs: A Commentary on Schools in Metropolitan Areas.* New York: McGraw Hill Book Co., Inc., 1961.

6. Leonard J. Duhl, Ed. *The Urban Condition: People and Policies in the Metropolis.* New York: Basic Books, Inc., 1963.

7. Arthur J. Goldberg. "Equal Justice for the Poor, Too," *New York Times Magazine Section,* March 15, 1964.

8. August B. Hollingshead and Frederick C. Redlich. *Social Class and Mental Illness; A Community Study.* New York: John Wiley and Sons, Inc., 1958.

9. Philip S. Laurence and Robert B. Fuchsberg. "Medical Care and Family Income," *Health, Education and Welfare Indicators,* May, 1964.

10. Henry A. Passow, Ed. *Education in Depressed Areas.* New York: Columbia University Press, 1963.

11. Ellen J. Perkins. "Unmet Need in Public Assistance," *Social Security Bulletin,* April, 1960.

12. Charles A. Reich. "Midnight Welfare Searches and the Social Security Act," *Yale Law Review,* 72 (May, 1963).

13. Alvin L. Schorr. *Slums and Social Insecurity: An Appraisal of the Effectiveness of Housing Policies in Helping to Eliminate Poverty in the United States,* Research Report Number 1, Division of Research and Statistics, Social Security Administration, United States Department of Health, Education and Welfare, Washington, D.C.: Government Printing Office, 1963.

14. Patricia C. Sexton. *Education and Income.* New York: Viking, 1961.

15. United States Department of Health, Education and Welfare, Welfare Administration. *The Extension of Legal Services to the Poor.* Conference Proceedings, Washington, D.C.: The Administration, 1964.

16. Elizabeth Wickendan. *Poverty and the Law—The Constitutional Rights of Assistance Recipients.* New York: The National Social Welfare Assembly, 1962.

17. Daniel Wilner, et al. *The Housing Environment and Family Life.* Baltimore: Johns Hopkins Press, 1962.

Chapter 5

The Values of the Poor

*The underprivileged worker lives in a different economic and
social environment from that in which the skilled and the middle-
class workers live. Therefore the behavior that he learns, the habits that are stimulated and maintained by his cultural group, are
different also. The individuals of these different socioeconomic
statuses and cultures are reacting to different realistic situations
and psychological drives. Therefore their values and their social
goals are different. Therefore, the behavior of the underprivileged
worker, which the boss regards as "unsocialized" or "ignorant,"
or "lazy," or "unmotivated" is really behavior learned from the
socioeconomic and cultural environments of these workers. In a
realistic view, we must recognize it to be perfectly normal, a
sensible response to the conditions of their lives.*

—From "The Motivation of the Underprivileged Worker" by Allison
Davis. Reprinted from *Industry and Society,* William Foote Whyte,
ed., New York: McGraw-Hill Book Co., 1946.

ONE READS A GOOD DEAL nowadays both in the popular and scholarly
publications about a "culture of poverty." The thesis is presented that
there exist neighborhoods, hamlets or larger geographical units where
there is an organized social life with a distinctive set of assumptions and
beliefs called "lower class values." The logical consequence of this thesis
is to suggest a social grouping that (1) does not share the basic assumptions of everyday life of the larger society and (2) has undergone a set of
experiences that is different from other groups in the community. The
"culture of poverty" is regarded as an adaptive series of responses
peculiar to the problems of low-income people. This is an interesting
thesis and deserves comment, if for no other reason than the fact that
assumptions about a culture of poverty become guidelines for programs
to reduce poverty.

Three points can be made about the "culture of poverty" thesis.
First, as Hylan Lewis has noted, present-day social science abounds
with the uncritical and loose usage of the culture concept. There is

reference to a "culture of the uninvolved," to a "culture of violence" and to a "culture of unemployment." The term *culture* is widely applied to numerous dimensions and components of aggregates, groups and persons. One common fallacy is to confuse *culture* with *class*. In a *culture* context we speak of norms and values which regulate behavior in some form of *organized social grouping*. In a *class* context, we refer to certain attitudes and motives that are *common to a category of individuals* sharing the same life chance or economic resources. In the latter case, workers may have the same beliefs but as a function of sharing like economic experiences rather than being socialized into certain beliefs in an organized social grouping. The offspring of the poor are not socialized into a *different* set of beliefs and assumptions about life but they are exposed at an early age to the lack and unpredictableness of economic resources and this exposure may be the important fact in structuring the irreducible assumptions about life. Thus, the cycle of poverty may refer to the intergenerational exposure to certain kinds of economic problems rather than exposure to a particular set of values and beliefs.

The second point to be made about a "culture of poverty" thesis is its utility as an explanatory variable in the behavior of the poor. The existence of a certain set of beliefs or behaviors tells us nothing about *why* these exist among the poor in contrast to other beliefs or behaviors. If we examine critically the explanations of poverty in the intellectual history of the western world, we observe a progression of stereotypes rather than logical, empirically-based explanations. Early explanations explain poverty as a failure to obtain salvation or as punishment for original sin. This explanation was replaced by a biologistic explanation —the poor have low intellectual endowment or physiological defects; or the poor are the "losers" in the natural ordering of society that follows the social Darwinist's struggle for survival. The "culture of poverty" explanation, largely proposed and championed by American intellectuals in the post World War I period, was essentially the replacement of previous stereotypes by others. Granted that the culture hypothesis is more intellectually satisfying than religious or biological explanations, has the case been proven that the behavior and values of the poor are reflections of culture rather than class?

Finally, a "culture of poverty" hypothesis must inevitably raise the question of the utility and worthiness of lower-class values in solving the poverty problem. Do we try to stamp out the values of the poor and try to socialize them to middle class values or do we try to strengthen what exists and respect the uniqueness and inviolability of cultural values? Is the solution to poverty to be found within the value framework of the poor or the value framework of the more affluent groups in the society? If we assume that the poor have the "wrong" values, the solution might be educational programs for the poor that emphasize the emergence of new values. On the other hand, if the assumption is that values reflect differentials in life chance, some effort would have to be made to change the opportunity structure. It may very well be that an anti-poverty program might emphasize both approaches.

In this chapter, Walter B. Miller presents a description of the main themes in lower class culture, emphasizing the distinctiveness of those values. Hyman Rodman presents an opposite point of view—there is no unique lower class subculture but rather a "value stretch." S. M. Miller, Frank Riessman, and Arthur A. Seagull examine some common stereotyped notions about the values of the poor. Finally, Herbert Gans discusses the existence of a lower class subculture and its relationship to the opportunity structure.

Focal Concerns of Lower-Class Culture

Walter B. Miller
Brandeis University School of Social Work

[Excerpted from the article, "Lower Class Culture as a Generating Milieu of Gang Delinquency" from the Journal of Social Issues, *March 1958, by permission of The Society for the Psychological Study of Social Issues, and the author.]*

THERE IS A SUBSTANTIAL SEGMENT of present-day American society whose way of life, values, and characteristic patterns of behavior are the product of a distinctive cultural system which may be termed "lower class." Evidence indicates that this cultural system is becoming increasingly distinctive, and that the size of the group which shares this tradition is increasing.[1] The lower class way of life, in common with that of all

---

[1] Between 40 and 60 percent of all Americans are directly influenced by lower class culture, with about 15 percent, or twenty-five million, comprising the "hard core" lower class group—defined primarily by its use of the "female-based" household as the basic form of child-rearing unit and of the "serial monogamy" mating pattern as the primary form of marriage. The term "lower class culture" as used here refers most specifically to the way of life of the "hard core" group; systematic research in this area would probably reveal at least four to six major subtypes of lower class culture, for some of which the "concerns" presented here would be differently weighted, especially for those subtypes in which "law-abiding" behavior has a high overt valuation. It is impossible within the compass of this short paper to make the finer intracultural distinctions which a more accurate presentation would require.

distinctive cultural groups, is characterized by a set of focal concerns—areas or issues which command widespread and persistent attention and a high degree of emotional involvement. The specific concerns cited here, while by no means confined to the American lower classes, constitute a distinctive *patterning* of concerns which differs significantly, both in rank order and weighting from that of American middle class culture. The following chart presents a highly schematic and simplified listing

CHART 1

FOCAL CONCERNS OF LOWER CLASS CULTURE

Area	*Perceived Alternatives* (*state, quality, condition*)	
1. *Trouble:*	law-abiding behavior	law-violating behavior
2. *Toughness:*	physical prowess, skill; "masculinity"; fearlessness, bravery, daring	weakness, ineptitude; effeminacy; timidity, cowardice, caution
3. *Smartness:*	ability to outsmart, dupe, "con"; gaining money by "wits"; shrewdness, adroitness in repartee	gullibility, "con-ability"; gaining money by hard work; slowness, dull-wittedness, verbal maladroitness
4. *Excitement:*	thrill; risk, danger; change, activity	boredom; "deadness," safeness; sameness, passivity
5. *Fate:*	favored by fortune, being "lucky"	ill-omened, being "unlucky"
6. *Autonomy:*	freedom from external constraint; freedom from superordinate authority; independence	presence of external constraint; presence of strong authority; dependency, being "cared for"

of six of the major concerns of lower class culture. Each is conceived as a "dimension" within which a fairly wide and varied range of alternative behavior patterns may be followed by different individuals under different situations. They are listed roughly in order of the degree of *explicit* attention accorded each, and, in this sense represent a weighted ranking of concerns. The "perceived alternatives" represent polar positions which define certain parameters within each dimension. As will be explained in more detail, it is necessary in relating the influence of these "concerns" to the motivation of delinquent behavior to specify *which* of its aspects it is oriented to, whether orientation is *overt* or *covert, positive* (conforming to or seeking the aspect), or *negative* (rejecting or seeking to avoid the aspect).

The concept "focal concern" is used here in preference to the concept "value" for several interrelated reasons: (1) It is more readily derivable from direct field observation. (2) It is descriptively neutral—permitting independent consideration of positive and negative valences as varying under different conditions, whereas "value" carries a built-in positive valence. (3) It makes possible more refined analysis of subcultural differences, since it reflects actual behavior, whereas "value" tends to wash out intracultural differences since it is colored by notions of the "official" ideal.

Trouble: Concern over "trouble" is a dominant feature of lower class culture. The concept has various shades of meaning; "trouble" in one of its aspects represents a situation or a kind of behavior which results in unwelcome or complicating involvement with official authorities or agencies of middle class society. "Getting into trouble" and "staying out of trouble" represent major issues for male and female, adults and children. For men, "trouble" frequently involves fighting or sexual adventures while drinking; for women, sexual involvement with disadvantageous consequences. Expressed desire to avoid behavior which violates moral or legal norms is often based less on an explicit commitment to "official" moral or legal standards than on a desire to avoid "getting into trouble," e.g., the complicating consequences of the action.

The dominant concern over "trouble" involves a distinction of critical importance for the lower class community—that between "law-abiding" and "non-law-abiding" behavior. There is a high degree of sensitivity as to where each person stands in relation to these two classes of activity. Whereas in the middle class community a major dimension for evaluating a person's status is "achievement" and its external symbols, in the lower class, personal status is very frequently gauged along the law-abiding-non-law-abiding dimension. A mother will evaluate the suitability of her daughter's boyfriend less on the basis of his achievement potential than on the basis of his innate "trouble" potential. This sensitive awareness of the opposition of "trouble-producing" and "non-trouble-producing" behavior represents both a major basis for deriving status distinctions, and an internalized conflict potential for the individual.

As in the case of other focal concerns, which of two perceived alternatives—"law-abiding" or "non-law-abiding"—is valued varies according to the individual and the circumstances; in many instances there is an overt commitment to the "law-abiding" alternative, but a covert commitment to the "non-law-abiding." In certain situations, "getting into trouble" is overtly recognized as prestige-conferring; for example, membership in certain adult and adolescent primary groupings ("gangs") is contingent on having demonstrated an explicit commitment to the law-violating alternative. It is most important to note that the choice between "law-abiding" and "non-law-abiding" behavior is still a choice *within* lower class culture; the distinction between the policeman and the criminal, the outlaw and the sheriff, involves primarily this one dimension; in other respects they have a high community of interests. Not infrequently brothers raised in an identical cultural milieu will become police and criminals respectively.

For a substantial segment of the lower class population "getting into trouble" is not in itself overtly defined as prestige-conferring, but is implicitly recognized as a means to other valued ends, e.g., the covertly valued desire to be "cared for" and subject to external constraint, or the overtly valued state of excitement or risk. Very frequently "getting into trouble" is multi-functional, and achieves several sets of valued ends.

Toughness: The concept of "toughness" in lower class culture represents a compound combination of qualities or states. Among its most important components are physical prowess, evidenced both by demonstrated possession of strength and endurance and athletic skill; "masculinity," symbolized by a distinctive complex of acts and avoidances (bodily tatooing; absence of sentimentality; non-concern with "art," "literature," conceptualization of women as conquest objects, etc.); and bravery in the face of physical threat. The model for the "tough guy"—hard, fearless, undemonstrative, skilled in physical combat—is represented by the movie gangster of the thirties, the "private eye," and the movie cowboy.

The genesis of the intense concern over "toughness" in lower class culture is probably related to the fact that a significant proportion of lower class males are reared in a predominantly female household, and lack a consistently present male figure with whom to identify and from whom to learn essential components of a "male" role. Since women serve as a primary object of identification during pre-adolescent years, the almost obsessive lower class concern with "masculinity" probably resembles a type of compulsive reaction-formation. A concern over homosexuality runs like a persistent thread through lower class culture. This is manifested by the institutionalized practice of baiting "queers," often accompanied by violent physical attacks, an expressed contempt for "softness" or frills, and the use of the local term for "homosexual" as a generalized pejorative epithet (e.g., higher class individuals or upwardly mobile peers are frequently characterized as "fags" or "queers"). The distinction between "overt" and "covert" orientation to aspects of an area of concern is especially important in regard to "toughness." A positive overt evaluation of behavior defined as "effeminate" would be out of the question for a lower class male; however, built into lower class culture is a range of devices which permit men to adopt behaviors and concerns which in other cultural milieux fall within the province of women, and at the same time to be defined as "tough" and manly. For example, lower class men can be professional short-order cooks in a diner and still be regarded as "tough." The highly intimate circumstances of the street corner gang involve the recurrent expression of strongly affectionate feelings towards other men. Such expressions, however, are disguised as their opposite, taking the form of ostensibly aggressive verbal and physical interaction (kidding, "ranking," roughhousing, etc.).

Smartness: "Smartness," as conceptualized in lower class culture, involves the capacity to outsmart, outfox, outwit, dupe, "take," "con" another or others, and the concomitant capacity to avoid being outwitted, "taken," or duped oneself. In its essence, smartness involves the capacity to achieve a valued entity—material goods, personal status— through a maximum use of mental agility and a minimum use of physical effort. This capacity has an extremely long tradition in lower class culture, and is highly valued. Lower class culture can be characterized as "non-intellectual" only if intellectualism is defined specifically in terms of control over a particular body of formally learned knowledge involving "culture" (art, literature, "good" music, etc.), a generalized perspective on the past and present conditions of our own and other societies, and other areas of knowledge imparted by formal educational institutions. This particular type of mental attainment is, in general, overtly disvalued and frequently associated with effeminacy; "smartness" in the lower class sense, however, is highly valued.

The lower class child learns and practices the use of this skill in the street corner situation. Individuals continually practice duping and outwitting one another through recurrent card games and other forms of gambling, mutual exchange of insults, and "testing" for mutual "conability." Those who demonstrate competence in this skill are accorded considerable prestige. Leadership roles in the corner group are frequently allocated according to demonstrated capacity in the two areas of "smartness" and "toughness"; the ideal leader combines both, but the "smart" leader is often accorded more prestige than the "tough" one—reflecting a general lower class respect for "brains" in the "smartness" sense.[2]

The model of the "smart" person is represented in popular media by the card shark, the professional gambler, the "con" artist, the promoter. A conceptual distinction is made between two kinds of people:

---

[2] The "brains-brawn" set of capacities are often paired in lower class folk lore or accounts of lower class life, e.g., "Brer Fox" and "Brer Bear" in the Uncle Remus stories, or George and Lennie in "Of Mice and Men."

"suckers," easy marks, "lushes," dupes, who work for their money and are legitimate targets of exploitation; and sharp operators, the "brainy" ones, who live by their wits and "getting" from the suckers by mental adroitness.

Involved in the syndrome of capacities related to "smartness" is a dominant emphasis in lower class culture on ingenious aggressive repartee. This skill, learned and practiced in the context of the corner group, ranges in form from the widely prevalent semi-ritualized teasing, kidding, razzing, "ranking," so characteristic of male peer group interaction, to the highly ritualized type of mutual insult interchange known as "the dirty dozens," "the dozens," "playing house," and other terms. This highly patterned cultural form is practiced on its most advanced level in adult male Negro society, but less polished variants are found throughout lower class culture—practiced, for example, by white children, male and female as young as four or five. In essence, "doin' the dozens" involves two antagonists who vie with each other in the exchange of increasingly inflammatory insults, with incestuous and perverted sexual relations with the mother a dominant theme. In this form of insult interchange, as well as on other less ritualized occasions for joking, semi-serious, and serious mutual invective, a very high premium is placed on ingenuity, hair-trigger responsiveness, inventiveness, and the acute exercise of mental faculties.

Excitement: For many lower class individuals the rhythm of life fluctuates between periods of relatively routine or repetitive activity and sought situations of great emotional stimulation. Many of the most characteristic features of lower class life are related to the search for excitement or "thrill." Involved here are the highly prevalent use of alcohol by both sexes and the widespread use of gambling of all kinds—playing the numbers, betting on horse races, dice, cards. The quest for excitement finds what is perhaps its most vivid expression in the highly patterned practice of the recurrent "night on the town." This practice, designated by various terms in different areas ("honky-tonkin' "; "goin' out on the town"; "bar hoppin' "), involves a patterned set of activities in which alcohol, music, and sexual adventuring are major components. A group or individual sets out to "make the rounds" of various bars or night clubs. Drinking continues progressively throughout the evening. Men seek to "pick up" women, and women play the risky game of entertaining sexual advances. Fights between men involving women, gambling, and claims of physical prowess, in various combinations, are frequent consequences of a night of making the rounds. The explosive potential of this type of adventuring with sex and aggression, frequently leading to "trouble," is semi-explicitly sought by the individual. Since there is always a good likelihood that being out on the town will eventuate in fights, etc., the practice involves elements of sought risk and desired danger.

Counterbalancing the "flirting with danger" aspect of the "excitement" concern is the prevalence in lower class culture of other well established patterns of activity which involve long periods of relative inaction, or passivity. The term "hanging out" in lower class culture refers to extended periods of standing around, often with peer mates, doing what is defined as "nothing," "shooting the breeze," etc. A definite periodicity exists in the pattern of activity relating to the two aspects of the "excitement" dimension. For many lower class individuals the venture into the high risk world of alcohol, sex, and fighting occurs regularly once a week, with interim periods devoted to accommodating to possible consequences of these periods, along with recurrent resolves not to become so involved again.

Fate: Related to the quest for excitement is the concern with fate, fortune, or luck. Here also a distinction is made between two states— being "lucky" or "in luck," and being unlucky or jinxed. Many lower class individuals feel that their lives are subject to a set of forces over which they have relatively little control. These are not directly equated with the supernatural forces of formally organized religion, but relate more to a concept of "destiny," or man as a pawn of magical powers. Not infrequently this often implicit world view is associated with a conception of the ultimate futility of directed effort towards a goal: if the cards are right, or the dice good to you, or if your lucky number comes up, things will go your way; if luck is against you, it's not worth trying. The concept of performing semi-magical rituals so that one's "luck will change" is prevalent; one hopes that as a result he will move from the state of being "unlucky" to that of being "lucky." The element of fantasy plays an important part in this area. Related to and complementing the notion that "only suckers work" (Smartness) is the idea that once things start going your way, relatively independent of your own effort, all good things will come to you. Achieving great material rewards (big cars, big houses, a roll of cash to flash in a fancy night club), valued in lower class as well as in other parts of American culture, is a recurrent theme in lower class fantasy and folk lore; the cocaine dreams of Willie the Weeper or Minnie the Moocher present the components of this fantasy in vivid detail.

The prevalence in the lower class community of many forms of gambling, mentioned in connection with the "excitement" dimension, is also relevant here. Through cards and pool which involve skill, and thus both "toughness" and "smartness"; or through race horse betting, involving "smartness"; or through playing the numbers, involving predominantly "luck," one may make a big killing with a minimum of directed and persistent effort within conventional occupational channels. Gambling in its many forms illustrates the fact that many of the persistent features of lower class culture are multi-functional—serving a range of desired ends at the same time. Describing some of the incentives behind gambling has involved mention of all of the focal concerns cited so far— Toughness, Smartness, and Excitement, in addition to Fate.

Autonomy: The extent and nature of control over the behavior of the individual—an important concern in most cultures—has a special significance and is distinctively patterned in lower class culture. The discrepancy between what is overtly valued and what is covertly sought is particularly striking in this area. On the overt level there is a strong and frequently expressed resentment of the idea of external controls, restrictions on behavior, and unjust or coercive authority. "No one's gonna push *me* around," or "I'm gonna tell him he can take the job and shove it. . . ." are commonly expressed sentiments. Similar explicit attitudes are maintained to systems of behavior-restricting rules, insofar as these are perceived as representing the injunctions, and bearing the sanctions of superordinate authority. In addition, in lower class culture a close conceptual connection is made between "authority" and nurturance." To be restrictively or firmly controlled is to be cared for. Thus the overtly negative evaluation of superordinate authority frequently extends as well to nurturance, care, or protection. The desire for personal independence is often expressed in such terms as "I don't need *nobody* to take care of me. I can take care of myself!" Actual patterns of behavior, however, reveal a marked discrepancy between expressed sentiment and what is covertly valued. Many lower class people appear to seek out highly restrictive social environments wherein stringent external controls are maintained over their behavior. Such institutions as the armed forces, the mental hospital, the disciplinary school, the prison or correctional institution, provide environments which incorporate a strict and detailed set of rules defining and limiting behavior, and enforced by an authority system which controls and applies coercive sanctions for deviance from these rules. While under the jurisdiction of such systems, the lower class person generally expresses to his peers continual resentment of the coercive, unjust, and arbitrary exercise of authority. Having been released, or having escaped from these milieux, however, he will often act in such a way as to insure recommitment, or choose recommitment voluntarily after a temporary period of "freedom."

Lower class patients in mental hospitals will exercise considerable ingenuity to insure continued commitment while voicing the desire to get out; delinquent boys will frequently "run" from a correctional institution to activate efforts to return them; to be caught and returned means that one is cared for. Since "being controlled" is equated with "being cared for," attempts are frequently made to "test" the severity or strictness of superordinate authority to see if it remains firm. If intended or executed rebellion produces swift and firm punitive sanctions, the individual is reassured, at the same time that he is complaining bitterly at the injustice of being caught and punished. Some environmental milieux, having been tested in this fashion for the "firmness" of their coercive sanctions, are rejected, ostensibly for being too strict, actually for not being strict enough. This is frequently so in the case of "problematic" behavior by lower class youngsters in the public schools, which generally cannot command the coercive controls implicitly sought by the individual.

A similar discrepancy between what is overtly and covertly desired is found in the area of dependence-independence. The pose of tough rebellious independence often assumed by the lower class person frequently conceals powerful dependency cravings. These are manifested primarily by obliquely expressed resentment when "care" is not forthcoming rather than by expressed satisfaction when it is. The concern over autonomy-dependency is related both to "trouble" and "fate." Insofar as the lower class individual feels that his behavior is controlled by forces which often propel him into "trouble" in the face of an explicit determination to avoid it, there is an implied appeal to "save me from myself." A solution appears to lie in arranging things so that his behavior will be coercively restricted by an externally imposed set of controls strong enough to forcibly restrain his inexplicable inclination to get in trouble. The periodicity observed in connection with the "excitement" dimension is also relevant here; after involvement in trouble-producing behavior (assault, sexual adventure, a "drunk"), the individual will actively seek a locus of imposed control (his wife, prison, a restrictive job); after a given period of subjection to this control, resentment against it mounts, leading to a "break away" and a search for involvement in further "trouble."

It would be possible to develop in considerable detail the processes by which the commission of a range of illegal acts is either explicitly supported by, implicitly demanded by, or not materially inhibited by factors relating to the focal concerns of lower class culture. In place of such a development, the following three statements condense in general terms the operations of these processes:

1. *Following cultural practices which comprise essential elements of the total life pattern of lower class culture automatically violates certain legal norms.*

2. *In instances where alternate avenues to similar objectives are available, the non-law-abiding avenue frequently provides a relatively greater and more immediate return for a relatively smaller investment of energy.*

3. *The "demanded" response to certain situations recurrently engendered within lower class culture involves the commission of illegal acts.*

A large body of systematically interrelated attitudes, practices, behaviors, and values characteristic of lower class culture are designed to support and maintain the basic features of the lower class way of life. In areas where these differ from features of middle class culture, action oriented to the achievement and maintenance of the lower class system may violate norms of middle class culture and be perceived as deliberately non-conforming or malicious by an observer strongly cathected to middle class norms. This does not mean, however, that violation of the middle class norm is the dominant component of motivation; it is a by-product of action primarily oriented to the lower class system. The standards of lower class culture cannot be seen merely as a reverse function of middle class culture—as middle class standards "turned upside down"; lower class culture is a distinctive tradition many centuries old with an integrity of its own.

The Lower-Class Value Stretch*

Hyman Rodman

Merrill-Palmer Institute

[Reprinted from Social Forces, December 1963, by the permission of the University of North Carolina Press.]

THERE ARE SHARP DISAGREEMENTS about the nature of the values held by members of the lower class, and correspondingly, about whether a society is based upon a common value system, or a class-differentiated

* Revision of a paper read at the annual meetings of the Eastern Sociological Society, April 1961. Although they do not necessarily agree with what I am saying, I gratefully acknowledge the help I received in writing this paper from Reinhard Bendix, Oswald Hall, George C. Homans, Everett C. Hughes, Frank E. Jones, Sally Snyder, Katherine Spencer, and Marvin B. Sussman. Talcott Parsons was especially helpful and encouraging. In addition, an unrestricted research grant from the Social Research Foundation provided the assistance needed to bring this paper to completion.

value system.[1] Some writers assert that the basic values of a society are common to all social classes within that society, while others assert that the values differ from class to class. Similarly, in discussing problems such as illegitimacy and juvenile delinquency, some writers assert that the lower-class values that center about these phenomena are similar to the middle-class values, while others assert that the lower-class values differ from those of the middle class. In this paper I propose to delineate these contradictory points of view, as well as to suggest that through a consideration of what I will refer to as the lower-class value stretch we can resolve some of the apparent contradictions.

A Common Value System. The assumption that a common value system underlies a system of stratification has been made by Parsons, as in his reference to "a single more or less integrated system of values" in any society.[2] Merton has also assumed that a society is based upon a common value system:

> "It is . . . only because behavior is typically oriented toward the basic values of the society that we speak of a human aggregate as comprising a society. Unless there is a deposit of values shared by interacting individuals, there exist social relations, if the disorderly interactions may be so called, but no society."[3]

When we turn to those who have dealt specifically with illegitimacy and juvenile gang delinquency we find that certain writers imply

---

[1] One could illuminate the discussion about a common or a class-differentiated value system by focusing upon any class rather than just the lower class. For example, do members of the upper class share the general values of society, or do they hold values unique to themselves? Indeed, the whole question of the parallels between the upper class and lower class deserves a good deal more attention. Deviations from the conventional standards of society are said to occur in both of them. And there are some related and interesting findings in small group research that both low-ranking and high-ranking members of a group have greater leeway, in certain respects, to deviate from the norms of the group: See John W. Thibaut and Harold H. Kelley, *The Social Psychology of Groups* (New York: John Wiley and Sons, 1959), pp. 250–251; George C. Homans, *The Human Group* (New York: Harcourt, Brace, 1950), p. 144; Henry W. Riecken and George C. Homans, "Psychological Aspects of Social Structure," in Gardner Lindzey, ed., *Handbook of Social Psychology*, Vol. II (Cambridge, Mass.: Addison-Wesley, 1954), pp. 793–794. For an excellent discussion of the subject, which I first read after writing the above, see George C. Homans, *Social Behavior: Its Elementary Forms* (New York: Harcourt, Brace & World, 1961), pp. 336–358 *et passim*.

[2] Talcott Parsons, "General Theory in Sociology," in Robert K. Merton, Leonard Broom, Leonard S. Cottrell, Jr., editors, *Sociology Today* (New York: Basic Books, Inc., 1959), p. 8.

[3] Robert K. Merton, *Social Theory and Social Structure*, revised and enlarged edition (Glencoe, Ill.: Free Press, 1957), p. 141.

the existence of a common value system by their contention that middle-class norms[4] are also effective within lower-class groups. For example, Blake and Goode have discussed illegitimacy in Jamaica and the Caribbean generally, and while taking note of a high rate of illegitimacy in the area (typically more than 50 percent) they nevertheless conclude that even from the point of view of the lower class this represents deviant behavior.[5] According to their interpretation the norm of legitimacy is the only norm to be found within the lower class as well as within the middle class. Although they do not address themselves to the question of whether a society is characterized by a common value system or a class-differentiated value system, we can nevertheless take their interpretation as indicative of a belief in the existence of a common value system.

In somewhat the same vein, a number of writers on juvenile gang delinquency have implied the existence of a common value system. Taft, for example, holds that juvenile delinquents share the basic values of our society.[6] Sykes and Matza have agreed with this viewpoint, but they also point out that through techniques of neutralization (e.g., projecting blame upon outside forces that propel one into action, or denying one's actions have harmed anyone) the delinquent is often able to

---

[4] No formal distinction is made in this paper between values, norms, aspirations, and (desirable) goals. I realize that they can be distinguished from each other and that several volumes could be devoted to the task. I realize also that some authors may complain, and with some justice, that by using their statements about norms, aspirations, or goals as an index of their position on "values" I am distorting their point of view. (Most authors, I should add, themselves use some of these concepts interchangeably). But it is because I want to focus on the common element of *desirability* that lies behind all these concepts, as I use them, that I am running that risk. At the same time, there is the advantage of being able to suggest that the "stretch" concept also applies to norms, aspirations, and goals, and does not necessarily have to be tied to the lower class. Since some of these points are incidental to this paper, which focuses upon the lower-class value stretch, I do want to state outright here a methodological point that is only implied in other parts of the paper. When a subject is asked for a single "value" (or norm, aspiration, goal) response among a number of alternatives, and he selects a single alternative, this cannot be taken as evidence that he holds only the selected value and no other values. Regardless of the care taken in constructing a questionnaire, value alternatives that are mutually exclusive in a psychological sense cannot be set up.

[5] Judith Blake, "Family Instability and Reproductive Behavior in Jamaica," *Current Research in Human Fertility* (New York: Milbank Memorial Fund, 1955), pp. 34–39; William J. Goode, "Illegitimacy in the Caribbean Social Structure," *American Sociological Review*, Vol. 25 (February 1960), pp. 21–30.

[6] Donald R. Taft, *Criminology*, revised edition (New York: Macmillan, 1950), pp. 181–182.

spare himself the anguish of guilt.[7] This position that the delinquents share the conventional values of the society can also be taken as evidence for a belief in the existence of a common value system.

A Class-Differentiated Value System. In contrast to the authors cited above, who support the notion that a common value system underlies a stratified society, there are others who support the notion that a class-differentiated value system underlies a stratified society. Herbert H. Hyman,[8] in a paper that is in considerable measure a reaction to Merton's paper "Social Structure and Anomie," gives empirical evidence that there are differences in the value systems of different classes. He examines the educational, income, and occupational aspirations of various classes, showing that, in general, level of aspiration is correlated with class level. Thus, he concludes that we have a class-differentiated value system.

Allison Davis has also, for a long time, been emphasizing the differentiated values that are to be found within a society, particularly as exemplified by lower-class persons who have adapted their values to their deprived circumstances. As he says, individuals of different classes are "reacting to different realistic situations. . . . Therefore their values and their social goals are different."[9]

In writing of illegitimacy in the Caribbean, Henriques has stated flatly that from a social point of view this does not represent deviance within the lower class. Rather, the values of the lower class differ from those of the middle class, and illegitimacy is acceptable and in no way stigmatized within the lower class. He believes that those who assess

---

[7] Gresham M. Sykes and David Matza, "Techniques of Neutralization: A Theory of Delinquency," *American Sociological Review*, Vol. 22 (December 1957), pp. 664–670. [Cf. Fritz Redl and David Wineman, *Children Who Hate* (Glencoe: Free Press, 1951), pp. 158–174.] In a more recent paper Matza and Sykes have taken a somewhat different tack. In the earlier paper their position was that the delinquents shared the conventional values. In this paper they address themselves to specifically delinquent values but stress the striking similarities of these to certain subterranean values that are to be found within the society at large. This raises the question of public versus private values and the greater efficiency of the higher classes in maintaining the privacy of their private values. David Matza and Gresham M. Sykes, "Juvenile Delinquency and Subterranean Values," *American Sociological Review*, Vol. 26 (October 1961), pp. 712–719.

[8] Herbert H. Hyman, "The Value Systems of Different Classes: A Social Psychological Contribution to the Analysis of Stratification," in Reinhard Bendix and Seymour M. Lipset, editors, *Class, Status and Power* (Glencoe: Free Press, 1953), pp. 426–442.

[9] Allison Davis, "The Motivation of the Underprivileged Worker," in William Foote Whyte, editor, *Industry and Society* (New York: McGraw-Hill, 1946), p. 104.

"the lower-class forms of the family" in terms of middle-class norms are committing a "fundamental error." [10]

In a similar vein, Walter Miller's major point about juvenile delinquency within the lower class is that it is congruent with the values to be found within the lower class, and that these lower-class values are very different from those to be found within the rest of the society. According to Miller, "the cultural system which exerts the most direct influence" upon members of delinquent gangs "is that of the lower-class community itself—a long established, distinctively patterned tradition with an integrity of its own." [11] Or again, with more clarity for our purposes, Miller states:

> "There is a substantial segment of present-day American society whose way of life, values, and characteristic patterns of behavior are the product of a distinctive cultural system which may be termed 'lower class.'" [12]

Here, too, it is clear that Miller does not specifically address himself to the general question of whether a society is characterized by a common or a class-differentiated value system, but we can readily see that he believes that values are differentiated by class.

Common or Class-Differentiated Values?

To what shall we attribute these different positions? Are we to believe that we have a common or a class-differentiated value system? That illegitimacy and juvenile delinquency are deviant or normative within the lower class? Should we go along with Parsons, Taft, and Goode, or with Davis, Miller, and Henriques?

I am certain that some of the writers will complain about the pigeonhole I have assigned them to, and in fairness to them it must be pointed out that they do not all fit comfortably into their assigned slots. By examining their writings carefully it can be seen that, from my point of view, most of them have second thoughts about their major position, or make statements that qualify their major position. For example, Parsons talks of "secondary or subsidiary or variant value patterns" [13] in

---

[10] Fernando Henriques, *Family and Colour in Jamaica* (London: Eyre & Spottiswoode, 1953), p. 162.

[11] Walter B. Miller, "Lower Class Culture as a Generating Milieu of Gang Delinquency," *Journal of Social Issues,* Vol. 14, No. 3, 1958, p. 5.

[12] See page 261.

[13] Talcott Parsons, *The Social System* (Glencoe: Free Press, 1951), p. 169. See also his discussion of the need for patterning as well as flexibility in adapting to changing situations: Talcott Parsons, "The Point of View of the Author," in Max Black, editor, *The Social Theories of Talcott Parsons: A Critical Examination* (Englewood Cliffs, New Jersey: Prentice-Hall, 1961).

addition to the basic value pattern. On the other hand, Allison Davis says that "each social class has developed its own differentiated and adaptive form of the basic American culture." [14] In these statements Parsons and Davis, who perhaps best exemplify the contrasting positions taken on this question, are practically in agreement. There must be something here that calls for further examination and clarification.

It will be useful to follow the progression of Merton's thoughts on these questions in some detail, for Merton, in his recent writings, has completely broken out of his assigned pigeonhole. In his first paper on "Social Structure and Anomie" Merton's tone strongly suggests that he once assumed the existence of a common value system. In this extremely influential paper Merton made the point that the basic problem faced by members of the lower class is that they are structurally in a position that makes it exceedingly difficult for them to attain the cultural goals of the society by legitimate means, and therefore "the greatest pressures toward deviation are exerted upon the lower strata." [15] This suggests that the members of the lower strata typically share the common values of the society,[16] and in the statement of Merton's that I have already quoted (p. 271) he becomes even more explicit about the existence of a common value system.

In fairness to Merton, however, it must be pointed out that even in his first paper, despite the strong inference that we can draw, he scrupulously refrains from stating outright that members of the lower class actually internalize the general values of the society. The cultural values are presented as external to the (lower-class) individuals, as in his following statement:

> "To say that the goal of monetary success is entrenched in American culture is only to say that Americans are bombarded on every side by precepts which affirm the right or, often, the duty of retaining the goal even in the face of repeated frustration." [17]

In his second paper on "Continuities in Social Structure and Anomie," Merton takes direct cognizance of the question as to whether all members do in fact share the same system of values:

> "But if the communications addressed to generations of Americans continue to reiterate the gospel of success, it does not follow that all

---

[14] Allison Davis, *Social-Class Influences Upon Learning* (Cambridge: Harvard University Press, 1948), p. 10.

[15] Robert K. Merton, *op. cit.*, p. 144.

[16] Cf. Herbert H. Hyman, *op. cit.*, p. 427: "It is clear that Merton's analysis assumes that the cultural goal of success is in actuality internalized by lower-class individuals."

[17] Robert K. Merton, *op. cit.*, pp. 136–137.

Americans in all groups, regions, and class strata have uniformly assimilated this set of values." [18]

Merton's conclusion on the question of common or class-differentiated values is that "it is a matter of inquiry," [19] which is, in effect, the same statement made by Lockwood with respect to Parsons' assumption of a common value system: it is "a matter for empirical investigation." [20] However, even when we turn to empirical studies the contradictions remain. In a secondary analysis of empirical data on illegitimacy in the Caribbean, Goode concludes that (in at least this area) members of the lower class share the general values of the society,[21] while Hyman, in a secondary analysis of data on educational, income, and occupational aspirations, concludes that the values differ from class to class.[22]

The Lower-Class Value Stretch

We can illuminate the contradictions, or apparent contradictions, that exist by focusing upon the reactions of the members of the lower class to their deprived circumstances. Even assuming similarly deprived circumstances for members of the lower class, we would not expect an unvarying response to their circumstances because of the known complexity of human behavior. Certain individual responses, such as neurotic or psychotic behavior, may result. Or group responses, such as revolution or the development of religious sects, may result. Walter B. Miller and Albert K. Cohen each discusses three different types of lower-class reactions; [23] Merton, Parsons, and Dubin, respectively discuss four, eight, and fourteen different types of (not necessarily lower-class) deviant reactions.[24] What I intend to do is to discuss an entirely different type of lower-class reaction that has been obliquely hinted at but for the most part overlooked by these writers, and that I believe constitutes the one most important reaction to be found within the lower class. That reaction is what I call the lower-class value stretch, and through a consideration of the lower-class value stretch I believe we can clear

---

[18] *Ibid.*, p. 170.

[19] *Ibid.*

[20] David Lockwood, "Some Remarks on 'The Social System,' " *British Journal of Sociology*, Vol. 7 (June 1956), p. 137.

[21] William J. Goode, *op. cit.*, pp. 21–30.

[22] Herbert H. Hyman, *op. cit.*

[23] Walter B. Miller, "Implications of Urban Lower-Class Culture for Social Work," *Social Service Review*, Vol. 3 (September 1959), p. 231; Albert K. Cohen, *Delinquent Boys* (Glencoe: Free Press, 1955), pp. 128–130.

[24] Robert K. Merton, *op. cit.*, pp. 141–157; Talcott Parsons, *The Social System*, pp. 256–267; Robert Dubin, "Deviant Behavior and Social Structure," *American Sociological Review*, Vol. 24 (April 1959), pp. 147–164.

up some of the contradictions that have appeared in the literature on the question of a common or a class-differentiated value system.

Merton has called attention to the problem of identifying the social mechanisms that minimize the strains that the (lower-class) person potentially faces—and the value stretch is one such mechanism. By the value stretch I mean that the lower-class person, without abandoning the general values of the society, develops an alternative set of values. Without abandoning the values placed upon success, such as high income and high educational and occupational attainment, he stretches the values so that lesser degrees of success also become desirable. Without abandoning the values of marriage and legitimate childbirth he stretches these values so that a non-legal union and legally illegitimate children are also desirable. The result is that the members of the lower class, in many areas, have a wider range of values than others within the society. They share the general values of the society with members of other classes, but in addition they have stretched these values, or developed alternative values, which help them to adjust to their deprived circumstances.

If I were to deal metaphorically with the development of a wider range of values within the lower class, my analysis, up to a point, would follow the position taken by Albert K. Cohen [25] on the development of a delinquent subculture. Lower-class persons in close interaction with each other and faced with similar problems do not long remain in a state of mutual ignorance. They do not maintain a strong commitment to middle-class values that they cannot attain, and they do not continue to respond to others in a rewarding or punishing way simply on the basis of whether these others are living up to the middle-class values. A change takes place. They come to tolerate and eventually to evaluate favorably certain deviations from the middle-class values. In this way they need not be continually frustrated by their failure to live up to unattainable values. The resultant is a stretched value system with a low degree of commitment to all the values within the range, including the dominant, middle-class values. This is what I suggest as the major lower-class value change, rather than a change in which the middle-class values are abandoned or flouted. [26]

---

[25] Albert K. Cohen, *op. cit.*, pp. 59–72 *et passim.*

[26] This is obviously only a very sketchy account of the development of the lower-class value stretch. Tracing the historical development of lower-class values is no simple matter, especially since, in Malthus's words, "the histories of mankind that we possess are histories only of the higher classes."

Important clues to the psychological processes that accompany the development of the lower-class value stretch can be found in the literature on learning theory that has come out of the fields of animal experimentation and small group

To continue in the metaphorical arena for a moment, I can perhaps clarify what I mean by the lower-class value stretch by referring
to the fable of the fox and the grapes. The fox in the fable declared
that the unattainable sweet grapes were sour: Merton's "rebellious" fox
renounces the prevailing taste for sweet grapes;[27] but the "adaptive"
lower-class fox I am talking about does neither—rather, he acquires a
taste for sour grapes.

If I am correct that the predominant lower-class response to its
situation is the value stretch, then we can immediately resolve many of
the apparent contradictions described earlier. Those who hold that the
basic values of the society are common to all classes are correct, because the members of the lower class do share these values with other
members of society. Similarly, those who hold that the values differ
from class to class are also correct, because the members of the lower
class share values unique to themselves, in addition to sharing the general values of the society with others. The theories are "both correct,
both incomplete, and complementary to one another."[28]

Values and Levels of Abstraction. Before turning to evidence
which can help us to substantiate the existence of the lower-class stretch
I want to dwell briefly upon another factor that complicates many discussions about values—the level of abstraction of the values involved.
The more concrete a value, the more differentiated a society may appear
with respect to it; the more abstract a value, the more integrated a society may appear. Some of the apparent contradictions about a common
or class-differentiated value system must therefore be attributed to the
confusion that results from the use of different levels of abstraction in
talking about values. Clyde Kluckhohn has made the apt comment that

> "much of the confusion in discussion about values undoubtedly arises
> from the fact that one speaker has the general category in mind, an-
> other a particular limited type of value, still another a different specific
> type."[29]

experimentation. For a demonstration of the applicability of such theory see George
C. Homans, *Social Behavior: Its Elementary Forms.* See also Allison Davis, *op. cit.;*
Genevieve Knupfer, "Portrait of the Underdog," *Public Opinion Quarterly,* Vol. 2
(Spring 1947), pp. 103–114.

[27] Robert K. Merton, *op. cit.,* p. 156.

[28] Homans makes this statement about what he refers to as the "social contract" theory and the "social mold" theory. George C. Homans, *The Human Group,*
p. 330. The argument between the egg enthusiasts and the sperm protagonists is
another particularly good example of the two warring sides mistaking part of the
truth for the whole of it: See N. J. Berrill, *Sex and the Nature of Things* (New
York: Pocket Books, 1955), pp. 1–11.

[29] Clyde Kluckhohn, et al., "Values and Value-Orientations in the Theory of

It should therefore be clear that those, like Parsons, who assume the existence of a common value system are talking about values at a high level of abstraction, and they may readily agree that at lower levels of abstraction there can be a great deal of differentiation.[30] Aberle, to cite another example, agrees that "a core of common values is an integrational principle of any viable social system,"[31] but he nevertheless also discusses "the diversification of values which in fact exists."[32] Even though Williams outlines a number of major American value-orientations, he nevertheless cautions that in a complex society "a common core of values that could be said to hold for even a plurality of the population would probably be quite thin and abstract."[33] These points are not altogether unlike the distinction that Aristotle makes in his *Ethics* between a "system of rules" and "the exigencies of the particular case." Because of this we can see that it is in theoretical discussions particularly that we may find contradictions about a common or class-differentiated value system that stem from the different levels of abstraction that are under discussion.

When we turn to such specific areas as delinquency and illegitimacy, however, we are presented with more substantial contradictions. Do juvenile delinquents and illegitimate mothers share the conventional values and regard their own acts as deviant? Or do they have values of their own such that delinquency and illegitimacy are normative rather than deviant acts? It is by referring to the lower-class value stretch that we can find the best general answer to these questions.

The Level of Aspiration. Let us now consider very briefly some evidence that can help us to substantiate the existence of the lower-class value stretch. Experimental as well as more qualitative data on the "level of aspiration" within different classes is potentially an important source of evidence. One problem with a great deal of the quantitative data is that the respondent is asked to give a simple, single response, and it is then impossible to tell exactly what the response means. As McClelland points out, it could represent a "level of defense," or a "level of expectation," as well as a "level of aspiration," and probably

Action," in Talcott Parsons and Edward A. Shils, editors, *Toward a General Theory of Action* (Cambridge: Harvard University Press, 1952), p. 412.

[30] Talcott Parsons, "General Theory in Sociology," in Robert K. Merton, Leonard Broom and Leonard S. Cottrell, Jr., editors, *Sociology Today*, p. 8.

[31] David F. Aberle, "Shared Values in Complex Societies," *American Sociological Review*, Vol. 15 (August 1950), p. 502.

[32] *Ibid.*, p. 497.

[33] Robin M. Williams, Jr., *American Society* (New York: Knopf, 1951), pp. 388–440; p. 385.

represents a varying combination of all three.[34] Even assuming that the response does represent a "level of aspiration," if we are interested in testing for the existence of a range of values (or aspirations), and if in fact such a range exists, then by forcing the respondent to give one reply we are in effect forcing him to select a response from within his range of aspirations. This means that such data are limited in their utility, despite the fact that they are quantitative and may cover a wide sample of respondents. For example, Hyman has done a valuable secondary analysis of survey data in which he concludes that there are differences in the level of educational, income, and occupational aspiration of the different classes. Hyman speaks somewhat deprecatingly of qualitative studies done in this area, but it is only by reference to qualitative matters that we can fully appreciate the fact that there are limitations to Hyman's study beyond those he mentions. On examination of Hyman's study, we find that *in every question from every survey that he uses in his analysis, the respondent was asked for only one response*.[35] It is therefore at least possible to interpret his findings in terms of the lower-class value stretch. That is to say that the lower-class person, having a wider range of aspirations than others, and selecting his response from within that downward-stretched range, would by chance alone appear to have a different and lower level (although in actual fact what he has is a wider range) of values.

A great variety of tasks has been used in level of aspiration experiments, and a great many different measures have been based on these tasks.[36] The task that has been most widely used is the Aspiration Board as described by Rotter,[37] or some minor variation of it.[38] It is an

---

[34] David C. McClelland, *Personality* (New York: William Sloane, 1951), pp. 563–568. Rotter also indicates that some of the earliest workers with the level of aspiration recognized the relevance of these three factors: Julian B. Rotter, "Level of Aspiration as a Method of Studying Personality: I. A. Critical Review of Methodology," *Psychological Review*, Vol. 49 (September 1942), pp. 467–468.

[35] Herbert H. Hyman, *op. cit.*, pp. 426–442.

[36] For a recent review of level of aspiration experiments see: James Inglis, "Abnormalities of Motivation and 'Ego-Functions,'" in H. J. Eysenck, ed., *Handbook of Abnormal Psychology* (New York: Basic Books, 1961), pp. 262–297.

[37] Julian B. Rotter, "Level of Aspiration as a Method of Studying Personality: II. Development and Evaluation of a Controlled Method," *Journal of Experimental Psychology*, Vol. 31 (November 1942), pp. 410–422.

[38] For example, see: Samuel F. Klugman, "Emotional Stability and Level of Aspiration," *Journal of General Psychology*, Vol. 38 (January 1948), pp. 101–118; Norman I. Harway, "Einstellung Effect and Goal-Setting Behavior," *Journal of Abnormal and Social Psychology*, Vol. 50 (May 1955), pp. 339–342; Kenneth C. Jost, "The Level of Aspiration of Schizophrenic and Normal Subjects," *Journal of Abnormal and Social Psychology*, Vol. 50 (May 1955), pp. 315–320; Joseph G.

individual task and a single response task (S is permitted to make only one response when asked for his level of aspiration). Although theoretically it has long been recognized that the level of aspiration is a complex variable, it is only recently that a variety of tests have been formulated which permit or require S to make more than one response.[39] These tests make it easier to isolate the various factors that go into making up a "single" level of aspiration, and they also point the way toward experimental tests of the ideas presented in this paper. Of exceptional interest in this connection I cite the study by Miller and Haller,[40] and even more so, the study by Clark, Teevan, and Ricciuti,[41] and I urge that their methods serve as a model for those experimenting further with the level of aspiration. Perhaps it will not be too much longer before Stouffer's suggestion that a social norm (or an aspiration) not be regarded as a point but as a range will be more widely accepted.[42]

An interesting study that lends support to the idea that there is a lower-class value stretch is presented by Rosen.[43] He studied the occupational aspirations of different ethnic and class groups and showed that certain ethnic groups and also the lower classes are characterized by a lower level of aspiration. This is because he follows the common and in some ways unfortunate habit of reducing his data to single aspiration scores. Nevertheless he correctly points out that "it is misleading to speak of the 'height' of vocational aspirations. For all groups have 'high' aspirations."[44] If we examine his data on ethnic group differences closely, we can see that certain ethnic groups have a wider range of aspirations, and we can safely infer that members of the lower class also have a wider range of aspirations—they express satisfaction rather than dissatisfaction over a wider range of occupational goals. Rosen's

---

Sheehan and Seymour L. Zelen, "Level of Aspiration in Stutterers and Nonstutterers," *Journal of Abnormal and Social Psychology*, Vol. 51 (July 1955), pp. 83–86.

[39] John R. Hills, "The Measurement of Levels of Aspiration," *Journal of Social Psychology*, Vol. 41 (May 1955), pp. 221–229; Sidney Siegel, "Level of Aspiration and Decision Making," *Psychological Review*, Vol. 64 (July 1957), pp. 253–262.

[40] I. W. Miller and A. O. Haller, "The Measurement of Level of Occupational Aspiration." Paper presented at the meetings of the American Sociological Association, St. Louis, Missouri, September 1961.

[41] Russell A. Clark, Richard Teevan, and Henry N. Ricciuti, "Hope of Success and Fear of Failure as Aspects of Need for Achievement," *Journal of Abnormal and Social Psychology*, Vol. 53 (September 1956), pp. 182–186.

[42] Samuel A. Stouffer, "An Analysis of Conflicting Social Norms," *American Sociological Review*, Vol. 14 (December 1949), pp. 707–17.

[43] Bernard C. Rosen, "Race, Ethnicity, and the Achievement Syndrome," *American Sociological Review*, Vol. 24 (February 1959), pp. 47–60.

[44] *Ibid.*, p. 60.

study, therefore, in an indirect way, demonstrates the existence of the lower-class value stretch in the area of occupational aspiration. . . .

Discussion

At the heart of our analysis lies the issue of when old values die and new values develop. It is precisely because old values never die, they only fade away, and because new values only gradually appear, that it may, at times, be difficult to state categorically that a particular value is effectively held by a particular individual, or shared by a particular group. All this is merely to say that people vary in their degree of commitment to a value. Despite the difficulties this poses for us, we can nonetheless see that it is entirely possible for a lower-class person to hold middle-class values only, to abandon middle-class values without developing any new values, or to abandon middle-class values while developing a new set of values.[45] I am certain that these are not merely possible but actual responses of many lower-class people to their deprived situation. But I am equally certain that the dominant response of the lower-class person is the lower-class value stretch. It is because the lower-class person, to a degree, typically shares the middle-class values and also holds values unique to the lower class that he is able to adapt to his circumstances without certain more specific phenomena, such as deviance or revolution, being more evident as actual or attempted responses within the lower class.

Once the lower-class value stretch has been developed the lower-class person is in a better position to adapt to his circumstances because

---

[45] The assumption made here, as elsewhere in the discussion of the lower-class value stretch, is that the dominant, conventional, middle-class values have relevance for all members of the society, including its lower-class members. Since many middle-class values, however, are inappropriate to the conditions of lower-class life, the members of the lower class are faced with a problem. Once this value problem has been solved within the lower class—as in the development of the value stretch—then this solution is learned by many in the next generation who therefore do not face the same problem all over again. But a different kind of problem now emerges, and it is perhaps the most serious problem that practitioners in the social welfare, health, educational, and vocational fields face: To what extent are lower-class individuals passing up realistic opportunities for better welfare, health, education, and jobs because of cultural resistances? And to what extent can or should these hard-to-reach lower-class individuals be induced to break away from these cultural resistances? An intriguing answer to these questions that deserves the serious attention of professional practitioners who work with lower-class individuals is given in S. M. Miller and Frank Riessman, "The Working Class Subculture: A New View," *Social Problems,* Vol. 9 (Summer 1961), pp. 86–97.

he has a wider range of values with which to operate.[46] Cultural resources, in a sense, come to compensate for his lack of social and economic resources. One aspect of what is involved in the lower-class value stretch is that the lower-class individual with the wider range of values must also have less commitment to each of the values within that range.[47] Goode has noted this point with respect to conventional values,[48] but insofar as the lower-class person stretches his values there would be a low degree of commitment to all values he holds. This is perhaps one factor which helps to explain the higher proportion of "don't know" answers to survey questions on aspirations within the lower class. The lower-class person with a low degree of commitment to a wide range of aspirations may find a question asking for his level of aspiration to be inane.[49]

---

[46] Members of the middle or upper class would not be under the same degree of environmental stress as lower-class members, and they would therefore not have to stretch their values to the same degree even if they did not adhere strictly to the conventional values. They would have access to resources that would permit them to retain their respectability and a seeming adherence to conventional values even in the face of deviance. Everett C. Hughes, for example, has suggested that any upper middle-class girl can get an abortion by some other name. He points out, in a personal communication, that no canon of behavior is absolutely adhered to, and that there must therefore be "a secondary set of canons of behavior—the rules which govern subsequent behavior after the first canon has been violated." This is an intriguing idea with manifold ramifications. The major comment suggested by a consideration of the lower-class value stretch is that secondary canons of behavior may interact with the primary canons in such a way that the primary canons are stretched.

A similar idea has been expressed by Reinhard Bendix: "Is not indeed every group in some measure engaged in a strategy of argument which seeks to maximize its self-respect in terms of the conventional standards from which behavior is bound to differ to some extent?" (personal communication).

[47] Cf. Albert J. McQueen, *op. cit.*, pp. 10–11.

[48] William J. Goode, *op. cit.*, p. 27.

[49] Speaking generally about the higher proportion of "don't know" responses in the lower class, such factors within the lower class as less knowledge and a feeling that one is less competent to judge undoubtedly account for a good deal of the difference between classes. See Genevieve Knupfer, *op. cit.*, pp. 103–114. On informational questions the factor of less knowledge is especially apparent. But it is interesting to speculate whether on questions of opinion, and especially on questions of level of aspiration, a considerable portion of the difference between the classes can be accounted for by the middle-class interviewer's questions rather than the lower-class respondent's personality. Under skillful questioning it may turn out that many lower-class respondents who "don't know" do know. A beautiful illustration of this point—and it is ironically an even better illustration because it deals with a middle-class sample—is given by Aberle and Naegele. They point out that

I have already expressed my conviction that the lower-class value stretch is the predominant response of lower-class individuals to their deprived situation, and that it is through an understanding of the lower-class value stretch that we can explain at least some of the apparent contradictions about a common or a class-differentiated value system. The conviction of the reader, of course, must depend upon his own familiarity with lower-class life, as well as upon additional research which seeks to test the existence of the lower-class value stretch.[50] In the meantime, I submit that some of the data pertaining to lower-class juvenile gangs and delinquency can be better understood in terms of the lower-class value stretch; I submit that a great deal of the data on lower-class family organization, and specifically illegitimacy in the Caribbean, is incomprehensible unless we assume the existence of the lower-class value stretch; I submit that responses such as mental disorder, juvenile delinquency, and rebellion would occur with greater

---

middle-class fathers always say initially that they have "no plans" for their sons' future occupation. This is clearly a "don't know" response. It turns out, however, that "further questioning always shows that 'no plans' means that any occupation is all right, *if* it is a middle-class occupation." David F. Aberle and Kaspar D. Naegele, "Middle-Class Fathers' Occupational Role and Attitudes toward Children," *American Journal of Orthopsychiatry,* Vol. 22 (April 1952), p. 371. In other words, the middle-class fathers have a wide range of occupational goals for their sons and they therefore reply that they have no plans for their sons' future occupation. But once the interviewers go beyond the initial question and initial "don't know" response they discover that the fathers do know and they are able to elicit from the fathers the range of desirable occupational goals these fathers have for their sons.

[50] In this paper I am adding to the concept of value (whether "dominant" or "basic") the concept of a "value stretch" and a "range of values." It is not the purpose of this paper to relate these concepts to other concepts that have been added to or opposed to the value concept, but I do wish to state, without comment, what some of these additions or oppositions have been. F. Kluckhohn has written about variant values and the range of value orientations to be found in all societies; Redl and Wineman have referred to "ranges" and "stretches" of "value sensitivity and value respect," by which they mean that individuals may show respect for the values of others and modify their behavior on that account; Yinger has referred to a contra-culture and counter-values, which are opposed to those of the surrounding society; others, like Wrong (and those he quotes), have suggested various ways of conceiving a non-normative situation in dialectic opposition to the concept of value.

See Florence R. Kluckhohn, "Dominant and Variant Value Orientations," in Florence R. Kluckhohn, Fred L. Strodtbeck, et al., *Variations in Value Orientations* (Evanston: Row, Peterson, 1961), pp. 1–48; Fritz Redl and David Wineman, *Children Who Hate,* pp. 203–205; J. Milton Yinger, "Contraculture and Subculture," *American Sociological Review,* Vol. 25 (October 1960), pp. 625–635; Dennis H. Wrong, "The Oversocialized Conception of Man in Modern Sociology," *American Sociological Review,* Vol. 26 (April 1961), pp. 183–193.

frequency within the lower class but for the existence of the lower-class value stretch; and finally, I submit that some of the survey and experimental work on the *"level* of aspiration" validates the existence of the lower-class value stretch, and that as greater attention is paid to a *"range* of aspirations" in these surveys and experiments, more data will accumulate to demonstrate the importance of the value stretch as a lower-class phenomenon.

Poverty and Self-Indulgence: A Critique of the Non-Deferred Gratification Pattern

S. M. Miller, *Syracuse University*
Frank Riessman, *Albert Einstein Medical College, Yeshiva University*
Arthur A. Seagull, *Michigan State University*

The history of this article is an interesting commentary on the development and dissemination of ideas. The basic outline of its concerns first appeared in Frank Riessman's unpublished doctoral dissertation, Class Differences in Attitudes Towards Participation and Leadership, *Columbia University, 1955. Miller and Riessman developed the ideas in a series of papers; one "The Critique of the Non-Deferred Gratification Image of the Worker" (1956), was exclusively devoted to the non-deferred gratification pattern. They were never able to find an academic journal willing to publish it. The article was privately circulated until the editors of this volume asked to publish it. Meanwhile, Arthur A. Seagull had worked with Miller and did his dissertation,* The Ability to Delay Gratification, *Syracuse University, 1964, on an experiment involving a test of the deferred pattern. Consequently, we were able to expand the article. One moral of this tale is that not only has the interest in poverty led to new work but that it also has disinterred neglected studies.*

THE OUTPOURING OF SOCIAL SCIENCE LITERATURE on social class differences has led to efforts to develop general themes which codify the scattered data and provide ways of thinking about class dynamics. One such theme is that of the deferred gratification pattern, which is thought to provide the basis for the social and economic advance of the middle classes. Its presumed absence in the non-middle classes is regarded as a barrier to improvement among this population, and, for some, an explanation of why the poor are poor.

In the absence of competing explanations of the varied data, the deferred gratification pattern (DGP) has been in the first rank of principles explaining "lower class behavior." Indeed, it is probably the most frequently used element in discussion of lower class life. The recent attention to poverty has renewed interest in the DGP. Our feeling is that it is a thin reed on which to hang analyses of behavior and that logical examination of the concept and appraisal of empirical materials do not confirm its usefulness as an all-explanatory theme.

While we believe that the DGP concern does point to some important problem areas, we do not have confidence that it is a satisfactory summation of the data, nor that it can be mechanically applied to interpret low income life. Since it affects social policy we believe it must be closely appraised.

The Concept of the DGP

The DGP is frequently discussed in the negative—that is, the characteristics which result from its absence in low income life. Schneider and Lysgaard[1] have provided the most compact summation of the non-deferred gratification pattern. They have concluded that in contrast with middle class life, lower class life is characterized by an inability to defer gratification by "impulse following" rather than "impulse renunciation." The catalogue of lower class, "impulse-following" non-deferred gratification behavior includes: "relative readiness to engage in physical violence, free sexual expression (as through intercourse), minimum pursuit of education, low aspiration level, failure of parents to identify the class of their children's playmates, free spending, little emphasis on being 'well-mannered and obedient,' and short time dependence of parents." On the other hand, "Middle class persons feel that they *should* save, postpone, and renounce a variety of gratifications."[2]

Allison Davis' approach[3] is central to the notion of ability to de-

---

[1] Louis Schneider and Sverre Lysgaard, "The Deferred Gratification Patterns: A Preliminary Study," *American Sociological Review*, 18 (April, 1953), pp. 142–49. We place a heavy emphasis on this article because it is a thoughtful effort to integrate a variety of studies.

[2] Sverre Lysgaard, "Social Stratification and the Deferred Pattern," *Proceedings,* World Congress of Sociology, Liege, International Sociological Association, 1953, p. 142.

[3] Allison Davis, *Social Class Influences Upon Learning,* Cambridge: Harvard University Press, 1949; Allison Davis and Robert J. Havighurst, "Social Class

lay, or its concomitant, "impulse renunciation." Davis felt that starting with early child rearing practices there was less emphasis on impulse control among lower class parents than middle class parents. He felt that, "Generalizing from the evidence . . . we would say the middle class children are subjected earlier and more consistently to the influences which make a child an orderly, conscientious, responsible and tame person."[4]

Considering the behavior of lower income adults, Davis stated that their propensity for choosing immediate reward was an adaptive response to the slum environment. "The lower class people look upon life as a recurrent series of depressions and peaks with regard to gratification of their basic needs. In their lives it is all or nothing. . . . The learned fears of deprivation drive lower class people to get all they can of other physical gratification, 'while the getting is good.'"[5]

The middle classes are believed to be distinguished by the presence and significant operation of the ability to defer gratification, to accept later rewards instead of immediate satisfactions, to bank their impulses, and to plan effectively for the future. The non-middle classes are believed to be characterized by the absence of these abilities. To some extent, then, the DGP statements are relative statements: the middle classes have more of the deferred patterns than do other classes (the upper classes are usually ignored in these discussions). Consequently, an examination must not only weigh the existence of these patterns among the poor but the degree of deficiency when compared with the middle classes.[6]

It is important to realize that an undertone of the DGP analysis is that the pattern is not temporary nor easily overcome. Indeed, the assumption is that the ability or inability to defer gratification is deeply

---

and Color Differences in Child-Rearing," *American Sociological Review*, II, 1946, pp. 698–710; Allison Davis, "Child Rearing and the Class Structure of American Society," in *The Family in Democratic Society*, Anniversary Papers of the Community Service Society of New York, New York: Columbia University Press, 1949.

[4] Davis and Havighurst, *op. cit.*, p. 707.

[5] Davis, *Social-Class Influence Upon Learning*, p. 27.

[6] We shall not discuss the social value of the deferred gratification patterns and the possible individual and social prices exacted by them. The avidly melancholy voice of Paul Goodman has been raised in question of the pain of impulse-renunciation. Indeed, some of those who pioneered the concept of deferred gratification like Allison Davis, were extremely critical of the price the middle classes paid for their impulse-renunciation, though feeling that it would be well for the less affluent to pay this price in order to advance. Nor do we question whether the DGP is a sine qua non for the development of occupational skills although we doubt that it is. See S. M. Miller, "Dropouts—A Political Problem," in David Schreiber, ed., *The School Dropout*, Washington: National Education Association, 1964.

embedded in the personality dynamics of the individual, performing an important role in the psychodynamic economy. The picture seems to be that the DGP or the non-DGP are developed through early life experience: they become incorporated in the personality and are relatively impervious to situational factors. We hasten to add that not all who espouse the DGP approach share the psychodynamic orientation or the notion of relative fixity. Perhaps, it is only ambiguous presentations which lead us to believe that most do.

Who Are the Non-Deferrers?

One of the difficulties in the discussion of the DGP is that the world is divided frequently into the middle classes and the non-middle classes. All in the middle classes are possessors of the ability to defer gratification, and those of the non-middle classes are bereft of this ability. Obviously, even among those who believe strongly in the dichotomous distribution of the deferring attributes, it is recognized at some level that it is not a 100 percent against a 0 percent distribution problem. Central tendencies are what are basically assumed—although some writing does not imply this—so that some middle class individuals do not possess the DGP and some non-middle class persons do.

Beyond the blurring of the distribution problem is the lumping of all who do not possess middle-level income or white collar jobs into the non-middle classes, frequently called "the lower class." We have previously indicated the inadequacy of lumping together regularly employed, skilled, blue-collar workers with irregularly employed, low-skill service workers.[7]

More recently it has been pointed out that there is considerable internal differentiation among those at the lower-income end of the lower class. Four sub-groups among the newly rediscovered poor have been denoted: the stable poor, the strained poor, the copers/skidders, and the unstable poor.[8] It is our suspicion that the kinds of attitudes and behavior which have been subsumed under the DGP term are most

---

[7] S. M. Miller and Frank Riessman, "The Working-Class Subculture: A New View," *Social Problems*, 1961. Reprinted in Arthur Shostak and William Gomberg, eds., *Blue Collar World*, Englewood Cliffs: Prentice-Hall, Inc., 1964, and in Frank Riessman, *The Culturally Deprived Child*, New York: Harper and Row, 1962.

[8] S. M. Miller, "The American Lower Classes: A Typological Approach," *Social Research*, 1964. Reprinted in Frank Riessman, Jerome Cohen and Arthur Pearl, eds. *Mental Health of the Poor*, New York: Free Press, 1964; in Shostak and Gomberg, *op. cit.*; in Shostak and Gomberg, eds., *Perspectives on Urban Poverty*, Englewood Cliffs: Prentice-Hall, Inc., 1965.

likely to be found among the unstable poor. It is misleading, then, to write as though all the poor have the same outlook as the unstable poor and will be benefited by the same social policies as might aid the unstable poor.

Since most analyses of attitudes and behaviors do not make fine distinctions within the poor or the lower classes, what might be real differences between the unstable poor and other groups of poor, near-poor and the middle classes do not appear in the available data.[9] Nevertheless, while we believe that some DGP elements may be more characteristic[10] of the unstable poor, we do not find the DGP concept a fully adequate way of understanding the behavior of the poor and of other non-middle class groups.

In investigations with no immediate middle-class comparison groups or in more general statements about the absence of the DGP among the poor, the middle classes are frequently explicitly or implicitly imaged in an out-moded way. They are regarded as delighting in hard work, frugally and carefully planning and budgeting every activity and expenditure, abjuring debt, and constantly foregoing the indulgence of present gain in order to reap future rewards. It is hard to recognize this "Protestant Ethic" pattern in the new middle classes possessed by "other direction" and pursuing the consumption euphoria of today. The rise of consumer debt among the middle classes, the refrain of "not being able to make ends meet" despite affluent income levels, the competition between work and the coffee break, suggest that important changes have taken place in many sections of the middle classes, or that the middle classes were never quite as described. Consequently, the comparisons with the middle classes are frequently of the actual behavior of the poor with "official norms rather than actual practice"

---

[9] Unfortunately the absence of refined social-class categories means that data on "the lower class" may in some studies we cite refer mainly to the upper working classes. We reluctantly and tacitly accept this group in the discussion of "the poor," because of difficulties in developing principles to include or exclude studies. Since the cited studies are used in buttressing the DGP position, we feel it important to raise questions about them.

We have used interchangeably terms like the non-middle classes, "the poor," "the lower classes," to refer to the groups which are being contrasted with the middle classes.

[10] By using "more" we mean to imply that the comparison is with the middle classes and that the unstable poor may not be "typically" characterized by these attributes. While more of the unstable may have these attributes, these practices may not characterize the overwhelming majority.

of the better-off.[11] Some official middle class norms may have changed as well, compounding the irreality of the comparison.

The Logical Basis of the DGP

Before proceeding to evaluate research on the class distribution of the DGP, it is important to note some problems in the formulation of this mode of analysis. In order for a valid interclass comparison to be made, certain conditions must be met:

1. *The two class groups must equally value the satisfaction that is being deferred.* If the object is less valued by the low income group, then obviously the interest in making immediate sacrifices is less.

2. *The two class groups must have an equal understanding and opportunity to defer an immediate gain for a future reward.* If one group is not presented with or is not aware of the opportunities of future gain, then we cannot infer from the fact that it has not deferred that it is unwilling to do so.

3. *The two class groups must suffer equally from the deferment.* If one class has many more other satisfactions, then it is difficult to equate the impact of the deferment. Or, if the penalty of postponement is greater for one of the groups, the comparison falls down.

4. *The two class groups must have the same probability of achieving the gratification at the end of the deferment period.* If one group has less risk than the other or has more confidence that the gratification will be forthcoming, then the comparison is not valid. Objective and subjective risk must be comparable.

Clearly, no research meets these conditions. Indeed, it is probably impossible in real life to find circumstances under which these conditions prevail in groups differently situated in the social structure. It was these doubts that made us first ponder the usefulness of the DGP. In most situations talked about in relation to the DGP, middle class or higher income groupings are more likely than lower-income groupings to value the object that is deferred (sometimes because they know more about it; sometimes because of value choices); or they are likely to suffer less from a deferment of gratification (largely because they have alternative rewards), or they are much more likely to be sure of getting the reward at the end of the deferment period.

---

[11] S. M. Miller and Frank Riessman, *op. cit.,* p. 90. For changes in child-rearing practices in the middle classes, see Urie Bronfenbrenner, "Socialization and Social Class through Time and Space," in Eleanor E. Maccoby, Theodore M. Newcomb, and Eugene L. Hartley, eds., *Readings in Social Psychology*, New York: Henry Holt & Company, 1958.

Furthermore, it is important to recognize that the same act can have quite different meanings and implications in the different settings of middle class and working class life. Deferment or non-deferment in the same situation may have different motivations in different groups. Caution must be exercised in order to avoid analyzing the behavior of the poor in terms of middle class experience without consideration of alternative explanations.

Nevertheless, class differences do exist. That one would expect differences between classes in their approach to life would seem incontrovertible, given differences in income, housing, education, and opportunities for upward mobility. It remains to be seen whether viewing these differences from a framework of "the ability to defer or to delay gratification," is helpful.

In our limited space, we cannot review every study that touches upon the DGP. We shall cite studies which question the appropriateness of the non-DGP for describing the behavior and attitudes of the poor. In a few studies, the investigators do not conclude that their data support the self-indulgence theme; in others, the investigators do conclude that their results support the non-DGP idea, but their data can be differently interpreted.[12]

We believe that data have been fairly consistently interpreted as supporting the non-DGP even where the results have been ambiguous. One purpose of this paper, therefore, is to free us to look in a more rounded way at the data and studies. By raising questions of interpretation, perhaps we shall begin to think of other alternative modes of analysis.

Spending and Savings

The ability to save—"to put money away for that rainy day," to forego the satisfactions of the immediate purchase, to resist "impulse buying"— are important elements in the DGP.[13] Schneider and Lysgaard studied the DGP by asking 2,500 high school students whether they thought that their parents had saved money to give them a start in life. In the middle class, over 80 percent thought that their parents had saved for them, as contrasted to over 70 percent in the non-middle class groups, be-

---

[12] In citing studies we do not wish to imply that the investigator himself necessarily believes in the value of the DGP analyses. Rather, his work has been interpreted as supporting evidence.

[13] This paragraph and the two following are based on Frank Riessman, *Workers' Attitude Towards Participation and Leadership, op. cit.*, pp. 94–96. In this analysis we have refrained from making methodological criticisms of studies.

cause differences were not controlled in the study. Although statistically significant, this difference between the upper and lower groups is not great when differences in income and hence available amounts for saving are considered. The non-middle class families—at least in the eyes of their children—were making efforts to help their children. And such efforts may have required more organization than in the middle class families of higher income.[14]

These findings of Schneider and Lysgaard are presented by them, however, to buttress the position that workers cannot defer gratifications as evidenced by the lower percentage reporting savings. Yet the same findings can be interpreted as indicating a restriction of consumption in order to save despite the obstacles of comparatively lower incomes.

Schneider and Lysgaard also observed class differences in response to the question, "If you won a big prize, say two thousand dollars, what would you do with it?" Again there is a small difference in the percentages of non-middle class and middle class students who indicate that they would "save most of it." They report this difference as indicative of less deferred gratification ability on the part of the worker. But over 65 percent of both class groups state that they would "save most of it," and the absolute class difference is less than 5 percent. Certainly, this small difference could be expected in terms of the likelihood that a larger proportion of the lower income group would need to spend more of its funds on direct economic necessities.

The difficulties of interpreting data are well revealed in William F. Whyte's findings that the corner boy shares his money with his friends.[15] Schneider and Lysgaard infer that ". . . the corner boys must share their money with others and *avoid* middle class thrift." (Italics ours.) This is considered to be an illustration of a negative attitude toward deferring gratifications. But since money shared with others is unavailable for personal gratification, sharing might be considered under the rubric of "renunciation," and hence a delay of gratification, although there may be some gain in status.

To infer a distinctive value or attitude pattern from this kind of data seems somewhat questionable. Particularly is this so in the light of the report of McConnell who described the "savings" orientation of

---

[14] The importance of impulse-buying among the middle classes suggests that the propensity to defer and save receives great competition from the propensity to consume even among the better off.

[15] William F. Whyte, *Street Corner Society*, Chicago: University of Chicago Press, 1958.

the blue-collar worker as "defensive savings" for a "rainy day" rather than as one focused toward status ascent.[16] This observation suggests that the savings practices of workers may fit into a different pattern than that of middle class individuals. Therefore, their low rate of savings may not be affected by the same psychological focus which would presumably be important among non-saving middle class individuals.

School

Schneider and Lysgaard interpret the fact that working class and lower class adolescents leave school earlier as evidence of their inability to defer gratification. Ely Chinoy has well expressed this point of view:

> The quick surrender of working class youth to the difficulties they face is not necessarily forced or unwilling. Although they are encouraged to focus their aspirations into a long future and to make present sacrifices for the sake of eventual rewards, they are chiefly concerned with immediate gratifications. They may verbally profess to be concerned with occupational success and advancement (as did fourteen working class boys who were interviewed), but they are likely to be more interested in "having a good time" or "having fun." They want to "go out," to have girl friends, to travel, to own a car or a motorcycle.[17]

While of course it is true that working class adolescents as a whole leave school earlier than do middle class youth, the question is whether the interpretation of this behavior is adequate. In addition to the school leaving statistics, at least three other items have to be considered:

1. The school situation, less enjoyable for the non-middle class youth than for the middle class youth because of its middle class structuring, teacher expectations, and utilization of class biased intelligence tests, is not comparable for the two—the strain of school is probably greater on the working class youth;[18]

2. Economic necessity undoubtedly contributes to the disproportionate withdrawal from school;

3. Lower income youth are, at least implicitly, being contrasted with the presumably deferred gratification middle class adolescent. A question therefore has to be raised as to whether today the latter typically give up spending money, good times, girl friends, travel, or a

---

[16] John McConnell, *The Evolution of Social Classes*, Washington: American Council on Public Affairs, 1942, pp. 144 ff.

[17] Ely Chinoy, *Automobile Workers and the American Dream*, New York, Doubleday and Company, 1955, p. 113.

[18] Riessman, *The Culturally Deprived Child, passim.*

car in order to go to school or college. Stern has asserted that certain schools are "fountains of knowledge where the students come to drink," i.e., enjoy themselves.[19]

The motivation of the behavior of an individual cannot be fully understood unless attention is paid to the particular pressures on him and to the means and resources available to him in a physical, financial and cultural sense. The imputed contrast between middle class and working class youth has to be studied in terms of these factors. For example, Beilin concludes that college education was the culmination of a desire of the working class student, and hence a gratification rather than a postponement. In his questionnaire study, he found no relationship between ability to delay gratification and upward mobility in his lower class sample.[20]

It is important to gather objective data concerning class differences in the area of education. Without a doubt, real class differences exist in attitude, dropout rate, and college attendance. One must be cautious, however, in ascribing a solitary motivation to a particular behavior, since individuals may react in an identical manner for very different reasons.

Sexual Experience

It is widely believed that differences between social classes in the amount of pre-marital sexual intercourse mirror differing ability to postpone immediate gratification and control "impulse following." The free and unrestrained sexual activity of non-middle class adolescents and adults is contrasted with that of their middle class counterparts. Allison Davis has presented a concise portrait:

> Like physical aggression, sexual relationships and motivation are far more direct and uninhibited in lower class adolescents. The most striking departure from the usual middle class motivation is that in much lower class life, sexual drive and behavior in children are not regarded as inherently taboo and evil.
>
> At an early age the child learns of common-law marriages, and extra-marital relationships by men and women in his own family. He sees

---

[19] G. G. Stern, "Characteristics of the Intellectual Climate in College Environments," *Harvard Educational Review*, 33, 1963, pp. 5–41.

[20] Harry Beilin, "The Pattern of Postponability and Its Relation to Social Class and Mobility," *Journal of Social Psychology*, 44, 1956, pp. 33–48. Unfortunately, Beilin defined "lower socio-economic group as those subjects 'whose fathers were in the lower middle class or below' (in such classification schemes as Warner's." Cf. Murray Straus, "Deferred Gratification, Social Class, and the Achievement Syndrome," *American Sociological Review*, 27, 1962, pp. 326–335.

his father disappear to live with other women, or he sees other men visit his mother or married sisters. Although none of his siblings may be illegitimate, the chances are very high that sooner or later his father and mother will accuse each other of having illegitimate children, or that at least one of his brothers or sisters will have a child outside of marriage. In his play group, girls and boys discuss sexual relations frankly at the age of eleven or twelve, and he gains status with them by beginning intercourse early.[21]

The Kinsey data are often cited to support the notion that the worker is sexually promiscuous and unable to defer gratifications.[22] While there are many limitations to the Kinsey studies which we cannot enter into here, it is worth noting, if the Kinsey material is to be offered in evidence, that much of it is self-contradictory, and that much of it does not support the usual interpretation of workers' sexual behavior.

For example, Schneider and Lysgaard cite the Kinsey reports as supporting the conclusion that "relatively 'lower' class persons indulge considerably in premarital intercourse; 'upper' class persons show relative deferment of gratification in this section of behavior."[23] Schneider and Lysgaard omit, however, from the Kinsey reference the report that middle class males pet and masturbate more. Apparently, Schneider and Lysgaard do not consider the middle class pre-marital pattern of erotic involvement without intercourse as a sexual experience, although Kinsey emphasized that this is itself a middle class attitude:

> The conflict [about sexual morality] is obviously one between two systems of mores, between two cultural patterns, only one of which seems right to a person who accepts the tradition of the group in which he has been raised. With the better educated groups, intercourse versus petting is a question of morals. For the lower level, it is a problem of understanding how a mentally normal individual can engage in such highly erotic activity as petting and still refrain from actual intercourse.[24]

The investigator's definition of what constitutes sexual experience is a crucial variable in determining whether a difference will be noted in the ability of either class to delay, and not the subject's behavior

---

[21] Allison Davis, "Socialization and Adolescent Personality," in Guy E. Swanson and Theodore H. Newcomb and Eugene Hartley, eds., *Readings in Social Psychology*, New York, Henry Holt and Company, 1955.

[22] A. C. Kinsey and others, *Sexual Behavior in the Human Male*, Philadelphia: W. B. Saunders, 1948. A. C. Kinsey and others, *Sexual Behavior in the Human Female*, Philadelphia: W. B. Saunders, 1953.

[23] Schneider and Lysgaard, *op. cit.*, p. 143.

[24] Kinsey, et al., *Sexual Behavior in the Human Male*, p. 541.

per se. Non-middle class and middle class males differ more in their manner of achieving sexual gratification than in the amount of sexual experience achieved, considering all sources.[25]

Even when using intercourse as the only criterion for sexual gratification, much of the data is contradictory and does not support the usual interpretation of the sexual behavior of the low income population:

1. While Kinsey reports that non-middle class males engaged in considerably more pre-marital intercourse than middle class males, no such class difference is reported for the females.

2. Kinsey finds that the middle class engaged in fellatio and cunnilungus to a much greater extent than did the non-middle class. He reported the latter as expressing disgust at these practices which are also violations of professed middle class mores. Thus, lower-income people avoided and condemned sexual practices which were not infrequent among middle class males, although they are counter to the usual middle class prescriptions.

3. Kinsey's data on nudity show that working class people are less likely to have intercourse without clothes than is true of middle class males.

Furthermore, according to Maccoby and Gibbs, lower class parents are much less likely to permit their children to walk around naked in the house, and they are also less likely to appear unclothed before their children.[26] What this means is not entirely clear, but we may tentatively hypothesize that it is related to problems of crowded living conditions and to some concern for the development of children's ideas with regard to sex.

The data on masturbation, to some extent, lend support to this hypothesis. The studies of Maccoby and Gibbs reveal that non-middle class families, far from encouraging indulgence of the child's sexual play with himself, are more concerned than are middle class parents to prevent sexual play. Now, this effort may be undesirable, but it certainly does not indicate any easy indulgence of the impulses of the

---

[25] In Kinsey's large sample, lower class males reported more premarital and extra-marital intercourse in the early years of marriage, and more intercourse with prostitutes, than did middle class males. Middle class males reported premarital petting and masturbation, and more extra-marital intercourse later in marriage. Can class-linked personality traits be legitimately inferred from these differences in sexual behavior when the definition of sexual experience is itself class related?

[26] Eleanor Maccoby, Patricia K. Gibbs, et al., "Methods of Child-Rearing in Two Social Classes," in William E. Martin and Celia Burns Stendler, eds., *Readings in Child Development,* New York: Harcourt, Brace and Company, 1954, pp. 380–96.

child. The low-income child is much more likely to be punished for masturbatory acts than is the middle class child (whose parents may be more attuned to the contemporary demands of permissive up-bringing).

Kinsey's data on adolescents and adults, which indicate less masturbation on the part of the lower class, could be interpreted in terms of the latter's greater outlet in sexual intercourse. The definite inhibition of masturbatory behavior in childhood on the part of the lower class cannot, however, be as easily explained in terms of the usual image of sexual "freedom." Moreover, the attitudes toward masturbation developed in childhood may provide a more adequate explanation of adolescent and adult rates of masturbation in the lower class.

Further evidence of the intricate regulation of working class sexual life rather than its unrestricted "freedom" is found in Whyte's analysis of the slum sex code of Cornerville.[27] Some have taken his study to reveal sexual licentiousness on the part of the Italian working class youth whom he describes. Yet, as the term "the slum sex code" suggests, their sexual behavior is strongly regulated by codes and traditions. As Whyte points out, it is clearly taboo to have intercourse with "good girls," i.e., virgins and relatives of friends. What kind of intimacy is acceptable and with whom is governed by strong community norms.

The data on illegitimacy have also been misunderstood. The presumption is that non-middle class populations have higher rates than middle class; this empirical observation is used by some to support the notion of easy sexual indulgence by the lower classes. Both the reports of data and their interpretation are questionable.

Early research sampled only public clinics and hospitals; the conclusion was that unwed mothers tended to come from lower socio-economic levels and from broken homes. When a more representative sample was employed, including private physicians and hospitals, Vincent concluded that, contrary to earlier beliefs, "the unwed mothers . . . were not predominantly of low socio-economic status, nor even predominantly of any particular socio-economic stratum."[28]

Furthermore, the illegitimacy rate by itself cannot be considered a behavioral measure of inability to delay, without controlling for "rate

---

[27] William F. Whyte, "A Slum Sex Code," *American Journal of Sociology*, XLIX, 1943, pp. 24–31, reprinted in Reinhard Bendix and Seymour M. Lipset, eds., *Class, Status and Power*, Glencoe: Free Press, 1953. We are indebted to David Matza for bringing to our attention the misleading interpretation of the Whyte data.

[28] Clark E. Vincent, *Unmarried Mothers*. Glencoe: Free Press, 1961, p. 64.

of illicit coitus"[29] and differential knowledge of contraceptive methods between classes.[30]

Knowledge of class-linked sexual behavior does not lend itself to an easy summary. But the limited evidence that we have brought together should question the facile acceptance of the notion that the sexual practices and outlook of the non-middle classes clearly support the DGP interpretation.[31]

Ability to Delay

We have examined some of the case studies and questionnaire investigations on the ability to delay gratification. We shall now survey some of the relevant experimental literature on class differences in the ability to delay gratification.[32]

Mahrer found that the expectancy that the "social agent" (E) actually would keep his word about bringing a delayed reward was an important cue for the choice of delayed or immediate reward.[33] His subjects were working class grade school children. He manipulated the level of their expectancy for reward in three different experimental groups by promising a delayed reward on each of four training trials, though keeping his promise none of the time in one group (low ex-

---

[29] *Ibid.*

[30] The importance of viewing alternative explanatory possibilities is shown in Cavan's explanation of why lower income groups have large families. (Ruth Cavan, *The American Family,* New York: Thomas Y. Crowell Company, 1953, pp. 182 ff.) In a sophisticated sociological discussion she reviews the effects of the larger number of Catholics in the non-middle classes, the expense and self-discipline involved in using contraceptives, the asset value of children as early wage earners (which, incidentally, is quite a long range deferred gratification view), and the lesser financial burdens that low-income children impose upon their families compared to the funds expended on middle class children. Some of the reasons stated by Cavan for large, low-income families are undoubtedly correct, but other, unmentioned reasons also exist. For example, the significance of the family as a crucial cooperative unit for many low-income groups is overlooked or the possibility of a positive feeling towards children and a desire to have a "big family" as a way of life.

[31] Lee Rainwater, *And the Poor Get Children,* Chicago: Quadrangle Books, 1960.

[32] Because of space limitations, we do not discuss the experimental literature or temporal orientation. In any case, the connection between temporal orientation and ability to defer gratification is not clear-cut. Cf. Levon H. Melikian, "Preference for Delayed Reinforcement: An Experimental Study Among Palestinian Arab Refugee Children," *Journal of Social Psychology,* 50, 1959, pp. 81–86; Walter Mischel, "Preference for Delayed Reinforcement and Social Responsibility," *Journal of Abnormal Social Psychology,* 1961, pp. 1–7. The discussion borrows from Seagull, *op. cit.*

[33] Mahrer, A. R., "The Role of Expectancy in Delayed Reinforcement," *Journal of Experimental Psychology,* 42, 1956, pp. 101–106.

pectancy); twice in the second group (moderate expectancy); and all four times in the third group (high expectancy). The fifth trial (test trial) was a choice between two toys—a less valued toy to be had immemediately or a more valued one obtainable after a day's delay.

He found that the "high expectancy" group differed significantly from the other two groups in choice of "delayed reinforcement." His results supported the position, at least for working class children, that it was the situation rather than the personality which determined whether they chose delayed or immediate reward.

He also found that neither the low, moderate, or high expectancy groups generalized from their experience with the E of the training trials (Ea) to a different E (Eb). ". . . the effects of training with Ea failed to generalize to Eb. Instead there were uniform reactions to Eb independent of the kind of training with Ea. . . . The implication is that delayed reinforcement behavior in general depends not only on the value of the reinforcements, but also on the expectancy for the occurrence of delayed reinforcement as related to the social agent involved."[34]

Such a position militates against uniform interpretations of the ability to delay as a class-linked personality variable, since it was clear that the choice of reward was determined by the particular interaction with the experimenter.

Shybut used a composite measure to explore the relationship between the ability to delay and certain psychological and demographic variables, including several measures relating to social class.[35] The first two components were behavioral measures—a vote for a "record hop" within a week, or a "band dance" with a well-known and much-liked band a month from the testing; and a "thank you ticket" worth 25c, 35c, or 50c in merchandise at a store, depending on how long the subject delayed cashing in the ticket. The third, a projective measure, was an essay about their personal reaction to obtaining a large windfall of money. A "Delayed Gratification Index" (DGI) was constructed from the responses to the three measures.

There was no significant relationship between the DGI and socioeconomic level as defined by any of the following criteria: paternal occupation, family income, an index of the number of people per room at home, or paternal education. Thus, on a well constructed, composite measure there was no indication that socio-economic classes differed in

---

[34] *Ibid*, p. 105.

[35] Shybut, J., *Delayed Gratification: A Study of Its Measurement and Its Relationship to Certain Behavioral, Psychological and Demographical Variables*, Unpublished Master's thesis, University of Colorado, 1963.

ability to delay. Ethnic groups, "Anglos" and "Non-Anglos" (Indians) did, however, differ, the Non-Anglos having a significantly higher DGI than the Anglos.

Seagull[36] investigated Mischel's hypothesis that the choice of delayed gratification might depend on the degree of trust the subject has for the E, rather than on the class affiliation. Children were given Mischel's choice between one bar of candy now or two bars in a week.[37] For the second and third sessions, however, the classrooms were randomly assigned to a trust condition (that E kept his promise about bringing the candy) and a Mistrust condition (where E did not). After the promise was kept or broken, the children again chose to delay or not.

The results were clear cut. The first week, when there was no experimental manipulation, no differences appeared between children from any social classes, or between white or Negro children. The second and third session, there was a large and significant difference between the Trust and Mistrust conditions in choice of delayed reward in the expected direction. It should be noted that there was no indication of a differential rate of sensitivity to trust or mistrust, since the rate of change was the same to or from a delay reward choice for the different social groups.

Thus, for those children whose socio-economic level was definable, there were no differences in ability to delay on the choice presented, while the differences in choice when they could trust the E or not were very large and significant.

The situational variable, then, rather than class affiliation determined the ability to delay. Though there are many other populations and choice stimuli to be sampled, the data do not support the hypothesis that the ability to delay is class-linked at least over the whole range of subjects and situations.

Conclusion

The studies that we have reviewed do not instill confidence in the sweeping conclusions of the DGP. Obviously, our interpretations of data can

---

[36] Seagull, *op. cit.*

[37] Walter Mischel's work has been influential. See his "Preference for Delayed Reinforcement: An Experimental Study of a Cultural Observation, *Journal of Abnormal Social Psychology*, 56, 1958, pp. 57–61; "Delay of Gratification, Need for Achievement and Acquiescence in Another Culture," *Journal of Abnormal and Social Psychology*, 62, 1961, pp. 543–552; "Father-absence and Delay of Gratification," *Journal of Abnormal and Social Psychology*, 63, 1961, pp. 116–124; "Reward as a Function of Age, Intelligence, and Length of Delay Interval," *Journal of Abnormal and Social Psychology*, 64, 1962, pp. 425–431.

be questioned. Our intention is not to foreclose discussion on the use-fulness of the DGP concept, but to encourage study of it and competing explanations.

We do feel that many lower-income people have a shorter time perspective than do many middle-income persons. The shorter time outlook may handicap many of the poor. But we are not sure that the shorter time perspective is *always* linked with an inability to defer gratification. More importantly, we do not view all those who seem to be unable to defer gratification as so psychodynamically constrained that the ability to delay is unavailable to them. For some, this is un-doubtedly true. But for others, situations which offer perceived hope do lead to postponement and planning.[38] They may not be able to over-come all the obstacles which face them, but they are not locked into self-indulgence.

The experimental studies on the importance of trust underline the significance of situational rather than psychodynamic variables. The former perspective leads us to provide situations which do, in truth, offer chances of payoff for postponement. Furthermore, by emphasizing nonpersonality variables, we have the possibilities of helping individuals to *learn* the kinds of patterns that may be important for their well-being. We do not doubt, for example, that lower income youth could have school experiences which work toward expanding the time in which the youth expect to get a return for their activities.

Many studies show that educational level is the major variable explaining different social class behaviorial/attitudinal patterns. This conclusion suggests that we are not dealing with outlooks that have an immutable quality; rather, they are affected by knowledge, and under-standing. They are subject, consequently, to influences and change.

The DGP emphasis leads to social policies which emphasize "re-habilitation" rather than expanding opportunity. Some of the poor obvi-ously need "rehabilitation" in order to take advantage of opportunity. For others, opportunity may reduce the need for "rehabilitation."

Our objections to the DGP emphasis do not rest with its social policy implications. At the level of social science analysis, the verdict on the DGP is "not proved." It is not adequate as the major, and some-times sole, variable in explanations of the behavior of the poor. By recognizing the limitations as well as the insights of DGP approach, we

---

[38] For a sophisticated approach to a situational analysis see the important article by Louis Kriesberg, "The Relationship Between Socio-Economic Rank and Behavior," *Social Problems*, 10, 1963, pp. 334–53; also in the Reprint Series of the Syracuse University Youth Development Center.

might move to search for alternative or supplementary explanations of the attitudes and behavior of that large slice of the American population who are not in the middle classes.

Subcultures and Class

Herbert J. Gans

[Reprinted from Chapter 11 of The Urban Villagers *(New York, 1962) by permission of The Free Press of Glencoe, A Division of the Macmillan Company. Copyright © 1962.]*

A Description of Working-Class, Lower-Class, and Middle-Class Subcultures

THE IDENTIFICATION OF THE PEER GROUP SOCIETY as a class phenomenon makes it possible to suggest some propositions about the working class that will distinguish it both from the lower and middle classes. These propositions rest on a specific definition of class.

Class can be defined in many ways, depending on the theoretical, methodological, and political orientation of the researcher.[1] Some sociologists have argued that class is a heuristic concept, nominalist in nature, which serves as a methodological device to summarize real differences between people in income, occupation, education, and related characteristics. Other sociologists have viewed classes as real aggregates of people who share some characteristics and group interests, who favor each other in social relationships, and who exhibit varying degrees of group consciousness. In the latter category, one school of sociologists has explained class mainly on the basis of occupational characteristics, on the assumption that work determines access to income, power, and status, and that it has considerable influence on an individual's behavior patterns.

Others see classes as more than occupational aggregates, that is, as strata in the larger society, each of which consists of somewhat—but

---

[1] The comments that follow are a highly oversimplified description of the various points of view, and serve only to introduce the hypotheses about class that follow below. More sophisticated discussions of the major "schools" in the study of class are available in Bernard Barber, *Social Stratification,* New York: Harcourt, Brace and World, 1957; Milton M. Gordon, *Social Class in American Sociology,* Durham: Duke University Press, 1958.

not entirely—distinctive social relationships, behavior patterns, and attitudes. The strata thus are composed of subcultures and subsocial structures. For the sake of brevity, however, I shall henceforth describe them
only as subcultures. While occupation, education, income, and other
such factors help to distinguish the subcultures, the exact role of these
factors is thought to be an empirical question. The strata are defined
as subcultures on the assumption that relationships, behavior patterns,
and attitudes are related parts of a social and cultural system. The word
"system" must be used carefully, however, for many similarities and
overlaps exist between them. Moreover, these systems are quite open,
and movement between them is possible, though—as I shall try to show
—not always easy. Considerable variation also exists within each stratum,
for social mobility and other processes create innumerable combinations
of behavior patterns.[2]

The heuristic conception of class, not being very productive for
social theory, need not concern us here. The two remaining ones each
have some advantages and disadvantages. The occupational conception
is most useful for understanding societies in the early stages of industrialization, when unemployment is great, and when an individual's job
is both a determinant of and an index to his way of life. But in a highly
industrialized society with considerable occupational variation and much
freedom of choice in jobs—as well as in other ways of life—too great a
concern with occupation, or any other single factor, is likely to lead the
researcher astray. For instance, when a blue-collar worker earns more
than a white-collar one, and can live by the values of the middle class,
it would be a mistake to classify him as working class. Similarly, when
a white-collar worker lives like a blue-collar one, even in a middle-
class neighborhood, one should not consider him middle class.

The great advantage of the subcultural conception is that it makes
no a priori assumptions about the major differences between the strata
or the determinants of these differences. It treats them rather as topics
for empirical research. Unlike the other approaches in which class is
defined in terms of easily researchable indices, the subcultural conception is harder to employ, however, for the characteristics and determinants of each class subculture must be carefully delineated.

The voluminous literature of class studies in America and elsewhere and the considerable similarity of the classes all over the industrialized world have made it possible to begin a delineation of the
principal class subcultures. While I shall not attempt this task here, I

---

[2] Even so, studies of status inconsistency have shown that many of these
combinations create marginality both in social position and cultural allegiances.

do want to suggest what seem to me to be some of the major "focal concerns"[3] of four of the subcultures: working class, lower class, middle class, and professional upper-middle class. These brief outlines are based on observations made in the West End and elsewhere, and on the research literature. For the most part, they describe the subcultures in America and in one period of the life cycle: that of the family which is rearing children.

Perhaps the most important—or at least the most visible—difference between the classes is one of family structure. *The working-class subculture* is distinguished by the dominant role of the family circle. Its way of life is based on social relationships amidst relatives. The working class views the world from the family circle, and considers everything outside it as either a means to its maintenance or to its destruction. But while the outside world is to be used for the benefit of this circle, it is faced with detachment and even hostility in most other respects. Whenever feasible, then, work is sought within establishments connected to the family circle. When this is not possible—and it rarely is—work is primarily a means of obtaining income to maintain life amidst a considerable degree of poverty, and, thereafter, a means of maximizing the pleasures of life within the family circle. The work itself may be skilled or unskilled; it can take place in the factory or in the office—the type of collar is not important. What does matter is that identification with work, work success, and job advancement—while not absolutely rejected—are of secondary priority to the life that goes on within the family circle. The purpose of education is to learn techniques necessary to obtain the most lucrative type of work. Thus the central theme of American, and all Western, education—that the student is an individual who should use his schooling to detach himself from ascribed relationships like the family circle in order to maximize his personal development and achievement in work, play, and other spheres of life—is ignored or openly rejected.

The specific characteristics of the family circle may differ widely —from the collateral peer group form of the West Enders, to the hierarchical type of the Irish, or to the classic three-generation extended family. Friends may also be included in the circle, as in the West Enders' peer group society. What matters most—and distinguishes this subculture from others—is that there be a family circle which is wider than

---

[3] I borrow this term from Walter Miller, who uses it as a substitute for the anthropological concept of value in his study of lower-class culture. See "Lower Class Culture as a Generating Milieu of Gang Delinquency," p. 261. I use it to refer to behavior as much as to attitude, and to phenomena of social structure as well as culture.

the nuclear family, and that all of the opportunities, temptations, and pressures of the larger society be evaluated in terms of how they affect the ongoing way of life that has been built around this circle.

The *lower-class subculture* is distinguished by the female-based family and the marginal male. Although a family circle may also exist, it includes only female relatives. The male, whether husband or lover, is physically present only part of the time, and is recognized neither as a stable nor dominant member of the household. He is a sexual partner, and he is asked to provide economic support. But he participates only minimally in the exchange of affection and emotional support, and has little to do with the rearing of children. Should he serve as a model for the male children, he does so largely in a negative sense. That is, the women use him as an example of what a man should not be.

The female-based family must be distinguished, however, from one in which the woman is dominant, for example, the English working-class family. Although this family may indeed revolve around the "Mum," she does not reject the husband. Not only is he a member of the family, but he is also a participant—and a positive model—in child-rearing.

In the lower class, the segregation of the sexes—only partial in the working class—is complete. The woman tries to develop a stable routine in the midst of poverty and deprivation; the action-seeking man upsets it. In order to have any male relationships, however, the woman must participate to some extent in his episodic life style. On rare occasions, she may even pursue it herself. Even then, however, she will try to encourage her children to seek a routine way of life. Thus the woman is much closer to working-class culture, at least in her aspirations, although she is not often successful in achieving them.

For lower-class men, life is almost totally unpredictable. If they have sought stability at all, it has slipped from their grasp so quickly, often, and consistently that they no longer pursue it. From childhood on, their only real gratifications come from action-seeking, but even these are few and short-lived. Relationships with women are of brief duration, and some men remain single all their lives. Work, like all other relationships with the outside world, is transitory. Indeed, there can be no identification with work at all. Usually, the lower-class individual gravitates from one job to another, with little hope or interest of keeping a job for any length of time. His hostility to the outside world therefore is quite intense, and its attempts to interfere with the episodic quality of his life are fought. Education is rejected by the male, for all of its aims are diametrically opposed to action-seeking.

The *middle-class subculture* is built around the nuclear family and its desire to make its way in the larger society. Although the family circle may exist, it plays only a secondary role in middle-class life.

Contact with close relatives is maintained, but even they participate in a subordinate role. Individuals derive most of their social and emotional gratifications from the nuclear family itself. One of the most important of these is child-rearing. Consequently, the middle-class family is much more child-centered than the working-class one and spends more of its spare time together. Outside social life takes place with friends who share similar interests. The nuclear family depends on its friends—as well as on some caretaking institutions—for help and support. Relatives may also help, especially in emergencies.

‒   The middle class does not make the distinction between the family and the outside world. In fact, it does not even see an outside world, but only a larger society, which it believes to support its aims, and in which the family participates. The nuclear family makes its way in the larger society mainly through the career of its breadwinner. Thus work is not merely a job that maximizes income, but a series of related jobs or job advances which provide the breadwinner with higher income, greater responsibility, and, if possible, greater job satisfaction. In turn his career enhances the way of life of the rest of the family, through increases in status and in the standard of living.

Education is viewed, and used, as an important method for achieving these goals. The purpose of education is to provide the skills needed for the man's career and for the woman's role as a mother. In and out of school, it is also used to develop the skills necessary to the maintenance and increase of status, the proper use of leisure time, and the occasional participation in community activities. Thus, much of the central theme of education is accepted. But the idea that education is an end in itself, and should be used to maximize individual development of the person, receives only lip service.

The subculture I have described here is a basic middle-class one; a more detailed analysis would distinguish between what is currently called the middle-middle class and the lower-middle class. The upper-middle-class subculture is also a variant of the basic middle-class culture. There are at least two such subcultures, the managerial and the professional. Since I shall be concerned with the latter, it is of primary interest here.

The *professional upper-middle-class culture* is also organized around the nuclear family, but places greater emphasis on the independent functioning of its individual members. Whereas the middle-class family is a companionship unit in which individuals exist most intensely in their relationships with each other, the upper-middle-class family is a companionship unit in which individuals seeking to maximize their own development as persons come together on the basis of common interests. For this subculture, life is, to a considerable extent, a striving for individual development and self-expression, and these strivings pervade many of its relationships with the larger society.

Therefore, work is not simply a means for achieving the well-being of the nuclear family, but also an opportunity for individual achievement and social service. Although the career, income, status, and job responsibility are important, job satisfaction is even more important, although it is not always found. Indeed, professional work satisfaction is a focal concern not only for the breadwinner, but often for the woman as well. If she is not interested in a profession, she develops an alternative but equally intense interest in motherhood, or in community activity. Child-rearing, moreover, gives the woman an opportunity not only to maximize her own individual achievements as a mother, but to develop in her children the same striving for self-development. As a result, the professional upper-middle-class family is not child-centered, but adult-directed. As education is the primary tool for a life of individual achievement, the professional upper-middle-class person not only goes to school longer than anyone else in society, but he also accepts its central theme more fully than do the rest of the middle class.

This concern with individual achievement and education further enables and encourages the members of this subculture to be deliberate and self-conscious about their choices. They are a little more understanding of the actions of others than the members of less educated strata. Their ability to participate in the larger society, plus their high social and economic status, also gives them somewhat greater control over their fate than other people, and make the environment more predictable. This in turn facilitates the practice of self-consciousness, empathy, and abstraction or generalization.

The possession of these skills distinguishes the upper-middle class from the rest of the middle class, and even more so from the working and lower class. For the latter not only lives in a less predictable environment, but they are also detached from the outside world, which increases their feeling that it, and, indeed, all of life, is unpredictable. In turn this feeling encourages a pervasive fatalism that pre-empts the optimism or pessimism of which the other classes are capable. The fatalism of the working and lower classes, as well as their lack of education and interest in personal development and object goals, minimizes introspection, self-consciousness, and empathy for the behavior of others.

Class: Opportunity and Response

The subcultures which I have described are *responses* that people make to the *opportunities* and the *deprivations* that they encounter. More specifically, each subculture is an organized set of related responses that has developed out of people's efforts to cope with the opportunities, incentives, and rewards, as well as the deprivations, prohibitions, and pressures which the natural environment and society—that complex of co-existing and competing subcultures—offer to them. The responses which make up a subculture are compounded out of what people have retained of parental, that is, traditional responses, the skill and attitudes they have learned as children, and the innovations they have developed for themselves in their own encounters with opportunity and deprivation.

These responses cannot develop in a vacuum. Over the long range, they can be seen as functions of the resources which a society has available, and of the opportunities which it can offer. In each of the subcultures life is thus geared to the availability of specific qualitative types and quantities of income, education, and occupational opportunities. Although I have used occupational labels to distinguish between the major subcultures,[4] a man's job does not necessarily determine in which of these he shall be placed. In the long run, however, the existence of a specific subculture is closely related to the availability of occupational opportunities. For example, the functioning of the family circle and the routine-seeking way of life in the working class depend on the availability of stable employment for the man. The lower-class female-based family is a response to, or a method of coping with, the lack of stable male employment. The goals of middle- and upper-middle-class culture depend on the availability of sufficient income to finance the education that is necessary for a career, and on the availability of job opportunities that will allow middle-class individuals to find the type of job satisfaction for which they are striving.

When these opportunity factors are lacking, the cultural responses made by people are frustrated. Should opportunities be deficient over a long enough period, downward mobility results. Should they disappear entirely, the subculture will be apt to disintegrate eventually. For example, working-class culture can function for a time in a period of unemployment, but if no substitute sources of stability are made available, people initially resort to protest. Eventually, the family circle be-

---

[4] It is relevant to note that the words I have used to label the class subcultures are somewhat misleading. For example, I describe the middle class not as a group in the middle of the economic and power structure, but as a subculture focally concerned with the nuclear family. Likewise, the working class obviously works no more or less than any other group. Only the lower-class label fits well, since this subculture is in so many ways a response to the deprivations to which it is exposed.

gins to break up under the strain, and its members adopt many if not all of the responses identified with the lower-class subculture.

Similar reactions take place in the other subcultures, although the ways in which they are expressed may differ. If job opportunities are lacking so as to frustrate the career desires of the middle class, or the professional desires of the upper-middle class, one reaction is to transfer aspirations elsewhere, for example, into non-work pursuits. Since upper-middle-class people are able and willing to act in the larger society, they may also develop social and political protest movements in order to create these opportunities, or to change society. Bourgeois socialist movements in America, taking their lead from the Marxist aim to "humanize" work so that it will provide quasi-professional job satisfaction to all people, are examples of such a reaction. Although downward mobility in the working class results in the adoption of lower-class responses, middle-class downward mobility does not bring about a working-class response. People may depend more on relatives as adversity strikes, but other differences between middle- and working-class subcultures remain in effect.

Downward mobility is also possible in the lower-class subculture. Since this culture is initially a response to instability, further instability can result only in family disintegration, total despair, and an increase in already high rates of mental illness, antisocial and self-destructive behavior, or group violence.

Conversely, when opportunity factors are increasingly available, people respond by more fully implementing their subcultural aspirations, and by improving their styles of life accordingly. For example, working-class people responded to the post-World War II prosperity by selecting from the available opportunities those elements useful for increasing the comfort and convenience of their way of life. They did not strive for middle-class styles. Nor did they reshape the family, adopt careers, or surrender their detachment from the outside world.

Periods of increased opportunity also encourage marginal members of each subculture to move into others to which they are aspiring. For example, lower-class women with working-class goals have been able to send their boys to school with the hope that they will be able to move into working-class culture. Whereas some of them have been able to make the move as adults, others have found that they could not summon the emotional and other skills necessary to succeed in school or job. In many cases, opportunities simply were not as freely available as expected, and sudden illness or other setbacks propelled them back into the lower-class culture.

Upward mobility that involves movement into another class sub-culture is relatively rare because of the considerable changes which people must make in their own lives, often against great odds. Thus the majority are content to improve the style of life within their own sub-cultures. They may, however, encourage their children to make the move in the next generation.

Although opportunities can increase or decrease rapidly and drastically over time, the subcultures I have described are relatively slow in changing their basic structure and content. In many ways con-temporary working-class culture is a continuation of European peasant cultures, and some features of the middle- and upper-middle-class sub-cultures can be traced back to the post-Renaissance and to the begin-nings of the urban-industrial revolution. Improvements and changes in the level of living take place all the time, as modern ideas, habits, and artifacts replace traditional ones. But the focal concerns of each sub-culture change more slowly.

Changes in the distribution and quality of opportunity factors do, of course, have significant effects. They influence the extent to which subcultural aspirations can be realized, and they help to determine the position of each subculture within the over-all class hierarchy. This in turn affects the political influence that each of them can exert on many matters in the national society, including the distribution of oppor-tunities itself.

Moreover, new opportunities and the need for new skills can in-crease the number of people found in any one subculture, just as the demise of opportunities can reduce it. For example, whereas the reduc-tion of temporary, unskilled labor is likely to shrink the lower-class sub-culture, the increased need for professionals has led to the enlargement of the middle and upper-middle class. In short, new opportunities bring higher incentives, which in turn encourage people to move into other subcultures, although a generation or two may pass before they adopt all of the primary focal concerns of their new way of life. At any one point in time, then, many people could be said to be living between subcultures. Radical changes in the society can even bring entirely new subcultures into being, although this has happened only infrequently in the course of history.

Selected Bibliography

1. Richard A. Cloward and Lloyd E. Ohlin. *Delinquency and Opportunities.* Glencoe, Illinois: The Free Press of Glencoe, 1960.

2. Elizabeth Herzog. "Some Assumptions About the Poor," *Social Service Review,* 37 (December, 1963).

3. Seymour M. Lipset. "Democracy and Working Class Authoritarianism," *American Sociological Review,* 24 (August, 1959).

4. S. M. Miller. "The American Lower Class: A Typological Approach," *Social Research,* 31 (Spring, 1964).

5. S. M. Miller and Frank Riessman. "The Working Class Subculture: A New View," *Social Problems,* 9 (Summer, 1961).

6. Hyman Rodman. "On Understanding Lower Class Behavior," *Social and Economic Studies,* 9 (December, 1959).

7. Leonard Schneiderman. "The Culture of Poverty: A Study of the Value Orientation Preferences of the Chronically Impoverished," Unpublished Doctoral Dissertation, University of Minnesota School of Social Work, 1963.

8. ———. "Value Orientation Preferences of Chronic Relief Applicants," *Social Work,* 9 (July, 1964).

Chapter 6

The Life of the Poor

Poverty not only has many faces, connections, and ramifications, but also different loci—and, therefore, it shows variations in behavioral symptoms, and calls for different diagnoses and prognoses. Poverty is endemic in the center city slum, and it is no accident that there occurs the classic convergence of poverty with other ills. Poverty in the city is obviously not confined to the slum, but the fact that it is embedded there with other ills makes it more difficult to treat than if it were in a non-slum setting. Nor do all slum dwellers present examples of poverty or require or want intervention or help beyond ordinary expectations. Although it may be related to time or duration, there is a difference between the pandemic poverty of Appalachia and the epidemic poverty of a Detroit hit a few years ago by automation or slackening car demand. For example, it is important to distinguish between the family or person relatively recently hit by an incident of unemployment or local epidemic of poverty and the long time Negro resident of the slums who has known nothing but endemic poverty and who refuses to be mouse trapped into any belief that significant change is forthcoming or possible by talk, exhortation, or misguided efforts to teach him middle-class values that may already be known and appreciated. Middle-class values, highly advertised as they are, indeed may be well-known. But that does not make them realizable. For many, particularly for the young poor, the distance between knowing and being able to achieve them is the rub.

—Quoted from "The Contemporary Urban Poverty Syndrome." Speech delivered by Hylan Lewis to Howard Medical School students, April 28, 1964.

OUR UNDERSTANDING OF LOWER-CLASS BEHAVIOR is hampered by a series of stereotypes and misconceptions about the poor. The mass media dramatize the sensational in lower class life—violence, brutalization and deviance—and this is often the only benchmark for viewing the behavior and attitudes of the poor. We must add to this the fact that the more affluent groups of the community rarely engage in close personal contact with the poor and consequently there are few challenges to the images of the poor that are presented in the mass media. If contact is made, it is apt to be in situations that reinforce these stereotypes—the panhandler on the street or the domestic in the home. The geographical confinement of the poor to the slum and the contact limitations afforded by the opportunity structure make the poor invisible to other groups in the community and it is this invisibility that sustains these misconceptions and stereotypes of lower-class life.

These stereotypes and misconceptions are of three kinds. First, lower-class life is seen as unorganized or disorganized. The middle-class individual may deplore the fact that the poor let their children run wild; or that the poor do not organize their finances well; or that the poor are promiscuous; or that people who would live in such deteriorated, disorganized surroundings must themselves lack organization or predictability. What is usually the case is that organization does exist in the slum but that it is organization of a kind that is not intelligible to the middle class observer. In his classic study of street corner society, William Foote Whyte showed that what appeared to be a disorganized slum was actually a highly organized community but that organization was on a different basis than what the middle class observer has come to expect from his own experiences. The failure to see organization in the slum does not stem from the fact that it does not exist but rather that such *kinds* of organization have no prototypes in middle class surroundings. Leadership exists but all too often it is the leadership that is unfamiliar or repugnant to middle class values (e.g. the leader of a rent strike). Few people are able to appreciate the tensions and anxieties of a poverty situation and fewer still appreciate the life styles that develop in these surroundings.

A second misconception is to attribute the behavior pattern to some imperfection in the individual rather than to the stresses that are generated by a particular poverty situation. In a society where emphasis is placed on the individual's ability to master his environment, little thought is given to the structuring of behavior by situational stress or to the existence of a particular opportunity structure. The individual behaves as he does because he is "lazy, dirty, or ignorant" or because he is "ambitious, polished, and intelligent." Only a little more than a century ago, little thought was given to the structuring of behavior by situational stresses or the existence of a particular opportunity structure. The profound contribution made by such researchers as Allison Davis is that the motivation of the underprivileged worker was to be found in terms of the opportunity and reward structure of the community. But old explanations die hard. Even in the 1960's, the solutions suggested to combat unemployment stress the retraining and rehabilitation of the individual rather than the changing or regulation of the job opportunity structure.

Finally, there is a misconception regarding the goals set by the poor as well as the means that they use in the attainment of these goals. Again, this reflects the fact that middle class people are not familiar with lower class living conditions. Goals tend to be fitted to the realities of situations. Where economic resources are unpredictable, greater emphasis is placed on subsistence rather than achievement. The latter is only possible where the former has been assured. Just as affluence sets the goals for the middle class child, so poverty becomes a limiting factor in setting the goals for the lower class child. The means are also a reflection of reality. The middle class child is surrounded by a world in which education pays off and where the successful serve as models. In lower class life where there is a general lack of successful work models, the child is apt to see the futility of an education in a second-rate educational system. Goal setting and the availability of means are circumscribed by the stresses and unpredictability brought about by a scarcity of economic resources.

But the most common misconception in understanding lower class life is to look for a single theme. Poverty is characterized by actual and sensed powerlessness as well as social isolation from the cues and rewards of the larger community. These are the end results of the lack and unpredictability of economic resources. Lower class life must be seen within this framework as a composite of many situations, many themes, and many experiences. In this chapter Warren Haggstrom begins by describing the power and the psychology of the poor. Family planning among the poor is reviewed by Frederick Jaffe. Hylan Lewis analyzes the child-rearing practices of low-income families in Washington, D.C. Martin Deutsch describes some of the deprivatory conditions under which the lower-class child engages in the learning process. Jeremy Larner discusses some of the self-perceptions of a particular group of lower-class school children against the context of the 1964 New York City school boycott. Joseph S. Himes then analyzes some stresses that are generated in the work situation for a group of lower-class Negro youths. The problems and potential for organizing the poor in community action are reviewed by George Brager. Mary Wright describes a typical day in the life of a welfare recipient and his anxieties and frustrations with bureaucracy. Finally, the inadequacy of budgets in fatherless families is discussed by Charles Lebeaux.

The Power of the Poor*

Warren C. Haggstrom

Syracuse University

[Reprinted from Mental Health of the Poor, *edited by Frank Riessman, Jerome Cohen, and Arthur Pearl (New York, 1964) by permission of the Free Press of Glencoe, A Division of the Macmillan Company. Copyright © 1964.]*

ON THE AVERAGE, the poor in the United States have bad reputations. They are regarded as responsible for much physical aggression and destruction of property; their support is alleged to be a heavy burden on the rest of the community; and they are said not even to try very hard to meet community standards of behavior or to be self-supporting. Poverty, it is said, is little enough punishment for people so inferior and so lacking in virtue.

Roughly speaking, these common opinions about the poor have some accuracy. Socially notorious varieties of deviancy and dependency do flourish in areas of poverty to a greater extent than in the remainder of our society. The middle classes, of course, have their own faults, which are sometimes perceptively observed and described by the poor. The relatively prosperous tend to use their verbal facility to conceal aspects of social reality from themselves and tend to use word-magic to make themselves comfortable about being in their generally undeserved positions of affluence, positions in which they manage to obtain the most pay and security for doing easy and interesting kinds of work.

Since the United States is a middle class society, those who emphasize the bad reputations of the poor are regarded as hard-headed realists, while those who stress the phoniness of the middle classes are considered rather extreme and overly suspicious. When a social worker reports that the lower classes tend in the direction of schizophrenia and character disorders, he is viewed as having made a sober report of the existing state of affairs. Or when a social scientist discovers that the poor are unsocialized, childlike, occupy an early category in *his* category system of degrees of socialization, his discovery is treated as an important basis for further scientific work. But suppose that a leader of the poor announces that social workers tend to be "phonies" and "half-queer" as well, or suggests in his own language that social scientists are

---

* Revised version of a paper prepared for presentation at the 71st Annual Convention of the American Psychological Association in Philadelphia, Pennsylvania, August 29–September 4, 1963.

usually fuzzy-minded and socially irrelevant. This invidious description is not seen as a suitable hypothesis for investigation and research; it is rather said (without benefit of evidence) to be a symptom of the ignorance or of the personal or political needs of the person making the statement.

We cannot, of course, simply shed the presuppositions which attach to our social positions, and those of us who see the poor from above are likely not to have viewed them from the most flattering perspective. But let us, in the following discussion, attempt to be critical and scientific by orienting ourselves to reasons and evidence rather than to common sense conceptual refinements of our current prejudices. We will first analyze a popular contemporary account of the psychology of poverty, and then advance a different orientation as a more precise explanation for available data.

Psychological Characteristics of the Poor

Social scientists have arrived at a rough consensus about the modal personality in neighborhoods of poverty:

(1)   The poor tend to have a keen sense of the personal and the concrete; their interest typically is restricted to the self, the family, and the neighborhood. There is a particular stress on the intimate, the sensory, the detailed, the personal. Not struggling to escape their circumstances, the poor often regard their ordinary lives as being of much intrinsic interest. This is related to their primary concern with the problem of survival rather than with the problem of moving up in society, and to the value which they attach to skills needed in coping with deprivation and uncertainty as distinguished from skills required to make progress. It has frequently been reported that persons in areas of poverty appear to be apathetic, to have little motivation, to be unable to cooperate with each other in the solution of problems which they regard as important, and to lack occupational and verbal skills and leadership traits; and are characterized by parochialism, nostalgic romanticism, and prescientific conceptions of the natural and social orders. Instead of having love for one another as fellow human beings, they achieve positive mutual attitudes through seeing themselves as all in the same boat together.

(2)   Caught in the present, the poor do not plan very much. They meet their troubles and take their pleasures on a moment-to-moment basis; their schemes are short-term. Their time perspective is foreshortened by their belief that it is futile to think of the future. Thus, when the poor use conventional words to refer to the future, those words tend to be empty of real meaning. They have little sense of the past and they go forward, but not forward to any preconceived place. Their pleasures and rewards are sought in the present; they find it difficult to delay gratification, to postpone satisfaction.

(3) There is much egoism, envy, and hostility toward those who prosper. There is a feeling of being exploited. There are many negative attitudes and few positive ones. The unity of the poor comes about through suspicion of and resentment toward outsiders, through opposition to common enemies and hostility to powerful groups. Disillusion about the possibility of advancement stems from a victim complex in relation to the powerful. There is a sense of inability to affect what will happen, a lack of conviction that it is within their power to affect their circumstances. The outside world cannot be trusted; it must be defended against. Outsiders and the outside are seen as risky, likely to injure you when you least expect it. Pessimism and fatalism about being able to affect one's own situation stems from a feeling of being victimized by superordinate, capricious, and malevolent natural and social forces. Their lives appear to them to be fixed by the immutable forces of fate, luck, and chance. While well-to-do people tend to attribute causality to inner forces, the poor tend to make external attributes of causality, seeing themselves as subject to external and arbitrary forces and pressures.[1]

The Social Problem of Poverty and Its Natural Solution

The poor, in short, are commonly seen as apathetic, childlike, not very competent, and hostile-dependent. Other research, emphasized in the past few years, has pointed out the extent to which the poor tend to occupy specific social categories (minority racial and ethnic groups, the elderly, ADC families, and the like), as well as the continuing large proportion of the population who have low incomes even in such an affluent society as the United States. It has been natural to get concerned about a large proportion of the population, the members of which have

---

[1] This summary social scientists' image of the psychological characteristics of the poor was prepared on the basis of a survey of articles and books relating to poverty published by social scientists during the past fifteen years. Any particular author would be likely to differ on one or more points and would probably want to add others not recorded here. For example, in *The Children of Sanchez* (New York: Random House, 1961), Oscar Lewis includes "a strong present time orientation with relatively little ability to defer gratification and plan for the future, a sense of resignation and fatalism based upon the realities of their difficult life situation, a belief in male superiority which reaches its crystallization in *machisme* or the cult of masculinity, a corresponding martyr complex among women, and finally, a high tolerance for psychological pathology of all sorts." (Pages xxvi–xxvii) Lewis, of course, restricted his account to urban Mexican poor.

behavior patterns and psychological characteristics that tend to place them in opposition to or dependence on the remainder of the community.

Poverty has therefore again become a publicly recognized social problem in the United States. The general perception of a social problem leads to a search for its solution. Since a lack of money is the most universal characteristic of poverty, and since a general increase of income for some social groups would automatically abolish poverty, it seems clear to many persons that certain known steps are suitable to end poverty in the United States. Their view is that public policies should be developed and implemented that emphasize provision of jobs, increased access to education that leads to jobs, and higher minimum wage levels and welfare payments. Scientists, according to this view, can contribute by learning how to measure poverty with greater accuracy and by studying its adverse psychological and other consequences, and they should seek to understand how these consequences might be controlled.

In this natural line of reasoning it is assumed rather than demonstrated that the major problem of the poor is poverty, a lack of money. But this assumption is essential to the associated recommendations for scientific work and social policy. It may be well, therefore, to inquire in a more searching fashion whether the problems of the poor primarily result from a lack of money.

There are a number of phenomena which one could hardly anticipate on the basis of such an assumption:

(1) A given level of real income has various consequences depending upon the circumstances in which a person receives the income.

Among the poor, there are many subgroups, the members of which do not display the presumed psychological consequences of poverty. These include most of that portion of the leadership of the poor which is itself poor, those low income families with high educational aspirations for their children, low income members of religious groups such as the Hutterites, university student families with little income, and the like. In the past, of course, members of the lower middle class have survived on real incomes below those received today by comparable public welfare families—and without losing their capacity to struggle in the pursuit of distant ends. Many from the intelligentsia today in such countries as India and Japan have incomes that, in the United States, would place them with the poor. They may differ from educated Americans in personality characteristics, but they do not have the alleged psychology of poverty either.

(2) Increases in income often do not lead to a diminution of the expected psychological consequences of poverty.

For example, the rise in real per capita public welfare expenditures in the United States has not had a demonstrated effect on the psychological functioning of welfare recipients.

(3) Differences in income between otherwise comparable groups of poor do not appear to be accompanied by differences in psychological functioning.

For example, states vary greatly in the size of their payments to comparable welfare recipient families. Comparable families appear to resemble one another in psychological orientation regardless of relatively major differences in their incomes.

(4) When income remains constant, but persons in a neighborhood of poverty become involved in successful social action on important issues, in their own behalf, their psychological orientation does extend over a greater period of time, their feeling of helplessness does lessen, their skills and activities do gradually change.

For example, no one could have predicted on the basis of articles in the relevant scholarly journals that lowly Negroes from areas of poverty would, with some help, begin to organize with such effect that they would carry timid and ultra-conventional members of the Negro middle classes along with them into a militant struggle for freedom. It has also been reported that many "lower class" Negroes who have become part of the Muslim movement have had their lives transformed in the direction of greater order and achievement.

During this past summer I gathered some data concerning The Woodlawn Organization (TWO), a primarily "lower class," predominantly Negro organization which was initiated about two years ago in Chicago with the assistance of Saul Alinsky and the Industrial Areas Foundation. The poor constitute the bulk of active members, and are an important segment of the leadership of this community organization, which has already demonstrated its effectiveness and power. For example, TWO has delivered a majority of the votes from a Negro area to elect a white alderman who takes a strong civil rights position; the unsuccessful opponent was a Negro from the regular political organization. It has been able to secure its own conditions for implementation of an urban renewal development proposed by the University of Chicago for part of the Woodlawn area. TWO has carried out rent strikes and has taken other successful actions against owners of dilapidated slum buildings; it has organized picketing of stores that sell merchandise to people who cannot afford the high interest on installments; it has organized successful city hall demonstrations of more than a thousand persons. Over this period of widespread involvement, the poor appear to have gradually acquired skills of organization, longer range planning, and other qualities contrary to those which reputedly characterize areas of poverty. I observed a similar process occurring in "lower class" white neighborhoods in Northwest Chicago, where the Northwest Community Organization, another Alinsky associated enterprise, has been in existence for less than two years.

(5) When members of some groups lose or give up their wealth, they do not thereby acquire the psychology of poverty.

One has only to consider the vows of poverty taken by members of some religious orders to illustrate this assertion.

Since the psychology of poverty obtains only under specific and describable circumstances, one cannot therefore use poverty as an explanation for these psychological characteristics which often are associated with poverty.

We might briefly mention other problems involved in the ready identification of poverty as the major problem of the poor. First, it is invalid reasoning to proceed without evidence from the fact that the poor have distinctive failings to the assumption that poverty is important in the etiology of these failings. It is incorrect simply to take the defining characteristics of a social category to which a group of people belong (the category "poverty" in this case) and use it without further evidence to account for the peculiar afflictions of that group of people. Second, even if *all* poor today were to exhibit the psychology of poverty, this may be merely an accidental connection, and the fact of having little money could remain only distantly related, for example, to feelings of being dominated by irrational external forces. One should not confuse an observed regularity with an inevitable regularity, a conventional law with a natural law. Third, when a scientist observes that a group of persons, the poor, have adopted their own patterns of behavior and system of beliefs, this does not mean that the behavior and belief patterns are cultural or subcultural or that these patterns represent durable characteristics of the people involved over a wide variety of social situations. The patterns and beliefs may be situational, not internalized, and may shift readily as the situation changes. Just when social scientists appear to be getting the poor firmly in mind, the poor are transformed. Thus, the "psychology of the poor" may be quite different from the psychology of a neurosis the basis of which *is* internalized.

It is therefore likely that the natural solution to the problem of poverty is naïve: it merely assumes the determinants of the psychology of poverty.[2]

---

[2] The personality characteristics of the poor may themselves be different from those reported. Much of the scientific literature is based on reports of verbal

The Self-Help Doctrine and Its Consequences for Dependent Persons

In rapidly industrializing societies in which there are many opportunities for individual advancement there typically arises some form of the doctrine of self-help. The common core of self-help views can be stated as follows: A person is good to the extent to which he has assumed responsibility for and accomplished the realization of his potentialities for maximum use of his native capacities in a long, sustained, and arduous effort to reach a distant legitimate goal. With enough effort any normal person can attain such goals; no special ability is needed.

In the older Western industrial nations a growing appreciation of the limitations of opportunity has provided increasing support for modification of the traditional doctrine, with the qualification that ability as well as effort is necessary to success, and that some persons have been born with more ability than others. Also, since the nineteenth century, the common legitimate goal has changed from entrepreneurship of a prosperous independent business to a high position in a large work organization, and the struggle begins in the institutions of learning before the transfer to a work setting.

According to the doctrine of self-help, *anyone*, given enough time and enough effort, could achieve success. Thus, to be poor could have either of two meanings. On the one hand, poverty was regarded as the original accompaniment of the highest development of character, the struggling poor who were later to become successful were most worthy of respect. On the other hand, poverty indefinitely prolonged might mean a character defect, a lack of will power. Poverty, therefore, was ambiguous; from it alone one could reach no conclusion about virtue. However, an economy with limited opportunities for success plus the belief in equal opportunity for success according to merit made inevitable an assault on the self-esteem of the permanently unsuccessful.

Officially defined dependency was not usually regarded as ambiguous. The person on welfare has left the struggle altogether and has sat back to allow others to furnish his sustenance. It is true that some persons, the crippled, the very young, the seriously ill, and so forth,

---

or other behavioral responses of the poor in the presence of researchers, usually middle class persons of much higher status and greater power than those being studied. It is not easy for a powerful person accurately to understand one who is weak since the behavior of the latter in the research situation may depend very much on the behavior of the former. The massive failure of intelligent and educated Southern whites to withstand Negroes with whom they had maintained years of presumably close relationship should provide reason for researchers to use caution in their claims based on a few hours' contact with persons much different from their usual associates.

clearly could not have avoided dependency. But as for the rest, the presumption of their ability to work and succeed if they only tried hard enough led to the inevitable conclusion that those who have left off trying are bad. The intensity with which this conclusion was known was also related to the fact that dependent persons were seen to be living at the expense of the rest of the community. Not only did the scoundrels manage to exist without honest labor, but they actually made of the rest of the community a duped partner to their idleness. Inexcused dependency became a social symbol communicating defective character, toward which there was a feeling of superiority tinged with contempt. Even in the best of circumstances professional helpers were automatically considered morally as well as materially superior to those helped, and thus the helping relationship became a concrete carrier of the general meaning of dependency: the unworthiness of the dependent.

In affecting the psychology of dependency, the self-help doctrine has also, of course, affected the *behavior* of persons who are in need. One way to evade the unpleasantness of being dependent is to avoid getting help at all in a dependent situation. Families in trouble, as was discovered in various studies, often hide away when they need help the most. The stigma attached to receiving assistance prevents the use even of available resources.

Official dependency in modern society is a residual category of persons unable to enter into the normal types of income-producing relationships. Such persons are unable to relate to the normal avenues for gaining support, and the presence and location of such avenues is therefore the major immediate condition or cause of dependency in modern society. Inability to relate to normal avenues of support symbolizes failure, and perception by a dependent person of his own dependency is sufficient to produce shame and guilt and their complications. Official dependency is fundamentally the perception of the use of relative social power within a superordinate-subordinate relationship; the doctrine of self-help in a contractual economy made financial dependency the focal point for this definition in modern society. The official assumption is that all working adults are equal in that they have entered into work contracts on an equal basis, contracts which they could have chosen to enter or not to enter.

The financially self-responsible person is assumed to be responsible also in other areas of his life. For this reason dependency can concern any area of superordinate-subordinate relationship, and there is always some stigma associated with any dependency relationship, even though there is often pleasure in divesting oneself of the burden of self-responsibility. Even the relationship of citizen to expert can be distasteful since it makes the citizen intellectually dependent on the expert.

The sharpest psychological impact of dependency has occurred where it is officially defined and therefore clearly perceived and sanctioned by the community. However, most dependency is not so explicitly defined; most of the poor are not "on welfare." Even so, the poor are generally perceived, however unclearly, as having failed, and this perception has hardened the community against them. In the latter case, the doctrine of self-help has intensified the feelings of hopelessness among the poor.

The extent of self-support is only one measure of the extent of dependency, a measure stressed only in connection with the doctrine of self-help. More generally, dependency is the placement of one's destiny in other hands. It is therefore especially characteristic of the areas of poverty, but also characterizes many other aspects of society, including the low echelons of large organizations, organization men at any echelon, and so forth. In a general sense dependency is also destructive, but more subtly so. If extent of self-realization is a measure of personality development, then dependency, which erodes self-realization with the loss of self-responsibility, is a measure of personality inadequacy. If the human personality develops as a decision process through self-responsible choices, then the taking away of self-responsible choices through assuming the subordinate position in a dependency relationship necessarily destroys personality.

The Social Situation of the Poor

Most of the poor are heavily dependent on outside forces. In many places, a poor person is much more likely to be subject to police interrogation and search, or to public identification as the object of police activity, than is a member of a middle class family. Urban renewal programs periodically disrupt the neighborhoods of poverty, scattering the families in several directions in accordance with standards which the poor do not understand or support. Schools function impervious to the concerns of the low income families whose children attend, or else schools may seek themselves to "lead" in the areas of poverty in which they are located, that is, they seek to impose school standards and definitions on the neighborhoods. Settlement houses run recreation programs that meet their own traditional criteria, but neighborhood youth often do not understand these criteria, often cannot engage in accustomed and legal modes of behavior and still participate in settlement house activities, often, involuntarily and without understanding, have to disperse friendship groups in order to participate in a recreation program.

Many families, having bought more than they can afford, especially through high-interest installment financing, have no way to know whether or when their furniture will be repossessed or their check garnisheed. Medical and psychiatric care are inadequate, inadequately understood, and uncertainly available, especially to the poor who do not have connections through welfare. The securing of general relief or categorical assistance is a humiliating experience at best for people imbued with self-help ideas, but the deliberate rudeness intended to discourage as many applicants as possible, the complex agency rules which are not so much bases for action as after-the-fact rationales to provide support for decisions already made, and the subjective and unpredictable decisions of social workers representing agencies to the poor, all combine to place the economic foundation of many families at the mercy of completely incomprehensible forces.

The poor who seek employment must find it in a dwindling supply of jobs available to unskilled and semiskilled persons (including domestics), often seasonal or temporary work. In addition, the landlords of the poor are frequently discourteous, seldom inclined to make adequate repairs on their buildings, and likely to blame the tenants for the condition of the ancient and crumbling structures for which high rents are charged.

In other words, the poor, by virtue of their situation, tend to be more dependent than other groups on a larger number of powerful persons and organizations, which are often very unclear about the bases for their actions and unpredictable in their decisions, and which further render the poor helpless by condescending or hostile attitudes, explicit verbal communications which state or imply the inferiority of the poor, and callousness or actual harassment. If we divide the powerful persons affecting the poor into two groups, the benevolent in intention on the one hand, and the callous or punitive on the other, we will find that the majority of both types of power figure treat the poor as inferior and reach down to relate to them.[3]

The situation of poverty, then, is the situation of enforced dependency, giving the poor very little scope for *action*, in the sense of behavior under their own control which is central to their needs and values. This scope for action is supposed to be furnished by society to any person in either of two ways. First, confidence, hope, motivation, and skills for action may be provided through childhood socialization

---

[3] It should be remembered that not all sections of the poor are so much at the mercy of outside forces. The stably employed working class poor are less dependent on mysterious, unpredictable, arbitrary, and capricious forces. There are degrees and kinds of poverty, and the differences among them will be set forth elsewhere to supplement the general description contained in this paper.

and continue as a relatively permanent aspect of the personality. Second, social positions are provided which make it easy for their occupants to act, which make it possible for decisions of their occupants to be implemented in their futures. Middle class socialization and middle class social positions customarily both provide bases for effective action; lower class socialization and lower class social positions usually both fail to make it possible for the poor to act.

Thus, the dependency of the poor is not primarily a neurotic need to occupy dependency positions in social relationships, but rather it results from a deprivation of those minimal social resources, at every period of their lives, which the poor need and therefore must seek. The poor are not victims of the social system in the sense that "organization men" are victims. They are rather, as Michael Harrington has emphasized, the *other* America, outsiders to the major society. In consequence, members of the majority society are usually outsiders to the poor.

The initial dependency and its consequences are reinforced by the hardening of a consensus in the majority community about the nature of the poor, stabilization of the patterns of behavior in areas of poverty, and partial internalization of ideas and patterns of behavior in the children who grow up in both communities. Thus, the positions of poor persons in relationship to superordinate forces are expressions of two communities, a superior and powerful community and an inferior and weaker community; two communities with institutionalized ways of living which prop up the superordinate position of the one in relation to the other.

People isolate and segregate those they fear and pity. The stronger of the two communities has traditionally acted to alleviate the results perceived to be undesirable without changing the relationship of the two communities or ending the division into two communities. Since persons designing and implementing such programs did not consider the consequences of the division for their aims, they were able to maintain an intention to bring the poor into their society. The recommendations have been for improved law enforcement; public welfare; public housing; social settlements; higher horizons educational programs; social work with "hard core" families; urban renewal, clean-up, paint-up, and fix-up programs; block and neighborhood organizations; and the like. All these plans and programs have usually shared two characteristics: (1) they are initiated and supported from outside the neighborhoods of poverty and imposed on the poor; and (2) they fail to make any lasting positive impact on neighborhoods of poverty. That is, although a few persons and families become affluent and leave the neighborhoods, the majority remain poor and continue in an atmosphere of apathy, disorganization, and hostility, toward the programs designed to rescue them. These programs, presupposing the inferiority of the people in the area, perpetuate and exacerbate the inequality. Definitions of the poor are carried by the institutionalized helping hands. Insofar as these agencies have any *social* impact, the definitions embedded in them become self-fulfilling. But, although the powerful external social agencies —powerful in relation to the poor—are not very effective in carrying out their official tasks in areas of poverty, they do enable the stronger community to believe that something is being done about the social problem of poverty, reducing guilt and shame to such an extent that there remains little motivation to develop some effective means to bring the poor into the larger society.

On the basis of this sketch of the dynamics of the situation of the poor, the following classification can be made of the sources of the "psychology of poverty."

(a) In any modern industrial society the overall amount of power of the society tends constantly to increase, although the rate of increase may vary. Although everyone in the society may secure ownership of additional *material* goods as a result of technological progress, the additional *power* tends to be secured only by those persons and social systems with preexistent power. The poor boy with strong internalized drives and skills for success and the large corporation with effective control over technological advances in its field both illustrate the tendency for socially created power to attract to itself additional power. But the poor most often have neither the power created through childhood socialization nor that to be secured through attachment to a strong social system in which they have influence. In some countries, the population is predominantly poor, and this populace may have some power through the political process. But, in the United States the poor are an unorganized or ineffectively organized minority, unable even to exert influence in the political sphere. Thus, increments in power tend to attach to those with power, and the balance of power in a country such as the United States tends naturally to tilt against the poor.

(b) The fact of being powerless, but with needs that must be met, leads the poor to be dependent on the organizations, persons, and institutions which can meet these needs. The situation of dependency and powerlessness through internal personality characteristics as well as through social position leads to apathy, hopelessness, conviction of the inability to act successfully, failure to develop skills, and so on.

(c) As a consequence of the self-help doctrine, this "psychology of poverty" arouses the anger of the affluent toward the poor. Thus, the affluent can avoid the necessity to alter the social situation of the poor by assuming that the poor are bad and deserve their situation. This additional meaning of poverty makes rigid the dependency aspects of the social situation of the poor, and, to some extent, the poor accept the prevalent view of themselves. However, since the poor are not together in an unambiguously clear social category, they, at the same time, may reject being placed in such a category subject to the assumption of their dependency and inferiority. For example, persons eligible to live in public housing are not affected only by the convenience, space, and other physical characteristics of their living quarters. A large proportion seem to prefer dilapidated private housing operated by an indifferent landlord to better maintained, less crowded, less expensive quarters in a public housing project in which the management is concerned with tenant needs. The meaning of living in such a project may offset the superiority of the physical living arrangements.

(d) Over time the dependency relationship of the poor becomes institutionalized and habits, traditions, and organizations arise in both the affluent community and in the neighborhoods of poverty, maintaining the relationship between them. The poor react in part to the institutionalization itself. For example, "lower class" delinquency does not only stem from the fact that the poor have few and drab job opportunities. There is also the perception that the conforming poor tend to remain indefinitely in low social positions as well as the angry rejection by the adolescent poor of attempts, through law enforcement and social agencies, to control and manipulate them without altering their situation.

Consequences of this social process for the poor have been indicated at several points in the preceding discussion; we will only briefly recapitulate some of them here.

First, people tend either to retreat from or to attack forces controlling their lives which they cannot affect and which are not inescapable. For this reason the poor typically stand aloof from settlement houses, get minimally involved with social workers, drop out of school. Only forces too omnipresent to be escaped may ensure normative affiliation through identification with aggressors. It is easy to see the poor as paranoid since they are so often hostile to and suspicious of powerful objects which they may perceive in a distorted fashion. However, paranoia presumably requires origins in early childhood, while the hostility and suspicion of the poor naturally arise from their social position and their necessarily over-simplified and naturally personified perceptions of it.

Second, with less of their selves bound up in their self-conceptions than is the case with other groups, the poor do not entirely accept these definitions of themselves, but protect themselves by various psychological strategies from fully accepting the implications of their situation.

The impact of the definitions then is primarily indirect; the definitions have consequences by creating the situation of the poor through the meaning of poverty to those who possess power. The situation gives rise to the typical absence of that hope which is associated with action and which give salience to intentions and attitudes. Thus, the poor frequently verbalize middle-class values without practicing them. Their verbalizations are useful in protecting their self-conceptions and in dealing with the affluent rather than in any pronounced relationship to non-verbal behavior. This does not imply deliberate falsification; a poor person may have the necessary sincerity, intention, and skill to embark on a course of action but there is so much unconscious uncertainty about achieving psychological returns through success that the action may never be seriously attempted. As has been discovered in social surveys, the poor may not only pay lip service to middle class notions, but may, for similar reasons, say to any powerful person what they believe he wants to hear. That is, much of the behavior of the poor does not relate primarily to their own basic values, beliefs and perceptions held by others about the poor. The poor are normally involved in partly involuntary self-diminution; their behavior may therefore be remarkably transformed when, as has happened through social action, they begin to acquire a sense of power, of ability to realize *their* aspirations. Thus, the so-called differential values of the poor, which are ill-defined at best, are more nearly comprehensible as the psychological consequences of a long continued situation of perceived powerlessness in contemporary industrial society. They become a subculture to the extent that the traditions, orientations, and habits of dependency become internalized.

Third, the situation of the poor, the inability of the poor to act in their own behalf, creates a less complex personality structure for them than is the case with affluent persons with more linguistic skills. This does not necessarily mean that the poor have less effective personalities, or are unsocialized in comparison, since the personalities of more highly educated persons are often partly constituted by social elaborated fantasies which conceal reality and rationalize avoidance of problem solving.

Fourth, awareness of their common fate typically leads the poor to engage in mutual aid activities, activities which, in spite of involving only very minor skills, are precursors to the joint social action which develops naturally as the poor acquire organizational skills and confidence in using them.

Fifth, because of the social situation of the poor and the fact that the majority society has relatively little normative basis for social control in areas of poverty, these areas are often characterized by high rates of publicly discernible types of deviance: juvenile delinquency, school dropouts, alcoholism, illegitimacy, mother-centered families, and the like.

Finally, there are differential consequences of institutionalized, uncompensated powerlessness for the poor who have various social positions within areas of poverty. For example, because of the greater expectation for men to be powerful and to be sources of power, the consequences of powerlessness for "lower class" men is usually greater than that for women.

All of this suggests that the problems of the poor are not so much of poverty as of a particularly difficult variety of situational dependency, a helplessness to affect many important social factors in their lives, the functioning or purpose of which they do not understand, and which are essentially unpredictable to them.

Not Enough Money Versus Situational Dependency

With increased money the poor could at least be better able to cope with such forces, could be less dependent on some. What, then, is the relationship between the poverty of the poor and their situational dependency?

Money is a generalized source of power over people through a right to control over goods and services. As such, money is one of many kinds of power. Poverty, therefore, is one of many kinds of powerlessness, of being subject to one's social situation instead of being able to affect it through action, that is, through behavior which flows from decisions and plans. Since there are several varieties of generalized power, an absence of money is often replaceable *insofar as the psychological reactions to powerlessness are concerned.* An American Indian who lives in poverty may have considerable influence through authority relationships traditional in his culture. Members of religious orders who have taken vows of poverty remain able to exercise influence through their order and through relationships of interdependence with colleagues. The college student with a very low income has influence through the expectations of his future social position. When the poor engage in successful social action they gain power, even when their incomes remain unchanged.

In other words, when social scientists have reported on the psychological consequences of poverty it seems reasonable to believe that they have described the psychological consequences of powerlessness. And many persons without money have, or get, other varieties of power, or else identify with powerful persons or groups and therefore fail to exhibit these consequences. Even the poor do not react entirely on the basis of the social definition of them. There are counter institutions and traditions (churches, unions, and clubs) which deflect the impact of the majority definition. Primary groups (family and peer) also mediate and modify the community definitions they transmit. The behavior of the poor may not, therefore, reflect their self-conceptions; we should not suppose that the poor feel as would middle class persons in their situations, or as their behavior suggests they feel. This very resistance of the poor makes it possible to attempt the otherwise herculean task of trying to get the major society to alter its relationship to poverty by helping the poor themselves to build a backfire, to become strong and effective enough to challenge the invidious definitions that have been made of them.

Human personality is a process of decisions and actions on the basis of decisions. One becomes fully human only through acting in important areas of one's life. All social arrangements which take responsibility out of the hands of the poor, which make decisions and action more difficult or operative over a more restricted area, feed the psychology of powerlessness which is so widely (and correctly) regarded as undesirable. For example, it is often noted that the poor lack a time perspective. But only through action (important decisions and behavior on their basis) does one acquire a history and, with the history, a practical concern with the future.

What consequences does the social situation of the poor have for programs to help the poor? We will next consider some general answers to this question.

Redefining the Social Situation of the Poor

We can reject two possible alternatives.

First, the solution most frequently suggested is to help the poor secure more money without otherwise changing present power relationships. This appears to implement the idea of equality while avoiding any necessary threat to established centers of power. But, since the consequences are related to *powerlessness,* not to the absolute supply of money available to the poor, and since *the amount of power purchasable with a given supply of money decreases as a society acquires a larger supply of goods and services,* the solution of raising the incomes of the poor is likely, unless accompanied by other measures, to be ineffective in an affluent society. Where the poor live in serious deprivation of goods and services, an increase in the supply of those goods and services would be an important source of power, that is, of access to resources which satisfy crucial needs. However, when the poor do not live in actual deprivation, increases in money make relatively little impact on the dependency relationships in which they are entangled. The opportunity to participate in *interdependent* relationships, as a *member* of the majority society, requires an increase in *power.*

Second, the *self-help* doctrine is normally related to conventional criteria of success, and persons who have not met these conventional criteria therefore are threatened with feelings of guilt and shame. One theoretically possible solution would seem to involve redefinition of success, allowing social support to lives which are now viewed as failures. This, however, presupposes an ability to meet some alternative criteria of success through action, a possible solution for philosophers, poets, or beatniks, but not now generally possible for the poor. It may, however, be that the meaning of the self-help doctrine could be adequately extended to reward the social action of the poor who can act successfully through their own organizations.

Along these lines the criteria for an effective solution are reasonably clear. In order to reduce poverty-related psychological and social problems in the United States, the major community will have to change its relationship to neighborhoods of poverty in such fashion that families in the neighborhoods have a greater stake in the broader society and can more successfully participate in the decision-making process of the surrounding community.

It is frequently said that we must provide opportunities for the poor. To render more than lip service to this objective demands more power and more skill and more knowledge than we now possess for the bureaucratic provision of such opportunities. For example, there are a finite number of jobs available, fewer than the number of people looking for work. There are severe limits to the extent to which the adult poor can be trained for existing openings. A large proportion of the poor have jobs which do not remove them from the ranks of the powerless. Any great shift in opportunities made available to the poor within the structure of the majority community will threaten more powerful groups with vested interests in those limited opportunities, and the proponents of creating opportunities for the poor cannot themselves affect the political or economic process enough to implement their good intentions.

It is important to develop opportunities in sensitive relation to the perception by the poor of their own needs. When this is not done, the poor are not likely to be able to use efficiently the opportunities created for them. And, most central of all, rather than to provide opportunities for the "lower class," the poor must as a group be helped to secure opportunities for themselves. Only then will motivation be released that is now locked in the silent and usually successful battle of the neighborhoods of poverty to maintain themselves in an alien social world. This motivation which will enable them to enter the majority society and make it as nurturant of them as it is at present of the more prosperous population.

The involvement of the poor in successful and significant social action provides both immediate and compelling psychological returns and also the possibility of initiative to help the bureaucratic organizations related to the poor to fulfill their officially stated purposes. The institutions of the major community can be forced to establish relationships of interdependence, not of dependence, with the poor; professionals can help by accepting professional roles as employees of the organizations of the poor.

In our society inner worth as expressed in action, striving, the struggle is held eventually to result in attainment of aspirations. If one is not successful, one is viewed as worthwhile so long, and only so long, as one struggles. The poor tend to be regarded as failures and not struggling, and hence as worthless. This perception of worthlessness is incorporated in the conception which others have of the poor and also, to some extent, in the conceptions which the poor have of themselves. One way in which the poor can remedy the psychological consequences of their powerlessness and of the image of the poor as worthless is for them to undertake social action that redefines them as potentially worthwhile and individually more powerful. To be effective, such social action should have the following characteristics:

1. the poor see themselves as the source of the action;
2. the action affects in major ways the preconceptions, values, or interests of institutions and persons defining the poor;
3. the action demands much in effort and skill or in other ways becomes salient to major areas of the personalities of the poor;
4. the action ends in success; and
5. the successful self-originated important action increases the force and number of symbolic or nonsymbolic communications of the potential worth or individual power of individuals who are poor.

The result of social action of this kind is a concurrent change in the view which the poor have of themselves and in the view of the poor by the outside world. There is a softening of the destructive social reality and immediate psychological returns to the poor, although not without hostile reactions from advantaged persons and organizations with known or hidden vested interests in maintenance of the areas of poverty.[4]

---

[4] The Syracuse University School of Social Work has developed a field placement in which graduate students are now receiving training in initiating social action projects by the poor to resolve problems of broad concern in neighborhoods of poverty. Experience indicates that social work students can learn to help the poor jointly to engage in efforts which meet these criteria. Social action efforts by the poor in areas of poverty have occurred in several places. For example, several

The only initial additional resources which a community should provide to neighborhoods of poverty should be on a temporary basis: organizers who will enable the neighborhoods quickly to create powerful, independent, democratic organizations of the poor. These organizations will themselves then seek from the rest of the community resources necessary to the neighborhoods for the solution of the problems they perceive. Agencies for the provision of training and education and opportunities can be developed under the control of the neighborhoods of poverty, thereby ensuring that the poor are in interdependent rather than dependent positions in relation to the agencies. This would meet the professed objectives of most communities since it would effectively motivate the poor to maximum use of opportunities, since the requirements of professional practice will ensure the quality of services rendered, and since the communities state their intention not to allow their help to become an instrument of domination.

The comment that "we know the needs of the poor" is accurate in a very general sense. But there is a great distance between this observation and a knowledge of how, in practice, those needs can be met. If a community is not merely giving lip service to meeting them, if a community wants to be effective as well as to have good intentions, then the way of meeting needs must be appropriate to the personal and social characteristics of those being helped. In this case, effectiveness requires that the only *unilateral* additional help be given at the outset and in the form of temporary assistance in the creation of democratic and powerful organizations of the poor. Through such organizations,

---

years ago, Hope and Dan Morrow moved with their family into a block in East Harlem, New York City. With their help, the families in the block organized themselves formally and informally for a number of important purposes ranging from keeping streets clean to reducing juvenile delinquency. On a larger scale, some of the social action organizations originated by Saul Alinsky of the Industrial Areas Foundation have involved large numbers of people in neighborhood improvement through a conflict process around crucial neighborhood issues. IAF organizations have enabled areas to decrease or end exploitation by some absentee landlords and unethical businesses. They have also ended police brutality and secured police protection, street cleaning, and other services which low income neighborhoods had not previously received at a level equivalent to that of the remainder of the community. Several of the IAF organizations are engaging in "self-help" nonfederally assisted urban renewal. It remains true, however, that most social action programs in low income areas do not meet the above criteria. Such programs frequently attempt to mobilize neighborhoods of poverty without jeopardizing any existing power arrangement, even temporarily, and thus pursue two contradictory objectives simultaneously. They may, in any case, perform such useful functions as providing symbolic satisfaction for the conscience of the majority community and jobs for some estimable persons.

the poor will then negotiate with outsiders for resources and opportunities without having to submit to concurrent control from outside. The outcome will be maximal motivation to take advantage of resources and opportunities which are sensitively tailored to their needs.

Summary

There are two alternative ways to understand the psychological characteristics of the poor. These characteristics can be naïvely understood as resulting from poverty. But there are a number of reasons why it is more precise to view them as the psychology of the *powerlessness* of the poor.

These alternative points of view have also different consequences for social policy. If the problem were only one of a lack of money, it could be solved through provision of more and better paying jobs for the poor, increased minimum wage levels, higher levels of welfare payments, and so on. There would be, in that case, no real need for the poor to undertake any social action on their own behalf. This view is consistent with the idea that the poor are unable to participate in and initiate the solution of their own problems.

However, since it is more likely that the problem is one of powerlessness, joint initiative by the poor on their own behalf should precede and accompany responses from the remainder of society. In practice this initiative is likely to be most effectively exercised by powerful conflict organizations based in neighborhoods of poverty.[5]

---

[5] Because of the nature of this paper there has been no attempt in it to marshal the data relevant to the various assertions made in the discussion of the psychology of areas of poverty as the psychology of powerlessness. This paper has not been designed as a contribution to science in the sense in which science is understood to be a body of verified statements. In the area under consideration there is no such body of statements now available. Contributions to science remain possible, but must be put forward as relatively tentative formulations in the early stages of a process which will move to the collection of additional data relevant to specific points. It is my hope that the above formulation can serve such a purpose.

Family Planning and Poverty

Frederick S. Jaffe

Planned Parenthood Federation

[Reprinted from the Journal of Marriage and the Family, *November 1964, by permission of the National Council on Family Relations.]*

THE MAIN FINDING of United States fertility studies during the last decade has been that many of the historic differentials are rapidly disappearing. Almost all Americans are coming to share a quite similar set of fertility values and practices. Some of the ancient differentials, such as those between urban and rural families, are narrowing considerably, and even the traditional inverse relationships between income (and related measures of socio-economic status) and family size have been reduced, and, for the most prosperous groups, even reversed.[1]

Yet within this over-all and clear trend toward uniformity, there remain many paradoxes which demonstrate that control over fertility has not yet been realized universally in America. Despite the progress of the last 20 years, many low-income families, and a disproportionate number of nonwhite families, still remain very significantly outside the area of effective fertility control.

Among the factors which are responsible for this situation are the institutional and social mechanisms which are amenable to modification and correction by the serving professions. First, some data are presented which will help to establish the parameters of the problem.

I. Family Size Preferences

A number of recent studies have shown, with remarkable consistency, that working-class Americans want as few children as, or fewer than, those of higher socio-economic status.

This is fully demonstrated in the 1960 Growth of American Families study,[2] which is a replication of the 1955 GAF study of a representa-

---

[1] Cf. especially the 1955 Growth of American Families study (Ronald Freedman, P. K. Whelpton, and Arthur Campbell, *Family Planning, Sterility, and Population Growth,* New York: McGraw-Hill, 1959), and the Princeton Study (Charles F. Westoff *et al., Family Growth in Metropolitan America,* Princeton, N.J.: Princeton University Press, 1961).

[2] The author is indebted to Dr. Arthur Campbell of the Scripps Foundation for Research in Population Problems for permission to cite data from completed sections of the 1960 GAF Study, the report of which will be published by Princeton University Press.

tive national sample of white wives in their childbearing years. Nonwhite as well as white wives were sampled in 1960, thus providing the first overview of recent nonwhite fertility attitudes and practices.

The GAF investigators found that nine out of ten American wives, white and nonwhite, thought two to four children is the "ideal" size family, with the average minimum number 3.4 and the average maximum 3.5. In this study, "ideal" is a slightly different concept than "wanted." The number wanted at the time of the interview was smaller than the ideal: The average minimum number for all wives was 3.1, the average maximum 3.4. Lower-income couples wanted somewhat smaller families than higher-income couples. While the average maximum number of children wanted by husbands with family incomes of $10,000 or more was 3.3, the average maximum among those with incomes under $3,000 was 3.1.

It is especially noteworthy that nonwhites wanted a significantly smaller average number of children than whites. White wives wanted a minimum of 3.1 and a maximum of 3.5, while nonwhites wanted 2.7 and 3.0. Forty-six percent of nonwhites wanted no more than two children, compared to 29 percent of whites.

In a similar manner, the recent Princeton study showed that white collar wives wanted 3.3 children, compared to 3.2 for blue collar wives.[3] And in a study by Bogue among Chicago families, the same preference of nonwhites for smaller families was shown. He found, for example, that 38 percent of nonwhites regarded one or two children as ideal, compared to 21 percent of whites.[4]

There is some evidence that these findings apply also to the most impoverished Americans—those who are on relief and those who depend on public health facilities. The Greenleigh study of ADC families in Chicago reported that 90 percent of mothers of out-of-wedlock children did not want to have the child.[5] A 1963 paper from the Florida State Health Department showed that 70 percent of more than 2,600 women attending maternity clinics wanted to have no more children. Two-thirds of this group were nonwhite, and they expressed a consistent desire to have fewer children than did white respondents.[6]

---

[3] Westoff et al., op. cit., p. 187.

[4] D. Bogue, "Experiments in Use of Mass Communication and Motivation To Speed Adoption of Birth Control in High Fertility Populations," presented at Sociological Research Association, 1962.

[5] Greenleigh Associates, Facts, Fallacies, and Future, 1960, p. 19.

[6] R. Browning and L. L. Parks, "Child Bearing Aspirations of Public Health Maternity Patients," presented at American Public Health Association, 1963.

Whether or not these findings can be regarded as definitive, they do tend to challenge some widely prevalent notions about lower-class fertility attitudes. Stycos has noted the remarkable similarity in many diverse societies of upper-class explanations for the high fertility of lower-class groups. The key proposition, he pointed out, is that ". . . the lower classes want many children . . . or do not care how many they have."[7] The same explanation is commonly offered in this country —and it appears to bear approximately the same relationship to reality as most other middle-class explanations of lower-class behavior.

II. Fertility Levels

If lower-class attitudes favor small families, however, it is quite clear from census data and recent research that the wish is not quite the deed. In 1962, 34 percent of the families with five children, and 44 percent of those with six, had incomes below $4,000, compared to 20 percent of the families with two children, and 22 percent of those with three.[8]

The 1960 GAF data show that one out of five couples with children have excess fertility, defined as those whose last child was unwanted by either husband or wife. Not surprisingly, the study found that ". . . the problem of unwanted pregnancies is most severe in the lower income and education groups." Among couples with excess fertility, it was found that those with lowest incomes expect more births than those with highest incomes (4.2 vs. 3.9) although those with lowest incomes want fewer (2.5 vs. 3.1). If the husband had an income of less than $3,000 and the last pregnancy was unwanted, the excess of births expected was 70 percent. Only 11 percent of the college-educated group fall into the excess fertility category, compared to 32 percent of the grade school group. The authors conclude: "A relatively high incidence of severe excess fertility in lower education and status groups explains most of the differences in expected family size between higher and lower status couples. In other words, lower status couples don't have more children . . . simply because they want more. They have more children because some of them do not use contraception regularly and effectively. If the wife has a grade school education and if the husband has an income of less than $3,000 a year, then 39 percent have excess fertility. . . . The judgment that their fertility is too high is their own opinion."

---

[7] J. M. Stycos, "Obstacles to Programs of Population Control—Facts and Fancies," *Marriage and Family Living*, 25: 1, February 1963.

[8] U. S. Census Bureau, *Current Population Reports—Consumer Income*, P-60, No. 41, Table 5, October 21, 1963.

III. Contraceptive Practices

Thus the fertility problems of impoverished Americans must be considered against the background of current family planning practices in the United States. Here the 1960 GAF findings are in the main familiar in that they reinforce and extend the results of the 1955 investigation.

In 1960, fertility control of some sort was favored by 96 percent of Protestants, 98 percent of Jews, and 85 percent of Catholics. Among whites, 81 percent had used *some* form of fertility control by 1960, six percent expected to begin practicing it some time in the future, and ten percent were subfertile. Thus almost everyone was practicing family planning after a fashion, although there still were some socio-economic differentials—e.g., 93 percent of college-educated wives had practiced fertility control or planned to, compared to 72 percent of grade school wives.

Data on nonwhite practices and the breakdown of methods employed by different classes are not yet available. In the 1955 study, however, lower-status (e.g., grade school) wives more often utilized such relatively unreliable methods as douching (32 percent vs. 23 percent) and less often used such reliable methods as diaphragms (16 percent vs. 52 percent) than higher-status (college) wives.

IV. The Gap between Aspiration and Performance

The gap between lower-class fertility aspirations and performance is usually explained by the fact that lower-class couples do not use contraception as regularly as higher-class couples, nor do they employ methods which are as effective. This, in turn, has led to studies, most notably by Rainwater,[9] of what is generally termed the "motivation" problem. These studies have been valuable in pointing up the partly different cultural settings of lower-class families, not to speak of the quite different living conditions. In so doing, they should reinforce the need for more extensive and intensive services to make fertility control a reality for low-income Americans.

Yet, by a curious inversion, these useful explorations have been distorted by some public health and welfare officials into a justification for failure to offer any contraceptive services to indigent families on the ground that "they won't use it anyway." More generally, the motivational analysis has been employed by some to obscure what would seem to be the first order of business—the study of the concrete conditions

---

[9] Lee Rainwater and Karol Kane Weinstein, *And the Poor Get Children*, Chicago: Quadrangle Books, 1960.

under which impoverished Americans receive their medical care, and the bearing that these conditions and other institutional factors may have on the availability of contraception to these families.

For example, 82 percent of married nonwhites in New York City between 1955 and 1959 delivered their babies in municipal hospitals or on ward services of voluntary hospitals, compared to 14.5 percent of whites;[10] in 1955, only 11.1 percent of nonwhite mothers had a private physician in attendance during delivery.[11] In a Washington, D.C. study published in 1961, 75 percent of nonwhite births were staff cases.[12] The 1961 report of the Obstetrical Statistical Cooperative, based on 66,000 discharges at approximately 20 hospitals in New York, New Haven, Hartford, Philadelphia, Denver, San Francisco, Baltimore, and Salt Lake City, showed that nearly 94 percent of nonwhite deliveries were on ward service, compared to 35 percent of whites.[13]

These figures make clear that the vast majority of nonwhite mothers do not have ready access to a private physician during the childbearing period. Most tax-supported hospitals still do not make contraceptive services routinely and easily available to their patients, and only the exceptional voluntary hospital operates a birth control clinic which ward patients can attend. Since the most effective methods of birth control are usually prescribed by private physicians for their private patients during the postpartum period, do not these related facts suggest a significant set of factors limiting the actual availability of effective fertility control measures for nonwhite families—and influencing their subsequent fertility performance? To what extent do similar considerations apply to impoverished whites?

Even before the advent of the oral birth control pills in 1960, contraception was acceptable to many low-income families. The 1960 GAF study, based still on conventional birth control methods, showed that the increase in contraceptive use over 1955 was greatest among couples in the lowest socio-economic group. The proportion of users of all forms of birth control among grade school graduates increased from 49 percent in 1955 to 66 percent in 1960.

It will be most interesting to see a study of the period after 1960,

---

[10] J. Pakter *et al.*, "Out-of-Wedlock Births in New York City, No. 1—Sociologic Aspects," *American Journal of Public Health,* 51:5 (May 1961).

[11] S. Shapiro *et al.*, "Further Observations on Prematurity and Perinatal Mortality in a General Population and in the Population of a Prepaid Group Practice Medical Care Plan," *American Journal of Public Health,* 50:9 (September 1960).

[12] E. Oppenheimer, "Population Changes and Perinatal Mortality," *American Journal of Public Health,* 51:2 (February 1961).

[13] *Obstetrical Statistical Cooperative—1961 Combined Report,* Table IV.

because there is considerable evidence that oral contraception has radically changed the picture. In Mecklenburg County, North Carolina, for example, the Health and Welfare Departments have been cooperating since 1960 in a joint project offering oral contraceptives free to a group consisting primarily of relief recipients. Of the 673 patients who enrolled in the clinic, 75 percent are still taking the pills regularly and effectively, and there have been no pregnancies in this group, although these patients previously had been quite prolific. Similar evidence of the acceptability of the oral pills among poor families comes from Bellevue Hospital in New York, where an active clinic serving a relief and impoverished population was established in 1959, and where more than 90 percent of the patients choose the orals.[14] In Planned Parenthood clinics throughout the country, 70 percent of the patients have incomes of under $4,000, and the pills have sparked a doubling of the patient load in the last five years. Between 1962 and 1963 alone, there was a 25 percent increase in contraceptive patients and a 60 percent increase in those on the pills.[15]

This recent experience should prompt the development of a more precise concept of the elements that go into motivation for family planning—and particularly of the relationship between ease of access to competent instruction and the level of motivation required for successful practice. Do all Americans today have equal access to fertility control? Would it not be fruitful to study the access problem of impoverished Americans realistically, to examine critically the obstacles society places in the way of effective fertility control guidance and instruction for poor families—and then to remove these obstacles? For it is certainly still true that most public hospitals, health departments, and welfare agencies either do not provide contraceptive service at all—or compel a couple to run an obstacle course in order to secure what everyone else in the society regards virtually as part of the Bill of Rights. In this connection, the significance of the fact should be pondered that in many public hospitals, it is considerably easier for an impoverished mother to be sterilized than for her to receive instruction and supplies for contraception.

Among these obstacles are those who manage to transform what has become an everyday practice for most American families into a traumatic experience, such as the caseworker who told a Planned Parenthood field worker not long ago, quite seriously, that she "wouldn't

---

[14] Personal communication from Dr. Hans Lehfeldt.

[15] A. F. Guttmacher, *1963 Annual Report*, Planned Parenthood Federation of America.

dream of suggesting birth control to a client unless the client had been in deep therapy for at least two years." [16] And, of course, there are the very physical arrangements of many public institutions, not to speak of the attitudinal problems of the serving professionals. How many middle-class couples would be practicing birth control effectively if it required first that the wife spend a half day in a dingy clinic waiting room, only to find that she has to defend her integrity against the indifference and hostility of a doctor who tells her that she ought to stop her sex life if she doesn't want children?

If that sounds extreme, it is useful to recall the story of Sadie Sachs which started Margaret Sanger on her work for birth control. As a public health nurse on New York's Lower East Side in 1912, Mrs. Sanger had carefully nursed back to life Mrs. Sachs, who was hemorrhaging after self-induced abortion. When Mrs. Sachs finally recovered, she asked the doctor to tell her how to keep from becoming pregnant. The doctor's immortal reply was: "Tell Jake to sleep on the roof." [17]

A half century later, in 1962, CBS did a telecast on the birth control situation in Chicago. The program contained the following equally immortal words from a white Tennessee mother of six who had delivered her last baby at Cook County Hospital. Like Sadie Sachs, she had asked the doctor for birth control information. "Well," she told CBS, "I asked him what I could do and he said that was up to me to decide. He said one thing that—the best thing for me to do would not be close to my husband, and if I didn't want to get that way, it was up to me to stay away from getting pregnant until I had the operation coming up in April. Well, I didn't like it, 'cause I figure my husband's a human being just like he is, and I don't think he'd like to be told that— to stay away from his wife, if he's married." [18]

---

[16] For a contrasting—and much more positive—view in the context of social work thinking, cf. *The Right to Birth Control Information in Family Planning*, Community Service Society of New York, 1964.

[17] L. Lader, *The Margaret Sanger Story*, New York: Doubleday, 1955.

[18] *CBS Reports on Birth Control and the Law*, May 10, 1962.

Child Rearing Among Low-Income Families

Hylan Lewis

Howard University

[Excerpted from Child Rearing Among Low Income Families. *Child Rearing Project, Health and Welfare Council of the National Capital Area. Washington, D.C.: The Washington Center for Metropolitan Studies, 1961.]*

MY COLLEAGUES AND I have been engaged in a field project with the operating title: "Child Rearing Practices Among Low Income Families in the District of Columbia." The focus of the project is on the relationships between the conditions of life in poorer families, and child neglect, parental inadequacy, and dependency. Stated simply, the aims in this phase of a planned two-part project are, first, to find out how different kinds of low-income families in different kinds of community situations are guiding the development of children; and, second, to discover what kinds of community programs involving the voluntary participation of lower income families are practicable.

This project, representing as it does a union of social science and social welfare techniques and experiences, is a pragmatic operation. It exists to provide a service for those who are confronted with practical, harsh, immediate problems.

While the central interest is in child rearing practices and community settings among low income "problem" families, material has been obtained, for comparative purposes, on low income families without "problems" and on "adequate" income families.

As of May, 1961, field observations had been made on a total of sixty-six families, of which fifty-seven are low income families, forty-nine non-white and eight white. Twenty-six, or slightly less than one-half of the low income families in the study population, are currently active with public welfare agencies; sixteen of these are families with Aid to Dependent Children grants.*

Field workers have been trained to observe and to report on people in their natural settings. The purpose is to get material in depth, to see as well as to listen.

The field documents illustrate wide variety in the concrete human

---

* The number of field contacts with families ranges from one to twenty-seven. The average number of contacts with low-income families was more than nine; the average number of hours of contact for these families was twelve.

styles of low income families. The fact that these documents were obtained indicates, among other things, an impressive willingness of these low income family heads to share their experiences over extended periods of time. One of the mothers volunteered that she was pleased to be "a part of a larger study," of a project that is "doing something that might be of help to other families like mine, so that they might not have to go through all the things we have been through."

My present purpose is not to summarize project accomplishments or findings—in fact, the analysis of the field materials is far from being completed; rather, it is to share some propositions and reflections that we think have relevance for family and child welfare programs, and for understanding the contemporary poor.

In general, our materials confirm the findings of other students that among low income families, unguided, unplanned influences outside of the family or household are relatively more important, and affect the socialization of the child relatively earlier, than among higher or adequate income families. Our initial analysis of the field materials has resulted further in a series of propositions about family and community influences on child rearing among low income families.

Among the propositions that we wish to share here are some that have to do with (1) parental control in low income families, (2) the relationship between the family values and the actual behavior of lower income parents, and (3) the quality of life in low income neighborhoods.

In many families studied, the effects of external influences are reflected in the strikingly early appearance of cut-off points in parental control and emotional support—in the falling off of parents' confidence in their ability, as well as in their will, to control and give attention to their children.

For practical purposes—and this reminds us of the recent news story about the seven-year-old veteran of vandalism and breaking in—the immediate point is that changes in parents' control, and in their self-estimates of ability to control, occur sometimes when the children are as young as five and six. In these instances I am talking about now, the factors associated with potential and actual child neglect are different from those in which neglect and inadequate care of infants and very young children are related to parental rejection. This latter type of situation is well understood, of course.

Here we are talking about the mothers who are not basically rejecting of, or hostile to, their children. Characteristically, for such mothers the care and control of younger children is not perceived as a real problem: the mothers show confidence, warmth, and ability to exercise effective control. As children grow older there seems to be a cut-off point at which parents express impotence and bafflement. Although there are anxieties, the fate of these growing children is often written off as out of parents' hands. There recurs in the records a mixture of hope and resignation: "I do hope they don't get in trouble. I tried to raise them right." "The Lord will have to look out for them." "I'm glad mine are little. I kinda hate to see them grow up. At least I can do something for them now."

Additional factors that seem to have something to do with the cut-off points are the size of the family and expectations about the child's work role. Mothers in low income, large family situations frequently set training and discipline goals in keeping with needs or demands for assistance in the household and in the care of other children; these goals are unrealistic in relation to growing children who are exposed progressively to extra-family influences. When mothers in such family situations fail to achieve their specific and immediate child rearing goals related to household functioning, they exhibit discouragement and bafflement. They describe their inability to cope with external factors which they say have stronger pulls on their children than maternal demands for good manners, respect, floor scrubbing, and supervision of the younger children.

A staff member's comments on some of the generalizations current about class factors in parental control should be considered:

> There is current in much of the literature on child rearing a belief that mature status for the child is granted relatively early on the lower socio-economic levels. Much is made of the idea that middle and upper class children envy the "freedom" of their lower class contemporaries. Our field materials suggest that this apparent freedom of the children in lower income families is not necessarily "granted." Frequently, it appears to be wrested from begrudging parents or parental substitutes.

The fact that the loss of parental control occurs so early in many of these families, whether due to parental abdication or the revolt of children, should be juxtaposed with the fact that the adolescent period is the socially accepted or expected period of revolt.

Much popular thinking, reinforced by some earlier studies, stresses presumed or demonstrated class differences in child rearing values. Our field materials suggest that the low income parents in this study group, whether they are adequate or inadequate, dependent or not dependent, tend to show greater conformity to, and convergence with, middle class family and child rearing standards in what they say they want (or would like to want) for their children and themselves, than in their actual child rearing behavior. This is evident in much of the material examined in relation to parental concerns and controls, self-appraisals of child rearing behavior, education of children, sex, marriage, and illegitimacy.

In both categories of low income families, the dependent and the non-dependent, are found parents who show a high degree of interest in children's health, education, and welfare. The persistence of positive concern, and of the willingness to sacrifice for children, despite deprivation and trouble, are features of the child rearing behavior of a good proportion of the low income families observed.

As other studies have shown, the low income mothers of this study group have relatively high educational aspirations for their children, and, above all, they want better housing and neighborhoods. The persistent themes are: "getting a good education," "getting enough education," "getting a good job." A staff member points out, however, that what constitutes a good job, or sufficient education, is not always specified.

> There is lack of knowledge or clarity as to how children are to obtain the goals projected; and there is very little indication that the parents know what to do themselves in order to motivate children. On the contrary, what seems to be an underlying theme is expressed in various ways in the idea that "you can lead a horse to water. . . ." There is communicated a combination of realism and pessimism, a kind of wise weariness that may appear to belie the very educational or career goals they express for at least some of their children.

Acute dissatisfactions cluster around housing, and the lack of proper places for children to play. Examples are:

> The first step I'm striving for is better housing . . . I just want to get out of all of this.
>
> The one thing I want, it's a backyard fenced in so my children don't play out in the street. I hope and pray some day to do better. But what can I do now?
>
> I would like a comfortable home for them, if I could give them anything.
>
> So we have the will, we're just waiting for the way. (With reference to moving out of the area.)

In the observations of parents in our study group of low income families, we have distinguished three varieties of parents classified according to concern: (1) those with high concern who demonstrated it in their behavior; (2) those with considerable verbal concern, but who exhibited inconsistent or contradictory behavior; and (3) those who expressed little or no concern and who are extremely neglectful.

The first type consists of parents whose high concern is exhibited in actions related to the welfare of children, in contrast to verbalizations. Working with what they have, they show high "copability," self-reliance, and self-respect. The way in which they face problems—that is, react to outside impersonal forces—indicates good mental health in this sense of the term.

The second type of parents includes those who are inconsistent in their concern and exhibit a borderline degree of parental control. They tend to be highly self-centered and demanding. Characteristically, parents of this type are persons who themselves recall unsatisfactory or deprived childhoods. They are reported as having difficulty in accepting the child as an individual. They tend to be impatient and they apply discipline inconsistently.

Parents of the third classification are the central adult figures in the classic picture of child neglect—children who suffer undernourishment, untreated physical ailments, exposure to violence, harsh treatment, and arbitrary punishment. There is a tendency among the parents who show a very low degree of concern and few parental strengths to use their children as scapegoats. Dependent and lacking in self-reliance themselves, they seem to resent their children for being dependent on them. They are rated low in self-confidence and self-esteem. It is probable that a good proportion of Junior Village children come from this type of parent.

The most inadequate and neglectful parents are the most reluctant to talk about the specifics of child rearing. Even the most neglectful parents, however, ascribe no virtue to inadequacy or neglectful behavior in themselves or in others, or to neighborhood disorganization. If there is any suggestion of approval of neglectful behavior or accentuation of the negative, it smacks of perverseness, defiance, bravado, or desperation of the "I-don't-care" type. The following field document illustrates this:

> When a neighbor commented to a mother that one of the mother's four children appeared to have a bad cold, the mother, referring to herself, calmly said, "Her mother don't care!" At the neighbor's expression of surprise that she would say such a thing, the mother, bridling at the implied criticism, countered with, "Well, that's the way it is so I might as well tell the truth."

In every category of low income families observed there are differences in hopes and expectations of changes for the better, and in the parents' estimates of resources they think they have, or can find, to effect changes in themselves. In other words, there are cutting points also in the optimism and confidence of many parents about the futures of their families—and in the belief that their efforts alone might affect them. This cut-off point in parental optimism and confidence is something that emerges, as one of the most insidious and eroding processes affecting child rearing. Confidence that is continuing, even though mixed or fluctuating, as much as anything, distinguishes low income families that are not now marked by neglect or dependency, from those that are "clinically" dependent or neglectful.

The "multi-problem" or "hard core" cases of inadequacy, dependency, and neglect are, to use medical terminology, "clinical cases," with unknown or varying potential for rehabilitation. As in types of heart disease and cancer, when the condition becomes known or public, it is frequently too late; prognosis for these cases is poor. "Clinical" dependency, that which is known to public and private agencies and health and welfare institutions, is costly, and provokes concern beyond the numbers involved.

Although it is necessary and important to seek improved ways of rehabilitation or containment, the long-range dividends are likely to be greater from research and demonstration programs that seek to identify and work with the highly vulnerable families, not yet publicly dependent or neglectful; that is, to examine the "pre-clinical" and "sub-clinical" aspects of dependency and neglect.

While there is a statistical relationship between illegitimacy and poverty, it is necessary to get behind the gross statistics, and to be discriminating in our judgments and conclusions. For example, any interpretation or programming based on the assumption that there is a distinctive population of unwed mothers, or that unwed mothers would rather be unwed, flies in the face of the facts.

Our materials support three propositions. First, the belief is not valid that broad categories of people, such as lower income groups, newcomers, and certain ethnic minorities, are not troubled about illegitimacy. Second, birth in wedlock is an important value; but in any given instance, it might be pre-empted by another important value, or its realization thwarted by practical considerations. Third, for program purposes, the salient values and practices related to illegitimacy are those reflected in the affirming of family support for the mother and child, "taking them in," or having and keeping the child in the face of possible community disapproval.

Pregnancy out of wedlock, particularly the first pregnancy, is commonly referred to as a "mistake." Identifying with her pregnant daughter, the mother of ten children differed with her husband who wanted to put his daughter out; she said:

> I told him she ain't the first one who ever made a mistake and I was going to let her stay right here with me. I told Esther we would take

care of her through this one, but no more babies before you're married.
I did this because I had made a mistake and got pregnant and I could
understand how anybody could make a mistake, at least once.

The idea of one's mistake being "human" or even a "right" is also
heard. Not unmindful of the fact that she did not marry until her second
pregnancy, another mother said:

Everybody has a right to one mistake, but two out of wedlock children
are no mistake—and three—the girl's just beyond herself!

The acceptance of the "first mistake" does not imply, however,
that there is no emotional upheaval on the part of the parents.

A grandmother, learning in court that her granddaughter's "mistake" had occurred in their own living room, said: "I just knew I was
going to die. I had tried so hard." A white mother who considered the
possibility of her daughter's becoming pregnant decided:

I don't know. Maybe I almost would have lost my mind, but I would
not turn her out. I just could not do it. I certainly would take care of
the baby. I would not permit the baby to be put for adoption.

A Negro mother of eight children concurred, saying:

I know it would hurt me an awful lot. But I wouldn't put her out.
A real mother wouldn't do that. But it would really hurt me . . . I
would not do that. But I wouldn't place the baby for adoption even
though I have so many children.

The field materials indicate a great deal of popular misunderstanding and some myth about the sex behavior and propensities of
lower income families and individuals from these families. There is a
striking incidence of parental shame and embarrassment about sex. (We
seriously doubt that this last is in itself a class trait, unique to this category of the population.)

Sex education is found to be a family matter to a very limited degree. Vague warnings and prohibitions constitute the bulk of sex training. Behavior and expressions of many mothers in relation to children's
curiosity about sex are reminiscent of a Victorian attitude. Their eva-
sions are reinforced by dismissal of talk about sex as "bad" and "nasty."
A mother in her early twenties who lives with her family in a housing
project said:

We knew nothing about sex the whole time we were growing up. Sex
was hush-hush. It was like the Dark Ages. It was sad. It really was.

A forty-two-year-old white mother of five children said:

No, we would never talk about such things to my mother. We had too
much respect for her.

A thirty-one-year-old mother in a housing project said:

> All my mother said to me was, "Tell your sister," when I started menstruating; and to this day that is all she said to me.

For the mothers in general, the onset of the menstrual cycle was the point at which the silence was broken by vague admonitions about keeping away from boys.

> My mother told me about "ministrating." She never told me about sex, nothing about a man and she say—after I got up the nerve to ask her— "You fool around with a boy, you get a baby" and that was all!

> My mother didn't talk to me when I was growing up. She would say, "If something happens to you, will you please let me know?" I used to wonder what she was talking about, but that's all she would say.

The woman whose mother referred her to her sister for explanation was told by the sister to read aloud a passage on menstruation from a medical book. She drew the conclusion that conception could occur automatically and was therefore expecting to become pregnant momentarily.

A young woman who married at eighteen said that she became pregnant three months later and, although she knew by then where the baby was, she was puzzled about how it was going to get out of her stomach.

The key problem, as in previous generations, seems to be embarrassment in talking about sex. Even some of the mothers who said they wanted to bring their children up differently, mentioned difficulty in overcoming this embarrassment. One of the mothers, when pressed for an explanation of why she said that she often got her sister to talk to her children, said:

> It was the way I was raised. I had a very strict mother and she never came out and talked to me about it and when they came to me I just couldn't.

This embarrassment in discussing any aspect of sex appeared to be widespread. A wife whose three children were born out of wedlock, blushed when any aspect of sex was mentioned, and said she "doesn't believe in that nasty talk."

Despite embarrassment and ambivalence, what to do about the sex training of children and the recognized threat of illegitimacy was seen as an acute dilemma by a good proportion of the low income mothers. Two of the more poignant examples are the mother who brought home condoms from the drugstore to explain their use to her twelve year old daughter, and another mother who requested a diaphragm from the birth control clinic for her fourteen year old daughter.

An important commentary on the matter of sex and illegitimacy among low income groups was the avidity with which women in four mothers' groups entered into a discussion of problems in these areas. A staff report said about these meetings:

> One got the impression of people anxious to share and exchange views and to learn. Tempers were riled, anxieties expressed, and personal confidences shared in brisk and lively sessions. . . . What was of particular importance was that so much interest was evidenced, even though it was clearly understood that our prime interest was in learning what they had to say and not in telling them what to do. Their reaction suggests that there is much more that can be done in this area on an educational level.

In spite of the fact that many homes do not have fathers or husbands, the lower income male and father is a key figure in gaining an understanding of child rearing in the lower income or dependent family. Of particular importance is the man's ability to support and stand for the family—to play the economic and social role wished of him, particularly by wives, mothers, and children. Some of the implications of this are suggested in the field document that describes a mother of six children chiding her husband for being afraid and not showing aggressiveness in looking for a second job to increase the family income. Showing his pay stub, she said: "This looks like a receipt for a woman's paycheck instead of a man's."

Although the analysis of our data is incomplete, the materials suggest that neither the quality of life in most low income neighborhoods nor the child rearing behaviors of low income families is to be interpreted as generated by, or guided by, what one student calls "a cultural system in its own right—with an integrity of its own." The behavior observed in these varying low income families does not represent the kind of organization or cohesion suggested by these phrases. Rather it appears as a broad spectrum of pragmatic adjustments to external and internal stresses and deprivations. In any event, programming might best focus on the facts of deprivation and the varied responses, rather than on presumably organized values that represent a preferred or chosen way of life.

Many low income families appear here as, in fact, the frustrated victims of what are thought of as middle class values, behavior, and aspirations. That this has its implications for child rearing is suggested in the separate comments of two mothers who blamed their parents for their childhood deprivations. "I don't think my parents should have sacrificed us to get a house." "My father ought not to have sacrificed us for a car."

Probably one of the more important contributions that can be made to thinking and research about the people who have in common the one trait of poverty is the stressing of the difference between the hard-core, "undeserving" poor—and the hard luck, "deserving" poor, as Dr. Thomas Gladwin did recently in a paper before the National Conference on Social Welfare. One of our difficulties is that this has not been done often or consistently enough; and one of the reasons is the false assumption about, or the image of, a homogeneous lower class culture. What many people mistakenly describe or imagine to be the attributes of the lower class, seem actually, to be the traits of a small segment, the so-called hard-core, of the whole category.

One danger from this confusion is that attempts to change or to penalize the hard core "undeserving" poor might divert our attention from, and unduly penalize a segment of, the poor population whose explicit behavior, if not values and preferences, is a result of not enough money, not enough work. Their exposure to harsh social, economic, and political realities can be a chronic and recurrent condition which they would rather not have to ameliorate or rationalize in the same terms that the hard core poor apparently do. We should not forget that money and work are sorely needed by many poor who are deserving by any test.

There are some assumptions about the contiguousness, the communication, the potentials for community organization among the hard core poor that need to be further examined in a number of different settings. Is there a community, a network, of the hard-core poor? Or do they exist in the cracks and crevices of larger communities of the poor and the more affluent? The practical point here is that the chronically dependent and not-yet dependent poor often live side-by-side in the same neighborhood or area; but often that is all that they do, or want to do together. Much community organization and block work assumes that, because they live in the same neighborhood or area, this in itself provides or connotes a sound basis for developing a more viable and organized community. The truth is that in our slums there are likely to be wide gaps between the hard core poor and the other core—the more respectable and deserving poor as it were. Too frequently the conventional community organization approach is geared to getting the respectable and non-respectable poor together. This represents built-in frustration. One frequent result is that all poor are written off, or condemned as hard-to-reach, because they will not cooperate, either with each other or the block organizers.

Even if homogeneous, continuing communities of the hard-core poor did exist in the past, the chances of finding them today are getting slimmer because of urban renewal, slum clearing, highway construction, etc. The chances are greater now that the poor people of all kinds will be scattered; they will live nearer and be more visible to us non-poor and not-so-poor people.

The lack of identification of the non-hard-core poor with the hard-core poor is graphically depicted in the following excerpts from two staff memos:

> Is there a representative Upton Square resident? In a sense there is not, since individuality and idiosyncrasies of character flourish here as they do not, at present, in conformist middle-class society.

> . . . we find a recurrent, underlying theme throughout a great deal of the "family" data, a theme which is corroborated by some of the generalized "participant-observations" . . . the reference is to the perception of "undesirable, anti-social behavior," not necessarily from the point of view of the broader society, but rather from the point of view of the milieu in question. These are frequently attributed to some vague, almost undefinable group called "the others" or those "others." Thus parents interviewed refer constantly, or almost so, to the "fussin" and "fightin," the bad language, and "cussin" and the "bad" manners of other families, of other children.

> The universe of the "winehead," the pimp and the whore seems to lie somewhere else than in the bosom of the household in question.

The first phase of our overall project concerned with child rearing among the poor has demonstrated, among other things, that all three types of lower income families—the "subclinical," the "pre-clinical," and the "clinical" dependents—are accessible for program participation. The willingness of families to cooperate appears to be related to an initial approach that stressed the contributions the families can make to a project larger than themselves—a project that they think will contribute something to the improving of child rearing—for themselves, if possible, for others certainly. Our experience shows the improving of child rearing to be a basic human value that is not confined by class lines, despite the fact that what some people themselves do about it, or are able to do about it, or even have the will to do about it, varies. As much as anything, the reasons we give for this variability have major consequences for social welfare practices and policy.

With your permission I will let four mothers sound the closing notes. Each one says something different about this "business of raising."

The first two comment on the neighborhoods in which they live; the second two tell about what they hope for their children.

The first said:

> I don't like the people here, because every place I live they just are wineheads and drink too much and use this bad cursing all the time.

The second mother had just moved into another area:

> The home owners don't pay much attention to you. But among those who live near me, people are all equals. They're all scuffling just like me. They ain't got nothing but a little furniture and nobody thinks she's any better than anybody else.

A young mother with several children, and now without a husband in the home, said with resignation:

> Like I said, you can't make no plans. I know I can't make no plans for myself until my children grow up and marry. Then I will be old. I have never thought too much about making any plans at all. I know I am going to have Welfare help until my children are able to look out for themselves. Maybe after that I can plan something for myself, but sometimes I don't see no use in trying to make plans because something is always happening to upset you.

And finally, with a restrained upbeat, the fourth said:

> When there are children, you usually have to watch out, because if you don't you'll have too many. And without education . . . and luck . . . you can't support your children. So that's why you should try to show your children that going to school and finishing school is for their good. Not so that you can hold up your head and brag and say, "That's my child. . . ." Because this world is getting weaker and wiser and it's going to take two parents to try and show a child the facts of life and the facts of marriage.

The Disadvantaged Child and the Learning Process

Martin Deutsch
Columbia University

[Reprinted from Education in Depressed Areas, *A. Harry Passow, Editor. Copyright © 1963 by Teachers College, Columbia University. Reprinted by permission of the Bureau of Publications, Teachers College, Columbia University. All rights reserved.]*

THIS PAPER WILL DISCUSS the interaction of social and developmental factors and their impact on the intellectual growth and school performance of the child. It will make particular reference to the large number of urban children who come from marginal social circumstances. While much of the discussion will be speculative, where appropriate it will draw on data from the field, and will suggest particular relationships and avenues for future investigation or demonstration.

Among children who come from lower-class socially impoverished circumstances, there is a high proportion of school failure, school drop-outs, reading and learning disabilities, as well as life adjustment problems. This means not only that these children grow up poorly equipped academically, but also that the effectiveness of the school as a major institution for socialization is diminished. The effect of this process is underlined by the fact that this same segment of the population contributes disproportionately to the delinquency and other social deviancy statistics.

The thesis here is that the lower-class child enters the school situation so poorly prepared to produce what the school demands that initial failures are almost inevitable, and the school experience becomes negatively rather than positively reinforced. Thus the child's experience in school does nothing to counteract the invidious influences to which he is exposed in his slum, and sometimes segregated, neighborhood.

We know that children from underprivileged environments tend to come to school with a qualitatively different preparation for the demands of both the learning process and the behavioral requirements of the classroom. There are various differences in the kinds of socializing experiences these children have had, as contrasted with the middle-class child. The culture of their environment is a different one from the culture that has molded the school and its educational techniques and theory.

We know that it is difficult for all peoples to span cultural discontinuities, and yet we make little if any effort to prepare administrative personnel or teachers and guidance staff to assist the child in this transition from one cultural context to another. This transition must have serious psychological consequences for the child, and probably plays a major role in influencing his later perceptions of other social institutions as he is introduced to them.

It must be pointed out that the relationship between social background and school performance is not a simple one. Rather, evidence which is accumulating points more and more to the influence of background variables on the patterns of perceptual, language, and cognitive development of the child and the subsequent diffusion of the effects of such patterns into all areas of the child's academic and psychological performance. To understand these effects requires delineating the underlying skills in which these children are not sufficiently proficient. A related problem is that of defining what aspects of the background are most influential in producing what kinds of deficits in skills.

Environmental Factors

Let us begin with the most macroscopic background factors. While it is likely that slum life might have delimited areas that allow for positive growth and that the middle-class community has attributes which might retard healthy development, generally the combination of circumstances in middle-class life is considerably more likely to furnish opportunities for normal growth of the child. At the same time, slum conditions are more likely to have deleterious effects on physical and mental development. This is not to say that middle-class life furnishes a really adequate milieu for the maximum development of individual potential: it doesn't. The fact that we often speak as though it does is a function of viewing the middle-class environment in comparison to the slum. Middle-class people who work and teach across social-class lines often are unable to be aware of the negative aspects of the middle-class background because of its apparent superiority over the less advantageous background provided by lower-class life. We really have no external criterion for evaluating the characteristics of a milieu in terms of how well it is designed to foster development; as a result we might actually be measuring one area of social failure with the yardstick of social catastrophe.

It is true that many leading personalities in twentieth-century American life have come from the slums, and this is a fact often pointed out by nativistic pragmatists in an effort to prove that if the individual "has it in him" he can overcome—and even be challenged by—his humble surroundings. This argument, though fundamentally fallacious, might have had more to recommend it in the past. At the turn of the century we were a massively vertical mobile society—that is, with the exception of certain large minority groups such as the Negroes, the Indians, and the Mexican-Americans who were rarely allowed on the social elevator. In the mid-twentieth century it is now increasingly possible for all groups to get on, but social and economic conditions have changed, and the same elevator more frequently moves in two directions or stands still altogether. When it does move, it goes more slowly, and, most discouragingly, it also provides an observation window on what, at least superficially, appears to be a most affluent society. Television, movies, and other media continually expose the individual from the slum to the explicit assumption that the products of a consumer society are available to all—or, rather, as he sees it, to all but him. In effect, this means that the child from the disadvantaged environment is an outsider and an observer—through his own eyes and those of his parents or neighbors—of the mainstream of American life. At the same time, when the child enters school he is exposing himself directly to the values and anticipations of a participant in that mainstream—his teacher. It is not sufficiently recognized that there is quite a gap between the training of a teacher and the needs, limitations, and unique strengths of the child from a marginal situation. This gap is, of course, maximized when the child belongs to a minority group that until quite recently was not only excluded from the mainstream, but was not even allowed to bathe in the tributaries.

What are some of the special characteristics of these children, and why do they apparently need exceptional social and educational planning? So often, administrators and teachers say, they are children who are "curious," "cute," "affectionate," "warm," and independently dependent in the kindergarten and the first grade, but who so often become "alienated," "withdrawn," "angry," "passive," "apathetic," or just "trouble-makers" by the fifth and sixth grade. In our research at the Institute for Developmental Studies, it is in the first grade that we usually see the smallest differences between socio-economic or racial groups in intellectual, language, and some conceptual measures, and in the later grades that we find the greatest differences in favor of the more socially privileged groups. From both teachers' observations and the finding of this increasing gap, it appears that there is a failure on some level of society and, more specifically, the educational system. Was the school scientifically prepared to receive these children in the first place? And, in addition, were the children perhaps introduced to the individual demands of the larger culture at too late an age—that is, in first grade?

Before discussing these psychological products of social deprivation, it is appropriate to look more closely at the special circumstances of Negro slum residents. In the core city of most of our large metropolitan areas, 40 to 70 percent of the elementary school population is likely to be Negro. In my observations, through workshops in many of these cities, I have often been surprised to find how little real comprehension of the particular problems of these youngsters exists as part of the consciousness of the Negro or white middle-class teachers. While in middle-class schools there is great sensitivity to emotional climates and pressures and tensions that might be operating on the child in either the home or the school, in lower-class schools the problems of social adaptation are so massive that sensitivity tends to become blunted.

In the lower-class Negro group there still exist the sequelae of the conditions of slavery. While a hundred years have passed, this is a short time in the life of a people. And the extension of tendrils of the effects of slavery into modern life has been effectively discouraged only in the last few decades, when there have been some real attempts to integrate the Negro fully into American life. It is often difficult for teachers and the personnel of other community agencies to understand the

Negro lower-class child—particularly the child who has come, or whose parents have come, from the rural South. There is a whole set of implicit and explicit value systems which determine our educational philosophies, and the institutional expectation is that all children participate in these systems. And yet for these expectations to be met, the child must experience some continuity of socio-cultural participation in and sharing of these value systems before he comes to school. This is often just not the case for the child who comes from an encapsulated community, particularly when the walls have been built by the dominant social and cultural forces that have also determined the value systems relating to learning.

A recent article in *Fortune* magazine asked why the Negro failed to take full advantage of opportunities open to him in American life. At least part of the answer is that the Negro has not been fully integrated into American life, and that even knowledge about particular occupations and their requirements is not available outside the cultural mainstream. Implications of this for the aspirations and motivations of children will be discussed later.

Another source of misunderstanding on the part of school and social agency people is the difficulty of putting in historical perspective the casual conditions responsible for the high percentage of broken homes in the Negro community. Implications of this for the child's emotional stability are very frequently recognized, but the effects on the child's motivation, self-concept, and achievement orientation are not often understood.

The Negro family was first broken deliberately by the slave traders and the plantation owners for their own purposes. As was pointed out earlier, the hundred years since slavery is not a very long time for a total social metamorphosis even under fostering conditions—and during that period the Negro community has been for the most part economically marginal and isolated from the contacts which would have accelerated change. The thirteen depressions and recessions we have had since Emancipation have been devastating to this community. These marginal economic and encapsulated social circumstances have been particularly harsh on the Negro male. The chronic instability has greatly influenced the Negro man's concept of himself and his general motivation to succeed in competitive areas of society where the rewards are greatest. All these circumstances have contributed to the instability of the Negro family, and particularly to the fact that it is most often broken by the absence of the father. As a result, the lower-class Negro child entering school often has had no experience with a "successful" male model or thereby with a psychological framework in which effort can result in at least the possibility of achievement. Yet the value system of the school and of the learning process is predicated on the assumption that effort will result in achievement.

To a large extent, much of this is true not only for the Negro child but for all children who come from impoverished and marginal social and economic conditions. These living conditions are characterized by great overcrowding in substandard housing, often lacking adequate sanitary and other facilities. While we don't know the actual importance, for example, of moments of privacy, we do know that the opportunity frequently does not exist. In addition, there are likely to be large numbers of siblings and half-siblings, again with there being little opportunity for individuation. At the same time, the child tends to be restricted to his immediate environment, with conducted explorations of the "outside" world being infrequent and sometimes non-existent. In the slums, and to an unfortunately large extent in many other areas of our largest cities, there is little opportunity to observe natural beauty, clean landscapes or other pleasant and aesthetically pleasing surroundings.

In the child's home, there is a scarcity of objects of all types, but especially of books, toys, puzzles, pencils, and scribbling paper. It is not that the mere presence of such materials would necessarily result in their productive use, but it would increase the child's familiarity with the tools he'll be confronted with in school. Actually, for the most effective utilization of these tools, guidance and explanations are necessary from the earliest time of exposure. Such guidance requires not only the presence of aware and educated adults, but also time—a rare commodity in these marginal circumstances. Though many parents will share in the larger value system of having high aspirations for their children, they are unaware of the operational steps required for the preparation of the child to use optimally the learning opportunities in the school. Individual potential is one of the most unmarketable properties if the child acquires no means for its development, or if no means exist for measuring it objectively. It is here that we must understand the consequences of all these aspects of the slum matrix for the psychological and cognitive development of the child.

Psychological Factors

A child from any circumstance who has been deprived of a substantial portion of the variety of stimuli which he is maturationally capable of responding to is likely to be deficient in the equipment required for learning.

Support for this is found in Hunt who, in discussing Piaget's developmental theories, points out that, according to Piaget, ". . . the rate of development is in substantial part, but certainly not wholly, a function of environmental circumstances. Change in circumstances is required to force the accommodative modifications of schemata that constitute development. Thus, the greater the variety of situations to which the child must accommodate his behavioral structures, the more differentiated and mobile they become. Thus, the more new things a child has seen and the more he has heard, the more things he is interested in seeing and hearing. Moreover, the more variation in reality with which he has coped, the greater is his capacity for coping."

This emphasis on the importance of variety in the environment implies the detrimental effects of lack of variety. This in turn leads to a concept of "stimulus deprivation." But it is important that it be correctly understood. By this is not necessarily meant any restriction of the quantity of stimulation, but, rather, a restriction to a segment of the spectrum of stimulation potentially available. In addition to the restriction in variety, from what is known of slum environment, it might be postulated that the segments made available to these children tend to have poorer and less systematic ordering of stimulation sequences, and would thereby be less useful to the growth and activation of cognitive potential.

This deprivation has effects on both the formal and the contentual aspects of cognition. By "formal" is meant the operations—the behavior —by which stimuli are perceived, encouraged, and responded to. By "contentual" is meant the actual content of the child's knowledge and comprehension. "Formal equipment" would include perceptual discrimination skills, the ability to sustain attention, and the ability to use adults as sources of information and for satisfying curiosity. Also included would be the establishment of expectations of reward from accumulation of knowledge, from task completion, and from adult reinforcement, and the ability to delay gratification. Examples of "contentual equipment" would be the language-symbolic system, environmental information, general and environmental orientation, and concepts of comparability and relativity appropriate to the child's age level. The growth of a differentiated additudinal set toward learning is probably a resultant of the interaction between formal and contextual levels.

Hypothesizing that stimulus deprivation will result in deficiencies in either of these equipments, let us examine the particular stimuli which are available and those which are absent from the environment of the child who comes from the conditions discussed above. This reasoning suggests also certain hypotheses regarding the role of environment in the evolving of the formal and contextual systems.

As was pointed out in the previous section, the disadvantaged environment as well as certain aspects of the middle-class circumstance offers the child, over-all, a restricted range of experience. While one does see great individual variability in these children, social conditions reduce the range of this variation; with less variety in input, it would be reasonable to assume a concomitant restriction in the variety of output. This is an important respect in which social poverty may have a leveling effect on the achievement of individual skills and abilities. Concomitantly, in the current problem of extensive under-achievement in suburban lower-middle-class areas, the over-routinization of activity with the consequent reduction in variety may well be the major factor.

In individual terms, a child is probably farther away from his maturational ceiling as a result of this experiential poverty. This might well be a crucial factor in the poorer performance of the lower socioeconomic children on standardized tests of intelligence. On such tests, the child is compared with others of his own age. But if his point of development in relation to the maturational ceiling for his age group is influenced by his experience, then the child with restricted experience may actually be developed to a proportionately lower level of his own actual ceiling. If a certain quantum of fostering experience is necessary to activate the achievment of particular maturational levels, then perhaps the child who is deficient in this experience will take longer to achieve these levels, even though his potential may be the same as the more advantaged child. It might be that in order to achieve a realistic appraisal of the ability levels of children, an "experience" age rather than the chronological age should be used to arrive at norms.

This suggests a limitation on the frequent studies comparing Negro and white children. Even when it is possible to control for the formal attributes of social class membership, the uniqueness of the Negro child's experience would make comparability impossible when limited to these class factors. Perhaps too, if such an interaction exists between experiential and biological determinants of development, it would account for the failure of the culture-free tests, as they too are standardized on an age basis without allowing for the experimental interaction (as distinguished from specific experimental *influence*).

Let us now consider some of the specifics in the child's environment, and their effects on the development of the formal, contextual, and attitudinal systems.

Visually, the urban slum and its overcrowded apartments offer the child a minimal range of stimuli. There are usually few if any pictures on the wall, and the objects in the household, be they toys, furniture, or utensils, tend to be sparse, repetitious, and lacking in form and color variations. The sparsity of objects and lack of diversity of home artifacts which are available and meaningful to the child, in addition to the unavailability of individualized training, gives the child few opportunities to manipulate and organize the visual properties of his environment and thus perceptually to organize and discriminate the nuances of that environment. These would include figure-ground relationships and the spatial organization of the visual field. The sparsity of manipulable objects probably also hampers the development of these functions in the tactile area. For example, while these children have broomsticks and usually a ball, possibly a doll or a discarded kitchen pot to play with, they don't have the different shapes and colors and sizes to manipulate which the middle-class child has in the form of blocks which are bought just for him, or even in the variety of sizes and shapes of cooking utensils which might be available to him as playthings.

It is true, as has been pointed out frequently, that the pioneer child didn't have many playthings either. But he had a more active responsibility toward the environment and a great variety of growing plants and other natural resources as well as a stable family that assumed a primary role for the education and training of the child. In addition, the intellectually normal or superior frontier child could and usually did grow up to be a farmer. Today's child will grow up into a world of automation requiring highly differentiated skills if he and society are to use his intellect.

The effect of sparsity of manipulable objects on visual perception is, of course, quite speculative, as few data now exist. However, it is an important area, as among skills necessary for reading are form discrimination and visual spatial organization. Children from depressed areas, because of inadequate training and stimulation, may not have developed the requisite skills by the time they enter first grade, and the assumption that they do possess these skills may thus add to the frustration these children experience on entering school.

The lower-class home is not a verbally oriented environment. The implications of this for language development will be considered below in the discussion of the contentual systems. Here let us consider its implication for the development of auditory discrimination skills. While the environment is a noisy one, the noise is not, for the most part, meaningful in relation to the child, and for him most of it is background. In the crowded apartments with all the daily living stresses, a minimum of non-instructional conversation is directed toward the child. In actuality, the situation is ideal for the child to learn inattention. Furthermore, he does not get practice in auditory discrimination or feedback from adults correcting his enunciation, pronunciation, and grammar. In studies at the Institute for Developmental Studies at New York Medical College, as yet unreported in the literature, we have found significant differences in auditory discrimination between lower-class and middle-class children in the first grade. These differences seem to diminish markedly as the children get older, though the effects of their early existence on other functioning remain to be investigated. Here again, we are dealing with a skill very important to reading. Our data indicate too that poor readers within social-class groups have significantly more difficulty in auditory discrimination than do good readers. Further, this difference between good and poor readers is greater for the lower-class group.

If the child learns to be inattentive in the pre-school environment, as has been postulated, this further diminishes incoming stimulation. Further, if this trained inattention comes about as a result of his being insufficiently called upon to respond to particular stimuli, then his general level of responsiveness will also be diminished. The nature of the total environment and the child-adult interaction is such that reinforcement is too infrequent, and, as a result, the quantity of response is diminished. The implications of this for the structured learning situation in the school are quite obvious.

Related to attentivity is memory. Here also we would postulate the dependence of the child, particularly in the pre-school period, on interaction with the parent. It is adults who link the past and the present by calling to mind prior shared experiences. The combination of the constriction in the use of language and in shared activity results, for the lower-class child, in much less stimulation of the early memory function. Although I don't know of any data supporting this thesis, from my observations it would seem that there is a tendency for these children to be proportionately more present-oriented and less aware of past-present sequences than the middle-class child. This is consistent with anthropological research and thinking. While this could be a function of the poorer time orientation of these children or of their difficulty in verbal, expression, both of which will be discussed, it could also relate to a greater difficulty in seeing themselves in the past or in a different context. Another area which points up the home-school discontinuity is that of time. Anthropologists have pointed out that from culture to culture time concepts differ and that time as life's governor is a relatively modern phenomenon and one which finds most of its slaves in the lower-middle, middle-middle, and upper-middle classes. It might not even be an important factor in learning, but it is an essential feature in the measurement of children's performance by testing and in the adjustment of children to the organizational demands of the school. The middle-class teacher organizes the day by allowing a certain amount of time for each activity. Psychologists have long noticed that American Indian children, mountain children, and children from other non-industrial groups have great difficulty organizing their response tempo to meet time limitations. In the Orientation Scale developed at the Institute, we have found that lower-class children in the first grade had significantly greater difficulty than did middle-class children in handling items related to time judgments.

Another area in which the lower-class child lacks pre-school orientation is the well-inculcated expectation of reward for performance, especially for successful task completion. The lack of such expectation, of course, reduces motivation for beginning a task and, therefore, also makes less likely the self-reinforcement of activity through the gaining of feelings of competence. In these impoverished, broken homes there is very little of the type of interaction seen so commonly in middle-class homes, in which the parent sets a task for the child, observes its performance, and in some way rewards its completion. Neither, for most tasks, is there the disapproval which the middle-class child incurs when he does not perform properly or when he leaves something unfinished. Again, much of the organization of the classroom is based on the assumption that children anticipate rewards for performance and that they will respond in these terms to tasks which are set for them. This is not to imply that the young lower-class child is not given assignments in his home, nor that he is never given approval or punishment. Rather, the assignments tend to be motoric in character, have a short-time span, and are more likely to relate to very concrete objects or services for people. The tasks given to pre-school children in the middle-class are more likely to involve language and conceptual processes, and are thereby more attuned to the later school setting.

Related to the whole issue of the adult-child dynamic in establishing a basis for the later learning process is the ability of the child to use the adult as a source for information, correction and the reality testing involved in problem solving and the absorption of new knowledge. When free adult time is greatly limited, homes vastly overcrowded, economic stress chronic, and the general educational level very low—and, in addition, when adults in our media culture are aware of the inadequacy of their education—questions from children are not encouraged, as the adults might be embarrassed by their own limitations and anyway are too preoccupied with the business of just living and surviving. In the child's formulation of concepts of the world, the ability to formulate questions is an essential step in data gathering. If questions are not encouraged or if they are not responded to, this is a function which does not mature.

At the Institute, in our observations of children at the kindergarten level and in our discussions with parents, we find that many lower-class children have difficulty here. It follows that this problem, if it is not compensated for by special school efforts, becomes more serious later in the learning process, as more complex subject matter is introduced. It is here that questioning is not only desirable but essential, for if the child is not prepared to demand clarification he again falls farther behind, the process of alienation from school is facilitated, and his inattentiveness becomes further reinforced as he just does not understand what is being presented.

It is generally agreed that the language-symbolic process plays an important role at all levels of learning. It is included here under the "contextual" rubric because language development evolves through the correct labeling of the environment, and through the use of appropriate words for the relating and combining and recombining of the concrete and abstract components in describing, interpreting, and communicating perceptions, experiences, and ideational matter. One can postulate on considerable evidence that language is one of the areas which is most sensitive to the impact of the multiplicity of problems associated with the stimulus deprivation found in the marginal circumstances of lower-class life. There are various dimensions of language, and for each of these it is possible to evaluate the influence of the verbal environment of the home and its immediate neighborhood.

In order for a child to handle multiple attributes of words and to associate words with their proper referents, a great deal of exposure to language is presupposed. Such exposure involves training, experimenting with identifying objects and having corrective feedback, listening to a variety of verbal material, and just observing adult language usage. Exposure of children to this type of experience is one of the great strengths of the middle-class home, and concomitantly represents a weakness in the lower-class home. In a middle-class home also, the availability of a great range of objects to be labeled and verbally related to each other strengthens the over-all language fluency of the child and gives him a basis for both understanding the teacher and for being able to communicate with her on various levels. An implicit hypothesis in a recent Institute survey of verbal skills is that verbal fluency is strongly related to reading skills and to other highly organized integrative and conceptual verbal activity.

The acquisition of language facility and fluency and experience with the multiple attributes of words is particularly important in view of the estimate that only 60 to 80 percent of any sustained communication is usually heard. Knowledge of context and of the syntactical regularities of a language make correct completion and comprehension of the speech sequence possible. This completion occurs as a result of the correct anticipation of the sequence of language and thought. The child who has not achieved these anticipatory language skills is greatly handicapped in school. Thus for the child who already is deficient in auditory discrimination and in ability to sustain attention, it becomes increasingly important that he have the very skills he lacks most.

The problem in developing preventive and early remedial programs for these children is in determining the emphasis on the various areas that need remediation. For example, would it be more effective to place the greatest emphasis on the training of auditory discrimination, or on attentional mechanisms, or on anticipatory receptive language functions in order to achieve the primary goal of enabling the child to understand his teacher? In programming special remedial procedures, we do not know how much variation we will find from child to child, or if social-class experiences create a sufficiently homogeneous pattern of deficit so that the fact of any intervention and systematic training may be more important than its sequences. If this is so, the intervention would probably be most valid in the language area, because the large group of lower-class children with the kinds of deficits mentioned are probably maturationally ready for more complex language functioning than they have achieved. Language knowledge, once acquired, can be self-reinforcing in just communicating with peers or talking to oneself.

In observations of lower-class homes, it appears that speech sequences seem to be temporally very limited and poorly structured syntactically. It is thus not surprising to find that a major focus of deficit in the children's language development is syntactical organization and subject continuity. In preliminary analysis of expressive and receptive language data on samples of middle- and lower-class children at the first- and fifth-grade levels, there are indications that the lower-class child has more expressive language ability than is generally recognized or than emerges in the classroom. The main differences between the social classes seem to lie in the level of syntactical organization. If, as is indicated in this research, with proper stimulation a surprisingly high level of expressive language functioning is available to the same children who show syntactical deficits, then we might conclude that the language variables we are dealing with here are by-products of social experience rather than indices of basic ability or intellectual level. This again suggests another possibly vital area to be included in an enrichment or a remedial program: training in the use of word sequences to relate and unify cognitions.

Also on the basis of preliminary analysis of data, it appears that retarded readers have the most difficulty with the organization of expressive language.

In another type of social-class-related language analysis, Bernstein (1960), an English sociologist, has pointed out that the lower-class tends to use informal language and mainly to convey concrete needs and immediate consequences, while the middle-class usage tends to be more formal and to emphasize the relating of concepts. This difference between these two milieus, then, might explain the finding in some of our recent research that the middle-class fifth-grade child has an advantage over the lower-class fifth grader in tasks where precise and somewhat abstract language is required for solution. Further, Bernstein's reasoning would again emphasize the communication gap which exists between the middle-class teacher and the lower-class child.

Though it might belong more in the formal than in the contextual area, one can postulate that the absence of well-structured routine and activity in the home is reflected in the difficulty that the lower-class child has in structuring language. The implication of this for curriculum in the kindergarten and nursery school would be that these children should be offered a great deal of verbalized routine and regulation so that expectation can be built up in the child and then met.

According to Piaget's theories, later problem-solving and logical abilities are built on the earlier and orderly progression through a series of developmental stages involving the active interaction between the child and his environment. This is considered a maturational process, though highly related to experience and practice. Language development does not occupy a super-ordinate position. However, Whorf, Vygotsky, and some contemporary theorists have made language the essential ingredient in concept formation, problem-solving, and in the relating to an interpretation of the environment. Current data at the Institute tend to indicate that class differences in perceptual abilities and in general environmental orientation decrease with chronological age, whereas language differences tend to increase. These might tentatively be interpreted to mean that perceptual development occurs first and that language growth and its importance in problem solving comes later. If later data and further analysis support this interpretation, then the implication would be that the lower-class child comes to school with major deficits in the perceptual rather than the language area. Perhaps the poverty of his experience has slowed his rate of maturation. Then by requiring, without the antecedent verbal preparation, a relatively high level of language skill, the school may contribute to an increase in the child's deficit in this area, relative to middle-class children. Meanwhile, his increased experience and normal maturational processes stimulate perceptual development, and that deficit is overcome. But the child is left with a language handicap. The remedy for such a situation would be emphasis on perceptual training for these children in the early school, or, better, pre-school, years, combined with a more gradual introduction of language training and requirements.

This theory and interpretation are somewhat, but by no means wholly, in conflict with the previous discussion of language. In an area where there is as yet much uncertainty, it is important to consider as many alternatives as possible, in order not to restrict experimentation.

In any event, whether or not we consider language skills as primary mediators in concept formation and problem solving, the lower-class child seems to be at a disadvantage at the point of entry into the formal learning process.

The other contentual factors that so often result in a poorly prepared child being brought to the school situation are closely interrelated with language. Briefly, they revolve around the child's understanding and knowledge of the physical, geographic, and geometric characteristics of the world around him, as well as information about his self-identity and some of the more macroscopic items of general information. It could be reasonably expected, for example, that a kindergarten or first-grade child who is not mentally defective would know both his first and last names, his address or the city he lives in, would have a rudimentary concept of number relationships, and would know something about the differences between near and far, high and low, and similar relational concepts. Much of what happens in school is predicated on the prior availability of this basic information. We know that educational procedures frequently proceed without establishing the actual existence of such a baseline. Again, in the lower-class child it cannot be taken for granted that the home experience has supplied this information or that it has tested the child for this knowledge. In facilitating the learning process in these children, the school must expect frequently to do a portion of the job traditionally assigned to the home, and curriculum must be reorganized to provide for establishing a good base. This type of basic information is essential so that the child can relate the input of new information to some stable core.

From all of the foregoing, it is obvious that the lower-class child when he enters school has as many problems in understanding what it is all about and why he is there as school personnel have in relating traditional curriculum and learning procedures to this child. Some reorientation is really necessary, as discussion of these problems almost always focuses on the problems the school has, rather than on the enormous confusion, hesitations, and frustrations the child experiences and does not have the language to articulate when he meets an essentially rigid set of academic expectations. Again, from all the foregoing, the child, from the time he enters school and is exposed to assumptions about him derived from experience with the middle-class child, has few success experiences and much failure and generalized frustration, and thus begins the alienating process.

The frustration inherent in not understanding, not succeeding, and not being stimulated in the school—although being regulated by it, creates a basis for the further development of negative self-images and low evaluations of individual competencies. This would be especially true for the Negro child who, as we know from doll-play and other studies, starts reflecting the social bias in his own self-image at a very early age. No matter how the parents might aspire to a higher achievement level for their child, their lack of knowledge as to the operational implementation, combined with the child's early failure experiences in school, can so effectively attenuate confidence in his ability ever to handle competently challenge in the academic area, that the child loses all motivation.

It is important to state that not all the negative factors and deficits discussed here are present in every or even in any one child. Rather, there is a patterning of socially determined school-achievement-related disabilities which tends initially to set artificially low ceilings for these children: initially artificial, because as age increases it becomes more and more difficult for these children to develop compensatory mechanisms, to respond to special programs, or to make the psychological readjustments required to overcome the cumulative effects of their early deficits.

It is also important to state that there are strengths and positive features associated with lower-class life. Unfortunately, they generally tend not to be, at least immediately, congruent with the demands of the school. For example, lack of close supervision or protection fosters the growth of independence in lower-class children. However, this independence—and probably confidence—in regard to the handling of younger siblings, the crossing of streets, self-care, and creating of their own amusements, does not necessarily meaningfully transfer to the unfamiliar world of books, language, and abstract thought.

School Conditions

Educational factors have of course been interlaced throughout this discussion, but there are some special features that need separate delineation.

The lower-class child probably enters school with a nebulous and essentially neutral attitude. His home rarely, if ever, negatively predisposes him toward the school situation, though it might not offer positive motivation and correct interpretation of the school experience. It is in the school situation that the highly charged negative attitudes toward learning evolve, and the responsibility for such large groups of normal children showing great scholastic retardation, the high drop-out rate, and to some extent the delinquency problem, must rest with the failure of the school to promote the proper acculturation of these children. Though some of the responsibility may be shared by the larger society, the school, as the institution of that society, offers the only mechanism by which the job can be done.

It is unfair to imply that the school has all the appropriate methods at its disposal and has somehow chosen not to apply them. On the contrary, what is called for is flexible experimentation in the development of new methods, the clear delineation of the problem, and the training and retraining of administrative and teaching personnel in the educational philosophy and the learning procedures that this problem requires.

In addition, the school should assume responsibility for a systematic plan for the education of the child in the areas that have been delineated here by the time the child reaches kindergarten or first grade. This does not mean that the school will abrogate the family's role with regard to the child, but rather that the school will insure both the intellectual and the attitudinal receptivity of each child to its requirements. Part of a hypothesis now being tested in a new pre-school program is based on the assumption that early intervention by well-structured programs will significantly reduce the attenuating influence of the socially marginal environment.

What might be necessary to establish the required base to assure the eventual full participation of these children in the opportunity structure offered by the educational system is an ungraded sequence from age 3 or 4 through 8, with a low teacher-pupil ratio. Perhaps, also, the school system should make full use of anthropologists, sociologists, and social psychologists for description and interpretation of the cultural discontinuities which face the individual child when he enters school. In addition, the previously discussed patterning of deficits and strengths should be evaluated for each child and placed in a format which the teacher can use as a guide. In the early years this would enable diagnostic reviews of the intellectual functioning of each child, so that learning procedures, to whatever extent possible, could be appropriate to a particular child's needs. New evaluation techniques must be developed for this purpose, as the standardized procedures generally cannot produce accurate evaluation of the functioning level or achievement potential of these children.

Possibly most important would be the greater utilization by educators in both curriculum development and teacher training of the new and enormous knowledge, techniques, and researches in the social and behavioral sciences. Similarly, social and behavioral scientists have in the school a wonderful laboratory to study the interpenetration and interaction of fundamental social, cognitive, psychological, and developmental processes. Close and continuing collaboration, thus, should be mutually productive and satisfying, and is strongly indicated.

References

1. Bernstein, B., "Language and Social Class," *Brit. J. Psychol.*, 11:271–76, September 1960.

2. Hunt, J. McV. *Intelligence and Experience.* New York: Ronald Press, 1961.

The New York School Crisis

Jeremy Larner

[Excerpted from the article, "The New York School Crisis," by Jeremy Larner with permission, from Dissent, *Spring 1964.]*

The Circumstances

UFT OFFICIAL: *Why is it we can get young people to volunteer for the Peace Corps to teach in Ghana, yet we can't get them to teach in public schools in Harlem? Answer: Because in Ghana, there's hope.*

LET ME START WITH SOME STATISTICS. There are 132 elementary schools and 31 junior high schools in New York City whose students are almost entirely (over 90% in the elementary schools; over 85% in the junior highs) Negro and Puerto Rican. In the past six years, while Negro and Puerto Rican enrollment has gone up 53%, white enrollment has fallen 8%, and the number of predominantly Negro and Puerto Rican schools has doubled. Of New York's one million schoolchildren, roughly 40% are Negro and Puerto Rican, 60% "other." Efforts of the Board of Education in the past six years to eliminate blatant gerrymandering and allow some voluntary transfers have reduced by a third the number of schools where Negroes and Puerto Ricans are less than 10% of enrollment. But the problem gets more difficult all the time, as is indicated by the fact that 52%—an outright majority—of the city's 1st graders are Negro or Puerto Rican.

The increase in segregated schools is due to three factors. First, rural minority groups are moving into the city and middle-class urban whites are heading for the suburbs. Second, discrimination, economic pressures, and lack of effective planning confine the newcomers to ghettoes. Third, cautious whites send their children to private or parochial schools rather than "risk" a neighborhood school where minorities predominate. Over 450,000 New York children attend private or parochial schools, a figure that would represent a staggering percentage even for an exclusive suburb.

Thus New York City suffers from an educational problem which it has come to describe as *de facto* segregation. The Board of Education says the facts are essentially beyond its control; the civil rights groups say they are the facts of a racist society, and must in all justice be eliminated by whatever means possible.

Segregation in ghetto schools is more than racial; there is segregation by economic class as well. Wherever Negro parents reach the middle class, at least some of them send their kids to private schools. Lower-class Negro kids find themselves isolated in schools which are understaffed, underequipped, overcrowded, demoralized, and conspicuously lacking in the mixture of cultural backgrounds which can make life in New York such an educational experience. Many of them are children of parents who are in effect first-generation immigrants from southern and rural areas; for of New York's 1,100,000 Negroes, 340,000 have arrived in the last ten years, 630,000 in the last twenty years. Most of the 600,000 Puerto Ricans have come in the past decade, while the white population has dwindled by 500,000.

Teaching middle-class children the ins and outs of a culture made for them is obviously easier than struggling with ghetto children, most of whom are members of a racial group which has never been allowed to recover from the effects of slavery. Some minority schools have annual teacher turnover rates of over 60%. Some teachers flatly refuse to take assignments in such schools; others drop out as the school year proceeds. Not only is one out of every two teachers a substitute, but some classes may stay without a regularly assigned teacher all year, defeating one temporary substitute after another. One can see that the atmosphere in minority schools is hardly conducive to learning. It is estimated that 85% of the 8th-grade students in Harlem are "functional illiterates," which means that their reading is not above 5th-grade level —in many cases it is much below.

Though some authorities, e.g. Kenneth Clark, disagree, it is hard to believe that the social conditions under which most New York Negroes live are not responsible for some of the difficulty. According to the Harlem Youth survey, whose figures many observers regard as conservative, only one-half of Harlem children under 18 are living with both parents, more than one-quarter of Harlem youth receives welfare assistance, and the rate of narcotics addiction in the area is ten times that for the rest of the city.

By the time they reach junior high school, ghetto children are well aware of their social situation, and it does not exactly give them a feeling of unlimited possibilities. Let me quote from two batches of essays which were gathered at different Harlem elementary schools from a 6th-grade class of "slow" readers (S) and a 6th-grade class of "fast" readers (F). I think the language shows as much about the children—their educational retardation and yet their straightforwardness and toughness—as about the conditions they describe.

> *6th-grade boy* (F): This story is about a boy namely me, who lives in a apartment in and around the slum area. I feel that other people should be interested in what I have to say and just like me, *try* to do something about it, either by literal or diatribe means. This book is only to be read by men and women boys and girls who feel deeply serious about segrigation and feel that this is no joke.

> *6th-grade girl* (S): I am not satifeyed with the dope addictes around our block. They take dope in our hallway every night. Another is they break in stores and bars. I am desatifed with the lady that live under us. she set fire to Doris's door. Some dope backs live under us. The lady under us robbed Teddy's aunt for $17.00's. One night a dope addict went cazey in our hally way. They are so many bums in our block. Please help to get and keep them out.

> *6th-grade girl* (S): I don't like people going around youing bad Lanugwsh around litter Kide a bearking in Store and fighting and youing dop. And Killing people. And drunk in hallwall. They should stop drink They are teacher the Kide how to Steel I see it alot of tim but I dont pay it no mind I am surrounded by them.

> *6th-grade boy* (S): Im not happy about the people who dink. wiskey and go to sleep And I not happy about the peole who come in my hallway and go up stairs and take a neals and. stick there themselve in the arm. I am not happy about the people who buy wine and wiskey and broke the bottle in the hallway

> *6th-grade girl* (S): the be out there in the hall taking dope and I be freighten.

> *6th-grade boy* (S): I deslike the peple being hit by cars, the car crashes, peple fighting, the peple jumping of roofes, stelling paper from the stores, peple picking pocketes, the peple with out thir cubs on dogs and stop peple from taking dop in this naborhood.

6th-grade girl (F): (True) *What a Block!* (true)

My block is the most terrible block I've ever seen. There are at lease 25 or 30 narcartic people in my block. The cops come around there and tries to act bad but I bet inside of them they are as scared as can be. They even had in the papers that this block is the worst block, not in Manhattan but in New York City. In the summer they don't do nothing except shooting, stabing, and fighting. They hang all over the stoops and when you say excuse me to them they hear you but they just don't feel like moving. Some times they make me so mad that I feel like slaping them and stuffing bag of garbage down their throats.

The fact that these kids have been encouraged to describe their surroundings is the first sign of hope that they will be able to change them. The school should represent that possibility; it should be a fortress of security in which the children are respected, accepted and developed. Otherwise they are surrounded, as the little girl says; drug addiction, for example, will begin to appear in their ranks while they are still in junior high school—and addiction is only the most dramatic form of withdrawal and defeat.

Looking around him, the young Negro boy will find few "father figures" to imitate; for the men of his world have not been accorded the honorable work men need to earn self-respect. Bitter, confused, withdrawn, violent against one another, lower-class Negro men do not usually last long with their women. The families are matriarchal, the children remaining with their mothers while a successions of "uncles" come and go. There is small hope of that masculine self-respect which is the traditional basis of family pride. The little boy is regarded as inferior to the little girl, and has less chance of survival—by which I mean simply less chance of getting through life without cracking up, without sliding into some form of self-obliteration.

Dismal to tell, the schools in many ways duplicate the situation of the homes. The classroom confronts the child with the same old arrangement: a woman with too many kids. Far too few of the elementary schoolteachers are men, let alone Negro men. The size of classes, usually around 30 pupils per class, makes individual attention—and thus the development of positive identity and incentive—as unlikely at school as it is at home.

When lower-class Negro children enter elementary school, they are already "behind" in several important respects. In crowded tenement apartments children are in the way from the moment they are born. While the adults of the matriachal clan unit work or wander, children are brought up by older children, who have reasons of their own to feel impatient or harassed. According to the teacher whose "fast" 6th-grade pupils I quoted above,

. . . middle-class Negro kids need integration. But what the lower-class kids need right now is that somehow we conquer the chaos they live in. They have no stability whatever—no family, no home, no one to talk with them. They live in a world without space or time. I mean that literally. Even by the time these kids reach the 6th grade, most of them can't tell time. You can't talk to them about the future—say, about jobs—because they won't know what you're talking about. And when you refer to concepts of space, why you can't talk about "somewhere else," tell how far away another city is, how long a river is, or simple facts of geography. Though they're fantastically sophisticated, more sophisticated than maybe they ought to be, about how adults behave, their mental orientation is almost utterly without abstract concepts. Look: they don't even know who pays the welfare! They don't even know what checks are!

Of course this particular teacher will get his kids talking and thinking about time and space and jobs and where the money comes from. But there aren't enough like him, and one year of a good teacher can dispel the chaos for very few. The class he has taken such pains with finds itself a year later without an assigned teacher, and the boy who last year wrote a brilliant autobiography is in danger this year of flunking at junior high, breaking down, and spending his high school years in and out of institutions.

Why don't teachers make more progress with these children? Because they are woefully short of books and materials, especially good readers based on the facts of urban life. Because they have to spend so much time on discipline.[1] Because they get poor support from their principals and from the rest of the top-heavy school bureaucracy. But the truth is that most of New York's teachers are too middle-class, too insensitive or too fragile to teach ghetto children successfully. Not that they are worse than teachers in other places, they are simply less suited to their jobs. Not all of them are bothered by their failure; some stay in slum schools because apparently it gives them a sense of security to blame the kids for what they fail to teach them. Others, with the best will in the world, are baffled by children who literally speak a different language. One young white teacher, extremely hard-working and perhaps more honest than most, told me after a grueling day,

I hate these kids. They're impossible. How did they get this way? I never thought I'd become so authoritarian.

---

[1] Discipline as opposed to socialization. The 6th-grade teacher quoted above reports that with a "slow" class he begins with checkers, and that it takes weeks to get the children to play together without turning over the board and having at each other. Then he brings out the readers.

Most of the teachers are conscientious: that's one of the hallmarks of the professional person. But the manner in which teachers are trained and chosen—which I will discuss below—is practically guaranteed to eliminate those possessing the imagination and flexibility to get through to slum children.

As for the curriculum, it is hopelessly inappropriate. The readers still current in practically every school are those insipid productions featuring Sally, Dick and Jane, the golden-haired cardboard tots from Sterilityville. One could go on by describing a series of tests and achievement-levels, but tests and levels are irrelevant to children who mostly do not pass or reach them. Let me quote Martin Mayer (from his book, *The Schools*) on what our young tenement-dwellers are supposed to be learning by the time they get to high school:

> In New York . . . the major Theme Center for tenth-grade "Language Arts" is "Learning to Live with the Family." . . . The curriculum guide suggests "round-table, panel, and forum discussions" on "questions relating to allowances, dating, working after school, selecting and entertaining friends, choosing a career, minding younger brothers and sisters, helping with household chores, contributing earnings to the family, decorating one's own room, choosing family vacation places, using the family car."

But what difference does high school make? The battle is lost long before then. Perhaps it's already lost by the time 1st graders move to the 2nd grade, when only 10% of them are on reading level.

Yet, when all is said and done, are not these conditions surmountable by individual effort? Is it not possible for the majority of these youngsters to pull themselves up by their own bootstraps, as so many of their 2nd-generation American teachers say that they or their parents did? Or is this problem unique somehow, does it have to do with the unprecedented oppression and separation of a group that has never in the history of this country been free? Is it really true, as the 1954 Supreme Court decision contends, that "Segregation of white and colored children in public schools has a detrimental effect upon the colored children. . . . A sense of inferiority affects the motivation of the child to learn"?

In the opinion of this observer, no one could sit for long in Harlem classes without seeing overwhelming evidence of the demoralizing effects of segregation. These children are treated as inferior, just as their parents and grandparents and great-grandparents were—and there is no sense of any possibility that such treatment is ending! In the classroom of a 1st-grade teacher who was a militant supporter of the boycott, I was surprised to find cut-out pictures of white children used almost exclusively as bulletin board illustrations. Later I found the purified faces of Sally, Dick and Jane beaming out at me in ghetto classrooms of teachers Negro or white, liberal or not: as if to say, these are what good children are like.

> *5th-grade Lower East Side boy* (F): I have a problem that I am colored. I would like to be handsom but I cant because other people have strait blond hair and they are handsom.

In a 2nd-grade Harlem classroom the teacher, a lively, intelligent Negro woman, has her kids acting out a nursery tale. In front of the class stands a shy, finger-sucking little girl, her hair in pigtails, absolutely adorable and black. From her neck hangs a large square of cardboard, on which an adult has painted the head of a white girl with abundantly flowing golden hair. Caption: "GOLDILOCKS."

In another 2nd-grade classroom, where well cared-for Negro children are industriously and quietly working under the direction of a Negro teacher, I glance up and see a row of self-portraits above the front blackboard. I count: of 23 portraits, 1 red, 1 green, only 2 brown, and 19 white as the paper they're drawn on.

The sense of inferiority runs deeper than skin-deep. I remember a junior-high-school social-studies teacher trying to discuss the school boycott with his 9th-grade "slow" pupils. Most of them are long since lost; they look as though they have drawn curtains across the inside of their eyeballs. It develops that they do not know the words "boycott" or "civil rights," and to them "discrimination" is something that happens down South. And oh the tortured embarrassment with which they answer questions! From beneath the embarrassment there slinks a kind of arrogance, thriving it seems on the mere fact that the teacher is trying to teach them—as if to say, imagine this fool, asking *me* a question! Whereupon they laugh. They have to. And we are all relieved.

Whether they know the word "discrimination" or not, these kids know they are not worth much to the world they live in. Some of them, all too many, are not worth much to themselves, and lash out in self-hating violence at the nearest target, usually someone who reminds them of themselves. Already the white people of America are beginning to dread the day when these children, as some day they surely must, will recognize their real enemies. As they are at last beginning to . . .

> *West Harlem 6th-grade boy* (F): Teacher! In the caveman days, if there were Negro cavemen, did the white cavemen use them as slaves? . . .

The Aftereffects

What effects did the 1964 New York City school boycott have? In terms of Negro self-respect, undoubtedly positive. In terms of its own objectives, too, it was successful, forcing a more definite integration plan than the Board of Ed would ever have volunteered.[2] But in other areas the effects were moot.

The Schools

Anyone who knows anything about the New York schools cannot help but be uneasy about the gap between the strategy of the boycott and the situation it attacks. The issue is by no means so simple as Galamison often made it out to be:

> We feel that if we desegregate the public schools, these other problems—like overcrowding, low curriculum, etc.—will go away. Like when you have an infection, and you take a shot of penicillin.

One problem that will not go away is that of money. In the 1964–65 state budget. New York City, which has 34% of the state's schoolchildren, is slated to receive only 25% of total state aid to schools. Due in part to the machinations of a rurally-dominated state legislature, the City and its residents pay 49.7% of all state taxes and get back only 37.3% in benefits. The rationale for low school aid is that New York has an abundance of taxable property with which to finance its schools; the catch is that the City also has stupendous upkeep expenses.

To be specific, the value of taxable property per pupil in New York City is $31,878, far above the state average of $26,600; and it is this ratio on which state aid is based. But whereas City taxes amount to $54.27 per $1000 of property valuation, the City spends $39.39 of that money for municipal purposes and only $14.88 for schools—which compares poorly with what is spent by surrounding districts. Even though the City tax rate is high, moreover, funds collected are minimized by the gross undervaluation of property holdings. Real estate in New York's five boroughs is currently valued at the bargain total of $35 billion; theoretically Manhattan is worth only $13.5 billion—but don't try to buy it if that's all you can raise. Furthermore, much of the non-school bite on New York's property taxes goes to pay for problems that only large cities have—such as the costs of tearing up streets and assigning extra police to direct traffic when property owners decide to pull down or put up new buildings for their private profit. And since current property taxes don't entirely cover the costs of municipal overburden, the City shifts the load to the public in regressive taxes such as the 4% city sales tax.

Financial shortages drastically affect the operation of the schools. According to a study of the New York schools sponsored jointly by the

---

[2] In September, 1964, however, the Board, under pressure from the well-financed P.A.T., ignored its "plan" and put into effect only two pairings.

PEA and the UFT, "30% of the daily instructional staff is made up of substitutes and other persons on similar temporary or emergency status."
The schools are short by 27,500 permanent staff members, including
12,500 "professionals" who would be required to bring the City up to
the *average only* of the school districts among which it once enjoyed
leadership. That leadership position was held in the early 1940's, before
suburban flight began in earnest, when the City spent more per child
than its suburbs did. Now it spends $200 per child less, which amounts
to about $200,000 per school and a total of $200 million per year simply
to bring the system up to par in staff, materials, textbooks and upkeep.[3]
The $200 million does not include extra funds urgently needed for
new construction.

At present, there is not enough room, time, or personnel to take
care of all the children. A major classroom problem is that one or two
children can disrupt an entire class and dissipate most of the teacher's
energy; and as one might expect, difficult children are more prevalent
in slum schools. According to one assistant principal,

> It's the 2–3% who are unteachable and uncontrollable—the ones with
> very deep emotional disturbances—who take so much time and trouble
> in the lower neighborhood schools. There's no place to put them. We
> can't even assign them to a "600" [special problems] school without
> their parents' permission. The "600" schools have no more room any-
> way. Sooner or later these kids are caught committing a serious crime:
> you send them to a judge and he sends them right back to school.

There are also curriculum problems which integration will not
necessarily solve. One of the most controversial is the practice of grouping the children according to reading level, and later, IQ test, so that
fast, "achieving" children are in a homogeneous group entirely separate
from the classrooms of the slow, "non-achieving" youngsters. One of the
effects of such grouping is that in schools where a small population of
whites remains, it is in effect segregated vertically in the advanced classrooms. So transporting kids from their neighborhoods will not by itself
guarantee them an integrated classroom experience; in fact, since most
Negro children lag in classroom skills, it might not do them much good
to be thrown in with white children of their own grade level—at least
not without drastic changes in the present set-up. Most experts now
agree, however, that homogeneous grouping leads to stereotyping of

---

[3] New York City school supplies and equipment are ordered from a purchasing manual through a central department which buys from designated contractors
at list price only—which is often two or three times the every-day retail price at
New York's discount houses.

individuals and is not desirable on the grade school level. To quote
Martin Mayer, "in New York, Wrightstone's study of comparative performance showed no significant advantage for bright kids grouped with
their fellows over bright kids scattered through the school at random."
But experts also agree that heterogeneous groupings cannot effectively
be taught unless class size is reduced to no more than 15 children, a
procedure which would require twice as many classrooms and teachers.
For the present, boycotters might take some satisfaction in a provision
of the February integration plan, wherein the Board agreed to eliminate IQ tests.

Also beyond the reach of the boycott is the teacher herself, who
is often unaware of her middle-class attitudes and the damage they do
her ability to teach. I remember one young teacher with an all-Negro
"slow" 1st grade, extremely conscientious and worried that she is not
more successful, yet unaware that her tone of voice is superior and hu-
morless. At any given moment, only about five of her children are paying attention, and at least three-quarters of the words she utters are
devoted to discipline. Let me give some flavor of her monologue:

> . . . well, why did you raise your hand if you had a pencil? I asked
> for only those who didn't have pencils to raise hands! That's not funny,
> Wilma! That's not funny! Boys and girls, we're not getting our work
> done and if we don't settle down we won't be able to have recess to-
> day. NOW I WON'T HAVE ANY MORE TALKING IN THIS ROOM! I'll start
> over again . . . we draw two lines across and that's the big A. Now
> I see that Freddy didn't hear me, Becky didn't hear me, Nicholas
> didn't hear me, Roger didn't hear me. And you're not looking! You
> can't learn to make the big A unless you're looking! Now can you
> make a big A? Let's see if you can. Raise hands if you need help. You
> don't have paper? Deborah, where is your paper? All right, I'll give
> you more . . .

After twenty minutes, a majority of the children are making big
A's. As the teacher starts on the little *a*, I do what most of the kids want
desperately to join me in: escape.

To give you an idea of these kids six years later, here is the teacher
of a 7th-grade English class.

> Now take a sheet of lined paper and write at the top "English notes."
> I want all of you to copy down right this second the facts I'm going
> to give you. Norman, would you be so kind as to put your hand down.
> Now your assignment is going to deal with this, so get these facts
> accurately. Hurry up, I haven't got too much time.

Unfortunately, teaching attracts types who enjoy relations where
they have undisputed superiority. Thus the effort to "understand the

disadvantaged child" turns out in practice to be the science of patron-
izing the slum-child without feeling guilty about it. For the disadvantaged child, of course, is really not that at all, no matter what it helps
one to know about his background: he is a person, and as such something splendid in his own right even before a teacher gets to him.

In every ghetto school I visited, teachers recommended a book
called *The Culturally Deprived Child* by Frank Riessman. Reading this
book, they told me, had helped them to understand the nature of the
children they had to deal with. Sure enough, I found Riessman's book
preaching "a sympathetic, noncondescending, understanding of the culture of the underprivileged." But neither Riessman nor the average
teacher realizes how un-noncondescending sympathy delivered from
the top can be:

> Moreover, self-expression and self-actualization, other aims of educa-
> tion, particularly modern education, are equally alien to the more
> pragmatic, traditional, underprivileged person.

No! You just can't talk that way about a child entering elementary school. Kids from "underprivileged" homes want to express themselves and realize themselves just as much as anyone else. Maybe the
most important thing for them is to have a teacher who will *expect*
something from them, let them know there is some authority who cares.
The best teacher I met in Harlem had taken a class of bright 6th graders
who up to that time were demoralized and undisciplined. Fortunately
he did not assume they weren't interested in self-expression. He assumed
that they had something to express, the fruits of their own experience,
which is in so many ways deeper and more demanding than that of
middle-class children. It was a long haul, after eleven years of neglect,
but eventually he got them writing and writing well. He read them
French translations and they wrote him parables and fables; it seems
Negro children are natural-born fable-writers, for—as we have seen—
they are not likely to pull their punches when it comes to the moral. He
read them Greek myths and stories, and they wrote him back their own
myths, classic transformations, and one boy even wrote an illustrated
history of the Trojan War. (One of the transformations begins, "I was
transformed from a poor little infant into a nice boy, and as I grew I was
transformed into a magnificent extraordinary deceiving nuisance to the
world.") Most of the children wrote novels, and one 11-year-old boy,
without having read a single modern novel, began a remarkable autobiography with the sentence, "I am dreaming and crying in my sleep."

This was an ordinary 6th-grade Harlem class; there were some
high IQ's, but it was not an "SP" (specially gifted) class and had attracted

no special attention to itself. The teacher disciplined them, yes, kept them in order, but did it not to triumph but to show them he cared. He respected them, which is something you can't learn from books. He visited their homes, which is absolutely unheard-of. He worked patiently with each child, and got them to work with each other.

Now it is a year later, the kids are dispersed into a notoriously depressing junior high, and most of them have lost what they gained. Some are flunking; their former teacher bitterly wonders how the life in them can survive. But for that one year they produced a body of work uniquely theirs.

The Grouping of Groupings

If conditions within the classroom are bad enough, to look beyond them is to find oneself in a jungle of stumbling and makeshift, where stentorian voices boom from the tops of trees, and clusters of officious missionaries rush about distributing memoranda on the cannibal problem.

First of all, there is the school bureaucracy. According to Martin Mayer, "New York City employs more people in educational administration than all of France." I believe I have alluded to the public relations men on the Board of Ed staff, but I have perhaps failed to mention the endless associations, commissions, sub-commissions, advisory committees, deputy directors, associate supervisors, district superintendents, coordinators, directors, foundations and independent consultants who must be involved in every policy decision. The trouble with such a set-up is that the basic concern on every level points up, toward impressing the higher-ups, rather than down, toward serving the classroom teacher. Would it be heresy to suggest equal salary for every school position? With the present system, the classroom teacher can be in a panic for materials she ordered three years ago, while the assistant superintendent is sincerely assuring the area superintendent that everything is all right in his sub-sector. In such a bureaucracy, the people who move toward the top are the yes-men, the round pegs, whom the public pays to rise away from the children.[4] They have a priority on operating funds, too; if they could not get their paperwork properly submitted and filed, the system would collapse. In fact, despite the teacher shortage, there are a number of employees listed on the Board of Ed budget as classroom teachers who never report to their assigned schools; they are clerks and typists working in the central offices. Ironically, the policy directives they type, like great portions of our public

---

[4] Gross's 1965 school budget included approximately $5 million to increase salaries for "Commissioners" who make curriculum revision recommendations.

school funds, may never filter down to the classroom; but they do reach the publicity department, from which they are carefully distributed to the newspapers, which in turn describe to us a school system that doesn't really quite exist. Nevertheless, its paper achievements will be proudly recounted by the functionary flown to a conference of "educators" at public expense. Life in the big city goes on somehow, though where it goes no one knows.

The gap between theory and practice is nowhere more striking than among the school principals. Many of them know little of what goes on in their own schools and make no effort to learn. The job of the principal is to spend his time in educational conferences, or addressing committees, or preparing reports for higher-ups who never come to check. At the Harlem school where the 6th-grade "slow" letters I have quoted were written, the principal assured me,

> I don't notice any demoralization on this level. The children are happy, well-behaved and eager to learn.[5]

Small wonder that one of the best teachers at this school could not get enthusiastic about the boycott:

> What if the boycotters are successful and get the Board to come up with a plan? Who has to implement it but these same shits!

Then there is the problem of the teachers themselves and their organization, the UFT. It would be unkind to expect too much of an organization so urgently needed and besieged with such difficulties as is the UFT. But it must be said that an excessive concern of teachers black and white is their own respectability. The most pressing practical issues are submerged in the desire to preserve their "professional image." For instance, a teacher's license in New York City cannot be obtained unless the applicant has passed the expensive and utterly idiotic education courses offered at teachers' colleges. I never talked to a single good teacher who claimed to have learned anything of value in these courses. Furthermore, they discourage many of the specially talented people gathered in New York City from seeking employment as public school teachers. Bright, educated people who want to try their hands at teaching children can't, not in New York, not even if they have PhD's, unless they are willing to go back to school for their "education credits."[6] Yet

---

[5] This principal did not bother to use up several thousand dollars of his allotted budget for equipment and supplies. The kids at this school are short on books and have no musical instruments whatever.

[6] Education courses are not the only obstacles in the paths of potentially valuable teachers. Teachers from the South or from Puerto Rico with advanced academic degrees may find themselves disqualified on the interview section of the teachers' license exam for "speaking English with an accent."

the union, although ambitious to work out a joint recruiting program with the Board aimed at attracting Negro teachers from the South, shows little interest in this question. The current teachers' pay scale is based on these pointless credits, and to upset it would invalidate years of useless course-taking.

Finally, there is the conglomeration of civil rights groups, divided and sub-divided within itself, spreading out towards too many separate targets with only the most general slogans to hold itself together. The structure of the rights organizations is chaotic beyond description. Let me say simply that the end effect is too often the mirror image of the bureaucracy they are arrayed against. And the boycott offered no program for the Negro children to realize their own particular talents, no social-action program with which to unite the Negro community in self-respect. Was not the boycott in some sense one more appeal to the great white father to do right by his poor black children?

No Ending

Have I captured the confusion? Here is New York City with a mass of black people, most of whom have never been allowed to partake of our civilization. Now they must be allowed that dubious privilege; for there is no other place for them. In previous eras of American life, there was some room for a variegated lower class, which took care of the dirty work and was not permitted entrance into the cultural mainstream. Little by little most groups surfaced into the middle class, leaving behind among unlucky remnants of themselves a permanent body of American Negroes, who, handicapped by years of slavery and oppression, remained what a Negro teacher describes to me as "a colonial people encapsulated *within* the colonial country." But now automation is chopping away at the colony; we see the natives in the street, shaking their fists. We must open the door and let them in.

The big question is, will they come in having truly changed and purified and reformed our social structure, as some say they must? Will we have to chip away at our stone walls to let them in, as the Trojans did for the Greek horse? Or will the Negro scrape through bloody, bitter and confused, ready to perpetuate the authoritarian ethic he has so far, to his unique credit, managed to evade?

The answer to this question depends in part on our schools. But all school systems are—and have always been—failures. Even Leo Tolstoy, with all his genius, his wealth, his command, and with not a single bureaucrat to hamper him, could not educate his peasants into free men. His failure, our failure . . . the failure is always the same: the failure to educate each man—not for a prestigious "function" or "role"—but to fulfill his own capacities for living, for being alive, for finding and making his own kind of beauty, for respecting the diversity of life without, in his frustration, turning to violence, self-suppression, and the worship of authority.

So what the boycotters are demanding, ultimately (and more power to them!) is a change in the nature of the lives we lead.

> *6th-grade Harlem girl* (S): I wish that the hold city can chage. and that the governor make new laws. that there to be no dirt on streets and no gobech top off and wish that my name can chage and I wish that whether can trun to summer.
>
> *6th-grade Harlem boy* (F): *Fable*
> Once upon a time there was two men who were always fighting so one day a wise man came along and said fighting will never get you anywhere they didn't pay him no attention and they got in quarrels over and over again. So one day they went to church and the preacher said you should not fight and they got mad and knock the preacher out
> Can't find no ending.

Some Work-Related Cultural Deprivations of Lower-Class Negro Youths

Joseph S. Himes
North Carolina College

[Reprinted from the Journal of Marriage and the Family, *November 1964, by permission of the National Council on Family Relations.]*

FOR LOWER-CLASS NEGRO YOUTHS just entering the labor market, three conditions are institutionally depriving: age, race, and social class. Since age tends to affect white and Negro youths alike, it may be omitted in the following discussion. Race and social class are, of course, not the same. For Negroes, however, race tends to determine class, and, in fact, the two are almost inseparable.

In the present discussion, cultural deprivation is understood to refer to residual personality characteristics that issue from socialization under specific institutionalized preconditions. In the case of lower-class Negroes, the significant institutionalized preconditions include, among others, color segregation, material discrimination, inferior or collateral social status, disparaging social evaluations, chronic social frustrations, and a substantively distinct subculture. From socialization under such preconditions, the individual emerges as a functioning member of his social world. Certain dimensions of the functional adjustment to his effective social world, however, constitute cultural deprivations in terms of the standards and demands of the larger world from which he is more or less excluded.

The work-related residual cultural deprivations of lower-class Negro youths taken at the point of entering the labor market have both judgmental and realistic dimensions. Judgmentally, deprivation refers to the absence or distortion of those knowledges, social graces, and levels of sophistication that "typical" young people are expected to exhibit. For example, culturally deprived young Negroes are said to be awkward and ill-at-ease, loud and boisterous, uncouth or gauche in manner, improperly dressed, limited in general knowledge, unsophisticated, and the like. These and similar phrases indicate that Negro youths differ in many respects from a generally accepted model or standard.

Stated judgmentally, deprivations signify cultural deviation rather than absolute cultural lacks. Lower-class Negro youths reveal the knowledge, social traits, and personality characteristics of the racial group and social class from which they emerge. Such characteristics seem to have more relevance for social acceptance than for specific job performance. For example, gauche manners or lack of sophistication may have little or no relevance for operating a machine or performing a technical task. However, such behavior may decisively influence the individual's chances of securing a job or his relations with associates in the work situation.

In terms of the reality dimension, some cultural deprivations represent genuine lacks as defined by minimal demands of the economy and specific occupations. For example, inability to read and to understand and follow directions is decisively handicapping for many modern jobs. Functional illiteracy of this kind is not limited, of course, to lower-class Negroes, although their race and social class make them peculiarly vulnerable to this cultural deprivation.

A number of studies have examined the nature, extent, and consequences of realistic cultural deprivations such as functional illiteracy, lack of basic education, inadequacy of mathematical and scientific skills, adolescent character defects, and so on.[1] Some other work-related cultural deprivations constitute incidental residual consequences of exclusion of Negroes from the basic work life of the economy. They

---

[1] Among other sources, see Michael Harrington, *The Other America*, New York: Macmillan, 1962; and James Bryant Conant, *The American High School Today*, New York: McGraw-Hill, 1959.

appear as group-linked, trained incapacities and function to handicap youthful Negroes when they enter the labor market.

Two local situations may serve to symbolize the institutionalized exclusion of Negro workers from important sectors of the national work force. In Piedmont, North Carolina, furniture and textile manufacture are basic, traditional industries. Historically, virtually no Negro workers are employed in production jobs in either industry. In Durham, within Piedmont, North Carolina, although some Negroes work as insurance executives and bankers in all-Negro concerns, none is employed as stock broker or advertising executive. The extent of Negro exclusion from the nation's work force is well known and has been documented elsewhere.[2] In the following paragraphs, three residual work-related cultural deprivations issuing from job exclusions of Negro workers are examined briefly.

Irrelevant Work Models. Lower-class Negro children are denied the experience of daily association with parents, relatives, neighbors, friends, and peers who manufacture textiles and furniture and who deal in securities or plan advertising campaigns. There is none of the casual talk and informal interaction that imperceptibly and inadvertently introduce the child to the role of the worker and the world of work in factory and office. Unlike their lower-class, poor white cohorts, such Negro children cannot, in routine socialization, acquire and identify with the roles of workers in factory and office. Rather they must rely on the formal institutions, the mass media and secondhand gleanings of Negro servants for glimpses into the world of work symbolized by the furniture factory and the brokerage office. In a revealing comment on transmission of the female role in American families, Talcott Parsons stresses the importance of the availability of the mother model in casual informal contacts with girl children in the home: ". . . it is possible from an early age to initiate girls directly into many important aspects of the adult feminine role. Their mothers are continually about the house and the meaning of many of the things they are doing is relatively tangible and easily understandable to a child. It is also possible for the daughter to participate actively and usefully in many of these activities. . . ."[3]

Excluded from casual though meaningful contacts with modern workers, the lower-class Negro child cannot identify by internal role

---

[2] See E. Franklin Frazier, *The Negro in the United States,* New York: Macmillan, 1957, Chapter XXIII; and Robert C. Weaver, *Negro Labor,* New York: Harcourt, Brace, 1946.

[3] Talcott Parsons, "Age and Sex in the Social Structure of the United States," *American Sociological Review,* 7 (October 1942), p. 605.

taking and anticipatory socialization with the worker models that are symbolized by the furniture maker and stock broker. Such experiences are as much beyond his social reach as if they were prohibited by law. Whatever knowledge and skill and character he may bring to the modern labor market, he cannot present those fringe cultural characteristics that come from being "bred to the job."

However, it must not be thought from the foregoing that the lower-class Negro youth comes to the job market culturally empty handed. He brings with him the residues of learning and the precipitates of identification with those occupational models that exist in reality within his racial and class world. For most, casual and informal childhood experiences have been with unskilled and service workers in city and country. But terms like "technology," "automation," and "white collar" tend to show how irrelevant this Negro youth's work-related cultural baggage is for the modern labor market.

Exclusion From Work Ethos. Workers who are restricted to the fringes of the occupational structure tend to be excluded from the tenets and rationalizations of the work ethos. They cannot perceive the linkage between effort and advancement. For example, the Negro janitors and maids in furniture factories and brokerage offices cannot expect to become production, office, or managerial workers as a result of hard work and self-improvement. The lower-class Negro child sees none of his parents, relatives, neighbors, friends, and peers moving up the occupational ladder. Hard work and extra effort may be a necessary condition of keeping a job. But neither hard work nor self-improvement leads to a promotion. What then is the value of hard work, extra effort, and self-improvement?

The work reserved for Negroes has no intrinsic goodness or importance. The worker does not have a sense of the relation of his job to any total scheme or large goal of the enterprise. Both he and his job are marginal to the aims of the business and to the philosophy of business. If he is loyal or dedicated, and many are, his reaction is likely to be personal rather than ideological. Such work is often uninspiring, fatiguing, and sometimes even deadening.

In family and neighborhood, Negro lower-class workers are prone to act out negative responses to the job. In casual talk and informal relations with their children, they say in effect that work is neither good nor promiseful of better things. In spite of the teachings of the social institutions and the mass media, they believe that work is simply work, an unpleasant though necessary condition of staying alive. They go to the job in the morning with reluctance and escape from it at day's end with relief.

Such workers and their children are often alleged to be "apathetic" or "lazy." But these words are social evaluations, not real explanations. From one perspective, they mean that lower-class workers and their children have not entered into the Protestant middle-class work ethos. They have not seen that work is good, that more education leads to greater opportunities, and that increased effort results in job advancements. From another perspective, such judgments reveal a pragmatic realism. The experiences of many lower-class Negroes demonstrate that self-improvement and increased effort tend to multiply and intensify their frustrations and unhappiness.

The lower-class Negro child relies upon the formal institutions, the mass media, and various adventitious personal experiences to acquire the tenets and rationalizations of the work ethos. In this respect, he is disadvantaged *vis à vis* his white cohort, whose childhood observations demonstrate the validity of hard work and self-improvement as preludes to advancement in the world of work. When he enters the labor market, therefore, the lower-class Negro youth is initially handicapped by a cultural deprivation with consequences which may accumulate with the passage of time.

Alienated From Job Ways. Family and neighborhood experiences of lower-class Negro children tend to alienate them from the distinctive ways of factory and office. They do not overhear relatives, neighbors, and friends in the "shop talk" about incidents, people, and things of the job. They cannot acquire familiarity with office and factory tools by playing with daddy's briefcase or tool kit. No casual talk and informal relations introduce them to the jargon, costumes, bearing, manners, and attitudes of office and shop. They have no childhood experiences that acquaint them with the general layout, daily routines, general atmosphere, and occupational *dramatis personae* of an industrial workshop or business office.[4]

Furthermore, lower-class Negro children cannot acquire from their occupationally marginal parents the ideologies and values of labor unions. Thus, they do not apprehend the sense of structured competition and cooperation that marks awareness of labor-management rela-

---

[4] I still remember vividly how alien and unprepared I felt the first days in the aircraft factory during the war. The overwhelming and incessant racket, the inescapable glaring lights, and the sense of frantic perpetual motion distracted and terrified me. Everything and everybody was strange. The jargon—socket wrench, bonding cable, duralium, lock nut, etc.,—was a foreign tongue. It took me days to find my way around and to feel at home in the factory. My experiences were duplicated by many other novices to the production line.

tions. They are not bred to that robust labor union conviction that the worker, if not his work, is good and dignified and important. These children are alien to the experience of group solidarity and secular collective destiny that distinguish the American labor movement. They cannot acquire from daily experience the definitions and justifications of legitimate individual and collective goals and values that are transmitted by the labor movement.

Finally, family patterns and daily habits of lower-class Negroes and their children are seldom conditioned by the long arm of production and office jobs. Work shifts, pay periods, overtime requirements, vacation schedules, and the like, seldom shape the routines of family life and daily activities. The climate of family relations is not affected by the vagaries of the politics of the job, for Negro workers are outside the occupational power system. These children and their families are passed by in the drama of the strike, the diversions of the industrial recreational program, or the securities and protections of pension systems.

Exclusion from these and other social extensions of the factory and office job tends to induce a further cultural deprivation among lower-class Negro youths. It appears as a trained unreadiness for smooth transition from family, school, and neighborhood to the social world and technical roles of work. For these youths, the workshop or the business office is a world apart, an alien and intimidating social milieu.

Conclusion. Race and class establish institutionalized preconditions under which lower-class Negro youths are socialized to certain work-related cultural deprivations. Some are judgmental in character and influence the individual's acceptance as a worker. Realistic deprivations, however, tend to handicap the individual in actual job performance. Exclusion of lower-class Negroes from important sectors of the work force constitutes one institutionalized precondition and eventuates in a series of work-related cultural deprivations. The three examined here briefly include socialization to irrelevant job models, exclusion from the prevailing work ethos, and alienation from the culture of the modern factory and office.

Organizing the Unaffiliated in a Low-Income Area

George Brager

Mobilization for Youth

[Excerpted from the article, "Organizing the Unaffiliated in a Low-Income Area," from Social Work, *Vol. 8, No. 2 (April 1963) pp. 34–40, with permission of the National Association of Social Workers, and the author.]*

COMMUNITY ORGANIZATION EFFORTS generally have one of three broad objectives. In the first instance a substantive area of community change —a needed reform—is emphasized, as, for example, attention to housing needs and inequities. Another goal is the co-ordinated and orderly development of services, as evidenced in the planning of a welfare council. The third focuses upon citizenship involvement, regardless of the issues that engage citizen attention, in order to heighten community integration. These three goals are not necessarily mutually exclusive, although it may reasonably be argued that this is more true than is generally realized. In any event, programs that do not develop objectives in some order of priority risk diffuse and ineffective performance, as well as the impossibility of focused evaluation. There is, of course, some advantage in this nondefinition. One of the three arrows may hit *some* mark, and, in any case, one need not face up to his failures if he has not specified his goals.

An encompassing delinquency prevention effort may rightly concern itself with all three objectives, although perhaps to some degree different programs need to be devised to achieve different objectives. In order to sharpen this discussion, however, focus will be placed only upon issues relating to citizenship participation.

In a study of two lower-income neighborhoods of similar socioeconomic levels it was found that in the more integrated neighborhood (in which people knew their neighbors, perceived common interests, shared common viewpoints, and felt a part of the community) delinquency rates were markedly lower.[1] Participation by adults in decision-making about matters that affect their interests increases their sense of identification with the community and the larger social order. People who identify with their neighborhood and share common values are-

---

[1] Eleanor Maccoby *et al.*, "Community Integration and the Social Control of Delinquency," *Journal of Social Issues*, Vol. 14, No. 3 (1958), pp. 38–51.

more likely to try to control juvenile misbehavior. A well-integrated community can provide learning experiences for adults that enable them to serve as more adequate models and interpreters of community life for the young. In short, participation in community-oriented organizations is highly desirable in delinquency reduction efforts.

A program must, however, involve significant numbers of representative lower-class persons.[2] Such an organization ought to enable what has been called the "effective community" of working-class youth— that is, the individuals, families, and groups with whom these youth interact and identify—to exert more positive influence on them.[3] The learning that accrues from the collective process can result in better opportunities or more effective models for potential delinquents only when large numbers of working-class adults are members of community organizations.

However, such membership is not very common among the lower class. A considerable number of studies indicate that formal group membership is closely related to income, status, and education; the lower one's income status and educational level, the less likely one is to participate in formal community groups.[4]

Furthermore, in every slum neighborhood there are adults who, in attitudes, strivings, verbal skills, and possession of know-how, are oriented toward the middle class. Although their children are less likely to experience strains toward deviance, these are precisely the parents who tend to join formal community organizations and to have faith and competence in the collective solution of social problems. In most organizations, therefore, persons who are in a minority among slum dwellers (*i.e.*, the upwardly mobile) unfortunately represent the majority of those working-class members who participate. Because lower-class persons tend to eschew formal organizations, organizers who set out to reach the effective community of the delinquent frequently settle for those slum dwellers who are easiest to enlist.

Although reports of failure only rarely find their way into the literature, the modesty of claims regarding the organization of the de-

---

[2] The word "representative" is used here in the sense of "typical of their group, *i.e.*, class" rather than in the political sense of "functioning or acting in behalf of others." Elsewhere in the literature it has been restricted to the latter use. *See* Chauncey A. Alexander and Charles McCann, "The Concept of Representativeness in Community Organization," *Social Work*, Vol. 1, No. 1 (January 1956), pp. 48–52.

[3] Derek V. Roemer, "Focus in Programming for Delinquency Reduction" (Bethesda, Md.: National Institutes of Mental Health, 1961). (Mimeographed.)

[4] Morris Axelrod, "Urban Structure and Social Participation," *American Sociological Review*, Vol. 21, No. 1 (February 1956), pp. 13–18.

prived population itself indicates a general lack of success. For example, in East Harlem in 1948 a five-block area was chosen for organization. Five trained social workers were assigned to organize these blocks and a program of social action was embarked upon, devoted to housing, recreational, and social needs of the neighborhood. Unfortunately, the East Harlem Neighborhood Center for Block Organization was able to attract only a limited number of participants during a three-year period. Subsequent research indicated that those who did participate were upwardly aspiring. Further, they were isolated from the rest of the community and therefore nonrepresentative.

Barriers to Community Integration

Characteristics of community life. Why are representative lower-income adults less likely to become closely involved in community affairs? The source of the barriers to their effective participation rests with all three elements of the interaction: the characteristics of community life, the nature of lower-income adults, and the structure of the community organization effort.

One such community characteristic is residential mobility. Local communities have been inundated by new migrants, many of them unfamiliar with the demands and opportunities of urban life. Although public housing mitigates some of the problematic aspects of slum life, the recruitment of single-family units from widely dispersed parts of the metropolitan area collects in one place thousands of deprived families, strangers to one another and to local community resources. Physical redevelopment programs and the consequent exodus of old residents have in many instances shattered existing institutions, so that they are unable to help in assimilation of the newcomers into the urban system. For example, the diminishing vitality of some local political machines, with their attentive political leaders, eliminates an important interpretive link to the new world.

Intergroup tensions are also a barrier to community integration, as are the bewildering operations of massive bureaucratic systems. The size, impersonality, concentrated power, and inflexibility of these large organizations makes them seem to local residents hardly amenable to their influence.

The community characteristic that may act as the major deterrent to involvement of lower-income people in community affairs, however, is the opposition of already entrenched organizations. New groups in a community—especially new minority groups—are often confronted with hostility from established groups whose positions of power are threatened by the possibility of forceful action by the newcomers.

There is evidence, for example, that some political machines will avoid registering minority group members, even under the impetus of national campaigns. This is so even though the minority group member is assumed to support the machine's national candidates. It is recognized that the new group will inevitably challenge the dominance of incumbent leadership.

This resistance of political parties, governmental agencies, and private organizations is never directly specified. Ordinarily it takes the form of statements such as "the minority groups are not really interested," they are "not ready," "they'll take positions we don't agree with," or they will be "controlled by the left-wing agitators." Whatever its form, the opposition of established community groups is a formidable obstacle to indigenous community participation.

　Lower-income life. The circumstances of lower-income life and the nature of lower-income persons constitute another set of obstacles. The realities of lower-class life, *i.e.*, the necessary preoccupation with the day-to-day problems of survival, hardly encourage attention to broad community matters. Furthermore, lower-class persons lack the verbal or literary requisites for organizational skills; neither do they tend to be comfortable with the formal methods of doing business in organizations. Their self-defeating attitudes also interfere with community integration. Lower-income groups tend to view life more pessimistically, with less hope of deliverance, and, as a consequence, they tend to retreat from struggle. A Gallup poll conducted in 1959 indicated that a higher percentage of respondents in the under-$3,000 income group expected World War III and a new depression than respondents in any other grouping. As one observer noted, "Seeing his chances for improvement as slim produces in the slum-dweller a psychology of listlessness, of passivity, and acceptance, which . . . reduces his chances still further." [5] Such defeatism, resulting in lack of participation, produces a loss of interest in changing their conditions.

　Structure of community organization. The community organization itself, while purportedly seeking the involvement of lower-income persons, offers certain obstacles, whether inevitable or otherwise. Most community activities, for example, are staffed by middle-class personnel. To the extent that lower-class people feel that they are being dominated, they are likely to withdraw from collective activities. The predominance of the middle class in community organizations has a number of sources. When community problems become so severe that

---

[5] Michael Harrington, "Slums, Old and New," *Commentary*, Vol. 30, No. 2 (August 1960), p. 121.

people are motivated to act, it is generally the middle-class element (or at least those who are oriented toward the middle class) that reacts first. Although lower-class persons may affiliate with the organization, its predominantly middle-class style soon becomes a subtle source of intimidation. Its leaders are likely to be businessmen, professionals, social welfare personnel, ministers, and other members of the middle class. The formality of the organization meetings, with predetermined agendas, concern with rules of procedure, and the like, tends to make the lower-class participant, unfamiliar with these matters, feel insecure and inferior.

Furthermore, organizers who insist on maintaining control of the activities and policies of the organization, subtly or otherwise, inevitably encourage the participation of lower-class persons whose values and skills are congenial with those of the middle-class organizer. Those whose values and skills differ, however, will gradually sense that such differences matter and that the organization exists to serve middle-class ends. They may, therefore, disassociate themselves.

It may be that, because of the disparity between lower- and middle-class "life styles," significant numbers of both groups cannot even be expected to participate together within the same organization. For example, a study conducted by the Girl Scouts, focused upon recruiting volunteers from working-class communities, was forced to conclude that the agency could offer no program suitable to both middle- and lower-class groups. As noted by the authors, lower-income adults are less interested in "the joys of fully integrated personality in a democratic society" than in the need to better their standard of living. They do not even object to their children being handled authoritatively if it serves such end.[6]

The tendency of social workers to emphasize the amelioration of conflict and the reduction of tension, while often appropriate and helpful, may, in effect, also discourage lower-income participation. With issues flattened rather than sharpened, differences minimized rather than faced, there may be little to arouse the interest of a group that already lacks the predisposition to participate. Matters sufficiently vital to engage slum residents are almost inevitably fraught with controversy or are challenging to some powerful community interest. If they are avoided by a community organization, it may be expected that the organization will be avoided in turn.

The sponsorship of the community organization effort will also

---

[6] Catherine V. Richards and Norman A. Polansky, "Reaching Working-class Youth Leaders," *Social Work*, Vol. 4, No. 4 (October, 1959), p. 38.

affect the character of participation. The primary interests of a sponsoring group will tend to determine membership selection, organizational form, objectives, and activities. Organizational maintenance requirements of the sponsor will inevitably limit the independence of an action-oriented affiliate. Further, its responsibility to a board of directors with widely variant views and connections to numerous community interest groups will limit a sponsor's freedom to encourage a free-wheeling community action program. When the sponsoring group is an already established community organization, it is likely to contain significant representation from groups that, as noted earlier, actively oppose the effective participation of lower-income and minority group people.

The formidable array of obstacles thus cited does not permit us to be sanguine about the success potential of any program oriented toward community action by representative lower-income adults. We may conclude, as a matter of fact, that the limitations to independence inherent in sponsorship by private or public social service organizations are hardly surmountable. Or we may discover that those obstacles least accessible to the social worker's means of intervention are most centrally required for program success. However discouraging, a specification of barriers is, nevertheless, a requirement of intelligent program planning. . . .

The Dusty Outskirts of Hope

Mary Wright

Council of the Southern Mountains

[Reprinted from Mountain Life and Work, *Spring 1964, by permission of the Council of the Southern Mountains, Inc.]*

I KNOW A MAN, I'll call him Buddy Banks. He lives in a ravine in a little one-room pole-and-cardboard house he built himself, with his wife, their six children, and baby granddaughter. Mr. Banks, 45 years old, is a sober man, a kindly man, and a passive man. He can read and write a little, has worked in the coal mines and on farms, but over the years he's been pretty badly battered up and today is "none too stout." Last fall, when he could no longer pay the rent where he was staying, his mother-in-law gave him a small piece of ground, and he hastened to put up this little shack in the woods before the snow came. If, as you ride by, you happened to glance down and see where he lives, and see his children playing among the stones, you would say, "White trash." You would say, "Welfare bums."

When the newspaper announced the new ADC program for unemployed fathers, I thought of Buddy Banks. There is not much farm work to be done in the wintertime, and Mr. Banks has been without a job since summer. Here in their ravine they can dig their coal from a hole in the hill, and dip their water from the creek, and each month he scratches together $2 for his food stamps by doing odd jobs for his neighbors, who are very nearly as poor as he is. Other than this there is nothing coming in. I thought, maybe here is some help for Buddy Banks.

Mr. Banks does not get a newspaper, nor does he have a radio, and so he had not heard about the new program. He said, yes, he would be interested. I offered to take him to town right then, but he said no, he would have to clean up first, he couldn't go to town looking like this. So I agreed to come back Friday.

On Friday he told me he'd heard today was the last day for signing up. We were lucky, eh? It wasn't true, but it's what he had heard and I wondered, suppose he'd been told last Tuesday was the last day for signing up, and I hadn't been there to say, well, let's go find out anyway.

Buddy Banks was all fixed up and looked nice as he stepped out of his cabin. His jacket was clean, and he had big rubber boots on and a cap on his head. I felt proud walking along with him, and he walked proud. (Later, in town, I noticed how the hair curled over his collar, and the gray look about him, and the stoop of his shoulders. If you saw him you'd have said, "Country boy, come to get his check.")

When we reached the Welfare Office it was full of people, a crowd of slouchy, shuffly men, standing around and looking vaguely in different directions. I followed Buddy Banks and his brother-in-law, who had asked to come with us, into the lobby, and they too stood in the middle of the floor. Just stood. It was not the momentary hesitation that comes before decision. It was the paralysis of strangeness, of lostness, of not knowing what to do. A girl was sitting at a table, and after a number of minutes of nothing, I quietly suggested they ask her. No, they told me, that was the food stamp girl. But there was no other. So finally, when I suggested, well, ask her anyway, they nodded their heads, moved over, and asked her. I wondered how long they might have gone on standing there, if I'd kept my mouth shut. I wondered how long the others all around us had been standing there. I had an idea that if I hadn't been right in the way, Buddy Banks just might have turned around and gone out the door when he saw the crowd, the lines, and that smartly-dressed food stamp girl bending over her desk.

Yes, he was told, and after waiting a few minutes, he was shown behind the rail to a chair beside a desk, and a man with a necktie and a big typewriter began to talk with him. They talked a long long time, while the brother-in-law and I waited in the lobby. (They had asked the brother-in-law if he had brought the birth certificates. No, he hadn't, and so they said there wasn't anything they could do, to come back next Tuesday. He said nothing, stared at them a moment, then walked away. He stood around waiting for us all day long and never asked them another question. He said he would tend to it some other time. Fortunately, they got Mr. Banks sitting down before they inquired about the birth certificates.)

I knew what they were talking about: I have talked long times with Mr. Banks myself, and they were going over it again, and again, and I could imagine Mr. Banks nodding his head to the question he didn't quite understand, because he wanted to make a good impression, and it would be a little while before the worker realized that he hadn't understood, and so they would go back and try again, and then Mr. Banks would explain as best he could, but he would leave something out, and then the worker wouldn't understand, so that, in all, their heads were bent together for almost an hour and a half. It seemed a long time to take to discover Buddy Bank's need—a visit to his home would have revealed it in a very few minutes, but of course twelve miles out and twelve miles back takes time too, and there are all those eligibility rules to be checked out, lest somebody slip them a lie and the editorials start hollering "Fraud! Fraud!" Actually, I was impressed that the worker would give him that much time. It takes time to be sympathetic, to listen, to hear—to understand a human condition.

At last he came out, and with an apologetic grin he said he must return on Tuesday, he must go home and get the birth certificates. Then they would let him apply. (How will you come back, Mr. Banks? Where will you get the $3 for taxi fare by next Tuesday? Perhaps you could scrape it up by Monday week, but suppose you come on Monday week and your worker isn't here? Then perhaps you won't come back at all . . .)

While Mr. Banks was busy talking, I was chatting with one of the other workers. Because I am a social worker too, I can come and go through the little iron gate, and they smile at me and say, "Well, *hello* there!" We talked about all the work she has to do, and one of the things she told me was how, often, to save time, they send people down to the Health Department to get their own birth records. Then they can come back and apply the same day. I wondered why Mr. Bank's worker never suggested this. Maybe he never thought of it. (Maybe he doesn't live twelve miles out with no car, and the nearest bus eight miles from home. And no bus fare at that.) Or perhaps he *did* mention it, and Mr. Banks never heard him, because his head was already filled up with the words that went before: "I'm sorry, there's nothing we can do until you bring us the birth certificates," and he was trying to think in which box, under which bed, had the children been into them . . . ?

So I tried to suggest to him that we go now to the Health Department, but he didn't hear me either. He said, and he persisted, I'm going to the Court House, I'll be right back, will you wait for me? I tried to stop him: let's plan something, what we're going to do next, it's almost lunchtime and things will close up—until suddenly I realized that after the time and the tension of the morning, this was no doubt a call of nature that could not wait for reasonable planning, nor could a proud man come out and ask if there might not be a more accessible solution. And so, as he headed quickly away for the one sure place he knew, I stood mute and waited while he walked the three blocks there and the three blocks back. I wonder if that's something anybody ever thinks about when they're interviewing clients.

Mr. Banks and I had talked earlier about the Manpower Redevelopment Vocational Training Programs, and he had seemed interested. "I'd sure rather work and look after my family than mess with all this stuff, but what can I do? I have no education." I told him about the courses and he said, yes, I'd like that. And so we planned to look into this too, while we were in town. But by now Mr. Banks was ready to go home. "I hate all this standing around. I'd work two days rather than stand around like this." It wasn't really the standing around he minded. It was the circumstances of the standing around. It took some persuading to get him back into the building, only to be told—at 11:30 —to come back at ten to one. (Suppose his ride, I thought, had been with somebody busier than I. Suppose they couldn't wait till ten to one and kept badgering him, "Come on, Buddy, hurry up, will you? We ain't got all day!")

I tried to suggest some lunch while we waited, but they didn't want lunch. "We had breakfast late; I'm not hungry, really." So instead, I took him around to the Health Department and the Circuit Court and the County Court, and we verified everything, although he needed some help to figure which years the children were born in.

At ten to one he was again outside the Welfare Office, and he drew me aside and said that he'd been thinking: maybe he should go home and talk this whole thing over a little more. He felt that before jumping into something, he should know better what it was all about. This startled me, for I wondered what that hour and a half had been for, if now, after everything, he felt he must return to his cronies up the creek to find out what it all meant. So we stood aside, and I interpreted the program as best I could, whom it was for and what it required, and what it would do for him and his family, while he stood, nodding his head and staring at the sidewalk. Finally, cautiously, almost grimly, he once again pushed his way into that crowded, smoke-filled lobby.

"Those who are to report at one o'clock, stand in this line. Others in that line." Mr. Banks stood in the one o'clock line. At 1:15 he reached the counter. I don't know what he asked, but I saw the man behind the desk point over toward the other side of the building, the Public Assistance side, where Mr. Banks had already spent all morning. Mr. Banks nodded his head and turned away as he was told to do. At that point I butted in. "Assistance for the unemployed is over there," the man said and pointed again. So I mentioned training. "He wants training? Why didn't he say so? He's in the wrong line." I don't know what Mr. Banks had said, but what *does* a person say when he's anxious, and tired and confused, and a crowd of others, equally anxious, are pushing from behind and the man at the counter says, "Yes?" I butted in and Mr. Banks went to stand in the right line, but I wondered what the man behind us did, who didn't have anybody to butt in for him.

While Mr. Banks was waiting, to save time, I took the birth certificates to his worker on the other side. I walked right in, because I was a social worker and could do that, and he talked to me right away and said, "Yes, yes, this is good. This will save time. No, he won't have to come back on Tuesday. Yes, he can apply today. Just have him come back over here when he is through over there. Very good."

At 1:30 Buddy Banks reached the counter again, was given a card and told to go sit on a chair until his name was called. I had business at 2:00 and returned at 3:00, and there he was, sitting on the same chair. But I learned as I sat beside him that things had been happening. He had talked with the training counsellor, returned to his welfare worker, and was sent back to the unemployment counsellor, after which he was to return once more to his welfare worker. I asked what he had learned about the training. "There's nothing right now, maybe later." Auto mechanics? Bench work? Need too much education. There may be something about washing cars, changing oil, things like that. Later on. Did you sign up for anything? No. Did they say they'd let you know? No. How will you know? I don't know.

At last his ADC (Unemployed) application was signed, his cards were registered, his name was in the file. Come back in two weeks and we'll see if you're eligible. (How will you get back, Buddy? I'll find a way.)

It was four o'clock. "Well, that's over." And he said, "I suppose a fellow's got to go through all that, but I'd sure rather be a-working than a-fooling around with all that mess." We went out to the car, and I took him home. "I sure do thank you, though," he said.

While I'd been waiting there in the lobby, I saw another man come up to the counter. He was small and middle-aged, with a wedding band on his finger, and his face was creased with lines of care. I saw him speak quietly to the man across the desk. I don't know what he said or what the problem was, but they talked a moment and the official told him, "Well, if you're disabled for work, then there's no use asking about training," and he put up his hands and turned away to the papers on his desk. The man waited there a moment, then slowly turned around and stood in the middle of the floor. He lifted his head to stare up at the wall, the blank wall, and his blue eyes were held wide open to keep the tears from coming. I couldn't help watching him, and when suddenly he looked at me, his eyes straight into mine, I couldn't help asking him—across the wide distance of the crowd that for just an instant vanished into the intimacy of human communion—I asked, "Trouble?" Almost as if he were reaching out his hands, he answered me and said, "I just got the news from Washington and come to sign up, and . . ." but then, embarrassed to be talking to a stranger, he mumbled something else I couldn't understand, turned his back to me, stood another long moment in the middle of the crowd, and then walked out the door.

Disabled or not disabled. Employed or not employed. In need or not in need. Yes or no. Black or white. Answer the question. Stand in line.

It is not the program's fault. You have to have questionnaires, and questionnaires require a yes or no. There is no space for a maybe, but . . .

Nor is it the people-who-work-there's fault, for who can see—or take time to see—the whole constellation of people and pressures, needs and perplexities, desires and dreads that walk into an office in the person of one shuffling, bedraggled man—especially when there are a hundred other bedraggled men waiting behind him? You ask the questions and await the answers. What else can you do?

Then perhaps it is the fault of the man himself, the man who asks —or doesn't quite know how to ask—for help. Indeed, he's called a lazy cheat if he does, and an unmotivated ignorant fool if he doesn't. It must be his own fault.

Or maybe it's nobody's fault. It's just the way things are . . .

Life on A.D.C.: Budgets of Despair

Charles Lebeaux

Wayne State University School of Social Work

[Reprinted with permission from New University Thought, *Winter 1963.]*

> *Editors' comment: One of the solutions to the state of poverty has been social welfare, but this article indicates the situation of those who are dependent on the help given within the present social ethic. Charles Lebeaux, who teaches in the School of Social Work of Wayne State University, undertook this study together with other faculty, social workers, and students — an indication of healthy concern within a much-derided profession.*

IN SEPTEMBER 1962 a grave crisis occurred in 6,000 needy families with children in Detroit. These families were recipients of Aid to Families with Dependent Children (AFDC), the aid program commonly known as ADC (Aid to Dependent Children) until its title was changed in 1962. In the early 1940's the Detroit welfare departments began supplementing AFDC grants out of general relief funds, because the Michigan state grant in AFDC was in many cases too small for the family to live on, and because it was often *less* than the same family would receive from general relief.[1] But due to Detroit's financial straits, about four years ago the city began cutting the amount of the supplement. In September 1962 the supplement was cut entirely. This last cut affected 6,000 of the city's 13,000 AFDC families—many more had been affected by earlier cuts. These many thousands of families are thus living below the minimum standards of health and decency, even as defined by this welfare program itself.

---

[1] AFDC is one of five categorical public assistance programs set up in the Social Security Act, in which the federal government shares costs with the states. These programs (AFDC, Old Age Assistance, Aid to the Blind, Aid to the Disabled, and Medical Aid to the Aged) are separate financially, and for the most part administratively, from general relief, which is run by the states and localities with no federal involvement. Detroit is in Wayne County where there are three relief offices: the Wayne County Bureau of Social Aid, which administers the categorical aid programs (including AFDC) for the entire county; the Detroit Department of Public Welfare, which handles general relief in Detroit; and the Wayne County Department of Social Welfare, which handles general relief in the rest of the county.

Few people in Michigan know about the plight of these families and even fewer seem to care. The AFDC mothers themselves, many without the clothes or carfare to go out of their homes, have almost no power to influence public policy or opinions. Although in the fall of 1962 members of the Detroit Chapter of the National Association of Social Workers (NASW) organized and supported efforts of some Negro organizations (primarily the Trade Union Leadership Council and the Federation of AFDC Mothers, a group of the mothers themselves), none of their appeals to rescind the cut, either to the mayor or the welfare department, were successful. When these efforts failed, the following survey of the families affected by the cut was made, in order to arouse the moribund consciences of the city and state.[2]

The People on AFDC

There are now about 7½ million people in the United States getting public assistance under all programs, special and general. Around four million of these are in AFDC families. There are about 33,000 AFDC families in Michigan; about 13,000 of these families with some 40,000 children, live in Detroit. AFDC is the most controversial of the public assistance programs, not only because of its size and persistent growth, but because of the social characteristics of the recipients. When the program started in the late 1930's, death of the father was the common cause for being in need of aid. Today, more than 60 percent of AFDC cases are due to estrangement of parents—divorce, separation, desertion, or unmarried motherhood. The American public regards these as bad or unworthy reasons to be in need, and is less inclined to give help.

Over 40 percent of AFDC families are Negro (compared to about 10 percent of the general population). In northern industrial cities, the caseload is largely Negro (about 81 percent in Detroit), and in cities

---

[2] After we were unable to obtain a list of the 6,000 from city, county or state agencies, which made a full random sample impossible, the NASW decided that it had to proceed on its own, and quickly. A list of some hundred odd names was supplied by the Federation of AFDC Mothers, and a questionnaire was devised by faculty and students of the Wayne State University School of Social Work. Twenty-five members of NASW and twenty-five social work students volunteered to do the home interviewing, which was accomplished in April 1963. Ninety-three usable interviews were held, and are the basis of this report.

Because we could not obtain the list of 6,000 supplement cut cases, we could not pick a statistically correct sample; but when a population is quite homogeneous with respect to the characteristic under investigation, just a few cases may represent all. So with the poverty aspect of our AFDC families. In fact, my guess is that our group is better off than the typical AFDC family, because women who participate in the Federation of AFDC Mothers also probably will be better managers than the average woman receiving AFDC.

like Detroit, the proportion of illegitimate children is unusually high (although less than one-quarter of all illegitimate children in the country receive AFDC assistance).

The federal law says that to qualify under AFDC a child must be in "need," but the states define that status and determine the actual amount of money that each child and his family receive. The Michigan AFDC law says that they shall receive enough to permit them to live with "health and decency," at a level below which something suffers—health, church and school attendance, or self-respect. However, most states, including Michigan, interpret a health and decency standard to mean "minimum subsistence."

Dollar costs of a minimum subsistence budget are determined by home economists and other experts in the Federal Department of Agriculture, the State Department of Social Welfare, and home economics departments in universities by adding together minimum amounts for food, shelter, utilities, clothing, household supplies, and personal incidentals. For example, on the scale prepared by the Family Budget Council of the Detroit Visiting Nurses Association, $266.21 per month was the minimum income required in January 1960, by a family consisting of a mother age thirty-five, a boy age fourteen, and two girls, nine and four, with rent assumed to be $55 per month. For the identical family, paying identical rent, the Michigan State Department of Social Welfare in January 1961, has $223.05 as the monthly amount required to meet basic needs.

In practice, the welfare worker on the case adds up the amount needed to meet basic needs of the family according to state standards, subtracts any income there may be, and the unmet need should be the amount of the AFDC check. But in most cases in Detroit that is *not what the family gets*. The state sets ceilings on what each family can get, no matter what the budget figures show they need, according to the 1963 formula shown in Table 1.

TABLE 1

Theoretical and Actual Grants

Family Size	Budget Requirements[1]	Maximum Grant
Mother and 1 child	$151	$120
Mother and 2 children	191	140
Mother and 3 children	228	160
Mother and 4 children	263	180
Mother and 5 children	300	200
Mother and 6 children	334	220
Mother and 7 children	368	240 (absolute) maximum)

[1] Includes food and incidentals allowance of $34 per person, $67 rent, and heat and utilities according to a standardized allowance based on family size.

How Are They Living?

Without important error, we can think of these families as living on the schedule of state ceiling grants. No income other than the relief grant was reported for seventy-nine families. This means that for 85 percent of the group, income is fixed by the state ceilings—$120 for a mother and one child, $140 for a mother and two children, and so on. Whenever income plus the ceiling grant exceeds the state subsistence standard for the family, the grant is reduced accordingly.

Court-ordered or voluntary support payments by the absent fathers of families on relief is the weakest of financial reeds. In many cases they are not actually forthcoming, and families dependent on them are chronically on the verge of utter destitution. Children over seventeen are excluded from the state-federal AFDC program, and since September 1962 are also eliminated from city welfare support. There are at least six families among our ninety-three with an unemployed child over seventeen living in the home with no provision for his support.

Out of the ceiling grant rent and utilities must get paid, usually first. Table 2 shows the combined cost of rent and utilities to these families in the month of March 1963.

TABLE 2

Combined Cost of Rent and Utilities—March 1963

Dollars	Public Housing	Private Housing	Type of Housing Not Ascertained
40-59	44	3	1
60-79	6	10	1
80-99	2	18	2
100-above	0	5	0
Total	52	36	4

Fifty-two of the families live in city public housing projects, thirty-seven in private housing. Living in public housing projects is cheaper—the median rent and utility cost is $56, compared with $86 in private housing, but few public housing units are large enough for the biggest families, who naturally pay more for bigger private quarters.

What do these reasonable rent and utility costs mean to an AFDC family? Consider a mother with two children. Say that rent and utilities are $70 per month. Out of their $140 grant that leaves $70. But the state welfare department says that three people need $102 a month for food and incidentals. It is clear that for these families "something suffers."

One mother, three days after receipt of her check (and twelve days before the next one would come), had 56c left. She had bought food and coal and paid the rent, but held off on the gas and electricity bills because there was no money to pay them. The gas and electricity may be cut off, she says, as they have been twice in the last two years. And what of school supplies, clothing, or carfare?

Sixteen mothers reported they were behind in rent. Half of these owed $50 or less, but one woman was $140 behind because her grant had stopped while the agency checked out a report that "a man was living with her." The lost income was never made up. Twenty-five families were behind in utilities; you need a roof overhead, at least in the winter, but you can exist without heat and light.

A surprising proportion of the mothers considered themselves not badly housed. In the words of the women:

> (Private housing): *"It's good because the rent is fair and it's near school, relatives and shopping. But the house is too small and the neighborhood is unfriendly."* (High-rise public housing project): *"It's cold in winter, causing excess use of electricity. It's too far from the children outside, too small, and the elevators are a problem. But it is burglar and fire proof, and there's a good incinerator."* (Also high-rise): *"It's too crowded, noisy, and too high,"* (woman has hypertension). *"But it's warm, fire proof, and the Neighborhood Service Organization has good programs for the kids."*

How Do AFDC Families Eat?

To get some detail on the quality of economic life on AFDC, we asked the mothers how much food they had on hand (meat, dairy products, and fresh or canned fruit). The information obtained was voluminous and interesting, but difficult to summarize and liable to misinterpretation. Just before check day, food stocks will naturally be low, and just after, there may be two weeks' supply of food newly purchased. Averages here would make no sense.

However, the trend of the information gathered indicated that hardly any mother had as much as a half-gallon of milk on hand, and very little meat. Often the meat listed was an inexpensive cut like neck bones, or a canned variety. There was a nearly universal report, "No fruit," "No fruit." And something we didn't inquire into was frequently volunteered: "No vegetables either." And in home economics courses in the schools they teach children about balanced diets!

Asked "Is your family adequately fed?" forty of the mothers answered "yes," six answered "sometimes," and forty-seven answered "no." "Never enough near the time the check is due. Hungry at other times too." "Before transfer to AFDC (from Detroit welfare) we ate well, but now food is inadequate." So the mothers respond who feel their families are inadequately fed. One mother had a doctor-prescribed high-protein diet (and TB too) that she has been unable to follow for two months.

Those that consider their families adequately fed have often given up something else. They say that they are getting behind in the rent, are without adequate clothing, and in one case without a phone, which was necessary because of a brain damaged child with frequent convulsions. Those who feel they are adequately fed usually go without fruit, and eat little meat and vegetables.

Food Stamps in the AFDC Program

For many years now the federal government has been disposing of some of the surplus foods accumulated under the farm subsidy program, by giving it to local relief agencies across the country who distribute it to poor people. In 1962 the food stamp program, which had been used before World War II, was started in a number of localities including Detroit to test whether it was a better way of distributing surplus foods. As a result, in Detroit surplus commodities are not now given directly to families, but food stamps are distributed by the City Department of Public Welfare to all low income people who wish to participate. The participant takes his cash to a stamp office and buys stamps which are worth more than the cash paid—for example, you may get $14 worth of stamps for $10. The amount one may purchase depends mostly on the size of the family, but most AFDC families qualify for less than a 50 percent bonus, e.g., for $30 cash, $43 in food stamps.

All AFDC families in Detroit are eligible to buy food stamps. Forty-seven out of our ninety-three families reported buying food stamps; forty-six did not. Most mothers who get the stamps say they are a great help. Those who do not get the stamps gave the following reasons (in order of frequency): not enough cash, restricts purchase selection, timing is off, and can't get to the stamp office.

Twenty-four families found the stamps restricted purchase selection. For example, the stamps don't buy soap, cleaning supplies, or toilet paper. They don't buy coffee or cocoa. These restrictions occur because the program, financed by the U. S. Department of Agriculture with farm subsidy funds, is designed to get rid of surplus food stores, not to help feed poor people. The resulting rules and procedures guard the interests of the farmers, who don't grow coffee or toilet paper, instead of the interests of the stamp users. Even a very careful home manager is penalized by the program's procedures; however, she still gains in dollars by using the stamps.

Not enough cash. This is the most important reason; and it causes all kinds of difficulties even for the families that buy food stamps. What happens is this: A family of mother and three children when receiving its semi-monthly AFDC check of $80 is certified to buy $30 worth of food stamps. But the rent of $55 is due and must be paid first; there is not enough left to get the food stamps. Suppose they pay only half the rent now (which many do); but some utility bills are due and a child must have a pair of shoes—again, not enough cash to buy the food stamps. They are not permitted to buy less than the amount they are certified for by the welfare department (this would be against the Department of Agriculture regulations). And they must buy regularly. Every time a family fails to buy the stamps at the appointed time, it is automatically decertified and must go through the application procedure again. If the family is very irregular in buying stamps, it becomes ineligible for the program for a while—a Department of Agriculture penalty to force regular participation. Thus those who most need the added food-buying power of the stamps are least able to get them.

Some find the "timing is off"—that the fixed time for buying stamps comes several days after (or before) the check comes. Meanwhile you have to eat, and there is then insufficient cash to buy stamps when the time comes. This problem is much less severe now than it was when the program was started because local relief officials, after fighting a long battle with Washington, have been able to get the check and stamp buying dates into approximate coincidence.

There are some cases where the mother wanted, and was able, to buy the stamps but couldn't get her relief worker to come out to certify her. Although occasionally workers are indifferent, the basic reason is that the Bureau of Social Aid is so understaffed that planned contacts with AFDC families have been made only once in every six to twelve month period. This period has been reduced under the 1962 welfare amendments. Yet when no worker comes around, the family doesn't get food stamps.

What Do the Children Wear?

As a further measure of the level of living on AFDC, information was obtained on the total wardrobe of the oldest school child in each family. As with the food data, the information obtained was voluminous and enlightening, but difficult to summarize and liable to misinterpretation. However, some startling facts emerged regarding what is one of the most critical problems in AFDC life, clothing for school children.

Only about half of the clothing is purchased, a good deal of it was bought before the supplement cut of September 1962, and a good deal of this purchased clothing is used. For the other half of their clothing the children depend on gifts, from relatives and neighbors, and from school teachers. About eight out of ten boys have but one pair of shoes; about half the girls have only one pair of shoes, and half have two pairs. About half the children have no rubbers or boots of any kind, and about three-fourths have no raincoats of any description. There is obviously no room in a state ceiling grant for clothing.

What Else Do They Spend Money On?

Although the grants hardly allow for it, the mothers are forced from time to time to spend money on things other than rent, utilities, and food. For the month prior to the interview they reported the following other expenditures—which, of course, are estimates from memory.

Sixty-nine had some expense for transportation, ranging in amount from under a dollar to $45 for a trip South to resettle a burned-out mother. Thirty spent one or two dollars, nineteen more spent three or four dollars. One woman said it cost $20 in carfare to make trips to the clinic for an asthmatic son. Twenty-four families apparently rode not at all.

A good deal of medical expense is reflected in the transportation figure, since the free clinic is their only medical provision. Many find Receiving Hospital care unsatisfactory because of long waits and responsibility for young children; thus we find thirty-one who had expenses for doctors, dentists, or medicines during the month. In twenty-four of these cases the amounts expended were less than $7, but one woman reported $48.68 for doctor and $4.25 for medicine, while another "pays what she can" on a $300 bill for braces for her son's teeth.

Eight families reported insurance premium payments of from $3 to $15 in the preceding month, and undoubtedly many more neglected to report such expenditures. Only ten families reported any expenditure for recreation, although all were specifically asked about this. Nine reported church expenses, from $1 to $6; nine had school expenses, from $1 to $10; eleven paid telephone bills; one paid $7.50 for house screens; one $2 for a horn mouthpiece for a child; one $3.09 for brooms and a mop; several had bought newspapers; one girl lost $10 from the sale of Girl Scout cookies and the mother had to make it good.

Life in Our "Affluent Society"

The significance of these other expenditures is twofold. First, that they should exist at all, since there is usually no allowance at all for them in the grim budgets of these families; and second, even more important, that they should be so few and so small considering that we live in a money economy. What does it mean that families should spend nothing at all for transportation for a whole month in a city like Detroit? That most should spend nothing at all for recreation in families averaging

over three children apiece? That with hundreds of school kids represented, only nine families reported expenses for school supplies?

As a refined measure of the economic situation of these families,
they were asked the combined value of cash and food stamps on hand,
and how many days until the next check came. AFDC checks are now
issued twice monthly, rather than once as formerly, to help families
spread their income over the entire month, although this interferes with
rent payment and purchase of food stamps. The essence of the financial
situation of these people is contained in the fact that thirty-one families
had between nothing and $4 on hand to last from three to fourteen days.
Asked if they ever ran out of money, they all answered yes.

When asked what they did about running out of money, two-
thirds said they borrowed, either from relatives and friends or store-
keepers, and one-third said they just "stayed run out." "Stay run out"
is the theme of their lives—and for those who borrow too, because the
loan must be paid back, and each month they sink a little deeper. Besides borrowing and staying run out, some found other ways to cope
with the continuing crisis: One "lets the bills go." (Where does this
end?) One cashes in bottles and borrows food. One cried in shame:
"The lady downstairs gives us food." One said, "If the children get sick,
I call the police to take them to Receiving Hospital."

One has been "borrowing" secretly from the funds of a Ladies'
Club of which she is treasurer. The club is her one meaningful adult
social contact. There is soon to be an election for new club officers and
she will be exposed. Her children ask: "Mama, why are you always so
sad?" Half crazy with worry, she feels sick; at Receiving Hospital they
have referred her to the psychiatrist.

One was in despair because a retarded son who delights in his
monthly visit home from the County Training School was coming tomorrow, and there was little food and no money or food stamps in the
house. One said bitterly: "A woman could always get $10 if she had to.
I prefer not to resort to this."

Consider our affluent society: in an economy generating wealth
sufficient to supply every family of four with nearly $10,000 per year
income, we reduce a family to cashing in pop bottles to get food, we
push a woman to thoughts of prostitution to feed her children, we force
an honest woman into theft and then provide her with $25 an hour
psychiatric treatment.

Impact of the Supplementation Cut

As noted above, only about two-thirds of the ninety-three families received a supplement cut in September 1962. The families that had been
cut were asked: Where did it hurt? What did you stop buying?

> *"No more clothes, fruit, milk. Clothes hurt most because mostly for school boy. Borrowed clothes to go to church." "Got behind in utilities—over $100." "Had to cut out food stamps. Hurt because came at time when children needed school supplies and clothing." "Shoes. Children have hard to fit feet so can't buy cheap shoes. Special treats cut out. We used to go as a family for small treats on holidays, but no more." "School clothing. They are ashamed of their ragged clothing. No spending money in school. This makes my children want to quit." "Boy dropped out of Boy Scouts. No shows, no getting away from the house."*

No clothing, no school supplies, no gym shoes, no church, no Boy Scouts, no movies, no little treats, no ice cream cones—nothing like this if you want to keep the roof overhead. But after a while you lose interest even in that, and you quit school, quit church, quit Boy Scouts, begin to steal, or perhaps take money from a boy friend. Every single family which has its supplement cut was seriously hurt by the income reduction—all gave stories like those above.

When the 6,000 AFDC cases were cut off supplemental relief in September 1962, it was expected at the welfare department that many would come to the department asking for reinstatement of supplementation. But few showed up. It was then suggested by some public assistance officials, "Maybe they are not so bad off as we thought. Maybe they don't really need it." As we have seen they are wrong.

But how many went, what happened, and why didn't the rest go? Actually thirty-one of the sixty-five mothers who had received a budget cut *did* go to the city welfare to ask for help. None got it. Why didn't the other thirty-four mothers go? Perhaps they were wiser in anticipating refusal; they decided to save the time, the carfare, and the effort. Of course, in refusing aid the intake workers are simply carrying out departmental policy. So often in the position of having to deny aid to people who in their heart they know need help, the workers tend to develop what one former worker calls "the culture of intake"—methods of denying aid without fully examining the circumstances of the family.

Social Poverty

These people are not starving or out on the street. But in our world lack of buying power, even when it is not so absolute as to lead to starvation or death, leads to a very real social starvation and social death.

Well-off people easily forget that almost all social relationships depend on the ability to spend some money. To go to school costs money —for books, notebooks, pencils, gym shoes, and ice cream with the other kids. Without these the child begins to be an outcast. To go to church costs money—for Sunday clothes, carfare to get there, and a little offering. Without these, one cannot go. To belong to the Boy Scouts costs money—for uniforms, occasional dues, shared costs of a picnic. Without these, no Scouts.

Poverty settles like an impenetrable prison cell over the lives of the very poor, shutting them off from every social contact, killing the spirit, and isolating them from the community of human life.

Selected Bibliography

1. Edwin W. Bakke. *The Unemployed Worker.* New Haven: Yale University Press, 1940.

2. M. Elaine Burgess and Daniel O. Price. *An American Dependency Challenge.* Chicago: American Public Welfare Association, 1963.

3. David J. Caplovitz. *The Poor Pay More: Consumer Practices of Low Income Families.* New York: Free Press of Glencoe, 1963.

4. Allison Davis. "Motivation of the Underprivileged Worker," *Industry and Society,* William F. Whyte, ed. New York: McGraw Hill, 1946.

5. Lenore A. Epstein. "Some Effects of Low Income on Children and Their Families," *Social Security Bulletin,* Vol. 24, February, 1961.

6. Herbert J. Gans. *The Urban Villagers.* Glencoe, Illinois: The Free Press, 1963.

7. Elizabeth Herzog. *Children of Working Mothers* (U.S. Children's Bureau Publication 383), Washington, Government Printing Office, 1960.

8. Genevieve Knaupfer. "Portrait of the Underdog," *Public Opinion Quarterly,* II (Spring, 1947).

9. Mollie Orshansky, "Children of the Poor," *Social Security Bulletin,* Vol. 26, July, 1963.

10. Lee Rainwater and Karol Kane Weinstein. *And the Poor Get Children.* Chicago: Quadrangle Books, 1960.

11. David Riesman, et al. *The Lonely Crowd.* New York: Doubleday and Company, 1953.

12. Frank Riessman. *The Culturally Deprived Child.* New York: Harper and Row, 1962.

13. Nicholas von Hoffman. "Reorganization in the Casbah," *Social Progress,* April, 1962.

14. William F. Whyte. "The Social Organization of the Slum," *American Sociological Review,* 8 (1944).

Chapter 7

Policies and Programs

To meet the problems effectively will require the concerted efforts of all segments of our national life—all levels of government working with labor and management and private community groups and organizations. With such coordinated, positive action, we are confident that, in overall terms, the total cost will be low when measured by the positive economic gains which will be generated throughout the total economy and also when measured by the resultant strengthening of the forces which produce an alert, productive, and democratic society.

—From Joint Economic Committee, 84th Congress, Second Session, Senate Report 1311.

Previous chapters have attempted to delineate the general prevalence of poverty, its specific incidence on certain groups and its causal roots and sustaining conditions in the American political economy. We then looked more closely at the value patterns, life styles and family situation of the poor, highlighting conditions of education, social and economic participation.

We can draw several generalizations from this varied material:

(1) Poverty does not exist at the periphery of an otherwise healthy social and economic order, but is the result of deficiencies in the way in which the society allocates resources, judges worth and rewards achievement.

(2) Poverty is not of a piece. While there are certain common roots, the problems of old people are different from those of youth or those of obsolete workers in depressed areas or those of mothers with dependent children. Remedies must be specific as well as general.

(3) Poverty will not gradually disappear with the advance of American prosperity. Trends in manpower needs coupled with high concentration of children among the poor, suggest a growing new generation of poor, without an expanding job market to offer opportunity for economic advancement.

(4) Poverty is not simply a matter of deficient income. It involves a reinforcing pattern of restricted opportunities, deficient community services, abnormal social pressures and predators, and defensive adaptations. Increased income alone is not sufficient to overcome brutalization, social isolation and narrow aspiration.

(5) Poverty is not something that just happens. There are groups in the society that make a profit from the poor. There are other groups whose profit or power would be threatened if the poor were to become secure economically and active as social and political participants.

The range of policies and programs included in this chapter was selected with a view to their relative agreement or disagreement with these general points of orientation. Seven criteria or dimensions might aid in assessing these proposals.

(1) Does the proposal assume no difficulty in eliminating poverty from our wealthy society (consensus model of social change), or does it assume conflicts, in attempts to eliminate poverty, between current values and the uncompromisable interest of some social groups (conflict model of social change)?

(2) Does the proposal see poverty in primarily income-economic terms or in social, quality-of-life terms? The income definition implies a need to rebuild the basis of economic self-sufficiency, whereas the wider, quality-of-life definition implies a need to reshape the entire opportunity structure of the poor; this involves value judgments as to which opportunities and experiences are relatively more important for the good life.

(3) Does the proposal focus on symptoms or causes? Treatment of cause requires an analysis of why poverty exists and how anticipated social changes of the next decades will affect poverty. Following this analysis, programs are designed to correct the root conditions—in the individual and in the society—that generate poverty. Treatment of symptoms seeks primarily to alleviate individual hardship, to dissipate "social dynamite" and to aid individuals in breaking the hold of poverty. It is thus akin to a clinical program of individual treatment and sponsored mobility in contrast to a social program of environmental reform and general uplift.

(4) Is it directed to aid the next generation of poor or the present poor? Some programs concentrate on the problems of youth or even pre-school children, while essentially writing off the present adult poor as beyond help except for symptomatic relief. Other programs seek generally to improve economic opportunities, seeing that this will aid both children and their parents; still other programs are more specific in designing both causal and symptomatic remedies for distinct age,

occupational and geographical groups. The issues are often how best to allocate scarce anti-poverty resources and how to minimize the social conflict which anti-poverty aid might foster.

(5) Does the proposal operate within the present framework of the affluent society or does it see anti-poverty action as a vehicle for broader social change? Some proposals affirm the status quo of welfare capitalism and limited democracy as a close approximation to the good society and assume that the poor should be aided toward full participation within this structure. Other proposals premise major failures in the status quo and see anti-poverty action as coordinated with such goals as the creation of participatory democracy, broadening the definition of productive work, deepening the quality of culture, or reducing manipulative pressures for mass consumption.

(6) Is the proposal paternalistic or democratic? Some programs plan out the needs to be met and opportunities to be offered in advance and then operate through a high level coordination of community services, welfare agencies and business leaders to most efficiently implement the plan. In these, the poor are largely passive recipients of aid or special opportunities. Other proposals would sacrifice a degree of efficiency and predictability in exchange for the democratic participation of the poor in the planning, staffing and administration of programs. The one sees the problems as primarily an organizational job of reallocating certain resources and opportunities, best handled by those with organizational experience and with direct control of the needed resources. The other view places greater trust in the poor and is concerned with the human goal of giving individuals some control over the conditions of their life, both to break patterns of passivity and dependence and to release their creative energies to the benefit of the whole community.

(7) Does the proposal identify the forces of resistance and develop a strategy for implementation? Some programs develop theoretical solutions while ignoring the political realities of social change. Others gear their vision to the limits of the immediately possible. Any serious proposal must analyze the interacting forces that would be potential antagonists to the program and those that would be the potential allies.

Each of these dimensions sets up a polarity, which roughly approximates minimal and maximal positions for dealing with poverty. The minimal position seeks to reduce hardship, mitigate poverty generated social problems and minimize disruptive social conflict. The maximal position seeks a wide range of social change where not only the life of the poor, but the whole society is transformed in terms of spiritual opportunities and economic realities of the next decade. It is on the conflict between these positions that the debate over poverty will focus in the coming years.

Approaches to the Reduction of Poverty

Robert J. Lampman

University of Wisconsin

[Excerpted, with permission of the American Economic Association, from "Approaches to the Reduction of Poverty," in the American Economic Review, *May 1965.]*

Why Poverty Persists

As background to . . . strategic decisions, it is useful to categorize the causes of poverty in today's economy. But perhaps it is necessary first to brush aside the idea that there has to be some given amount of poverty. Most economists have long since given up the idea that a progressive society needs the threat of poverty to induce work and sobriety in the lower classes. Similarly, one can consign to folk-lore the ideas that some are rich only because others are poor and exploited, that if none were poor then necessary but unpleasant jobs would go undone, that the middle class has a psychological need to exclude a minority from above-poverty living standards, and that poverty is a necessary concomitant of the unemployment which necessarily accompanies economic growth.

Why, then, is it that there remains a minority of persons who are involuntarily poor in this affluent society? How does our system select the particular members for this minority? To the latter question we offer a three part answer.

(1) Events external to individuals select a number to be poor.
(2) Social barriers of caste, class, and custom denominate persons with certain characteristics to run a high risk of being poor.
(3) The market assigns a high risk of being poor to those with limited ability or motivations.

One cannot look at the data on who are the poor without sensing that many are poor because of events beyond their control. Over a third of the 35 million poor are children whose misfortune arises out of the chance assignment to poor parents. In some cases this poverty comes out of being members of unusually large families. Among the poor adults, about a third have either suffered a disability, premature death of the family breadwinner, or family dissolution. A considerable number have confronted a declining demand for services in their chosen occupation, industry, or place of residence. Some have outlived their savings or have lost them due to inflation or bank failure. For many persons who are otherwise "normal" poverty may be said to arise out of one or a combination of such happenings.

A second factor that operates in the selection of persons to be poor is the maintenance of social barriers in the form of caste, class, and custom. The clearest example of this, of course, is racial discrimination with regard to opportunities to qualify for and to obtain work. (It is perhaps worth emphasizing here that only a fifth of the present poor are non-white, and that only a minority of the non-whites are presently poor.) Similar types of arbitrary barriers, or market imperfections, are observable in the case of sex, age, residence, religion, education, and seniority. They are formalized in employer hiring procedures, in the rules of unions and professional and trade associations, in governmental regulations concerning housing and welfare and other programs, and are informally expressed in customer preferences. Barriers, once established, tend to be reinforced from the poverty side by the alienated themselves. The poor tend to be cut off from not only opportunity but even from information about opportunity. A poverty subculture develops which sustains attitudes and values that are hostile to escape from poverty. These barriers combine to make events non-random, e.g., unemployment is slanted away from those inside the feudalistic walls of collective bargaining, disability more commonly occurs in jobs reserved for those outside the barriers, the subculture of poverty invites or is prone to self-realizing forecasts of disaster.

The third factor involved in selecting persons out of the affluent society to be poor is limited ability or motivation of persons to earn and to protect themselves against events and to fight their way over the barriers.[1] To the extent that the market is perfect one can rationalize the selection for poverty (insofar as earnings alone are considered) on the basis of the abilities and skills needed by the market and the distribution of those abilities and skills in the population. But we note that ability is to some extent acquired or environmentally determined and

---

[1] For an insight into the relative importance of this factor see James N. Morgan, Martin H. David, Wilbur J. Cohen, and Harvey E. Brazer, *Income and Welfare in the U.S.*, 1962, pp. 196–198.

that poverty tends to create personalities who will be de-selected by the market as inadequate on the basis of ability or motivation.

Countering "Events"

Approaches to the reduction of poverty can be seen as parallel to the causes or bases for selection recounted above. The first approach then is to prevent or counter the events or happenings which select some persons for poverty status. The poverty rate could be lessened by any reduction in early death, disability, family desertion, what Galbraith referred to as excessive procreation by the poor, or by containment of inflation and other hazards to financial security. Among the important events in this context the one most relevant to public policy consideration at this time is excessive unemployment. It would appear that if the recent level of over 5 percent unemployment could be reduced to 4 percent the poverty rate would drop by about one percentage point.[2] Further fall in the poverty rate would follow if—by retraining and relocation of some workers—long-term unemployment could be cut or if unemployment could be more widely shared with the non-poor.

To the extent that events are beyond prevention, some, e.g., disability, can be countered by remedial measures. Where neither the preventive nor the remedial approach is suitable, only the alleviate measures of social insurance and public assistance remain. And the sufficiency of these measures will help determine the poverty rate and the size of the poverty-income-gap. It is interesting to note that our system of public income maintenance, which now pays out $35 billion in benefits per year, is aimed more at the problem of income insecurity of the middle class and at blocking returns to poverty than in facilitating exits from poverty for those who have never been out of poverty. The non-poor have the major claim to social insurance benefits, the levels of which in most cases are not adequate in themselves to keep a family out of poverty. Assistance payments of $4 billion now go to 8 million persons all of whom are in the ranks of the poor, but about half of the 35 million

---

[2] Unemployment is not strikingly different among the poor than the non-poor. Non-participation in the labor force is more markedly associated with poverty than is unemployment. However, it seems that about 1 million poor family heads experience unemployment during the year. (Census Population Reports, P-60, No. 39, February 28, 1963, Tables 15 and 16.) If half of this group were moved out of poverty by more nearly full employment, then the poverty rate would be one percentage point lower. Another way to estimate this is as follows. The national income would be $30 billion higher than it is if we had full employment. And a $30 billion increase in recent years has generally meant a full percentage point drop in the percent of families in poverty.

poor receive neither assistance nor social insurance payments. One important step in the campaign against poverty would be to re-examine our insurance and assistance programs to discover ways in which they could be more effective in helping people to get out of poverty. Among the ideas to be considered along this line are easier eligibility for benefits, higher minimum benefits, incentives to earn while receiving benefits, ways to combine work-relief, retraining, rehabilitation, and relocation with receipt of benefits.

Among the several events that select people for poverty the ones about which we have done the least by social policy are family breakup by other than death and the event of being born poor. Both of these could be alleviated by a family allowance system, which the U. S., almost alone among western nations, lacks. We do, of course, have arrangements in the federal individual income tax for personal deductions and exemptions whereby families of different size and composition are ranked for the imposition of progressive rates. However, it is a major irony of this system that it does not extend the full force of its allowances for children to the really poor. In order to do so, the tax system could be converted to have negative as well as positive rates, paying out grants as well as forgiving taxes on the basis of already adopted exemptions and rates. At present there are almost $20 billion of unused exemptions and deductions, most of which relate to families with children. Restricting the plan to such families and applying a negative tax rate of, say 20 percent, to this amount would "yield" an allowance total of almost $4 billion. This would not, in itself take many people out of poverty but it would go a considerable distance toward closing the poverty-income-gap, which now aggregates about $12 billion.

It would, of course, be possible to go considerably further by this device without significantly impairing incentive to work and save. First, however, let me reject as unworkable any simple plan to assure a minimum income of $3,000. To make such an assurance would induce many now earning less than and even some earning slightly more than $3,000 to forego earnings opportunities and to accept the grant. Hence the poverty-income-gap of $12 billion would far understate the cost of such a minimum income plan. However, it would be practicable to enact a system of progressive rates articulated with the present income tax schedule.[3] The percent rates fall from 70 percent at the top to 14 percent at income just above $3,700 for a family of five, to zero percent for income below $3,700. The average negative tax rates could move, then, from zero percent to minus 14 percent for, say, the unused ex-

---

[3] C.f. Milton Friedman, *Capitalism and Freedom*, 1962, pp. 192–193.

emptions that total $500, to 20 percent for those that total $1,000 and 40 percent for those that total $3,700. This would amount to a minimum income of $1,480 for a family of five; it would retain positive incentives through a set of grants that would gradually diminish as earned income rose.

The total amount to be paid out (interestingly this would be shown in the Federal budget as a net reduction in tax collections) under such a program would obviously depend upon the particular rates selected, the definition of income used, the types of income-receiving units declared eligible, and the offsets made in public assistance payments. But it clearly could be more than the $4 billion mentioned in connection with the more limited plan of a standard 20 percent negative tax rate. At the outset it might involve half the poverty-income-gap and total about $6 billion. This amount is approximately equal to the total federal, state, and local taxes now paid by the poor. Hence it would amount to a remission of taxes paid. As the number in poverty fell the amount paid out under this plan would in turn diminish.

Breaking Down Barriers

The approaches discussed thus far are consistent with the view that poverty is the result of events which happen to people. But there are other approaches including those aimed at removing barriers which keep people in poverty. Legislation and private, volunteer efforts to assure equal educational and employment opportunities can make a contribution in this direction. Efforts to randomize unemployment by area redevelopment and relocation can in some cases work to break down "islands of poverty." Public policy can prevent or modify the forming of a poverty sub-culture by city-zoning laws, by public housing and by regulations of private housing, by school re-districting, by recreational, cultural, and public health programs. It is curious that medieval cities built walls to keep poverty outside. Present arrangements often work to bottle it up inside cities or parts of cities and thereby encourage poverty to function as its own cause.

Improving Abilities and Motivations

The third broad approach to accelerated reduction of poverty relates to the basis for selection referred to above as limited ability or motivation. The process of economic growth works the poverty line progressively deeper into the ranks of people who are below average in ability or motivation, but meantime it should be possible to raise the ability and motivation levels of the lowest. It is interesting that few children, even those of below average ability, who are not born and raised in poverty, actually end up in poverty. This suggests that poverty is to some extent an inherited disease. But it also suggests that if poor children had the same opportunities, including pre-school training and remedial health care, as the non-poor (even assuming no great breakthroughs of scientific understanding), the rate of escape from poverty would be higher. Even more fundamentally, we know that mental retardation as well as infant mortality and morbidity have an important causal connection with inadequate pre-natal care, which in turn relates to low income of parents.

A belief in the economic responsiveness of poor youngsters to improved educational opportunities underlies policies advocated by many educational theorists from Bentham to Conant. And this widely shared belief no doubt explains the emphasis which the Economic Opportunity Act places upon education and training. The appropriation under that Act, while it seems small relative to the poverty-income-gap, is large relative to present outlays for education of the poor. I would estimate that the half-billion dollars or so thereby added increases the national expenditure for this purpose by about one-seventh. To raise the level of educational expenditure for poor children—who are one-fifth of the nation's children but who consume about a tenth of educational outlay—to equal that of the average would cost in the neighborhood of $3 billion. Such an emphasis upon education and training is justified by the fact that families headed by young adults will tend, in a few years, to be the most rapidly increasing group of poor families.

Summary

Past experience provides a basis for the belief that poverty can be eliminated in the U. S. in this generation. The poverty-rate has been reduced at the rate of one percentage point a year; the poverty-income-gap is now down to 2 percent of gross national product.

Preventing and countering the "events" which select people for poverty can help to maintain or accelerate the rate at which we have been making progress against poverty. For example, by returning to the 4 percent "full employment" rate of unemployment, we would instantaneously reduce the poverty rate by one percentage point. For another example, we could make a great stride toward early closing of the poverty-income-gap by modifying the income tax to pay out family allowances.

Another broad approach to the elimination of poverty is to break down the social barriers which restrict opportunities for the poor. Examples of this are legislating against practices of discrimination and making plans to bring the poor into the mainstream of community life.

The third approach is to make progressively greater investment in improving the abilities and motivations of the poor. Substantial increase in outlays for education and training is a promising example of this approach.

Reduction of poverty hinges on the attainment of other goals such as economic growth, full employment, income security, and equal opportunity. But it also turns upon the reduction of poverty itself since poverty to an important degree causes itself. Hence, any favorable break in the circle makes the next step easier. More nearly full employment makes barriers less meaningful; lower barriers shrink differences in motivation. Similarly, higher incomes for the poor work to reduce both acquired and at-birth limitations of ability.

But any one of the approaches will involve costs and it would be valuable to know their comparative cost-benefit ratios. It is on this that, by theoretical and empirical research—including inter-country study, social scientists can make a distinctive contribution to the long-dreamed of, but now explicitly stated, goal of eliminating poverty.

President Johnson's Message on Poverty to the Congress of the United States, March 16, 1964

[*Reprinted from* The War on Poverty: The Economic Opportunity Act of *1964, Senate Document No. 86, Washington, D. C., 1964.*]

To the Congress of the United States:

We are citizens of the richest and most fortunate nation in the history of the world.

One hundred and eighty years ago we were a small country struggling for survival on the margin of a hostile land.

Today we have established a civilization of free men which spans an entire continent.

With the growth of our country has come opportunity for our people—opportunity to educate our children, to use our energies in productive work, to increase our leisure—opportunity for almost every American to hope that through work and talent he could create a better life for himself and his family.

The path forward has not been an easy one.

But we have never lost sight of our goal—an America in which every citizen shares all the opportunities of his society, in which every man has a chance to advance his welfare to the limit of his capacities.

We have come a long way toward this goal.

We still have a long way to go.

The distance which remains is the measure of the great unfinished work of our society.

To finish that work I have called for a national war on poverty. Our objective: total victory.

There are millions of Americans—one-fifth of our people—who have not shared in the abundance which has been granted to most of us, and on whom the gates of opportunity have been closed.

What does this poverty mean to those who endure it?

It means a daily struggle to secure the necessities for even a meager existence. It means that the abundance, the comforts, the opportunities they see all around them are beyond their grasp.

Worst of all, it means hopelessness for the young.

The young man or woman who grows up without a decent education, in a broken home, in a hostile and squalid environment, in ill health or in the face of racial injustice—that young man or woman is often trapped in a life of poverty.

He does not have the skills demanded by a complex society. He does not know how to acquire those skills. He faces a mounting sense of despair which drains initiative and ambition and energy.

Our tax cut will create millions of new jobs—new exits from poverty.

But we must also strike down all the barriers which keep many from using those exits.

The war on poverty is not a struggle simply to support people, to make them dependent on the generosity of others.

It is a struggle to give people a chance.

It is an effort to allow them to develop and use their capacities, as we have been allowed to develop and use ours, so that they can share, as others share, in the promise of this Nation.

We do this, first of all, because it is right that we should.

From the establishment of public education and land-grant colleges through agricultural extension and encouragement to industry, we have pursued the goal of a nation with full and increasing opportunities for all its citizens.

The war on poverty is a further step in that pursuit.

We do it also because helping some will increase the prosperity of all.

Our fight against poverty will be an investment in the most valuable of our resources—the skills and strength of our people.

And in the future, as in past, this investment will return its cost many fold to our entire economy.

If we can raise the annual earnings of 10 million among the poor by only $1,000 we will have added $14 billion a year to our national output. In addition we can make important reductions in public assistance payments which now cost us $4 billion a year, and in the large costs of fighting crime and delinquency, disease and hunger.

This is only part of the story.

Our history has proved that each time we broaden the base of abundance, giving more people the chance to produce and consume, we create new industry, higher production, increased earnings, and better income for all.

Giving new opportunity to those who have little will enrich the lives of all the rest.

Because it is right, because it is wise, and because, for the first time in our history, it is possible to conquer poverty, I submit, for the consideration of the Congress and the country, the Economic Opportunity Act of 1964.

The act does not merely expand old programs or improve what is already being done.

It charts a new course.

It strikes at the causes, not just the consequences of poverty.

It can be a milestone in our 180-year search for a better life for our people.

This act provides five basic opportunities:

It will give almost half a million underprivileged young Americans the opportunity to develop skills, continue education, and find useful work.

It will give every American community the opportunity to develop a comprehensive plan to fight its own poverty—and help them to carry out their plans.

It will give dedicated Americans the opportunity to enlist as volunteers in the war against poverty.

It will give many workers and farmers the opportunity to break through particular barriers which bar their escape from poverty.

It will give the entire Nation the opportunity for a concerted attack on poverty through the establishment, under my direction, of the Office of Economic Opportunity, a national headquarters for the war against poverty.

This is how we propose to create these opportunities.

First, we will give high priority to helping young Americans who lack skills, who have not completed their education or who cannot complete it because they are too poor.

The years of high school and college age are the most critical stage of a young person's life. If they are not helped then, many will be condemned to a life of poverty which they, in turn, will pass on to their children.

I therefore recommend the creation of a Job Corps, a work-training program, and a work-study program.

A new national Job Corps will build toward an enlistment of 100,000 young men. They will be drawn from those whose background, health, and education make them least fit for useful work.

Those who volunteer will enter more than 100 camps and centers around the country.

Half of these young men will work, in the first year, on special conservation projects to give them education, useful work experience, and to enrich the natural resources of the country.

Half of these young men will receive, in the first year, a blend of training, basic education, and work experience in job training centers.

These are not simply camps for the underprivileged. They are new educational institutions, comparable in innovation to the land-grant colleges. Those who enter them will emerge better qualified to play a productive role in American society.

A new national work-training program operated by the Department of Labor will provide work and training for 200,000 American men and women between the ages of 16 and 21. This will be developed through State and local governments and nonprofit agencies.

Hundreds of thousands of young Americans badly need the experience, the income, and the sense of purpose which useful full or part-time work can bring. For them such work may mean the difference between finishing school or dropping out. Vital community activities from hospitals and playgrounds to libraries and settlement houses are suffering because there are not enough people to staff them.

We are simply bringing these needs together.

A new national work-study program operated by the Department of Health, Education, and Welfare will provide Federal funds for part-time jobs for 140,000 young Americans who do not go to college because they cannot afford it.

There is no more senseless waste than the waste of the brain-power and skill of those who are kept from college by economic circumstance. Under this program they will, in a great American tradition, be able to work their way through school.

They and the country will be richer for it.

Second, through a new community action program we intend to strike at poverty at its source—in the streets of our cities and on the farms of our countryside among the very young and the impoverished old.

This program asks men and women throughout the country to

prepare long-range plans for the attack on poverty in their own local communities.

These are not plans prepared in Washington and imposed upon hundreds of different situations.

They are based on the fact that local citizens best understand their own problems, and know best how to deal with those problems.

These plans will be local plans striking at the many unfilled needs which underlie poverty in each community, not just one or two. Their components and emphasis will differ as needs differ.

These plans will be local plans calling upon all the resources available to the community—Federal and State, local and private, human and material.

And when these plans are approved by the Office of Economic Opportunity, the Federal Government will finance up to 90 percent of the additional cost for the first 2 years.

The most enduring strength of our Nation is the huge reservoir of talent, initiative and leadership which exists at every level of our society.

Through the community action program we call upon this, our greatest strength, to overcome our greatest weakness.

Third, I ask for the authority to recruit and train skilled volunteers for the war against poverty.

Thousands of Americans have volunteered to serve the needs of other lands.

Thousands more want the chance to serve the needs of their own land.

They should have that chance.

Among older people who have retired, as well as among the young, among women as well as men, there are many Americans who are ready to enlist in our war against poverty.

They have skills and dedication. They are badly needed.

If the State requests them, if the community needs and will use them, we will recruit and train them and give them the chance to serve.

Fourth, we intend to create new opportunities for certain hard-hit groups to break out of the pattern of poverty.

Through a new program of loans and guarantees we can provide incentives to those who will employ the unemployed.

Through programs of work and retraining for unemployed fathers and mothers we can help them support their families in dignity while preparing themselves for new work.

Through funds to purchase needed land, organize cooperatives, and create new and adequate family farms we can help those whose life on the land has been a struggle without hope.

Fifth, I do not intend that the war against poverty become a series of uncoordinated and unrelated efforts—that it perish for lack of leadership and direction.

Therefore this bill creates, in the Executive Office of the President, a new Office of Economic Opportunity. Its Director will be my personal chief of staff for the war against poverty. I intend to appoint Sargent Shriver to this post.

He will be directly responsible for these new programs. He will work with and through existing agencies of the Government.

This program—the Economic Opportunity Act—is the foundation of our war against poverty. But it does not stand alone.

For the past 3 years this Government has advanced a number of new proposals which strike at important areas of need and distress.

I ask the Congress to extend those which are already in action, and to establish those which have already been proposed.

There are programs to help badly distressed areas such as the Area Redevelopment Act, and the legislation now being prepared to help Appalachia.

There are programs to help those without training find a place in today's complex society—such as the Manpower Development Training Act and the Vocational Education Act for youth.

There are programs to protect those who are specially vulnerable to the ravages of poverty—hospital insurance for the elderly, protection for migrant farmworkers, a food stamp program for the needy, coverage for millions not now protected by a minimum wage, new and expanded unemployment benefits for men out of work, a housing and community development bill for those seeking decent homes.

Finally there are programs which help the entire country, such as aid to education which, by raising the quality of schooling available to every American child, will give a new chance for knowledge to the children of the poor.

I ask immediate action on all these programs.

What you are being asked to consider is not a simple or an easy program. But poverty is not a simple or an easy enemy.

It cannot be driven from the land by a single attack on a single front. Were this so we would have conquered poverty long ago.

Nor can it be conquered by government alone.

For decades American labor and American business, private institutions and private individuals have been engaged in strengthening our economy and offering new opportunity to those in need.

We need their help, their support, and their full participation.

Through this program we offer new incentives and new opportunities for cooperation, so that all the energy of our nation, not merely the efforts of government, can be brought to bear on our common enemy.

Today, for the first time in our history, we have the power to strike away the barriers to full participation in our society. Having the power, we have the duty.

The Congress is charged by the Constitution to "provide . . . for the general welfare of the United States." Our present abundance is a measure of its success in fulfilling that duty. Now Congress is being asked to extend that welfare to all our people.

The President of the United States is President of all the people in every section of the country. But this office also holds a special responsibility to the distressed and disinherited, the hungry and the hopeless of this abundant Nation.

It is in pursuit of that special responsibility that I submit this message to you today.

The new program I propose is within our means. Its cost of $970 million is 1 percent of our national budget—and every dollar I am requesting for this program is already included in the budget I sent to Congress in January.

But we cannot measure its importance by its cost.

For it charts an entirely new course of hope for our people.

We are fully aware that this program will not eliminate all the poverty in America in a few months or a few years. Poverty is deeply rooted and its causes are many.

But this program will show the way to new opportunities for millions of our fellow citizens.

It will provide a lever with which we can begin to open the door to our prosperity for those who have been kept outside.

It will also give us the chance to test our weapons, to try our energy and ideas and imagination for the many battles yet to come. As conditions change, and as experience illuminates our difficulties, we will be prepared to modify our strategy.

And this program is much more than a beginning.

Rather it is a commitment. It is a total commitment by this President, and this Congress, and this Nation, to pursue victory over the most ancient of mankind's enemies.

On many historic occasions the President has requested from Congress the authority to move against forces which were endangering the well-being of our country.

This is such an occasion.

On similar occasions in the past we have often been called upon to wage war against foreign enemies which threatened our freedom. Today we are asked to declare war on a domestic enemy which threatens the strength of our Nation and the welfare of our people.

If we now move forward against this enemy—if we can bring to the challenges of peace the same determination and strength which has brought us victory in war—then this day and this Congress will have won a secure and honorable place in the history of the Nation, and the enduring gratitude of generations of Americans yet to come.

Waging War on Poverty*

A.F.L.–C.I.O. Executive Council Statement

[Reprinted with permission from The American Federationist, *April 1964.]*

THE A.F.L.–C.I.O. HAS LONG SOUGHT to focus public attention on the paradox of poverty in the midst of America's plenty. We have spelled out steps which must be taken to end it and we have sought to implement this program through both public and private action.

Our concern is not only the magnitude of poverty remaining in the United States—the fact that 35 million Americans still live in families with incomes of under $3,000, before tax. We are even more concerned because progress towards eradication of this cancer has slowed down almost to a halt in the past decade of spreading unemployment and underemployment. What is more, success in winning civil rights and dignity for Negroes and other minority groups is inseparably linked with our success in effectively waging war against want.

President Johnson now must reverse nearly ten years of stagnation in the effort to reduce the prevalence of poverty. Moreover, the Administration's anti-poverty campaign in 1964 must be viewed as hardly a first, small step. Bold measures and substantial funds will have to be added to achieve meaningful progress in this worthy national crusade.

No nation in the history of the world has a greater capability of lifting all of its people above the level of want. The test we now face is our will to do it.

---

* The A.F.L.–C.I.O. Executive Council issued this statement on February 21, 1964, following the President's "State of the Union" address.

If we now engage in merely a token effort—a mere skirmish instead of a war—we will be deluding the millions of impoverished and frustrating the expectations of the nation and of the world.

On the other hand, the victory that will result from a genuine crusade will not only benefit those now in want. It will increase the self-respect and wellbeing of every American and it will give added meaning to the reality of the American way of life.

The Nature of the Problem

From early New Deal days until the mid-1950s, substantial progress was made in lifting the incomes of our neediest families—and this progress was not accidental. New Deal social and economic programs, like minimum wages and fair labor standards, social insurance and welfare aids for the aged, survivors, unemployed and indigent were purposely designed to help the neediest. Simultaneously, encouragement of the rapid growth of unions helped lift the earnings of millions of the underpaid. Then the impact of the war in generating full employment— within the framework of wartime price-control and tax policies which effectively prevented a regressive income shift—further speeded inroads on poverty.

Rising postwar production and employment until the mid-1950s helped continue this trend. Despite the adverse effect of price inflation and profiteering, families with cash incomes of less than $3,000, in 1962 dollars, dropped from 32 percent of the total to 23 percent, from 1947 to 1956.

Since the mid-1950s, however, the portion of our families still impoverished has remained practically stationary. This misfortune is rooted in the spread of unemployment and underemployment and in government policies excessively concerned with the welfare of corporations and the already well-off, rather than the needs of our fellow citizens most in want. Despite the continuing rise in the wellbeing of most Americans, families with incomes below $3,000 dropped only to 20 percent of the total by 1962. In fact, between 1956 and 1962 the share of total personal income going to the neediest fifth of our families actually went down.

If we are indeed determined to wage war against poverty, this wrong-way income distribution trend must be reversed. In 1961, the poorest 20 percent of our families received only five percent of total after-tax personal income. The top five percent of our families with the highest incomes, on the other hand, received 17.7 percent of the total, which is considerably more than what was received by the 40 percent of our families at the bottom.

A renewed effort to quickly raise the income share of the lowest 20 percent need not jeopardize the affluence of those at the top. As personal income continues to go up, we must simply direct a greater portion of this growth to the families who need it most. Surely, as President Franklin Roosevelt said thirty years ago: "The test of our progress is not whether we add to the abundance of those who have much; it is whether we provide enough for those who have too little."

Studies of poverty in the United States reveal that over half of the families affected have members who are employed or are seeking work. Often their breadwinners are unemployed because of displacement due to automation, discrimination, lack of adequate skills or simply because jobs are not available in this period of persistent and rising unemployment. Many others are compelled to work part-time or for relief-level wages.

Persons 65 years of age or older head the families of almost one-third of our neediest. One-quarter of the most impoverished are families without any breadwinner at all because of disability, death, desertion or old age. Non-white Americans comprise over 20 percent of those most in want, although they account for only about 10 percent of all families. Most of the poorest can be found in metropolitan area slums and in our large number of distressed industrial and rural areas across the country. Generally, the educational opportunities of those most in need have been low.

In now launching all-out war on poverty, adequate measures to immediately alleviate human suffering are imperative. The food-stamp plan and other measures to provide an adequate diet for all needy families should be improved and extended. But at the same time that such humanitarian efforts are being pursued, fundamental measures must deal with the basic causes of poverty at their roots. In planning these actions, four major areas of responsibility in which the federal government must lead—but in which state and local governments and private groups must cooperate—are evident.

Measures to Create Jobs and Aid the Jobless

First, it is clearly self-evident that the long and persistent trend of rising unemployment and under-employment must be reversed if any significant progress is to be made in eradicating poverty. Achievement of the national goal of jobs at decent pay for all Americans who are able and willing to work must underlie any realistic anti-poverty program.

The stubborn persistence of poverty since the mid-1950s—during a period in which the majority of Americans have continued to improve their living standards—is substantially rooted in the rising trend of unemployment and part-time work. What is more, if this deplorable situation is allowed to continue—as a consequence of labor displacement at a time when new jobseekers are increasing faster than ever before—we will experience spreading poverty rather than its reduction. If national economic policy continues to enthrone greater productive efficiency and higher profits as the top-priority goals, rather than fulfillment of the promises of the Employment Act of 1946, a crusade against poverty—no matter how well intended—will show only scant results.

National policies to sharply increase employment for the jobless and underemployed, for the victims of discrimination, for the young flocking into the labor force and for those who will be displaced by automation are the essential foundation of an anti-poverty program. Through the rest of this decade at least, the American economy must create over 4 million job opportunities a year—more than 80,000 a week—in order to keep Americans at work. To the extent that we fail, want will grow.

On the basis of the record, this objective will not be reached without bold, far-reaching leadership by the federal government.

One of the major needs at this time—in addition to other long-range job-expanding actions—is a vast increase in federal outlays for job-creating public works. This will quickly create jobs—including substantial employment opportunities for unskilled and semi-skilled workers—and at the same time provide vitally-needed public improvements of permanent worth. Toward this end, the now expiring Public Works Acceleration program should be extended with a $2 billion appropriation and similar measures should be enacted which would create jobs, producing schools, hospitals, housing, urban redevelopment and other improvements that all communities urgently need.

Special programs should be enacted to provide young people with useful employment opportunities, including jobs in the conservation of natural resources as well as part-time job opportunities in schools and community services for high school and college students to encourage young people to continue their education. Such youth employment measures, however, should be civilian programs, with civilian management and supervision.

These and other job-creating measures can succeed in sustaining full employment only if they are accompanied by effective adjustment procedures to the labor-displacement and community disruption of automation, defense cutbacks and, frequently, foreign imports.

In addition, special measures to assist the jobless and the underemployed are essential parts of the campaign to eliminate poverty. These include improvement of the federal-state unemployment compensation system through the application of federal standards, implementation of the national manpower program in a manner that upgrades skills while safeguarding worker standards, a more effective nationwide public employment service, relocation allowances to aid the jobless to move to areas where work is available, enactment of effective fair employment practices legislation and strengthening the area redevelopment effort. Such measures are vitally important to aid jobless and underemployed workers to improve their incomes and opportunities.

Programs to Lift Wages

Second, programs to lift the incomes of low-paid workers must be an integral part of the campaign to eradicate the sources of poverty.

Extension of minimum wage coverage and an increase in the minimum hourly rate are essential, as well as special aids for our tragically exploited farm workers, including termination of the bracero importation program. These actions are essential to raise the income standards of the millions of impoverished employed workers and their families.

The federal government also must vigorously support the right of all wage and salary earners to organize and sustain effective unions and engage in collective bargaining—in agriculture as well as in industry and commerce. It is no accident that poverty is usually most prevalent among groups in which union organization is weak or nonexistent and in areas where trade unionism is compelled to function against the handicap of hostile state legislation. The experience of the 1930s clearly indicates that effective labor organization and collective bargaining are vital parts of an effort to help low-paid workers improve their economic status.

Aid Against Unavoidable Hazards

Third, a meaningful attack on the causes of want must deal effectively with the need for adequate income maintenance when unavoidable hardships destroy a family's ability to be self-supporting. This is particularly true in the case of most of the aged, broken families generally headed by a woman with children in her care and families in which the breadwinner has died or is incapacitated.

No war against poverty can be meaningful unless adequate family income protection is provided for those who cannot be self-sustaining, even in a full employment economy, because of such hazards. To meet the problems of these families, a whole series of special aids are vitally necessary.

A hospital insurance program for the aged, under social security, should be immediately adopted. Social security benefits for retirees, survivors and the disabled should be substantially increased.

The benefit and coverage levels of all state social insurance and welfare programs must be brought up to date. Moreover, public assistance payments must be increased to meet the family needs of the 1960s and improvements of community welfare programs are required.

To provide decent safeguards for the families of those who are injured or killed at work, federal standards are needed to upgrade the archaic workmen's compensation systems of the states.

Income maintenance when ill and the means to meet the rising costs of adequate medical care are problems confronting most families, but particularly those with the lower incomes. Insurance for the families of breadwinners separated from payrolls by illness—now limited to four states and the railroads—must be improved and extended nationally.

Education, Housing and Personal Adjustment

Fourth, in the effort to conquer poverty a substantially increased effort must be launched to meet special problems of the poor in the areas of health, education, housing and personal adjustment. Particularly, increased and improved opportunities for education must be made available for the children of the poor if the cycle of poverty is to be broken.

The war on poverty requires a vast increase in the quantity and improvement in the quality of education, health care, low-cost public housing, consumer counseling and personal guidance services for the members of low-income families. Without such efforts, their avenues toward higher living standards will also be blocked.

Improvement in the educational opportunities available to the children of low-income families, including federal aid for school construction and extension of free public education to the college level, must be viewed as basic public investments in the nation's future. Through supplemental federal aid for school districts where the need is greatest, the spread of junior colleges, substantial increases in the availability and amount of college scholarships and revival of the National Youth Administration idea of the 1930s, greater educational opportunities for these children can be achieved, the cycle of poverty can be broken and the entire nation can be enriched.

Successful war against poverty will automatically do more for American Negroes than for the population as a whole because they are such a disproportionately large part of our families still in want. But more than that, by taking the measures necessary to end poverty, we will create the conditions and climate that will enable us to end more quickly the ugly fact of discrimination in American life.

Action to achieve employment opportunities at decent wages for all Americans able and willing to work must be viewed as the primary underpinning of the anti-poverty program. This is true not only because so many impoverished families have a member who is, or could be, employed and the possession of a decent job is the best way to raise their income status and personal dignity; but, also, the restoration of a full employment, maximum-production economy is also of paramount importance because, as we rapidly raise our national income by effectively utilizing now-wasted resources, America will be even more able to meet the social costs of its anti-poverty crusade on every front.

Moreover, achievement of sustained full employment depends on success in rapidly reducing the prevalence of poverty. The expansion of jobs requires raising the buying power of the millions of low-income families since they are a vast potential market for the goods and services the economy can produce.

President Johnson's pledge to lead the nation in unconditional war on poverty lays down a long overdue challenge to the conscience of the American people. Already substantial public interest has been aroused but, if we really mean to wage this war, victory will not come easily. Offensives must be mounted on many fronts. Long-entrenched attitudes must change. A vast amount of effort and money will have to be expended.

Planning a Long-Range Balanced Effort

Leon H. Keyserling

Conference on Economic Progress

[Reprinted with permission from Progress or Poverty *by Leon H. Keyserling (Washington, D. C., 1964).]*

The Most General Measures:
National Fiscal and Monetary Policies

Federal tax policy. For economic and social reasons, any further tax reduction should concentrate upon enlarging the after-tax income of low- and lower-middle-income families and unattached individuals. This could be accomplished by lifting exemption credits in the personal income tax structure—these ought to be approximately doubled—and by reduction of Federal excise or sales taxes on necessities as distinguished from luxuries.

Federal spending policies. Increased Federal spending should take high precedence over further tax reduction. Wisely directed spending is obviously more helpful to the poor. And viewing the new technology and automation, spending can also do much more to help everybody—and especially the poor—because of its much greater stimulus to those types of output which will add most to employment opportunity and economic growth. Federal *per capita* outlays for all domestic purposes should be lifted from less than $181 in the original fiscal 1965 Budget to almost $251 by calendar 1970, and to about $256 by calendar 1975. Over the same period of time, Federal *per capita* outlays for all purposes should be lifted from about $483 to $639, and then to about $677. The total Federal Budget should be lifted from 97.9 billion dollars to 135 billion, and then to 156 billion. With optimum economic growth, these increases would result in a *smaller* Federal Budget in ratio to total national production, and a very much smaller national debt when measured similarly.

Monetary policies. The monetary policy prevalent since 1952 has been highly regressive in its income effects, as higher interest payments have penalized low-income groups. And tight money has worked severely against adequate employment and economic growth. The policies of the Federal Reserve Board should be drastically revised—by Congressional and/or Presidential intervention—toward a more liberal expansion of the money supply from year to year, with lower interest rates.

Measures to Reshape the Structure of Job Opportunity: Prime Importance of Housing and Urban Renewal

Because of the new technology and automation, the rate of productivity gains in agriculture and in many branches of industry is extremely rapid. Even though a greatly increased demand for the products of these types of economic activity is essential toward lifting the consumption standards of the poor and deprived, feasible increases in such demand are unlikely to outrun by much the further productivity gains in agriculture and in these branches of industry. This means relatively small opportunities for expansion of employment in these types of economic activity. By far the most promising opportunities to expand employment—especially among the unskilled and semi-skilled—are in the types of economic activity where our unmet nationwide needs call for expansion of goods and services far in excess of the likely technological advances in such types of activity. And in addition to the employment benefits which would result from vast expansion of such types of activity, the goods and services which such types of activity would turn out would also be exceedingly helpful to the poor as consumers. This calls for vigorous measures to reshape the entire structure of production, demand, and job opportunity.

Housing and urban renewal is by far the most important of these areas quantitatively, and as important as any qualitatively. We need to lift housing starts from 1.6 million (almost all for middle- and high-income groups) in 1963 to about 2.2 million by 1970, with almost half of these starts divided equally between lower-middle and low-income groups. This effort will require more favorable credit terms, including lower interest rates, to stimulate private investment in housing; for the poverty-stricken people in the slums, it will require a vast increase in public outlays at all levels, especially by the Federal Government. This housing expansion should be accompanied by enormous programs of urban renewal. *Per capita* Federal outlays for housing and community development should rise from a negative figure of $1.56 in the original fiscal 1965 Budget (when the Government is expected "to make money" on these programs) to more than $15½ by calendar 1970, and about $16½ by calendar 1975. In the aggregate, these Federal outlays should rise from a negative of 317 million dollars to 3.3 billion, and then to 3.8 billion.

Conventional-type public works, to serve genuine needs and to reduce unemployment, should receive at least a billion dollars a year of additional Federal support.

Direct Income-Reinforcement Programs

Minimum wage protection. The glaring deficiencies in coverage under the Federal Fair Labor Standards Act should be remedied promptly, and the minimum wage floor in general should be lifted to $2.00 an hour. Overtime premiums should be extended and liberalized.

Unemployment insurance. By combined State and Federal action, including higher Federal standards and some Federal contributions, unemployment insurance should as soon as feasible become the right of all those unemployed through no fault of their own, for as long as they are unemployed, and at average benefit payments of at least half the average full-time working wage. Regular insurance benefits should be reinforced by special revolving funds and installment payments to laid-off workers. With increased Federal aid, disability coverage under public assistance and OASDI should be as broad as the broadened coverage under unemployment insurance, and disability benefits should be lifted to adequate standards as to amounts and duration.

Farm-income improvement. The whole national farm program needs drastic reconstruction, to focus more effectively upon the goal of income parity rather than price parity for farmers, and to get more of the income increases to those farmers who need them most, with accent

upon the family-type farm. Hired farm labor should be covered by minimum wage and unemployment insurance legislation, and should have
the right to organize and bargain collectively. The highest concentration of effort should be upon expansion of domestic consumption, including surplus food distribution programs aimed toward adequate nutrition
for the millions of poor Americans who still lack it. Our exports of farm
products to the underdeveloped peoples still scourged by starvation
should be enlarged. Special efforts should be directed toward overcoming the exceptionally large deficiencies in education, health services, and
housing in those relatively poor States where agriculture and other rural
living are also highly concentrated. This calls for enlarged application
of the Federal "equalization" principle.

Old age insurance and pensions. These programs, almost everywhere are woefully behind the times, and this has grave effects upon
the lives of the poor. Within about five years, the average benefits under
OASDI should be approximately doubled, taking into account not only
retired workers but also their spouses or survivors and other dependents.
Emphasis should also be placed upon earlier retirements in general,
special forms of early-retirement benefits, and pension reinsurance plans.
Because of the regressive nature of payroll taxes, Federal contributions
financed by general taxation should assume a large part of the costs of
benefit payments under OASDI. With increased Federal aid, the same
retirement and income objectives should be sought for our senior citizens and their families who are helped by pensions rather than insurance, and for those who for one reason or another receive neither. There
is room for very large improvement in those aspects of OASDI which deal,
not with old age benefits proper, but with other types of help—including
medical—to those in great need.

Workmen's compensation. There is urgent need for very large
improvements in benefits and coverage under State workmen's compensation laws; the time has come to consider Federal standards and
aid to expedite this process.

Special and general public assistance. One of the greatest trage-
dies of our national life is the pitiful inadequacy of all types of public
assistance (both monetary and in kind) to broken families in need, to
families headed by women who cannot work, and to many other types
of family groups living in poverty. This calls for enlarged Federal assistance to those special types of State and local public assistance now
aided Federally to a degree, coupled with initiation of Federal aid to
general public assistance. *Per capita* Federal outlays for public assistance
should rise from $14.15 in the original fiscal 1965 Budget to more than

$21 by calendar 1970, and more than $23 by calendar 1975. In the aggregate, the increase should be from 2.9 billion dollars to 4.5 billion, and then to 5.4 billion.

Programs to Build Our Human Resources

These programs would have the same double-barrelled effects as the proposed housing programs. They would serve immediately and directly the needs of the poor. And because the needed increases in output in these areas would far exceed the rate of technological gains in these areas, these programs would do most to enlarge employment opportunity, and, in their construction aspects, would do most to increase employment opportunity for the unskilled and semi-skilled.

Education. In the public schools alone, we need from now through 1970 about 100,000 new classrooms a year, compared with actual building programs averaging about 60,000. We need to recruit about 100,000 teachers a year for the public schools, or about 50 percent more than recent and current recruitment levels. Teachers still need large salary increases, especially in the poorer States. Specialized programs to deal with the school dropouts should be pushed vigorously. In higher education, very large increases are needed in scholarships, student loans, and physical plants. Even if the States and localities continue to strain their resources to the utmost, and even with the highest foreseeable private outlays, Federal outlays for education should increase on a *per capita* basis from $8.35 in the original fiscal 1965 Budget to more than $33 by calendar 1970, and about $39 by calendar 1975. In the aggregate, they should be lifted from 1.7 billion dollars to 7 billion, and then to 9 billion.

Medical care. Prompt enactment of "Medicare" is essential, along with expansion of other types of public medical assistance to the needy regardless of age. We need approximately to double the average annual rate of hospital construction during the next ten years, along with vast increases in the numbers of doctors and nurses, and their improved distribution throughout the country. Medical research has made great strides, but it needs far more support. On a *per capita* basis, Federal outlays for health services and research should be lifted from $8.55 in the original fiscal 1965 Budget to close to $23 by calendar 1970, and more than $30 by calendar 1975. In the aggregate, they should be lifted from 1.7 billion dollars to 4.8 billion, and then to 7 billion. With more adequate health facilities and personnel as a foundation, a Federal system of universal health insurance should be established, financed in part by payroll taxes and in part by general taxation.

Training and Retraining Programs

The very encouraging projection of training and retraining programs for the poor and deprived under the Economic Opportunity Act of 1964 leaves many needs untouched. Handicapped workers need more attention. Federal aid in the form of relocation allowances is essential. In the broad category of labor and manpower and other welfare services, Federal *per capita* outlays should be increased from $6.07 in the original fiscal 1965 Budget to about $9.50 by calendar 1970, and increased slightly further by 1975. In the aggregate, they should be increased from 1.2 billion dollars to 2 billion, and then to about 2.2 billion.

Conservation and Improvement of Our Natural Resources

We have been experiencing a long drawn-out neglect in this whole field. In some areas, water and power supplies are lagging far behind very rapid population growth and corresponding industrial growth. The rivers flowing through some of our most congested urban areas are polluted. The air hanging over many of our industrial areas is dirty and foul. Recreational facilities and areas are inadequate and inaccessible, certainly for many of the poor and deprived. Atomic energy research and development for industrial purposes should be quickened, with more emphasis upon public control or regulation in the public interest. Such investment is an essential part of the expansion of employment opportunity, especially for the lesser-skilled who comprise so large a portion of those who are poor, young, and jobless. This is basically a national responsibility. Federal *per capita* outlays for resource development should be lifted from $12.77 in the original fiscal 1965 Budget to about $15 by calendar 1970, and more than $15.50 by calendar 1975. In the aggregate, they should be lifted from 2.6 billion dollars to 3.2 billion, and then to 3.6 billion.

Programs for the Distressed Areas

Our approaches thus far to the shocking conditions in Appalachia and elsewhere are mere nibbling on the fringes. With appropriate modifications, we need to apply to these areas the same boldness and practical imagination, and the same comprehensiveness of effort, which went into the making of TVA. Our country now sorely needs many "TVA's."

Redressing Dislocations Caused by Government Programs

Shifts in the size and location of national defense activities, as well as in Government procurement activities arising under other programs, result in major changes in employment opportunity. The Government should make every effort to reduce dislocating effects to a minimum, including placement of new plants and other activities in labor surplus rather than in labor shortage areas, and curtailment of plants and other activities in labor shortage rather than in labor surplus areas. Similarly, the international trade and tariff policies of the United States have a short-range adverse impact upon some industries and employment therein. As these international policies are in the national interest, their economic costs should be borne by the nation rather than by specific groups, and compensatory action of the proper kind should be taken to prevent these policies from impacting with excessive severity upon these particular groups.

The War Against Discrimination in All Its Forms

We cannot rest on our oars with respect to civil rights and liberties. These rights and liberties are precious for their own sake; their denial in any degree is evidence of the man-made oppression and neglect which also filter through the whole problem of poverty and deprivation in our country. Further, the whole crusade for civil rights and liberties needs to be allied with the whole crusade against poverty; for even when people become entirely free, they will still struggle to be well-fed and well-housed. Other forms of discrimination, while less talked about, are also on the scene. Despite passage of highly desirable legislation by the Congress in 1964, women are still grossly discriminated against—in their education and training opportunities, their chances to get jobs, and their pay when on the job. Through combined action at all levels, this type of discrimination should be stamped out. The same comments apply to the irrational and unjust aspects of discrimination based on age.

The Range of State and Local Responsibilities

Superficially, it might seem that the foregoing listing would impose too heavy a share of the war against poverty upon the Federal Government. But to date, the States and localities have made Herculean efforts to expand their services, in sharp contrast with inadequate action at the Federal level. In an article in the September 1964 *Harper's*, Edmund G. Brown, the Governor of our most populous State with one of the most intricate combinations of every kind of social and economic problem, sets forth courageously and admirably the fallacy of denying that such problems as medical care, poverty, and education are national in scope, or asserting that they fall within "the province of the city or State just because they occur in the city or the State." Governor Brown points out that we live in a time of "jet-age federalism and it is here to stay, no matter how fervently its detractors invoke the Founding Fathers."

Despite all this, many of the proposals in this study involve combined action at all levels of government. The projections in this study urge that the annual rate of Federal outlays for goods and services be lifted to a 1975 level about 41 billion dollars above the 1963 level, and that over the same period of time the annual rate of State and local outlays for goods and services be lifted about 36 billion. *Thus, the proposed increases at the State and local levels are more than six-sevenths as large as those proposed for the Federal Budget.*

The Range of Private Responsibilities

There is nothing in this study which indicates the prospect or desirability of any shrinkage in the traditional role and responsibilities of private enterprise. While the study urges, comparing 1975 with 1963, an increase of 77.4 billion dollars in the annual rate of outlays for goods and services by governments at all levels, it projects an increase of 103.6 billion in gross private investment (including net foreign), and an increase of 335 billion in private consumer expenditures, adding up to an increase of 516 billion in the annual rate of total national production. And within the private sector, many adjustments in prices, wages, and profits are needed to achieve a more workable balance between the advance of our productive capabilities and the advance of effective demand for ultimate products.

Further, the proposals for expansion of social security, to the extent adopted, would impose additional obligations in the form of payroll taxes upon employers and workers in the private sector, even though Federal legislation would continue to provide the framework.

Effective implementation of these proposals would require many changes in the methods by which national economic and social policies are developed and applied, beginning with the Employment Act of 1946.

The Need for Improved Utilization of the Employment Act of 1946

The very real problem is how we may obtain the knowledge and consents required for the best attainable blend of private and public efforts at all levels. The Employment Act of 1946 is admirably suited to this purpose. But operations under this Act, while rewarding in many respects, require further improvement.

The Economic Reports of the President should include the types of goals set forth in this study but not as yet adequately spelled out in these *Reports.* They should contain a *Job Budget,* looking at least five and probably ten years ahead. As part of their analysis of purchasing power, and of the policies needed to maximize it, they should embrace the objective of *a minimum adequacy level of living for all American families, and include goals for the rate of the reduction of poverty in America.* Only these *Reports* can carry to a logical conclusion the co-ordination of the war against poverty intended by the responsibilities vested in the Director under the Economic Opportunity Act of 1964; the programs under his purview are at best limited segments of a total war against poverty. The *Economic Reports* should include the equivalent of the *American Economic Performance Budget* used throughout this study to develop balanced goals. The Federal Budget should become an integral part of this *American Economic Performance Budget* —for national fiscal policy is only an implement of national economic and social policy—and so should our other basic national economic programs, such as Social Security, housing, and monetary policies.

Proper Limitations on "Planning" in a Free Society

The methods just recommended would represent neither top-heavy concentration of responsibility, nor excessive "planning" alien to our institutions and values. They do not envisage governmental encroachment upon the traditional functions of our private economic groups. They do not even envisage major additional *types* of public functions, although they would result in quantitative increases in many of these functions. And our national economic policies, under these methods, would be guided by the same managerial integration and purposefulness which mark large business enterprises; one of the important by-products would be that the Government could slough off or reduce many of its rapidly proliferating activities by doing a few essential things better.

And while this suggested procedure would not improperly mingle private and public responsibilities, the general goals embodied in it would offer extremely useful information to the private sector of the economy. The goals for employment, production, and purchasing power, accompanied by meaningful analysis of our potentials and needs, would be helpful to private enterprise in somewhat the same manner as the "Postwar Market" surveys made by the Government and others toward the end of World War II. Moreover, by providing a better *rationale* for recommended public policies, the procedure would enlarge private understanding of needed public action. This in itself would tend to reduce greatly the ultimate determination of public policies by "compromise" of competing group pressures; it would bring to the fore the long-range mutuality of real interests which should override the short-range or superficial conflicts. Developed through consultation and cooperation between private economic leadership and the Government, this procedure would help toward that larger degree of unity under freedom which is the fundamental answer to the totalitarian challenge.

In many respects, this procedure—modified to comport with our own institutions—would be similar to the "indicative planning" which has sparked the remarkable performance of some countries in Western Europe during the past decade. It would help us to steer more effectively between the Scylla of doctrinaire statism and the Charybdis of doctrinaire *laissez-faire*. Nothing much short of this can meet our own needs in the second half of the 20th Century.

The Triple Revolution: An Appraisal of the Major U.S. Crises and Proposals for Action

The Ad Hoc Committee on the Triple Revolution

THIS STATEMENT IS WRITTEN in the recognition that mankind is at a historic conjuncture which demands a fundamental reexamination of existing values and institutions. At this time, three separate and mutually reinforcing revolutions are taking place:

THE CYBERNATION REVOLUTION: A new era of production has begun. Its principles of organization are as different from those of the industrial era as those of the industrial era were different from the agricultural. The cybernation revolution has been brought about by the combination of the computer and the automated self-regulating machine. This results in a system of almost unlimited productive capacity which requires progressively less human labor. Cybernation is already reorganizing the economic and social system to meet its own needs.

THE WEAPONRY REVOLUTION: New forms of weaponry have been developed which cannot win wars but which can obliterate civilization. We are recognizing only now that the great weapons have eliminated war as a method for resolving international conflicts. The ever-present threat of total destruction is tempered by the knowledge of the final futility of war. The need of a "warless world" is generally recognized, though achieving it will be a long and frustrating process.

THE HUMAN RIGHTS REVOLUTION: A universal demand for full human rights is now clearly evident. It continues to be demonstrated in the civil rights movement within the United States. But this is only the local manifestation of a world-wide movement toward the establishment of social and political regimes in which every individual will feel valued and none will feel rejected on account of his race.

We are particularly concerned in this statement with the first of these revolutionary phenomena. This is not because we underestimate the significance of the other two. On the contrary, we affirm that it is the simultaneous occurrence and interaction of all three developments which make evident the necessity for radical alterations in attitude and policy. The adoption of just policies for coping with cybernation and for extending rights to all Americans is indispensable to the creation of an atmosphere in the United States in which the supreme issue, peace, can be reasonably debated and resolved.

Interaction of the Three Revolutions

The Negro claims, as a matter of simple justice, his full share in America's economic and social life. He sees adequate employment opportunities as a chief means of attaining this goal: the March on Washington (August, 1963) demanded freedom *and* jobs. The Negro's claim to a job is not being met. Negroes are the hardest-hit of the many groups being exiled from the economy by cybernation. Negro unemployment rates cannot be expected to drop substantially. Promises of jobs are a cruel and dangerous hoax on hundreds of thousands of Negroes and whites alike who are especially vulnerable to cybernation because of age or inadequate education.

The demand of the civil rights movement cannot be fulfilled within the present context of society. The Negro is trying to enter a social community and a tradition of work-and-income which are in the process of vanishing even for the hitherto privileged white worker. Jobs are disappearing under the impact of highly efficient, progressively less costly machines.

The United States operates on the thesis, set out in the Employment Act of 1946, that every person will be able to obtain a job if he wishes to do so and that this job will provide him with resources adequate to live and maintain a family decently. Thus job-holding is the general mechanism through which economic resources are distributed. Those without work have access only to a minimal income, hardly sufficient to provide the necessities of life, and enabling those receiving it to function as only "minimum consumers." As a result the goods and services which are needed by these crippled consumers, and which they would buy if they could, are not produced. This in turn deprives other workers of jobs, thus reducing their incomes and consumption.

Present excessive levels of unemployment would be multiplied several times if military and space expenditures did not continue to absorb 10% of the Gross National Product (i.e. the total goods and services produced). Some 6–8 million people are employed as a direct result of purchases for space and military activities. At least an equal number hold their jobs as an indirect result of military or space expenditures. In recent years, the military and space budgets have absorbed a rising proportion of national production and formed a strong support for the economy.

However, these expenditures are coming in for more and more criticism, at least partially in recognition of the fact that nuclear weapons have eliminated war as an acceptable method for resolving international conflicts. Early in 1964, President Johnson ordered a curtailment of certain military expenditures. Defense Secretary McNamara is closing shipyards, airfields, and army bases, and Congress is pressing the National Space Administration to economize. The future of these strong props to the economy is not as clear today as it was even a year ago.

The Nature of the Cybernation Revolution

Cybernation is manifesting the characteristics of a revolution in production. These include the development of radically different techniques and the subsequent appearance of novel principles of the organization of production; a basic reordering of man's relationship to his environment; and a dramatic increase in total available and potential energy.

The major difference between the agricultural, industrial and cybernation revolutions is the speed at which they developed. The agricultural revolution began several thousand years ago in the Middle East. Centuries passed in the shift from a subsistence base of hunting and food-gathering to settled agriculture.

In contrast, it has been less than 200 years since the emergence of the industrial revolution, and direct and accurate knowledge of the new productive techniques has reached most of mankind. This swift dissemination of information is generally held to be the main factor leading to widespread industrialization.

While the major aspects of the cybernation revolution are for the moment restricted to the United States, its effects are observable almost at once throughout the industrial world and large parts of the non-industrial world. Observation is rapidly followed by analysis and criticism. The problems posed by the cybernation revolution are part of a new era in the history of all mankind but they are first being faced by the people of the United States. The way Americans cope with cybernation will influence the course of this phenomenon everywhere. This country is the stage on which the Machines-and-Man drama will first be played for the world to witness.

The fundamental problem posed by the cybernation revolution in the United States is that it invalidates the general mechanism so far employed to undergird people's rights as consumers. Up to this time economic resources have been distributed on the basis of contributions to production, with machines and men competing for employment on somewhat equal terms. In the developing cybernated system, potentially unlimited output can be achieved by systems of machines which will require little cooperation from human beings. As machines take over production from men, they absorb an increasing proportion of resources while the men who are displaced become dependent on minimal and unrelated government measures—unemployment insurance, social security, welfare payments. These measures are less and less able to disguise a historic paradox: that a growing proportion of the population is subsisting on minimal incomes, often below the poverty line, at a time when sufficient productive potential is available to supply the needs of everyone in the United States.

The existence of this paradox is denied or ignored by conventional economic analysis. The general economic approach argues that potential demand, which if filled would raise the number of jobs and provide incomes to those holding them, is under-estimated. Most contemporary economic analysis states that all of the available labor force and industrial capacity is required to meet the needs of consumers and industry and to provide adequate public services: schools, parks, roads, homes, decent cities, and clean water and air. It is further argued that demand could be increased, by a variety of standard techniques, to any desired extent by providing money and machines to improve the conditions of the billions of impoverished people elsewhere in the world, who need food and shelter, clothes and machinery and everything else the industrial nations take for granted.

There is no question that cybernation does increase the potential for the provision of funds to neglected public sectors. Nor is there any question that cybernation would make possible the abolition of poverty at home and abroad. But the industrial system does not possess any adequate mechanisms to permit these potentials to become realities. The industrial system was designed to produce an ever-increasing quantity of goods as efficiently as possible, and it was assumed that the distribution of the power to purchase these goods would occur almost automatically. The continuance of the income-through-jobs link as the only major mechanism for distributing effective demand—for granting the right to consume—now acts as the main brake on the almost unlimited capacity of a cybernated productive system.

Recent administrations have proposed measures aimed at achieving a better distribution of resources, and at reducing unemployment and underemployment. A few of these proposals have been enacted.

More often they have failed to secure Congressional support. In every case, many members of Congress have criticized the proposed measures as departing from traditional principles for the allocation of resources and the encouragement of production. Abetted by budget-balancing economists and interest groups, they have argued for the maintenance of an economic machine based on ideas of scarcity to deal with the facts of abundance produced by cybernation. This time-consuming criticism has slowed the workings of Congress and has thrown out of focus for that body the inter-related effects of the triple revolution.

An adequate distribution of the potential abundance of goods and services will be achieved only when it is understood that the major economic problem is not how to increase production but how to distribute the abundance that is the great potential of cybernation. There is an urgent need for a fundamental change in the mechanisms employed to insure consumer rights.

The Cybernation Revolution—Facts and Figures

No responsible observer would attempt to describe the exact pace or the full sweep of a phenomenon that is developing with the speed of cybernation. Some aspects of this revolution, however, are already clear:

> the rate of productivity increase has risen with the onset of cybernation;
>
> an industrial economic system postulated on scarcity has been unable to distribute the abundant goods and services produced by a cybernated system or potential in it;
>
> surplus capacity and unemployment have thus co-existed at excessive levels over the last six years;
>
> the underlying cause of excessive unemployment is the fact that the capability of machines is rising more rapidly than the capacity of many human beings to keep pace;
>
> a permanent impoverished and jobless class is established in the midst of potential abundance.

Evidence for these statements follows:

1. The increased efficiency of machine systems is shown in the more rapid increase in productivity per man-hour since 1960, a year that marks the first visible upsurge of the cybernation revolution. In 1961, 1962, and 1963, productivity per man-hour rose at an average pace above 3.5%—a rate well above both the historical average and the post-war rate.

Companies are finding cybernation more and more attractive. Even at the present early stage of cybernation, costs have already been lowered to a point where the price of a durable machine may be as little as one-third of the current annual wage-cost of the worker it replaces. A more rapid rise in the rate of productivity increase per man-hour can be expected from now on.

2. In recent years it has proved impossible to increase demand fast enough to bring about the full use of either men or plant capacities. The task of developing sufficient additional demand promises to become more difficult each year. A thirty billion dollar annual increase in Gross National Product is now required to prevent unemployment rates from rising. An additional forty to sixty billion dollar increase would be required to bring unemployment rates down to an acceptable level.

3. The official rate of unemployment has remained at or above 5.5 percent during the Sixties. The unemployment rate for teenagers has been rising steadily and now stands around 15 percent. The unemployment rate for Negro teenagers stands about 30 percent. The unemployment rate for teenagers in minority ghettoes sometimes exceeds 50 percent. Unemployment rates for Negroes are regularly more than twice those for whites, whatever their occupation, educational level, age or sex. The unemployment position for other racial minorities is similarly unfavorable. Unemployment rates in depressed areas often exceed 50 percent.

These official figures seriously underestimate the true extent of unemployment. The statistics take no notice of under-employment or feather-bedding. Besides the 5.5 percent of the labor force who are officially designated as unemployed, nearly 4 percent of the labor force sought full-time work in 1962 but could find only part-time jobs. In addition, methods of calculating unemployment rates—a person is counted as unemployed only if he has actively sought a job recently—ignore the fact that many men and women who would like to find jobs have not looked for them because they know there are no employment opportunities. Underestimates for this reason are pervasive among groups whose unemployment rates are high—the young, the old, and racial minorities. Many people in the depressed agricultural, mining and industrial areas, who by official definition hold jobs but who are actually grossly underemployed, would move if there were prospects of finding work elsewhere. It is reasonable to estimate that over 8 million people are not working who would like to have jobs today as compared with the 4 million shown in the official statistics.

Even more serious is the fact that the number of people who have voluntarily removed themselves from the labor force is not constant but increases continuously. These people have decided to stop looking for employment and seem to have accepted the fact that they will never hold jobs again. This decision is largely irreversible, in economic and also in social and psychological terms. The older worker calls himself "retired"; he cannot accept work without affecting his social security status. The worker in his prime years is forced onto relief: in most states the requirements for becoming a relief recipient bring about such fundamental alterations in an individual's situation that a reversal of the process is always difficult and often totally infeasible. Teenagers, especially "drop-outs" and Negroes, are coming to realize that there is no place for them in the labor force but at the same time they are given no realistic alternative. These people and their dependents make up a large part of the "poverty" sector of the American population.

Statistical evidence of these trends appears in the decline in the proportion of people claiming to be in the labor force—the so-called labor force participation rate. The recent apparent stabilization of the unemployment rate around 5.5% is therefore misleading: it is a reflection of the discouragement and defeat of people who cannot find employment and have withdrawn from the market rather than a measure of the economy's success in creating jobs for those who want to work.

4. An efficiently functioning industrial system is assumed to provide the great majority of new jobs through the expansion of the private enterprise sector. But well over half of the new jobs created during the period 1957–1962 were in the public sector—predominantly in teaching. Job creation in the private sector has now almost entirely ceased except in services; of the 4,300,000 jobs created in this period, only about 200,-000 were provided by private industry through its own efforts. Many authorities anticipate that the application of cybernation to certain service industries, which is only just beginning, will be particularly effective. If this is the case, no significant job creation will take place in the private sector in coming years.

5. Cybernation raises the level of skills of the machine. Secretary of Labor Wirtz has recently stated that the machines being produced today have, on the average, skills equivalent to a high school diploma. If a human being is to compete with such machines, therefore, he must at least possess a high school diploma. The Department of Labor estimates, however, that on the basis of present trends as many as 30% of all students will be high school drop-outs in this decade.

6. A permanently depressed class is developing in the United States. Some 38,000,000 Americans, almost one-fifth of the nation, still live in poverty. The percentage of total income received by the poorest 20% of the population was 4.9% in 1944 and 4.7% in 1963.

Secretary Wirtz recently summarized these trends. "The confluence of surging population and driving technology is splitting the American labor force into tens of millions of 'have's' and millions of 'have-nots.'

In our economy of 69 million jobs, those with wanted skills enjoy opportunity and earning power. But the others face a new and stark problem—exclusion on a permanent basis, both as producers and consumers, from economic life. This division of people threatens to create a human slag heap. We cannot tolerate the development of a separate nation of the poor, the unskilled, the jobless, living within another nation of the well-off, the trained and the employed."

Need for a New Consensus

The stubbornness and novelty of the situation that is conveyed by these statistics is now generally accepted. Ironically, it continues to be assumed that it is possible to devise measures which will reduce unemployment to a minimum and thus preserve the overall viability of the present productive system. Some authorities have gone so far as to suggest that the pace of technological change should be slowed down "so as to allow the industrial productive system time to adapt."

We believe, on the contrary, that the industrial productive system is no longer viable. We assert that the only way to turn technological change to the benefit of the individual and the service of the general welfare is to accept the process and to utilize it rationally and humanely. The new science of political economy will be built on the encouragement and planned expansion of cybernation. The issues raised by cybernation are particularly amenable to intelligent policy-making: cybernation itself provides the resources and tools that are needed to ensure minimum hardship during the transition process.

But major changes must be made in our attitudes and institutions in the foreseeable future. Today Americans are being swept along by three simultaneous revolutions while assuming they have them under control. In the absence of real understanding of any of these phenomena, especially of technology, we may be allowing an efficient and dehumanized community to emerge by default. Gaining control of our future requires the conscious formation of the society we wish to have. Cybernation at last forces us to answer the historic questions: What is man's role when he is not dependent upon his own activities for the material basis of his life? What should be the basis for distributing individual access to national resources? Are there other proper claims on goods and services besides a job?

Because of cybernation, society needs no longer to impose repetitive and meaningless (because unnecessary) toil upon the individual. Society can now set the citizen free to make his own choice of occupation and vocation from a wide range of activities not now fostered by our value system and our accepted modes of "work." But in the absence of such a new consensus about cybernation, the nation cannot begin to take advantage of all that it promises for human betterment.

Proposal for Action

As a first step to a new consensus it is essential to recognize that the traditional link between jobs and incomes is being broken. The economy of abundance can sustain all citizens in comfort and economic security whether or not they engage in what is commonly reckoned as work. Wealth produced by machines rather than by men is still wealth. We urge, therefore, that society, through its appropriate legal and governmental institutions, undertake an unqualified commitment to provide every individual and every family with an adequate income as a matter of right. This undertaking we consider to be essential to the emerging economic, social and political order in this country. We regard it as the only policy by which the quarter of the nation now dispossessed and soon-to-be dispossessed by lack of employment can be brought within the abundant society. The unqualified right to an income would take the place of the patchwork of welfare measures—from unemployment insurance to relief—designed to ensure that no citizen or resident of the United States actually starves.

We do not pretend to visualize all of the consequences of this change in our values. It is clear, however, that the distribution of abundance in a cybernated society must be based on criteria strikingly different from those of an economic system based on scarcity. In retrospect, the establishment of the right to an income will prove to have been only the first step in the reconstruction of the value system of our society brought on by the triple revolution.

The present system encourages activities which can lead to private profit and neglects those activities which can enhance the wealth and the quality of life of our society. Consequently national policy has hitherto been aimed far more at the welfare of the productive process than at the welfare of people. The era of cybernation can reverse this emphasis. With public policy and research concentrated on people rather than processes we believe that many creative activities and interests commonly thought of as non-economic will absorb the time and the commitment of many of those no longer needed to produce goods and services. Society as a whole must encourage new modes of constructive, rewarding and ennobling activity. Principal among these are activities such as teaching and learning that relate people to people rather than people to things. Education has never been primarily conducted for profit in our society; it represents the first and most obvious activity inviting the expansion of the public sector to meet the needs of this period of transition.

We are not able to predict the long-run patterns of human activity and commitment in a nation when fewer and fewer people are involved in production of goods and services, nor are we able to forecast the overall patterns of income distribution that will replace those of the past full employment system. However, these are not speculative and fanciful matters to be contemplated at leisure for a society that may come into existence in three or four generations. The outlines of the future press sharply into the present. The problems of joblessness, inadequate incomes, and frustrated lives confront us now; the American Negro, in his rebellion, asserts the demands—and the rights—of all the disadvantaged. The Negro's is the most insistent voice today, but behind him stand the millions of impoverished who are beginning to understand that cybernation, properly understood and used, is the road out of want and toward a decent life.

The Transition*

We recognize that the drastic alterations in circumstances and in our way of life ushered in by cybernation and the economy of abundance will not be completed overnight. Left to the ordinary forces of the market such change, however, will involve physical and psychological misery and perhaps political chaos. Such misery is already clearly evident among the unemployed, among relief clients into the third generation and more and more among the young and the old for whom society appears to hold no promise of dignified or even stable lives. We must develop programs for this transition designed to give hope to the dispossessed and those cast out by the economic system, and to provide a basis for the rallying of people to bring about those changes in political and social institutions which are essential to the age of technology.

The program here suggested is not intended to be inclusive but rather to indicate its necessary scope. We propose:

---

* This view of the transitional period is not shared by all the signers. Robert Theobald and James Boggs hold that the two major principles of the transitional period will be (1) that machines rather than men will take up new conventional work openings and (2) that the activity of men will be directed to new forms of "work" and "leisure." Therefore, in their opinion the specific proposals outlined in this section are more suitable for meeting the problems of the scarcity-economic system than for advancing through the period of transition into the period of abundance.

1. A massive program to build up our educational system, designed especially with the needs of the chronically undereducated in mind. We estimate that tens of thousands of employment opportunities in such areas as teaching and research and development, particularly for younger people, may be thus created. Federal programs looking to the training of an additional 100,000 teachers annually are needed.

2. Massive public works. The need is to develop and put into effect programs of public works to construct dams, reservoirs, ports, water and air pollution facilities, community recreation facilities. We estimate that for each $1 billion per year spent on public works, 150,000 to 200,000 jobs would be created. $2 billion or more a year should be spent in this way, preferably as matching funds aimed at the relief of economically distressed or dislocated areas.

3. A massive program of low-cost housing, to be built both publicly and privately, and aimed at a rate of 700,000–1,000,000 units a year.

4. Development and financing of rapid transit systems, urban and interurban; and other programs to cope with the spreading problems of the great metropolitan centers.

5. A public power system built on the abundance of coal in distressed areas, designed for low-cost power to heavy industrial and residential sections.

6. Rehabilitation of obsolete military bases for community or educational use.

7. A major revision of our tax structure aimed at redistributing income as well as apportioning the costs of the transition period equitably. To this end an expansion of the use of excess profits tax would be important. Subsidies and tax credit plans are required to ease the human suffering involved in the transition of many industries from manpower to machine-power.

8. The trade unions can play an important and significant role in this period in a number of ways:

   a. Use of collective bargaining to negotiate not only for people at work but also for those thrown out of work by technological change.

   b. Bargaining for perquisites such as housing, recreational facilities, and similar programs as they have negotiated health and welfare programs.

   c. Obtaining a voice in the investment of the unions' huge pension and welfare funds, and insisting on investment policies which have as their major criteria the social use and function of the enterprise in which the investment is made.

d. Organization of the unemployed so that these voiceless people may once more be given a voice in their own economic destinies, and strengthening of the campaigns to organize white-collar and professional workers.

9. The use of the licensing power of government to regulate the speed and direction of cybernation to minimize hardship; and the use of minimum wage power as well as taxing powers to provide the incentives for moving as rapidly as possible toward the goals indicated by this paper.

These suggestions are in no way intended to be complete or definitively formulated. They contemplate expenditures of several billions more each year than are now being spent for socially rewarding enterprises, and a larger role for the government in the economy than it has now or has been given except in times of crisis. In our opinion, this is a time of crisis, the crisis of a triple revolution. Public philosophy for the transition must rest on the conviction that our economic, social and political institutions exist for the use of man and that man does not exist to maintain a particular economic system. This philosophy centers on an understanding that governments are instituted among men for the purpose of making possible life, liberty and the pursuit of happiness and that government should be a creative and positive instrument toward these ends.

Change Must Be Managed

The historic discovery of the post-World War II years is that the economic destiny of the nation can be managed. Since the debate over the Employment Act of 1946 it has been increasingly understood that the Federal Government bears primary responsibility for the economic and social well-being of the country. The essence of management is planning. The democratic requirement is planning by public bodies for the general welfare. Planning by private bodies such as corporations for their own welfare does not automatically result in additions to the general welfare, as the impact of cybernation on jobs has already made clear.

The hardships imposed by sudden changes in technology have been acknowledged by Congress in proposals for dealing with the long and short-run "dislocations," in legislation for depressed and "impacted" areas, retraining of workers replaced by machines, and the like. The measures so far proposed had not been "transitional" in conception. Perhaps for this reason they have had little effect on the situations they‧ were designed to alleviate. But the primary weakness of this legislation is not ineffectiveness but incoherence. In no way can these disconnected measures be seen as a plan for remedying deep ailments, but only, so to speak, as the superficial treatment of surface wounds.

Planning agencies should constitute the network through which pass the stated needs of the people at every level of society, gradually building into a national inventory of human requirements, arrived at by democratic debate of elected representatives.

The primary tasks of the appropriate planning institutions should be:

——— to collect the data necessary to appraise the effects, social and economic, of cybernation at different rates of innovation;

——— to recommend ways, by public and private initiative, of encouraging and stimulating cybernation;

——— to work toward optimal allocations of human and natural resources in meeting the requirements of society;

——— to develop ways to smooth the transition from a society in which the norm is full employment within an economic system based on scarcity, to one in which the norm will be either non-employment, in the traditional sense of productive work, or employment on the great variety of socially valuable but "nonproductive" tasks made possible by an economy of abundance; to bring about the conditions in which men and women no longer needed to produce goods and services may find their way to a variety of self-fulfilling and socially useful occupations.

——— to work out alternatives to defense and related spending that will commend themselves to citizens, entrepreneurs and workers as a more reasonable use of common resources.

——— to integrate domestic and international planning. The technological revolution has related virtually every major domestic problem to a world problem. The vast inequities between the industrialized and the underdeveloped countries cannot long be sustained.

The aim throughout will be the conscious and rational direction of economic life by planning institutions under democratic control.

In this changed framework the new planning institutions will operate at every level of government—local, regional and federal—and will be organized to elicit democratic participation in all their proceedings. These bodies will be the means for giving direction and content to the growing demand for improvement in all departments of public life. The planning institutions will show the way to turn the growing protest against ugly cities, polluted air and water, an inadequate educational system, disappearing recreational and material resources, low levels of medical care, and the haphazard economic development into an integrated effort to raise the level of general welfare.

We are encouraged by the record of the planning institutions both of the Common Market and of several European nations and believe that this country can benefit from studying their weaknesses and strengths.

A principal result of planning will be to step up investment in the public sector. Greater investment in this area is advocated because it is overdue, because the needs in this sector comprise a substantial part of the content of the general welfare, and because they can be readily afforded by an abundant society. Given the knowledge that we are now in a period of transition it would be deceptive, in our opinion, to present such activities as likely to produce full employment. The efficiencies of cybernation should be as much sought in the public as in the private sector, and a chief focus of planning would be one means of bringing this about. A central assumption of planning institutions would be the central assumption of this statement, that the nation is moving into a society in which production of goods and services is not the only or perhaps the chief means of distributing income.

The Democratization of Change

The revolution in weaponry gives some dim promise that mankind may finally eliminate institutionalized force as the method of settling international conflict and find for it political and moral equivalents leading to a better world. The Negro revolution signals the ultimate admission of this group to the American community on equal social, political, and economic terms. The cybernation revolution proffers an existence qualitatively richer in democratic as well as material values. A social order in which men make the decisions that shape their lives becomes more possible now than ever before; the unshackling of men from the bonds of unfulfilling labor frees them to become citizens, to make themselves and to make their own history.

But these enhanced promises by no means constitute a guarantee. Illuminating and making more possible the "democratic vistas" is one thing; reaching them is quite another, for a vision of democratic life is made real not by technological change but by men consciously moving toward that ideal and creating institutions that will realize and nourish the vision in living form.

Democracy, as we use the term, means a community of men and women who are able to understand, express, and determine their lives as dignified human beings. Democracy can only be rooted in a political and economic order in which wealth is distributed by and for people, and used for the widest social benefit. With the emergence of the era of abundance we have the economic base for a true democracy of participation, in which men no longer need to feel themselves prisoners of social forces or of decisions beyond their control or comprehension.

From Protest to Politics:
the Future of the Civil Rights Movement

Bayard Rustin

A. Philip Randolph Institute

[Reprinted from Commentary, *February 1965, copyright © 1965 by the* American Jewish Committee.]

> *There are 50 million poor in this country. And the Negro poor will never rise up until there is no more poverty. I hate to say this to young Negro people, but it is blindness to say anything else. We are sending them down a blind alley to pretend that by some hook or crook we can deal with slums on our own and with a few isolated whites. Or that somehow we can really deal with the housing problem, or that we can deal with the school problem or with jobs. Now there must be a great revolution in this country which is prepared to turn things upside down on these fundamental questions.*
> *The war on poverty is a contribution of the Negro struggle to the American revolution. . . . We have to see that we have an American revolution and not simply a civil rights movement in isolation. . . . Let some of the white students who are so happy to go to Mississippi . . . put on old clothes and go into the ghettoes of Detroit and Chicago and take on the really tough task of finding the leadership among the white poor and educating them and getting them marching in the streets. . . . For the civil rights movement, life now depends on whether other segments of the society can adopt a political platform, program, and broad movement to deal with the poor of this country, black and white.*
>
> —From a speech to the Michigan Regional Conference of the Congress of Racial Equality, May 1, 1964.

I

THE DECADE spanned by the 1954 Supreme Court decision on school desegregation and the Civil Rights Act of 1964 will undoubtedly be recorded as the period in which the legal foundations of racism in America were destroyed. To be sure, pockets of resistance remain; but it would be hard to quarrel with the assertion that the elaborate legal structure of segregation and discrimination, particularly in relation to public accommodations, has virtually collapsed. On the other hand, without making light of the human sacrifices involved in the direct-action tactics (sit-ins, freedom rides, and the rest) that were so instrumental to this achievement, we must recognize that in desegregating public accommodations, we affected institutions which are relatively peripheral both to the American socio-economic order and to the fundamental conditions of life of the Negro people. In a highly industrialized, 20th-century civilization, we hit Jim Crow precisely where it was most anachronistic, dispensable, and vulnerable—in hotels, lunch counters, terminals, libraries, swimming pools, and the like. For in these forms, Jim Crow does impede the flow of commerce in the broadest sense: it is a nuisance in a society on the move (and on the make). Not surprisingly, therefore, it was the most mobility-conscious and relatively liberated groups in the Negro community—lower-middle-class college students— who launched the attack that brought down this imposing but hollow structure.

The term "classical" appears especially apt for this phase of the civil rights movement. But in the few years that have passed since the first flush of sit-ins, several developments have taken place that have complicated matters enormously. One is the shifting focus of the movement in the South, symbolized by Birmingham; another is the spread of the revolution to the North; and the third, common to the other two, is the expansion of the movement's base in the Negro community. To attempt to disentangle these three strands is to do violence to reality. David Danzig's perceptive article, "The Meaning of Negro Strategy," correctly saw in the Birmingham events the victory of the concept of collective struggle over individual achievement as the road to Negro freedom. And Birmingham remains the unmatched symbol of grass-roots protest involving all strata of the black community. It was also in this most industrialized of Southern cities that the single-issue demands of the movement's classical stage gave way to the "package deal." No longer were Negroes satisfied with integrating lunch counters. They now sought advances in employment, housing, school integration, police protection, and so forth.

Thus, the movement in the South began to attack areas of discrimination which were not so remote from the Northern experience as were Jim Crow lunch counters. At the same time, the interrelationship of these apparently distinct areas became increasingly evident. What is the value of winning access to public accommodations for those who lack money to use them? The minute the movement faced this question, it was compelled to expand its vision beyond race relations to economic relations, including the role of education in modern society. And what also became clear is that all these interrelated problems, by their very nature, are not soluble by private, voluntary efforts but require government action—or politics. Already Southern demonstrators had recognized that the most effective way to strike at the police brutality they suffered from was by getting rid of the local sheriff—and that meant political action, which in turn meant, and still means, political action within the Democratic party where the only meaningful primary contests in the South are fought.

And so, in Mississippi, thanks largely to the leadership of Bob Moses, a turn toward political action has been taken. More than voter registration is involved here. A conscious bid for *political power* is being made, and in the course of that effort a tactical shift is being effected: direct-action techniques are being subordinated to a strategy calling for the building of community institutions or power bases. Clearly, the implications of this shift reach far beyond Mississippi. What began as a protest movement is being challenged to translate itself into a political movement. Is this the right course? And if it is, can the transformation be accomplished?

II

The very decade which has witnessed the decline of legal Jim Crow has also seen the rise of *de facto* segregation in our most fundamental socio-economic institutions. More Negroes are unemployed today than in 1954, and the unemployment gap between the races is wider. The median income of Negroes has dropped from 57 percent to 54 percent of that of whites. A higher percentage of Negro workers is now concentrated in jobs vulnerable to automation than was the case ten years ago. More Negroes attend *de facto* segregated schools today than when the Supreme Court handed down its famous decision; while school integration proceeds at a snail's pace in the South, the number of Northern schools with an excessive proportion of minority youth proliferates. And behind this is the continuing growth of racial slums, spreading over our central cities and trapping Negro youth in a milieu which, whatever its legal definition, sows an unimaginable demoralization. Again, legal niceties aside, a resident of a racial ghetto lives in segregated housing, and more Negroes fall into this category than ever before.

These are the facts of life which generate frustration in the Negro community and challenge the civil rights movement. At issue, after all, is not *civil rights*, strictly speaking, but social and economic conditions. Last summer's riots were not race riots; they were outbursts of class aggression in a society where class and color definitions are converging disastrously. How can the (perhaps misnamed) civil rights movement deal with this problem?

Before trying to answer, let me first insist that the task of the movement is vastly complicated by the failure of many whites of good will to understand the nature of our problem. There is a widespread assumption that the removal of artificial racial barriers should result in the automatic integration of the Negro into all aspects of American life. This myth is fostered by facile analogies with the experience of various ethnic immigrant groups, particularly the Jews. But the analogies with the Jews do not hold for three simple but profound reasons. First, Jews have a long history as a literate people, a resource which has afforded them opportunities to advance in the academic and professional worlds, to achieve intellectual status even in the midst of economic hardship, and to evolve sustaining value systems in the context of ghetto life. Negroes, for the greater part of their presence in this country, were forbidden by law to read or write. Second, Jews have a long history of family stability, the importance of which in terms of aspiration and self-image is obvious. The Negro family structure was totally destroyed by slavery and with it the possibility of cultural transmission (the right of Negroes to marry and rear children is barely a century old). Third, Jews are white and have the *option* of relinquishing their cultural-religious identity, intermarrying, passing, etc. Negroes, or at least the overwhelming majority of them, do not have this option. There is also a fourth, vulgar reason. If the Jewish and Negro communities are not comparable in terms of education, family structure, and color, it is also true that their respective economic roles bear little resemblance.

This matter of economic role brings us to the greater problem—the fact that we are moving into an era in which the natural functioning of the market does not by itself ensure every man with will and ambition a place in the productive process. The immigrant who came to this country during the late 19th and early 20th centuries entered a society which was expanding territorially and/or economically. It was then possible to start at the bottom, as an unskilled or semi-skilled worker, and move up the ladder, acquiring new skills along the way. Especially was this true when industrial unionism was burgeoning, giving new dignity and higher wages to organized workers. Today the situation has changed. We are not expanding territorially, the western frontier is settled, labor organizing has leveled off, our rate of economic growth has been stagnant for a decade. And we are in the midst of a technological revolution which is altering the fundamental structure of the labor force, destroying unskilled and semi-skilled jobs—jobs in which Negroes are disproportionately concentrated.

Whatever the pace of this technological revolution may be, the *direction* is clear: the lower rungs of the economic ladder are being lopped off. This means that an individual will no longer be able to start at the bottom and work his way up; he will have to start in the middle or on top, and hold on tight. It will not even be enough to have certain specific skills, for many skilled jobs are also vulnerable to automation. A broad educational background, permitting vocational adaptability and flexibility, seems more imperative than ever. We live in a society where, as Secretary of Labor Willard Wirtz puts it, machines have the equivalent of a high school diploma. Yet the average educational attainment of American Negroes is 8.2 years.

Negroes, of course, are not the only people being affected by these developments. It is reported that there are now 50 percent fewer unskilled and semi-skilled jobs than there are high school dropouts. Almost one-third of the 26 million young people entering the labor market in the 1960's will be dropouts. But the percentage of Negro dropouts nationally is 57 percent, and in New York City, among Negroes 25 years of age or over, it is 68 percent. They are without a future.

To what extent can the kind of self-help campaign recently prescribed by Eric Hoffer in the *New York Times Magazine* cope with such a situation? I would advise those who think that self-help is the answer to familiarize themselves with the long history of such efforts in the Negro community, and to consider why so many foundered on the shoals of ghetto life. It goes without saying that any effort to combat demoralization and apathy is desirable, but we must understand that demoralization in the Negro community is largely a common-sense response to an objective reality. Negro youths have no need of statistics to perceive, fairly accurately, what their odds are in American society. Indeed, from the point of view of motivation, some of the healthiest Negro youngsters I know are juvenile delinquents: vigorously pursuing the American Dream of material acquisition and status, yet finding the conventional means of attaining it blocked off, they do not yield to defeatism but resort to illegal (and often ingenious) methods. They are not alien to American culture. They are, in Gunnar Myrdal's phrase, "exaggerated Americans." To want a Cadillac is not un-American; to push a cart in the garment center is. If Negroes are to be persuaded that the conventional path (school, work, etc.) is superior, we had better provide evidence which is now sorely lacking. It is a double cruelty to harangue Negro youth about education and training when we do not know what jobs will be available for them. When a Negro youth can reasonably foresee a future free of slums, when the prospect of gainful employment is realistic, we will see motivation and self-help in abundant enough quantities.

Meanwhile, there is an ironic similarity between the self-help advocated by many liberals and the doctrines of the Black Muslims. Professional sociologists, psychiatrists, and social workers have expressed amazement at the Muslims' success in transforming prostitutes and dope addicts into respectable citizens. But every prostitute the Muslims convert to a model of Calvinist virtue is replaced by the ghetto with two more. Dedicated as they are to maintenance of the ghetto, the Muslims are powerless to affect substantial moral reform. So too with every other group or program which is not aimed at the destruction of slums, their causes and effects. Self-help efforts, directly or indirectly, must be geared to mobilizing people into power units capable of effecting social change. That is, their goal must be genuine self-help, not merely self-improvement. Obviously, where self-improvement activities succeed in imparting to their participants a feeling of some control over their environment, those involved may find their appetites for change whetted; they may move into the political arena.

III

Let me sum up what I have thus far been trying to say: the civil rights movement is evolving from a protest movement into a full-fledged *social movement*—an evolution calling its very name into question. It is now concerned not merely with removing the barriers to full *opportunity* but with achieving the fact of *equality*. From sit-ins and freedom rides we have gone into rent strikes, boycotts, community organization, and political action. As a consequence of this natural evolution, the Negro today finds himself stymied by obstacles of far greater magnitude than the legal barriers he was attacking before: automation, urban decay, *de facto* school segregation. These are problems which, while conditioned by Jim Crow, do not vanish upon its demise. They are more deeply rooted in our socio-economic order; they are the result of the total society's failure to meet not only the Negro's needs, but human needs generally.

These propositions have won increasing recognition and acceptance, but with a curious twist. They have formed the common premise of two apparently contradictory lines of thought which simultaneously nourish and antagonize each other. On the one hand, there is the reasoning of the New York *Times* moderate who says that the problems are so enormous and complicated that Negro militancy is a futile irritation, and that the need is for "intelligent moderation." Thus, during the first New York school boycott, the *Times* editorialized that Negro demands, while abstractly just, would necessitate massive reforms, the funds for which could not realistically be anticipated; therefore the just demands were also foolish demands and would only antagonize white people. Moderates of this stripe are often correct in perceiving the difficulty or impossibility of racial progress in the context of present social and economic policies. But they accept the context as fixed. They ignore (or perhaps see all too well) the potentialities inherent in linking Negro demands to broader pressures for radical revision of existing policies. They apparently see nothing strange in the fact that in the last twenty-five years we have spent nearly a trillion dollars fighting or preparing for wars, yet throw up our hands before the need for overhauling our schools, clearing the slums, and really abolishing poverty. My quarrel with these moderates is that they do not even envision radical changes; their admonitions of moderation are, for all practical purposes, admonitions to the Negro to adjust to the status quo, and are therefore immoral.

The more effectively the moderates argue their case, the more they convince Negroes that American society will not or cannot be reorganized for full racial equality. Michael Harrington has said that a successful war on poverty might well require the expenditure of $100 billion. Where, the Negro wonders, are the forces now in motion to compel such a commitment? If the voices of the moderates were raised in an insistence upon a reallocation of national resources at levels that could not be confused with tokenism (that is, if the moderates stopped being moderates), Negroes would have greater grounds for hope. Meanwhile, the Negro movement cannot escape a sense of isolation.

It is precisely this sense of isolation that gives rise to the second line of thought I want to examine—the tendency within the civil rights movement which, despite its militancy, pursues what I call a "no-win" policy. Sharing with many moderates a recognition of the magnitude of the obstacles to freedom, spokesmen for this tendency survey the American scene and find no forces prepared to move toward radical solutions. From this they conclude that the only viable strategy is shock; above all, the hypocrisy of white liberals must be exposed. These spokesmen are often described as the radicals of the movement, but they are really its moralists. They seek to change white hearts—by traumatizing them. Frequently abetted by white self-flagellants, they may gleefully applaud (though not really agreeing with) Malcolm X because, while they admit he has no program, they think he can frighten white people into doing the right thing. To believe this, of course, you must be convinced, even if unconsciously, that at the core of the white man's heart lies a buried affection for Negroes—a proposition one may be permitted to doubt. But in any case, hearts are not relevant to the issue; neither racial affinities nor racial hostilities are rooted there. It is institutions—social, political, and economic institutions—which are the ultimate molders of collective sentiments. Let these institutions be reconstructed *today*, and let the ineluctable gradualism of history govern the formation of a new psychology.

My quarrel with the "no-win" tendency in the civil rights movement (and the reason I have so designated it) parallels my quarrel with the moderates outside the movement. As the latter lack the vision or will for fundamental change, the former lack a realistic strategy for achieving it. For such a strategy they substitute militancy. But militancy is a matter of posture and volume and not of effect.

I believe that the Negro's struggle for equality in America is essentially revolutionary. While most Negroes—in their hearts—unquestionably seek only to enjoy the fruits of American society as it now exists, their quest cannot *objectively* be satisfied within the framework of existing political and economic relations. The young Negro who would demonstrate his way into the labor market may be motivated by a thoroughly bourgeois ambition and thoroughly "capitalist" considerations, but he will end up having to favor a great expansion of the public sector of the economy. At any rate, that is the position the movement will be forced to take as it looks at the number of jobs being generated by the private economy, and if it is to remain true to the masses of Negroes.

The revolutionary character of the Negro's struggle is manifest in the fact that this struggle may have done more to democratize life for whites than for Negroes. Clearly, it was the sit-in movement of young Southern Negroes which, as it galvanized white students, banished the ugliest features of McCarthyism from the American campus and resurrected political debate. It was not until Negroes assaulted *de facto* school segregation in the urban centers that the issue of quality education for *all* children stirred into motion. Finally, it seems reasonably clear that the civil rights movement, directly and through the resurgence of social conscience it kindled, did more to initiate the war on poverty than any other single force.

It will be—it has been—argued that these by-products of the Negro struggle are not revolutionary. But the term revolutionary, as I

am using it, does not connote violence; it refers to the qualitative transformation of fundamental institutions, more or less rapidly, to the point
where the social and economic structure which they comprised can no
longer be said to be the same. The Negro struggle has hardly run its
course; and it will not stop moving until it has been utterly defeated
or won substantial equality. But I fail to see how the movement can be
victorious in the absence of radical programs for full employment, abolition of slums, the reconstruction of our educational system, new definitions of work and leisure. Adding up the cost of such programs, we can
only conclude that we are talking about a refashioning of our political
economy. It has been estimated, for example, that the price of replacing
New York City's slums with public housing would be $17 billion. Again,
a multi-billion dollar federal public-works program, dwarfing the currently proposed $2 billion program, is required to reabsorb unskilled
and semi-skilled workers into the labor market—and this must be done
if Negro workers in these categories are to be employed. "Preferential
treatment" cannot help them.

I am not trying here to delineate a total program, only to suggest the scope of economic reforms which are most immediately related
to the plight of the Negro community. One could speculate on their
political implications—whether, for example, they do not indicate the
obsolescence of state government and the superiority of regional structures as viable units of planning. Such speculations aside, it is clear that
Negro needs cannot be satisfied unless we go beyond what has so far
been placed on the agenda. How are these radical objectives to be
achieved? The answer is simple, deceptively so: *through political power.*

There is a strong moralistic strain in the civil rights movement
which would remind us that power corrupts, forgetting that the absence
of power also corrupts. But this is not the view I want to debate here, for
it is waning. Our problem is posed by those who accept the need for
political power but do not understand the nature of the object and therefore lack sound strategies for achieving it; they tend to confuse political
institutions with lunch counters.

A handful of Negroes, acting alone, could integrate a lunch
counter by strategically locating their bodies so as *directly* to interrupt
the operation of the proprietor's will; their numbers were relatively
unimportant. In politics, however, such a confrontation is difficult because the interests involved are merely *represented.* In the execution
of a political decision a direct confrontation may ensue (as when federal
marshals escorted James Meredith into the University of Mississippi—
to turn from an example of non-violent coercion to one of force backed
up with the threat of violence). But in arriving at a political decision,

numbers and organizations are crucial, especially for the economically disenfranchised. (Needless to say, I am assuming that the forms of political democracy exist in America, however imperfectly, that they are valued, and that elitist or putschist conceptions of exercising power are beyond the pale of discussion for the civil rights movement.)

Neither that movement nor the country's twenty million black people can win political power alone. We need allies. The future of the Negro struggle depends on whether the contradictions of this society can be resolved by a coalition of progressive forces which becomes the *effective* political majority in the United States. I speak of the coalition which staged the March on Washington, passed the Civil Rights Act, and laid the basis for the Johnson landslide—Negroes, trade unionists, liberals, and religious groups.

There are those who argue that a coalition strategy would force the Negro to surrender his political independence to white liberals, that he would be neutralized, deprived of his cutting edge, absorbed into the Establishment. Some who take this position urged last year that votes be withheld from the Johnson-Humphrey ticket as a demonstration of the Negro's political power. Curiously enough, these people who sought to demonstrate power through the non-exercise of it, also point to the Negro "swing vote" in crucial urban areas as the source of the Negro's independent political power. But here they are closer to being right: the urban Negro vote will grow in importance in the coming years. If there is anything positive in the spread of the ghetto, it is the potential political power base thus created, and to realize this potential is one of the most challenging and urgent tasks before the civil rights movement. If the movement can wrest leadership of the ghetto vote from the machines, it will have acquired an organized constituency such as other major groups in our society now have.

But we must also remember that the effectiveness of a swing vote depends solely on "other" votes. It derives its power from them. In that sense, it can never be "independent," but must opt for one candidate or the other, even if by default. Thus coalitions are inescapable, however tentative they may be. And this is the case in all but those few situations in which Negroes running on an independent ticket might conceivably win. "Independence," in other words, is not a value in itself. The issue is which coalition to join and how to make it responsive to your program. Necessarily there will be compromise. But the difference between expediency and morality in politics is the difference between selling out a principle and making smaller concessions to win larger ones. The leader who shrinks from this task reveals not his purity but his lack of political sense.

The task of molding a political movement out of the March on Washington coalition is not simple, but no alternatives have been advanced. We need to choose our allies on the basis of common political objectives. It has become fashionable in some no-win Negro circles to decry the white liberal as the main enemy (his hypocrisy is what sustains racism); by virtue of this reverse recitation of the reactionary's litany (liberalism leads to socialism, which leads to Communism) the Negro is left in majestic isolation, except for a tiny band of fervent white initiates. But the objective fact is that *Eastland and Goldwater* are the main enemies—they and the opponents of civil rights, of the war on poverty, of medicare, of social security, of federal aid to education, of unions, and so forth. The labor movement, despite its obvious faults, has been the largest single organized force in this country pushing for progressive social legislation. And where the Negro-labor-liberal axis is weak, as in the farm belt, it was the religious groups that were most influential in rallying support for the Civil Rights Bill.

The durability of the coalition was interestingly tested during the election. I do not believe that the Johnson landslide proved the "white backlash" to be a myth. It proved, rather, that economic interests are more fundamental than prejudice: the backlashers decided that loss of social security was, after all, too high a price to pay for a slap at the Negro. This lesson was a valuable first step in re-educating such people, and it must be kept alive, for the civil rights movement will be advanced only to the degree that social and economic welfare gets to be inextricably entangled with civil rights.

The 1964 elections marked a turning point in American politics. The Democratic landslide was not merely the result of a negative reaction to Goldwaterism; it was also the expression of a majority liberal consensus. The near unanimity with which Negro voters joined in that expression was, I am convinced, a vindication of the July 25th statement by Negro leaders calling for a strategic turn toward political action and a temporary curtailment of mass demonstrations. Despite the controversy surrounding the statement, the instinctive response it met with in the community is suggested by the fact that demonstrations were down 75 percent as compared with the same period in 1963. But should so high a percentage of Negro voters have gone to Johnson, or should they have held back to narrow his margin of victory and thus give greater visibility to our swing vote? How has our loyalty changed things? Certainly the Negro vote had higher visibility in 1960, when a switch of only 7 percent from the Republican column of 1956 elected President Kennedy. But the slimness of Kennedy's victory—of his "mandate"—dictated a go-slow approach on civil rights, at least until the Birmingham upheaval.

Although Johnson's popular majority was so large that he could have won without such overwhelming Negro support, that support was important from several angles. Beyond adding to Johnson's total national margin, it was specifically responsible for his victories in Virginia, Florida, Tennessee, and Arkansas. Goldwater took only those states where fewer than 45 percent of eligible Negroes were registered. That Johnson would have won those states had Negro voting rights been enforced is a lesson not likely to be lost on a man who would have been happy with a unanimous electoral college. In any case, the 1.6 million Southern Negroes who voted have had a shattering impact on the Southern political party structure, as illustrated in the changed composition of the Southern congressional delegation. The "backlash" gave the Republicans five House seats in Alabama, one in Georgia, and one in Mississippi. But on the Democratic side, seven segregationists were defeated while all nine Southerners who voted for the Civil Rights Act were reelected. It may be premature to predict a Southern Democratic party of Negroes and white moderates and a Republican Party of refugee racists and economic conservatives, but there certainly is a strong tendency toward such a realignment; and an additional 3.6 million Negroes of voting age in the eleven Southern states are still to be heard from. Even the *tendency* toward disintegration of the Democratic party's racist wing defines a new context for Presidential and liberal strategy in the congressional battles ahead. Thus the Negro vote (North as well as South), while not *decisive* in the Presidential race, was enormously effective. It was a dramatic element of a historic mandate which contains vast possibilities and dangers that will fundamentally affect the future course of the civil rights movement.

The liberal congressional sweep raises hope for an assault on the seniority system, Rule Twenty-two, and other citadels of Dixiecrat-Republican power. The overwhelming of this conservative coalition should also mean progress on much bottlenecked legislation of profound interest to the movement (e.g., bills by Senators Clark and Nelson on planning, manpower, and employment). Moreover, the irrelevance of the South to Johnson's victory gives the President more freedom to act than his predecessor had and more leverage to the movement to pressure for executive action in Mississippi and other racist strongholds.

None of this *guarantees* vigorous executive or legislative action, for the other side of the Johnson landslide is that it has a Gaullist quality. Goldwater's capture of the Republican party forced into the Democratic camp many disparate elements which do not belong there, Big Business being the major example. Johnson who wants to be President "of all people," may try to keep his new coalition together by sticking close to the political center. But if he decides to do this, it is unlikely that even his political genius will be able to hold together a coalition so inherently unstable and rife with contradictions. It must come apart. Should it do so while Johnson is pursuing a centrist course, then the mandate will have been wastefully dissipated. However, if the mandate is seized upon to set fundamental changes in motion, then the basis can be laid for a new mandate, a new coalition including hitherto inert and dispossessed strata of the population.

Here is where the cutting edge of the civil rights movement can be applied. We must see to it that the reorganization of the "consensus party" proceeds along lines which will make it an effective vehicle for social reconstruction, a role it cannot play so long as it furnishes Southern racism with its national political power. (One of Barry Goldwater's few attractive ideas was that the Dixiecrats belong with him in the same party.) And nowhere has the civil rights movement's political cutting edge been more magnificently demonstrated than at Atlantic City, where the Mississippi Freedom Democratic Party not only secured recognition as a bona fide component of the national party, but in the process routed the representatives of the most rabid racists—the white Mississippi and Alabama delegations. While I still believe that the FDP made a tactical error in spurning the compromise, there is no question that they launched a political revolution whose logic is the displacement of Dixiecrat power. They launched that revolution within a major political institution and as part of a coalitional effort.

The role of the civil rights movement in the reorganization of American political life is programmatic as well as strategic. We are challenged now to broaden our social vision, to develop functional programs with concrete objectives. We need to propose alternatives to technological unemployment, urban decay, and the rest. We need to be calling for public works and training, for national economic planning, for federal aid to education, for attractive public housing—all this on a sufficiently massive scale to make a difference. We need to protest the notion that our integration into American life, so long delayed, must now proceed in an atmosphere of competitive scarcity instead of in the security of abundance which technology makes possible. We cannot claim to have answers to all the complex problems of modern society. That is too much to ask of a movement still battling barbarism in Mississippi. But we can agitate the right questions by probing at the contradictions which still stand in the way of the "Great Society." The questions having been asked, motion must begin in the larger society, for there is a limit to what Negroes can do alone.

Appalachia: the Heart of the Matter

Robb K. Burlage

Tennessee State Planning Commission

[Excerpted with permission from "The 'War on Poverty': This Is War?" from New University Thought, Summer 1964.]

JOHN KENNEDY held a can of "Mollygrub" (surplus food) before a nationwide TV audience during his debate with Hubert Humphrey in the West Virginia Primary and declared that he would never forget these faces. Lyndon and Ladybird Johnson in the summer campaign of 1960 poignantly told of the "Save-a-Meal Plan" they had learned about from a West Virginia child—one meal a day being skipped by the children so they could at least have one decent meal. The Johnsons promised that the people of Appalachia would never be neglected again.

Since then, Appalachia has not lacked for attention. But it has lacked for action to meet its needs. We put this discussion forth with the assumption that a growing indigenous movement in the mountains, starting with the Committee for Miners, can without apology carry its own program proposals to the Courthouse, to the Statehouse, and to the Nation.

The list of mountain troubles is endless. It would not be valuable here to repeat too much of what the volumes and treatises say. In Hazard the troubles are many and the solutions are difficult. The issue is not just unemployment, although there is 50 percent unemployment among the miners. There is a total failure of the community and region to provide a liveable situation for its people. What connects Harlem, an island in the midst of urban plenty, with Hazard, an urban island in a sea of rural isolation, is "community decay": this Culture of Poverty. Unemployment, it must be remembered, is both a cause and a symptom of this decay, this neglect, this inexcusable blot on our society.

Appalachia needs upwards of 500,000 new jobs right now; Eastern Kentucky needs upwards of 100,000. Many of the smaller "ribbon towns" face ghost futures in the next decade. Migration is both an escape valve and a further depressant, because more and more of the migrants are bouncing back. Those that make it—the younger ones, the potential local leaders—leave high rates of dependency behind them in the mountains. Coal production is down due to coal seam exhaustion and the competition of other fuels; and firms are hiring less per ton to produce that due to automation. The rugged terrain is generally not good for farming; the non-coal counties are *worse* off in income than the more dramatically collapsing coal counties. There are few industrial complexes and truly metropolitan areas, and most of these are on the edges of Appalachia. In an area that has always depended on exploitation of natural resources, the harvest is thinning. The timber stands and live-stock herds, supposedly the "new hopes" of the mountain in the eyes of some developers, are generally scrawny. The larger plots of land are largely absentee-owned. The smaller plots are too small to add up to anything without a "collectivist" revolution unheard-of among the highly independent mountaineers, who are in characteristic American fashion (and then some) "self-reliant" about their pea patches and conspiratorial about their Welfare.

The people reflect the inadequacy of their environment. They are generally two years behind in educational attainment, not to mention *quality* (Harlan County's 80 percent draft rejectees among the 17–35 age bracket is a flagrant example). Even most of the "skilled" are hung up in an obsolete corner, mining. Lacking the land or capital for self-venture, the only homegrown solution for many is to bid down wages or to compete for the political Welfare. This, Harry Caudill, author of *Night Comes to the Cumberlands,* tells us, is the grim catalyst of court-house politics. The people cling on for dear life to their Welfare Fund hospitals, one of the few signs of provision for the future, re-opened in response to miners' protest and pickets with funds bootlegged from the Area Redevelopment Administration after the UMW shut them down.

Results of Past Attention

Individual states of Appalachia have initiated interesting programs in recent years with assistance from federal and private resources: North Carolina's Ford Foundation sponsored drive against "educational poverty"; West Virginia's community work program; Pennsylvania's campaign against strip mine waste and pollution; Tennessee's pioneering local and regional planning assistance program.

But all persons familiar with the hardest core problem areas of Appalachia know that without immediate massive outside assistance, Appalachia will become one large ghost region, inhabited by people who have chosen to die not in city slums but in their family graveyards. And everyone knows that the only source of outside assistance is the federal government.

Proposed Federal Appalachia Program

Three devastating floods in Eastern Kentucky in five years, massive out-migration, the ghosting of more hamlets, the closing of welfare hospitals, wage and union-busting in the mines, acute rates of unemployment and underemployment—this is the picture. Unless solid assistance is brought to the mountains in the next few years, the whole community-life structure of most of Appalachia will be completely collapsed.

"PARC" is the President's Appalachian Regional Commission, which recently reported the results of more than a year of formulating on an intensive "single-focus team effort" for the development of the Appalachian region.* In defining the problems of Appalachia, the Report uses vivid language to describe this "Other Country" within America. But PARC's analysis fails in its emphasis: (a) No hint is given of diversities in the region (farms and mines, plateaus and mountains, and even some viable towns and cities as well as rural wasteland); (b) The interrelationships with the national economy are forgotten in the stress on regional uniqueness; thus, the close relationship between national trends, e.g. automation and unemployment, and the deepening of these trends in the region are ignored; and (c) Unmentioned is the need to guarantee the welfare of all the people of the area regardless of economic means necessary, rather than to develop the region and hope for the best trickle-down effects possible.

The Report is totally geared to providing some form of makeshift economic development based on the existing natural resources, which will bring Appalachia "into the free enterprise orbit" of the American economy at large. This, of course, fails to deal with the fact that the "free enterprise orbit" as presently structured is manufacturing depressed areas such as Appalachia's rural and urban slums throughout the country.

PARC's aim in Appalachia is to build a basic infrastructure and encourage certain promising industries in addition to the other national War-on-Poverty policies. Based solidly on a framework of "cooperative federalism" (no program may be imposed on an unwilling state), what actually gets achieved will depend on the cooperation, financial and otherwise, of state and local leaders. PARC pretends not to have a precise formula, but a "variety of programs . . . brought into coordinated attack to lay the preconditions . . . not as a solution but as the indispensable groundwork for a solution" for development of (a) human resource with supporting infrastructure and (b) natural resource capability and employment opportunities.

Limitations of PARC Approach

The vision of developing improved communities, industrial complexes, and "up-graded," healthy, and well-fed human beings in Appalachia

---

* The Report of this committee was used as the basis of the Appalachian Bill Regional Development Act of 1965.

dominates the rhetoric of the PARC Report, but the specific program recommendations (and, more importantly, budget requests) fail to take
even the first steps in these directions in most cases. The emphasis on
roads, dams, timber, cattle, and training as the specifics of this vision
leaves too much to the unseen hand, a hand which has maimed the people, scarred the hillsides, polluted the rivers, and moved on. Though
the PARC Report acknowledges the existing economic death in Appalachia, it fails to do more than prescribe smelling salts to lure private
capital to the area. Though the PARC Report acknowledges the scarring
of people in Appalachia, it fails to cope with the total problem of what
it will take to give them equality in American society, whether they
choose to stay in the hills or migrate to the cities.

This is not only a failure of nerve, a failure to see political resources that could be used to achieve a program that can honestly transform the region and the people within the region. It is especially a poverty of imagination, it is a loss of a great opportunity to project new
approaches to solving the total needs of the individuals and their communities. Instead, PARC has exercised a conservative discretion in making its progress recommendations. In probably sincere hopes of getting
a foot in the door, and therefore being able to do something for the
people of the area, they have failed to stand up and declare what is
really needed for these people. All the controversial issues are dodged:
direct public industrial and power investment, widespread powers of
public planning and development, direct public creation of totally new
or rebuilt communities, direct substitution for the technical and administrative inadequacies and roadblocks on the state and local levels, massive federal aid for education and medical care, directly created jobs or
directly provided income for those persons who cannot be immediately
"placed," humane "planned resettlement" for those persons who choose
it. Thus PARC may have carefully ruled itself irrelevant. By putting most
of their imagination into recommending clever ways of primarily financing agricultural development projects for marginal employment and
income (timber, livestock), those who created the PARC Report denied
themselves the forum they needed to make bolder proposals.

Now it is time for PARC to answer for its modest proposals and its
more obvious oversights:

Wouldn't the provision of cheap public power in all Appalachia
be as strong an inducement to region-wide industrial development as
the Tennessee Valley Authority has been in its more limited area?

Can it be demonstrated that the expansion of land-intensive commercial activities (timber and livestock) will provide sufficient income
and employment in the rural areas of Appalachia when most of the

poverty-stricken are very small landholders on generally very poor land and when the majority of land is owned outside the region? With agriculture a shrinking share of national production and fewer persons needed in it, can clear opportunities for agricultural income (expansion of sufficient national demand and "employment opportunities") be demonstrated?

Isn't a policy of federally subsidized conversion from cropland to pasture and timber just a way of setting up small landowners for the kill—either by inadequate scale to meet competition or by land-speculators to buy their lease in their name and controlling the spoils? By essentially ignoring the landless and steering the small-landed into unproductive traps, is this just a more subtle way of forcing hopeless migration in the name of development?

Although recreational and tourist development in the area meets an important national need, can this kind of development be counted on to provide significant income and employment to reach many of the rural poverty-stricken in the region?

Can new uses and new markets for coal possibly catch up with the automatic process in coal extraction and provide new jobs in mining?

Isn't the race for labor-intensive production locations abating with the rise of automated competition, especially in unionized areas; and, except for certain waterfront or mineral-source locations, isn't the relative industrial attractiveness of the urban and urbanizing areas becoming even more pronounced? If so, isn't the only feasible economic solution to provide sufficient comparative advantage and economics-of-scale through direct public investment in those areas where Appalachia can be competitive among national growth industries?

Raising no other question about the PARC program than "Will it work?", we see the pitfalls that timid and marginal public proposals face in the area. Is not the most "pragmatic" approach to the problem a dramatic program which tells the truth about what's needed?

And yet we cannot fully blame the President's Commission for its hesitation. It is operating in an environment of political timidity. It is making its report as part of a total federal effort which seems preoccupied not with the size of the flood but with how to get its feet wet. Perhaps the only way to "free" the staffs and commissions and to allow them to talk honestly about the tasks before us, is to urge that the people formulate their own program proposals and then confront the policy-makers and the program-pushers themselves.

Vision at the Base—To Break the Logjam at the Top

In the absence of a national leadership to carry out a program to fulfill the needs of the people of Appalachia, the people themselves, starting with the organized miners and hopefully including all the forgotten people of Appalachia, must make their own demands. What is needed is a New Society for Appalachia, a model for all America: *New Vision, New Politics, New Towns, New Industries, New Lives.*

New Vision: (1) There must be a new definition of the problems of "regional poverty" and a new vision for its solution. The problems of Appalachia must be seen in terms of national structural problems— automation, stagnation, and neglect.

(2) The need is for democratic national planning and massive public expenditures to correct the society's poverty-making processes.

(3) The need is for a shift in national investment patterns, away from defense, private waste, and excess profits, and toward meeting the most felt human needs.

(4) The need is to guarantee a decent life situation for all Americans, regardless of place or race, skill or age. Americans must agree upon a decent "floor" to be built under income and basic standards of life for all Americans: a decent home in a decent community, at least a high school education for all, adequate health care, full participation in economic and political decision-making, and meaningful employment in the ongoing processes of the society, social as well as productive.

This must be more than rhetoric. The government must honestly intend to guarantee such standards. Just as the (Full) Employment Act of 1946 was passed with clear national consciousness of a basic national goal (though it has been eroded since that time), a new national standard should be set. This might be called a *National Full Opportunity Act,* guaranteeing specific basic living standards for all Americans. Just as the Council of Economic Advisors was created in 1946 to pursue policies guaranteeing full employment, so a "Council of Social Advisors" might be created in 1964 to pursue policies guaranteeing that all Americans enjoy standards of living which are considered commensurate with national full opportunity. What is important, however, is the achievement, not just the pursuit. Perhaps the most important single step toward fulfilling full opportunity is to achieve the statutory promise of the original Full Employment Act!

New Politics: Instead of simply an Appalachian development group, there should be a National Development Administration with regional units such as Appalachia to coordinate intensive efforts in particular areas. At present, Appalachia is the tail that must wag the dog, since there is no comprehensive national effort in this direction. Such a national program would cooperate with the states but would rely heavily on direct federal financing and control. Large federal staffs supplement and encourage local efforts. Regional "units of government" organized by the federal catalyst would administer programs either cooperatively with local governments or directly, if necessary. Such a national agency would have large discretionary investment powers, and the power of eminent domain and land purchase and allocation. Inherent in a national emphasis of this sort is not only direct regional investment power, but also coordination with national controls on interest rates, money supply, aggregate consumption levels, and so on.

The Appalachian program could be an example for "opening up" the depressed regions of the whole South, as well as urban slums and depressed areas of the North and West. The present Appalachian program involves parts of Virginia, North Carolina, Georgia, Tennessee, and Alabama, all of the Old Confederacy. A federal commisson to study the Southeast River Basin (parts of Alabama, Florida, Georgia, South and North Carolina) recently recommended a $5.5 billion program for land and water resource development alone in that area. Parts of Southwest Georgia, North Florida, and South Alabama are as seriously depressed as many areas of Appalachia. Such regional developmental emphasis in the South should reach as well to the depressed areas of the Eastern Shore of Maryland and Virginia, the Delta country of Arkansas-Tennessee-Louisiana-Mississippi, the Big Thicket of Louisiana-Texas, the Mexican borderlands of Texas.

New Towns: Through carefully selected and planned community development efforts, as many persons as possible should be guaranteed decent community life as close to their existing homes as possible. President Johnson has approved the notion of "new towns" in his speech on community development; Appalachia is a perfect place to experiment with such a program. If war and the Cold War can build in Appalachia the planned "new city" of Oak Ridge and cause tenfold increase in the city of Huntsville, Alabama (where Marshall Space Flight Center is located) why can't a site like Hazard be selected for reconstruction featuring aspects of community life selected by the people themselves? Just as Brazil carved out Brasilia in the jungle as a new national, cultural, and convention center, so America could turn to Appalachian new towns. This means the rehabilitation of potentially decent existing areas as well as starting from scratch. It also means making new towns of the "Appalachian" quarter of Chicago, Cincinnati, and Detroit as well, another policy which starts unraveling the national as well as the regional ball of twine. Tracing down the poverty-stricken Appalachians who are now living in urban slums across th country and providing them with decent community situations would be like initiating a nationwide new towns program. Well, why not?

New Industry: The key question that must be asked of all economic development programs is: Will they seriously help in meeting the job and income gap, given the demands of the automating national economy? Are the industrial proposals stop-gaps or growth operations? The limits of resource extraction are clear, because the "exporter" generally pays more for "value added" in the finished products which he imports than he receives for the raw material which he exports. Breaking out of this colony status in relation to the rest of the American economy will take selective policies to develop high-wage, high-growth industry in the region. Once the initial elements of industrial complexes are constructed, often they become "self-expanding," in adding more industries because of newly-discovered "economies of scale," interlocking use of inputs-outputs, etc. This will take more than adequate preparation of potential industrial sites with decent processing water and public facilities. It calls also for public support for power development, labor force in-training at decent wages, and direct investment in needed products. This is what is done in wartime if adequate private investment cannot be found.

What needs of the society are not now being fulfilled by private industry and private research? Development of cheaper sound construction materials for pre-fabricated housing? Fabrication of processes for desalinization and depollution of water supplies? Experiments could be made in simulating "underdeveloped country" bottlenecks (use of labor-intensive production processes with relatively skilled workers) to demonstrate here in America how they could be solved. New techniques of production could be tried out as a challenge to existing industries, while keeping wages at good levels, just as TVA has pioneered in the development of new fertilizers.

New Lives: First things first demands that the Congressional log-jams be broken on federal aid to education and medical care. Without a thorough breakthrough on underprivileged education, efforts to help both the young and the older, real progress in human development will be stymied. "Compensatory Universities" could be built throughout Appalachia to serve as cultural centers and training centers for teachers, and community leaders. These could be built around existing college centers or at new locations.

The way to develop Appalachia as a recreation haven is to publicly develop low-cost recreation, training, and "retreat" sites for private organizations and industries from throughout the country. As the leisure revolution becomes more predominant (the potential human good of job-killing automation) in America, these wilderness areas will be left less to tourist-promotion chances "rest and relaxation" areas, and will be guaranteed the "trade." This is important not only because Appalachia needs service jobs to fill its employment gaps, but because America will need more and more wilderness recreation area in the coming years.

Many of the detailed recommendations of the Committee for Miners' "Program for Eastern Kentucky" are excellent. More specific demands for change in each community should be formulated. Such demands must stem from a view held by the people themselves that there are certain expectations which are reasonable for them as American citizens to have. There are many possible development strategies for Appalachia, but the strategy that cannot be allowed is the present one of neglect and tokenism.

Selected programs can help many areas prove adequate to their residents' needs. For other individuals the only path is to live in a viable urban community, in or out of Appalachia. For others, their best life-chance is in the development of new towns built around new industry where their lives will no longer sink into the total neglect and squalor of the other America again. Nothing less than a new society must be the expectation—and insistence—of the people of Appalachia.

Notes on Strategy

The Hazard miners and their Eastern Kentucky allies have already shown their willingness to stand up for their rights and hopes. By picketing at home demanding reopening of the Welfare hospitals and picketing the White House seeking a meaningful federal development program, the miners have made sure that the local, state, and national power structures have been confronted by their determination. The nation has been made aware of their plight. The parents of a depressed Appalachian town, Clairfield, Tennessee, recently followed suit with one of the first Appalachian school boycotts. The very existence of a federal Appalachian program, regardless of its content, will bring constant attention to the area and provide a great number of opportunities to raise the demands.

It is important to remember that Appalachia as currently defined is an area stretching from central Pennsylvania to northwest Alabama. The opportunities for alliance in every state with liberal-labor-Negro-political forces, particularly the equally insurgent and insistent Student Non-Violent Coordinating Committee and other community-based movements, should not be overlooked. The significance and limitation in the new federal approach to Appalachia is in the willingness of states like Virginia, Georgia, Tennessee and Alabama (although with some balking from Virginia and Alabama) to join with northern states and the federal government in accepting responsibility for the problem of poverty in their areas. Therefore, strong pressures must be applied on the states and local communities as well as the federal government to follow through on the Appalachian program.

It is also important to remember that some national "interests" dwell in Appalachia who are directly concerned for the welfare of the poverty-stricken. Their national voices can be important, particularly on poverty. The National Farmers Union and Sharecroppers Fund back "developmental" agricultural programming. Many marginal Appalachian farmers live outside the coal counties and must be counted as potential for the movement if possible. "Citizens for TVA" and the National Rural Electric Cooperative Association are for expansion of public power.

The miners can have considerable influence by exerting their power on local leadership. To do more than spotlight their problems on higher levels, however, they must find alliances and coalitions on the state, regional, and national level with those who desire the best kind of development for Appalachia. Much of what will be done for the region will depend on re-allocation of national resources for that purpose.

Where inadequacies or phoniness in the programs exist, they must be dramatically pointed out: jamming the retraining programs, for instance, to show the limited opportunities; or picketing an ARA motel boondoggle which isn't providing jobs.

The "Migration is Salvation" myth must also be met head-on. Hazard or Eastern Kentucky "alumni associations" might be organized on at least an informal basis in the Appalachian "quarters" of cities which are already being organized (e.g., Students for a Democratic Society full-time unemployment project in Chicago and projected summer projects in Louisville, Detroit, Cleveland, Philadelphia, etc.). These "alumni groups" could hold solidarity demonstrations or sympathy pickets to show that the problems of Eastern Kentucky and Appalachia are mobile and national.

Most federal programs provide for "local participation" in decision-making. Because few plain people call their hand on it, the local power structure still usually manages to run things. However the ARA, Manpower Development and Training program (Dept. of Labor), Agriculture Extension Service, and Rural Areas Development (Agriculture) programs, to mention a few, all have local supervisory committees which are by law supposed to have a "diversity of representation." Miners and other forgotten people should demand their right to representation; once seated on these committees, more details of local policy can be learned. Just keeping track of local programs on how (and to whom) their funds are expended can be an important function. Irregularities should be reported immediately to Washington. In addition, public hearings held by Bureau of Public Roads or Corps of Engineers, for instance, should be attended and group demands made clear.

Local groups can fruitfully formulate counter-plans and work for their implementation. With a little bit of technical assistance, the groups can formulate their own ideas about how, where, when, and for whom schools should be built and present their plan to the School Board. What they believe should be involved in urban renewal and housing programs can be presented to the local Planning Board or Urban Renewal group. The projects they feel can be most helpful to the local people can be presented to local Industrial Development Committees.

The demonstration can present the strong feelings of the forgotten and raise an issue in a dramatic way. Local school boycotts, such as in Clairfield, can demand better educational conditions. Some persons have suggested picketing the Selective Service offices to indicate opposition to proposed "school drop-out" conscription instead of jobs at home. Local mass tax strikes have been suggested to dramatize the need for the improvement of public services, living conditions, and employment opportunities.

Even applications for federal projects could be formulated by a protest group as a means of expressing the needs of the people. Application for participation in agricultural projects could be made by all the people, whether or not they have any land or capital, noting in each application that what is needed is sufficient land and income even to make a start on such a venture. Groups of miners could charter independent "districts" or "development associations" and get direct federal financing for water and sewerage systems, establish "industrial sites" and seek federal technical assistance grants for feasibility studies. It has even been suggested that unemployed miners form a "craft group" and apply for assistance from the State crafts program in Kentucky and then "sell" things along the highways with signs on their stands: "We Want Decent Jobs."

As part of mobilizing people in communities of Appalachia, it should be realized that unionization can be a great catalyst for unified social action in many different economic situations—from organizing marginal garment plants in the farm counties to assisting workers' organization in all the plants of the more diversified industrial areas (e.g., Ashland).

All opportunities to express community-based sentiments in cooperation with others should be seized: Some strategists insisted that a large contingent of miners at the Kentucky State Civil Rights March on Frankfurt would have helped build new alliances and reach new audiences.

How Does It All Fit Together?

How do people move from "demands" to "dreams"—from local gripes to steps toward achieving the sort of democratic society in which they really believe?

Attaining a meaningful national "Full Opportunity" program will take a concerted political drive among those very people who are now denied the opportunity to be fully "political" and "economic" in the American society. These people are found in every area of America, for America in terms of its human potential is a national depressed area. In some areas, they are the majority.

These people must confront the operative political and economic system at all levels. Although the most immediate felt needs are usually the spark to their total awakening, they must demand not only the solution to their immediate problems; they must also seek the realization of their greatest aspirations—a new vision of a better society.

The forgotten people of Hazard and their alumni in Chicago, the neglected people of Mississippi and their alumni in Harlem, all Americans who feel the bite of poverty or the shame of national neglect must work together. This issue goes to the heart of the American political and economic process, and it must be kept alive until the society is transformed. Not only must the needs of the people be met, but the people must be involved in the basic fabric of life and decision-making, so that they gain control, through cooperation, over the forces that rule their lives.

A Way to End the Means Test

Edward E. Schwartz

University of Chicago

[Reprinted with permission of the National Association of Social Workers, from Social Work, *Vol. 9, No. 3 (July 1964), pp. 3–12.]*

THE KENNEDY-JOHNSON war on poverty is avowedly aimed at the abolition of poverty. The grand strategy as revealed thus far is *prevention* through increased provision of gainful employment.

The social work profession has long been committed to the objectives of this war and to the strategy of prevention. Social workers strongly support measures for increasing the demand for employment and for preparing young persons and displaced workers better to meet the demands of the labor market through improved educational, health, and other community services. Yet at any given time not all persons and families will—or necessarily should—be related to a payroll. To insure victory the attack on unemployment must be supported by a system of defense that will assure the maintenance of income for all families. The treatment of poverty, like the treatment of other ills, through alleviation, reduction, and control, is in itself a necessary form of prevention against the spread and perpetuation of the problem. This may seem obvious to social workers, but it is also obvious that this fact has to be repeated frequently.

The current chief defense against poverty is, of course, the social security system; the last line of this defense is public assistance. A most notable aspect of the public assistance programs in the United States today is the dissatisfaction expressed toward them by all parties concerned—the applicants for and the recipients of assistance, the rank-and-file of public assistance staff, legislators, and the public at large—and it is hardly possible to exaggerate the extent and depth of this dissatisfaction. The *treatment* aspect of the war on poverty will require a more effective operation than can be provided through our battered, tired public assistance programs. The public assistance programs will not be good enough even though they be pasted together with surplus-food stamps, glossed over with pseudo-service amendments, or even braced up with Kerr-Mills old age medical payments.

Like many other groups in the population, social workers have become increasingly critical of the public assistance programs, but for their own reasons. They have shown their skepticism of the possibilities of providing high-standard professional services within the framework of public assistance agencies clearly, but chiefly silently, by staying away in droves from employment in these programs. More recently a few lonely academics, crying in the wastelands, have publicly raised important questions and given vent to righteous indignation about the vagaries and inequities of the treatment of the poor.[1]

The recent social work literature of this country appears to offer no specific proposals that would be better suited to contemporary society than is public assistance for maintaining the income of the millions of impoverished families who are untouchable ("not covered") by the "social insurances." Recently Walter C. Bentrup inveighed, feelingly and effectively, against the archaic public assistance means test approach and challenged the social work profession ". . . to visualize the char-

---

[1] *See* Eveline M. Burns, "What's Wrong With Public Welfare?" *Social Service Review*, Vol. 36, No. 2 (June 1962), pp. 111–122; and Alan D. Wade, "Social Work and Political Action," *Social Work*, Vol. 8, No. 4 (October 1963), pp. 3–10.

acteristics of a better one."[2] The purpose of this article is to propose an income maintenance program that would involve neither a means test nor contributions to an earmarked insurance fund and to discuss some of the salient features of this plan.

Family Security Program

The proper treatment of poverty in the United States today is for the federal government to guarantee to every family and person in this country, as a right, income sufficient to maintain a level of living consonant with American standards for the growth and development of children and youth and for the physical and mental health and social well-being of all persons. The right to a livelihood must be recognized and guaranteed as a constitutional civil right. The most satisfactory way to implement such a guarantee is through a modification and expansion of the present mechanism for the collection of the federal income tax.

Every person who is either the head of a family or is not a member of any family would file each year a financial statement of his anticipated income for the coming year, as well as a statement of his income for the past year, and information on the number of his dependents. If his anticipated income for the coming year is below his Federally Guaranteed Minimum Income (FGMI) he may then file a claim for a Family Security Benefit (FSB) in the amount of the difference. If his anticipated income is above his FGMI he will pay an income tax as under present tax law and procedures. After the first year of operation of the Family Security Program, reports of a family's income for the past year and any changes in the number and kinds of dependents will be used to revise prior statements of anticipated income and to make adjustments of Family Security Benefits received for the past year.

Reports of income on which benefits are based will be made in the same style used for individual income tax returns. Methods of checking and auditing of claims for FSB will be developed as expansions of present methods for processing individual income tax returns. This includes field investigation of a sample of cases and of all cases that are highly complex, questionable, or involve large sums. Procedures for checking and auditing will include those recently instituted by the Internal Revenue Service for charging to the individual account of each taxpayer all payments to him of wages, salaries, and other income now subject to identification by a social security number. The kind of automatic data processing equipment now installed at Morgantown, West Virginia, for checking income tax returns against collated information

---

[2] "The Profession and the Means Test," *Social Work*, Vol. 9, No. 2 (April 1964), pp. 10–17.

on income payments to individuals can be used as well for checking the validity and accuracy of claims for FSB.

The level of the FGMI for families of different size will be established by a presidential commission. Provision will be made in the legislation for annual automatic adjustments of dollar amounts on the basis of changes in an appropriate cost-of-living index and for decennial adjustments to reflect changes in standards of living as indicated by appropriate research.

To what extent should FGMI be adjusted to differences in family maintenance costs related to characteristics of members of the family such as age and sex, or to place of residence, regional or urban-rural? Although the use of computers and automatic data processing makes possible increased flexibility in the design of a plan, it should also be recognized that each elaboration increases the complexity of administration and should be adopted only after the net advantages are clearly established.

A problem likely to generate popular interest is involved in the making of FSB payments to families with limited current income but substantial non-income or low-income producing assets. Should FSB payments be made to an aged couple, for example, whose income is below their FGMI but who have $60,000 invested in tax-free municipal bonds yielding 3 percent per annum? Or the widow who lives in her own home in which she has an equity of $30,000? A solution to this problem is suggested by the finding that the median net worth of the fifth of all spending units (roughly equivalent to the total of families and unrelated individuals) having the lowest incomes in 1962 was only $1,000, mostly in the form of equity in dwellings.[3] Persons claiming FSB could be required to include in their annual reports of income a statement of their net worth. Families having a net worth of, perhaps, not over $13,000 of equity in their own dwellings or $2,000 exclusive of sole equity would then not be eligible for benefits.

Can the Nation Afford This?

In discussing the problem of poverty in America the President's Council of Economic Advisers selected the figure of $3,000 (before taxes and expressed in 1962 prices) as the minimum income for a decent life for a non-farm family of four.[4] The council noted a study made by the Social Security Administration that defines a "low-cost" budget for a non-farm family of four and finds its cost in 1962 to have been $3,955.

---

[3] *Economic Report of the President* (Washington, D.C.: U.S. Government Printing Office, 1964), p. 67.

[4] *Ibid.*, p. 58.

The Bureau of Labor Statistics City Workers' Budget, also designed for a family of four, but described as neither "minimum maintenance" nor "luxury" but rather as "modest but adequate" when last priced (1959), exclusive of allowances for the payment of taxes and insurance ranged from $4,622 for Houston to $5,607 in Chicago.[5] For the country as a whole, $5,000 is taken here to represent the cost of a "modest but adequate" annual budget for a family of four.

Using these standards as rough guides the following equally rough estimates may be made of the general order of magnitude of total national payments of FSB at the following levels: minimum maintenance level, $3,000 = $11 billion per annum; economy level, $4,000 = $23 billion per annum; modest-but-adequate level, $5,000 = $38 billion per annum.

The economic feasibility of a proposal for a Family Security Program at the minimum maintenance level is specifically attested to by the Council of Economic Advisors in the following terms:

> Conquest of poverty is well within our power. About $11 billion a year would bring all poor families up to the $3,000 income level we have taken to be the minimum for a decent life. The majority of the Nation could simply tax themselves enough to provide the necessary income supplement to their less fortunate citizens. The burden—one fifth of the annual defense budget, less than 2 percent of GNP—would certainly not be intolerable.[6]

The council's report goes on to express a preference for a solution to the problem of poverty that would permit Americans "to *earn* the American Standard of Living." However, the report further states:

> We can surely afford greater generosity in relief of distress, but the major thrust of our campaign must be against causes rather than symptoms. We can afford the cost of that campaign too.[7]

The gross national product of the United States is now about $600 billion per annum. If the Federally Guaranteed Minimum Income for a family of four were set at the $5,000 per annum modest-but-adequate level the *gross cost* would be less than 7 percent of the gross national product—still quite tolerable. At whatever level the FSB is set the *net cost* of benefit payments would of course depend on the extent to which these were offset through reductions in expenditures of existing welfare programs.

All public welfare payments under present federal, state, and

---

[5] Helen H. Lamale and Margaret S. Strotz, "The Interim City Worker's Family Budget," *Monthly Labor Review*, Vol. 83, No. 8 (August 1960), pp. 785–808.

[6] *Economic Report of the President, op. cit.*, p. 77.

[7] *Ibid.*

local programs including public assistance, veterans' benefits, unemployment compensation, and old age and survivors insurance benefits, but excluding health and education, now total about $33 billion. Public assistance payments alone are close to $5 billion and almost the entire amount could be taken immediately as an offset against payments of Family Security Benefits. Savings from other welfare programs would be dependent on the extent and rate at which they could be "phased out." Appreciable savings would also be effected through the substitution of modern accounting and auditing techniques and the use of automatic data processing for the present costly, slow, and labor-consuming procedures for determining initial and continuing eligibility of each family through office interviews, home visits, investigation of each family's income and resources, and computation of individual budgets and budget deficits on a case-by-case basis.

A fresh and useful perspective on how much this country can afford to spend for welfare measures may be gained by a look abroad. Data gathered by Gordon show public welfare expenditures in various nations as a percent of national income in 1950, 1953, and 1957.[8] In each year the United States ranked lower than any of the sixteen western and eastern European countries reported, and lower than Canada, Chile, Australia, New Zealand, and Israel. The only nations reported that are outranked by the United States in this "measure of welfare effort" are Guatemala, four Asian, and three African and Middle Eastern countries.

In a recent analysis of the share of industrial production allocated to the beneficiaries of governmental welfare programs, Colm selected for comparison Sweden as the western European country most advanced toward the "welfare state" and Germany as that which is often considered the nearest approximation to a "free enterprise" country. He found that the relative size of social welfare expenditures was about the same in both countries and considerably higher than in the United States. He declares that there is a great deal of unfinished business in the development of our social welfare programs and concludes:

> With the technical knowledge of our age we will have the material means available for eliminating poverty as a mass phenomena [sic]. We can only hope that we will also develop the attitudes necessary to use these resources for the benefit of those who will not automatically benefit from economic growth and rising incomes *and from the conventional security and welfare programs.* [Author's italics.][9]

---

[8] Margaret S. Gordon, *The Economics of Welfare Policies* (New York: Columbia University Press, 1963), pp. 15–16.

[9] Gerhard Colm, "The Economic Base and Limits of Social Welfare," *Monthly Labor Review*, Vol. 86, No. 6 (June 1963), pp. 695–700.

Now that our war on poverty blows hot we should be able to find the wherewithal to wage it.

Origins of the Proposal

Schemes for a redistribution of income have a long and interesting history and in fact and in fancy constitute a substantial portion of Utopian literature.[10] Utopian ideas represent leaps—sometimes highly creative and fruitful leaps—into the future. Proposals for social policy, such as this modest one, are more likely to be simply a drawing together and reformulation of existing ideas about a state of affairs deemed more desirable than the existing situation and one that may be achieved by a series of specified actions, that is, through a plan. An examination of the origins of the essential ideas brought together in this proposal for a Family Security Program will serve to point up some of the issues that will have to be faced in considering a plan of action.

The present proposal derives somewhat from the literature and history of family allowances, but more directly from the writings of Lady Rhys Williams. Her proposal is for a new social contract

> . . . whereby the State would acknowledge the duty to maintain the individual and his children at all times and to assure for them all of the necessities of a healthy life. The individual in his turn would acknowledge it to be his duty to divert his best efforts to the production of the wealth whereby alone the welfare of the community can be maintained.[11]

Under this contract a benefit would be paid to every person who is employed or unemployable, or, if unemployed, is willing to accept suitable employment. Benefits would be paid in addition to earnings and income from other sources. Financing would be through a flat rate income tax that, when combined with per capita benefit payments, would produce the net effect of a progressive income tax.

The social contract is designed to solve the following problems: (1) the distribution of wealth, (2) the freeing of the unemployed to undertake part-time work for profit, (3) the maintenance of a stable

---

[10] *See,* for example, Lewis Mumford, *The Story of Utopias* (New York: Boni and Livewright, 1922). In the present atomic-space age it is easy to forget that the earliest form of science fiction was social-science fiction and that this genre too had its uses. Shall we also think on why latter-day social-science fiction (e.g., Huxley's *Brave New World,* Orwell's *1984*) is not Utopian but "Dystopian"?

[11] Lady Juliet Rhys Williams, *Something to Look Forward To* (London, England: MacDonald and Company, 1943), p. 145. This book is, unfortunately, out of print, but a short selection from it appears in William D. Grampp and Emanuel T. Weiler, *Economic Policy, Readings in Political Economy* (Homewood, Ill.: Richard D. Irwin, 1953), pp. 284–292.

price level, (4) the ending of opposition between taxpayers and state beneficiaries, (5) the complete abolition of the means test, without involving state bankruptcy, (6) the maintenance of full employment, without resort to compulsory labor. Considering the number and magnitude of its objectives, the social contract idea seems disarmingly simple, but when subjected to analysis turns out to be amazingly powerful. The Beveridge plan which relies heavily on the social insurance principle and was developed contemporaneously with *Something to Look Forward To,* won immediate political interest and support. Subsequent critiques by competent British economists point to distinct advantages in the new social contract.[12]

In this country, Friedman and Theobald recently proposed ways of treating poverty that are reminiscent of Lady Rhys Williams' writings.[13] The similarity of Friedman's and Theobald's proposals is noteworthy in view of the marked variations in their general stance and economic philosophies.

Friedman identifies himself as a liberal, in the nineteenth-century meaning of that term. He is committed to political decentralization and to economic reliance on private voluntary arrangements arrived at in the marketplace. He believes that the most desirable way of alleviating poverty is through private charity, but recognizes that government action is necessary, at least in large impersonal communities. Friedman's proposal, which he terms "a negative income tax," is that if an individual's income is less than the sums of his exemptions and his deductions he would receive from the government as an income subsidy a percentage of the difference. The levels at which subsidies would be set would be determined by how much taxpayers are willing to tax themselves.[14]

If Friedman's philosophy is characterized as the liberalism of the nineteenth century, then Theobald's can safely be placed in the twentieth century—if not later. Theobald's proposal for basic economic security is as follows:

> One of the fundamental principles of the present United States tax system is the "exemption" of a part of an individual's income from

[12] Alan T. Peacock, *The Economics of National Insurance* (London, England: William Hodge & Company, 1952), p. 94 *ff. See also* Denstone Berry, "Modern Welfare Analysis and the Forms of Income Distribution," in Alan T. Peacock, ed., *Income Redistribution and Social Policy* (London, England: Jonathan Cape, 1954), pp. 41–51.

[13] Milton Friedman, *Capitalism and Freedom* (Chicago: University of Chicago Press, 1962); Robert Theobald, *Free Men and Free Markets* (New York: Potter, C. N., 1963).

[14] Friedman, *ibid.,* pp. 190–192.

taxation. At its inception, this exemption insured that taxes would not be paid on that portion of income required to provide a reasonable standard of living. However, the Government lost sight of this aim when increasing the tax load to pay for World War II, and the value of this exemption has been further reduced since the end of World War II by the effects of inflation. The original aim of the federal tax exemption should be raised immediately to a level which would guarantee an un-taxed income adequate for minimum subsistence. Those whose incomes from earnings or from capital did not reach this level would then be entitled to receive further government payments sufficient to raise the incomes to this level and assure their basic economic support.[15]

Theobald points out that the provision of medical care as well as education as a community responsibility would simplify the establishment of appropriate levels of basic economic security. A consulting economist, he is primarily concerned with the effects of technology, especially cybernetics, the combination of automation and computers, on the distribution of income and on the labor market. He believes that because of the increased productive capacity of our economy it is not only unnecessary but impractical to attempt to make everyone's livelihood dependent upon his working. He accepts the position that Galbraith developed in *The Affluent Society* that we are in an economy of abundance rather than in an economy of scarcity and asserts that an absolute constitutional right to a "due income" is not only possible but essential for the future of the economy.[16]

The Incentive to Work

Arguments against the treatment of poverty through the use of taxes represent a curious congerie of theories, ideas, and biases. Some are of historic interest only, some persist over time, and still others may be of more recent coinage.[17] For example, the early attacks against the Elizabethan Poor Laws launched by Malthusian enthusiasts: in its current form this movement has, of course, been diverted from criticisms concerning support by the state of the "spawning poor" to the support of birth control programs. The banner of Social Darwinism has long been raised against the puny forces of poor relief in this country, and garnished by the symbols of racial prejudice it is still flaunted in the benighted backwoods around certain state capitals.

---

[15] Theobald, *op. cit.*, pp. 192–193.

[16] John Kenneth Galbraith, *The Affluent Society* (Boston: Houghton-Mifflin Co., 1958).

[17] Samuel Mencher, "The Changing Balance of Status and Contract in Assistance Policy," *Social Service Review*, Vol. 35, No. 1 (March 1961), pp. 17–32.

Some of the disadvantages of the direct treatment of poverty cited by some contemporary economists are (1) it must be done over and over again and (2) productivity may be inhibited by (a) diverting money from capital formation and from investment in the nation's industrial plant to taxes and (b) reducing the incentive to work, and especially to work as much as possible.[18]

The only comment that will be made here about the criticism listed first is that, although true, it can also be leveled against eating. The current curious and unique phenomenon of universally bullish economic indicators together with the recent tax reduction should help to mute although not inhibit continued expressions of anxiety about the tax burden.

The chief argument against the present proposal and in favor of the retention of the means test is also one that can be expected to persist over time and that is based on the theory that by insuring everyone a livelihood and removing the whiplash of hunger "most folks won't work"—and that this will be not only demoralizing for the general populace but ruinous of the economy. Social workers and others familiar with modern dynamic psychology may contend that this fear and the argument as a whole derive from an outmoded, simplistic view of human behavior. We can also oppose our professional ethic of ameliorism against what may appear to us to be an unduly pessimistic view of human nature and we can, if need be, produce a considerable amount of clinical evidence to show that mature individuals strive to be productive. However, perhaps the best that can be hoped for here is a verdict of "not proved," for there appears to be an absence of the kind of data needed for policy formulation.

Lady Rhys Williams posits the necessity of providing economic incentives for work as one of the basic tenets of the social contract. Her proposal, like state unemployment compensation laws, provides for payment only if persons accept suitable employment. At the other extreme, Theobald's basic economic security plan is focused on the problem of too few jobs rather than on the problem of too few takers, and it seems likely that increasing numbers of people will agree with his contention that it is unjust to insist that a person work or starve if no one will give him a job.

Friedman says of his proposal:

Like any other measures to alleviate poverty it reduces the incentive of those helped to help themselves but it does not eliminate that incen-

---

[18] Allen G. B. Fisher, "Alternative Techniques for Promoting Equality in a Capitalist Society," in Grampp and Weiler, *op. cit.*, pp. 277–278.

tive entirely as a system of supplementing incomes up to some fixed minimum worth. An extra dollar earned always means more money available for expenditure.[19]

This effect is gained under Friedman's proposal because the subsidies granted are a fraction of the sum of personal exemption and deductions, which in turn may or may not equal the required income. Friedman's built-in incentive feature is therefore obtainable only at the expense of sacrificing the assurance that all families will receive the income they need.

A work incentive feature can be incorporated into the present proposal for a Family Security Program without sacrificing the guarantee of a minimum income merely by reducing Family Security Benefits by a percentage of earnings. Assuming a family of four and a Federally Guaranteed Minimum Income of $3,000 the effects of reducing FSB by a percentage that would increase with each earnings bracket is demonstrated in Table 1.

TABLE 1

Earned Income	FSB/Taxes	Total Income
$ 0—$ 999	$3,000—$2,400	$3,000—$3,399
1,000— 1,999	2,399— 1,700	3,399— 3,699
2,000— 2,999	1,699— 900	3,699— 3,899
3,000— 3,999	899— 0	3,899— 3,999
4,000— 4,499	0	4,000— 4,499
4,500 and above	Tax on amounts above $4,500	4,500+

The net effect in this illustration would be that in addition to receiving a $3,000 FSB, families earning up to $1,000 would retain up to 40 percent of such earnings. If family earnings were between $1,000 and $1,999 the family would retain between 35 and 40 percent of this income in addition to their FSB, and so on. An extension of the work incentive feature is gained by fixing an income bracket within which a family could not claim FSB but would be tax exempt. Families earning from $4,000 to $4,500 would receive no FSB and would pay no taxes. Families earning above $4,500 would receive no FSB and would pay taxes only on income above $4,500.

Total national expenditures for FSB payments including incentive allowances for earnings if the FGMI were set at $3,000 for a family of four would of course fall between previous estimates of $11 and $23

---

[19] *Op. cit.*, p. 192.

billion. Substantial additional costs, however, would arise from narrowing the present tax base as a result of exempting family income up to $4,500, in the form of reduced revenues from the income tax.

The Law of Parsimony, the dictates of administrative simplicity, and the social work ethic would all argue against including the incentive feature in the FSB plan, unless and until experience indicates the need for it. However, this is the kind of issue that, if properly structured, may provide reasonable men with grounds for agreement. And those who feel strongly about the necessity of a work incentive should have the opportunity of considering the payment of the additional cost.

FSB and Social Welfare Manpower

Of the 105,000 social welfare workers in the United States, 35,000 or one-third are employed in state and local public assistance agencies.[20] The overwhelming proportion of the time of public assistance staffs goes into the mechanics of eligibility determination and the handling of details of financial assistance and precious little into the provision of restorative, rehabilitative, therapeutic, integrative, socializing services. Suggestions have been made from time to time that one way of achieving a better balance in public assistance programs between the provision of financial service and other welfare services would be to establish functionally specialized staff units for each type of service in the same agency or possibly in two separate agencies.[21] The weakness of this type of proposal is that it does not go far enough. As long as the two functions—the administration of financial service and of other welfare services—appear to require the same kind of activity (e.g., interviewing, traveling, home visiting) by the same kind of staff and with the same clientele it seems highly unlikely that many administrative takers will be found. Contrast with this the evident and substantial gains in the efficient utilization of manpower that would be made available by the adoption of the policies and procedures possible under the federal Family Security Program.

The establishment of a federal Family Security Program would enable state and local public welfare agencies to change the focus and emphasis of their programs in the direction so presciently indicated by the change in the name of the federal Bureau of Public Assistance to

---

[20] *Salaries and Working Conditions of Social Welfare Manpower in 1960* (New York: National Social Welfare Assembly, undated), p. 20. Figures given are exclusive of recreation workers.

[21] See Editor's Page, *Social Work*, Vol. 7, No. 1 (January 1962), p. 128; and Eveline M. Burns, *op. cit.*, p. 122.

the Bureau of Family Services. Poverty is, of course, sometimes preceded by psychological, emotional, health, and other problems of the individual. However, social workers will testify that of far greater import is the effect chronic, hopeless, and grinding poverty, produced by massive external social and economic forces, has on the appearance and exacerbation of problems in the individual and his family. These effects may persist even after financial support is provided and are likely to be of an order that require and respond to social work treatment, fortified by a strong battery of community welfare services.

An important part of a plan to transfer the income maintenance function of the public assistance programs to a federal Family Security Program would be to extend and expand the extremely limited range of state and local welfare services now provided through public assistance agencies, and to fashion them into a comprehensive flexible program of public services for families. Together with our developing public child welfare service programs we would then have an organizational base for a well-rounded public welfare service available to all the people. Freed of the incubus of the means test and properly selected and equipped and well related to the community and to the social work and other professions, state and local public welfare staffs would have a fair and rare opportunity of making a great contribution to the war against poverty.

Political Realities

Politicians as well as caseworkers know how to "partialize," and among the kinds of questions that will be asked about the present proposal sooner or later will be, "Do you have to have all of this?" and "What part of this is most important?" One possible ploy will be, "Let's start with children or better yet the aged—they vote."

Almost two decades ago the writer suggested that the unfolding of the Canadian experience with family allowances could be observed with benefit by those in the United States who are concerned with social security and child welfare.[22] Over the years social workers, when overwhelmed by public assistance bureaupathology, are wont to murmur rather wistfully that perhaps they ought to start thinking about family allowances. It is, of course, possible that the present proposal to abolish the means test may not seem to be overly modest to some people and we may be forced to settle at this time for a family allowances program. But this should be resisted even by those of us who think children are

---

[22] Edward E. Schwartz, "Some Observations on the Canadian Family Allowance Program," *Social Service Review*, Vol. 20, No. 4 (December 1946), pp. 451–473.

the most important people but who would also like to prevent further "hardening of the categories" and increased complexity in the intricate mosaic or crazy-quilt pattern that characterizes our present social security and welfare nonsystem. The case for starting a noncontributory Family Security Program for the aged might have political appeal, but the fact is that parents of children vote too.

Temporizing is another technique of practical politics and, in a form that social workers themselves have been known to use, includes the appeal to "demonstration and research." We must have research and we must also be clear about the function of research and how it differs from careful planning, detailing, documentation, and justification of proposals for social policy.

Nevertheless, consideration may well be given to the desirability of a geographically limited demonstration of some aspects of the proposal for an FSB plan. For example, through use of federally available research and demonstration funds a state welfare agency might develop a procedure for checking the feasibility of a central mechanical check of eligibility through the use of data processing equipment after the necessary arrangements were made for social security or other numerical identification of all salary, wages, and other types of income payments within the state.

This kind of jurisdiction-limited demonstration would appear to be feasible in a state having a small daily commuting population and an effective state income tax law. Financing of assistance payments in this kind of demonstration would not require new federal legislation inasmuch as nothing in the present public assistance titles of the Social Security Act requires the kind of means test currently used and states are free to submit their own plans for determining need. One of the points of administrative interest in such a demonstration would be a check on possible differences in the completeness of social security identification of income in low- as compared with middle- and upper-income brackets. Other administrative problems such as the frequency of FSB payments and methods of adjusting reports of anticipated income to subsequent experience could also be tested in practice on a restricted demonstration basis. Necessary research on an FSB program would of course be expedited if there is clear evidence of interest in abolishing the means test.

If a Family Security Program can be administered on a state basis, why go to a centralized federal program? The answer to this, in part, is that not all states meet the conditions necessary for a demonstration and that in a population as mobile as ours, national administration would appear to be an administrative prerequisite. A more fundamental reason is simply that the experience of the past three decades clearly points to the greater probability of meeting the most essential elements of a Family Security Program—*the right to an adequte and equitable income*—through a federally administered program than through a federal-state grant-in-aid scheme. Some of the disadvantages of the public assistance approach have been documented as follows:

> In theory, public assistance should take care of all current need, coming into play when all other sources of income fall short of socially acceptable minimum levels and underpinning all other income-maintenance programs. How far short of this standard the existing public assistance programs fall can be measured in several ways.
>
> One recent study used as a standard of need twice the amount of a low-cost food budget as calculated, with regional variations, by the Department of Agriculture.[23] A standard under which 50 percent of total income must go for food is minimal indeed. Yet in 1958, to meet this standard, assistance payments for families receiving aid to families with dependent children would have needed to be increased for the country as a whole by 72 percent. . . . In the West a 27-percent increase would have brought actual expenditures to the level where they would meet the standard, and in the South a 149-percent increase would have been required.
>
> . . . It was estimated that to provide an income of twice the cost of a low-cost food budget to all persons on the public assistance rolls in 1958 would have required expenditure of $1 billion more than the $3 billion actually spent for public assistance by all levels of government in that year. . . .
>
> The Michigan study referred to earlier found that less than one-fourth of the families living in poverty in 1959 were receiving public assistance.[24]
>
> Public assistance is a Federal-State program, with levels of assistance and conditions of eligibility determined by the individual States. For this reason the raising of standards for public assistance is a far more complex and difficult problem than it is for a national insurance program. It must be noted, also, that Federal financial aid is available only for selected categories; general assistance is financed entirely by State and local funds and in many places entirely by local funds. It is important to keep in mind these structural barriers to the transfer of resources released by disarmament.[25]

---

[23] Ellen J. Perkins, "Unmet Need in Public Assistance," *Social Security Bulletin,* Vol. 23, No. 4 (April 1960), pp. 3–11.

[24] James M. Morgan *et al., Income and Welfare in the United States* (New York: McGraw-Hill Book Co., 1962).

[25] Ida C. Merriam, "Social Welfare Opportunities and Necessities Attendant on Disarmament," *Social Security Bulletin,* Vol. 26, No. 10 (October 1963), pp. 10–14.

The possibility of obtaining equitable and adequate support for families in all the states through the federal-state public assistance program may well be more remote—and in that sense more Utopian—than through a conversion to the proposed federal Family Security Program.

Social Work's Contribution

Assuming that the reader has quickly adjusted to the idea of standing the income tax on its head and that he has perceptively grasped the economic and administrative feasibility of a federal Family Security Program, as well as the compelling logic and inherent social justice of this modest proposal, he should now have no difficulty in recognizing the appeal it will have not only to prospective beneficiaries, but to fair-minded, democratic voters in general. He will also recognize that insuring the civil right to a livelihood is inextricably bound up with protecting the civil rights of ethnic minorities, and the drive for each must be mutually supportive.

Social workers have here the ingredients for effective social action —a cause to which they can dedicate themselves without reserve—a friendly administrative atmosphere, opportune timing in relation to the beginning reduction in expenditures for armament, and the "seed corn" resources to get things started. The National Association of Social Workers is now a larger, more complex organization than many of us are used to being in or using. By the same token, it has the potential resources in finances and structure to serve as at least the "secondary mover" in the process of obtaining favorable public consideration of this proposal.

The prime movers in social action to abolish the means test and establish the right to a livelihood as a constitutional guarantee must be the individual members of the association, who can instruct their chapter and national officers, representatives, and delegates in the association to declare that as a result of the war on poverty the social work profession is in a state of emergency. Social work's contribution to the waging of this war can be fixing the highest program priority and the greatest possible focus of association financial and personnel resources on winning the battle to abolish the means test and to guarantee a fair livelihood to all the people of the nation.

We are aware that substantial gains in human welfare that require expenditures of public funds are hard to come by, but, if social workers do not fight for them, who will? And, if someone else does and we do not, then what are we?

Poverty and Social Change

S. M. Miller, *Syracuse University,* and
Martin Rein, *Bryn Mawr School of Social Work*

[Reprinted from the March 1964 issue of American Child, *published quarterly by the National Committee on Employment of Youth, 145 East 32nd Street, New York, New York, 10016.]*

THE REDISCOVERY of the once invisible poor has rapidly captured public interest. Poverty is sloganized into political glamor by the use of military metaphor. The gaping needs of today rivet attention so that a way of thinking about poverty does not seem necessary. Unfortunately, narrow perspectives lead to narrow programs.

The concept of poverty is neither fixed nor precisely measured. As society advances, the notions of need, adequacy and subsistence must be looked at in new ways. Nor can the concepts of inequality and dependency be ignored. The inadequate conceptualization of poverty leads to an inadequate formulation of action alternatives in the present "war on poverty."

A brief review of the American experience is useful here. Economic theories of the 18th century assumed that real wages were fixed by a natural law and helped earn for economics the unhappy name of "the dismal science." Man was caught in limited possibilities; improvement of the position of the poor was impeded by the inexorable requirements of the economy. But by the mid-20th century, everyone's income was increasing, and the poor's most rapidly of all. Kuznets seemed to provide statistical proof that the income pyramid was being flattened. In a spirit of "dazed euphoria," American social scientists formulated a new natural law of income equalization.

This theory went as follows: The expansion of production and productivity resulted in a much greater economic pie. The graduated income tax, expanded welfare services, and education were more equitably distributing this larger pie. Continued increase in aggregate economic wealth would invariably filter down, more or less equitably, to all income groupings. Marginal economic groups, it was assumed, would in time "gracefully succumb" to continued economic growth and that small residual group not covered by expanding welfare and social security programs would be handily cared for by the traditional public dole.

Facts seem to bear the theory out. The standard of living had substantially increased during the post-World War II era. The G.I. Bill provided many working-class youth, who would never have achieved technical and advanced education, an opportunity for upward occupational mobility. Indeed, the traditional income pyramid seemed to be slowly changing into a giant barrel-shaped distribution. The residual groups also seemed to be slowly dwindling, especially as old people increasingly came to be covered by old age and survivor's insurance.

But these remarkable results were not the product of some natural economic law. We had entered a period of full employment in the war and postwar periods, producing a shortage of labor. Special factors accentuated the shortage—the low birth rate of the great depression, the war demands for many able-bodied men, and the postwar concentration on further education through the G.I. Bill of Rights. These conditions helped create a vacuum which sucked disadvantaged groups into the labor force.

One important result of the operation of these forces was a change in the character of the labor force. The labor vacuum pulled into the labor force a large number of women, so that by 1957 almost 30 percent of all families in the United States had two wage earners. In addition, many wage earners had more than one job as moonlighting expanded. (Interestingly enough, families with both husband and wife in the paid labor force were concentrated among the upper income fifth of American families. Sixteen percent of those in the lowest income fifth had a husband and wife in the paid labor force in 1957 as compared to 41 percent of those in the upper income fifth.)

"Pockets of poverty" were, of course, present, and occasional public recognition was given to the plight of migrant laborers, tenant workers, old workers and other groups. But these groups were considered as special cases. Galbraith's term of "case poverty" seemed to cover them. By particularizing the poor, we avoided an overall summation of the groups in poverty, so that the scope was not comprehended in its totality.

By the late 1950's and early 1960's the suction power of the economy began to weaken. Our economy moved into a new industrial revolution, the cybernetic age. In this period, as the demand for labor increases, we can no longer depend on a corresponding reduction of unemployed and unemployable groups. This latest industrial revolution has created a labor demand aimed chiefly at the skilled and educated.

The theory that expanding aggregate production will funnel down to all income groups has collapsed as the gross national product has soared to an unprecedented half a trillion dollars. Production has continued to mount but so has unemployment. Six percent of the labor force are unemployed, with twice this rate of unemployment among the low-educated and unskilled and triple this rate for youth entering the labor force. Unemployment and poverty are not simple reciprocals of

Selected Agencies and Organizations from which Additional Information Can Be Obtained

American Jewish Committee
165 East 56th Street
New York, New York

Association on American Indian
Affairs
475 Riverside Drive
New York 27, New York

Center for the Study of Democratic
Institutions
Box 4068
Santa Barbara, California

Citizens' Crusade Against Poverty
132 Third Street SE
Washington, D. C. 20003

Committee for Economic Development
1001 Connecticut Avenue NW
Washington, D. C.

Committee for Miners
1165 Broadway
New York, New York 10001

Committee on Pockets of Poverty
1020 Connecticut Avenue NW
Washington, D. C. 20036

Conference of Economic Progress
1001 Connecticut Avenue NW
Washington, D. C., 20036

Congress of Racial Equality
38 Park Row
New York, New York

Economic Research and Action
Project
1100 West Ainslie
Chicago, Illinois

Grey Areas Project
Ford Foundation
477 Madison Avenue
New York, New York 10022

Industrial Areas Foundation
8 South Michigan Avenue
Chicago 3, Illinois

Industrial Union Department
A.F.L.–C.I.O.
815 16th Street NW
Washington, D. C. 20006

Institute for Policy Studies
1900 Florida Avenue NW
Washington, D. C. 20090

Jewish Labor Committee
25 East 78th Street
New York, New York

League for Industrial Democracy
112 East 19th Street
New York, New York 10003

National Advisory Committee on
Farm Labor
112 East 19th Street
New York, New York 10003

National Association for the Advancement of Colored People
20 West 40th Street
New York, New York

National Committee for Children and
Youth
1145 19th Street NW
Washington, D. C.

National Committee for Full
Employment
Box 232, Village Station
New York, New York 10014

National Committee on Employment
of Youth
145 East 32nd Street
New York, New York

National Consumers League
1029 Vermont Avenue NW
Washington, D.C.

National Planning Association
1606 New Hampshire Avenue NW
Washington, D. C.

National Sharecroppers Fund
112 East 19th Street
New York, New York 10003

National Urban League
14 East 48th Street
New York, New York

Research Department
A.F.L.–C.I.O.
815 16th Street NW
Washington, D. C. 20006

Southern Regional Council
5 Forsythe NW
Atlanta, Georgia

Student Non-violent Coordinating
Committee
360 Nelson Street NW
Atlanta, Georgia

United States Office of Economic
Opportunity
1156 15th Street NW
Washington, D.C.

The W. E. Upjohn Institute for
Employment Research
709 South Westnedge Avenue
Kalamazoo, Michigan

employment and production. The power of the unregulated economy to siphon off a large part of expanding production to the low-income groups has been reduced.

Our changing economy has to be related to the changing nature of poverty. Poverty is traditionally related to the cost of a fixed basket of goods and services that are required for survival. But as Galbraith has so aptly said, "people are poverty stricken when their income, even if adequate for survival, falls markedly behind that of the community . . . they are degraded, for in the literal sense, they live outside the grades or categories which the community regards as acceptable."

Poverty is thus not a fixed point. It is a moving escalator, reflecting the values of a society. Our conceptualization of poverty has been too narrowly limited to a dollars and cents standard. A more embracing standard is needed to include the distribution of non-monetary resources, of education, recreation, medicine, old age protection, and similar services.

Moreover, we have tended to disregard the issue of inequality by giving too much importance to the fact that people were receiving more than they were getting before. Clearly, the shoring up of incomes does not mean that we are also automatically improving the relative position of low-income holders. For example, the average earnings of the non-white male increased from $1,800 in 1950 to over $3,000 in 1960. But these figures represent a slight drop in the percentage of Negro income, compared to the average white man's income, from 61 to 60 percent.

The recent tendency in American society has been to raise the absolute level while increasing inequality. The percentage of the total pie going to the bottom 20 percent has slightly declined in the post-World War II period. As Myrdal has observed, this trend results in widening the class chasms and stiffening the class structure.

We cannot presume that the tax structure operates to reduce inequalities and to redistribute income. The differences in the distribution of income before and after tax are amazingly slight. Tax evasion is partly to blame. The poor pay more of their income for taxes than families five times as rich since state and local taxes rely on regressive taxes such as the sales tax. The *Wall Street Journal* recently reported that "28% of family incomes under $2,000 a year is paid out in taxes." Increasingly, tax exemptions, fringe benefits, expense accounts, pension plans serve as hidden multipliers of economic advantage. Macauley estimates that a quarter of payroll costs in the United States are in the form of fringe benefits.

Today, little emphasis is placed on the direct redistribution of income as a means of reducing poverty and inequality. Education is increasingly seen as the important escape hatch and the Johnson "war on poverty" will likely emphasize education as the answer to poverty. A cult-like devotion to the magical aid of a high school diploma is developing. As educational achievement rather than family connections became more important in determining occupational possibilities, it was believed that inequalities and poverty could be reduced by expansion of educational attainments.

Education today does not seem to be effectively reducing the occupational and income inequalities in society, at least for youth coming from the lowest income families. The long-term neglect of schools in the low-income areas is only now slowly beginning to be rectified. Despite the additional investments in low-income schools, the relative per capita expenditures in better off areas of the United States is still much greater. A recent Pennsylvania study by Rein and Hare reveals that in poor counties welfare expenditures are high and educational outlays low. In better off counties the pattern is reversed. Suburban per capita expenditures for white middle class children usually far outdistance those spent for low-income white and Negro children living in center cities. Thus, present investments in low-income areas may serve only to increase the absolute level without strengthening the relative educational position of the poor.

The educational level needed for jobs which provide decent income and security is constantly moving upward. As low-income youth increase their absolute level of educational achievement, the educational achievements of the rest of the population also continue to rise. The best that can be hoped for is that low-income youth will maintain the same relative position. Maintaining the same relative position may in time represent a decline in opportunity as the overall volume of jobs declines in relation to a growing labor force and as educational credentials for jobs increase. The use of an absolute standard such as high school graduation as a national goal can be deceptive, because the meaning of this standard changes over time. Increasingly, high school graduation will be inadequate to gain a secure foothold in the American occupational structure.

An underlying assumption is that if we bring people up to a certain level in education, there will continue to be jobs for them. Despite expanded production, there simply may not be enough jobs to cover the rapidly growing labor force. Expanding educational achievement which leads to no work can be disillusioning for a young person. An educated, discontented, and deprived population is the kind of incendiary substance from which revolutions are formed. We have to re-think poverty and inequality in a cybernetic, affluent society.

The following principles are crucial in developing a successful strategy for reducing poverty and inequality today. Clearly, these suggestions do not represent detailed programs but broad organizing principles based on the reconceptualization of poverty.

Present programs are acting as though poverty is a short-run problem aimed at raising family income to some absolute standard. When the changing character of poverty is recognized, these short-term, remedial programs appear limited. It is necessary to institutionalize these programs rather than define them as a temporary injection of limited funds to solve a short term problem. *The present form of ad hoc tinkering with minor demonstration programs will not meet the long-range requirements.* It is unlikely that if we rely on fragmented remedial programs we can educate people as fast as industry's educational level is moving up. What is needed is a broad-scale, permanent program. For example, a program designed to provide a guaranteed college education for all low-income youths, much like the G.I. Bill's provision of a guaranteed college education for veterans, should be given thoughtful attention. The distribution of educational opportunity should be extended not only to selected groups such as those who have served their country in war, but to all individuals by virtue of citizenship in American society.

In place of short-term programs we need a broad redistributive program aimed at reallocating income and services. One step would be providing higher benefit levels for social insurance and public assistance that would directly and immediately aid many of the poor.

As we have suggested, poverty must be conceptualized to include the quantity and quality of services. Consequently, redistributing housing, educational, medical, recreational and other services would be important. And these services should be quality services.

The broadened concept of poverty antiquates the rigid *ideology of the minimum* in public welfare services which permeated nineteenth century economic liberalism. It was feared that the expansion of public provision would kill incentive to participate in the main economy. In a similar fashion our present emphasis on short-term programs is continually guided by the fear that a comprehensive approach to poverty would reduce incentives and destroy freedom. Consequently, in retraining programs, for example, we stop at retraining and neglect the important tasks of getting job and worker together. In economically distressed areas we do not provide subsidies to families to enable them to move, to locate a place to live and to secure a definite job. Implicit in these apprehensions is the assumption that unemployment in an affluent society is a result of personal inadequacy. Our present formulation of strategies of change continues to be chained to a 19th century ideology, of minimum help to the "laggards," rather than to a 20th century notion of *adequate help* to the victims of society who frequently need pervasive aid to manage in the changing society.

Existing service-dispensing institutions have failed to alter the relative position of the disadvantaged. Many social institutions have ignored or dealt inadequately with the poor. Therefore, it will not be sufficient to simply provide these *institutions of failure* with more funds —to continue doing what they have always done in the past. *It is necessary to change social institutions so that they are more effectively responsive to the needs of the poor.* Changes in the programs of educational and welfare institutions and in the styles of professional intervention are needed.

Professionals must turn more to a concept of service, with less emphasis in the guild function of their professions. Hamlin at the Harvard School of Public Health recently recommended that voluntary agencies be made accountable to a public review board. In a similar fashion we think that it is important that independent sources of accountability be developed which would encourage and pressure welfare and educational institutions to be more responsive to the needs of low-income families. More services are not enough; they have to be changed and improved.

The operation of our economic system needs priority consideration. The growth of poverty and inequality may well be interpreted as free enterprise on trial. Present programs have avoided a confrontation on this issue. The favored action programs today are those directed at the machinery for inducting individuals into the labor force or retreading those who are already in the work market but unable to hold a job or compete for a new one. Free enterprise and the operation of our economy remain a privileged sanctuary in American society. It is acceptable to criticize voluntary agency programs, schools, and public welfare, but criticism of the economy is conspicuously absent. Long-range economic planning is neglected; public attention is concentrated on short-range issues designed to promote private consumption. As Galbraith has proposed, more attention needs to be paid to collective consumption. We need to reverse the equation of public squalor and private affluence. To do this we need to modify our traditional suspicion about increasing public budgets and we should be ready to make a very substantial investment in public expenditures for schools, hospitals, welfare services, roads and other forms which would expand collective consumption.

It is important to extend monetary and fiscal policy to include not only a broad investment in the public sector but also a greater investment in specialized industries. In an economy committed to promoting labor-saving industries by devices such as generous depletion allowances, a parallel investment needs to be made in the expansion of labor-intensive industries. Many low-skilled individuals—and there will continue to be many—will not be employable in the industries of the future. In this context, the expansion of the role of the sub-professional, as pointed out by Marcia Freedman in the January 1964 issue of *American Child*, warrants special consideration as a device for expanding job opportunities. Labor shortages among the helping profession are acute.

Finally, we need to consider changes in social values. This calls for a two-pronged program aimed both at the present and the future. As far as the present is concerned, we must develop a broader view that permits us to see welfare programs not only as devices for creaming off those who are most able to participate in the economy but also for those who are not economically mobile. The true test of the humanity of a society is what it does with people who cannot participate directly or effectively in the economy. As for the society of the future, in which there may be a greatly lessened need for traditional work assignments, we must find new, socially respectable ways of getting financial support for families. Today, only people who make an economic contribution are assumed to have any value. The concept of work needs to be re-examined and new standards for the definition of social utility developed. We need new standards by which to measure *the moral equivalent of an economic contribution.*

Poverty cannot be studied and changed without studying and changing society.

Selected Bibliography

1. Edgar S. and Jean C. Cahn. "The War on Poverty: A Civilian Perspective," *Yale Law Journal*, 73 (July, 1964).

2. Joel Cogen and Kathryn Feidelson. "Rental Assistance for Large Families," *Pratt Planning Papers*. Brooklyn: Pratt Institute, June, 1964.

3. Rennie Davis. "The War on Poverty: Notes on Insurgent Response," Economic Research and Action Project, Ann Arbor, Mich., 1965.

4. Economic Opportunity Act of 1964. Hearings before Select Committee on Poverty of the Committee on Labor and Public Welfare, United States Senate, June, 1964.

5. Economic Opportunity Act of 1964. Report of the Committee on Labor and Public Welfare together with minority and individual views, Report Number 1218, July, 1964.

6. Milton Friedman. *Capitalism and Freedom*. Chicago: University of Chicago Press, 1962.

7. Herbert Gans. "Some Proposals for Government Policy in An Automating Society," *The Correspondent*, 30 (January–February, 1964).

8. Hubert H. Humphrey. *War on Poverty*. New York: McGraw Hill, 1964.

9. David Komatsu. "Mr. Johnson's Little War on Poverty," *New Politics*, Spring, 1964.

10. Martin Oppenheimer. *Disarmament and the War on Poverty*. American Friends Service Committee, 1964.

11. Mobilization for Youth, Inc. *A Proposal for the Prevention and Control of Delinquency by Expanding Opportunities*. New York: Mobilization for Youth Inc., 1961.

12. Ben Seligman, Ed., *Poverty as a Public Issue*. New York: Free Press of Glencoe, A Division of the Macmillan Company, 1965.

13. Robert Theobald. *Free Men and Free Markets*. New York: Potter, C. N., 1963.

14. Adam Walinsky. "Keeping the Poor in Their Place," *New Republic*, July 4, 1964.

Appendixes

The Economic Opportunity Act of 1964:
A Summary

[Reprinted from Legislative Notes, *Office of Education, March 16, 1964.]*

THE BILL ESTABLISHES the Office of Economic Opportunity in the Executive Office of the President. The Director of the Office is provided with coordinating powers with respect to existing Federal agency poverty-related programs, and with authority to carry out new programs to attack poverty. Operating functions of the new programs, except for the Job Corps, the community action program and the volunteers for America program, will be performed by other departments and agencies. Funds will be appropriated to the Director; it is anticipated that the first year program allocations will be:

Program Summary

		Millions
Total		$962.5
I.	Youth opportunity programs	412.5
	A. Job Corps	190.0
	B. Work-training program	150.0
	C. Work-study program	72.5
II.	Urban and rural community action programs	315.0
III.	Rural economic opportunity programs	50.0
IV.	Employment and investment incentives	25.0
	A. Incentives for employment of unemployed	25.0
	B. Small business loans	(1)
V.	Family unity through jobs	150.0
VI.	Volunteers and administration	10.0

The bill contains six titles:

---

[1] Utilizes existing funding authority.

Title I.—Youth Programs

Part A.—Establishes a Job Corps within the Office of Economic Opportunity, with responsibility for administering a program of education, work experience, and vocational training for youths aged 16 through 21. Two kinds of programs are envisaged—conservation camps providing useful work and basic education and residential training centers providing basic education and job training programs to increase employability.

Part B.—Authorizes the Director to enter into agreements with State and local governments or nonprofit agencies to pay part of the costs of part- or full-time employment for young men and women aged 16 through 21 to enable them to resume or continue their education or to increase their employability. This part of the program will be administered by the Department of Labor.

Part C.—Authorizes the Director to enter into agreements with institutions of higher learning to pay part of the costs of part-time employment for undergraduate, graduate, or professional students from low-income families in order to enable them to pursue courses of study at such institutions. This part of the program will be administered by the Department of Health, Education, and Welfare.

Title II.—Urban and Rural Community Action Programs

Authorizes the Director to encourage and support community action programs which mobilize community resources to combat poverty and which are conducted by a local government unit or an organization which is broadly representative of the community. Elementary or secondary school education programs which receive Federal assistance will be administered by the public school system, and such programs must be open to all children regardless of whether they are regularly enrolled in the public schools. Assistance may be provided to communities in advance of the completion of the plan. Technical assistance in preparing and administering community programs may be furnished. Financial assistance from the Federal Government under this title will be 90 percent of the costs of the programs for the first 2 years and 75 percent thereafter. The Director will establish criteria for equitable distribution of Federal funds; not more than 12½ percent of total funds may be used within one State in any one year. Programs will be administered by the communities and will incorporate assistance from various Federal departments and agencies.

Title III.—Special Programs to Combat Poverty in Rural Areas

Authorizes grants up to $1,500 to low-income rural families where such grants are likely to effect a permanent increase in the income of such families, and loans up to $2,500 to finance nonagricultural income-producing enterprises for the same purpose. The Director may also provide assistance to nonprofit corporations to acquire land to be reconstituted into family farms, and make loans to cooperatives. Program will be administered by the Department of Agriculture.

Title IV.—Employment and Investment Incentives

Part A.—Authorizes the Director to make, participate in, or guarantee loans for investments which will employ hard-core unemployed or members of low-income families. These investments may be outside designated surplus labor areas, if they are part of a community action plan. Program will be administered by the Area Redevelopment Administration.

 Part B.—Authorizes the Director to make, participate in, or guarantee loans to small businesses not in excess of $15,000 on more liberal terms than the regular loan provisions of the Small Business Administration. Program will be administered by SBA.

Title V.—Family Unity through Jobs

Authorizes the Director to transfer funds to HEW to pay costs of experimental, pilot or demonstration projects designed to stimulate the adoption in States of programs providing constructive work experience or training for unemployed fathers and other members of needy families with children.

Title VI.—Administration and Coordination

Establishes the Office of Economic Opportunity. Authorizes the Director to recruit, select, and train volunteers, and to refer them to programs at the State or local level, or to utilize them, with appropriate allowances and benefits, in specified mental health, migrant, Indian, and other Federal programs, including the Job Corps. Establishes an Economic Opportunity Council made up of Federal officers, and a National Advisory Council of citizens appointed by the President to consult with and advise the Director. Also authorizes the Director to assist the President in coordinating the antipoverty efforts of all Federal agencies and requires other agencies, to the maximum extent feasible, to carry out poverty-related programs in a manner which will assist in carrying out the purposes of this bill. Provides that the President may direct that programs of Federal agencies be carried out, to the extent consistent with other applicable law, in conjunction with or in support of programs authorized by the bill. Requires heads of agencies, where possible, to give preference in their programing to community action programs. Authorizes the Director to take steps to insure that adequate information concerning all relevant Federal programs is readily available to public officials and other interested persons.

The War on Poverty

Sargent Shriver

Director of the Office of Economic Opportunity

[From the opening statement to the Ad Hoc Subcommittee on Poverty of the House Committee on Education and Labor, April 12, 1965.]

FIRST, the War on Poverty is an attempt to help individuals—thirty-five million of them—get out of poverty. But it is *not* just aimed at individuals. It embraces entire neighborhoods, communities, cities and states. It is an attempt to change institutions as well as people. It must deal with the culture of poverty as well as the individual victims. Second, the War on Poverty embraces a cluster of government programs. But it is *not* just a governmental effort. It involves and must involve all sectors of the economy and all the American people. Third, it is a program which must and will produce results, quantifiable results, numerical results. But it is *not* simply a series of numerical results. It is also a process of arousing, of mobilizing, of harnessing the moral energies of the American people.

Let's take one at a time. The War on Poverty does reach out to individuals—one by one. When I was at the Job Corps Center in Ouchita, Arkansas, I saw it reach out to a strapping six-foot 17-year-old who just the day before had read the first two sentences in his life. Do you know what the book he read from looked like? One side of the page was a tiny picture of an ant, and just below it was a small picture of a human being. And those first two sentences of text said:
"I am not an ant."
"I am a man."

The War on Poverty starts with individuals—with a man, a woman, a child—taking them one by one. But it does not stop there, because poverty is not just an individual affair. It is also a condition, a relationship to society, and to all the institutions which comprise society. Poverty is need. It is lack of opportunity. But it is also helplessness to cope with hostile or uncaring or exploitive institutions. It is lack of dignity. And it is vulnerability to injustice. The treatment the poor get, at the hands of bureaucrats and politicians, at the hands of private industry, at the hands of landlords and merchants and agriculturalists is more than the sum of the individuals involved. A pattern of response, a way of reacting to and treating the poor has become entrenched, and institutionalized.

Poverty is personal. But it is also a terrifyingly impersonal and dehumanizing condition, imposed on thirty-five million Americans. Both dimensions of poverty come through in this statement by Mrs. Janice Bradshaw of Pueblo, Colorado. It says a whole lot:

Poverty is a personal thing!

Poverty is taking your children to the hospital and spending the whole day waiting with no one even taking your name, and then coming back the next, and the next, until they finally get around to you.

Poverty is having a landlady who is a public health nurse who turns off the heat when she leaves for work in the morning and turns it back on at six when she returns. It's being helpless to do anything about it because by the time the officials get around to it, she has turned the heat back on for that day and then it will be off the next.

Poverty is having the welfare investigators break in at four o'clock in the morning and cut off your welfare check without an explanation, and then when you go down and ask, they tell you it is because they found a pair of men's house slippers in the attic, where your brother left them when he visited a month ago.

Poverty is having a child with glaucoma and watching that eye condition grow worse every day, while the welfare officials send you to the private agencies, and the private agencies send you back to the welfare, and when you ask the welfare officials to refer you to this special hospital, they say they can't—and then when you say it is prejudice because you are a Negro, they deny it flatly and they shout at you: "Name one white child we have referred there." And when you name twenty-five, they sit down, and they shut up, and they finally refer you but it is too late then, because your child has permanently lost eighty percent of his vision—and you are told that if only they had caught it a month earlier, when you first made inquiry about the film over his eyes, they could have preserved his vision.

And that is why the War on Poverty is more than a program to help individuals—one by one. It is a program to help institutions and entire communities view and treat poor people in a very different way—as citizens, as Americans.

Our General Counsel would tell you that the War on Poverty—or at least the community action phase of it—is a program under which an entire city, or neighborhood, or county, or state enters into a binding agreement to pull itself up by its bootstraps. In effect, it means that communities are applying to us for a new type of corporate charter. They are incorporating themselves as a new enterprise, a new business, the business of creating opportunity for the very poor. This job can't be done piecemeal. This new enterprise—the community action program—

will have to design and tool up for a new model: Opportunity—1965 style.

Each of the component parts—education and training, experience and motivation, confidence and health, hope and self-reliance—has to be designed afresh. We have to go back to the drawing boards because for thirty-five million Americans the old product has not been selling. It isn't reaching the consumer—the poor themselves. And so, we have to engage in a new kind of market research. We have to find out why the old product didn't appeal to the consumer—to one-fifth of the market. And only the poor—the consumer—can tell us.

The War on Poverty is not a hand-out program or an individual casework program. It is a part of that effort to fashion a world where, in President Johnson's words: "The meaning of man's life matches the marvels of man's labors."

And that is why the Congressional presentation, with its rundown on each specific program, is not a full description of the War on Poverty. Look at the Table of Contents and you will see the programs, the new programs which the Office of Economic Opportunity is charged either with managing or supervising and with coordinating. We are asking you, today, to renew and reauthorize each of these programs.

The point needs to be made over and over again that these programs, including the many other federal programs which help the poor —that all of the programs taken together are NOT the War on Poverty. If the War on Poverty were just a governmental program, it would be doomed. Because no matter how big the federal payroll or budget may become, it can't get big enough to reach out to all the poor and to enlist all America in a war which will determine the future and shape of our society. And perhaps one of the most important and exciting things about the War on Poverty is that all America is joining in. Religious groups, professional groups, labor groups, civic and patriotic groups are all rallying to the call.

That is a major part of the War on Poverty. And so, when we come before you to ask for our renewal of programs, we are, in effect, saying, continue not just these programs, but reaffirm a national commitment to fight an all-out battle on all fronts, by all segments of society.

And this brings me to my last point about what the War on Poverty is. It is a set of production goals, a series of specific target goals and production quotas. We are meeting those goals. With your go-ahead, we'll continue to meet them.

But beyond these specific results, these particular numerical target figures, the War on Poverty is a catalytic force. And the effectiveness of the programs you have been asked to continue and enlarge must be judged, not only in terms of their specific, tangible results—but equally, in terms of their catalytic effect.

For we are beginning to find out:

> that the processes we set in motion are at least as important as the direct results we achieve;
>
> the energies we release are at least as important as the specific production goals we attain;
>
> the attitudes we affect, the concerns we generate, the myths we destroy are at least as important as the number of salaries we pay, directly or indirectly.

Let me be even more specific—because this applies on every level. There are five-year-olds who don't even know how to hold a book or how to listen to a sentence with more than two or three words. When we teach one of these children those things, we aren't making him "employable." But we will have begun to supply the missing ingredient—the catalyst—so that our regular school system won't lose that child along the way. And with that child, that five-year-old, we will have set in motion a process, a possibility, a chance which in our time, in our generation, can spell the end of poverty.

The same is true when we train a teen-ager in one of our Job Corps Centers. Suppose we teach him how to repair a car engine or operate a tool-cutting machine. We can't guarantee that next year's cars won't change to turbine engines, or that that particular machine will always be in use. But we can say that that boy will feel different about himself and about work. He'll have a new sense of dignity, of self-confidence—because for what may be the first time in his life, he'll have proven that he can learn, and that he can succeed.

That's a form of "poverty-proofing" that won't wear off. And this catalytic effect works on communities as well as individuals.

When we fund a local antipoverty program—like the one in Washington (UPO) or in Chicago or St. Louis, or Detroit or Atlanta—there may be about fifteen or twenty or thirty parts: pre-kindergarten classes, literacy classes, consumer education, job training, counseling, placement, legal services, health services. We don't know and they don't know if every single one of those programs will work. Or if that particular assortment of programs is exactly the right combination to eliminate poverty today, or tomorrow or the next day. What counts, what *really* counts, is that there is an organization like UPO—

> that for the first time, an entire community has pulled together to worry about the poor, and to find out about the causes of poverty;

that for the first time government has pooled resources with private agencies in a special kind of partnership;

and that for the first time, the poor have a forum in which they are represented, in which their voice will be heard.

And this perhaps is the final lesson—and the ultimate dimension of the War on Poverty—the spiritual dimension. Because for us, for all America, the War on Poverty is a movement of conscience, a national act of expiation, of humbling and prostrating ourselves before our Creator.

And when all is said and done, what the War on Poverty will have achieved is to have gained for an entire people an appreciation of those words attributed to St. Vincent de Paul:

> Before you go out and help the poor,
> you must first beg their pardon.

And this is what the War on Poverty is really all about.

Selected Agencies and Organizations from which Additional Information Can Be Obtained

American Jewish Committee
165 East 56th Street
New York, New York

Association on American Indian
  Affairs
475 Riverside Drive
New York 27, New York

Center for the Study of Democratic
  Institutions
Box 4068
Santa Barbara, California

Citizens' Crusade Against Poverty
132 Third Street SE
Washington, D. C. 20003

Committee for Economic Development
1001 Connecticut Avenue NW
Washington, D. C.

Committee for Miners
1165 Broadway
New York, New York 10001

Committee on Pockets of Poverty
1020 Connecticut Avenue NW
Washington, D. C. 20036

Conference of Economic Progress
1001 Connecticut Avenue NW
Washington, D. C., 20036

Congress of Racial Equality
38 Park Row
New York, New York

Economic Research and Action
  Project
1100 West Ainslie
Chicago, Illinois

Grey Areas Project
Ford Foundation
477 Madison Avenue
New York, New York 10022

Industrial Areas Foundation
8 South Michigan Avenue
Chicago 3, Illinois

Industrial Union Department
A.F.L.–C.I.O.
815 16th Street NW
Washington, D. C. 20006

Institute for Policy Studies
1900 Florida Avenue NW
Washington, D. C. 20090

Jewish Labor Committee
25 East 78th Street
New York, New York

League for Industrial Democracy
112 East 19th Street
New York, New York 10003

National Advisory Committee on
  Farm Labor
112 East 19th Street
New York, New York 10003

National Association for the Advancement of Colored People
20 West 40th Street
New York, New York

National Committee for Children and
  Youth
1145 19th Street NW
Washington, D. C.

National Committee for Full
  Employment
Box 232, Village Station
New York, New York 10014

National Committee on Employment
of Youth
145 East 32nd Street
New York, New York

National Consumers League
1029 Vermont Avenue NW
Washington, D.C.

National Planning Association
1606 New Hampshire Avenue NW
Washington, D. C.

National Sharecroppers Fund
112 East 19th Street
New York, New York 10003

National Urban League
14 East 48th Street
New York, New York

Research Department
A.F.L.–C.I.O.
815 16th Street NW
Washington, D. C. 20006

Southern Regional Council
5 Forsythe NW
Atlanta, Georgia

Student Non-violent Coordinating
Committee
360 Nelson Street NW
Atlanta, Georgia

United States Office of Economic
Opportunity
1156 15th Street NW
Washington, D.C.

The W. E. Upjohn Institute for
Employment Research
709 South Westnedge Avenue
Kalamazoo, Michigan

Contributors

ALAN BATCHELDER is an assistant professor of economics at Kenyon College.

FAY BENNETT is the executive secretary of the National Sharecroppers Fund.

GEORGE BRAGER is a special assistant to the Manpower Administration, United States Department of Labor. He was formerly co-director of Mobilization for Youth.

LEE G. BURCHINAL is the deputy director, Division of Educational Research, Bureau of Educational Research and Development, United States Office of Education.

ROBB K. BURLAGE is a graduate student in economics at Harvard University. He is on leave from the Tennessee State Planning Commission.

DAVID CAPLOVITZ is an associate professor of sociology at Columbia University and a member of the staff of the Bureau of Applied Social Research.

MARTIN DEUTSCH is the director of the Institute for Developmental Studies and a professor in the Department of Psychiatry at New York Medical College.

HERBERT J. GANS is an associate professor of sociology and education at Columbia University. He is a frequent contributor to both professional and popular magazines and journals.

WARREN C. HAGGSTROM is a senior research associate at the Youth Development Center, Syracuse University; and an assistant professor in the Syracuse University School of Social Work.

MICHAEL HARRINGTON is chairman of the board of the League for Industrial Democracy. He is the author of *The Other America* and *The Accidental Century*.

JOSEPH S. HIMES is a professor of sociology at North Carolina College at Durham. He is the author of *Social Planning in America*.

FREDERICK S. JAFFE is the vice-president for program planning of the Planned Parenthood Federation of America. He is a co-author of *Planning Your Family—The Complete Guide to Contraception and Fertility* and *The Complete Book of Birth Control*.

TOM KAHN is the executive secretary of the League for Industrial Democracy. He was the administrative assistant to Bayard Rustin for the Civil Rights March on Washington in August 1963.

LEON H. KEYSERLING is a former chairman of the Council of Economic Advisors. He is now president of the Conference on Economic Progress.

CHARLES C. KILLINGSWORTH is a professor of labor and industrial relations at Michigan State University. He has served as a labor dispute arbitrator and a consultant to both labor and industry.

ROBERT J. LAMPMAN is a professor of economics at the University of Wisconsin. He is a former staff member of the Council of Economic Advisors and the author of *The Low Income Population and Economic Growth.*

JEREMY LARNER recently won the Delta prize for his novel, *Drive, He Said.* He is also a co-author of *The Addict in the Streets.*

CHARLES LEBEAUX is a professor in the school of social work at Wayne State University. He is a co-author of *Industrial Society and Social Welfare,* and *Studies in Renewal and Change in an Urban Community.*

SAR A. LEVITAN is affiliated with the W. E. Upjohn Institute for Employment Research. Among his works is *Vocational Education and Federal Policy.* He is a co-author of *Programs in Aid of the Unemployed.*

HYLAN LEWIS is a professor of sociology at Howard University.

EDWIN J. LUKAS is the director of national affairs of the American Jewish Committee. He is a lawyer by profession and a contributor to many professional journals.

DWIGHT MACDONALD is presently a staff writer for *The New Yorker.* His works include *Henry Wallace: The Man and the Myth,* and *Memoirs of a Revolutionist.*

SAMUEL MENCHER is a professor of public welfare and social work research at the University of Pittsburgh. He is currently completing a book entitled, *The Development of Economic Security Policy.*

S. M. MILLER is a professor of sociology at Syracuse University and a senior research associate at the Syracuse University Youth Development Center. His works include *Comparative Social Mobility,* and *Dynamics of the American Economy.*

WALTER B. MILLER is an assistant research professor at the Boston University School of Social Work and a staff consultant of the President's Committee on Juvenile Delinquency and Youth Crime Projects.

OSCAR ORNATI is a professor on the graduate faculty of the New School for Social Research. He is presently on leave from the New School, working for the Office of Economic Opportunity as chief of the Economic Development Section of the Community Action Program.

MOLLIE ORSHANSKY is an economist with the Social Security Administration of the United States Department of Health, Education and Welfare.

MARTIN REIN is an associate professor in the Department of Social Work and Social Research at Bryn Mawr College. He is currently writing a book on poverty with S. M. Miller.

FRANK RIESSMAN is an associate professor in the Department of Psychiatry at the Albert Einstein College of Medicine of Yeshiva University. His works include *The Culturally Deprived Child, Mental Health of the Poor,* and *New Careers for the Poor.*

HYMAN RODMAN is a senior research associate with the Merrill Palmer Institute. He is the author of the forthcoming book, *Marriage, Family and Society.*

BAYARD RUSTIN was the chief organizer of the August 1963, Civil Rights March on Washington. He is the director of the A. Philip Randolph Institute, a newly formed civil rights organization.

ALVIN L. SCHORR is a family life specialist with the United States Department of Health, Education, and Welfare and acting director of the Long Range Research Division of the Social Security Administration.

EDWARD E. SCHWARTZ is a professor of social science and social work administration at the University of Chicago.

ARTHUR SEAGULL is an assistant professor of clinical psychology at Michigan State University. He is also a consultant with the Lansing, Michigan, Board of Education on programs for emotionally disturbed children.

PATRICIA CAYO SEXTON is a professor of educational sociology at New York University. She is the author of *Education and Income,* and *Spanish Harlem.*

HILDA SIFF is a social science analyst with the Welfare Division of the United States Department of Health, Education and Welfare.

GUS TYLER is the assistant president of the International Ladies Garment Workers Union and director of its Department of Politics, Education, and Training. He is the editor of *Organized Crime in America* and a contributor to many periodicals and anthologies.

ELLEN WINSTON is the first United States commissioner of welfare. She is a co-author of *Seven Lean Years* and *Foundations of American Population Policy.*

MARY WRIGHT is a caseworker with the Presbyterian Child Welfare Agency in Buckhorn, Kentucky. She has been intimately connected with the Appalachian region for many years.

Index